Emperor of the West

Emperor of the West

Hywel Williams

Quercus

First published in Great Britain in 2010 by
Quercus
21 Bloomsbury Square
London
WC1A 2NS

A CIP catalogue record for this book is available
from the British Library

ISBN 978 1 84916 190 9

10 9 8 7 6 5 4 3 2 1

Typeset by Ellipsis Books Limited, Glasgow
Printed and bound in Great Britain by Clays Ltd, St Ives plc

TO THE MEMORY OF
WILLIAM RAYMOND WILLIAMS
11 January 1927–21 July 2009

*Fy enaid, bendithia yr Arglwydd: a chwbl sydd
ynof ei Enw sanctaidd ef.*
Psalm 103:1

Contents

Preface   VII
Maps   IX
Introduction   XII

1   Gods, Kings and Franks   1

2   From Prince to King   47

3   The Kingdom at War   68

4   Crown Imperial   139

5   Aristocratic Power and Carolingian Calculation   190

6   Charlemagne and the Institutions of Carolingian
    Government   229

7   The Economic Basis of a Civilization   270

8   The Carolingian Cultural Renaissance   303

9   The Survival and Revival of Empire   355

    Primary Source References   382
    Secondary Source References   397
    Index   445
    List of Illustrations   457

Preface

Those who write about the past stand on the shoulders of their predecessors. A bibliography of secondary literature indicates the extent of my indebtedness and includes some classic works in the corpus of literature dealing with this period. Ferdinand Gregorovius's history of medieval Rome for example, first published in 1859-72, remains a magnificent achievement, supplemented by the more recent works of Richard Krautheimer which show such refinement in relating architectural history to political and cultural developments. Contemporary thinking on Charlemagne's reign inevitably takes Rosamond McKitterick's biography of the emperor as a major point of departure with its marvellously detailed account of the reign's surviving literary sources. I do not share some features of her scepticism about the significance of Charlemagne's coronation as an emperor, but I have been guided by her learned account of palace society and by her analysis of Charlemagne's techniques of government which shows the extent to which this was a personal form of rule. Students of early medieval Europe are the beneficiaries of Dame Jinty Nelson's acute insights and lucid scholarship, and my description in particular of aristocratic life and influence has been shaped by her conclusions on these matters as well as by those of Stuart Airlie. The penetrating originality of the late Patrick Wormald's publications has led to a major re-evaluation of the role of law in Anglo-Saxon England, but his panache as an historian was not confined to insular developments. In thinking about issues of command and obedience in post-Roman western Europe, a period when tribes and chieftains were transmuted into nations and monarchs, I have been deeply influenced by Wormald's work.

Staff at the British Library, the London Library and the German Historical Institute gave me invaluable assistance in the course of my researches. I am grateful to all those at Quercus who prepared *Emperor of the West* for publication, and particularly so Georgina Difford and Josh Ireland. Helen Campbell's very sure touch showed why she is so widely admired as a copy editor, and the book's structure benefited greatly from the detailed comments of my editor, Richard Milbank. It is, as always, a particular pleasure to thank my literary agent Georgina Capel for the wisdom of her advice and the constancy of her encouragement, and to express my gratitude to Anthony Cheetham, an inspirational figure in British publishing and whose idea it was that I should write about Charlemagne. I reserve my greatest debt to the last. Conversations with my late father about Christianity's early history formed a stimulating background to my writing. His lively erudition, elegant exposition and dynamic character influenced the lives of many, and I therefore dedicate this book to his memory with a more than filial *pietas*.

Hywel Williams

Maps

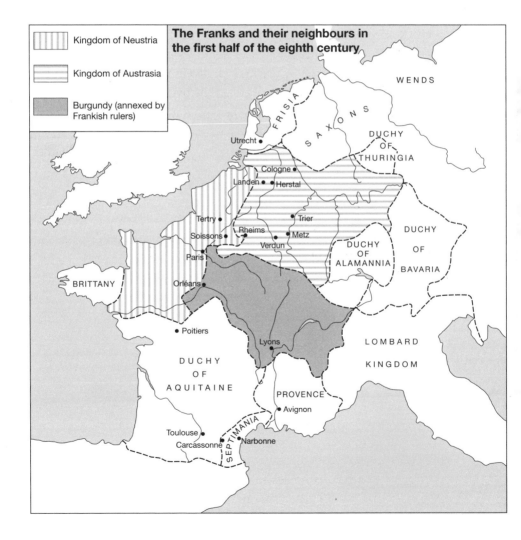

Kingdom of Neustria

Kingdom of Austrasia

Burgundy (annexed by Frankish rulers)

The Franks and their neighbours in the first half of the eighth century

WENDS

FRISIA

SAXONS

DUCHY OF THURINGIA

Utrecht

Cologne

Landen • Herstal

Tertry

Rheims • Trier

Soissons • Metz

Verdun

Paris

DUCHY OF ALAMANNIA

DUCHY OF BAVARIA

BRITTANY

Orléans

Poitiers

Lyons

LOMBARD KINGDOM

DUCHY OF AQUITAINE

PROVENCE

Avignon

Toulouse

Carcassonne • Narbonne

SEPTIMANIA

The Carolingian empire at the death of Charlemagne, 814

Iona
Lindisfarne
NORTH SEA
ULSTER
PICTS
Jarrow
Wearmouth
Clogher
Armagh
NORTHUMBRIA
FRIESLAND
FRISIANS
MEATH Tara
Kildare
Dublin
LEINSTER
Bangor
GWYNEDD
Njimegen
Münster
Verden
OFFA'S DYKE
Severn
Ouse
EAST ANGLIA
St. David's
DYFED
Thames
London
Cologne
ATLANTIC OCEAN
WESSEX
KENT
Canterbury
Winchester
Hamwic
SUSSEX
Hastings
Boulogne
Quentowic
Tournai
Herstal
Aachen
AUSTRASIA
Rhine
Valenciennes
St. Riquier
Amiens
Corbie
Trier
Moselle
BRITTANY
Bayeux
Rouen
Noyon
Quierzy
Laon
Metz
BRETON MARCH
Angers
Seine
Paris
(St. Denis)
Soissons
Reims
Meaux
Ponthion
Strasbourg
Meuse
Tours
Orleans
NEUSTRIA
Troyes
Rhine
Loire
Bourges
Saône
BURGUNDY
St. Maurice
Poitiers
Angoulême
Lyons
Great St. Bernard Pass
Vienne
Mt. Cenis
Turin
Po
BAY OF BISCAY
Bordeaux
AQUITAINE
Dordogne
Loire
Garonne
Agen
Albi
Nimes
Avignon
PROVENCE
Nice
GASCONY
Toulouse
SEPTIMANIA
Béziers
Narbonne
Marseille
Toulon
GALICIA
ASTURIAS
Roncesvalles
BASQUES
Pamplona
NAVARRA
SPANISH MARCH
Roussillon
Burgos
Huesca
Ebro
Zaragoza
Barcelona
Tarragona
Douro
Toledo
EMIRATE OF CORDOBA
Valencia
MINORCA
MAJORCA
Cordoba
Seville
Guadalquivir
Granada
MEDITERRANEAN
Tangier Ceuta
Rhône

SWEDEN

DENMARK

BALTIC SEA

Danevirke

Reric
Hamburg
ABODRITES
Elbe
WILTZI
POMERANIA
Oder
Vistula
Warthe
Gniezno
POLES

SAXONY
WEST-
PHALIANS
EAST-
PHALIANS
Magdeburg
Dorstadt
Paderborn
Lippe
Diemel
Weser
SORBS
Elbe
Oder

THURINGIA

Fulda

Prague

BOHEMIA

Frankfurt
Mainz
Ingelheim
Worms
Würzburg
Main
FRANCONIA
Regensburg
MORAVIA
Eichstätt
Rhine
ALAMANNIA
Passau
Danube
Vienna
AVAR
CONFEDERATION

Reichenau
BAVARIA
Enns
The Ring of
the Avars?
St. Gallen
RHAETIA
Brenner Pass
CARANTANIANS
CARINTHIA
PANONNONIA
Danube
Drava

MARCH OF FRIULI
Aquileia
CROATS
Sava
Danube
Milan
Brescia
Verona
Torcello
KINGDOM OF THE LOMBARDS
Pavia
Po
DALMATIA
SERBS
BULGARS
Bobbio
FORMER
EXARCHATE
OF RAVENNA
Bologna
Ravenna
Genoa
PATRIMONY OF PETER
Lucca
Florence
Ancona
Pisa
Arno
TUSCANY
Perugia
ADRIATIC SEA
Spoleto
DUCHY
OF
SPOLETO
CORSICA
Ostia
Rome
Monte
Cassino
Bari
DUCHY OF PETER
Capua
Benevento
Naples
DUCHY OF
BENEVENTO
APULIA
Otranto
Salerno

SARDINIA

TYRRHENIAN
SEA

CALABRIA

IONIAN
SEA

SEA

Trapani
Palermo
Taormina
SICILY
Catania
Syracuse

Hippo
Carthage
Tunis

Introduction

This is the story of a king who became an emperor. It is also a history of the dynasty which is named after him since Charlemagne's achievements need to be understood in the context of the Carolingian family whose members ruled the kingdom of the Franks. The term *Karlinger* or Carolingian seems to have been coined in the tenth century over a hundred years after the emperor's death in 814, and it would therefore have meant little to Charlemagne himself, his dynastic predecessors or immediate successors on the throne. Surnames, however, had yet to be established at this stage in Europe's history and 'Carolingian' is therefore the most convenient way of referring collectively to the members of a dynasty whose history starts over a century before Charlemagne became a king of the Franks in 768.

In striking a balance between what is known about Charlemagne and the details of the wider Carolingian picture, I have sought to portray the successful early medieval struggle to restore order and civility in western Europe during the centuries following the Roman imperial collapse. But though the canvas is so broad, the reign of one ruler remains in the foreground. Knowledge of the imperial past, awareness of present political and military opportunity, and a conviction that God's providence would bless the Franks' future: all combined to lend an unusual range and depth to Charlemagne's ambitions, and this book's chapters detail the vision as it worked out in practice.

The Franks were the most significant of all the tribal forces that succeeded in turning themselves into nations during the immediate post-Roman centuries. 'Gods, Kings and Franks' describes the evolution of the early Frankish monarchy under the Merovingians, the emergent influence of those Carolingians who were Charlemagne's ancestors, and the nature of the Germanic kingdoms that developed in western Europe in the wake of the western Roman empire's dissolution. Power politics supposedly blessed by sacramental agency is the emperor Constantine's fateful legacy, and it acquired a new lease of life among the Franks. The fact, however, that the Frankish leaders called themselves kings shows the arrival of a new element in the justifications of power that were current in the immediate post-Roman world. The dynamic nature of monarchy meant that it was more than just a development of past Roman autocracy, and the excitement generated by kingship right across western Europe was evident most of all among the Franks.

Charlemagne was not born a prince, and only became one when his father Pippin III engineered the coup d'état of 749–50 which deposed the Merovingian dynasty. His boyhood and youth were therefore spent at a court where the idea of 'sacral kingship' was giving a new depth and authority to the rulers of Francia, and the account of the years from 750 to 771 reveals the pattern of diplomatic activity involving the papacy and the Frankish throne. Following the death of Pippin III in 768 Charlemagne and his brother Carloman reigned in Francia as co-rulers. After Carloman's sudden death at the end of 771 Charlemagne ruled as sole king of the Franks, and the militarist emphases of his reign gained an early expression with the conquest and occupation of Lombardy in 774.

The discussion of Charlemagne's military campaigns in Chapter 3, 'The Kingdom at War', follows a broadly chronological narrative and is divided into the main theatres of armed conflict in Lombardy, Saxony and northern Spain. The takeover of the duchy of Bavaria was mostly effected by diplomatic bullying, and the federation of peoples known as the Avars seems to have collapsed largely as a result of internal strains almost as soon as the Carolingian army came into view. Killing as many Saxons as possible, and forcing the survivors to become Christians, was a major preoccupation of Charlemagne's reign. The military thrust worked in tandem with the religious campaign to extirpate paganism, and Saxony's assimilation was the central event in the making of medieval Germany. The Saxon campaign had another long-term consequence since it is the first major example of the crusading instinct at work, although it would be another three centuries before that cause was formally adopted by the papacy and endorsed by Christian kings.

Few contemporary visual representations of the emperor survive, and the bust engraved on the coinage Charlemagne issued in 812 reveals a porcine profile. One detail of that coin, however, is charged with meaning since the laurel wreath that adorns Charlemagne's head is a feature of Roman imperial portraiture. As king and emperor he ruled over most of what had once been the western half of the Roman empire, and that fact has guided my overall interpretation of Charlemagne's significance. His imperial style had been evident long before the coronation ceremony conducted by Pope Leo on Christmas Day, 800. Ancient and medieval political thought was at pains to point out that only emperors ruled more than one kingdom, and in adopting *Rex Francorum et Rex Langobardorum* as his formal ascription in all official documents issued from 774 onwards Charlemagne was already pointing out that he was an exceptional kind of ruler. The creation of a new kingdom was a right reserved to emperors, and the kingdoms Charlemagne created in Aquitaine and Italy in 781 showed him exercising a distinctive imperial prerogative. Charlemagne's intimate involvement in the affairs of the Christian Church harked back to the imperial prerogatives exercised by Constantine. He appointed bishops and abbots, took steps to ensure the adoption of the Roman liturgy within his empire, and at Frankfurt in 794 he presided over a council of the Church which settled questions of doctrine.

The reality of Charlemagne's power had therefore been exercised in a manner associated traditionally with an emperor since the early years of his reign. Nonetheless, it is right to see the coronation which is described in Chapter 4, 'Crown Imperial', as a ground-breaking event. The last imperator to exercise any legitimate power in the west was Flavius Julius Nepos who had to flee from Italy to Dalmatia after he was deposed in 475 by Flavius Orestes, one of his own military commanders, and the arrival of a new emperor 325 years later was a point at which certain truths of power became increasingly explicit. From 812 onwards even the Byzantines acknowledged Charlemagne's title and qualified their own in a highly revealing way. Constantinople's official documents now start to add as a matter of course the word '*Romaion*' to the term '*Basileus*' to signify that the emperor was the ruler of the Romans of the east or, as we would refer to them, the Greeks. Before 812 this was only rarely done; afterwards it became the necessary and limiting formula.

A discussion of the issues surrounding Charlemagne's coronation on Christmas Day of that year leads into a portrayal of the European scene at that time. He was now the dominating figure in western European political and diplomatic life, and his victories in battle had secured him a military prestige unparalleled in that region since the reign of Constantine the Great. The year 800 also supplies us with a perspective from which we can view the evolution of the city of Rome itself as a Christian capital of the world, that 'caput orbis' which is central to an understanding of Charlemagne.

Charlemagne mobilized an entire kingdom for war, and all his subjects both in Francia and within the lands he conquered were liable for military conscription. He was able to do this because of a rigorous overhaul of the system of government, and the two chapters devoted to his power base approach this issue from complementary angles.

Chapter 5, 'Aristocratic Power and Carolingian Calculation', describes the palace society which was Charlemagne's domestic milieu as well as a focus for the regal, and subsequent imperial, administration. The palaces were also home to the royal family, a large and disparate collection of individuals, as well as a place of rendez-vous for the Frankish aristocracy who came to wait in attendance on the king. This chapter therefore shows how Charlemagne ruled through the aristocracy, and my account broadens out into a description of aristocratic life and influence in other regions and kingdoms of Europe during the early Middle Ages.

'Charlemagne and the Institutions of Carolingian Government' describes the more formal and institutional aspects of Charlemagne's administration including the documentation, especially the capitularies, which were produced by court officials, the various assemblies which were summoned by the king, the importance of ritual ceremonies as an expression of regal *auctoritas*, and the courts of law which delivered the king's justice. Locally based counts were an important means of communication between the king and his subjects, but the *missi dominici* enjoyed substantial powers since they were sent from court and instructed to enforce certain orders at the king's express command. The variety of surviving ninth-century sources enables us to grasp the dynamic of Carolingian government as a whole both during Charlemagne's reign and in the subsequent decades.

In 'The Economic Basis of a Civilization' I describe a *renovatio* which accompanied and made possible the political, military and cultural advances. The emergence of north-west Europe as a politically powerful, economically vibrant and culturally expansive region is a key feature of the history of the eighth century. It involved an orientation of European civilization's most progressive elements away from the Mediterranean base which had been predominant within that culture since classical antiquity. The great Belgian scholar Henri Pirenne started one of the major historical debates of the twentieth century when he stated that 'without Mohammed Charlemagne would have been inconceivable'. It is certainly true that the victories of the Arab armies in north Africa and the Middle East, and the subsequent loss to Christianity of Syria, Egypt and Palestine, had a major impact on the configuration of power and the distribution of wealth within the European continent from the seventh century onwards. Long-established patterns of trade with the Middle East were disrupted, and with the Mediterranean looking as if it might become a Muslim lake, European civilization developed an alternative dynamic, one that looked to the north and west. If ever there was a *longue durée* then this is surely it, but however impersonal this great historical force may have been, it remains a shift of resources and a change of attitudes in which the actions of individuals mattered. The options available to Charlemagne in this regard, and the decisions he took, show how central he was to this momentous reorientation of Europe.

The story of land is also a story of power, since its possession was basic to the exercise of authority, and kings in western Europe generally from the eighth century onwards were managing their domains more rigorously, extracting more work from their peasantry, and increasing dues owed in kind as well as in cash. Kings had to be resourceful in this regard since the Roman system of land-based taxation had disappeared and monarchs were therefore heavily dependent on their own estates for the means which enabled them to exercise their kingship. Conquest and territorial expansion might still give rulers an opportunity to augment their resources through loot and plunder. That dynamic had been the raison d'être of the barbarian kingdoms, with a ruler's authority being affirmed through his ability to expand his territory and distribute the proceeds of conquest among his followers. This institutional instability, paradoxically enough, was the basis of a king's order. Charlemagne's acquisition of Avar treasure, part of which he then redistributed as a form of largesse, shows that this venerable tradition of early medieval kingship was still in operation right at the end of the eighth century. By then, however, looting was becoming less common, and the emergence of relatively fixed frontier zones meant that rulers were concentrating on maximizing the resources they could obtain within the area of their agreed and legitimate authority.

Carolingian culture was an aspect of Carolingian power, and the renaissance to which Charlemagne lends his name was a pragmatic affair. My discussion emphasizes the degree of nation-building that was involved in the revival of learning which was evident in Francia from the end of the eighth century onwards. Clarity of expression, as in the famous example of the Carolingian script's introduction, meant that thought attained greater precision. This in turn helped to improve communication levels within Charlemagne's realm so that the king's commands could be more easily understood and implemented. Charlemagne was fundamental to the programme of cultural recovery in another way as well since this was a society without any universities, and the intelligentsia was therefore dependent on the Church–State axis and its powers of patronage. Close association with royal policy elevated the social standing of the learned in a culture which remained infused by the warrior ethic, and the vocational aspect to this intellectual work explains the renaissance's strongly hierarchical nature. It was directed by a fairly narrow class of mostly clerical professionals and it propagated the idea that the Frankish society, with the king at its head, was a nation of the elect chosen by God and sanctified by Him. A more generous appreciation of what was achieved culturally is possible, however, if we take a chronologically wider perspective. My account of the Carolingian renaissance relates it to the culture of late antiquity and describes the strategies that had enabled the arts and letters to survive during the early medieval period.

*

Charlemagne dominated the battlefields of his own age, but in the twelve hundred years since his death the emperor's reputation has often been taken hostage by different national camps who had their own wars to wage. The question of whether Charlemagne was 'French' or 'German' may indeed presuppose categories that make no sense in the context of his own time. He was a king of the Franks and they considered themselves to be a proudly individual *gens* or people. Nonetheless, sharp cultural differences evolved quite rapidly to the east and west of the Rhine in the generation after Charlemagne's death. The Treaty of Verdun's territorial division of the Carolingian empire in 843 reflected the new cultural configuration. Two separate kingdoms now emerged, those of the eastern and of the western Franks, and they were separated by a middle kingdom extending from the North Sea coast to northern Italy. During the period of their ninth- and tenth-century evolution, therefore, both the French and the German kingdoms could claim with equal plausibility that Charlemagne was their founder.

The debate about Charlemagne's true identity and aims, once started, never went away in subsequent centuries. French republicanism and Bonapartism alike were enthused by Charlemagne's consolidation of Francia and its subsequent expansion towards and beyond the Rhine. Here was an imperial adventure on the grand scale, and French national history in the nineteenth century, and for some decades afterwards, regarded Charlemagne as a ruler who anticipated Napoleon. This was Napoleon's own view of the matter too and his propagandists drew the appropriate parallels. The rocks of the St-Bernard Pass, painted in Jacques Louis David's portrait *The Emperor Crossing the Alps*, are inscribed with the names of Napoleon, Charlemagne and Hannibal. Charlemagne had associated his rule with the revival of ancient Roman notions of empire, and Napoleon in a rather similar act of aggrandizement appropriated some of the symbols of early Frankish monarchy. Cloisonné jewellery shaped in the form of a bee was a distinctive feature of Merovingian royal adornment. Brooches of that design, with the deep-red mineral known as garnet being encased in gold, were among the objects found in the grave of the late fifth-century monarch Childeric I when it was excavated in 1653. The treasure trove eventually came into the possession of Louis XIV in 1665, and the cloak used during Napoleon's imperial coronation was covered in embroidered bees like the ones thought to have been present on Childeric's cape. Another rare and precious survival of Merovingian kingship is the throne of the early seventh-century ruler Dagobert I. It remained in Paris at St-Denis, the abbey established by the king, until the French Revolution, after which time it was appropriated by Napoleon. He used it when he was First Consul during the siege of Boulogne in 1802 and on the occasion when he presided over the inauguration of the order of the Legion of Honour.

Charlemagne the national hero of the French meets his match in the figure captured by the historiography of the Germans and who emerges as Kaiser Karl, their first emperor. His native tongue after all was probably a dialect of Old High German. And his major campaigns were directed towards the east, most importantly so in the case of Saxony. It has been all too easy to draw a parallel with the German emperors and generals of later centuries, and with their own *Drang nach Osten*, that striving towards the east which in their case attempted the assimilation through conquest of the Slavic peoples. My account of Charlemagne's legacy in Chapter 9, 'The Survival and Revival of Empire', stresses the degree to which the German emperors of the tenth century were inspired by his memory. The Reich that they established, later to be named the Holy Roman Empire, bore the imprint of that combination of secular and spiritual authority which had been fundamental to Charlemagne's own revival of the imperial title over a century and a half previously.

Charlemagne's contested legacy is therefore basic to the Franco-German divide which was a central issue in the politics, diplomacy and warfare of western European history until the second half of the twentieth century. But if the emperor inspired competing forms of nationalism his memory could also be used to transcend those same divisions. The original signatories to the Treaty of Rome all represented countries which had been part of the Carolingian empire, and Charlemagne was soon enrolled as the founding father of the movement which led to the eventual emergence of the European Union. Not all of this was mere propaganda mouthed by politicians keen on a self-dignifying association with a respectably antique past. Many of the palaces that provided Charlemagne with an institutional base for the imperial administration were located in an area straddling the modern boundaries of France,

Belgium and the former West Germany. This is essentially the territory of the ancient Frankish kingdom of Austrasia, and since it is also home to the European Commission based in Brussels and the European Parliament located in Strasbourg there was a real basis to the belief that western Europe was recovering its Carolingian origins in the second half of the twentieth century.

The debate about Charlemagne has therefore been well-nigh continuous from his time to ours, and the facts about his life merge imperceptibly with the many and varied interpretations of the emperor's significance. His dramatic imprint on his own time and his profound influence on subsequent generations and centuries make him the founding father of the many different kinds of Europe that have dominated the imaginative longings of those whose lives have been lived on the continent. The interpretation of Charlemagne is the very stuff of Europe's history and the subject matter of this book.

CHAPTER 1

Gods, Kings and Franks

AUTHORITY WITHIN FRANCIA

The history of 'Frank' as a word begins in the fourth century when it was used by Roman writers to describe all those people they came across to the north of the imperial frontier on the Rhine. It was therefore a foreigner's very rough and ready attempt at establishing a single convenient category, and it is very doubtful if any of these peoples actually called themselves 'Franks' during the history of the later empire. History identifies the Salians and the Ripuarians as the two predominant tribal groups among those Franks who came to settle west of the Rhine. Convenience and convention dictate that these are the Franks that matter as the ancestors of those of Charlemagne's subjects who lived in Austrasia and Neustria. But there were other groupings who were also called Franks by the Romans and whom they came across originally on the northern frontier. The Chamavi and the Batavians, the Bructeri and the Chatti survive only dimly in the historical record. But they too are among those who were still being welded together into a people by the Merovingian ruler Childeric and then by his son Clovis at the beginning of the sixth century. It was not just their name therefore which was imposed upon the Franks by the Romans. The empire's literate elite also attributed to them a sense of ethnic identity which simply was not there to begin with and had to be invented at a much later stage.

The authority of the Frankish crown extended across three regions, each of which had its own history as a subordinate kingdom: Austrasia,

Neustria and Burgundy. Austrasia or 'the eastern land' formed the north-eastern part and straddled the modern-day frontier between eastern France and the western part of Germany, while also including much of the land belonging to the contemporary Belgian and Dutch states. Metz was the major regional centre. Neustria or 'new western land' was a territory with its own distinctive identity since the early sixth century, and it extended from Aquitaine to the English Channel. Paris and Soissons were the main cities and the core territories lay between the Seine and the Loire. Burgundy was conquered by the Franks in the early sixth century and its population shared with the Franks a common origin in the Germanic culture of those 'barbarian' kingdoms which had emerged at the time of the fifth-century dissolution of Roman imperial authority in western Europe. The term 'Francia' was sometimes used towards the beginning of our period to describe Austrasia on its own, and this was the Carolingian house's original power base. But Austrasia's amalgamation with Neustria and Burgundy was one of the dynasty's great achievements, and in this book 'Francia' will be used to describe collectively these core components of the kingdom. They are thereby distinguished from the territories and countries which were subsequently conquered and assimilated within the wider Carolingian empire.

The first Carolingian to be crowned king was Charlemagne's father Pippin III (714–68) who masterminded the coup of 750–51 which removed Childeric III (r. 743–51), the last of the Merovingian rulers, from the throne of the Franks. This action relegated the dynasty and its members to subsequent obscurity. But for at least a century before then the great men of the Carolingian family in its successive generations had already been exercising the substance of royal power by occupying the office of 'mayor of the palace' in Austrasia, the job held by the kingdom's senior administrator and supreme generalissimo. In describing the relationship between the kings and their mayors a useful, if limited, analogy can sometimes be drawn with the position of constitutional rulers and their chief ministers. The history of the Franks had therefore been shaped from the late seventh century onwards by the three great mayors who were Charlemagne's direct ancestors: his great-grandfather and grandfather, Pippin II (c. 635/45–714) and Charles Martel (686–741), followed by Martel's son Pippin III. These men behaved like kings and, together with their predecessors and Charlemagne's successors, they constitute a dynasty with a continuous history.

Interpretation of Charlemagne was current right from the beginning of his reign. He enjoyed success in war and brought a new élan to the business of being a king. Contemporaries were alerted and wanted to find out more about what made him tick. Many also noticed that Charlemagne did not come out of a vacuum, and that his family had been similarly driven for over a century before him. This book is an attempt at finding some answers in that search for Charlemagne and the Carolingians. The quest begins with the early history of the Franks during the period when they were ruled by the Merovingian royal house.

Propaganda comes between us and the Merovingians. The guidelines of the official story were laid down by those ninth-century chroniclers and compilers of official annals who were beholden to the new dynasty, and these Carolingian apologists therefore presented the later Merovingian rulers as feeble figureheads who deserved their eventual fate. Later historiography followed the same line of interpretation. The influential school textbooks produced by the French Third Republic (1870–1940) delighted in satirizing the so-called *rois fainéants*, and anti-monarchical sentiment lumped the Merovingians with the Bourbons as examples of rulers who had to be got rid of in order to ensure progress and guarantee modernity. But even the later Merovingian kings were often, as we shall see, more effective than the conventional narrative allows them to have been, and even after that time their role was not always limited to the merely ceremonial and decorative aspects of power. So who were the Merovingians?

THE HISTORY OF THE MEROVINGIAN ROYAL HOUSE

Dynastic alliances established through marriage determine the facts of power, or who can do what to whom, in all societies governed by aristocrats. That principle was particularly at work in western Europe in the early Middle Ages, and it contributed to an unusual fluidity in the dispersal of power. Boundaries between different kingdoms and provinces had yet to emerge in anything like the relatively fixed form of later centuries. Aristocratic hegemony prevailed, however, right across western Europe, and new patterns of power could therefore emerge fairly suddenly as a result of the alliances established by marriages whose arrangements indicated a convergence between powerful nobles, their interests and ambitions. Family relationships are therefore basic to an understanding of this period, although it is important not to interpret that fact in too mechanical a way, and the genealogical zeal displayed by some historians in recent years runs the risk of missing the wood for the family trees. Not everything in life can be reduced to the fact of a shared lineage, even in early medieval Europe. In what follows I shall concentrate on the essentials.

Clovis I (c. 466–511) was the effective founder of the Merovingian dynasty, and he belonged to the particular tribe of the Franks known as the Salians. His father was Childeric I (c. 440–c. 481), who ruled the Salian Franks from his capital at Tournai, and whose paternity was ascribed by the Frankish chroniclers to Merovech, a semi-legendary figure of the early fifth century who gave his name to the Merovingian dynasty. After conquering the neighbouring Frankish tribes who, like the Salians, were established along what is now the French–Belgian border, he became the first Frankish king to unite all of the Franks under one ruler. He also converted to Christianity, and absorbed into his kingdom almost the entire region comprising the ancient Roman region of Gaul. The subsequent history of his kingdom and of the Merovingian dynasty was, however, one of division since the rights of succession to the kingdom of the Franks were governed by the principle of partible inheritance. A king's male heirs succeeded on his death to the lands they were allocated and which they ruled as kings in their own right. Partible inheritance was designed to promote a system of collective Frankish leadership, with the rulers of the individual kingdoms or sub-regna upholding the collective unity of the regnum – the kingdom of Francia – as a whole. On occasions the sub-regna might coalesce under the leadership of one king. But partible inheritance was a tricky system to operate, and during the Merovingian period in particular it often promoted disunity rather than a kingly consensus, as the story of Clovis's four sons illustrates. Their centres of power and capitals were concentrated in and around north-eastern Gaul, the area which was the real Frankish heartland. Reims was the capital of Theuderic I (c. 485–533/4) and Chlodomer (c. 495-524) ruled in Orléans which also became the centre from which the kingdom of Burgundy was governed. Childebert I (c. 496–558) reigned in Paris and Chlothar I (c. 497–561) in Soissons.

Chlodomer, however, died young and his lands were then divided among his brothers. Theuderic died in 534 and was succeeded by his son Theudebert I (c. 500–547/8) who proved to be a highly effective ruler whose expansionist policies enabled him to exercise suzerainty over lands in northern Italy and within what is now Austria and Bavaria. Theudebert's death led to his kingdom being allocated to his uncle Chlothar who, after the death of Childebert in 558, reigned alone as king of the Franks.

The period of recovered unity in Francia was, however, brief and when Chlothar I died in 561 the kingdom was divided between his four sons. A series of internecine Frankish conflicts ensued in the decades that followed, with the brothers and their heirs pursuing their ambitions and vendettas at each other's expense. These wars preoccupied the Merovingian kings and the ruling elite for the best part of half a century and it was during this period that the three kingdoms of Austrasia, Neustria and Burgundy started to emerge as distinctive units within Francia.

Charibert I (c. 517–67) had inherited the kingdom centred on Paris and his influence extended across to western Gaul, while Guntram (c. 532–92) ruled Burgundy and adjacent territories to the west from his base in Orléans. Sigebert I (c. 535–c. 575) was the ruler of the north-eastern territories which were now being identified as those of Austrasia, with Reims and Metz as its chief centres. Both he and Guntram were also allocated lands in Aquitaine. Chilperic I (c. 539–84) was the youngest son, and his kingdom at Soissons, although the smallest, provided the nucleus for the subsequent development of Neustria. He was a significant beneficiary on the death of Charibert in 567 since Chilperic inherited his brother's lands in western Gaul.

THE MEROVINGIAN BLOOD FEUD: CAUSES AND CONSEQUENCES

The family feud that plunged these sub-regna into wars had its origins in a royal murder. Galswintha was Chilperic's queen but he also had a mistress named Fredegunda. The king was involved in his wife's murder in 568 following which Fredegunda, a former serving girl, sat on the throne of Neustria as Chilperic's consort. Brunhilda (c. 543–613) was the sister of Galswintha and since she was also Sigebert's queen she used her influence to avenge the murder by instigating a series of wars between Austrasia and Neustria.

Fredegunda's social origins might have been lowly but she soon showed her mastery of some of the bloodier techniques used by Frankish sovereigns in order to attain and retain their thrones. Her hand has been detected in the assassination of Sigebert I in 575, and she also plotted to murder both Brunhilda and the queen's young son who now reigned in Austrasia as Childebert II (570–95). The long period of Brunhilda's regency had now begun and she proved to be a resolute and skilful defender of her interests and those of her child. The alliance she formed with Guntram meant that he pledged himself to protect Childebert II, and when Guntram died in 592 Childebert succeeded him as Burgundy's king. Fredegunda had in the meantime been ruling in Neustria as regent following the death of her husband Chilperic I in 584. Their child, who would reign as Chlothar II (584–629), was not yet born when his father died, and the period of Fredegunda's regency lasted for thirteen years until her own death in 597.

Brunhilda's implacable hatred for her enemies continued to wreak its destructive effects long after the death of Fredegunda. Her son Childebert II died in 595, and the king's sons divided his lands according to the principle of partible inheritance: Theudebert II (595–612) took the bulk of Austrasia and Theuderic II (587–613) inherited Burgundy. They were also heirs to the lands in Aquitaine which Childebert had inherited both as the son of Sigebert I and as Guntram's beneficiary, and these territories too were divided between the two brothers. Their goal was to deprive their cousin Chlothar II of his throne, and they enjoyed substantial success in the military campaigns they waged to secure that end.

By 599 the brothers had conquered most of the Neustrian kingdom though they failed to capture their cousin. It was at this point, however, that they turned against each other, and here again the influence of their grandmother Brunhilda was detectable. Theudebert had forced her to leave his court and Brunhilda sought revenge by allying herself with Theuderic who was now plotting against his brother. The quarrel became fratricidal, and in 612 Theuderic killed Theudebert. As a result the expansive royal domain which had been ruled by their father Childebert II was once again ruled by one king. But Theuderic had barely a year to savour the fruits of his success in Austrasia, and in 613 he died while preparing a new campaign against Chlothar.

Theuderic's son and heir Sigebert II (601–13) was barely two years old when his father died, and Brunhilda exercised the powers of regent on behalf of her great-grandson. It is at this stage in Francia's history that an ancestor of Charlemagne first appears. Pippin I (c. 580–640) was one of the great magnates of Austrasia and his career as the kingdom's mayor of the palace provides the earliest examples of the family drive and ambition. In 613 the leading aristocrats of Austrasia and Burgundy decided to abandon their support of Brunhilda. They turned instead to Chlothar II of Neustria and recognized him as the boy-king's regent and guardian. Sigebert was killed in the ensuing hostilities and Brunhilda, then about seventy years old, was captured by her enemies. A history of the Franks written just over a century later describes her as having been tied to the feet of wild horses and then torn limb from limb. This may be gleeful, and retrospective, wish-fulfilment on the part of the chroniclers, but there is little doubt that Brunhilda was killed and that the manner of her death displayed a typically Frankish delight in vengeance. Chlothar II had been faithful to the memory of his mother Fredegunda and pursued her foe Brunhilda to the grave. The Merovingian blood feud had ended.

Chlothar II re-established a degree of Frankish unity which was based on the Neustrian centre in Paris and extended to all three kingdoms. He appointed his son Dagobert I (603–39) to rule in Austrasia. After Dagobert himself succeeded to the Merovingian throne (629–39) he sent in turn his own son Sigebert III (630–56) to govern the Austrasians. Pippin I was central to these developments. He had to wait some ten years before being rewarded by Chlothar but the honour when it came was a great one. In 623 he was appointed mayor of the palace in Austrasia, and at the same time Pippin's close friend and political ally Arnulf of Metz (582–640), that see's bishop, became an adviser to young Dagobert I. Six years of high office and influence followed until, in 629, Pippin left the court and retired to his estates for a decade. This is unlikely to have been a voluntary act since resigning an honour and giving up on power were not the kind of thing that Carolingians did off their own bat. Nonetheless, after this prolonged hiccup Pippin was back on the scene as mayor in the very last year of his life (639–40) and at a time when Sigebert III was still ruling in Austrasia.

Sigebert's brother Clovis II (637–58) had now become the Merovingian king of Neustria and Burgundy, with his stepmother Nanthild ruling as regent on his behalf. The period of a king's minority often saw plotting and counter-plotting in early medieval courts, and it was this time of Neustrian weakness which was exploited by the next bearer of the Carolingian power gene. Grimoald (616–56) was the son of Pippin I and there is every indication that he was an unusually persuasive and forceful character. He is said to have saved the life of Sigebert III during a major revolt of the Thuringians, a Germanic people who were the Franks' neighbours and had been dominated by them since the early sixth century. The king certainly seems to have fallen under Grimoald's influence. Sigebert was initially childless and he was persuaded to adopt Childebert, Grimoald's son, as his own. The eventual arrival of an heir, in the form of the future Dagobert II, seems not to have changed the pecking order, and the unfortunate child was sent out of the kingdom. His place of exile is uncertain – an Irish monastery and the cathedral school at Poitiers are both possible locations – and Dagobert would resurface in the Merovingian story in 676 when he returned from exile to enjoy three brief years as a monarch in Austrasia before being murdered.

When Sigebert died in 656 Grimoald acted quickly and placed his son, 'Childebert the Adopted', on the Austrasian throne. He had failed, however, to take into account the reaction of Clovis II, now an adult ruler and bent on Merovingian revenge. Clovis marched into Austrasia and, according to one version of events, in 657 seized and murdered both the usurper and the scheming father. Another account claims that Austrasia was annexed in 661, and that both Childebert and Grimoald were executed at about that time. By then Clovis's eldest son and successor Chlothar III (652–73) was sitting on the Merovingian throne. Whichever narrative is true, it is certain that by this stage Neustria had gained the upper hand.

Grimoald's story matters, and in two ways. It gives us the earliest example of an ancestor of Charlemagne having family designs on a throne and not being too fussy about Merovingian sensitivities. And his story left its mark on later Frankish history and consciousness. Childebert might have been 'the usurper' but the *Liber Historiae Francorum*, compiled in c. 727, gives a noticeably dusty account of Clovis II's reign and that of his son Chlothar. Clovis is said to have 'brought ruin to the kingdom of the Franks . . . He was a seducer and a debaser of women, a glutton and a drunk.' Was Clovis therefore a *roi fainéant*? Those who were in charge of writing up Frankish history in the 720s certainly presented him as such. And yet Clovis was clearly vigorous enough to be involved somehow in the restoration of Neustrian influence in Austrasia, regardless of whether or not he actually killed Grimoald and Childebert. But by the time the *Liber* was being written Charlemagne's direct ancestors were running the show, and the reputation of Clovis II suffered accordingly. Grimoald was after all one of the family. And this was a dynasty which was determined to control the past as well as the present.

HOW THE CAROLINGIANS ROSE TO POWER

Real Carolingian glory starts with Pippin II (635/45–714), sometimes known as Pippin of Herstal. He was the son of Begga, the daughter of Pippin I, and of Ansegisel, whose father was Pippin I's colleague Arnulf. Pippin II was therefore the product of a union arranged between two great interest groups, and his ancestry carried with it a fair bit of baggage. His father Ansegisel was the brother-in-law of Grimoald and probably involved in the plot that had put 'Childebert the Adopted' briefly on the throne in Austrasia. Ansegisel may have paid the price and was certainly assassinated at about the time Neustrian forces re-established themselves there. Blood would have blood here, in time.

9

History records Pippin II as the supreme commander of Austrasia and its mayor of the palace. He was also astonishingly long-lived: Pippin's survival into probably his early seventies, and possibly for a few years longer, was quite a record in a society which regarded forty-somethings as venerable. His great-grandson Charlemagne must have inherited the same tough constitution since he enjoyed exceptional health throughout his life and remained a physically active ruler in his mid sixties. A good deal had happened in Pippin II's life. He had searched out and killed his father's assassin who is named as Godoin, a Merovingian hit man, and that retaliation singled out Pippin II as a man with leadership potential so far as Frankish mores were concerned. He is celebrated in the family chronicle, and in the history of the Franks, as the victor of the battle of Tertry in 687 which settled the contest for predominance between Neustria and Austrasia. Pippin led his forces into battle against Neustria whose king, Theuderic III (c. 650–91), was nominally king of all the Franks at that time, and the Austrasian victory confirmed Pippin's authority.

Theuderic had his own mayor of the palace and that position was held by the very ambitious Ebroin, until his assassination in 681, and then by Berthar. Pippin II forced the resignation of Berthar, and he then became mayor in all the three Frankish kingdoms of Austrasia, Neustria and Burgundy. He allowed Theuderic III to continue to rule as king with what an obliging annalist calls 'unimaginable faithfulness . . . lest he should seem to exercise tyranny or cruelty. But he retained the right to judge cases in the placitum [the judicial court], the governance of the whole kingdom, the royal treasure and the command of all the army.' In other words he had everything except the title of king. Charles Martel, his son, would make much the same concession to Chilperic II (c. 672–720) after his battle success of 718. There were two other sons, one of whom was called Grimoald II. Names are never just names in Carolingian history. They are indicators of policy and a record of solidarity. And the baptism of this particular Grimoald affirmed the continuing ambition of those who stood in the lineage of a turbulent forebear. Pippin II would eventually send Grimoald to Neustria to serve as mayor, and another son, Drogo, performed the same role in Burgundy. Both sons were in effect his viceroys. Berthar had now fled the kingdom and his wife Anstrude decided to throw in her lot with the conquerors. In an astute move she opted to marry Drogo.

We shall often see in this book just how important royal and aristocratic women could be as power-brokers. They were the educators of their children, and that instruction included transmission of the family history, its patterns of loyalty, victory and revenge. That was an important role in a society so heavily influenced by genealogy, and it could lead to power itself. Pippin II's mother Begga, for example, had adapted swiftly after the assassination of her husband Ansegisel. She is thought to have taught her son how to govern and is described as helping him subsequently to run the kingdom. She may well have been some kind of regent for a while. Plectrude, Pippin II's first wife, was another powerful and determined aristocratic woman, well versed in politics and not afraid to protect her interests. She was the mother of Drogo and Grimoald II, both of whom predeceased their father, and Plectrude may well have wished to rule the kingdom herself thereafter through Grimoald's very young son Theudoald. She therefore apparently persuaded Pippin II to disinherit his surviving, and illegitimate, son. This was a plan as unwise as it was bold since that son was Charles 'Martel', the dominating figure of the age as Austrasian mayor of the palace, and whose nickname, 'The Hammer', had been gained on the field of battle.

After a brief civil war Martel gained victory in 718, and he then ruled an undivided kingdom, with Chilperic II being allowed to continue on the throne. When a later Merovingian king, Theuderic IV, died in 737 Martel did not even bother to find a royal successor and left the throne empty. He himself died in 741, and two years later Martel's sons and heirs Carloman and Pippin III, mayors of the palace in Austrasia and Neustria respectively, placed Childeric III (743–51) on the throne. A Merovingian king still seems to have been useful to them, therefore, at this stage in their careers despite Childeric's irrelevance to their own power base.

There are some murky features to the politics of the 740s which culminate in Carloman's decision to retire to a monastery in 747 and leave his brother in sole charge. To these we shall return. It is enough to note here that Carloman and Pippin III had a half-brother called Grifo who was Martel's son by his second marriage. Martel may well have wanted all three sons to rule in some form of condominium but Grifo found himself imprisoned in a monastery by his brothers. At about the time of Carloman's withdrawal from public life Grifo escaped to Bavaria and he may have tried to take over the duchy. This was an opportunity for Pippin to assert himself. Duke Odilo of Bavaria died in January 748 (or in late 747) and his infant heir Tassilo III, having been installed by Pippin, reigned under a form of Frankish overlordship. Forty years later Charlemagne would initiate the duchy's complete assimilation within the Carolingian empire, but it is important to note how Pippin III had already shown the kind of ambitious territorial expansionism which would typify the reign of his son Charlemagne.

Christianization through conquest was another dynastic goal which was evident long before Charlemagne. Pippin II's conquest of Frisia had opened up the area to Christian missionaries such as the Northumbrian Willibrord who was given permission to preach in the region and allowed to establish an episcopal see in Utrecht. The early Carolingians' relationship with the English missionary Boniface was a particularly close one. In 723 Charles Martel took Boniface under his formal protection and in a letter written sometime in 742–6 Boniface says that he could not have done his work without Martel's support and the fear he inspired. The fluid situation immediately after Martel's death must have worried Boniface since he wrote to Grifo and asked for an assurance that support would continue for his work in the mission field in Thuringia. Church–State co-operation was fundamental to the Carolingian cultural renaissance as well as to the conversion of the pagans, and this power axis also achieves an early anticipation when, in 742–3, a Concilium Germanicum was held and presided over by Boniface and Carloman.

Carloman and Pippin III were being referred to as *principes* in the 740s, long before the formal deposition of the Merovingians in 750–51, and they displayed few scruples in the pursuit of their ambitions. Amiability was never a Carolingian characteristic, as this sketch has perhaps demonstrated, and right from the outset of the dynasty's history the lives of its members display a ferocious intensity in the search for power and position. The transmission of that ambition from one generation to the next culminated in the achievements of Charlemagne. Boniface was praising Martel's memory when he described his ability to frighten people, and that characteristic takes us right to the heart of what was involved in being a really successful ruler in early medieval Europe. The *furor* these men displayed was no mere bout of bad temper but a technique which was integral to their method of government and personal survival. Their contemporaries viewed the capacity to strike a precisely calculated terror into the hearts of others as an entirely positive attribute in a king, and rulers who knew how to be terrifying were highly regarded for that reason. Carolingians more than qualified on that score. But power, if it was to be exercised really effectively, still needed to be justified and somehow made to appear legitimate. Anger was a necessary skill when it came to securing the obedience of subjects but royal power in the kingdom of the Franks was also surrounded by a sense of the sacred. These monarchs did not rule just because they were experts in violence and frightening behaviour. The obedience they elicited was also awestruck, since the Franks were convinced that a sacred power upheld and endorsed the authority exercised by their kings. How therefore did this idea of the holy come to make its appearance, not just in Francia but in other early medieval kingdoms as well?

IMPERIAL DISSOLUTION AND CHRISTIAN CONSOLATION

One of the great issues of this period is the way in which Christianity, a religion whose original principles inclined to pacifism and quietism, was assimilated by the warrior ethic of a militarized aristocracy. Christianization and militarization are the two pre-eminent and distinguishing features of European society in the second half of the first millennium, the one marching hand in hand with the other. This in part is the story of the legacy of the emperor Constantine whose acceptance of the new religion encouraged its diffusion among the ruling orders of later Roman imperial society. Christianity ceased therefore to be an underground movement and lost much of its original dissenting edge when it was adopted by those who ruled. Frankish justifications of power built on that particular legacy. But kings of the Franks were considered to be sacred for some time before Clovis's conversion to Christianity. 'Sacral kingship' was in its origins a pagan belief which had enjoyed currency not just in Francia but in most of the other barbarian kingdoms that emerged in the wake of the Roman empire's dissolution in western Europe. The vogue for kingship in the early medieval west therefore saw an originally pagan custom being adopted by a Christianized society, and the holy power of kingly warriors would also be upheld by arguments derived from classical culture. A consensus about why kings should be obeyed was thereby created. Charlemagne and the Carolingians were the beneficiaries of that new orthodoxy which would be used thereafter to sanctify and justify the power of monarchs in medieval and early modern Europe. But this new style of Christian kingship and its conviction that it ruled by a divine dispensation were in fact surprising developments so far as western Europe was concerned. We need to capture a sense of just how unusual this must have seemed originally, and in order to do so we travel first of all to the north Africa of the early fifth century where a bishop is writing a book.

Sometime during the year 413 Aurelius Augustinus, bishop of Hippo Regius in the Roman province of north Africa, started to write *De Civitate Dei contra Paganos*, the masterpiece which would occupy his few leisure hours during the next thirteen years. The immediate background to the composition of *The City of God* and its attack on paganism was the sack of the city of Rome by the Germanic tribe of the Visigoths in 410, an event which had encouraged some vigorous polemicism on the part of orthodox pagans who blamed Christianity for that disaster. Rome as both republic and empire had flourished – so went the critique – during the centuries when her citizens and subjects had been loyal to the old gods, and, according to the resentful propagandists, it was the failure to worship those divinities which explained the empire's enfeebled condition in the early fifth century.

Christianization had spread rapidly among the Roman governing elites in the fourth century in the wake of the emperor Constantine's decision to privilege the new faith. The Edict of Milan (313) granted toleration to Christians and restored property which had been confiscated from them during the period of persecution under the emperor Diocletian. Further legislation outlawed the murder of slaves and abolished crucifixion as a punishment. Saints' days were officially recognized and in 321 Sunday work was forbidden by law. The emperor's personal donations to the Christian Church were on a lavish scale but it was the privileges granted to the Christian clergy which struck the severest blow against the position enjoyed by pagan religion as an endorser of public-spiritedness and civic-minded solidarity.

The notion of an esprit de corps sustained and protected by the old rites had been transplanted from the city-states of classical Greece to the Roman republic, and its communal impulses continued to sanctify the cause of the *patria* as it evolved into an imperial power. The traditional religion of the Romans had of course been used to express private hopes as well as to further public policy, and the very wide range of gods included within its pantheon offered their individually appropriate expertise when it came to the resolution of human difficulties. Those who worshipped and brought their sacrifices to the pagan temples and altars were impelled to do so by reasons which might range from the wish for a successful harvest or a delivery from sickness to the need for a victory in the law courts or in battle at the expense of an opponent who might also have made a sacrifice to a favourite divinity in order to gain his own advantage. The notion that an appropriate sacrifice could produce a tangible benefit to the worshipper by, as it were, return of post would be castigated by Christian apologists as a materialist view of religion. It certainly presupposed that the gods were open to persuasion and that they were quite as jealous in temperament and prone to partiality as the humans who approached them for individual favours. Roman piety was therefore used to justify aspirations and consequences which varied widely and often contradicted one another.

Nonetheless, taken as a whole, the old religion with its structure of temples, priestly networks and ancestrally approved ways of offering sacrifice and expressing praise did hang together. The pantheon embraced its own contradictions, including the gods' family quarrels, to become a necessary part of the whole Roman social fabric as well as constituting a fundamental feature of the society's collective mentality. The rejection of pagan religion *tout court* first by the Jews and then by the Christians marked them out as profoundly un-Roman, not least because they were dismissing religious attitudes which were as typical of the illiterate masses as they were of the governing elites. Their refusal in particular to bend the knee to emperor worship and their rejection of that cult as a particularly ludicrous form of religious decadence showed just how detached the Jews and Christians were from the society in which they found themselves. The idea that humans might be gods provided Jewish satire with some of its earliest and best jokes.

As a result of Constantine's new dispensation those who had previously refused to play by the team rules of a social religion now found themselves accommodated, recognized and legitimized within a fast-evolving Christian society. Financial and legal privileges were extended to the Christian clergy and they were also freed from having to perform civic duties. Constantine did not make Christianity the official faith of his empire and neither did he outlaw pagan religion, preferring – and hoping – that the ancient practices would simply wither away as a result of neglect. But the scale of the immunities enjoyed by the Christians was equivalent to a series of opt-out clauses in the name of conscience, and these concessions to private judgment amounted in effect to the creation of a new religious establishment.

Discontented pagans still attached to the old ways therefore turned to this comparatively recent apostasy in order to explain what might be presented as an equally novel phenomenon – the indifference of the old gods to the fate of the empire and their refusal to lift so much as a single divine finger to protect the city of Rome against the Visigoths. Rome herself might be in the process of becoming a more provincial place – and especially so after Constantine's decision to remove the imperial capital to Constantinople. Both the economic currents and the intellectual life of the empire were moving east – to the great centres of Alexandria and Aleppo, to Antioch and Damascus as well as to Constantinople itself, a city built in a hurry and the façades of whose churches and palaces often concealed some shoddy workmanship as a result. This was the great age of the Christian city in the region that would later be termed the 'Middle East' and before the impact on that area of expansionist Arab armies and Islamic mission from the mid-seventh century onwards. But despite this eastward shift of power the original city of the seven hills by the banks of the Tiber remained a powerful symbol of the imperial and Roman past. Its fate was a question of consequence in a traditionalist society which equated antiquity with wisdom and in which innovation therefore had to be presented as continuity if it was to stand any chance of being accepted. The events of 410 had to be explained, and not least to Christians whose self-confidence had taken a beating since their identification with the cause of the later Roman empire was so profound.

BARBARIAN ARRIVALS

Shortly after Augustine had finished writing his book there was a further Germanic incursion on imperial territory, and one which affected the bishop directly since the tribe known as the Vandals had now moved across the straits of Gibraltar after a brief period of settlement in southern Spain, and arrived in north Africa. The initial Vandal wave of invasion into Spain had occurred in 407–9, and the first response of the Roman state was to employ them as officially recognized *foederati* – a military and mercenary force which could be used to help maintain imperial order on the furthermost boundaries. Ostrogoths, Visigoths and Franks were among the many other German tribes who had played a similar role at various times during this period of protracted imperial decline. Repenting rapidly of their Vandal association, the Romans then turned to the Visigoths who were themselves enrolled as federated allies and given land in Gallia Aquitania, the province which became their base for an anti-Vandal campaign. The decision to settle the Visigoths in the region had a serious long-term consequence – the emergence of an independent Visigothic kingdom of Toulouse, an entity which embraced Spain, Aquitaine and Gallia Narbonensis (modern-day Provence). The victory of Clovis's Frankish army at the battle of Vouillé in 507 detached Aquitaine from the control of the Visigothic crown and, apart from its retention across the Pyrenees of a Narbonne-centred strip of coastal territory (Septimania), the successor kingdom of Toledo was confined to its Iberian base. Nonetheless, it hung on until 711 when the kingdom fell to the advancing Arab forces.

It was the vagaries of another opportunistic strategy on the part of an insecure Roman colonialism which had given the Vandals their chance in north Africa. Boniface, the area's Roman governor, had invited them to cross the frontier in 429 in order to protect his position, since he thought the ruling imperial family of the west regarded him with suspicion. As soon as he believed himself restored to favour Boniface repented of his Vandal initiative but by then it was too late to turn back the tide.

By the spring of 430 the now hostile invaders had advanced to the walls of Hippo Regius which, after Carthage, was the second most important city of the Roman diocese of Africa, and it was during the subsequent siege of just over a year that Augustine died on 28 August. Carthage itself fell to the Vandals in 439 and the independent kingdom that they went on to establish in north Africa lasted for almost a century until the forces led by General Belisarius re-established Byzantine imperial control in 534. The military thrust which was directed from Constantinople in the early sixth century enjoyed astonishing success on its campaign by both sea and land in order to recover the empire's western territories. But the fifth-century dissolution of Roman authority in those regions had been so profound that it proved beyond Constantinople's capacity to maintain its campaign in the long term, and the Vandals' economic impact on Italy was especially calamitous. Both Rome and the peninsula were more or less totally dependent on north African grain imports in order to secure supplies of bread, a commodity whose scarcity could always be relied upon to produce urban tension and political instability. Having developed rapidly into a resourceful maritime power, and thereby incorporated Sardinia as well as Corsica within their kingdom, the Vandals were able to cut off exports of north African grain supplies across the central Mediterranean trade routes. It is that economic blockade and its calamitous consequences which explain the bitterness of the Roman polemic against the Vandals in the surviving sources and which has ensured the tribe's subsequent reputation for senseless destruction – although in fact, just like other Germanic tribes, they could be adept at establishing co-existence, albeit on their own terms, with the conquered native population.

THE APPEAL OF ARIAN CHRISTIANITY

For a Catholic Christian such as Augustine there was, however, one crucial fact about the Vandals which did justify the view of them as barbaric outsiders, a species of enemy who could not possibly be accommodated within the late Roman empire's religious and political settlement. The strength of the Vandals' attachment to Arianism made them Christians but of a type deemed to be particularly heretical by the Catholic orthodoxy which had attained its most luminous definition in the writings of Hippo's bishop. Arianism took its name from the teachings of Arius (250–336), a Greek theologian who spent most of his life in Alexandria – a city notorious for the vigour and street violence of its religious disputes. This was the single most powerful form of early Christian dissidence and the Church establishment – starting with Constantine presiding in his imperial role over the council specially convened at Nicaea in 325 – found it next to impossible to get rid of Arianism permanently within its own ranks.

North African Christianity had always been notable for its passion, as Augustine's own writings demonstrate. The myth of Dido, Queen of Carthage, enjoyed prestige in the region long before Virgil gave it literary expression in the *Aeneid* with his description of her all-consuming and ultimately suicidal desire for the wanderer Aeneas. And a similar kind of intensity at the level of both the heart and the mind marked the quarrels between the followers of Arius and his opponents – disputes which claimed the lives of many as they spread from Alexandria in Egypt across the Maghreb to the west as well as to the Levantine shores in the east. But many Germanic tribesmen, or at the very least their leaders, also claimed to be inspired by Arianism and its picture of the relation between God, Christ and humanity. At a technical level Arianism stood for the rejection of the idea that Christ the Son was 'of one substance' with God the Father – a formula hammered out during the discussions at Nicaea. But in the Arian view God was unique, infinite and self-contained. His nature was not to be confused with that of Christ, a human figure who, precisely because he was God's son, must have been created within time and was therefore finite.

Wulfila, consecrated in 341 as a bishop of the Gothic Christians by Eusebius of Nicomedia, bishop of Constantinople, is a key figure in the history of early north European Christianity. He shared Eusebius's Arianism and preached its doctrines during the 340s as a missionary to the Goths who were settled north of the Danube. Any discussion of exactly why Arian Christianity had such an impact on the Germanic tribes is bound to be speculative. Perhaps this picture of an awesomely unique God so clearly defined beyond the apex of all other hierarchies appealed to warrior societies and their chains of command. This was God as the supreme chieftain. But there was another aspect to Arianism which might also have made sense in a barbarian context. Although considering Christ to be human and therefore separated from God's nature, Arians also thought that he was a true Son of God and should certainly be worshipped as such. Catholic orthodoxy shuddered at the introduction of this frame of reference. Did not this turn Christ into a kind of subordinate god rather than part of the real thing? Was this not tantamount to the return of polytheism? But if that was really so it may have been exactly why Arianism appealed to tribes who were only a few generations away from the worship of the Teutonic gods in all their diversity.

Whatever the reason for its popularity, Arianism certainly struck a deep Germanic chord and one which carried on resonating for a very long time. The Visigoths who were settled in Spain remained attached to the creed until the conversion to Catholicism of their king Reccared. The third Council of Toledo, held in 589, was the official moment at which the Visigothic nobility of Spain decided to follow their king's example and renounce Arianism, a heresy which defined the colonial ruling elite and had served a social purpose by distinguishing that caste from its mostly Catholic subjects. In north Africa the Vandals stuck to their chosen faith and their kingdom witnessed regular waves of officially approved persecution. Catholic laymen were excluded from public office and their priests subjected to a variety of punishments including exile, deposition and murder.

AUGUSTINE OFFERS AN ANSWER

Cultural confusion, political chaos and personal danger: Augustine had to explain the emergence of these threats after the collapse of a social order which had once enabled human beings to find their way in the world, to plan for the future and prepare for the hereafter. In doing so he turned to the idea of the city – an analogy which formed part of the mental furniture of any educated person in the culture of late antiquity.

It was also a picture which made sense to the less educated whose daily lives were so often framed by the physical walls which defined city existence.

The *civitas terrena* and the *civitas dei* that Augustine describes in *The City of God* stand for two kinds of human experience which may overlap with each other in the course of a lifetime but are nonetheless entirely different in content, aspiration and impact. The earthly city is the domain of power politics in the world as we experience it in the here and now. It is concerned with relationships of command and obedience, the injunctions of law and the decrees of governors. Augustine draws on his experience of the later empire when describing this earthly city. But his aim is broader since he is also offering a typology of power – a characterization of the impulses which lie behind all governments as they try to bring order to human affairs. Subjects and citizens, he says, are necessarily constrained by the earthly city and have to obey its commands. But the Christians for whom Augustine is writing are also afforded occasional visionary glimpses of another kind of city – the one which is their true home.

The *civitas dei* can never be realized in this life and although a Catholic and sacramental Church can lead to the heavenly city it is not its equivalent. Force, punishment and law: these are the necessary hallmarks of the earthly city's power arrangements. But the city of God described by Augustine exists at the level of a tantalizing ideal which seizes the heart and the imagination. Once experienced, however fugitively, it redirects a whole life and turns Christians into pilgrims – the *peregrini* who recur in his pages. From now on they are travelling through a landscape of earthly power which they have to recognize but from which they are also detached since they know its inherent limitations. This disenchanted analysis set out to undermine the pretensions of even the greatest governments and rulers. What are all states in essence, asks Augustine in one of his most striking phrases, but *magna latrocinia* – great bands of robbers? The allusion would have struck home with early fifth-century north Africans who had suffered their own experiences at the hands of such criminals. But Augustine's ambitions extended further than a mere description of the disorder in his own native region.

The idea that the state existed in order to administer justice had been a commonplace of classical antiquity ever since the writings of Plato and Aristotle had inaugurated that particular trend in political thought. Cicero's idealization of the virtues of a *res publica* had revived the tradition in the dying years of the old Roman republic. Constantine's transformation of the empire had pressed these old ideas into new service and put a Christian gloss on them. The *Church History* written by Eusebius of Caesarea (c. 265–340), the bishop who was a member of Constantine's inner circle, sees the close association between Church and empire as Christianity's natural evolution – a development ordained by providence and one which served the common good. Augustine, by contrast, writing a century later than Eusebius, rejects this view of power as mere wishful thinking and is as dismissive of the idea of an official Christian government as he is of the classical city-state or empire with its claim to represent an even-handed justice. From his perspective there was therefore nothing surprising in the fact of the early fifth-century collapse since this was the necessary fate of all such power arrangements. Force was their raison d'être and was therefore bound to be their nemesis as well. Talk of the state as the guarantor of justice, whether indulged in by Christian apologists or their pagan equivalents, was either self-delusion or unedifying propaganda.

The City of God made sense to a world adrift, one in which paradise was forever postponed, but its insights continued to influence thought and action during the early medieval centuries of recovery, a period when the imperial and Roman heritage assumed new forms. Its dramatic picture of the contrast between this world and the next, of the tension between human impulses and divine intent, mattered especially in western Europe, a region where ecclesiastical and secular rulers would clash repeatedly and violently on the issue of their respective rights and powers. In the making of that world there was one Germanic tribe, once pagan and subsequently Christianized, which mattered above all others. It is therefore to the distinctive history of the *gens Francorum* that we must now return.

THE FRANKS: RECOMMENDED BY GOD

By the middle of the eighth century Frankish kings, courtiers and churchmen were asserting that the people or *gens* to which they belonged enjoyed a special place in the divine dispensation. The Franks had been chosen by God and that divine endorsement was surely illustrated by their political successes and military victories. Theirs was an imperial and providential destiny and it was therefore the Franks who were the true heirs of ancient Rome. Charlemagne's achievements constitute the apex of that Frankish success story and his biographer Einhard claims that Charlemagne's favourite reading was *The City of God*, a book whose hostility to paganism matched the king's own. The series of wars (772–804) that Charlemagne directed against the Saxons were the first example since the Romans' Carthaginian campaign of a European power attaining colonial dominance by ethnic cleansing and mass extermination. The brutality shocked Charlemagne's contemporaries and the savagery was a consequence of the desire to convert the Saxons from their native religion. But Augustine's rejection of the idea that any dynasty or prince, state or empire can claim to be an adequate Christian power finds no echo in Charlemagne's view of his role. The same is true of his predecessors and successors in the lineage of Carolingian rulers. Here it is the differences from Augustine that matter.

The frescoes that decorated the walls of the throne room at Ingelheim, the palace built by the Carolingians near the river Rhine and on what had been the Romans' northernmost frontier, survive in the description of them by a court poet writing during the reign of Charlemagne's son and successor, Louis the Pious. A sequence of paintings represented first the biblical heroes followed by those of classical antiquity and succeeded in turn by the Romans' Christian emperors. Then came the glories to which the Franks had been led by the Carolingians. Charles Martel was portrayed at his moment of victory over the pagan Frisians and his son Pippin III was to be seen defeating the Aquitainians. Charlemagne himself was painted securing the defeat and conversion of the Saxons. This triumphalist imagery demonstrated the Carolingians' religious and imperial sense of mission – an enterprise which enabled them to lay claim to the past as well as the present. The historical process into which they had inserted themselves was presented as a dynamic, dramatic and purposeful force. It consisted of a series of divine disclosures which granted victories to some and ensured defeats for others. These were the prophetic anticipations of Frankish dominion and of the Carolingian dynasty's privileged role as an agent of the divine intent.

This Frankish self-assurance would have been evident in all the other Carolingian palaces as well, at sites such as Paderborn and Quiercy, Frankfurt and Aachen. These palaces were built to impress and their visual impact contributed to their effectiveness as regional power centres. In their earlier warrior history the Frankish aristocracy's face-to-face encounters with their kings had been largely restricted to periods of military campaigning. The new palaces, however, enabled the aristocracy to regularly congregate around the king, to play their part in the rituals of a more established and less itinerant type of court life, and to consolidate thereby the Carolingian might. This dynastic concentration of political and military power, allied with an immense cultural and religious self-confidence, is the dominant fact in the history of eighth-century Europe. Augustinian pessimism about the possibility of a Christian civilization was swept away and in its place came *renovatio*. This was the term used by the Carolingians themselves, their chroniclers and poets, soldiers, courtiers and priests, in order to define the dynasty's achievements and aspirations. It was a world restored, one which saw itself as a continuation of Constantine's legacy. But this was also a forward-looking process, and the Franks' sense of their own exceptional destiny had been obvious ever since their evolution from pagan tribe to Christian nation.

THE SIGNIFICANCE OF CHILDERIC'S GRAVE

In c. 481 the body of Childeric, king of the Merovingian dynasty and ruler of the Franks, was interred in a grave at Tournai in what is now Belgium. It was probably Clovis, Childeric's son and heir, who supervised the burial, and its lavish nature would have been intended as an assertion of dynastic legitimacy as well as a demonstration of the dead chieftain's personal prowess. The grave was discovered in 1653, and the magnificence of the objects uncovered during that first excavation would be used to illustrate the profound roots of monarchy on French soil. Like the Valois before them, the Bourbons saw themselves as heirs to the specifically Christian notion of divinely approved kingship exemplified by the Merovingians. However, at the time of the burial Clovis, just like his father before him, was a pagan, and the fact that Childeric was buried with a horse, along with a harness embellished with gold and covered in cloisonné bees, shows the warrior values of a pre-Christian society.

Horse burial was a rare event in fifth-century Gaul, the territory which would evolve into Francia, and Church leaders both then and later condemned it consistently as an example of paganism. A few other contemporary examples of the practice are to be found on sites scattered between the Rhine, Elbe and Danube rivers and they invariably show how this particular gesture was usually reserved for the obsequies of significant military leaders. Recent archaeology, however, has uncovered another twenty-one horses buried in the three graves which lie near Childeric's and which can be dated, using radiocarbon evidence, to the period 460–520. Located probably at the foot of a mound which was raised over the king's grave, these burial sites taken together provide evidence of a degree of royal power concentrated in this area of northern Gaul and attracting thereby the allegiance of a warrior aristocracy.

Burial of regalia, artistic ornaments and weapons of war alongside the bodies of dead leaders is a widespread phenomenon in most ancient civilizations and not just in classical antiquity. Those objects which were found in Childeric's grave are very similar, both in terms of style and origin of manufacture, to the ones discovered in burial sites of the same period in the region of the Danube river valley and along the shores of the Black Sea. Childeric belonged to an international network of barbarian warriors many of whom were able to establish local kingdoms as a result of the power vacuum which emerged in the fifth century following the collapse of Roman imperial authority. The kind of objects which went into his grave would therefore have looked familiar to the Goths and Vandals who were the Franks' barbarian cousins. And the affinities do not end there. The ultimate stylistic influence on much of the ceremonial war gear and ornamental objects may well be that of the Huns whose powerful force of westward expansion impacted on the Germanic tribes.

The goods with which the king was buried, along with the horse, evoke therefore a world beyond the frontier. But Childeric's grave also belongs to the last phase in the history of Gaul, a territory which had formed part of the Roman empire and whose cultural influences included those of classical, Graeco-Roman, antiquity. Three hundred coins, the latest dating from 476–7, were discovered within the site as well as the king's brooch, one of a type usually worn only by senior officers in the Roman army. The greatest single find, from a political point of view, was Childeric's seal-ring. This was the object which enabled the grave to be identified unambiguously as the king's and it showed that this war-lord probably had to authenticate public documents in the manner of a Roman provincial governor. Tournai itself was a settlement of key strategic significance in the empire's control of northern Gaul and the grave's location, by the side of an important Roman road, shows that we are dealing with a chieftain who worked within the context of Roman-ized power politics.

Barbarian kingdoms had emerged as a result of their leaders' con-tacts with Rome and often because of an initial agreement to serve imperial interests. Childeric was one such barbarian and the mix of influences revealed within his grave shows that the Frankish chroniclers were not just indulging in providentialist propaganda when they claimed that the Franks were heirs to the Romans. Frankish kings did more than just rule in a territory which was once Roman. They did so in a way which was framed by imperial practice and which continued to be moulded by those precepts long after the final withdrawal of the legions and the end of Roman civilian administration in Gaul.

Like all Merovingian rulers, the king would have worn his hair long, a custom which was originally a sign of miracle-working kingly charisma and one that survived the dynasty's conversion to Christianity. This was no mere antiquarian gesture. Early medieval kings had to be visible to their close retinue, the war band on which they were dependent. Sym-bolism of power therefore needed to be tangible and obvious, just as the rewards offered by kings to their followers, most often in the form of booty looted on campaigns, had to be immediate and generous. Childeric's grave goods in all their magnificence were another such collection of symbols and a material sign of his effectiveness as ruler of the Franks. Their deposition by Clovis was also a visual statement of his own intentions and amounted to a promise that the son would maintain the father's legacy of prosperity and success – a resolution he would fulfil in abundant measure. In driving towards that success Clovis and his successors were able to exploit the powerful appeal of kingship, a system of command which was carrying all before it.

MONARCHY: AN EARLY MEDIEVAL SUCCESS STORY

The spread of kingly rule in western Europe in the centuries immediately after the withdrawal of Roman imperial authority from the region is a fact which needs some explaining. Classical culture, still an object of veneration to the minority who were educated, had been notably sceptical about methods of government which concentrated power in the hands of a single individual. Isidore of Seville, author of the *Etymologiae* which provided a key compendium of knowledge for the sixth and seventh centuries, derived *rex* from *regere* which, he wrote, meant doing right (*recte facere*) and putting right (*corrigere*) rather than just ruling. Kings who lived up to such a self-advertisement were as admirable as they were, in his view, rare. 'Hence the ancient proverb,' he wrote, 'you will be king if you do right; if you do not, you will not.' Rome's republic had been introduced in order to avoid the pride in dominance (*libido dominandi*) which, true to his classical sources, Isidore attributed to her early kings. Biblical evidence was also unenthusiastic about monarchy. Early medieval monarchs looked back to the Old Testament whose kings of Israel from Solomon onwards provided them with convenient epitomes of the just ruler. But the Book of Kings and the thundering of the prophets convey a powerful contempt for monarchic pretension and perfidy.

Against this unpromising background one-person rule had nonetheless succeeded in establishing itself by the year 700 as an almost universal norm in the territories which had once formed part of the Roman empire. The Umayyad dynasty was the caliphs of Islam and its latest representative, 'Abd al-Malik, ruled over the court in Damascus. Justinian II occupied the throne of Constantinople, where he reigned over an eastern Roman empire although facing widespread rebellions against his right to legitimate authority as the last of the Heraclian dynasty. In the Balkans, previously ruled by Byzantium, the Mongolian–Turkic invaders known as the Avars had established their centre of power in the region of modern-day Belgrade and were subject to rule by a single *khagan*, a term which was the Avar equivalent to the Persian *shahanshah* or 'king of kings'. Bulgars, of similar provenance, were in control south of the Danube and their ruler, Asparuch, was also probably a *khan* of some kind. Both Avars and Bulgars claimed suzerainty over a variety of Slavic peoples settled in the Balkans and whose fluctuating tribal groupings provide an exception to this picture of an increasingly consolidated monarchical authority.

In western Europe kingship was the early eighth-century norm and precursor to the region's future history of monarchical power. Byzantium's surviving north Italian toehold in Ravenna was precarious and its weakness clearly prefigured the final withdrawal of half a century later, although the eastern empire's authority in the south of the peninsula and in Sicily remained considerable. But it was the Lombards, chronologically the last of the successive wave of Germanic invaders, who were established across most of northern Italy by 700. In that year Cunipert, ruling from the dynastic base at Pavia, was the Lombard king. He was meeting sustained opposition from the rulers of the duchy of Benevento, another Lombard power and one normally enjoying a semi-autonomous relationship with the court at Pavia. Cunipert's claim to authority remained considerable. He had been the first Lombard ruler to issue gold coinage and he did so in a style which was a deliberate imitation of Byzantine models.

The Lombard experience showed some of the tensions which could arise between monarchic power and the ambitions of military aristocracies in the event of a king showing signs of weakness – a problem which had also surfaced further west in Spain. Here the Visigothic kings had seriously neo-Roman pretensions and, just like the Lombard rulers, they had adopted Flavius (one of Constantine's names) as a component part of their official title. The gesture failed to impress aristocratic dissidents and King Egica, ruling in Toledo since 687, was the latest of his line to experience difficulties. The king was the son-in-law of Ervig, his predecessor on the throne, and it was the usual Visigothic custom for a likely successor to marry into the family of the ruling monarch once he was judged to have a solid base of support. Aristocratic ambitions, it was hoped, might be appeased and accommodated by the introduction of this marital career route. Its practical effect, however, amounted to an aggravation of the problem, with palace intrigue becoming an endemic and debilitating feature of Visigothic kingship.

Egica managed to ensure, unusually, the succession of his own son in 702 after a period of joint rule. But Wittiza (r. 702–10) was succeeded by a mid-seventh-century king's grandson whose own period on the throne would be plagued by the rebellions of other dynastic claimants. In order to maintain its dynamism early medieval kingship needed clear rules of succession as well as an established pattern of success. Rulers incapable of providing that thrust tended to be replaced by those who could. The Visigoths' failure in this regard had a major cultural and political consequence, the Islamicization of early medieval Spain. In 711 an invasion force consisting mostly of Berber tribesmen along with a number of Syrians and Yemenis was launched from Tangiers and landed in southern Spain before marching on Toledo and Cordoba which were then seized and occupied.

Beyond the Pyrenees, Childebert III now reigned in Frankish Gaul and in the two centuries which had elapsed since his ancestor's burial the Merovingian domain had extended far beyond its original northern base to cover most of the territory we now call France (excepting Aquitaine in the south-west) as well as significant parts of the modern Netherlands and western Germany. Like many Merovingian kings after him, this latest Childebert had come to the throne as a boy – a fact which shows that kingship was now necessarily a hereditary institution in western Europe. But the phenomenon of Merovingian child-kingship meant that actual power was exercised by a new class of senior courtiers, the 'mayors of the palace' whose role originally was that of regent during a king's minority. The increasingly attenuated nature of the Merovingian kings' personal authority also ensured that these figures tended to retain their power even after the king had attained his majority.

Pippin II was the most influential mayor of the palace and exercised his power in the region of Austrasia which, covering the north-eastern part of the kingdom, was distinguished from Neustria to the north-west. His direct heirs and successors as rulers, the dynasty of the Carolingians, would halt Islam's advance beyond the Pyrenees and establish their control over the Frankish and Lombard kingdoms. In 700 the scale of the Franks' ambitions was already leading them to assert a claim to territories beyond the Rhine where, at this stage, there were still independent rulers who called themselves kings. Radbod, ruling in Frisia, is downgraded to a 'duke' in the Frankish documents but the Anglo-Saxon missionary Boniface, a more neutral figure in this regard, calls him a king. Alamanns, Bavarians and Thuringians were ruled by dukes who prized their autonomy but whose independence would fall victim to the Carolingians' eastern thrust. The Franks' northern neighbours included the two peoples who would be their most significant late eighth-century enemies, the Danes and the Saxons. There's no evidence of a single king emerging at any stage to assume leadership among the diverse tribes of the Saxons. Denmark's equally pagan society, however, was certainly a consolidated kingship and one whose degree of concentrated authority enabled it to build a massive defensive fortification at the southern frontier.

The British Isles of this period reveals a complex mosaic of kingship in action. South-eastern England c. 700 contained the realms of Essex, Kent and Sussex – regions where kingship's powers were often shared – but the kingdom of the East Angles, north of the river Thames, was undoubtedly an independent power as was Wessex, a substantial regal domain with the river Tamar forming its western border. England's two other kingdoms impressed contemporaries by virtue of their size. Mercia, ruled by Aethelred, comprised the English midlands and extended to the Welsh border, while Northumbria, ruled by Aldfrith, stretched from the Humber estuary to the Firth of Forth. Within south-east Wales the previously separate kingdoms of Glywysing (modern Glamorgan) and Gwent now formed a single regal power under Morgan ap Athrwys, while Idwal, Gwalluc and Cadwgan were the respective rulers of the country's other kingdoms, Gwynedd, Powys and Dyfed.

Ireland contained what was easily Europe's greatest concentration of figures who claimed the title of king. In 697 the abbot of Iona issued a list containing no fewer than forty-four Irish rulers whose authority and legal powers meant that clerics could rely on them for protection in times of war. The kings of Connacht, Leinster, Meath, Munster and Ulster were Ireland's regional super-powers, and the leaders of the Ui Neill clan claimed a regal overlordship within the island. An Irish kingdom had also been established in the Western Isles and Argyll, while in the north-east of what would one day be called Scotland the rules of succession within the royal house which governed the Picts may well have been matrilineal. Iona's abbot thought that clerics fearful of disorder on Pictish soil could rely on the powers of 'Bridei, son of Derilei', an official title linking the king with the mother from whom he probably derived his legitimacy.

THE APPEAL OF KINGSHIP: ROMAN INSPIRATION AND EAST-WEST PARALLELS

In the early eighth century, therefore, systems of kingship varying greatly in their authority, but all of them showing the defining features of monarchical rule, were in place right across the vast expanse of territory which extended from the Atlantic coast in the European west and towards the region which stretched inland from the Levant in the east. Most of this area had been affected in some way, either directly or indirectly, by Rome at varying stages during the preceding 700 years. Early medieval kings therefore drew on the experience of that autocratic form of monarchy which was in fact, if not in constitutional theory, the essence of the Roman emperors' power. This had been the predominant and most recent governmental influence in the history of their respective areas, and it therefore provided them with precedents on which they could build. In the year 700 Constantinople, the 'New Rome', was the fulcrum of that imperial authority's latter form and its rulers showed how, just as in the past, an emperor's *auctoritas* required both a military and a civilian dimension. It was the command of an army, along with the victories proclaimed in the name of an emperor, which lay at the heart of the introduction of autocratic rule into Roman government under Augustus, and the imperial title retained its military associations in the centuries that followed. Iconography linked the imperator with the force of arms, and the coins which were issued with a portrait of the emperor on the obverse carried on their reverses military symbols such as a vengeful Mars, a winged Victory or a defeated barbarian.

Roman emperors, however, were rarely front-line commanders, and for two centuries from the 390s onwards, a time when the empire experienced waves of sustained attack, they did not go on campaign at all. Generalship on its own rarely led directly to the throne between 306 and 602 and it was only in the last two decades of the western empire's history that field commanders were able to make and unmake emperors. Justinian presided as emperor (r. 527–65) over a series of military victories in the west but was nonetheless rarely seen outside his palace in Constantinople. The emergence of a major Persian threat after 610 forced Heraclius to assume the role of an emperor leading his army into battle. His aim was the recapture of Jerusalem and the recovery of the True Cross, an inspiration which is probably recorded in the set of silver plates commissioned at this time and which record scenes from the life of David. But this intrusion of an Old Testament theme of heroic militancy was a rare event. Byzantine emperors frequently led their armies on military campaigns but only rarely were they at the head of the army when it actually came to warfare. Those who sat on the throne either in Rome itself or in Constantinople later were necessarily generals, but throughout the history of their office the emperors were also members of a cultivated and aristocratic governing class. In order to be acceptable to that class it was therefore necessary that they should display that ruling order's civilian, and civilizing, features, and an emperor's role as a judge was at least the equal in significance to his function as a soldier. As Justinian expressed the matter when explaining the need to compile the Roman civil law code, the *Corpus Iuris Civilis*, 'Imperial Majesty should not only be distinguished by arms but also armed by laws . . . so that the Roman emperor . . . should appear as devout in justice as triumphant over defeated enemies.'

Law was the single intellectual activity which, above all others, defined Roman thought, and the intellectuals of the Greek east invariably accepted that in this regard Latin culture was possessed of a greatness comparable to that of the Hellenes in philosophy. The *Corpus* collected in Justinian's name comprised all the surviving *constitutiones* or imperial pro-nouncements having the force of law dating back to the time of the emperor Hadrian. But Roman law, and the emperors' role in its for-mulation, owed much to the initiatives taken by the populations of Hel-lenistic cities in approaching the emperors and asking them for judgment. This was a region with a long history of monarchical rule in the cen-turies following the death of Alexander the Great and its peoples regarded the new Roman rulers in the same light as they had viewed, for example, the Seleucid kings in the past. Roman emperors were therefore over-whelmed with petitioners, a large number of whom expected their ruler to adjudicate on specific legal grievances. Having exercised the right to make an 'appeal to Caesar', the petitioners received a '*rescript*', and the incorporation of these individual replies in Justinian's code shows how these responses came to be seen as law during the earlier centuries of Roman authority in the Greek east.

Constantine's reign marks a point at which the style of the emperors' legal formulations changed, since the Theodosian Code (418) took 311 as its starting point and was defined as only containing laws which had a 'sacred generality'. A new official, the 'Quaestor of the Sacred Palace', had emerged as the imperial spokesman under Constantine, and the holder of that office, though legally trained and fulfilling the role of a minister of law and justice, was also a specialist in rhetoric. Legal peti-tioners, like all Roman subjects when addressing their emperor, invari-ably used an elaborate literary style and the responses of the Quaestors observed the same courtesies. This amounted to a major change in legal formulation since the emperors were now responding to individual griev-ances by issuing general-sounding pronouncements, and it was that style of response which contributed to the idea that Roman emperors defined their role as that of makers of law. The generalizing tone also accounts for the misleading impression of an implacable imperial machine using law to impose its will on a subject population. In fact, however, the imperial bureaucratic machine was as much a passive as an active force in this regard, since in both the earlier and the later periods it was responding to petitioners who exerted a constant pressure and demand for action.

The Hellenic milieu of the east produced not only petitioners but also jurists who were intimately involved in the creation of Justinian's *Corpus*. Tribonian, for example, who wrote the constitutions which introduced and summarized the project's various stages, was born in Pamphylia, a thoroughly Hellenized area of southern Asia Minor. He worked on the *Institutes* (a smaller and separate law book), as well as on a revision of the first *Codex* of imperial *constitutiones*, and his collaborator in both projects was Dorotheus, a professor in the law school at Beirut which counted many Greeks among its students and teachers. Tribonian was also the jurist who was chiefly responsible for the *novels* (or *Novellae Constitutiones*), changes in the laws as a result of Justinian's own judgments during the last thirty years of his reign. Most of the *novels* were written in Greek, a fact which shows how the Hellenic intelligentsia was bringing its own cultural background to bear on the correct interpretation of Roman law. Greek culture had a further impact on Roman imperial authority when the emperor Heraclius formally adopted the word *basileus* to describe his title in 629. Although its literal meaning was 'king', Greek speakers had long since used the term to describe an emperor and its adoption shows the way in which the traditions of the Latin west were being reshaped by the Hellenes of the east.

The emergence of a new kind of palace culture shows the same trend towards greater elaboration, display and ritual. Situated on the Palatine, and deriving its name from that Roman hill, the Roman emperors' first such palace was an undeniably magnificent aristocratic house, but the imperial complex in Constantinople was on an entirely different, and very public, scale. By the fifth century it covered 300,000 square yards and was the place of work for an officialdom which was running into four figures compared to the fewer than 200 who were in attendance on the early emperors. This was now a proper governmental machine, one which could raise revenue on a more systematic basis than in the past and which had the space to collect documents which could then be stored in official archives. As the later Roman empire evolved into 'Byzantium' the palace structure integrated ambitious and educated provincials into the imperial service and provided them with careers, just as had happened in the case of the aristocracy who had now become a true service elite.

Ritual played a fundamental role in this display of power and already by the sixth century, as Peter the Patrician's contemporary *De Magistro Officiorum* demonstrates, imperial coronations showed some of the ritualized style which would later be seen as typically 'Byzantine', with the patriarch crowning the senior emperor who, in turn, was responsible for an associate emperor's crowning. Diplomatic protocols were also acquiring many of the details which would be dismissed in future centuries as fussily pretentious by western European powers but which may have been more acceptable to the Byzantines' Persian neighbours, while in the Hippodrome, an adjunct to the imperial palace, emperors staged the public ceremonies which enabled the city's population to acclaim their rulers in a style which was prescribed by an official *Book of Ceremonies*.

Religious belief and practice were the area in which the emperors of eastern Rome anticipated most obviously the Carolingian dynasty's ambitions. Constantine had debated the theological details of the Trinity with the bishops assembled at the Council of Nicaea and was buried as *isapostolos* (the equal of the Apostles) in the Church of the Twelve Apostles. Ever since then his successors had followed Constantine's example and committed themselves to the defence of orthodox doctrine as well as the more general protection of the Church's interests. The idea that rulers' responsibilities included the need to ensure the correct belief of their subjects, a duty for which they were answerable to God, had therefore a Hellenic root. Imperial *laudes* were chanted to mark the beginning of the ecumenical councils of the Church held in the sixth and seventh centuries, and the Quinisext Council, held in 691–2 and showing signs of Justinian II's personal initiative, specified the details of what might count as a Christian society. The emperors' aim might have been to preserve peace rather than to get embroiled in the details of theological debate, but since Church doctrine was such a major cause of civil disorder the one object was not easily distinguished from the other. It was this specifically Byzantine view of imperial rule which inspired Carolingian rulers and, as developed by them, that notion of sacral power would remain an important aspect of European kingship until the secularizing impact of the eighteenth-century Enlightenment.

Islam's caliphs also operated in a context and in regions where the influence of Roman hegemony survived as a model and an inspiration to both rulers and subjects. The sheer speed of the Arab conquest meant that many of the old structures of government remained in place across the Fertile Crescent and its inhabitants had much the same expectations of their new rulers among the Umayyad dynasty as they had of their former Roman masters. Caliphs, just like later Roman emperors, were absorbed within a palace milieu and were rarely seen on the field of battle. The similarity extends to systems of law, since the Quran's admiring remarks about Solomon and David prefigured the judicial role of the Caliphs whose edicts, expressed in a familiar imperial style, marked a continuity with the Middle East's Roman and colonial past. Caliphs were not themselves prophets but the legitimacy of their rule was derived from the belief that Allah required a deputy on earth, one who would implement the details of the divine intention in the ages following the death of Muhammad. By these means an originally religious authority acquired a political dimension and the subsequent mingling of the two forms of power is analogous to the way in which the Byzantine emperors' originally political dominance merged with their religious role.

Those peoples who bore down on Byzantium from the north and whom the Franks confronted to their east were ruled in a kingly manner and it was that style of authority which enabled them to achieve a degree of consolidated power. The *Strategicon*, a military manual attributed to the Byzantine emperor Maurice (r. 582–602), contains information about the Avars (against whom Maurice campaigned) and describes them as having 'a monarchical form of government'. The khanate of the Avars was an institution whose ambitions and chains of command were typical of power arrangements on the steppe. One of their rulers claimed, according to the seventh-century Byzantine historian Theophylact Simocatta, that 'there existed no one, even as far as the sun extended its gaze, who would be able to confront him'. Bulgars shared the characteristic ambitions of steppe powers and were equipped with *khans* who led their armies in person. Influenced not just by what they knew of Persian autocracy but also, probably, by Chinese government, both these nomadic powers acquired a focus of unity and identity which forced Rome to deal with them as equals. But where the Slavs are concerned the evidence of the *Strategicon* confirms the view that their war bands were unable, or did not wish, to coalesce into units governed by kings. The author describes their 'many kings [*rhegon*] . . . always at odds with one another' but was only using a term (*rhex*) which, in the context of a Latin or Germanic culture, seemed the right one to denote a ruler of any kind. *Knez*, meaning a local lord, seems to have been the word used by the Slavs themselves to describe their headmen, figures who would have found any of the various features of kingly rule to be entirely alien.

Ireland in the seventh and the eighth centuries produced, in the form of the annals compiled by the scribal class termed the *filid*, a substantial body of literature describing those whom the Irish called their *ri* or kings. There were some pre-Christian strands at work here, far more than in the barbarian notions of kingship which were developing at the same time on the western European mainland and in other parts of the British Isles. The functions of the *filid* as recorders of genealogies and sagas, of laws and the deeds of rulers, have affinities with those of the druids of pre-Roman Britain and Gaul. Nonetheless, by the time the *filid* were expressing themselves in writing they were merging with Ireland's monastic clergy. *Ri* is cognate with the Latin *rex* and the Sanskrit *raj*, and a hint of pre-Christian sacral power therefore attaches itself to the word. But by the seventh century Ireland's traditions were thoroughly Christianized and the kind of justice which its kings were expected to deliver followed Old Testament precepts of judgment.

One Irish source on the duties of kingship states that 'the word of a king is a sword for beheading, a rope for hanging, it casts into prison, it condemns to exile'. But the Old Testament could be used to justify resistance to an unjust king, and the abuse which Columbanus handed out to Frankish kings may reflect a more widespread Irish readiness to be awkward and rebel when a king failed to live up to expectations. Irish monarchs at least had an alternative they could turn to since, to a far greater extent than their Germanic equivalents, they often resigned their thrones in order to enter a monastery. It was perhaps the very extent and depth of Ireland's Christianization which made their position so insecure. The fact that there is no record of an Irish Church council being presided over by a king may reflect ecclesiastical suspicion of the aura of pagan charisma which possibly still lingered around the kingly presence. The sheer number of Irish kings limited the power which could be exercised by any single one of them, and conflicts resulting in high casualty rates seem to have been endemic as a result of this monarchical profusion. Taking the seventh century as a whole, the *Annals of Ulster* list at least fifty kings who died in battle during that period in just one region. Estimates for the total number of kingdoms (referred to, appropriately enough, in Irish as *tuatha* or tribes) vary between eighty and 185, and extensive hierarchical systems prescribed how any individual *ri* was subject to a *riuri* ('great king') who in turn owed obedience to a *ri riuirech* 'king of great number' who might be ruler of one of the five great provinces. Precisely because kingship was so small in scale other and rival sources of authority were able to flourish. Poets, prophets and lawyers were more powerful than kings in early medieval Ireland. Nonetheless, by the high Middle Ages the structures of kingly power in Ireland had broken through these barriers and, just as in Wales and Scotland by that stage, they were corresponding to the west European norm of an ascendant and elaborate royal power.

THE DISTINCTIVE POWER OF GERMANIC KINGS

The Germanic kings who ruled in the former Roman dioceses of Italy, Spain, Gaul and Britannia are so called because their own names and/or that of the people they ruled are derived from languages categorized as 'Germanic' by philologists. Rulers such as these, together with their followers, had been influenced by Rome long before their emergence as a population settled in independent barbarian kingdoms, and those who describe them in the surviving sources were either Romans themselves or influenced by Romanizing habits of thought. The mingling of influences was so profound and long-term that it is therefore difficult to disentangle the customs native to the barbarians from the Roman ones that they adopted and made their own. Authors such as Tacitus, seeking to typify the behaviour of barbarians, describe how they fixed an enemy's head on a stake, and how leaders gave gold rings or military equipment to their followers. But these were also practices which had long since been current among Roman emperors and generals. Germanic rulers and subjects absorbed customs which they had originally learnt from their imperial neighbours and then re-expressed them in their own vivid way. Roman writers and observers of the Germanic north may have wanted to convey an impression of a world which was alien and un-Roman. But, when it came to the selection of evidence to describe that strangeness, they were inevitably drawn to patterns of behaviour which they could understand.

The translation of biblical writings into Gothic by Ulfila in the fourth century provides hints of what may have been distinctively pre-Roman forms of Germanic rule. He is the inventor of the Gothic alphabet which he devised partly from Latin but primarily from Greek, and by 381 Ulfila had translated large parts of the Bible from Greek into Gothic, including the Gospels and the Pauline epistles. Significantly, he uses the word *reiks* to describe the role of the chief Pharisees and also that of Nicodemus, a ruler of the synagogue. The Gothic noun has widespread derivatives including the highly resonant *Reich* in German. Procopius, the Byzantine historian of the age of Justinian, says that *rhex* was the word used to describe Theoderic the Ostrogoth and 'was what barbarians were wont to call their leaders'. *Rix* was also a word used on Ostrogothic coinage. Theoderic's title was therefore distinctively Germanic and in a line of development whose origins can be traced back to the *reiks* of the age of Ulfila well over a century earlier.

Tacitus in his *Germania* makes a famous claim about leadership: 'they take kings for their high birth, war leaders for their courage' (*reges ex nobilitate, duces ex virtute sumunt*). It has therefore been supposed that Germanic kings were not war leaders. Caesar in his writings on the Gallic Wars does not even bother to refer to any kings whom he may have encountered on campaign. But Tacitus's formulation tries to express in a fixed way what was in fact a fluid situation – one which is described elsewhere in his writings and in Caesar's as well. The picture both writers give of early Germanic society is one in which chieftains attract followers by giving them hospitality as well as a share of the loot and weapons seized as a result of successful campaigning. Warfare was widespread from the late second century onwards, and predominance came to the *duces* who might have been initially chosen for their courage and had to carry on displaying it but who were then able to solidify their base of support and turn themselves into *reges*. Traditional tribal structures could therefore be torn apart and reconstituted with new leaders emerging to become the focus of identity for the followers who comprised their 'kin'. The vocabulary of kingship was developed among the Germanic peoples to describe those warriors who had succeeded in this task of expressing a new tribal identity, one which was concentrated on their person.

HOW TO ROMANIZE A BARBARIAN

The influence of Rome was paramount in the evolution of barbarian leaders who combined kingship with war leadership. Some earlier barbarians might have encountered Roman emperors as their battlefield opponents and eventually a large number of them served in the Roman army. But the overwhelming majority never saw an emperor in person and for them it was the iconography carved on triumphal arches and reproduced on coins as well as medals which was most influential in communicating an idea of supreme military command which could then be re-expressed in a barbarian idiom. The Lombard king Agilulf is therefore represented on his helmet-plate as a figure enthroned between winged Victories and with defeated supplicants emerging from towered cities. But this was now a world in which Germanic kings had the upper hand, and the motifs borrowed from the Roman past in order to portray a victory ritual had to co-exist with non-Roman elements. Agilulf's long hair and beard are distinctively barbarian and he also carries a sword – a rare posture in the iconography of Roman emperors and one which pinpoints the difference between the civilian nature of their aristocratic lives during the later empire and the martial ambience of barbarian kingship.

It was the need to find warriors who would be successful in battle which elevated Germanic leaders. This was a culture saturated in a military ethic and the names that aristocrats gave themselves contained elements which evoked the field of battle such as *brand* (sword) and *brunn* (breastplate), *grim* (helmet) and *gunt* (fight), *sige* (victory) and *vig* (war or warrior). The ethic of loyalty was fundamental to the values of this warrior society and the Frankish law codes contribute their own distinctive term, *antrustiones*, to describe those who were closest to the king. Clovis, Childebert's son and the Franks' first Christian king, seems to have understood the value of the term and the need for what it signified. Gregory of Tours, in his *History of the Franks*, describes how Ragnachar's followers complained to Clovis that he had used fake gold to win them over and met with the king's dusty response that this was their just desert since they had abandoned their lord.

Germanic kings needed to rely on the solidarity of their immediate war band because they were exposed to near-constant levels of danger. Of the eight kings who ruled Northumbria down to 685 only Oswiu died in his bed. But the followers themselves also came to sense the need for the distinctive *nobilitas* of a kingly leader, and perhaps for reasons they could only intuit rather than express in obvious definition. Procopius tells the story of the Heruli, a Germanic tribe who had decided to get rid of their *rhex*. Repenting of their deed and deciding that they needed after all some kind of 'ruler or general', they sent emissaries to Scandinavia to find someone of 'royal blood' who could fill that role. A belief in kingship's characteristic mystique is also evident in Bede's account of how the East Anglians, faced with a Mercian attack, dragged their former king Sigeberht from the monastery to which he had retired 'in the hope that soldiers would be less . . . ready to flee if they had one who was once their most vigorous . . . leader'. That retired East Anglian king's contemporary, and near-namesake, Sigebert III, king of the Franks, was only a child, but he knew that it was his duty to be on the battlefield when Thuringian rebels advanced towards the army under his command.

The slaughter of Sigebert's army was immense, leaving the boy 'seated on his horse weeping unrestrainedly for those he had lost'. Charisma was a potent weapon in the armoury of Frankish kingship, just as with other barbarian monarchs, but its wonder-inducing qualities also needed to be visibly effective. Sigebert's defeat opened the way for the ascendancy of the mayors of the palace as leaders of the military aristocracy and led to the eventual replacement of his own Merovingian dynasty.

When it comes to legal arrangements, those Roman officials who remained *en poste* helped Germanic kings to perform the new range of duties which were now devolved upon them. The *Variae* of Cassiodorus, Quaestor and Praetorian Prefect for Italy's Ostrogothic rulers, shows that the issues requiring an adjudication were much the same as they had always been. Slaves who had escaped, sexual offences, sorcery, murder, property rights: such cases would have been familiar to the two generations of Cassiodorus's family who had done the job of Quaestor before him. The writings and letters of Sidonius Apollinaris, a Gallo-Roman aristocrat of the fifth century who was bishop of Auvergne and the son of Gaul's Praetorian Prefect, reveal the same process at work with Roman administrators showing the Visigothic and Burgundian invaders how to rule in Gaul. Isidore of Seville describes how under King Euric the Goths started to have 'institutes of law in writing, for before they were governed by tradition and custom alone'. Germanic rulers concerned themselves with the laws governing their Roman subjects as well as with law codes relevant to their own people, and Alaric II went so far as to issue a Breviarium of Roman law. Cassiodorus distinguishes law suits between Goths which were subject to regal edict from those between Goths and Romans which were to be decided 'by fair reason in association with a Roman jurist-consul'. Cases in which both sides to the dispute were Romans were decided according to the parties' own legal traditions. All these legal codes, however, operated under the jurisdiction of a Germanic kingship which had replaced Rome's emperors as makers of new laws on Italian soil.

The Visigothic law issued by Chindasuinth and Reccesuinth in mid-seventh-century Spain was published in twelve books, an arrangement which reveals the dominating influence of the Twelve Tables despite the code's formal abolition of Roman law. The fact that the council of the Spanish Church published Reccesuinth's code shows the close association of Church with State in Visigothic law, a feature which parallels Byzantine developments and finds its culmination in Carolingian kingship. The legal edict issued by the Lombard king Rothari, at about the same time as the Visigothic law books' composition, claimed to be stating 'the ancient law of the Lombards'. Laws relating to feuding may indeed show the antiquity of the edict's original material but its comprehensiveness marks it out as a thoroughly Roman document, one which was written in order to enable the Lombards to relate to the Roman legal culture which they discovered on arriving in northern Italy.

Lex Salica was the defining legal statement of the Franks and is ascribed, with a high degree of probability, to Clovis himself. An early prologue to that law, however, attributes it to four unnamed men who came 'from beyond the Rhine'. This seems an obvious attempt to relate the *Lex Salica* to the Franks' pre-invasion past, and their other law code, the *Lex Ribuaria*, lacks a regal attribution. The reason for this may lie in the possibility that earlier Germanic leaders were cautious about the notion of kings as lawmakers and that they wished to retain some idea of tribal solidarity. But if the Franks did have hesitancies of this kind at one time, those doubts would be put to one side once they came into contact with peoples whose minds and expectations had been shaped by the Roman traditions. Kings who make laws are a sign of Romanization at work. The distinctive symptoms of that process are evident right across Europe in the early Middle Ages and the Franks are no exception to the general rule.

Romanization was never as widespread in northern Europe as in the south and not every *lex* referred to in earlier Frankish law suits had been written down. The fact that a king's declaration of law often remained an oral affair also meant that his association with justice remained highly personal. The Frankish belief in that personal connection may already have been ancient by the time Clovis composed the *Lex Salica*. His successors, rulers of new subject peoples who expected their kings to act and defend their legal rights, were subject however to the same kind of pressures that the inhabitants of Hellenistic cities had brought to bear on Roman emperors. These kings of the Franks responded therefore by becoming explicit legislators, and the laws that they declared in order to safeguard Church interests and further Christianization showed the degree to which they also took an activist view of their legal function. Childebert II, for example, legislated against work on Sundays and forbade the taking of revenge. Charlemagne's legislation would mark the most sustained development of Frankish law in this regard.

WESTERN EUROPE'S NEW CHRISTIAN ELITE

The paring-down of officialdom to a point at which bureaucracy all but disappeared is one of the defining features of early medieval monarchy in the west. Barbarian kings lived in their 'hall' rather than in a palace and the architectural confinement explains the term '*domesticus*' used to describe a Merovingian noble retainer. Pavia was admittedly a genuine capital city for the Lombards, as Toledo was for the Visigoths, and Spain saw some self-conscious attempts at imitating Byzantium. Isidore describes the Visigoth ruler Leovigild (r. 568–86) as being the 'first to sit openly in royal garb upon the throne' and the king may have indulged himself with crown-wearing ceremonies on such occasions. Leovigild's issue of gold coins in his own name and bearing his image is a clear aping of Byzantine practices. Germanic kings may also have tried to imitate Constantinople's Hippodrome rituals and to present themselves to their subjects in a similarly theatrical and public manner. Agilulf, for instance, proclaimed his son's succession in the theatre in Milan, and the amphitheatres built by the Frankish ruler Chilperic in Arles and Soissons may be a sign of his interest in the choreography of power. Cassiodorus's *Variae* show how Theoderic the Ostrogoth tried to preserve the late Roman machinery of palace government in Italy. He was trying to please the senatorial class which enjoyed its role in such matters and Theoderic was well placed in this regard since plenty of palaces survived in his kingdom. But the gulf between any system of western rule at this time and the elaborate sophistication of Constantinople's courtiers is vast. If there is any kind of relevant Roman parallel it is provided by the very earliest emperors who, like many early medieval kings, were mostly itinerant and therefore lacked bureaucratic resources.

Western royal officials were now not just greatly reduced in number, they were also less civilian and more military in status and function. The young aristocrats who attended the king at his table and for the hunt were being trained for a predominantly military career. Their seniors at court, such as the 'seneschal' (a Germanic term for one who served) and the 'mayor of the palace', had earned their position because of battlefield success. These were the martial imperatives of the western European situation and in the process the late Roman distinction between military and civilian values was swept away. The Ostrogothic kingdom collapsed because it tried to preserve that distinction in the form of a division between barbarians and Romans. But the success of the kingdom of the Franks is measured in terms of the ability of its kings and aristocrats to engineer an elite which was unified, which was congregated around the figure of its chief, and which had a supreme disregard for officialdom. The success which came to such a Germanic kingship and aristocracy had a further and crucial consequence. Barbarian kings did not have the kind of governmental hierarchies which might have allowed them to raise taxes as emperors had once done. As a result they were dependent on an aristocracy whose notion of patronage was not office but land. Noble followers might enjoy the hospitality afforded them by their king at his table in the royal hall but, like his predecessors, a *rex* who wanted to be obeyed still needed to demonstrate in tangible ways the *virtus* of his courageous leadership as well as the *nobilitas* of his blood.

The particular form of the Roman imperial tradition which was adopted by barbarian rulers included Christianity as a matter of course, and especially (once they had abandoned a hereditary Arianism) the style of the faith which was associated with Constantine. It is not surprising, therefore, that Clovis should have called his first ecclesiastical foundation the Church of the Holy Apostles, and it was at that same site in Paris that his great-grandson, Chlothar II, convened the great Church council of the Merovingians in 614. Augustine had wanted to teach the western Church that the kingdoms of this world were always bound to be ambiguous allies. But there were few takers for that kind of scepticism in these Christianized barbarian kingdoms. Royal martyrs may have made the difference by showing that kings could be sincere Christians, and that association with kingly rule was therefore the Church's best bet. Sigismund, the king of the Burgundians killed by the Franks in 523, was a significant royal martyr and so was Oswald (605–42), the king of Northumbria who had been educated at Columba's monastery in Iona and who fell in battle against Penda, Mercia's pagan king. Horribly mutilated in death and with his separated limbs set up on stakes, Oswald was the genuine article as a holy royal martyr. He is said to have broken up a silver dish at an Easter feast in order to provide relief for beggars and is one among many rulers who provided a practical justification for 'sacral kingship' by linking it with the needs of his most abject subjects. St-Denis in Paris was the necropolis of the Merovingians but Clovis II had no hesitation in stripping the apse of its silver in order to relieve the needs of the poor. Monarchical gestures of this kind linked kings with their subjects. They are an important counterpoint to the renewed Church–State axis whose magniloquence might otherwise be dismissed as yet another example of the pomposity of rulers.

CHAPTER 2

From Prince to King

A DYNASTY IS DEPOSED

Sometime in the winter of 749–50 the abbot of St-Denis in Paris and an Anglo-Saxon missionary working in Wurzburg arrived in Rome with a question they wished to put to the pope. Was it right that the Frankish throne was occupied by monarchs who did not have 'kingly power'? The identity of the person who had sent Abbot Fulrad and Bishop Burchard to Rome was not disclosed but easy enough to guess. A leading question produced the desired answer: 'Pope Zacharias instructed Pippin that it was better to call him king that had power than him who remained without royal power.' By 751 the deed was done. Pippin III, hitherto mayor of the palace, was 'elected king according to Frankish custom, anointed by the hand of Archbishop Boniface . . . and elevated by the Franks to the kingdom . . . while Childeric, who was falsely called king, was tonsured and sent to a monastery'.

The unmistakable sound of Carolingian gloating can be heard at this great moment in the history of the Franks. A family which had long since been royal in style had now acquired the regal reality. Triumphalism was the order of the day. But before we investigate the acclamation it is best to pause and look in some detail at just how Pippin III managed to pull it off.

All Carolingians were supposed to be glorious, at least in their own eyes, but some of them thought they should be more glorious than their relatives. Prizes in that contest tended to go to those who were not too fastidious about the means which had to be deployed in pushing their way to the top. Pippin III's career, along with that of his brother Carloman, shows the sharpness of their elbows and the keenness of their swords. Their father, Charles Martel, had probably envisaged them sharing power with Grifo, his son by a second marriage. Carloman and Pippin moved quickly to secure their inheritance after Martel's death in 741 and established themselves as mayors of the palace in Austrasia and Neustria respectively. Grifo was then imprisoned by his half-brothers in a monastery, and during the 740s the two mayors of the palace were already being called *principes*.

The monastic life awaited Carloman as well in a few years' time. In 746 he announced that he was going to resign as Austrasia's mayor of the palace. Soon afterwards he was tonsured and then became a member of the community at Monte Cassino. Why should a Carolingian in his prime do such a thing, and especially Carloman who after all was ruling in Austrasia which was his family's historic power base? He was certainly interested in Church administration, but that specialist expertise need not imply a particularly lively spiritual life. Boniface, that ecclesiastical busybody, had quickly latched on to Carloman after the death of Martel. The two of them presided at the *Concilium Germanicum* of 742, the first major synod of the Church in the German territories, and the major monastic foundation of Fulda would be raised on land given to Boniface by Carloman. It was not Carloman the churchman, though, that the Alamannic leadership came up against in the 740s. Their people had originally been conquered by Clovis some two and a half centuries previously, but the Alamannic desire for independence was not so easily crushed and the early eighth century witnessed frequent rebellions against the Frankish overlords. Like any Carolingian warlord, Carloman was keen on winning, and he had a rough and ready solution to the Alamannic problem. In 746 he invited the region's aristocratic leadership to a council he had convened at Cannstatt in the Neckar valley, and a few thousand of them obliged him by turning up. What happened next is known to history as the 'Blood Court at Cannstatt'. Carloman's *Blutgericht* involved the arrest of his guests on grounds of high treason and he then had them executed. The Alamannian duchy was extinguished and direct rule was imposed with Frankish counts being introduced throughout the area.

Carloman therefore had had a busy time of it during the five years since he came to power but relations with his brother could well have become difficult. He had of course his own Austrasian region to look after, but viewed in the context of Francia as a whole he was joint ruler with Pippin and, like any coalition government, that kind of arrangement could lead to friction. Carloman's resignation may also have been intended to benefit his son Drogo. Pippin III was still without issue when Carloman announced his withdrawal from public life, and the plan may have been calculated to elevate Drogo's position as the putative heir to a united Austrasia and Neustria. Perhaps Carloman could not rule in quite the way he wanted. In that case he might well have been determined to take every step possible to ease his son's advancement towards that same goal. If this was indeed the plan it was shot to pieces in 747–8 when Charlemagne was born, and Pippin's marriage to Bertrada, the mother of his son, in 749 legitimized the infant's status as his heir. Drogo probably operated as mayor of the palace in Austrasia for a year after his father's removal from the scene. He certainly resisted Pippin's subsequent annexation of Austrasia, and continued with that campaign until his capture and imprisonment in 753.

Any great dynastic schemes that Carloman might have entertained had therefore unravelled completely. Safely ensconced in the seclusion afforded him in Monte Cassino, he engaged in diplomacy with the Lombards and hoped thereby to destabilize the position of his brother Pippin. That Lombard association would be his undoing. In 754 Pope Stephen II asked Pippin to send in his troops to protect the papacy against the Lombards. Carloman decided to return to Francia, and to present the case against military intervention in person to his brother. He may well have wanted to protect his recently captured son as well. Pippin promptly had him imprisoned in Vienne, and Carloman died in captivity shortly afterwards.

Grifo re-emerges in the family story at about the time of Carloman's resignation. In 747 he managed to escape from his monastic prison, and turned up in Bavaria where he was welcomed by Odilo, the duchy's ruler. This is not entirely surprising since Odilo can have had little liking for the Carolingian main line. Pippin and Carloman had waged a military campaign against him in 742–3 and despite the heavy losses incurred by the Franks during that offensive Bavaria remained within the ambit of Frankish hegemony. Grifo launched a coup to take over the duchy when Odilo died a few months after his arrival. He was well placed to do so since his mother, Martel's second wife, had herself been a Bavarian. And there was another family connection too since Odilo's wife Chiltrude was Martel's daughter by his first marriage. But if the fugitive was relying on his half-sister to help him then he was very much mistaken. Chiltrude's full brother was Pippin III, now the sole mayor of the palace for all of Francia, and she played an important role in his plans for the duchy of Bavaria. Pippin ensured the succession of Tassilo, the duke's infant son by Chiltrude, and she then became regent. Frankish overlordship was therefore re-established in Bavaria. Grifo survived and continued to try to foment rebellion against Pippin but in increasingly forlorn circumstances. He is last recorded as operating in the valley of the river Arc in the Savoy region and it was here that he was killed in battle in 753.

CAROLINGIAN CONTROL: PAST AND PRESENT

The story of Grifo, like that of Carloman and Drogo, shows that Pippin III had to work in order to get his crown. His success was hardly pre-ordained. From the Carolingian point of view, though, it was important that all possible steps were taken to ensure that their rise to power looked both necessary and inevitable. Making the Merovingians look silly was an important part of that project.

Merovingian kings claimed to represent the divine will but they had never been consecrated either by popes or by papal representatives. Carolingian chroniclers and historians made sure that the dynasty's deposition was explicitly associated with papal policy, and the coup would eventually be presented as the necessary prelude to Charlemagne's commanding and centralizing style of kingship. Einhard, the most gifted of these polemicists, ridiculed the later Merovingian kings in his *Life of Charlemagne*. His unforgettable portrayal of the ceremonial processions of the long-haired kings, mounted in carts which were dragged along by oxen, achieved its parodic effect. These were the *rois fainéants*, shadow kings whose antiquated ways had rendered them both absurd and irrelevant to the future glory of the Franks. The Merovingians' long hair was a token of the kingly charisma or sacred power, and though Christianized, the tradition's roots were pagan. Einhard's attention to that detail makes the kings look thoroughly reactionary. Pippin III would have looked entirely different since, following the Frankish custom in these matters, his hair had been ceremonially cut for the first time in the rite which marked a youth's passage to manhood. But the *Vita Karoli Magni*, completed by the late 820s, records the past in order to justify what came afterwards. By no means all the subjects of the later Merovingians thought they were as ineffective or as foolish as Einhard makes them out to be.

The *Liber Historiae Francorum* was written by a Frankish aristocrat during the 720s and he describes a dynasty which was still playing a necessary role in ensuring the glory of his race. He thought Childebert III (695–711) had been particularly successful in this regard and the Merovingians he describes are perfectly competent rulers who exercise their power in a traditionalist way. They adjudicate impartially in the disputes that arise between great aristocrats and they secure the realm's stability by dispensing patronage in a way which recognizes the balance of power within its boundaries. These were the essential functions of early Germanic kingship wherever it is found and the Merovingians were within that tradition of rulership.

Carolingian power was a good deal more centralizing, and its dynamo was supplied by a tough-minded brand of Christian kingship. Pippin III's success, followed by that of Charlemagne, meant that this would be seen as the path to the future and they set the pattern followed by later European monarchs in the Middle Ages. But there were other ways of being a king or ruler in the seventh and eighth centuries, and these examples show that the Carolingian way of doing business was not necessarily how things had to be. Saxony is a case in point. It is the paganism of the Saxons which is usually adduced as the reason for their ferocious resistance to Charlemagne's campaigns of conquest. That view respects the Carolingians' own version of events although there is evidence of Christian practices having already penetrated into Saxony even before the armies of Francia marched over the border. Christian beliefs may have co-existed with the region's pagan religion in some areas and perhaps even merged with those rites. Worshippers at that earlier stage may not have distinguished at all clearly between the two sacred effects. Saxony's subsequent conversion on Carolingian terms certainly involved the drawing of sharp distinctions between what was, and was not, Christian. But Saxon rulers would have had an additional reason to resist. They were the products of a system in which the equivalent of 'kingly power' was allocated by casting lots and, being exercised temporarily, it was the polar opposite to Carolingian dynasticism.

The form of sacred kingship associated in particular with Charlemagne's reign aimed at a hierarchical stability which would be the earthly and militant counterpart to celestial order. But other views about how to judge the holiness of kings were still current in the eighth century. A belief in strong kingship as a method of government was a distinctively English motif of this period. Bede, for example, says that his native Northumbria declined in the early eighth century because its kings were too feeble. Nonetheless, it is also clear that one of the English kings Bede admired the most was Ine, the ruler of Wessex who abdicated in 726 and made a pilgrimage to Rome. He spent the remaining two years of his life there and established a hospice for English pilgrims to the city. Ine would be buried in Rome but the reign which preceded his ultimate act of penitence had been a vigorous affair. He led an offensive campaign against the kingdom of Kent as well as against the west Britons of Cornwall, and in Wessex he had got rid of sub-kings, replacing them with ealdormen who were more pliant to his will. The west Saxon law codes were compiled during Ine's reign and, surviving as an appendix to the laws later issued by Alfred, they represent the first stage in the development of English common law as well as testifying to the king's determination in building up the resources of royal authority. But it was that final act of self-denial which earned him Bede's respect, despite the fact that in other respects the historian's knowledge of Wessex politics was pretty patchy. Augustine's disenchanted view of earthly power was clearly still relevant. It is the reason why Bede thought that Ine was such a fine king. Cadwalla (Cadwalader) was Ine's immediate predecessor on the throne of Wessex and he pursued a similar path of renunciation after a reign notable for the brutality of its invasions of Sussex, Kent and the Isle of Wight. A sudden conversion to Christianity in 688 was the prelude to Cadwalla's abdication and a journey to Rome where he received baptism, died and was buried in 689.

There was therefore a powerful strain of thought which led some kings to reject the world of power. That of itself could lead to self-doubt in the minds of yet other rulers and ensure that in many cases the exercise of kingship was hedged around with ambiguity. It is also possible that the dim recollection of tribal assemblies in the barbarian traditions may have been another way in which kingly power found itself subject to qualification and limitations.

It was nonetheless Pope Zacharias's answer which won the day in 750–51 and his clarity swept aside all the ambiguities which might otherwise have surrounded the power emanating from a Christian throne. Kings had to be the real thing if they wanted to be obeyed. It is not surprising that this particular pope thought in the way that he did. Fourteen out of the twenty popes elected between 644 and 772 were Greek speakers and Zacharias, who came from Byzantine Calabria, was one of them. Familiarity with the idea of a *basileus* and knowledge of how such a ruler had to conduct himself were bred in his bones, and Byzantium had long since decided that a *basileus* ought to rule like a Roman imperator. The alliance between the see of Peter and the throne at Aachen was more than just a convergence of diplomatic interests and political ambition. It also tried to emulate what had been achieved in Constantinople, and the pact was built on the recognition that so glittering an allure was the hallmark of the kinds of ruler who were acknowledged as God's vice-regents on earth.

HOLY OIL: WHY ANOINTMENT MATTERED

The *Annales Regni Francorum* record that Pippin III was 'raised to the kingship by the Franks in the city of Soissons'. Whoever wrote that entry did so in the 790s. Retrospection may play a misleading role here since it is questionable whether Soissons was the actual location for such a key event. Reims would have been the more obvious choice since the city was the site of Clovis's baptism and therefore enjoyed pre-eminence in the choreography of that sacred power claimed by his successors. The fact that Soissons was where Carloman, Charlemagne's younger brother, had been crowned king in 768 may have misled the annalist into making an assumption. But it is the reference to Pippin's anointment which shows the arrival of a whole new set of assumptions about the source of legitimate power, since that ritual had never been followed before during the ceremonies marking the elevation of a king of the Franks. Election was no longer enough, and by the 790s the reference to it in the annalist's description of Pippin's enthronement must have seemed a quaintly antiquarian evocation of the tribal past.

The pouring of consecrated oil, or unction, on the head of a new king was a custom which could claim a biblical precedent since kings of ancient Israel were anointed. But in the circumstances of eighth-century Francia it was a novelty. Consecration of rulers had happened in the kingdom of the Visigoths during the late seventh century. But the Carolingian dynasty is unlikely to have looked to the records of that now defunct kingdom when seeking a way to show that they were kings of a rather special kind. Their source of inspiration is more likely to have been the papacy itself – the only other mid-eighth-century European institution whose rulers regularly used the rite of unction. The *Annales* give only a brief indication of the details of the ceremony which made Pippin king. The *Liber Pontificalis*, the collection of papal biographies compiled by officials working in Rome, makes no mention at all of Pippin becoming king. That fact has led some to doubt whether Boniface did in fact perform an act of consecration. But there's no doubt that Pippin, his queen Bertrada and their two sons Carloman and Charlemagne were all anointed by Pope Stephen II when he visited Francia in 754. And in the case of Pippin's accession some three years earlier there is a high probability that the new dynasty opted for a rite of consecration on that occasion as well. An ancient usage in a new setting would have been a very royal form of renewal.

Byzantium's influence explains why the ecclesiastical and the secular were so thoroughly intermeshed in Carolingian Francia. The key idea here was that of a *ministerium*: an office and a duty whose varying expressions were modulated to suit the different orders of society, including the king himself, but which was also an overarching concept uniting an entire kingdom in its quest for the salvation of all Christian peoples. Bishops and counts therefore had their own ministry which in turn was derived from the ruler's. This idea of a society of different, but complementary, orders acquired a classic expression in 806 when four counts who were also *missi dominici*, officials charged with the implementation of the king's legislation, wrote to their colleagues: 'Devote all your energy to everything pertaining to your ministry, [regardless of] whether this concerns the cult of God, the service of our lord [Charlemagne] or the salvation and care of the Christian people.'

Later centuries would divide the 'religious' from the 'secular' but Carolingian practice blended them together, and as a result it was not just bishops and popes who made a ruler sacred and lent legitimacy to his rule. The lay aristocracy, leaders of the *gens Francorum*, mattered as well, and the fact that they were often closely related to the bishops and senior clergy who might be their brothers, uncles or nephews deepens the impression of an integrated elite. Nobles were therefore called upon to play their own part in the rituals which bestowed kingship's powers on a ruler. Old Testament texts supplied useful precedents in this respect. Bishops identified themselves with the prophets and especially with Samuel since he had, according to the Scriptures (I Samuel 16: 1–13), anointed David. The fact that 'David' was a favourite nickname at court for Charlemagne shows how a sacral power could also be an intimate one. There was Old Testament evidence (I Chronicles 11: 1–9) that the elders of Judah had also played a role in anointing David, and the Frankish aristocrats could identify with these magnates of an earlier age as their precursors in the whole business of king-making.

It was therefore the *gens*, the entire nation of the Franks led by its lay aristocracy, which was the focus of the mid-eighth-century transformation of the kingly office, and this emphasis on the people as a whole, bonded together as ruler and ruled, is a distinctive feature of Carolingian kingship. The Old Testament was a potent source of authority because it could be used to show how the tribes of ancient Israel, that earlier example of a privileged *gens*, anticipated the present condition of the Franks as the *beata gens* (blessed people) of Alcuin's description. The only contemporary Frankish account that survives of Pippin's accession, *The Continuator of Fredegar*, reflects these priorities since it emphasizes that it was 'with the consent of the Franks' that Pippin sent his mission to Pope Zacharias. All the elements that went into the making of a Carolingian ruler are present in the document's insistence that 'by the election of all the Franks to the throne of the kingdom, by the consecration of bishops and by the acknowledgment of lay magnates, with Queen Bertrada as the rules of ancient tradition require he [Pippin] was elevated into the kingdom'.

THE NEW POWER BASE

The new kind of authority bestowed on Francia's kings bears the mark of careful preparation. The pope had written to Pippin and the Frankish magnates three years before the king's delegation arrived in Rome anticipating how in Francia as well as in Italy 'their fighting and our praying' could combine in order 'to save the province'. A monk specializing in the drafting of charters describes the welfare-state obligations which devolved on Pippin as a result of his consecration's infusion of divine grace: the king was now a sublime *rector*, and in discharging that preaching role God expected him to govern and educate the needy and powerless.

This reconstitution of government brought about a new, and very special, relationship not just between the pope and the royal house but also between St Peter and the Franks. The terms in which Pope Stephen II, Zacharias's successor, addressed Pippin, his queen and their two sons after he had consecrated them in 754 make this very clear with a quotation from the first epistle of Peter (2:9): 'You, dearest ones, you, "a holy *gens*, a royal priesthood, a special people", whom the Lord God of Israel has blessed, rejoice and be glad, for the names of your kings and your names are written in heaven.' There was a further allusion contained in Stephen's reference to the inscription of names. It was a common contemporary practice to write down individuals' names in monastic Books of Life. Thus recorded, they would be remembered and prayed for so that they might gain prosperity in this world and salvation in the next. Pippin and his kin were therefore being promised, on papal authority, temporal success and eternal joy.

The mood of fervour and heightened expectation meant that *Lex Salica*, the Frankish code of traditional laws first compiled in the reign of Clovis between about 507 and 511, needed to be updated. *Legisla-*

tores working at Pippin's court therefore drafted the law's new prologue which, added in 763–4, exulted in the fact that 'the bodies of holy martyrs, which the Romans burned with fire, and mutilated by the sword, and tore apart by throwing them to wild beasts: these bodies the Franks have found, and enclosed in gold and precious stones'. So great a devotion was proof, according to the draftsmen, of a vivid faith, and it was that fidelity which explained God's recent decision to privilege the 'illustrious people of the Franks . . . founded by God' (*gens Francorum inclita . . . auctore Deo condita*). Pippin and his people had surpassed the Romans and deserved the divine approval. *Vivit qui Francos diligit Christus*: 'Christ lives who loves the Franks.'

Religious triumphalism was therefore now combined with Frankish national assertion and Carolingian dynastic confidence. This convergence of effects was a novelty in the history of western Europe and it also meant that the influence of the Old Testament's *Vetus Lex* was being supplemented in a new and significant way.

The fact that the 'old law' was so ancient continued to make it a venerable source of authority in a society which valued tradition. This sacred history moreover was a daily reality as a source of texts which, regularly quoted and commented upon, explained the present. Israel's formation of a kingdom through royal anointing was, as we have seen, used by the Frankish clergy, intelligentsia and nobility as a source of reference to guide them in the creation of an early medieval political identity. They also turned to the Old Testament for guidance on issues such as the levying of tithes, Sunday observance, and fair weights and measures. But there was a very influential light-entertainment side to the sacred book as well. The Heptateuch and the Books of Kings record tales of war and adultery, which is why St Benedict, fearing their influence on 'those of feeble understanding', forbade his monks to read them just before bedtime. But adventures such as these may well have been among those 'deeds and histories of the ancients' which were read to Charlemagne at his dinner table. They would have co-existed quite happily with the traditional stories and songs recounting the Franks' own tribal past.

The Old Testament would always be important to the Franks, but the events of 750–51 and the papal consecration or anointment of 754 also meant that they transcended the *Vetus Lex*. Theirs was supposed to be after all the supreme example of a Christian society in operation and, as such, it represented the fulfilment of the law of the 'earlier people' rather than its literal-minded imitation. The point now was to move forward, and in the legitimation of that *renovatio* there was another past which counted quite as much as that of the Jews. Frankish national vitality and identity were now appropriating the history of the early Christians who were portrayed in the Acts of the Apostles and whose faith was witnessed in the glorious sufferings of the martyrs. This too was a history which could be used to prefigure and justify the successes of the Frankish present. That is why the prologue added to the *Lex Salica* emphasizes not only the Franks' devotion to the martyrs but also their courage in shaking off the Roman yoke. By defeating those who had once been the persecutors of Christians the Franks had vindicated the martyrs and the cause for which they had died.

The regal milieu of the Carolingians and the nation at their command seemed therefore to be the culminating expression of the meaning embodied in the histories of ancient Judaism, of imperial Rome and of early Christianity. Franks had been set apart by God because they, and they alone, represented the quintessence of these august traditions of thought and endeavour. This was the heady atmosphere which surrounded Charlemagne in the years of his childhood and youth. As an education in the arts of kingship, the justification of power and the techniques of solidarity, it took some beating.

Papal approval of Carolingian ambitions was dictated by papal strategy. Stephen's offer of anointment came at a time when the Lombards under their king Aistulf were threatening Rome and he therefore needed the Franks' military support. Byzantium's foreign policy was also happy to see the Franks in Italy since Constantinople's emperors needed allies in the prosecution and defence of its own interests in the peninsula, first against the Ostrogoths and then against the Lombards. Meanwhile, the division between the Greek empire and the western Church over the worship of icons was deepening, and when the emperor Leo III (717–41) embarked on an iconoclastic policy, the papacy found another reason to support the Franks. Pippin III's invasions of Italy in 755 and 756 were therefore a practical consequence of the new authority bestowed upon him by the papacy, but the challenges to his authority within Francia would claim his attention soon afterwards. Large areas of the duchy of Aquitaine had reverted to independent status soon after the death of Charles Martel, and from 760 onwards Pippin was embroiled in a series of annual campaigns to restore his dynasty's authority in the south-west. By the spring of 768 Waiofar, duke of Aquitaine, was on the run and on 2 June he was murdered by some of his own former supporters. Pippin had precious little time to savour his victory before falling ill during the summer's campaign. He was taken from Aquitaine to St-Denis, just north of Paris, in whose great abbey he died on 24 September.

THE EDUCATION OF A PRINCE

Charlemagne's childhood showed him being prepared for power from an early age. He was born in either 747 or 748, and would therefore have been three or two years old when his father seized the throne. His first public duty was performed in 753–4 when Pope Stephen II visited Francia, and Charlemagne's involvement meant that he became familiar from a very young age with sacral power both as an idea and as a specific ceremony. The papal visit was, as we have seen, a major event in the history of the relationship between the papacy and the Frankish crown. The deposition of the Merovingians had been supported by the papacy and Pippin may already have been episcopally anointed back in 751 following his coronation. He was eager, however, to have further confirmation of his position, and that of his family, as legitimate rulers and the pope travelled across the Alps to provide that reassurance. In January 754 the royal family assembled before the pope at St-Denis, and Stephen proceeded to anoint not just Pippin but also his wife Bertrada and their sons Charlemagne and Carloman. The protocol involved in the visit was elaborate. Abbot Fulrad of St-Denis and Duke Rothard had travelled to St-Maurice d'Agaune near the Alpine passes in order to greet the pope and accompany him on the rest of his journey to the palace of Ponthion near Paris. The six- or seven-year-old Charlemagne had a particularly important job to do. Accompanied by some of the senior nobility, he was sent to meet the pope at a location some 100 miles beyond Paris where Charlemagne then joined the official escort. This was a high responsibility for so young a prince but Pippin was evidently eager to establish the principle of dynastic continuity and Charlemagne's very public role during the papal visit was a good way of doing so.

There are no details known of Charlemagne's education and of the means by which he acquired that love of culture and respect for learning which would be so evident during his reign. His father had been formally educated at the abbey of St-Denis but there is no record of Charlemagne receiving any instruction there. Like many another early medieval prince, therefore, it is probable that he was educated at court, and his mother would have played an important role in that process. We know that Bertrada was cultivated and that she enjoyed the company of the learned. She assembled a circle of scholars at her court and these men would have influenced the young prince. It is significant that Charlemagne's sister Gisela, who would also have been educated at court, was herself a person of scholarly interests. She knew Alcuin of York, the scholar of Northumbrian and British origins who played an important role in Charlemagne's cultural programme, and was herself an active supporter of his work.

THE AQUITAINE CAMPAIGN: CHARLEMAGNE'S TRAINING IN WAR

The education of a prince included as a matter of course a training in the arts of war. 760 is the year when, according to the law of the Franks, Charlemagne attained his majority. In the spring of the following year he gained his first practical experience of war by joining his father at the head of a military campaign which aimed to quell the independence movement spreading in Aquitaine. The duchy was contiguous with the Franks' original power base and only assimilated by them with some difficulty. The policies adopted in Aquitaine by first the Merovingian dynasty and then the Carolingians follow principles which we shall see in operation in other border areas which became part of the greater Francia. *Duces* of Frankish origin had been installed here by the Merovingians to rule in their name by the mid-sixth century, as well as in the neighbouring Basque region between the Pyrenees and the Garonne, an area later known as Gascony. A similar policy was followed with regard to those Germanic peoples established east of the Rhine and who had been conquered by the Merovingians, such as the Thuringians and Alamanns. The roots of Aquitainian identity, however, were exceptionally strong and its indigenous Roman culture came to exert a hold over the dukes who had been sent to rule there. Ducal rule became hereditary and the dukes intermarried with the inhabitants native to the region. By the early eighth century Aquitaine had enjoyed an effective independence from the Frankish crown for some half-century. Charles Martel re-established control of the duchy, but after his death a resurgence of Aquitainian resistance posed serious problems for both his sons who now governed as mayors of the palace. Similar problems in the Frankish duchies elsewhere seem to have been quickly dealt with. Alsace had been effectively independent for some decades and its local ruling family was deprived of power in the early 740s. The same happened in Alamannia in 746, and we have already seen the rapidity with which a Frankish hegemony was established over the dukedom of Bavaria. Aquitaine, however, was a tougher nut to crack.

Chunoald, the son of Eudo, the former duke, rebelled on Martel's death, and Pippin III's period as ruler and then as king was dominated by a series of attempts at restoring the hegemony of the Frankish crown over the duchy. Pippin was taken ill at the Aquitainian town of Santes, having secured the region's submission in 768, and then travelled north in order to regain his health. A stop at Tours must have been well-nigh inevitable for this was the location of the shrine of St Martin, a figure of special importance to the Frankish royal house. A Roman soldier of the fourth century, Martin had torn his cloak or *cappa* in two and given one half of it to a beggar in order to relieve his distress. The other half became a special relic in the possession of the royal house of the Franks and frequently accompanied the monarch when he went on military campaign. Martin's bones were to be found at the shrine dedicated to his memory in Tours, and it was here that Pippin offered his prayers before resuming his journey to Paris. Having died at St-Denis at his own request, he was buried there just as Martel had been. That wish tells us much about the Carolingians' desire to establish themselves not just as legitimate kings but also as rulers who offered continuity with the Merovingian past. As a place of prayer and of scholarship St-Denis was the spiritual power house of the Frankish royal line and of Francia as a whole. Charles Martel and Pippin III had a special relationship with the abbey, and Pippin established the family tradition of asking the monks to pray for both the royal family and the kingdom. But this was also the burial place of Merovingian rulers, and St-Denis had become especially noteworthy as the last resting place of the seventh-century king Dagobert I. It was not coincidental that Charlemagne and Carloman were crowned kings in succession to their father on St Denis's feast day, 9 October 768. The short period of joint rule had begun and following Carloman's unexpected death in 771 Charlemagne would rule alone.

CHARLEMAGNE'S JOINT KINGSHIP WITH CARLOMAN: 768-71

For the first three years of his reign Charlemagne shared the throne with his younger brother Carloman. The sharing of authority between male successors was common practice in the Germanic kingdoms, but as might be expected the experience of 768–71 was one of division, following the separate and simultaneous coronations of Charlemagne and of Carloman at, respectively, Noyon and Soissons on Sunday, 9 October 768. Charlemagne's power base was in the former Austrasia, while his brother exercised authority in Burgundy, Provence, Septimania, Alsace and Alamannia. Aquitaine, now once again under Frankish rule, was divided between the two of them as was, possibly, Neustria in the northwest. It would be wrong, however, to see this as a hard-and-fast territorial division and there was a substantial degree of overlap between the two brothers' areas of influence. Sporadic resistance in Aquitaine required joint action by the two rulers in 769 and it was during the course of this campaign that some kind of disagreement about their respective roles arose between them. Charlemagne was certainly in the lead when it came to the pursuit of Duke Chunoald II, who was probably Waiofar's son, out of Aquitaine and into the Basque territories south of the Garonne. Charles Martel had organized these lands into a duchy in the 730s and its ruler Lupus now handed the rebel over to the Carolingian force, after which time Chunoald and his lineage disappear from history. The notion of Aquitainian independence had been crushed but it was the Italian dimension to Frankish foreign policy which now threatened to disturb the domestic politics of Francia.

In the summer of 770 Pope Stephen III (768–72) wrote to Francia's new kings and urged them to ensure the observance of 'the rights of the Prince of the Apostles'. The Lombard king Desiderius (757–74) was failing to honour a commitment made by his father to return to papal rule those five coastal towns to the south of Ravenna and which were known as the Pentapolis: Rimini, Pesaro and Fano, Sinigaglia and Ancona. Pippin III had extracted that promise during his Italian expeditions in 755–6. It was now time for his sons to enforce the deal. Moreover, the Lombards had been instrumental in enabling a dissident cleric to claim the Archbishopric of Ravenna for himself and against the wishes of Rome. Charlemagne and Carloman were obliged to act but in doing so they also sowed the seeds of further discord between each other. Carloman had his own close contacts at the papal court in the form of Christopher and his son Sergius who, as *Primicerius* and *Secundicerius*, were leading officials of the papal bureaucracy and pursuers of a strongly anti-Lombard policy. They were also, however, closely associated with the previous regime, that of Pope Paul I (757–67), and therefore detached from the current incumbent who viewed them with suspicion. Charlemagne and his immediate circle for their part saw Pope Stephen's appeal as an opportunity to establish their own credentials with the papacy.

The role in these machinations of Bertrada, Pippin's widow and mother of the two kings, remains both controversial and uncertain. By now she was a nun – a common enough vocation for a royal widow but not one that stopped her from playing an active role in public affairs. We know that early in 770 she held talks with Carloman 'in the interests of peace', and it has been assumed that she was a supporter of Charlemagne in the quarrel between her two sons. Later that year she was on the move, travelling through Bavaria and into Italy where she visited the tombs of the Apostles in Rome. That journey has been associated with the subsequent marriage alliance contracted between Charlemagne and a daughter of the Lombard king Desiderius. Another of Desiderius's daughters was already married to Duke Tassilo III of Bavaria (748–88), and the route taken by Bertrada suggests that she may have been brokering this diplomatic deal. As a result of this initiative Charlemagne put aside Himiltrude, described as a concubine by subsequent Frankish annalists keen to legitimize his action, but who was almost certainly the king's wife.

The new alliance might have seemed initially to be a Frankish rejection of papal concerns, and Pope Stephen sent a letter of protest at the prospect of a Carolingian alliance with so 'barbaric' a race. Charlemagne's position was nonetheless strengthened by this diplomatic recognition of his authority, and the ploy was possibly designed to weaken Carloman's power base. But the deal also offered certain advantages to the papacy, as Bertrada may have explained when she visited Rome. The negotiations now concluded between Charlemagne and the Lombards allowed for the return of the Pentapolis to papal control, and Ravenna's egregious archbishop would be ejected in favour of a candidate to be approved of by the papacy. Christopher and Sergius, together with their circle, were intended to be the chief casualties of this diplomatic *bouleversement*, and Desiderius accordingly marched on Rome at the head of his Lombard force to confront them. Pope Stephen made evident his lack of support for the two officials by suggesting that they enter a monastery, and that was the option they agreed to, having been abandoned by their supporters and taken prisoner. It was, however, a plan which their enemies were determined to forestall. Paul the papal chamberlain made the necessary arrangements to remove Christopher and Sergius from the basilica of St Peter's where they were being kept under guard and they were taken to another location where they were blinded. At the time of the abduction the pope was conveniently elsewhere and celebrating a mass for King Desiderius within the city walls of Rome. Christopher died three days later. Sergius lingered on until the opening weeks of 772 when he was put to death.

The papacy and Charlemagne, the Lombards and the Bavarians, were now parties to an alliance which seemed to benefit all concerned. Its chief feature, however, was the designed encirclement of Carloman, and his sudden death on 4 December 771 deprived the arrangement of its usefulness. And when Pope Stephen III himself died soon afterwards on 24 January 772 the entire scheme was thrown into disarray. Charlemagne no longer needed a Lombard alliance in order to demonstrate his authority and he was now Francia's sole ruler. He repudiated his Lombard wife and sent her back to Italy, and Pope Hadrian I (772–95) reversed his predecessor's policy of a rapprochement with the Lombards. Paul the papal chamberlain was killed – probably on Hadrian's orders but in a way which did not implicate the pope. The remains of Christopher and Sergius were disinterred and given a dignified funeral in St Peter's in order to make amends for the indignities heaped upon them at the end of their lives. The rupture in Franco-Lombard relations led to Carloman's widow and two children taking refuge at Desiderius's court. Since he had been only twenty at the time of his death Carloman's offspring must have been mere infants and his circle therefore transferred their allegiance to Charlemagne rather than coalescing around the possible succession of Pippin, the dead king's eldest son. Negotiations about the future roles of Carloman's former courtiers must nonetheless have been an urgent matter. Alamannia had been a key component of Carloman's inheritance, and Charlemagne's meeting with two of the region's leading aristocrats, Warin (d. 774) and Adalhard (762–86?), is recorded in the *Annales Regni Francorum*. By the end of the winter of 771–2 Charlemagne had chosen Hildegard (758–83), the daughter of Count Gerold and granddaughter of the last duke of the Alamanns, to be his new wife. A concern to incorporate the Alamannic nobility within the new power structures is also evident in the appointment of the new queen's brother, Gerold (d. 799), to be Prefect of Bavaria when that dukedom was incorporated within the Carolingian kingdom in 788.

Charlemagne's takeover of his dead brother's inheritance seems to have been effected with relative ease. We know of only two voices that were raised in objection to the abandonment of the Lombard alliance. Both these individuals were, however, significant. Queen Bertrada's criticisms of the move are recorded in Einhard's *Life* and her dissent is unsurprising given her probable involvement in the original negotiations. The *Life* of Adalhard (752–826) claims that this influential and learned nobleman considered Charlemagne's repudiation of his Lombard bride to be an immoral act. Adalhard was a member of the monastic community at Corbie in Picardy, and what he thought mattered since his father was Bernard, Charles Martel's son by his mistress and there-fore a half-brother of Pippin III. It may have been religious scruple that motivated him, and we know that shortly after Charlemagne's assump-tion of sole rule Adalhard left Francia and Corbie for Italy where he entered the monastery of Monte Cassino. A generation had passed since the retreat of Charlemagne's uncle Carloman to this same foundation. This time, however, the arrival at Monte Cassino of yet another disen-chanted Carolingian was not going to be tolerated for long.

When Charlemagne conquered Lombardy in 774 he took advan-tage of his new authority in Italy and the agents he sent to Monte Cassino were charged with bringing Adalhard back to Francia. The young count returned to Corbie where he eventually became abbot. A distinguished career beckoned. Adalhard was reconciled to Charle-magne who made him a chief counsellor to his son Pippin who reigned as king in Italy. Charlemagne's successor Louis was suspicious of his influence and in 814 exiled Adalhard for some seven years until repenting of his mistake and inviting him back to become one of his key advisers. Adalhard's greatest single bequest to posterity was his decision, made in the early 820s, to found a daughter house of Corbie, and the Benedictine foundation of Corvey in Westphalia would become one of the greatest of all European centres of learning during the Middle Ages. Its scholars had a continental reputation, and abbots of Corvey were ranked as princes of the empire. The foundation's library pre-served the first five books of Tacitus's *Annals* and it was here that Widukind wrote his magisterial history of the Saxons. But Corvey was more than a centre of scholarship. Its location placed it on the north-ernmost frontier of evangelization, and the monks of Corvey, including St Ansgar, the apostle of Scandinavia, were in the vanguard of Chris-tianity's further penetration into northern Europe in the ninth and tenth centuries.

Adalhard's long life merged religion with politics, the claims of God and his Church with those of the dynasty and its territorial extension, in a typically Carolingian style. It was a career and a pattern of achieve-ment made possible by the ruler to whom he became reconciled, since it was Charlemagne's fixity of purpose in peace and war which created the matrix for the advance of a civilization. In 772 the king sat alone on his throne and the scene was set. It is time to consider the military means by which he consolidated his kingdom and extended its boundaries to an effect which was truly imperial.

CHAPTER 3

The Kingdom at War

THE SINEWS OF WAR

Charlemagne developed the most effective war machine seen in western Europe since the later Roman empire, and its logistical prowess secured the expansion of his kingdom's original boundaries. But the armies which achieved Charlemagne's victories in so many different theatres of war were by no means composed exclusively of his own Franks. The expansionist Francia of Charlemagne's day was sustained by its martial ethos, and military service was therefore imposed on subjects in every region of the Frankish empire. Victories in war meant that the conquered populations became Charlemagne's subjects and that increase in the number of possible conscripts made further military adventures possible. Ethnic assertion and religious zeal were intrinsic to the king's personal sense of mission and central to the way in which he defined and justified his rule. Military policy was infused with those two priorities, and a kingdom designed for war needed therefore to carry on winning.

The numbers who were called up varied according to the demands of particular campaigns, and military service would have been a very effective way of ensuring that soldiers drawn from the conquered areas were culturally assimilated within the Frankish hegemony. The official records nonetheless continued to use the traditional national and regional labels when describing the armies' composition. Burgundians, Bavarians, Lombards and men from Septimania are numbered as being among those who went on campaign with Charlemagne to Spain in 778, and the army which went on the offensive against Bavaria in the 780s included Frisians, Saxons, Ripuarian Franks and Thuringians.

A prodigious amount of care went into the finer details of military mobilization, and in 802–3, for example, the counts were instructed to make sure that each soldier reporting for duty had a lance and shield, a breastplate and helmet. The same precision is evident in the instructions Charlemagne gave in April 806 to Abbot Fulrad of St-Quentin near Amiens. Fulrad had raised a body of local men to serve in the army and was responsible for conveying them from their native Picardy to eastern Saxony where the assembly was being held that year and where instructions would then be given as to where the army would be congregating. The horsemen that Fulrad provided each had to have a shield and lance, a sword and dagger, as well as a bow and a quiver filled with arrows. The abbot also had to make sure that utensils which his men would find useful while on campaign, such as spades, shovels and trenching tools, were loaded on to carts so that they might be transported from Picardy to the army's encampment.

Equipping and provisioning Charlemagne's army was a major organizational feat, and each count had to set aside part of his district's fodder so that it could be used to feed the army. Periods of acute danger led to the adoption of emergency measures, such as the universal conscription which applied in the area beyond the Seine as a result of the acute famine of 806–7. Arrangements for the mustering of troops c. 807 showed a typical administrative zeal: 'If it shall be necessary to furnish aid against the Saracens of Spain or the Avars, then five of the Saxons shall equip a sixth, and if it be necessary to bear aid against the Bohemians, two shall equip a third; if, indeed, there is a need to defend the native country against the Sorbs, then all shall come together . . .' Charlemagne's armies transformed the map of western Europe. But equally their very existence changed the way in which the Franks themselves were governed, and the administrative apparatus which served the army's needs also suited Charlemagne's purpose as a highly interventionist civilian ruler.

CHARLEMAGNE AND THE SAXONS

THE BACKGROUND TO THE FRANKISH-SAXON CONFLICT

Saxons and Franks had, as we have already seen, a lot in common. Both these groups of Germanic peoples had emerged into the light of recorded history in north-west Europe as a direct result of the collapse of Roman imperial power along the lower Rhine in the mid-fourth century. Those identified as the Salian Franks had moved to the west across the Rhine and into the area known as Toxandria, a low-lying region between the river Meuse and the Channel coast. It was here that they settled, and in 358 the future emperor Julian, at that time Caesar of the western empire, bought peace by handing over Toxandria to the Salian Franks who then became Roman allies and provided the imperial army with troops for frontier defence.

The Saxons had no such history of immediate frontier involvement with the Roman empire since their original zone of settlement lay in an area to the east of the river Elbe and south of the Danish peninsula. But the Franks' successes brought in their wake substantial opportunities for the Saxons who, along with Angles and Jutes to the east and north, were also now able to migrate westwards and did so from the early fifth century onwards. South-east Britain's penetration by these Germanic peoples was one consequence of this new fluidity, as was the Saxons' own involvement in the internal power struggles in northern Gaul where they engaged in warfare against combined Frankish-Roman forces.

By the late fifth century, and under Clovis's leadership, the Franks had established their predominance over most of Gaul between the Loire and the Channel coast. They would have continued to come across some scattered Saxon settlements in this region. But by now most Saxons were to be found east of the Rhine where they became the subject peoples of the Frankish kingdom of Austrasia whose power bases were in Reims, Metz and Cologne. The Austrasia which was ruled by the Frankish monarch Theuderic I (c. 511–33) and then by his son Theudebert I (533–48) was able to enforce its authority on a number of subject peoples east of the Rhine, including Thuringians and Jutes as well as Saxons, though that hegemony was often under threat. Gregory of Tours records, for example, a major revolt of the Saxons in this region during the reign of Chlothar I (c. 511–61). Some Saxons also joined forces with Alboin, king of the Lombards, during his 568 invasion of north Italy and were then able to launch raids on Provence in the following year.

For most of the time during the sixth and seventh centuries the Franks were able to extract tribute payments from the Saxons, usually in the form of horses, as well as some military service, and they proved especially useful in defending the north-east frontier against the Slavic people known as the Wends. Austrasia's Merovingian rulers, however, were confronted by a major challenge among their tributary peoples in 639 when the Thuringians mounted a large-scale rebellion as a result of which their leader, Duke Radulf, was able to claim the title of king. The child-king Sigebert III (634–56) is supposed to have wept in the saddle after Radulf's forces defeated his army, and the collapse of Austrasian authority east of the Rhine was a serious blow to Merovingian prestige. The fact that Charles Martel and Pippin II were able to restore Frankish hegemony over the Thuringians contributed greatly to the Carolingians' fast-growing reputation for military competence. But it was Saxonia which first claimed Martel's attention after he led Austrasia to victory over Neustria in the civil war of 715–17. His campaign of 718 was the first of a series of offensives he launched against the Saxons, with further onslaughts in 720, possibly in 733 or 734, and then again in 738, leading to the re-establishment of the Franks' dominance. Charlemagne's father, Pippin III, took to the field of battle against the Saxons in 747 and 753, just as his uncle Carloman had done in 744.

The long history of Frankish–Saxon relations was, in terms of warfare, the most vital aspect of Charlemagne's inheritance. The question of what to do about the Saxons, how to respond to their military challenges and how to control them most effectively, had recurred in the reigns of most of his predecessors on the throne of the Frankish kingdom. Charlemagne thereby inherited the assumption that Saxons ought to be somehow dependent on the Franks, as indeed they had occasionally been at various periods since the sixth century. The fact that these long-term neighbours were so similar to the Franks lent an added urgency to the question of how to deal with them. These were not remote 'barbarians' but a people whose level of civilization in the mid-eighth century was comparable to that of the Franks. Their weapons were at least as good, and their jewellery and domestic equipment were of an equal sophistication. What is more, they had consistently proved themselves to be as vigorous in war as any of their opponents. Numerous and widely dispersed across different European regions, the Saxons were an international phenomenon.

Modern-day estimates tend to minimize the numbers involved in the migration to south-east Britain but, taken together with the Saxons established in northern Francia and the main body of their number to the east of the Rhine, the undeniable impression remains of a substantial grouping of peoples who shared a distinctive identity. Only a people with an expanding population base could have established themselves so successfully in so many different areas, and the Saxons' involvement in the Lombard invasion of Italy is a further illustration of that fact. Rising population levels would have put pressure on the marshy territory north of the Lippe which was the original Saxonic heartland, and that provided one motive for expansion. Another reason for the Saxons' increasing mobility could have been the impact on them of Frisians from further north and of the Wends from the north-west since both these peoples were themselves expanding their population base. Pippin III's army of 747 discovered that many Frisians and Wends had united with the Saxons to form a powerful anti-Frankish alliance.

Merovingian rulers of the Franks, together with their Carolingian successors, had plenty of reasons therefore to be at best wary, and more often hostile, towards the Saxons. Domestic difficulties within Francia could be exploited by this resourceful enemy, as happened during the civil war of 715–17, and Frankish rebels often found that Saxonia was a good place to which to flee in order to round up support for their cause. Pippin III's half-brother Grifo was one such malcontent following his failure to get a share of the kingdom in 741 and, having escaped from prison in the Ardennes, he first of all joined the Saxons before trying his luck with the Bavarians. Little wonder then that the Frankish sources were so insistent on portraying the Saxons as a faithless and unreliable people whose oaths could not be relied upon. Saxons would have sworn their oaths on their weapons, and the fact that they remained at this stage a pagan people was an additional reason for the suspicions of the Christian Franks. During the course of the long campaign to sub-jugate them the Franks had many opportunities to observe their en-emies' strange customs. Saxons burnt the corpses of the dead rather than burying them straight away, and the ashes of the deceased were then interred in mounds. Those suspected of witchcraft were also burned – probably alive – and their flesh was then eaten. Human sacrifices seem to have been a regular feature of Saxon religion, with prayers being offered at springs and trees deemed to be sacred.

Strategic threat, rather than cultural difference, was however the main justification for the Franks' hostility towards the Saxons as they pushed south of the river Lippe in their search for higher and drier ground. Flowing from east to west where it then joins the Rhine, the Lippe formed a valley which had been an important zone of fortification cen-turies earlier. A whole network of forts was built along the valley in the time of the emperor Augustus, and although these had long since been dismantled the area retained its strategic significance. A further Saxon push to the south of here would imperil those areas east of the Rhine which were under Frankish control as well as the Franks' present set-tlements in the lower Rhine valley. At the outset of Charlemagne's reign the situation looked ominous and the Saxons had already penetrated as far south as the valley of the river Diemel where they constructed a fortress at Eresburg, a site which frequently changed hands in the years of war that lay ahead.

Frankish determination to subjugate the Saxons merged ineluctably with the campaign to Christianize them, and from 723 onwards Boni-face, the apostle to the Germans, had enjoyed the protection of Charles Martel in his missionary work. Martel had founded the four Bavarian dioceses of Regensburg, Salzburg, Passau and Freising, and transferred them to Boniface in the saint's capacity as metropolitan over all of Ger-many east of the Rhine, with Mainz as his metropolitan see. Boniface may well have been aware of the need to use the Carolingian connec-tion rather than being simply a tool of the dynasty. He kept his links with other royal houses such as the Agilolfing rulers of Bavaria, and was always mindful of the fact that it was the papacy, in the person of Pope Gregory II, who had originally charged him in 719 with the task of converting the Germans. Boniface had after all had experience of the way in which Frankish militarism could cut across his plans: his earlier campaign of 716, when he had sought to convert the Frisians, had to be suspended because of the virulent conflict between their king Radbod and Martel.

During a visit to Rome in 732 Boniface was given the *pallium* and named archbishop with jurisdiction over the whole of Germany, and during a subsequent visit in 737–8 he was named papal legate to the territory. His concern for the Church's independent jurisdiction is manifest throughout his career: he organized provincial synods within the Frankish Church and appointed his own followers to be bishops. But the Bavarian sees which were founded after his 737–8 visit to Rome could not have developed as they did had it not been for the support of Martel. From fairly early on in the eighth century the Carolingian offensive carried with it the expectation that conquered Saxons had to convert to Christianity and in 738 Martel was already campaigning on the Lippe against the Saxon forces. The presumably enforced baptism of captured Saxons was a feature of the 744 campaign conducted by Carloman, Martel's son. Those who surrendered to Pippin III in 747 are supposed to have asked to be baptized, a request which indicates Saxon recognition of the fact that defeat necessarily involved conversion even though many reverted to their familiar gods when circumstances were more propitious.

A missionary Church operating in close association with the conquering Carolingians was therefore an established feature of dynastic policy even before Charlemagne's ascent to the throne. It was Carloman who signed the grant allowing the establishment of the abbey of Fulda which, located at a frontier outpost in what is now Hesse, played a key role in Boniface's strategy and supplied many of the missionaries who accompanied Charlemagne's armies in their anti-Saxon campaigns. In the years following his coronation Pippin III went to war twice against the Saxons and during the first of these campaigns, in 753, Archbishop Hildegar of Cologne was killed by the enemy. Five years later, however, the Franks were able to extract a substantial tribute of 500 horses, and in reaching the confluence of the Weser and the Werne Pippin had advanced further into Saxon territory than any of his predecessors.

CHARLEMAGNE'S SAXON WARS: THE EARLY YEARS

The first military campaign launched by Charlemagne in 772 as sole king of Francia was against the Saxons. Complaints about the enemy's perfidy and the breaking of oaths are the usual prelude to a Frankish campaign against the Saxons, and the absence of such pretexts as a justification for war on this occasion may indicate that it was the Franks who were the aggressors after a fourteen-year period of peace. Every known feature of Charlemagne's campaign certainly indicates a seriousness of intent and a new scale of ambition when it came to dealing with the Saxons. His first act was to seize the fortress at Eresburg on the river Diemel, and he then directed his forces to the Irminsul, a sacred shrine erected close to the border by the Saxons. The Irminsul contained an idol which, along with the rest of the site, was completely destroyed by the Carolingian force. Water was the means used, according to the *Annales Regni Francorum*, and the Irminsul may therefore have been flooded by diverting a nearby stream or river. The fact that the shrine also contained a substantial amount of gold and silver deposited there for safe-keeping by the Saxons made the site doubly attractive. Europe's early medieval rulers used the profits of war in order to defray their military expenses and Charlemagne, being no exception to that general rule, duly seized the treasure. But the attack on the Irminsul also had an undeniable religious significance. This is the first recorded evidence of the Franks planning a specific attack on a Saxon religious centre and the event showed a marked escalation in the nature of the conflict between the two forces. Retaliatory raids and ad hoc responses to the Saxon southern push were being replaced by a sustained and long-term offensive whose aims were cultural and religious as well as territorial and political.

The Saxons certainly responded accordingly and a year later, in 773, they retaliated by raiding the church built by Boniface at Fritzlar, in northern Hesse, half a century earlier. It was here, in 723, that Boniface had felled the local oak dedicated to Thor and used its wood to build a Christian chapel. Fritzlar was the place which marked the beginning of German Christianization, and the Saxons' attack therefore had a tremendous symbolic significance. For whatever reason, the Saxons failed to burn the church and in 774 Charlemagne returned to do battle. He had spent the preceding winter at his villa in Quierzy and while he was there he must have done some serious thinking about future strategy. The relevant annalist records that Charlemagne came to the conclusion that he needed not only 'to attack the treacherous and treaty-breaking tribe of the Saxons' but also 'to persist in this war until they were either defeated and forced to accept the Christian religion or entirely exterminated'. The genocidal note was a new one and an appropriate prelude to the major invasion of 775, a campaign which was led by Charlemagne himself.

The king's force first advanced along the Ruhr valley and seized the Saxon fortress at Syburg before making for the Diemel valley where the Carolingian army regained Eresburg, a fortification which may have been recaptured by the Saxons two years earlier. Charlemagne then led his army to the Weser valley where he defeated a Saxon army at Braunsberg, and divided his force in two. Those troops which were led by the king in person travelled to the east and at the river Oker Charlemagne received the formal submission of two groups of Saxon tribes termed the Austreleudi and the Angrarii. The other Carolingian force, however, was attacked by the Saxons as it continued northwards in the borderland territory along the Weser. This was marshy terrain and it would have been difficult for the Franks to manoeuvre when they were exposed to a surprise attack by the Westphalian grouping of Saxons. Joining his imperilled troops, Charlemagne reunited his army, and enforced submission on the Saxons of this border area who as a result had to give hostages to their enemy.

Part of Charlemagne's difficulties in dealing with the Saxons lay in the fact that he had to deal with several simultaneous strategic threats. He was perhaps fortunate that there were no signs of Saxon restiveness while he was dealing with the Aquitainian issue during the period of his joint rule with Carloman, but the Saxons' attack on Hesse in 773 came at a time when he was campaigning in Italy. In 776 they returned to the offensive while Charlemagne was once again away in the peninsula, regaining Eresburg for a second time and then attacking Syburg. The king's hasty return from Italy at the head of a large army led to a new stage in Saxon–Frankish relations and the onset of a major programme of colonization. A Frankish garrison was established in Eresburg, and a new fortress, the origin of the later city of Paderborn, was built on the Lippe. It was at this latter site that the assembled Saxons were forced to accept Christian baptism en masse. Charlemagne returned to Paderborn during the following year of 777 and it was there that he convened the great annual assembly of the Franks known as the *Marchfeld*, a term derived from the *Campus Martius* which was ancient Rome's city centre and a major place of public assembly. The Paderborn fortress would develop into a major Carolingian palace, and the settlement was the southern Saxon base for the Frankish policy of imposed assimilation. A systematic programme of colonization was now clearly in operation. It is at this point that the annals record the first appearance of a Saxon leader called Widukind, and his northern redoubt would provide a focus for further resistance to the Franks.

WIDUKIND'S LEADERSHIP OF THE SAXON RESISTANCE

The heirs of Widukind, who often bore the same name, would play a long and distinguished role in the future history of the Saxons as a Christian people. But there are some indications that even in the age of his great rebellion against Charlemagne in the late eighth century Widukind's lineage was already important. We have seen how, before Charlemagne's reign, the Franks had embarked on occasional retaliatory campaigns against the Saxons. Charlemagne's policy of outright colonization was certainly a new departure. But the Merovingian dynasty, though involved in military campaigning, had also used other techniques to pacify their unruly neighbours. Ducal dynasties, most probably Frankish in their origins, had been imposed upon those peoples east of the Rhine who came under the Franks' hegemony. Some of these same families' leaders, however, started to identify themselves with the subjugated peoples and even took the lead in organizing opposition to Frankish rule. This is what had happened in Thuringia, Alamannia and Bavaria, and it is probable that this is also the background to Widukind's assumption of leadership and rebellion. The names Widukind and Theoderic recur in the kinship group to which the Saxon leader belonged. A Saxon leader called Theoderic led his people's resistance in Westphalia to the campaigns waged there by Carloman and then by Pippin in 743 and in 744. Widukind may therefore have belonged to a dynasty with a habit of rebelling and it would not be surprising if he was himself of ducal status.

Widukind proved his worth as a national leader in 778. Charlemagne at this stage had left for his expedition to northern Spain, having received a plea for help from local Arab leaders opposed to the growing predominance of the Umayyad dynasty of Cordoba. This was a major military offensive and in embarking on it Charlemagne must have felt confident that he could afford to divert his energies away from the theatre of war in Saxony. But the scale of the Saxon uprising of 778 posed a major threat to the Frankish kingdom, with the enemy raiding the valley of the lower Rhine and reaching as far as the area of Cologne. While withdrawing from these territories they were confronted by an army composed of eastern Franks and Alamanns who had been ordered by Charlemagne to inflict vengeance. The Franks' historians record a great defeat for the Saxons at a site near Leisa in the Eder valley, but two further major campaigns were necessary to ensure their temporary subjugation. In 779 the Saxons of Westphalia sustained a series of defeats during the military engagements conducted along the Lippe and Weser valleys, and in the following year Charlemagne gained his greatest victory yet in the Frankish–Saxon wars.

The king started his campaign of 780 by once again holding the *Marchfeld* in Saxony, this time at the source of the Lippe, and that triumphalist gesture was followed by a major penetration of Saxon territory in the east. We are told that the Saxon inhabitants of the Bardengau and many of the grouping termed the Nordeludi were baptized at a spot on the river Oker. Charlemagne was now driving hard towards the Elbe and its demarcation of the frontier zone between the Saxons and the Slavs further east. The Frankish army had by now covered some 250 miles since its original point of departure on the Rhine, and Charlemagne's command was benefiting from his experience of conducting complex long-distance military campaigns in northern Italy and Spain. The success gained in Saxony enabled him to contemplate the future pattern of Frankish government in what was now a colony rather than just an area to be raided and plundered.

With Saxony now appearing quiescent, Charlemagne travelled to Italy towards the end of 780 and spent Easter of the following year in Rome. When he returned to the region in 782 he held a major assembly, once again at the source of the Lippe, and this was attended, according to the chroniclers, by 'all of the Saxons except for Widukind' as well as by representatives of the Danish king Sigifrid. This is the background to the First Saxon Capitulary, which was issued shortly afterwards and whose thirty-four clauses prescribe the new laws which were to apply to the conquered Saxons. It is also a major document in the history of religious persecution since pagan observances and anti-Christian actions became punishable by death. It is unsurprising that the murder of priests and acts of arson against churches were deemed to deserve the death penalty. But the eating of meat in Lent and burial by cremation also became capital offences, and provisions such as these are uniquely severe compared to other early medieval law codes in Europe.

COLONIZATION AND MASSACRE

Charlemagne's reign saw the start of a distinctively Christian element to the colonization of Saxony with the Church being integral to the conquered territory's administration. The churches that were built in increasing numbers in Saxony from the 780s onwards were the frontier outposts of an expansionist power, and they were therefore highly vulnerable to attack by the original population who were no longer allowed to worship their own gods. It would have made sense therefore for the earliest of these churches to have been built within the Frankish fortresses whose manpower and defences protected them from attack. The capitulary of 802 also provided Saxony's fledgling Christian Church with an economic base, and the military arm of Frankish might would have enforced those provisions. Saxony was now being divided into ecclesiastical units: inhabitants of each area had to provide the land on which their church would be built. The supply of local slaves to serve church needs was also raised by the local population and calculated in proportion to the population density. Some of this labour supply may have included the Saxon magicians and soothsayers who had been enslaved under the terms of the capitulary. Each church received ten per cent of all fines incurred locally as well as a tenth of the free inhabitants' move-able wealth and income.

These were tough provisions and it would be unrealistic to assume that their implementation was an easy matter. Indeed, the Saxons' paganism may in fact have been strengthened for a while as a result of attacks which forced them to define their religious identity in a more explicit way than in the past. Religious belief provided the Franks with an ideological raison d'être for the warfare they conducted on Saxon soil, and their enemies may well have decided to follow suit. The Irminsul was the Saxons' national shrine, and the fact that it was raised right on the frontier with Francia could well record a readiness to see the con-flict as a clash between competing cultures.

The first Saxon capitulary would be the basis of the colony's subse-quent Frankish government but the immediate response to it was hos-tile. Charlemagne was also now imposing military service on the Saxon population, and his army certainly needed extra soldiers in order to press on to the east where the king now had the Slavs in his sights. He paid the price for his ambitions when, perhaps in direct response to the issuing of the 782 capitulary, Widukind raised an army of national resist-ance. By the spring of 783 rebellion was widespread across Saxony. Three Frankish commanders who were to have led the campaign against the Slavs were forced instead to confront the Saxon rebel force which was massing in the area just north of the Suntel mountains. Adalgis, Gailo and Worad went into battle without waiting for Count Theoderic, a rel-ative of the king, to join them since, quite possibly, they wanted the glory of a victory for themselves alone.

If that was indeed their aim it was a major miscalculation and the battle ended in a major humiliation for both the Franks and their king. Most of the Frankish army were killed, including four counts and some twenty other noblemen as well as Adalgis and Gailo.

Charlemagne inflicted a savage reprisal. He returned with a better-prepared force and summoned the Saxon leaders to a renewal of their submission, Widukind having fled in the meantime to seek safety among the Danes. His absence meant that the Saxon leadership could blame Widukind for instigating the revolt, and their capitulation seems to have been complete since the 4,500 Saxon soldiers who were deemed to have taken part in the fatal battle in the Suntel mountains were surrendered to the Franks. In the course of a single day all were beheaded at Verden, a location near the river Aller. Ethnic slaughter on this scale may not have been entirely novel in the history of the Carolingian dynasty. Charlemagne's uncle Carloman inflicted a similar vengeance on the Alamanns in 746. It was, however, the massacre at Verden which would resonate in future German history, and the SS commander Heinrich Himmler, himself a Saxon and one who empathized with the region's pagan past, would raise a monument to those killed in 782 on Charlemagne's command.

Ten years had now passed since Charlemagne's instigation of a major military offensive against the Saxons, and the vengeance inflicted at Verden records the moment at which both sides recognized the reality of their engagement in a long-term conflict, a bloody *Kulturkampf* without parallel in the previous history of either of these northern European peoples. Even the Verden massacre failed to frighten the Saxons into submission and by the spring of the following year rebellion against Frankish rule was again widespread throughout the region. The continuing Saxon–Frankish war in 784–5 witnessed unremitting brutality on both sides as well as the determination of the Saxon resistance movement.

Bad weather hampered Charlemagne's progress in the unfamiliar Saxon terrain in 784. He had first attacked the Westphalian Saxons of the west, but his subsequent progress beyond the Weser valley was blocked by severe flooding and the mass of rebels in the north were thereby saved from attack. Instead, the king left part of his army in Westphalia under the command of his son Charles the Younger while he executed an intriguing military formation. He led his men first in a south-eastern direction and passed through Thuringia before then returning to Saxony and marching along the Elbe and the Saale where he systematically destroyed the inhabitants' crops and burnt their settlements. This was the ominous prelude to the winter months of 784–5, a period when, despite the conventional military practice of the age, the king continued to march his men into battle. His policy now was one of well-nigh continuous destruction of Saxon property and land as well as standard military engagements in battle formation. This was the terror he had unleashed along the Elbe in 784 and he resolved to continue the same methods, to the evident satisfaction of one of the Frankish annalists: 'he gave the Saxons a winter of discontent indeed, as he and the *duces* whom he sent out ranged here, there and everywhere and threw everything into disorder with killings and burnings. By ravaging in this fashion throughout the whole period of the winter he inflicted immense destruction on well-nigh all the regions of the Saxons.'

WIDUKIND'S SURRENDER AND CONVERSION

At the end of that terrible winter Charlemagne held an assembly at Paderborn and then travelled to the Elbe where he had been reliably informed that Widukind and his force would be found. Rather than terrorizing them, however, he started negotiations, promised clemency, and handed over hostages to the Saxons as a security guarantee. The anti-Saxon campaign was suspended. After Charlemagne's return to Francia, Widukind and the other leading dissidents including one called Albio travelled to the king's villa at Attigny in what is now the Ardennes. It was here that Widukind and Albio, along with other leading former rebels, were baptized as Christians. The ceremony was part of the formal deal concluding hostilities and amounted to an extraordinary volte-face coming so soon after the savagery of just a few months earlier. Charlemagne stood as godfather to Widukind at his baptism, thereby cementing the personal nature of the alliance between them.

The battle-weary Saxons had been forced to negotiate because of the terror unleashed on them but the agreement was still something of a gamble for both parties. In order to make a lasting peace Widukind would have to demonstrate his authority over the great mass of the Saxon population. Charlemagne himself was also risking a good deal, given the extent of suffering among the Frankish population. Those living in the eastern territories of Francia had been exposed to sustained Saxon raids throughout the 770s, and most of the troops killed in the battle of 782 in the Suntel mountains came from that endangered frontier region. A desire for vengeance rather than peace may well have been predominant among these people of the east, and later in 785 leading aristocrats in Thuringia would be plotting to murder Charlemagne. The conspiracy was discovered and those involved were either blinded or exiled, but the gravity of the threat to the king's position showed that his peace plan was a high-risk strategy.

By 785 Charlemagne had put in place the structures which would eventually enable Saxony to be governed less as a colony and more as an integral part of his kingdom. His determination to impose Christianity on the Saxons had evolved from 772 onwards and was now achieving its institutional goal in the form of a Frankish system of Church government erected on Saxon soil. Pushing towards the east had always been the most obvious way for Francia to extend and securitize its border zones, as the history of both the Merovingians and the earlier Carolingians had demonstrated. But the territories to the south of Charlemagne's kingdom also provided him with opportunities, and the push into Saxony had to be balanced against the strategic needs, dangers and policy options which presented themselves in northern Italy and in Spain.

LOMBARD OPPORTUNITIES AND SPANISH DANGERS

THE HISTORY OF FRANKISH–LOMBARD RELATIONS

The Lombards, rather like the Saxons, had for a long time been a people familiar to the Franks. Here again, there was a common Germanic milieu and a shared experience: both peoples had emerged as nations in the period of the Roman imperial breakdown. It was the emperor Justinian I (527–65) who had allowed the Lombards to settle in what was once the Roman province of Pannonia, south of the Danube. Justinian wanted some kind of buffer zone in place between his eastern empire and the Franks who, during the reign of their king Theudebert I (533–48), had been threatening to expand into the Balkans. A Lombard kingdom which had found the Byzantines to be so helpful and accommodating might just do the trick. Strategies of this kind had been part of the ancient Roman policy mix on the frontiers for centuries. The Franks for their part wanted the Lombards within their own zone of influence. Dynastic deals could help in that regard and the Frankish princess Chlodosuinth married the Lombard king Alboin (d. 572) in the mid-560s. By then the Lombards had been established on the Pannonian plain for some twenty years but the scale of their ambitions was such that they were not going to hang around there for very much longer. In 568 Alboin led his people on their famous march to the south and across the Alps. The Byzantines lost control of northern Italy and most of the peninsula's centre as a result of that onslaught, and the Lombards replaced them as the supreme regional authority.

The Lombards of the sixth century were either still attached to their ancestral pagan rites or they were Christians of an Arian variety, and their eventual acceptance of Catholic Christianity was a very long-term development during the seventh century. Marriage to Chlodosuinth, the granddaughter of that celebrated convert Clovis, was designed to ensure Alboin's own conversion and to further the irradiation of Frankish political and cultural influences among his people. Even after their remarkable success in establishing themselves in Italy, the Lombards remained exposed to threat from the Franks. The Greeks, now reduced to their outpost in Ravenna and keen to regain their Italian possessions, were not slow to exploit that fact. Both militarily and diplomatically, there was often a Frankish dimension to the Byzantines' manoeuvrings in Italy, as witnessed in the series of expeditions launched against the Lombards by the Merovingian ruler Childebert II (575–96). The Lombard king Authari (584–90) allowed Childebert some kind of overlordship and also made tribute payments to the Frankish king. Although neither of these arrangements survived into the seventh century, relations during that period between Lombards and Franks remained cordial, aided perhaps by the fact that the Lombards were at that time ruled by the Agilolfings, a family whose origins lay among the dynasty, of Frankish origins, who ruled Bavaria.

We have already seen how the revival of Frankish ambitions in mid-eighth-century Italy was initially prompted by the papacy's appeal to Pippin III. The city of Ravenna had finally capitulated to the Lombards in 751 and as a result the Byzantines had been expelled from northern Italy. A frightened papacy stood exposed to the Lombard threat and needed military help. The new king was indebted to the papacy for its role in enabling him to depose the Merovingian dynasty, and he had sidelined the domestic opposition to that transfer of power.

Pippin's nephew Drogo, the son of Carloman, was no longer a serious threat and would be incarcerated by 753, while his half-brother Grifo, the dissident son of Charles Martel, was now dead. One source claims that Grifo was killed while travelling to join the Lombards, and the possibility that the Lombard king Aistulf was intriguing with Pippin's enemies would have supplied another motive for Carolingian intervention. Another possible Lombard attempt at the manipulation of internal Carolingian family disputes is better documented. Aistulf was involved in the decision taken by Pippin's brother Carloman, then a monk at Monte Cassino, to return to Francia and present the case against an Italian campaign in person to the king. Pippin, however, ensured that Carloman, once he had crossed the border, was kept in custody at Vienne under the supervision of Queen Bertrada until his death in 754.

Pippin proceeded with the invasion of north Italy in 755 after he, together with Bertrada, Carloman and Charlemagne, had been anointed by Pope Stephen in the previous year. But the invasion's results were inconsequential. Pippin first laid siege to Pavia and then returned to Francia after Aistulf undertook to transfer to the papacy all those territories and towns of north-east Italy which had been annexed by the Lombards. His failure to keep those promises led to the second Frankish invasion in 756 which saw Pippin occupying Ravenna and the territories surrounding the city. As the Exarchate of Ravenna, this had of course been the outpost of the Byzantine empire on Italian soil, but rather than returning it to the emperor in Constantinople Pippin handed the region over to papal control. Aistulf renewed his pledge concerning the other cities of the north-east conquered by the Lombards, but both he and his successor Desiderius (757–74) continued to resist implementation of that commitment to the papacy.

Charlemagne therefore inherited a long-term situation in which the Lombards played an important part in Frankish calculations and strategy. His father, Pippin, was preoccupied with the Aquitainian issue in the 760s and played no further role in Italian affairs. During the period of joint rule with Carloman an alliance between Charlemagne and the Lombard royal house came to play, as has been shown already, an important role in Francia's domestic politics. But the formal dissolution of Charlemagne's marriage to King Desiderius's daughter was the start of a period in which the Franks once again viewed the Lombards as both a problem and an opportunity. Frankish dissidents such as Carloman's widow Gerbera and her children, as well as Charlemagne's relative Adalhard, had sought refuge among the Lombards whose urban centres and wealth were tempting to the Franks. Francia's domestic and foreign policy alike dictated that Charlemagne would want to assert his interests against the Lombards. All he needed was a pretext.

It was late in the campaigning season of 773 when Pope Hadrian I (772–95) made a formal appeal to Charlemagne, asking for military and diplomatic assistance to ensure the Lombards' withdrawal from the cities they had occupied in north-east Italy. Desiderius was also making some very threatening noises in relation to the security of the city of Rome itself. Charlemagne had already arrived at his villa in Thionville, near Metz, when the papal message was delivered; he had intended to spend the winter there. His first instinct was to opt for diplomacy rather than war. He offered Desiderius the substantial sum of 12,000 gold *solidi* to withdraw from the contested towns, but the Lombard rejection of that initiative meant that Charlemagne had to go to war. His strategy involved crossing the Alps and dividing his army in two. One detachment was led by Charlemagne across Mont Cenis where Desiderius tried, and failed, to halt his advance, while another Frankish force made its way through the St-Bernard Pass. Faced with this dual attack, the Lombards retreated to Pavia, and Charlemagne laid siege to the city throughout the rest of the winter and on into 774.

It was a risky strategy for the Franks since the winter snows had now fallen and a retreat through the Alpine passes was therefore an impossibility. Charlemagne's army would have been trapped in the event of the Lombards being able to relieve the siege of Pavia. Pippin's awareness of the need to return to Francia before the first falls of snow in the Alps is the probable reason why he decided to abandon the siege of Pavia in 755 and agree on the treaty whose terms Aistulf failed to fulfil. Charlemagne's gamble paid off, however – his forces must have been unusually resilient. By Easter the king was able to leave the siege and travel to Rome for his first meeting with Hadrian I, a pope with whom he established an unusually warm friendship that lasted until the pope's death in 795.

CHARLEMAGNE'S CONQUEST OF LOMBARDY

Charlemagne would have gained a ready papal approval for any plans he might have presented to Hadrian that Easter for the future government of the Lombard kingdom. By June 774, following Desiderius's surrender of both his person and the city of Pavia, Charlemagne was able to start implementing his policy for the region. The major Lombard urban centres took their cue from Desiderius and also made their submission. It is doubtful, however, if Desiderius could have had any inkling of the full scale of Frankish ambitions. He and his family were forced into exile in Francia and the kingdom itself ceased to exist as an independent polity. Later that summer Charles had himself proclaimed *Rex Langobardorum* in a move which must have been planned some time beforehand. It was a very unusual course of action. Succession disputes and rivalries among the local dukes had been an endemic feature of Lombard politics from at least the late seventh century onwards. That fact helped Charlemagne and the new regime, since there would have been a local presumption in favour of recognizing the authority of whoever had gained a monopoly of force. Lombard history dictated that a new king needed the assent of the people and the dukes, and there are no indications of any further resistance once Pavia had fallen. But the idea that a victorious ruler should actually take over the title of another and use it himself was a novelty at this period in European history, and the absorption of one kingdom within another by military means had few precedents.

By the end of the summer Charlemagne was back in Francia and administering his kingdom from his base in Worms. The Lombards' north Italian kingdom had long since been a conglomeration of regions each run by their dukes, none of whom could attain the military might and political authority required in order to assert predominance over the others. Such a balance of power would have eased the assertion of a Carolingian hegemony, and Charlemagne seems to have confirmed the authority of a large number of local *duces* and officials. During that same summer the papacy launched its own military campaign against its neighbour, the Lombard duchy of Spoleto, whose rulers were independent of the kings reigning in Pavia. This was Pope Hadrian's revenge for the duchy's involvement in the faction-ridden politics of the papal court in recent years, and after removing Duke Theodicius from power he replaced him with a more amenable local claimant. But the more significant Lombard duchy of Benevento in southern Italy retained its independence despite the hostility of both the papacy and the Franks. Papal nervousness would have been increased by the actions of the Beneventan ruler, Desiderius's son-in-law Arichis II (758–87), who proclaimed himself a prince in 774 and started minting gold coins in his own name.

Charlemagne's absences in Francia and in Saxony played into the hands of the Lombards' factional leaders in the northern kingdom. Hrodgaud, the duke of Friuli, may have proclaimed himself king and was certainly at the heart of the conspiracy supported by other *duces* within the Lombard kingdom in 775. He may also have been negotiating with his fellow Lombards who were ruling in Spoleto and Benevento, an eventuality which would have heightened the traditional papal fear of a territorial encirclement. Charlemagne's further intervention in northern Italy was launched in the early months of 776 when he led an army into the peninsula through the duchy of Friuli. Hrodgaud was killed during the campaign and a more effective system of direct rule was imposed with Charlemagne appointing Frankish counts to govern in the cities he had seized.

The swift collapse of the Lombard kingdom in 773–4 had presented Charlemagne with the opportunity, eagerly seized, to extend his kingly power. But the problems associated with the extension of such power over long distances were also emerging by the mid- to late 770s. The Lombard north of the peninsula was now Charlemagne's new kingdom but the continued independence of Spoleto and, more significantly, that of Benevento posed problems for the Franks. And any resolution of these questions had to be balanced against the strategic demands of the wars in Saxony. In the summer of 776, for example, the king had to return quickly to Francia in order to plan a response to the Saxon uprising of that year, and he was therefore unable to take any further steps to deal with the situation in Spoleto and Benevento.

Moreover, the city of Rome and its adjacent territories in central Italy were now themselves something of a Carolingian problem. This entire area had once been an imperial duchy governed as part of the eastern, or Byzantine, empire. But the imperial authority's representatives based in Ravenna had been unable to defend this central Italian region from Lombard attacks. From at least the time of the papacy of Gregory the Great (590–604) onwards the see of Rome had therefore been building up its own authority as a secular ruler in this region. What is more, despite the theological disputes between Rome and Constantinople and including the often virulent iconoclastic controversy, the pope was still at least in name a subject of the emperor. This meant that any lands controlled by the papacy formed part of the imperial territory. It was as subjects of the emperor that the popes laid claim to rule in the former imperial territories of the north-east (including Ravenna) after these were seized by the Lombards. Hadrian I would therefore have expected all of these lands to be transferred to the papacy after Charlemagne had conquered the Lombard kingdom. But the king chose not to do so, and Ravenna, together with the other former imperial towns of the north-east, would be ruled as part of the new Carolingian kingdom in Italy.

The papacy had been relieved of the immediate Lombard threat as a result of Charlemagne's military campaign and conquests, but the question of who should rule in the north-east of the peninsula anticipated the heady disputes of later medieval history between the popes and the emperors of the west, between a sacral power with temporal pretensions and a temporal power which regarded itself as divinely ordained.

Both Charlemagne and his successors had their work cut out in trying to define the relationship between pope and emperor, though he and they respected the papacy's freedom of action within its territories. The see of Rome was clearly operating a de facto independent government in central Italy, but it was in fact extremely unclear what kind of state the papacy actually was in constitutional terms. *Respublica Sancti Petri* was one of the many terms used by this entity when describing itself institutionally, but the title hardly denoted the existence of a 'Republic' with a constitution to match. Perhaps the phrase was being used in a loose sense and indicated no more than the sum total of scattered landed estates owned by the Church of Rome, but the lack of definition made for a fluid and uncertain situation. Moreover, Byzantium was still ruling some parcels of land in mainland southern Italy as well as Sicily, an island which contained important papal estates before it was seized from the Greeks by the Arabs in a gradual process of conquest which started in the 830s and whose completion took over a century.

Carolingian authority within those areas of Italy lying beyond the region of the former Lombard kingdom would only acquire a real definition in the decades following Charlemagne's imperial coronation in 800. But the history of his Italian campaigns showed that blend of ambition and pragmatism which typified his responses in other regions where military opportunities and challenges presented themselves. In northern Italy Charlemagne took over the existing structures of government, and it was only the Lombard revolt in 775–6 which forced his hand and led to the imposition of some major administrative changes in the region. But the appointment of Frankish counts to run some of the northern Lombard cities did not herald the arrival en masse of officials from Francia. The core territories of his kingdom claimed priority on Charlemagne's time as an administrator, and Saxony was always the most important theatre of war. When the opportunity of an expansion into the Iberian peninsula presented itself during the late 770s Italy had to take second place.

The main business of the assembly that Charlemagne held in Paderborn in 777 was the formal submission of the Saxons of Westphalia. This was the first *Marchfeld* to be held on Saxon territory and, with the military situation in the region appearing to be increasingly under control at that time, the prospects for a swift and complete subjugation must have looked good. While the *Marchfeld* was in session that spring envoys from the Arab rulers of north-eastern Spain arrived in Paderborn requesting military assistance and Charlemagne's personal intervention in the affairs of their region. His ready acquiescence shows that he thought he could now afford to divert his forces and campaign elsewhere. That was of course an optimistic assessment of Charlemagne's prospects in Saxony, but it would prove to be an equally costive judgment about the opportunities that now seemed to be unfolding before him in the Iberian peninsula.

THE BACKGROUND TO CHARLEMAGNE'S SPANISH OFFENSIVE

The Frankish kingdom's involvement in the affairs of northern Spain was of long standing. Over two and a half centuries earlier Clovis's victory at the battle of Vouillé (507) had led to the dissolution of the Visigothic kingdom in southern Gaul. Subsequent Frankish leaders in the sixth century had tried to remove the Visigoths from Septimania, the coastal strip which was their last remaining enclave north of the Pyrenees. The Franks had also sought to establish themselves just south of that mountain range and especially so in the Ebro valley. But any sustained Frankish intervention in Spain was an impossibility during the seventh century partly because of the Franks' own internal divisions, and the Visigothic kingdom of Spain proved adept at consolidating its position.

It was the Arabs who finally conquered Septimania in 720 following their invasion of Spain nine years earlier, and their arrival in the peninsula had the paradoxical effect of strengthening the position of Frankish rulers. The attacks of Arabs, as well as those launched by Berbers, on first of all Aquitaine in the 720s and then on Provence in the 730s weakened two regions which at that time stood outside the area of Frankish rule. Leaders in those localities were forced to call on Martel for help despite their opposition to his ambitions within the now emerging Francia, and he was able to impose his authority on the duchy of Aquitaine in 735 and then on that of Provence four years later. His son Pippin III had his own expansionist ambitions in the south. The Arabs' internal Iberian divisions as well as their conflicts, both within Spain and in north Africa, with the Berber tribesmen gave Pippin the chance to fulfil some of those aspirations. In 752 the Visigothic ruler of Nîmes, Agde and Béziers surrendered the towns to Pippin, and in 759 the Frankish king seized Narbonne itself, once the capital of Visigothic Septimania.

The immediate background to Charlemagne's intervention is to be found in the Ebro valley of northern Spain whose local Arab rulers were contesting the growing power of the Umayyad emirate of Cordoba, established just over twenty years earlier by 'Abd al-Rahman I (756–88). His family, the Umayyads, had been ejected c. 750 from Damascus, the power base of an empire extending across the Middle East and north Africa. Al-Rahman, however, was able to secure a continuation of Umayyad influence in Spain after arriving there from north Africa. He defeated Yusuf ibn 'Abd al-Rahman, the governor of the province of al-Andalus who was in effect the area's independent ruler despite owing nominal obedience to the Caliph. But although Umayyad authority was established quickly enough in Cordoba, the new ruler encountered resistance in the rest of Spain. Partisans of the Abbasid dynasty that had displaced the Umayyads in the east, followers of Yusuf, especially in Toledo, Berbers in the grip of a series of messianic movements and who controlled most of central Spain: all were able to resist the expansion of the Cordoban emirate for some twenty years. By the late 770s 'Abd al-Rahman had defeated these opponents and was extending his authority to the north-east of the Iberian peninsula where, following Yusuf's overthrow, various local Arab leaders were contesting the right to local predominance. It was these regional overlords, and especially the ones who had emerged in Barcelona, Zaragoza and Huesca, who had sent envoys to Charlemagne at Paderborn.

HUMILIATION AT RONCESVALLES

Later Carolingian propaganda would make much of the fact that the subjects of these Arab rulers in north-east Spain were Christians. The decision of a Christian king to lead an army into Spain could thereby be rationalized as part of his religious mission. But Charlemagne's decision to dispatch two armies to come to the aid of the Arab rulers was an opportunistic one, and the intervention was in the long-term tradition of Frankish eagerness to exploit divisions in areas bordering the Pyrenees. The army led by Charlemagne crossed the mountain range at the Roncesvalles pass, took Pamplona, and then marched down the Ebro valley towards Zaragoza. A second Frankish army crossed the eastern Pyrenees, marched towards Barcelona, which it failed to take, and then made a rendez-vous with Charlemagne's army at Zaragoza, a city which the king's forces failed to take either by siege or by storm. The two cities were supposed to be under the control of Arab leaders who had invited the Frankish army into Spain, but in both locations the Arab and Berber garrisons refused to admit an army which was supposed to be allied with them. The expedition had taken a disastrous course for reasons which remain mysterious.

We know that one of the two local leaders in Zaragoza who had appealed to Charlemagne had been murdered by his colleague, and there may well have been second thoughts among the original grouping who had once considered the Franks to be the answer to their problems. Having seen two Frankish armies marching towards them, the Arab leaders may well have concluded that they were in danger of substituting one possible tutelage for another and ending up as no more than a Carolingian colony.

A fate far worse than the mere loss of face involved in withdrawal was visited on Charlemagne's army as, now united, it retreated in the summer of 778 through the Ebro valley, destroyed the fortifications at Pamplona, and then embarked on its journey home to Francia through the Roncesvalles pass in the Pyrenees. The king's men were now in Basque country, a frontier territory inhabited by one of Europe's most enigmatic and dissident peoples. On or about 15 August the rearguard of Charlemagne's army was attacked by the Basques, detached from the rest of the force and then massacred. The Basques also looted the army's baggage train. Those who were killed included the Seneschal Eggihard, Anshelm, the Count of the Palace, and Hruodland who, as *praefectus* of the Breton March, had been in charge of the border area between Brittany and western Neustria. These were grave losses which touched Charlemagne intimately since Anshelm and Hruodland were members of the palatine aristocracy, those nobles who waited in daily attendance on the king at court, and many of his other intimate courtiers were also slaughtered.

The massacre would live on in a literary form, with Hruodland becoming the central figure of the eleventh-century *Chanson de Roland*, a work destined to become a centrepiece of the European cult of chivalric values. The Roland of the poem falls during a heroic confrontation, one waged between a heavily outnumbered Frankish force and a Muslim army, rather than being felled in the Basque raid of recorded history. Roland's valour in battle and against the odds becomes emblematic of

the superior qualities of the Christian knight, and Charlemagne's expedition in the *Song* (as retold in the course of the Middle Ages) seemed
to be an anticipation of the European crusades. But in 778 the king had
been humiliated. His Muslim allies had betrayed him, some of the
courtiers closest to Charlemagne had been killed, and the king's absence
in Spain had encouraged the Saxons to raid and plunder on expeditions
which had even extended into the Rhineland. And since the Basques
had disappeared so quickly after their raid Charlemagne was unable to
avenge the deaths of his courtiers, an important and shaming failure in
a warrior society. It is unsurprising that he never again visited the Spanish
frontier.

ITALIAN OPPORTUNITIES AND PAPAL CEREMONIES

By the late 770s, therefore, it was obvious on the basis of experiences
in Italy and in Spain that expeditions on these borders were a good deal
more problematic than might have appeared at first. There were, however, signs that things might be going Charlemagne's way in Italy since
Duke Hildeprand of Spoleto visited Charlemagne in 779, probably in
the course of the Frankish assembly being held at Duren that year, and
made his submission to the king. Hildeprand was by now something of
an anti-papal malcontent though he had once been a beneficiary of
Hadrian I's patronage. During his years of exile from Spoleto he had
lived in Rome, and it was Hadrian who had engineered his return to
the duchy after papal forces conquered the territory and deposed the
previous ruler, Duke Theodicius. Saxony was the urgent problem
demanding Charlemagne's immediate attention after his return from
Spain. But after two years of campaigning there he travelled to Italy
again towards the end of 780, and this time round he arrived in the
peninsula without an army. The king and his entourage celebrated
Christmas in Pavia before then going on to Rome where they had arrived
by Easter in April 781. Charlemagne's intentions on this particular Italian
journey might not have been military but they were nonetheless pregnant
with significance so far as the survival of his kingdom and the security of
his dynasty were concerned.

*

In the week after Easter the pope baptized Charlemagne's second son by his marriage to Hildegard, and gave him the name Pippin. The boy had until then been known as Carloman, a name which had probably fallen out of favour among the Carolingians who would soon be blackening the reputation of Charlemagne's dead brother of the same name. Pippin, by contrast, was a name of ancient and distinguished lineage among the family's male members, including of course Charlemagne's own father. A papal baptism also served to emphasize the Holy See's close association with the dynasty. Pippin III had been the first Frankish ruler to receive the title *Patricius Romanorum* from the papacy, an honour which conferred no power on the holder but was nonetheless a sign of papal respect as well as signifying a pretension to continuity with the ancient and imperial past. The latest Pippin to be baptized would have his own special association with the papacy since Hadrian I now became the child's 'spiritual father', an honour which bound the pope in a relationship of special amity to Charlemagne as well as to the king's son. The entire visit amounted to a determined assertion of dynastic authority, with the pope crowning the boy Pippin and his younger brother Louis as, respectively, king of the Lombards and king of the Aquitainians. The announcement at the same time of an engagement between Charlemagne's daughter Rotrud and the infant emperor of Byzantium, Constantine VI (780–96), showed the Carolingian dynasty's emerging awareness of its own pan-European role and of the consequent need to reach out to the rulers of Constantinople.

The king was now a ruler in his prime, proven in war and battle-hardened. His successes had yielded new territories which were now related to the core Carolingian royal domain in a variety of ways: by outright annexation and absorption as well as by tribute payment and assertion of overlordship. It was therefore natural that Charlemagne should now start to consider the question of his succession, and these arrangements for his legacy provide some of the best evidence available for Charlemagne's conception of his own role as king. He was clearly concerned to restrict the succession to his children by his present queen, Hildegard, although he had a son, himself called Pippin, by a probable earlier marriage to Himiltrude, a Frankish noblewoman. Einhard describes him as a hunchback, and although the disability could have been real enough, the historian's more probable motive in highlighting any disability was to explain this son's exclusion from the succession. Charlemagne wanted his first-born surviving son to be regarded as illegitimate, and the later rebellion of 'Pippin the Hunchback' was a direct consequence of that mistreatment. The king's eldest son by Hildegard was called Charles after his father and, though not mentioned in any account of the dynastic settlement in 781, it is a fair assumption that he was intended to succeed in the core Carolingian territories within Francia and also in Saxony, with his brothers reigning in the more outlying regions.

A papal ceremony affirming these plans, while useful for purposes of public display, was by no means necessary, and one annalist notes that Charlemagne had already 'divided up his kingdoms between his sons' in 780. In other words, Charlemagne had made known his intentions in the previous year, and although there was a strong connection between the Frankish monarchy and the papacy he was not conceding any of his domestic and political authority to the see of Peter. These were long-term previsions of the future and they related to sons who had only recently been born. With the local Lombard dukes now proving to be quiescent, it is also possible that the prospect of a king, albeit a Carolingian one, ruling in their midst was designed to appease them. A permanent court in north Italy, rather than government by a largely absentee king, might be a good way of massaging the self-esteem of the Lombard aristocracy. Even more importantly, such a centre would have kept a wary eye on local Lombard officials and would also have been useful in invigilating arrangements across the vital frontier area between Francia and north Italy.

The Lombard kingdom had a genuine, possibly ethnic-based, identity and its survival as a distinctive unit owed much to the strength gained from the population's collective historical experience. Aquitaine, however, had always been a pretty amorphous entity, and calling the duchy a 'kingdom', as Charlemagne now chose to do, did not lend this parcel of territories any greater cohesion. By the middle of the ninth century the kingdom of Aquitaine would dissolve as an institutional unit. But Charlemagne's establishment of a local Carolingian court did at least mean that the challenging terrain on the Pyrenean border would now be more effectively patrolled than in the past, and Aquitaine as a whole could be supervised more closely. Charlemagne of course retained overall control of both north Italy and Aquitaine, and from a military point of view the limited devolution that he granted had the great advantage of enabling him to raise armies which were locally based. Rather than going into action at the head of an entire Frankish army, he could now instruct that a local force be raised to deal with localized problems. Although, for example, Charlemagne was campaigning in Saxony in 785, he could still arrange for the raising of an Aquitainian army which then went on to occupy Genoa, a city which had been controlled by the Lombards for over a century. The Frankish takeover was easily effected, especially since it was supported by the local population, and Genoa became the centre of a new countship on the frontier.

SOUTHERN ITALY: FROM SUCCESS TO FAILURE

Towards the end of the following year Charlemagne would return in person to Italy, having secured the apparent conquest of the Saxons, and he spent the Christmas of 786 in Florence before moving on to Rome. By now he was intent on the subjugation of the principality of Benevento, a substantial territory ruled by Arichis II and extending over most of the southern Italian mainland down to Apulia and Calabria, which were for the most part still Byzantine-controlled. Here again the submission seems to have been secured rapidly and without bloodshed. Charlemagne advanced to Capua, and Arichis, having withdrawn to the port town of Salerno, submitted to the king of the Franks and surrendered hostages, including his younger son Grimoald. Formal oaths of allegiance were now becoming an established feature of Charlemagne's government, and these were imposed on Arichis and the leading figures of Beneventan society.

The capitulation of Benevento in 787 involved sending *missi* into the territory in the name of Frankish regal government, and it had been one of Charlemagne's easiest victories. He was issuing charters in Capua on 22 and 24 March, and by the end of the month he was back in Rome where he prepared to celebrate Easter. But he had also benefited from the contemporary interplay of power politics involving Byzantium and its southern Italian interests. Had the Greeks wished to support Arichis, a real and bloody conflict in south Italy would have been well-nigh inevitable. But their interests now lay with the prospect of a Frankish alliance. The engagement of Charlemagne's infant daughter Rotrud in 781 to the infant emperor Constantine VI had been a deal brokered by the boy's mother, Irene, the widow of the emperor Leo IV (of the Khazar dynasty) who died in 780. A reminder of obligations incurred under that agreement came in 787 while Charlemagne was in Capua. It was here that he received Byzantine envoys who requested that Rotrud be sent to Constantinople in order to prepare her for her imperial role. The Frankish–Greek diplomatic entente also involved an attempted east-west theological concordat. Irene stood apart from the wave of iconoclasm which had been unleashed in Byzantium during the reigns of Constantine V (741–75) and Leo IV (775–80). One ecumenical council of the Christian Church had already been held in Constantinople in 786 and had attempted to restore the veneration of icons, but a mutiny by Iconoclasts among the imperial guards had frustrated that goal. A second council was convened the following year and representatives of the western Church needed to be present if it was going to achieve its declared aim of settling the iconoclastic issue. And since the Franks were the papacy's most powerful political ally, Charlemagne was an all-important link in Irene's strategic aim of securing religious peace within the Byzantine empire.

Arichis was an initially unwilling subordinate to the Frankish hegemony in Italy. Faced with the advance of Charlemagne's army towards Capua, he had entered into secret negotiations with Irene and even offered to recognize Byzantine suzerainty in return for military aid. It was Pope Hadrian I who, somewhat sneakily, told Charlemagne of these discussions after Arichis had made his submission to the Franks. The papacy was regularly on its guard against the ambitions of its southern neighbour, and amity between Benevento and the Frankish kingdom was not something that Hadrian would have wished to encourage.

Following the death of Arichis in 787, his heir Grimoald, who had hitherto been kept in custody by the Franks as a hostage, was released and allowed to succeed to the throne in the following year. An alarmed pope warned Charlemagne of Grimoald's unreliability, but Frankish policy would have been dictated by the need to keep the Beneventans quiet and allowing them to be ruled by Arichis's heir helped to achieve that end. Charlemagne insisted that Grimoald's subordinate status as a ruler had to be made explicit on both the Beneventan coinage and the principality's charters, but from the papal point of view things were going badly wrong in south Italy. Hadrian thought that he had secured two Beneventan towns as a result of Charlemagne's assertion of supremacy in the region in 786, but that deal was clearly no longer on the cards after the rapprochement between the king and Grimoald. Charlemagne was also mindful by now of the fact that he needed as widespread a base of support as possible in Benevento following a deterioration in his relations with Byzantium. He had refused to agree to the Byzantines' request of 787 that Rotrud be sent to Constantinople and, the terms of the proposed marriage alliance having now been broken, Irene retaliated by ordering an army into Italy. The occupation of Benevento was the aim of the force which was commanded by John the Military Logothete and supported by Theodore, the governor of Sicily, which still remained part of the Byzantine empire. That expedition of 788 ended in a Greek disaster, however, when the Beneventan army, aided by the Lombards of Spoleto, inflicted a heavy defeat on the invaders at a battle fought in Calabria.

Many humiliations lay ahead for the Greeks in the long story of their enforced withdrawal from Sicily as Arab forces gradually gained the upper hand during the ninth century. Their authority in Capua and Calabria would also evaporate during the same period. But in the late eighth century their position in these regions remained substantial enough for it not to be undermined by a single defeat. Besides which, Benevento's prince, now reigning as Grimoald III, was tiring of his Frankish association. By 791 he had dropped references to his overlord Charlemagne on the local coinage. Even more gravely, he was now negotiating with Constantinople, and the pattern of manipulating Franks and Greeks against each other was one that Grimoald would follow to his own advantage for the rest of his reign.

Charlemagne seems to have done little to bring Grimoald to heel in the 790s but his return to Italy in 800 led to some significant attempts at subjugating Benevento's unreliable prince. The king's son Pippin led two expeditions into the region in 800 and 801 though neither seems to have been successful in re-establishing Carolingian authority. In 802 Grimoald was on the offensive, besieging Winigis, duke of Spoleto and a key Frankish ally, in the town of Lucera and forcing his capitulation. Winigis had been Charlemagne's *missus* during the highly successful Beneventan campaign of 787 and shortly afterwards succeeded Hildebrand as Spoleto's ruler. His ejection after a long period in power removed a major Frankish ally from the Italian scene and was a major reversal for Charlemagne. The king only achieved a settlement in Benevento right at the end of his reign and in 812 Grimoald agreed to pay a tribute of 25,000 gold *solidi*. Even then the understanding between the two rulers only became possible as part of an extensive pattern of diplomatic agreements arrived at between the Franks and the Byzantines.

THE FRANKISH ARMY RETURNS TO SPAIN

Charlemagne's initial success in southern Italy had given way to significant failures but in Spain this pattern was reversed. Although he never returned to the country after the debacle at Roncesvalles, the Frankish counts and courtiers established at the Aquitainian court seized many an opportunity to extend the *imperium* of the Frankish crown along the frontier region to the south and along the Pyrenees.

The Arab ambition to push northwards had not faded away as a result of the defeat inflicted by Charles Martel at Poitiers in 732, significant though that event would turn out to be in retrospect. In 793 the Cordoban emirate launched a major raid on the Aquitainian kingdom, penetrating as far as Narbonne and taking at least 45,000 prisoners. But the period immediately following the death of 'Abd al-Rahman I (756–88) was one of dynastic dispute over the succession, and this pattern was repeated after the early death of his son and successor Hisham I (788–96). The Franks saw their opportunity and could now embark on a highly significant alliance with the kingdom of the Asturias, a Christian outpost in the mountains but one which had expanded to include most of eastern Galicia and part of the Basque country on the Pyrenean fringe.

Many Christians had fled to the Asturias as a place of refuge following the Arab invasion of the rest of Spain in the mid-eighth century, and the kingdom was itself of fairly recent foundation, having come into being as a result of a local revolt c. 720. Its survival in the face of the Arab threat was one of the most astonishing features of Iberian civilization in the eighth century and the discovery of the supposed tomb of St James the Apostle in Santiago de Compostela in the early ninth century would turn the kingdom and the town into a centre of European pilgrimage second only to Rome itself during the Middle Ages. In the 790s, however, just like the Aquitainian kingdom of the Franks, the Asturias was being subjected to raids from the Cordoban emirate, and the capital city, Oviedo, would be sacked twice during the decade. A serious defeat was inflicted on the army of the Asturias in 791 and the local nobility, having concluded that they needed a more vigorous defender of the realm, deprived King Vermudo I the Deacon (788–91) of his throne. He was replaced by his relative Alfonso II the Chaste (791–842), who was probably responsible for issuing an appeal to Charlemagne for military assistance.

Alfonso may have come to regard himself as Charlemagne's dependant, which is why Einhard uses the word *proprius* to describe the Asturian king's status. The gifts that he sent Charlemagne in 797 certainly signified some kind of diplomatic recognition of his subordinate status, and Alfonso had plenty of reasons to be grateful after the successes of the combined Frankish and Asturian forces during that year. The Cordoban emirate was itself running into difficulties at this time, with the emir waging military campaigns against his great-uncles and also against rebels in Toledo and Zaragoza. Barcelona had practically seceded from the emirate and was being run as his own domain by Zatun, a member of the local nobility who came to Aachen in the summer of 797 to pledge his allegiance to Charlemagne. As a result of this accretion of power Charlemagne ordered his son Louis of Aquitaine to raise an army and to lead it over the Pyrenees in an expedition which led to the fall of Huesca.

There was another Muslim supplicant who came to Aachen during that year asking for Charlemagne's intervention in Spanish affairs. 'Abdallah ibn 'Abd al-Rahman had originally been forced into north African exile after he was discovered to be conspiring against the emir

Hisham I. He seems to have been quite chronically dissident and 'Abdallah now wanted help in order to get rid of the present ruler in Cordoba, his great-nephew al-Hakam I. At the beginning of the winter Charlemagne authorized him to travel with Louis of Aquitaine's army to the Spanish border where he hoped to raise a rebellion in the Ebro valley. Not all the successes of 797 were attributable to the Frankish intervention, and it was the Asturian army which was responsible for the raid which led to the capture of the ancient Roman town of Olisipo (modern Lisbon).

While these opportunities were opening up for the Franks in the Spain of 797 Charlemagne had to keep to his main priority, the prosecution of the Saxon wars, and the Frankish response to the situation in the south was much more cautious than it had been in 778. Roncesvalles was still a powerful memory and, almost twenty years on, Charlemagne and his advisers were not quite so credulous about the claims made by the local Muslim rulers in Spain when they came seeking help. 'Abdallah was launched on his rebellion by Louis in 798, but there is no evidence of the Franks involving themselves any more deeply in his campaign, and the rebel was forced to recognize al-Hakam I's authority. By the year 800 Huesca was once again being run by rival gangs of Arab chieftains, and Barcelona's surrender to the Franks, though much prophesied, did not happen during this earlier campaign. It was another expedition from Aquitaine, led by King Louis, which would take advantage of the Umayyads' dynastic instability and finally capture Barcelona in 801. The city became part of the Carolingians' 'Spanish March' and the centre of a county. Its capture provided a suitable apotheosis to Charlemagne's ambitions, coming as it did just a few months after his coronation in Rome.

A PLOT IN BAVARIA

THE IMPORTANCE OF BAVARIA TO FRANCIA

The rewriting of history by the Franks often involved its deliberate falsification, and the annalists who recorded the reigns of Charlemagne and of his successors could be unscrupulous in their determination to portray the king's enemies in the worst possible light. The case of the

Bavarian duchy which was assimilated into the Frankish kingdom following the elimination of its ruling dynasty in 788 is a particularly good example of the ruthlessness which was evident both in the initial deed and then in the use of words which recorded and justified depredation.

Bavaria's population and its rulers had been of particular interest to the kings of the Franks from Merovingian times onwards. Just as in the case of the Lombards and Saxons there was a question of shared Germanic origins, the Bavarians were in large measure the descendants of tribes which had migrated to the west and to the south, and had subsequently settled in what had once been the Roman province of Rhaetia. It is probable that the population mix of the eighth century also contained a number whose lineage connected them with the original Roman population, supplemented perhaps by those whose ancestors had fled from the adjacent province of Norricum, a territory whose Celtic kings and population had been conquered by the Romans. Towards the southern half of Bavaria there were also distinct signs of Slavic penetration from the sixth century onwards. But the dominant impression by the mid-eighth century is of a duchy whose distinct sense of its own individual identity had developed over some centuries.

Geography meant that Bavaria was an area of exceptional strategic importance in military terms since it covered the upper Danube basin, linking the area of the upper Rhine and Thuringia with the northern Balkans and the Hungarian plains. This was an all-important central European corridor whose control was desirable for a western-based power with pronounced eastern ambitions, and Bavaria's own eastern border zone fronted on the territories under the dominion of the Avar confederacy. To the south lay the Brenner, one of many such mountain passes giving access to Italy and the European south. These north–south and east–west axes of communication made Bavaria central to the Franks' ambitions. There were other important advantages to be seized here as well. Salt mining was a major Bavarian trade, and as a result the Roman centre of Iuvava had been renamed Salzburg or 'Salt-town', with food processing and preservation becoming basic to the agricultural wealth of the duchy. A population increase accompanied this economic prosperity and impelled the Bavarians to expand towards the south-east. By the 740s the Slavic people known as the Carantanians had been brought under the Bavarian hegemony, and that control was asserted more vigorously from 772 onwards following an attempted rebellion in that year by these subjected Slavs.

The process by which the Bavarians came under the overall lordship of the Franks corresponds to a pattern common among the Germanic peoples east of the Rhine such as the Thuringians and the Alamanns. By the middle of the sixth century the Bavarians had been provided with a ruling dynasty of Frankish origin, and its chief, or *dux*, ran the duchy under the overall hegemony of the Merovingian kings to the west. This was the dynasty known to history as the Agilolfings, one of the very grandest of all Frankish families, and their ambitions extended well beyond the core Bavarian territories.

THE LOMBARD-BAVARIAN CONNECTION

Garipald is the first Agilolfing ruler whose name is recorded, and the Lombard historian Paul the Deacon was sufficiently impressed to give him the title of king. No other evidence survives of Garipald's kingly title, but both marriage and descent certainly gave him a regal association. His wife Walderada was the daughter of the Lombard king Wacho I (c. 510–40) and she had been married previously to Theudebald, king of the Franks (548–55). Tassilo I, who was probably the son of Garipald and Walderada, may well have been made king c. 593 by the Merovingian monarch Childebert II (584–96), though the pages of Paul the Deacon's *History of the Lombards* record him as having been a duke at the time of his death.

The fact that the Agilolfing rulers of Bavaria had a pedigree going straight back to the ancient and royal Lombard lineage had a major political consequence. Later Lombard rulers did not have that dynastic link, and they were therefore very keen to have alliances with the Bavarian rulers. In 589 the Agilolfing noblewoman Theodelinda (d. 627), who was Tassilo I's sister, married the Lombard king Authari (584–90). She outlived her husband. But she must have enjoyed the Lombard royal experience since she married his successor Agilulf (590–616), a duke of Turin who had seized the throne in the absence of a direct heir. King Adaloald (616–26) was the son of this second marriage but was deposed on account of his supposed insanity. The nobleman who succeeded him on the throne was Arioald (626–36), another ambitious duke of Turin. Since he was married to Adaloald's sister Gundiberga the Agilolfing connection continued. Her distinguished lineage, however, did not save the poor queen from being locked up in a monastery after her husband accused Gundiberga of plotting against him.

Theodelinda's Agilolfing genes produced yet another Lombard king in the form of Aripert I (653–61) the son of her brother Gundoald. The 'Bavarian dynasty' of Lombard rulers who traced their origins back to either Theodelinda or Gundoald was deposed in 712 by Liutprand (712–44). He proved to be a powerful Lombard ruler as well as a long-lived one, and he was careful to buttress his position by making sure that he had an Agilolfing wife. The Agilolfings showed an equal zeal for the alliance: the wife of Tassilo III, duke of Bavaria (748–88), was the daughter of the Lombard king Desiderius (757–74).

THE BACKGROUND TO THE ANNEXATION OF BAVARIA

These powerful and long-lived associations made the Agilolfings of Bavaria the natural allies of successive Lombard ruling houses. At the same time, however, they had to be mindful of the fact that they were subject to a more powerful hegemony, that of the Merovingians and their Carolingian successors. The Bavarian rulers also needed to keep an eye on certain domestic rivals, some of whom were themselves of Frankish origin and therefore ready to play that particular card when quarrelling with the Agilolfings. Charlemagne's elimination of the Bavarian ruling house in 788 certainly suited the interests of these powerful families, and his subsequent partition of the duchy into a number of smaller counties gratified their localized ambitions.

There are also signs that elements within the Church in Bavaria, and especially its bishops, were wary of the Agilolfings and their increasingly active role in ecclesiastical policy. Bavaria's dukes were keen on the reorganization of their Church domestically and also involved themselves with the missionary activity which was being directed towards the Slavs on their eastern frontier. Regensburg, Freising and Salzburg were all dioceses established by the Agilolfings whose patronage also extended to the founding of monasteries such as San Candido in 769 and Kremsmunster in 778.

The eighth century was of course a period of vigorous Church reform right across central and western Europe, and the Carolingians were especially associated with the cause of renewing the Frankish Church. Bavarian bishops were similarly appreciative of the need to update Church structures to keep in step with the new missionary impulses of the age. But they were also very conscious of the need to protect their own position, and when Boniface, that ecclesiastical agent provocateur operating under Frankish protection, tried to get involved in the Bavarian diocesan reorganization in the 740s he was repulsed. The Frankish monarchy itself, however, was another matter. Bavarian churchmen may well have preferred a long-distance association with the Carolingians rather than having the Agilolfings breathing down their necks.

Charlemagne's Bavarian annexation was the culmination of tensions which had developed earlier in the century. Under the later Merovingians the duchy, like other territories east of the Rhine, had been able to assert some kind of de facto independence of the Frankish kingdom. Carolingian foreign and military policy took a dim view of this development and strove to reassert the long-established hegemony. Charles Martel campaigned in Bavaria in both 725 and then again three years later, and the fact that he did not need to return to Bavaria after 728 implies that he achieved the local acceptance of his authority. A Bavarian noblewoman called Beletrude and her niece Swanachild accompanied Martel home and his subsequent marriage to Swanachild would have been a further sign of the Frankish hegemony. The succession to Martel, however, was no smooth transfer of power from one generation to the next, and his sons Pippin III and Carloman had, as we have seen, a fight on their hands in Aquitaine. They probably had to assert themselves pretty vigorously in Bavaria as well, and in 743 the brothers launched a campaign against Duke Odilo who had married their own sister, Chiltrude. The Frankish army had to return home after suffering heavy losses on that occasion. Odilo's death in January 748, however, led to the creation of a set of circumstances which would allow Charlemagne to achieve, in the next generation, his goal of a final elimination of the Bavarian problem.

The son of Charles Martel and Swanachild was called Grifo, and his mother's ancestry gave him some kind of a claim to the Bavarian dukedom. Although initially kept in captivity by Carloman and Pippin III, he had managed to escape and by 747 was to be found among the Saxons who had granted him refuge. In the course of the next year Grifo launched a coup in Bavaria with the help of a local count called Suidger, thereby dispossessing Duke Tassilo, the infant heir of Odilo and Chiltrude. Tassilo's supporters would have included a number of powerful local noblemen, and it was they who now issued an appeal to Francia for assistance. Pippin III duly obliged, recognizing the opportunity this gave him for a powerful reassertion of his dynasty's hegemony in an area which had become troublesome but remained vital for the realization of Frankish interests.

Pippin's army captured Grifo and returned the dukedom to young Tassilo who was obliged to accept his uncle's authority in explicit terms. Tassilo and his heirs would now be expected to provide military assistance to the Frankish kingdom and its rulers. The earliest example of this subordination would come in 756 when the Bavarian ruler was ordered by Pippin to participate in a military expedition against the Lombards, and Tassilo was at his side as the force marched towards Pavia. Oath-taking ceremonies of a highly detailed kind are also meant to have been held at Compiègne in the following year, in the course of which Tassilo is supposed to have promised to bear allegiance to Pippin, his sons Charlemagne and Carloman, 'as a vassal should to his lords'.

The Compiègne ceremonies may well be a fiction, or at least an elaboration of what actually happened. The annalist concerned may have invented the details at a later date in order to provide a justification of Charlemagne's deposition of Tassilo, but the account does at least give us an indication of the Frankish ruling circle's opinion of the duke's inferior status. The Frankish sources get to work again on the issue of Tassilo when describing his failure to accompany Pippin on his fourth Aquitainian expedition in 763: 'Tassilo brushed aside his oaths and all his promises and sneaked away on a wicked pretext, disregarding all the good things which King Pippin his uncle had done for him. Taking himself off, with lying excuses, he went to Bavaria and never again wanted to see the king face to face.' That last phrase is a strong indication that the entire entry must have been written after Pippin's death in 768. Tassilo may well not have been present on the Aquitainian campaign but the annalist's interpretation of his absence captures the mood of Charlemagne and his courtiers at a much later date when any and every evidence of Tassilo's supposed perfidy was being used, and invented, to justify the ruthless measures that had been taken against him.

If Pippin was outraged by Tassilo's ingratitude he nonetheless took no action against him during his remaining years on the throne, and there is every indication of Bavarian forces being prepared to play their allotted role in the waging of war on behalf of the Carolingian dynasty. Bertrada certainly thought it worthwhile to visit Bavaria on her way to Italy in 770, and the speculation concerning her role in the construction of a diplomatic alliance involving the dukedom and the Carolingian dynasty has already been touched upon. The Tassilo who emerges in some annals covering this period is far from being the resentful plaything of Frankish power as recorded in the *Annales Regni Francorum*. His victory over the Slavic Carantanians on the Bavarian borders in 772 as well as his active promotion of the Slavs' Christianization are both fairly well documented, while his foundation of the monastery of San Candido (at Innichen), another frontier site, shows an activist ruler intent on the conversion of the Slovenes, another Slavic grouping.

THE SUBMISSION OF DUKE TASSILO

In 781 Charlemagne held an assembly at Worms, and he was keen that Tassilo should attend. The duke accepted and an exchange of twelve hostages on each side was agreed upon in order to ensure Tassilo's safety. The mutuality of that exchange shows that Charlemagne knew that he was not dealing with a mere dependant and also demonstrates that the duke's attendance at the annual Frankish assembly was an unusual event. It was an important year for the king. Sub-kingdoms had just been established in Italy and Aquitaine, and this assembly was the first opportunity for the Frankish nobility to come together and pay homage to young Pippin and his brother Louis, the boy-kings whose regal careers had been anticipated by a papal coronation, and whose titles anticipated a secure future for the Carolingian dynasty. Legitimacy was the issue here, and its public acknowledgment. Tassilo's presence at this great event signified the intimacy of his own family's connection with the Frankish royal house. Besides which, Bavaria was a dukedom of acute strategic significance to the new kingdom of Italy and it was important to bind Tassilo into Charlemagne's decisions about the shape of the Carolingian future.

It would be some years yet before Charlemagne would act against Tassilo, but when the moment came it involved a degree of stage management and, as we might expect, a fair amount of papal support. In 787 Charlemagne was in Italy and, after he had secured the submission of the Beneventans, spent Easter in Rome. While he was there Charlemagne, together with Pope Hadrian I, received two Bavarian emissaries, Bishop Arn of Salzburg and Abbot Hunric of Mondsee, both of whom bore a message from Tassilo. Would the pope act as an intermediary in the dispute which had recently arisen between Charlemagne and Tassilo? The details of the dispute are unknown but the fact that the churchmen are named gives credence to the annalist's story, and the background of Frankish ambition with regard to Bavaria makes a quarrel at least plausible. Hadrian's readiness to broker a deal would have been a natural response. It is the Frankish annalist's account of what happened next which suggests some calculated plotting, while also giving us another insight into the mentality of a dynasty on the make.

Charlemagne is said to have been ready to agree to peace terms which would then be negotiated by the pope, and the two ambassadors are supposed to have claimed that they lacked the authority to agree to such a deal there and then. If that was indeed what the bishop and the abbot told Hadrian and Charlemagne, it was a natural enough response. No ruler could have been expected to be bound by treaty arrangements arrived at by his emissaries and without reference to his own ultimate authority. That was not the way of princes in eighth-century Europe. Nor is there any indication of any previous negotiations having taken place before this particular meeting. It was at this point, however, that the pope lost his temper and accused the ambassadors of bad faith. He threatened to anathematize Tassilo and his supporters if the duke did not start to behave according to the terms of his undertaking, made on oath, to obey Pippin and his heir Charlemagne. Were this not done,

Charlemagne's army, according to the pope, would be freed of any contaminating sin were it to take retaliatory action. It could attack Bavarian territory with all that might entail, including the taking of human life and the burning of property. The anger was clearly contrived: after all, there is no evidence of Tassilo having launched any aggressive action against the Franks at any stage. But the episode, together with its emphasis on oaths pledged and broken, was designed to play an important role in justifying what was to come. Charlemagne and his papal accomplice had decided on their course of action and were casting around for convenient reasons to justify what they were going to do in any event.

The king's next step was to call an assembly in Worms on his return to Francia. Senior ecclesiastics and the nobility congregated there would have heard his account of the recent Italian expedition, and also an explanation of 'what had been done concerning Tassilo'. Charlemagne was preparing them for his solution to the Bavarian question. He issued an order commanding Tassilo to attend the assembly 'in order that all should be fulfilled according to the order of the Apostolic [pope] and as was only just . . . that he should be obedient and faithful to the lord king . . . and to his sons and to the Franks'. *Missi* were sent to Bavaria to effect this command, with no hostages either offered or exchanged to secure Tassilo's safety. The duke, who must by now have been thoroughly alarmed, refused to come to Worms. Charlemagne was thereby supplied with a pretext for war.

The Frankish commanders organized a tripartite assault on Bavaria from west, north and south: Charlemagne's own army of Franks marched from Worms, a combined assault force consisting of Saxons, Thuringians and eastern Franks assembled on the Danube at a point between Ingolstadt and Regensburg, while a third army was raised in Italy and marched towards Bolzano. Tassilo submitted immediately and, in the gleeful account offered by the annalist, he met Charlemagne and 'returned the dukedom that had been given to him by the lord king Pippin [III] and acknowledged himself to have sinned in all things and to have acted evilly'. He was required to take an oath of vassalage and, having surrendered thirteen hostages who included his own son Theodo, the duke was officially pardoned and allowed to leave. But Charlemagne had not finished with him yet.

Tassilo was now a royal vassal and his attendance at the next assembly of the Franks, held in Ingelheim in 788, was mandatory. New accusations were brought against him during the meeting and various anonymous Bavarians accused him of conspiring with the Avars and against Frankish interests. He was also supposed to have uttered treasonous remarks concerning Charlemagne. Once again the records obsess about oaths and their violation, and Tassilo was supposed to have engaged in hostile acts subsequent to his submission at Worms in the previous year. The annalist records that the duke 'ordered his *homines* to make mental reservations when they were swearing oaths and to swear deceitfully; what is more, he confessed to having said that even if he had ten sons he would rather lose every one of them than accept that the agreements should remain as they were or allow what he had sworn to stand'. This may well be an accurate record of the accusations brought against Tassilo, and he may even have confessed to them as the *Annales Regni Francorum* insist that he did. But he surely had little choice in the matter. Another source records that Tassilo was only charged after his wife and children, 'together with their treasures and household, extremely numerous', had also been brought to Ingelheim. If this report is correct, the duke's entire family were already being kept under custody, a fact which would surely have impelled him to plead guilty to the trumped-up charges.

Bavaria's duke was formally sentenced to death by the Frankish assembly, but the sentence was not carried out and Charlemagne ensured instead that Tassilo was tonsured as a monk. He was then sent to the monastery of Jumièges in what is now Normandy. His sons Theodo and Theodebert were also forced to become monks and his wife Liutperga, daughter of the Lombard ruler Desiderius, was sent into exile. Where exactly they were sent we do not know but Charlemagne could rest content in the knowledge that he had abolished the ducal line and that there would be no future heirs to raise the banner of Bavarian identity. Other leading Bavarians were also sent into exile and the duchy itself was divided into countships with overall control resting with a *praefectus*.

Charlemagne's first nominee to this prefectorial post was his own brother-in-law Gerold, an aristocrat from Alamannia, and that appointment signified the determination to subject Bavaria to dynastic control. It was a policy which was unrelenting in its application, and the following year Charlemagne took an army into Bavaria in order to obtain the explicit acknowledgment of his authority by its subject population. An assembly of the Bavarians congregated at Regensburg gave him the formal submission that he wanted, and the populace handed over hostages as a guarantee of their future quiescence.

The unfortunate Tassilo re-emerges in the historical record just one more time when he was obliged to attend the Council of Frankfurt in 794. This was a Church council convened by Charlemagne under papal authority and its main purpose was to condemn as heretical the belief labelled 'adoptionism'. This particular heresy had acquired a certain following in eighth-century Spain, with its portrayal of a Christ who had been born entirely human and only became divine at a later stage in his life as a result of his adoption by God. This drive in favour of a universal orthodoxy can be seen as a counterpart in the realm of belief to the Carolingian assertion of political unity, and Tassilo was expected to play a very public role in this regard when he appeared before the assembled ecclesiastics. Having been brought from his monastery to Frankfurt, he was 'reconciled with the lord king, renouncing and handing over to the lord king all the rights which he had in Bavaria'. He had of course no such rights left to transfer, but this was still an important moment since it publicized Charlemagne's successful absorption of Bavaria within a victorious Francia.

The Frankish accusation that Tassilo had been conspiring with the Avars was clearly a trumped-up charge. When writing up their account of what happened in 788, the annalists claimed that the truth of the charge was confirmed by the launch of an Avar offensive later in the same year. But that was a campaign conducted against the Bavarians themselves, and it was repulsed by them in a frontier engagement some time before Charlemagne's arrival in Regensburg. The Franks' absorption of the duchy, however, did mean that from now on there was no territory which might serve as a buffer zone between themselves and this significant foe from the east. The Bavarian–Avar border zone had become the new eastern frontier territory of Charlemagne's enlarged Francia, and the king now turned his attention to the new kind of military threat which was to be found on this new and unexplored outpost of his realm.

EASTERN ADVENTURES

WHO WERE THE AVARS?

Alarmist stories and sensationalizing rumours about the Avars had been circulating in western Europe ever since the middle of the sixth century, the time of their first appearance in the literary sources of that part of the continent. But the Greek empire had been familiar with their style of swift warfare waged on horseback for rather longer, since these nomads were already dominating the plains north of the Danube during the fifth century. Their ultimate origins lay in central Asia, and the motivation for their move to the west lay in the disturbance and conflicts among other tribal confederations located on the border with China. The Huns are the most celebrated of these groups, and the vigorous Chinese consolidation of their own borders forced these nomadic warriors to abandon their original homelands. A subsequent domino effect, set in motion by the Huns, forced the Avars on their travels westward. Their initial European impact was experienced in the middle Danube valley, a region whose control was being hotly contested between three Germanic peoples: the Gepids, the Heruls and the Lombards.

There may have been some form of Avar–Lombard alliance directed against the Gepids, whose subsequent annihilation could have been a consequence of that military action. And there is reliable evidence that the Avar tribes went on to occupy what had once been Gepid-controlled territory. Whatever advantage the Lombards may have gained by their alliance was soon dispelled, since their new neighbours proved to be more powerful adversaries than the Gepids. The Lombards' own traditions maintained that their decision to move south from their original territories and to invade Italy in 568 was due to the hostile pressure placed on them by the Avars. By the beginning of the seventh century the Avars had become a significant central European power able to exert their hegemony over the Slavic peoples located north of the Danube and in the Balkans. From these areas they were able to pose a threat to

Byzantium and in 626 the Avars, aided by their Slav dependants, launched an assault against the city walls of Constantinople itself. They were foiled in that attempt, and subsequent decades saw their gradual displacement as a significant power along the lower Danube basin by the Bulgars, another nomad confederacy which grew to greatness and became Byzantium's powerful adversary. Even so, and well into the period of Carolingian expansion, the Avars remained a powerful force towards the west, especially in the region surrounding Lake Balaton (in modern Hungary), as well as in the south beyond the Danube to the Sava valley and also in the south-west to the Morava valley.

Nomadic speed enabled the Avars to inflict a series of defeats over centuries on civilizations which were more sophisticated but less adroit at agile retaliation. In the process they garnered considerable amounts of loot and imposed annual tributes. The Avars' wealth in gold and silver was also hugely boosted as a result of their frequent deployment as mercenaries by the Byzantines. It has been estimated that by 626 payments to the Avars in gold and other goods amounted to a total value of some 200,000 *solidi*. That sum would have outstripped the resources available to the treasury of any other contemporary European power with the exception of Byzantium itself.

The same restless agility which secured their triumphs also meant that the Avars had little interest in establishing a consolidated empire. Their relation with the Slavic tribes that they conquered is a case in point. These peoples became the settled populations of the Balkans while the Avars remained north of the Danube, exercising a very remote form of overall hegemony over them and exacting payments in tribute. The Slavs conquered by the Avars seem to have been used as guarantors of frontier security since they occupied zones which were at the furthermost edge of the Avar hegemony. It was the Bavarians' expansion to the south-east, therefore, and their associated subjection of the Slavic Carantanians in the 740s, that brought the duchy into confrontation with the Avars. Charlemagne's deposition of Tassilo in 788 meant that he also succeeded the duke in his role as a protagonist in the Bavarian region's most important military conflict. These circumstances practically invited an Avar–Frankish war.

THE ONSET OF FRANKISH–AVAR HOSTILITIES

In 788 three battles ensued between the two powers: one was waged in Friuli in the Italian north-east, and the others took place on Bavarian soil. The fact of an Italian dimension is interesting, and may indicate a degree of encouragement being given to the Avars by Byzantium, a power with a history of employing these peoples of the steppes as mercenaries when it suited Constantinople's strategic interests. In the southern Italy of 788 hostilities had broken out between the Byzantines and the Lombard dukes of both Spoleto and Benevento after these rulers' submission to Charlemagne in 779 and 787 respectively. A Frankish army, under the command of a reliable *missus* called Winigis, had been sent to Italy as a relief force to aid these Lombard rulers, and the Avar attack in Friuli may have been inspired by the Byzantines as a way of distracting the Carolingian force. The Bavarian attacks, however, surely sought to exploit the power vacuum within the duchy in the months following Tassilo's removal from power. Avar alarm on seeing the emergence to their west of a major power in the form of Charlemagne's Francia can also be guessed at. They were a scattered collection of tribes and chronically prone to fragmentation, but the evidence suggests that they did have a reliable system of intelligence gathering and they had probably got wind of the scale of Frankish military success since Charlemagne's succession to the throne.

All three Avar attacks failed but it would be another three years before Charlemagne pressed home his advantage, and at the Regensburg assembly of 791 he formally proposed a campaign to avenge injuries inflicted on 'the Christian people'. The Avars were ethnically diverse but the one characteristic which did help to define them (at least in Frankish eyes) was their paganism. They probably had information about the Christian missions to the conquered Slavs which had been sponsored by both Bavarians and Franks, and the prospect of that kind of proselytizing would have ensured the Avars' animosity. This cultural and religious dimension to the Avar–Frankish conflict seems to have been present right from the beginning. When Charlemagne's army arrived at that point on the river Enns, in eastern Bavaria, which marked the start of its journey into Avar-controlled territory, the king ordered his soldiers to spend three days in observance of various Christian rites. From 5 to 7 September the Frankish force fasted, prayed, recited penitential litanies and took part in liturgical services. Special masses were said and the clergy recited fifty psalms. Charlemagne's letter describing these preparations to his queen, Fastrada, suggests that elements in Francia's population, and perhaps especially the royal household and aristocracy, were also expected to engage in a three-day fast as a supplication for victory in the struggle ahead.

Charlemagne's disposition of his forces ensured an initial approach along both banks of the river Danube: to the south marched the division of the army led by the king in person, while on the northern bank a second force, which included Saxons and Frisians, was led by Count Theoderic and by Meginfred, the Royal Chamberlain. This was a major expedition and the fact that it was going into battle so very late in the normal campaigning season perhaps indicates the degree of preparation undertaken during the preceding summer months. The additional presence of a fleet which carried the baggage and supplied a chain of communication across the Danube made this one of the greatest of all Frankish expeditionary forces. No pitched battles are recorded and the Avars seem to have dissolved away rather than deciding to stand and fight. It is possible, of course, given their particular style of warfare, that they wanted to avoid a pitched battle, and that the Avars' plan was to lure the Frankish force deeper into their own territory and into a terrain where they would enjoy a greater advantage over their adversary. The evidence suggests, however, that they were having serious difficulties in asserting control over their own forces by this point.

Having advanced some 150 miles east of the original point of departure at the river Enns, Charlemagne called a halt and led his troops back to Regensburg, while Theoderic and Meginfred made their way back to Francia through the territories of the Bohemian Slavs. The king had gained his victory although he had only penetrated into the very periphery of the area within overall Avar control, and Charlemagne seems to have decided that a deeper penetration into the enemy's territory would be necessary in order to achieve the kind of knock-out blow that would signify the enemy's explicit submission. 793 was probably the year he chose for the launch of just such an expedition, but a major attack launched by the Saxons at a point on the river Weser and against the northern army under Theoderic's generalship meant that the campaign had to be abandoned. Charlemagne apparently took some care to stop the news of this disaster from spreading since he feared its possible impact on the Avars and any plans they might have been harbouring. But they were not the only enemy he had to fear in this regard. The Arabs in Spain had learnt of the king's intention to launch a major campaign against the Avars and, judging that Charlemagne would be preoccupied with that grand strategy, they launched in 793 an opportunistic, and highly successful, raid across the Pyrenees on Frankish-controlled Septimania.

THE CONSEQUENCES OF THE AVAR DISSOLUTION

There would in fact be no full-scale military confrontation between the Franks and the Avars, whose dominion along the middle Danube and on the Hungarian plain simply dissolved away during the 790s. Why this should have been so remains uncertain and any possible answer is more a matter of hints and guesswork than reliable evidence. But we do know of an unexpected development in the course of 795 while Charlemagne was campaigning against the Saxons. He was at a point on the river Elbe when a major Avar figure travelled to see him and asked for arrangements to be made for his Christian baptism. The source gives this Avar leader the otherwise unexplained title of 'Tudun', and his decision to become a Christian amounted also to a political submission which was formalized in a ceremony held at Aachen in the following year. Was the action of this dissident related to the internal conflicts which we know had broken out at about the same time among the Avar leadership? The overall leader, whose office was that of 'Khagan', and another official who held the title of 'Jugur' are described as being at war with each other, and in the course of that conflict both were killed by their own followers.

This was clearly a moment of great opportunity for the Franks, and Eric, duke of Friuli, was well placed to seize the moment as the man who had been appointed to run this crucial frontier territory. In 796 he sent an expedition commanded by a Slav leader called Wonomir deep into the territory controlled by the Avar federation and further than any enemy force had ever been before. There he found the 'Ring' or *Hringum*, a system of concentric layers of earthworks which served as the command centre of the confederation and also accommodated its leadership. Right at the heart of the structure, and previously carefully guarded, Wonomir's men discovered an immense amount of treasure which would have consisted for the most part of the tribute exacted by the Avars (mostly in the form of gold *solidi*) and also of loot seized by them. This, we should remember, would have been the sum total of some century and a half of successful warrior activity both as enemies and as mercenaries, and as a still-nomadic people with no tradition of settled civilization the Avars would have had precious little need to spend any of this treasure. It was this treasure which, having been conveyed to Aachen, would transform the Frankish royal finances in the last decade of Charlemagne's reign and enable him to embark on some of the artistic, literary and architectural achievements that characterize the 'Carolingian renaissance'. The start of work on the additions to the palace complex at Aachen, for example, is datable to the period following the arrival of the Avar treasure. Charlemagne also gave some of the treasure to other rulers. Such gestures of largesse were typical of early medieval European rulers who wanted to display their success – and some of these riches were sent by Charlemagne to Rome and the court of the new pope Leo III.

The treasure was so abundant that not all of it could be carried back to Francia in one journey, and later that year an expedition under the command of Pippin, king of Italy, was sent to seize the rest of the booty and then to demolish the Ring. When they arrived at the Ring Pippin's men found that the remaining treasure was still in place in the middle of the earthworks, and the fact that the Avars had taken no steps for its protection or transfer elsewhere for safer custody suggests that their military organization and defensive capacity had by now collapsed entirely.

The *Tudun's* baptism had been followed by that of his immediate followers, and his office probably denoted some kind of regional military governorship. His own manoeuvrings would have been dictated by internal Avar rivalries in the context of a federation in full decline, and this particular *Tudun* would soon renege on his alliance with Charlemagne. Another holder of the same office is described by the Frankish annalist covering the year 811 as exercising command over those Slavs who lived along the Danube. The *Tudun* of 795 could therefore have been enjoying a similar range of powers, ruling on behalf of the central authority and governing the subjected population. If he was coming over to Charlemagne's side he would surely therefore have been offering to transfer to overall Frankish control a substantial territory occupied by Slavs. The history of the Germanic tribes themselves had shown how kings had to maintain their position by showing their prowess as effective war leaders. The *Khagan* had been the Avars' leader at a time when, for the first time in their history, a large-scale foreign army had been able to penetrate the federation's outer territorial defences and then strike right at the heart of its power structure. He would therefore have lost much of his authority and power to command, and the *Jugur* documented as fighting the *Khagan* in 796 may well have been a dissident 'subordinate'. Given these circumstances, it is not difficult to envisage a regional overlord, viceroy or *Tudun* manoeuvring for position.

Charlemagne's Frankish monarchy was therefore the beneficiary of the Avars' internal dissolution. That process had been going on before he launched his first campaign against them and the military action he took revealed the extent of that malaise rather than being a decisive blow inflicted on a major military power. His victory, though, was certainly an important element in the aura of invincible power which surrounded the king in the years immediately preceding his coronation as emperor in 800. For at least a century and a half the Avars had been a thorn in the side of successive emperors of Byzantium, and the credit for their defeat would be attributed to the new Carolingian power which dominated western Europe. But Charlemagne himself did not view his success in the former Avar-controlled territories as an excuse for imperial expansion into the lands of the steppe and south of the Danube. The wealth that he seized from the Ring was used for domestic cultural projects and his own diplomatic ends rather than providing a basis for direct colonial rule and systematic settlement. He had consolidated Frankish authority in what had once been considered a contested frontier, and

the border zone of effective Christianization had therefore shifted east-
wards. Missionary work among the Avars was certainly part of Charlemagne's responsibility as a Christian ruler and, since such ventures were
being directed from 796 onwards by Bishop Arn of Salzburg, Pope Leo
III acceded to the king's request that the see's status be raised to that of
an archbishopric. But beyond the new frontier there was now a power
vacuum, and various Slav populations emerged to take charge of their
own destinies within the territories once dominated by their Avar masters. One of the most significant of these developments was the establishment of the ninth-century Slav kingdom termed Great Moravia. Its
precise location and possible identification with the valley of the river
Morava flowing through the Czech republic remain debatable, but the
kingdom's defeat by invading Magyars would be an enduring memory
in the development of Slav cultural consciousness.

Meanwhile, what became of the once mighty Avars? In 799 an Avar
force defeated Gerold, the governor of Bavaria who was also Charlemagne's brother-in-law, but this is the sole evidence we have of their
retaining any kind of offensive capacity. The fact that the Avars were
never a distinctive grouping in ethnic terms means that they could have
assimilated fairly easily with the Slav population, and when another
Tudun submitted formally to Charlemagne in Regensburg in 803, his
retinue is described as a mixture of both Avars and Slavs.

For at least a few years into the new Carolingian hegemony over the
region there were some Avars who remained loyal to the *Khagan* and
submitted to his authority within the lands he had been allocated by
the Frankish monarchy. In 805 the *Khagan*, who had converted to Christianity and taken the name of Theodore at his baptism, went to see
Charlemagne with a complaint. He and his people could no longer live
on the lands given to them by the king because of its subsequent 'infestation' by Slavs. Could they instead move to an area south of the Danube?
The land Theodore had his eye on lay between the two settlements which
would evolve subsequently into the towns of Szombathely in modern
Hungary and of Petronell which is located on the river Danube and
within contemporary Austria. Charlemagne agreed, and the Avars who
lived in this area on the extreme westernmost edge of the Hungarian
plain became an outpost of Carolingian power. Their rulers operated

under Charlemagne's patronage and their function was to protect access into Bavaria via the Danube valley. When Theodore died later in 805 his successor sent a leading Avar to the king asking for his permission to rule. Conversion to Christianity would appear to have been part of the deal allowing this to happen. The new *Khagan* was accordingly baptized in the river Fischa and took the name of Abraham.

Theodore's complaint about Slav 'infestation' shows that some Avars were resisting assimilation right at the beginning of the ninth century. In 811 Charlemagne had to send in an army to deal with Avar–Slav disputes, and its commanders sent one Avar leader and some Slav ones to Aachen in November of that year in order to confer with the king. By then, however, the Slavs were ensuring the Avars' elimination, both through warfare and by cultural and ethnic assimilation. We know that in 822 the Avars living south of the Danube sent presents and envoys to Louis the Pious, Charlemagne's son and successor. But after that date there is no further record of the Avars existing anywhere, and by then the future of large areas of the territories they once dominated lay with the Slavs who were migrating and expanding in ever greater numbers.

Part of the reason for that Slavic expansion lies in the western Balkans where the rulers of Byzantium were having increasing success in reasserting control of areas they had previously lost. In the late eighth century the Greeks reoccupied an area extending from south of the Balkan mountains to the Aegean coast, and during the reign of Nicephorus (802–11) they followed this up with a swift advance to the west across the Balkans and into western Greece. This brought Byzantium to a confrontation with the Bulgars who launched a highly effective military retaliation. The impact of both these protagonists on the Slav population of the central and western Balkans was severe and this motivated them to migrate northwards into the Danube region and the former Avar territories. Theodore's characterization of the Slav menace as an 'infestation' suggests that he was complaining about this migrant wave rather than referring to a specific military defeat. This is the context for the emergence of the Bohemians or *Beheimi* as a distinctive Slav confederation established to the north-west of the remaining Avar rump. Their land is mentioned for the first time in 791 when Charlemagne, at the end of that year's campaign against the Avars, ordered the Saxon and Frisian elements of the military expedition to travel home through Bohemia.

It was not just the Avars who had to contend with the consequences of the Slav migration and self-assertion. The Franks also came into conflict with this new element in central Europe, and in 805 the campaign authorized by Charlemagne, and which was under the command of his son Charles the Younger, ravaged the Bohemians' entire territory and secured the death of their leader, Lecho. In the following year Charlemagne followed this up with a second military expedition against the Bohemians, this time with a force raised in Burgundy, Bavaria and Alamannia. Another chapter had opened. The Carolingian kings of east Francia who were Charlemagne's successive heirs, followed in turn by their tenth-century successors, the Ottonian kings and emperors, would all struggle with the question of how to deal with the Slavs.

NORTHERN CONSEQUENCES
AND IMPERIAL CONCLUSIONS

CHARLEMAGNE'S MILITARY PRAGMATISM

The emergence of a greatly expanded Francia ruled by a king who became an emperor has been portrayed as a result of a consistent geopolitical strategy, one embarked upon by Charlemagne at the outset of his reign and pursued thereafter in order to promote a revival of ancient Roman notions of empire within a Christian dimension. But the reality of what happened as a result of campaigns waged and of battles both won and lost is a good deal more ambiguous, as this survey has suggested. Charlemagne's military responses were pragmatic when they needed to be as well as opportunistic when circumstances allowed them to be so. He was first and foremost a king of the Franks, and much of what he achieved on the borders of the original Francia – that blend of Austrasia and Neustria with Burgundy – was consistent with the ideas and policies pursued by his father, Pippin, and his grandfather, Charles Martel, as well as by their Merovingian predecessors as Frankish rulers. But although Charlemagne was not especially original in the scope of his ambitions, or in the set of assumptions which guided his military strategy, he was uniquely effective when it came to their implementation. His success in this regard made his legacy a daunting one for his immediate successors, and the Carolingian dynastic rulers of the ninth century struggled to emulate Charlemagne's achievements in the less propitious circumstances of the eastern and western Francia of their time. But it was inevitably the local context within which he operated that determined the scope and nature of Charlemagne's victories rather than the impulse of an idealism cast in the mould of an expansionist grand strategy.

It is his land campaigns which make the emperor so important a figure in the history of warfare, but Charlemagne also had an assertive naval policy and his fleets were notably successful in the western Mediterranean and the Adriatic. In 799 the Carolingian navy defeated a Muslim flotilla off the Balearic Islands. An expeditionary military force was then able to land on the islands which, following the submission of the occupying Saracens, duly became part of the Carolingian empire. The reign's last decade records much naval activity, which includes a series of successes enjoyed over the Byzantine navy in the Adriatic between 806 and 810 as well as victories over the Muslims off the coasts of Corsica, Sardinia and Majorca in, respectively, 806, 807 and 813. River navigation would play an important part in Charlemagne's land warfare, and in 793 he started work on the construction of a canal linking the Rhine with the Danube. Bad weather forced the abandonment of that work but traces of the massive engineering enterprise can still be seen. The canal would have provided the Carolingian military machine with a continuous river highway extending from western Europe to the Black Sea, and its planning shows the ambitious scope of Charlemagne's military strategy.

There were just four theatres of war that really mattered to Charlemagne in the course of his long years on the throne: those areas of northern Italy that were ruled by the Lombards; the duchy of Bavaria; the Avar-controlled territories which became contiguous with his expanded eastern frontier, and Saxony. The first three areas were eliminated as sources of opposition and absorbed with relative ease. Saxony is the exception, and the reason behind its successful long-term resistance pinpoints the difference between Charlemagne's Saxon wars and all his other military campaigns. The Lombard kingdom was an advanced civilization and its sophisticated monarchy enjoyed a pre-eminent position in relation to the very widespread regional centres of influence within the realm. As the new *Rex Langobardorum* Charlemagne was the heir to the same kind of pre-eminence, and the transfer of power was therefore a relatively smooth process. Lombard dukes might have been motivated to oppose this takeover but they were unable to form a coalition of those unwilling to accept Carolingian rule. None of them enjoyed anything like the equivalent of that preponderance of military power which had accrued to Charlemagne in Lombard north Italy and which enabled him to impose his will on the region. The Avars and the Bavarians illustrate a similar situation since the tribal federation of the former society and the aristocratic elite that governed the latter were subject to internal strains and divisions which, in turn, facilitated the Carolingian takeover. None of these conditions obtained in Saxony, and that fact ensured that the Franks faced a persistent problem in asserting and maintaining control despite the ten-year period of peace which followed the three-year period of continuous and intense warfare between 782 and 785.

THE RESURGENCE OF SAXON RESISTANCE AND CHARLEMAGNE'S FINAL SOLUTION

Part of the difficulty confronting the Franks was the sheer degree of Saxon internal organization. The existence of representative bodies for each Saxon regional community or *pagus*, each with its own elected leader, is fairly well attested. All the representatives of these communities would meet annually to discuss laws, deliver judgments on legal cases, and either plan next season's military campaigning or debate the details of the management of peace. The evidence suggests we are dealing here with large numbers of individuals, with each community being represented by a sum total of thirty-six people, twelve for each of the three social classes: the aristocracy, the free, and the half-free or *lati*. There is no indication that the Franks tried to get rid of such assemblies, on either the regional or the national level. Nor was there any great invasion of Frankish settlers into the conquered Saxony from 785 onwards, and Charlemagne's efforts at legislative renewal and religious reform had to be directed from a small number of fortresses which were outposts of Frankish culture within an inhospitable Saxon milieu and terrain. In those first few years of awkward peace the Franks did, however, make certain military demands. Saxon soldiers were called upon to do their duty and join Charlemagne's army when it attacked Bavaria in 787. They were also enrolled in the offensives that were launched against the Slavic Wiltzi in 789 and also the Avars during the 790s.

The first inklings of a serious recurrence of the Saxon question came in 793 when a *missus* attending the general assembly of the Franks held that year in Regensburg reported that 'a general defection of the Saxons' might be imminent, and concern had already been expressed that the Saxons were reneging on their promises to become Christians. The following year saw Charlemagne leading his army into Saxony. No pitched battle was fought and the enemy surrendered quickly, handing over hostages and taking further oaths of loyalty. But the king remained suspicious. The next assembly that he held was in 795 at Kostheim am Main, a location convenient for the launch of a Saxon offensive, and it was there that Charlemagne learnt that the Saxon troops he had ordered to present themselves for military service had failed to turn up. Refusal to obey such a command was a sure indication that the Saxons were getting ready to attack, and the king now looked for allies who could be co-opted for a pre-emptive strike.

It was the Slavic peoples known as the Abodrites who emerged as the Frankish army's companions-in-arms, a role they had already performed with some effectiveness during Charlemagne's earlier campaign of 789 against their fellow Slavs, the Wiltzi. A Saxon attack on an Abodrite force during the offensive launched in 795, and the killing of their king Witzan, is supposed to have spurred Charlemagne on to 'the swifter crushing of the Saxons' and to have 'provoked him to greater hatred of that perfidious people'. Certainly every available report of this last phase of the Frankish–Saxon wars lasting up to 802 indicates a cycle of attack and counter-attack motivated by a renewed ethnic hatred and genocidal fury.

Since the western Saxons had been in large measure disposed of as an effective enemy by 785, a good deal of the fighting of the late 790s took place in northern Saxony and within the area of the Elbe and the Weser. This was a region which had not been penetrated previously by the Frankish armies, and it had witnessed none of the mass Christian conversion which had accompanied Charlemagne's militant advance elsewhere in Saxony. The expeditions launched in 795–6 showed that Saxon disaffection was in fact widespread throughout their territory, and the reports of vigorously repressive measures adopted by the Franks prove that they were encountering profound hostility. Charlemagne's campaign of 797 took his army right up to Saxony's North Sea coast and to a point between the estuaries of the Elbe and the Weser. The fact that he took both Saxon and Frisian hostages at this location indicates that there may have been some kind of co-operation between the two peoples.

It was now a quarter of a century since Charlemagne had first gone to war against the Saxons as sole king of the Franks, but his determination to crush 'that perfidious people' was unabated and he decided to spend the winter of 797–8 in Saxony. His army would be quartered in locations right across the region, both north and south, with the explicit aim of cowing the rural population. The king himself and his entourage made their headquarters at a point near the confluence of the Weser with the Diemel, a location Charlemagne would christen *Heerestelle*, 'the Army's Meeting Place'.

Saxon retaliation was not slow in coming and in the early spring, before the Franks could obtain the supplies of fodder needed to get their horses moving and thereby attain military mobility, a group of dissidents to the east of the Elbe captured a number of Frankish nobles, killing some and holding others to ransom. Emboldened by this success, the same Saxon grouping launched an attack on the Abodrites, who remained the Franks' allies, and succeeded in defeating them in battle at Bornhoved near the North Sea coast. The Frankish commander who was in charge of part of the Abodrite force reported 4,000 Saxons killed during the first encounter alone. Another source revises the figure of the slain down to 2,901, but whichever figure is closer to the truth, this was clearly an exceptionally bloody encounter. Meanwhile Charlemagne, furious on account of the killing of his Frankish nobles, was laying waste to a large area of territory between the Weser and the Elbe.

The year was 799 and Saxony, Charlemagne's longest-lasting theatre of operations as a military commander, was now providing the background to that movement in Italian politics which would lead to his coronation a year later. He was in Paderborn and overseeing the imposition of a harsh peace settlement on the Saxons when news arrived from Rome of the physical attacks on Leo III. Charlemagne's move southwards would not have been possible had he not brought the Saxon situation under control by 799–800, and concern about Saxony continued in the period after his coronation. The first military action he took as emperor involved raising in 802 an army composed of pro-Frankish Saxons, who were then dispatched across the river Elbe in order to fight their less pliant compatriots within the last area of stubborn Saxon resistance to Carolingian rule. Charlemagne's ultimate offensive in Saxony therefore showed him dividing the Saxons in order the better to rule them. *Divide et impera* had been the strategy imputed to the Roman imperial commanders of classical antiquity, and now this latest heir to their legacy visited a final devastation on the Saxon people.

From 799 onwards Charlemagne had been expelling the Saxon population from its native territories, which he then appropriated as a prelude to settling his own Frankish soldiers on those lands. Here too there was surely an ancient Roman precept at work since the victorious generals of both the republic and the empire had rewarded their faithful veterans by granting them land. A network of loyal clients was thereby created, one which was supportive of their patrons' interests while these leaders manoeuvred for power in the domestic politics of Rome. Charlemagne's land grants fulfilled a similar purpose so far as the maintenance of his own power was concerned, and the *clientalia* he formed was composed of great aristocrats as well as the more humbly born soldiers who had marched in his armies. Those Saxons who were pushed off their land were then sent to work as unfree labourers in other parts of the Frankish empire, where they survived in that condition of modified slavery which would be categorized as serfdom at a later stage in the history of medieval Europe. In 804 the emperor in person led an army to the Saxon lands east of the Elbe and there he rounded up as many of the local population as he could get his hands on. Charlemagne then sent these dispossessed individuals back to Francia and 'dispersed them within his kingdom where he saw fit'. The newly empty lands beyond the Elbe were handed over to the reliably loyal Slavic Abodrites who, having been settled in their new homes and territories by the emperor, were happy to regard him as their patron. In the reign's last decade there were simply no Saxons left who might cause any trouble. The few surviving references to a once formidable foe merely record their presence as members of the Frankish army which was ensuring Charlemagne's hegemony over the Avars on the eastern front of his empire.

THE LIMITS TO EMPIRE: DANISH AND SLAVIC FRONTIER ZONES

During the 790s Francia's territorial expansion by military means came to an end. This halt probably reflected a conscious judgment arrived at by Charlemagne, his advisers and military commanders. His kingdom could not absorb any more new peoples and territories, and any military action taken on the expanded frontier zones had to safeguard those areas rather than expand them further. There were also limits to the Frankish religious mission and during Charlemagne's reign the Slavic tribes were not subjected to the kind of systematic conversion campaign which had been implemented in Saxony.

The river Elbe was the empire's eastern limit and it formed a boundary beyond which no system of direct rule was imposed. Even so, the very extent of this new empire and the external threats to which it was subjected meant that its ruler often had to intervene in areas lying beyond the border zones in order to protect his own military and political interests. The Abodrites are a case in point. Charlemagne not only gifted them the lands he had conquered to the east of the Elbe, he also nominated one of their leaders to be king. Thrasco, previously a *dux*, was clearly intended to be the ruler of a client-state which would be friendly to Frankish interests. There is a clear parallel here with the position of those Avars who had fled from the migrating Slavs and were then settled by Charlemagne in an area just south of the Danube. Charlemagne's attempt at sponsoring institutional change may not have worked in the case of the Abodrites, since by 808 Thrasco was once again being referred to as *dux* rather than *rex*. Nonetheless, the situation on the imperial boundaries as a whole showed that there were few neighbours who could insulate themselves from the external consequences of Francia's domestic, and Carolingian, transformation.

At the end of Charlemagne's reign it was Denmark which would supply the latest example of that domino effect, and this last phase in the story of Frankish militarism is also the beginning of a new period in the history of European warfare, one which would be dominated by the Viking warriors of Scandinavia.

DENMARK'S CHALLENGE

Towards the end of the late eighth century the Danes became increasingly concerned about the extension of Frankish influence in areas that were so close to their kingdom. There was something of a history of nervousness along the frontier zone which separated these two societies and that wariness extended as far back as the early sixth century. The reign of the Merovingian king Theuderic I (c. 511–33) had seen Frankish power making itself felt in the area to the north-east of the Rhine, and when the Danes launched a naval attack on that coastal area they were repulsed. Charlemagne's penetration into Saxony would have revived the Danes' fears, but to the south at least they were well protected by the *Danevirke*. Extending for nearly twenty miles along the south of the country from the marshes of the west to the port town of Schleswig on the coast of the Baltic Sea, the *Danevirke*'s system of defensive earthworks is one of the most impressive surviving fortifications of the early Middle Ages. In the earliest phase of its construction it may also have been a canal providing a shipping lane. It was certainly in place by the middle decades of the eighth century and the *Danevirke* would play an important role in Denmark's defensive strategies right up until the country's defeat by Prussia and Austria in the war of 1864. Only a country with a formidable degree of centralized power could have marshalled the workforce and amassed the technology needed to build this structure. Its very existence would have demonstrated to the Franks of the age of Charlemagne that the civilization which neighboured them to the north, though pre-literate, was capable of a high degree of organization.

The hospitality extended to the rebel Saxon leader Widukind when he fled to Denmark seeking refuge in 777 showed that King Sigifrid at least was not intimidated by Charlemagne and the evident scale of Frankish ambitions. Ten years later, however, the danger posed by Francia, its culture and armies alike, must have seemed painfully near with the establishment in 787 of a new episcopal see at Bremen close to the Danish frontier. The bishopric of Bremen enjoyed Frankish protection and its location would have aroused Danish suspicions of a full-scale mission intent on their conversion from paganism to Christianity. By this stage other areas of Europe provided plenty of evidence that the missionary enterprise of the Frankish Church tended to mirror the expansionist thrust of the Frankish monarchy, and Bremen became a very lively Christian centre. The career of the see's first occupant showed the kind of international links which had turned Christianity into such a formidable force among the Germanic peoples.

Willehad was an Anglo-Saxon missionary sent originally by the Northumbrian Church into Frisia c. 770 to Christianize the local population. His links across the North Sea ensured that his style of evangelism reflected the cultural and religious traditions exemplified in the career of Boniface. That intellectual and spiritual lineage, as well as his Frisian experiences, made Willehad well qualified for the Saxon mission, and in 780 Charlemagne instructed him to evangelize the area between the Weser and the Elbe. Widukind's uprising of 783 interrupted that endeavour and Willehad then retreated to the congenial atmosphere of the abbey at Echternach (in modern Luxembourg), a foundation established by the Northumbrian missionary Willibrord and continental Europe's first Anglo-Saxon monastery. Charlemagne's father, Pippin, had been baptized there and the emperor always took a close interest in the abbey's affairs and its scholarly activities. Echternach's scriptorium was one of Francia's busiest, and Willehad immersed himself in the business of transcribing the epistles of St Paul while also assembling a new missionary team. By 785 he was back at work converting the Saxons, and two years later he was made Bremen's first bishop.

The arrival of this well-connected and dynamic character right on the Danish frontier was a sign that Frankish energies were being directed towards that border and probably beyond it. Willehad's death in 789 after contracting a fever did not diminish the religious zeal associated with his name. Miraculous cures were supposed to take place at his tomb, which consequently became a major place of pilgrimage. Anskar, the monk who wrote an account of those miracles, became the effective inheritor of Willehad's mission as the great apostle to both the Danes and the Swedes during the reign of Louis the Pious.

The link between the Cross and the sword, between authority in its spiritual and temporal guises, was a defining attribute of Carolingian power. Charlemagne and those who acted in his name were at pains to make this explicit, and those who fought the Franks knew that military defeat leading to the imposition of direct rule necessarily involved Christian conversion as well. This had been the pattern followed in Saxony, and although evangelism in that area would turn out to be a very long-term project it is probable that Charlemagne and his circle saw the Christianization of the Danes (and perhaps also of the Slavic Wiltzi and Wends) as a natural extension of the same enterprise. The establishment of a bishopric in Bremen, followed by another in the Saxon settlement of Hamburg in 804, was surely an explicit cultural and political threat to the Danes and to those Slavs who lived beyond the Elbe. But the way the Danes responded to that challenge set them apart from many Slavs.

Some Slavic tribes had accepted the logic of the Frankish hegemony and were prepared to convert since this gave them the advantage of a reliable Frankish alliance in their struggles against many of the Saxons. And Charlemagne also benefited from the internal divisions among the various Slavic peoples since some of them regarded a Frankish alliance as a way of beating fellow Slavs belonging to other tribes. Among the Danes, however, there were no internal divisions of the kind used elsewhere by the Franks in order to 'divide and rule'. This was a compact, well-defined territory and one with a keen sense of its own cultural and political integrity, which is why the Danes viewed the Franks with such consistent hostility. The Franks' zealous linkage between religious culture and military policy meant that they were regarded as a straightforward threat to the very survival of Danish identity rather than as a neighbour that might be negotiated with and appeased.

It was the invasion of Saxony that aroused fears in the Danish peninsula, and Charlemagne had his first recorded diplomatic encounter with the Danes in 782 when he met King Sigifrid's envoys at the source of the river Lippe. Five years had passed since Widukind's flight to Denmark and the exile of this Saxon insurgent would have demonstrated to his hosts the reality of the Frankish menace. By 798, when Charlemagne sent his representative Godescalc to talk to Sigifrid, the Bremen bishopric had been established and the Franks were a visible and present danger. The Danish response would open a new theatre of war and by 800 we have the first reports of raiding and acts of piracy being committed by the *Nordmanni*, as the annals usually describe these northerners. This was why Charlemagne had to undertake a military inspection of the Channel coast just before travelling south to Rome for his coronation, and the fleet of ships that he had commissioned was now charged with the task of protecting that coastline.

Charlemagne's final anti-Saxon measures of 804 destabilized Denmark's international position by eliminating the Saxons east of the Elbe and giving a boost to his allies, the Slavic Abodrites. A new Danish king called Godefred raised a naval force and a cavalry unit, both of which were based at Schleswig right on the frontier between his kingdom and Saxony. Negotiations followed between the two kings' envoys, and the annalists record Charlemagne's determination to achieve the return of certain 'fugitives' who may have been escaped Saxons. At the time of this negotiation he was at Hollenstedt on the Elbe, the river which had become his imperial boundary to the east. But the Elbe was also close to the Danish frontier, and to the east of the river lay the Abodrites whose status as his allies made them vulnerable to a Danish attack.

In 808 Godefred, who was now allied to the Slavic Wiltzi, led a joint attack on the Abodrites. He forced their leader Thrasco to flee and may also have arranged for the hanging of another of their chief men, Godelaib, as a suitable sacrifice to Odin. Godefred's campaign led to the capture of a large number of Slav fortresses and as many as two-thirds of the Abodrites may have been taken hostage by the Danes. The greater humiliation, though, was the one inflicted on the Franks who, despite being allied to the Abodrites, had been unable to prevent this catastrophe, one moreover which would be allowed to go unavenged. Charles the Younger, Charlemagne's son, did lead an expedition across the Elbe against the Smeldingi and the Linones, minor Slavic peoples who had become Danish allies, and he proceeded to lay waste to their territories before retreating to Saxony. But the Danes themselves escaped any punishment and now started to consider their future options with regard to the king of the Franks, whose imperial crown combined allure with menace to so potent an effect.

DENMARK DESTABILIZED

The solution adopted by Godefred was broadly autarkic. Denmark's economic development and self-sufficiency would be promoted by controlling and restricting the movement of merchants in and out of the country. A tighter invigilation of border traffic in general was intended to further the Danes' military, cultural and political interests. When Godefred returned from campaigning against the Abodrites he destroyed their trading post on the Baltic, which the Danes called Reric, and the merchants of that settlement were forced to travel with him to the Danish port of Sliesthorp. He already had the *Danevirke*, of course, but Godefred also built another system of earthwork fortifications which extended from the Baltic to the river Eider's north bank. Provided with just one gateway to control the movement of peoples passing through it, this formidable structure gave Denmark a new defensive boundary to the south.

The scale of the Frankish involvement in the southern Baltic region had nonetheless destabilized the entire region, and Denmark's interests were ill-served by a simple policy of withdrawal. Frankish and Danish interests clashed partly because the two powers' frontier regions were now contiguous. But they also conflicted because each had its own allies among the Slavic and Saxon populations of the southern Baltic. Charlemagne and Godefred were therefore drawn into conflicts which were already endemic to these peoples. The Danish king realized that he was exposed to a retaliatory attack from the Franks as a result of his successful campaign against the Abodrites. In 809 Godefred sent a message to Charlemagne claiming that he had only attacked the Franks' allies because they had broken the terms of a treaty arrived at in 804. Representatives of the two kings then met on the Elbe–Danish frontier, and there must have been some kind of rapprochement between Godefred and the Abodrites since their leader Thrasco surrendered his son as a hostage to the Danes. Any agreement arrived at was soon undermined, however, as a result of Thrasco's subsequent campaign against the Slavic Wiltzi who were Denmark's allies. This was not Thrasco's only act of provocation since he also gained the support of some of the Saxons in order to attack another Slavic ally of Denmark's, the Smeldingi. So flagrant an act of aggression could not be ignored and rather than mounting a full-scale anti-Abodrite campaign Godefred arranged for Thrasco's murder.

The inter-Slavic conflict between the Abodrites on the one hand and the Wiltzi and Smeldingi on the other may well have ended up weakening all of them. At first sight, Charlemagne seems the most obvious beneficiary of these southern Baltic struggles. Godefred's actions could be presented as anti-Frankish provocation and Charlemagne's forces advanced into the frontier zone of Frisia where he built a fortified settlement just under twenty miles from the Danish border. In 810 a marked escalation of hostilities brought the two countries to the very brink of outright war. A Danish naval raid involving about 200 ships devastated some of the islands off the coast of Frisia, and Godefred's land army inflicted a heavy defeat on the Frisians. Charlemagne raised an army which started to advance through Saxony and towards the Danish border. At this stage in the reign, thirty-eight years after his emergence as sole ruler of the Franks, Charlemagne was not often to be seen campaigning at the head of his army. But there was a strong personal dimension to this last conflict and the king had heard that Godefred wanted to face him on the field of battle.

Even as these military preparations were reaching their final stages, however, they were being overtaken by political developments within Denmark. Godefred's promotion of a siege economy and his closing of the border had aggravated his country's difficulties and weakened the king's domestic position. Far from insulating Denmark from danger, his policies had exposed the country to a greater military threat than it had ever experienced in its history. The disruption of normal trade is one probable reason why so many Danes, along with other Scandinavians, were now resorting to piracy and migrating by sea beyond their original homelands. Godefred would pay the price for these failures and before the end of 810 he was murdered by a member of his own entourage.

In the same year Danish troops were withdrawn from Frisia, and Gode-fred's successor, Hemming, started the negotiations which led to a formal peace accord with the Franks in 811.

THE LOGIC OF EMPIRE

During the few remaining years of Charlemagne's reign Denmark no longer posed a challenge to the Frankish empire. To that extent the actions he had taken to deal with the threat from the north must be regarded as a success. Denmark continued to be plagued by internal discontent and political factionalism during the early ninth century, and some of the claimants to the throne who emerged during this period sought military help and dynastic recognition from the Franks. At the same time it is debatable whether Charlemagne's strategy in the southern Baltic was at all relevant to his kingdom's true interests, especially when viewed within its newly acquired imperial context. The expansion to the Elbe turned out to be a process which had raised a whole new set of military problems and political dilemmas rather than an achievement which might neatly round off Francia's borders and thereby establish what was, or was not, in the legitimate dynastic interest.

Charlemagne's campaigns in Lombardy, Bavaria and Saxony had shown him to be a pragmatic militarist. In these areas there were prece-dents for his interventions since the history of each territory revealed a long-established pattern of Frankish involvement, and that fact made all the difference. Like any military commander he made calculations about where and when to strike to maximum advantage, and he exe-cuted his moves in these regions at the moment when he thought for-tune could be prevailed upon to smile on him. But where Lombards, Saxons and Bavarians were concerned, Charlemagne also had the his-torical experience of his *gens*, the Frankish people and their leaders, to guide him. The endeavours of the past, and the experiences thereby gained, supplied him with a reliable context and helped lead him to suc-cess. But in areas where the precedents for intervention were more ambiguous, as in the case of northern Spain, or where they barely existed at all, as in the southern Baltic, his military strategies were more oppor-tunistic and therefore lacking in clear focus and sense of direction. The

Franks' successes in Saxony, hard-fought and maintained in often precarious circumstances, created a whole new set of military problems which eventually came to centre on the Danish question. And Denmark's consequent implosion was a major component in the development of that ninth-century Viking activity which plagued Charlemagne's successors on the thrones of the eastern and western Frankish kingdoms.

A tremulous kind of peace descended on Francia in the last three years or so of Charlemagne's reign, and the aged emperor's scepticism about the chances of its survival is reflected in his commissioning of the new fleet which was built in Boulogne and on the Scheldt in 810–11. The Danes nonetheless seemed eager enough to please and their emissaries caught up with Charlemagne while he was travelling back to Aachen, having been denied his battle with Godefred. It was Charlemagne's counts, led by his cousin Wala, who had negotiated the peace deal, and the Danish embassy wanted to express their country's peaceful intentions to the emperor in person. Danish raids did indeed stop for over twenty years, but the country's disintegration was a long-term process and the disorder which started within Denmark's borders and then spread to the seas was a development beyond the control of the country's political leaders. In 834 the raiders returned, ready to inflict their damage at the worst of times. By then the Frankish empire was in disarray and Charlemagne's heir Louis the Pious was engaged in a civil war fought against his own quarrelsome sons. An imperial legacy gained by the force of arms had been undermined and although it would be revived a century hence by the Ottonian dynasty of Saxon emperors, the strength of that wondrous recovery was beyond the prevision of any ninth-century prophet.

The reign's military campaigns recall the unfinished business of the Roman army, since it was Charlemagne who revived the expansionist thrust pioneered by the emperor Augustus and then abandoned after three imperial legions were slaughtered by an indigenous German force at the battle of the Teutoburg Forest in the year AD 9. That disaster ended the Roman military's attempt at a northward penetration beyond the river Rhine. What Charlemagne and his armies did in Saxony as they marched towards the east, and along a terrain which Roman generals had sought to gain, is best seen as a resumption of the original policy goal of Augustus. Whether this was a conscious design on his part we cannot know, but he had the sources at hand which would have given him and his military advisers some good information about what had happened eight centuries previously. Suetonius's *Twelve Caesars* circulated widely in Charlemagne's milieu, but the *History* written by Velleius Paterculus may be of even greater importance since it too was well known in the Carolingian court and is a work full of useful detail concerning the military strategies adopted by the Roman army during its German campaigns in the first century AD. The global reach of Charlemagne's interests would have been well served by another text to which he had access, the *Map of the World*, which had been commissioned by the emperor Theodosius in c. 435 and whose measurements of distances between certain key strategic points made it exceptionally valuable in terms of military logistics. Einhard describes an engraved table-top map of the world owned by Charlemagne and its details may well have been based on the Theodosian text.

Memories of Rome would also have been evoked by the *Notitia Dignitatum*, a substantial work which was produced by officials working in the Imperial Chancery in Rome and which provides a detailed picture of the western empire's civilian and military organization in c. 420. The section dealing with the eastern half was compiled earlier and its account of the bureaucracy and army dates from about the year 395. Those consulting the copy of the *Notitia* which existed at the Carolingian court in the late eighth century would not just have learnt about the offices held right across the empire in the late fourth century, they would also have come across the names of places, of natural features such as mountains and rivers, and of structures such as castles and frontier walls. Did Charlemagne use it? It would be surprising if he had not done so, and the text which was available to him was so well thumbed that a new copy had to be made in about 825.

Throughout his career of military activity and strategic thinking Charlemagne remained a general who responded to contemporary needs and circumstances. No man was ever less likely to suppose that success would automatically come to those who stepped into dead men's shoes and sought to follow past formulae. *Reformatio* and *renovatio* were the key ideas in the Carolingian programme as a whole, in politics, administration and diplomacy, in programmes of cultural initiative and religious renewal, as well as in the arts of war. Reform and renewal meant looking forward and shaping the future rather than just pouring new wine into old bottles. Charlemagne needed no insistent or obvious reminders of the Roman heritage since it lay all around him in the fabric of daily life, in the architectural style of his palaces and the stones of still-functioning imperial roads, in the survival of Latin as a spoken and written language as well as in the liturgy of his Church, in the names of places and the titles of his courtiers' offices. The question was how to use the imperial legacy of thought and deed in the circumstances of his own time and make it amenable to his own ambitions. His strategies in war, therefore, may well have learnt from the past but they always bore the imprint of his own mind and understanding. Charlemagne was creating a new and Frankish Rome, not re-creating an old one.

CHAPTER 4

Crown Imperial

On the morning of Christmas Day in the year 800 Pope Leo III celebrated mass at St Peter's, the great basilica raised on the Vatican Hill in
Rome by the emperor Constantine almost five centuries earlier. From
the last hours of Christmas Eve onwards Leo and his retinue had been
making their way between the other basilicas which now dominated the
city's skyline and where the pope was expected to preside at a series of
masses to celebrate the birth of Christ. A demanding schedule had been
followed through the hours of winter darkness and its culmination arrived
in the middle of the morning as Leo approached St Peter's, for this was
the church built on the site of the tomb of the Apostle whose authority
was meant to be the rock-like basis of the papal office. All popes, as
bishops of Rome, claimed to be Peter's direct successors and that transmitted Petrine authority was the key to their role as interpreters of the
Christian faith and defenders of the Christian Church. Those prerogatives were reflected in the liturgy and prayers of the Roman churches,
and nowhere more than in St Peter's where the Christmas mass followed
its prescribed ritual as Leo celebrated the sacred mysteries.

On this particular morning, however, an additional ceremony was
performed. Leo placed an emperor's crown on the head of Charlemagne,
the king of the Franks, who was kneeling before him as a member of
the congregation. Now in his early fifties, western Europe's premier
warrior-king was an imposing figure who needed no finery in order to

demonstrate his power, and it was only on feast days that he wore the jewellery and embroidery which usually signified Frankish aristocratic status. He had been christened 'Carolus' or 'Karolus', a Latin derivation from the Germanic word *karl* meaning a free man. Posterity would conflate *Carolus Magnus* or Charles the Great to produce 'Charlemagne', the name by which this king-emperor is known to history. But in his own time he was referred to in speech and in writing by his birth name, and something of that word's sense of attributed independence is conveyed in a courtier's account of the king's insistence on simplicity of dress. Charlemagne almost invariably wore the kind of clothes which typified his own people, the Franks: shirt and breeches both made of linen, a tunic fringed with silk, hose fastened by bands to cover his lower limbs, a cloak which in his case was usually blue in colour, and a close-fitting winter coat made of otter or marten skins to protect him from the cold. There was little in all of this to distinguish Charlemagne from many thousands of his subjects, but it was in part his physique which set him apart. When the emperor, now crowned, rose to his feet before the altar of St Peter's he would have towered over the rest of the congregation. Standing at well over six feet tall, with a short neck and a rather prominent nose, Charlemagne's fitness and robust health were the wonder of contemporaries during a reign which, at any time, would have been noteworthy for its longevity but was especially remarkable in the Europe of the early Middle Ages. A paunch had developed during his middle years – perhaps because of the roast meat to which he was addicted – but the eyes remained large and animated in the years of his maturity, and Charlemagne's hair, once blond and now white, was still abundant and flowing. There were very few occasions when he was prepared to wear foreign clothes, but even Charlemagne had had to concede the need to mark the significance of this particular day, and those within the basilica who now acclaimed to choreographic effect the imperial majesty of this 'Carolus Augustus' could see that a tunic and a *chlamys* or cloak, both ancient Roman in style, covered his sturdy frame.

The coronation has been seen as the culminating event of Charlemagne's reign, a recognition of his successes in a career devoted to military conquest and political integration in western Europe, and as the inaugura-

This fourth century head of Freyr, Norse god of fertility, was found in Arras (ancient *Nemetacum*). His local worshippers were probably Germanic immigrants enrolled in the Romans' frontier army and therefore allowed to celebrate their rites.

The visionary gaze of Flavius Valerius Constantinus, sole ruler of the Roman empire (324–37) and Christian convert. Early medieval Europe's imperial revival referred back to Constantine's blend of religious authority with temporal power.

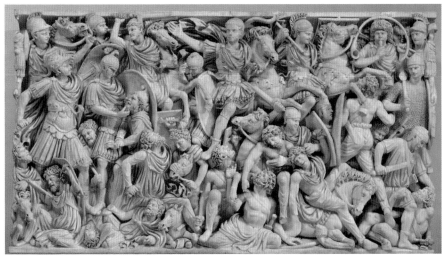

A mid-third century Roman view of submissive, possibly Ostrogothic, barbarians. Some are brave but their uniform hairiness shows them to be irrational and primitive. Romans impose ordered reason's benefits on the maelstrom.

The basilica at Trier
built by the emperor
Constantine in
c. 310. Seated in state,
the emperor
transacted official
business within this
aula palatina or
palace hall. Basilicas
with their apses were
easily adapted to
Christian church use.

Probably made in Constantinople,
the 'Achilles' shield' of c. 400
illustrates episodes from the Iliad.
This ceremonial plate travelled to late
Roman Gaul, and was discovered in the
river Rhône near Avignon in 1656.

Flavius Honorius, Western Roman Emperor (395–423), is portrayed on these ivory diptytch panels. The triumphalist imagery includes a banner (*labarum*), the globe symbolising universal power and surmounted by a winged Victory, a sceptre, pearl diadems and halos. Visigoths nonetheless sacked Rome in 410.

Treasures buried with the Merovingian king Childeric I in c. 481 include brooches, a bracelet, buckles, weaponry, and items for harnessing a horse. The hoard's ornaments and accessories are in solid gold, sometimes with cloisonné decoration, as seen here. Bee-shaped jewellery typified Merovingian royal adornment.

Left: The *cathedra* or throne of Maximianus, archbishop of Ravenna (546–556), consists of ornate ivory plates. Old and New Testament scenes are framed and divided by bands with tendrilled motifs and animals.

Below: The seal ring of the Merovingian king Childeric I would have been used to transact business devolved on him as a fifth century Roman ally. His long hair signifies the sacral powers of a still pagan king.

The mausoleum of Theoderic the Ostrogoth (eastern Goth) whose army took Ravenna in 493 evokes both Roman and Germanic traditions. As Italy's king (493–526) Theoderic allowed local aristocrats to administer while Goth warriors retained military control.

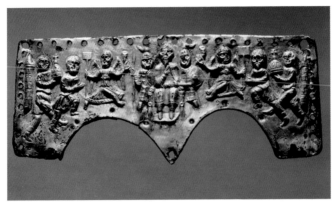

The glittering brow piece of the 'helmet of Agilulf' shows north Italy's Lombard king (590–616) apeing a Roman emperor. Two winged Victories present homage-bearing subjects to Agilulf, enthroned and flanked by warriors.

This exquisite mid-seventh-century gold cloisonné casket of Merovingian workmanship is a portable reliquary. It contained the bones of St. Maurice, a third century Egyptian soldier martyred by the Roman army in an Alpine pass.

The celebrated Iron Crown of the Lombards, with its narrow band of iron beaten out of a nail supposedly used at the Crucifixion, was used at Charlemagne's coronation as king of the Lombards.

The lower part of this throne, originally a folding stool, dates from the Merovingian king Dagobert I's early-seventh-century reign, and it was used by Charlemagne. Panther heads crown the four uprights ending in stylised animal paws.

The votive crown of Reccesuinth, the Visigoth (western Goth) who was Spain's king (649–72). Such crowns were offered to the Church as a symbolic demonstration of support, though this one may also have been worn.

A rare survival: a seal for the transaction of business in Charlemagne's chancery with his features seen in profile.

A Carolingian seal: Charlemagne dedicates the Palatine Chapel, Aachen to the Virgin Mary.

Below right: The reliquary bust of Charlemagne contains his skull and was donated to Aachen cathedral in 1349 by the Holy Roman Emperor Charles IV. Fleurs-de-lys and single-headed eagles symbolise, respectively, French kingship and the empire.

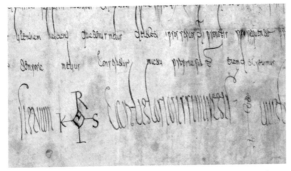

Above: Charlemagne's monogram consisting of the combined letters KAROLUS: the consonants are on the outside of the diamond form and the vowels (with U represented by V) inside it.

An eighteenth century copy of the original mosaic of 798/9 on the wall of the Lateran Palace's *triclinium* (a formal dining hall): St. Peter enthroned hands the *pallium* to Pope Leo III and a banner to Charlemagne, who is not yet an emperor.

Charlemagne's throne of marble slabs, dating from c. 800, was placed in the gallery of Aachen's Palatine Chapel. That unusual position emphasised the emperor's combination of religious authority with temporal power.

tion of a revival of ancient Roman notions of imperial overlordship. But the kind of authority thereby bestowed on Charlemagne was open to interpretation, and the debate about the coronation both among his contemporaries and subsequently reflects the fact that imperial rule meant different things to different people. For some theologians Charlemagne was a Christian emperor ruling a Christian empire whose domain in this world reflected the divine order. Others regarded him as the natural heir to the emperors of ancient Rome, and many admirers had concluded that the scale of his victories in battle was such that he had transcended the mere title of king. But for Pope Leo himself this new emperor was, first and foremost, a protector.

ROME'S STREET VIOLENCE

The background to the day's events was one of violence. On 25 April 799 Leo had been attacked by a gang of thugs in a Roman street near the church of St Lawrence in Lucina. The ringleaders were members of the local Roman nobility: Paschalis and Campulus were related to Hadrian, Leo's predecessor as pope, and they were high officials in the papal hierarchy, while Maurus of Nepi was a military aristocrat and a neighbour of Hadrian's family. Aristocratic factionalism was a key feature of Rome's ecclesiastical politics in the late eighth century and it is clear that Leo, who was not of noble birth, had alienated powerful individuals whose coup d'état was intended to restore their blue-blooded predominance in the see of Peter. Leo was thrown to the ground and while he was half-alive an attempt was made to mutilate him. He was subsequently imprisoned in the Roman monastery of SS. Stephen and Sylvester, and then in that of St Erasmus, from where he escaped with the help of a loyal papal official who escorted him to the safe-keeping of two prominent individuals: Wirundus of Stavelot, a local administrator who was one of Charlemagne's counts, and Duke Wingis, ruler of the neighbouring duchy of Spoleto. The pope was then able to flee across the Alps and made his way to Paderborn where he was received by Charlemagne.

At the time the king was engaged in the latest of his numerous campaigns against the Saxons whose ancestral paganism was being gradually undermined as a result of their conversion to Christianity, a change of faith imposed upon them by the Frankish military machine and at Charlemagne's express command. The Franks' thrust to the east, towards the conquest of Saxony and its incorporation within an expanded Francia, was the central military mission of Charlemagne's reign, and the series of campaigns which had started over a quarter of century earlier encountered severe and prolonged resistance. But by 799–800 a final settlement was in sight and Charlemagne was able to devote his energies to a resolution of the pope's problems in Italy. He first sent messengers to Rome but they were unable to provide any more information about the nature of the difficulties in which Leo found himself. Towards the end of 799 Leo, accompanied by a Frankish escort, was able to return to Rome, and in August of the following year the king himself arrived in the city. Charlemagne's close adviser Alcuin, a cleric of Northumbrian and British origin, may have been influential in persuading him that his presence was needed there in order to protect the pope in person and restore the dignity of the papal office. On 1 December 800 Charlemagne presided at a legal tribunal but none of Leo's opponents would come forward with specific accusations of wrongdoing. Three weeks later Leo made a public declaration of his innocence and the imperial crowning followed two days afterwards. Shortly after Christmas Charlemagne condemned to death those guilty of the attack on Leo, but the pope persuaded him to commute the sentence to one of exile.

Leo had appealed to Charlemagne as an ally, and the king had responded accordingly although it took him a year and a half to actually get to Rome and intervene in person. The military priorities in Saxony may account in part for the delay but Leo's case also presented some real problems for Charlemagne. In the first place he had no clear legal right to intervene in the city of Rome since, as part of the papal lands, it lay beyond his territorial jurisdiction and he could not pass judgment on local Romans since they were not his subjects. Besides which, and initially, the possibility had to be faced that Leo was actually guilty of some kind of offence. There were also clear signs of unease within Charlemagne's circle at the prospect of putting a pope on trial. Alcuin had written to his friend Bishop Arn of Salzburg, one of those deputed to accompany Leo back to Rome, and expressed the view that no one had the right to sit in judgment on the pope. The conviction expressed a high view of the papal office rather than a vote of confidence in Leo's own merits, and Alcuin took care to destroy a report about the pope which Arn had sent him. The bishop and his associates had held an inquest into the affair after they arrived in Rome but failed to discover any specific details which might resolve the issue. Charlemagne was forced therefore to intervene, but the initial proceedings he held in Rome took the form of a Roman synod rather than a secular tribunal – a fact which shows him operating within an ecclesiastical context and avoiding a legal intervention on Roman territory. Once again, however, no one came forward to admit culpability, and before the great event of 25 December Charlemagne did not have the legal power to pronounce judgment.

PAPAL HONOURS AND RITUALS

An emperor's crown was not the first honour to have been bestowed on the *Reges Francorum* by a pope. In 754 Stephen II had declared Charlemagne's father, Pippin, to be 'Patrician of the Romans', a hereditary title and one which signified the papacy's recognition that Frankish kings would henceforth be the officially recognized protectors of the Holy See. The origins of the title were Byzantine and high dignitaries at the court in Constantinople were often called patricians, a largely honorific dignity which was in the sole gift of the emperor. The addition of an ethnic component, however – as in *patricius Romanorum* – was a papal innovation and Stephen had acted on his own initiative when bestowing the honour on Pippin, his heirs and successors. From 754 onwards successive popes would find these kings of the Franks to be reliable allies, and especially when it came to defending the integrity of the papal states against the Lombards who ruled adjacent territories within the Italian peninsula. The patrician title was part of that diplomatic fabric governing relations between Francia and the papal territories. Charlemagne and all the Franks were seen as the pope's *amici*; they were friends who could be expected to help him fight his enemies and play their allotted role in the propagation of the Christian faith as understood by the Church in Rome. Like his father before him, Charlemagne was respectful of papal independence: he collected no taxes within the papal territories and he never summoned any of the pope's subjects to serve in his armies. Neither he nor his father interfered in a papal election or asserted any right to do so. Before 800 the king did not intervene in any judicial proceeding within the republic, and when Charlemagne came to do so during 800–01 it was, as we shall see, at the behest of the pope and with the intention of strengthening Leo's authority.

Public ritual governing the relations between rulers underlines this impression of careful respect. St Peter's was located just outside the city walls, and while visiting the basilica on an earlier trip to Rome in 774 Charlemagne asked the pope's formal permission before being allowed to enter the city of Rome where he then spent Easter at the Lateran palace. The ritual observed by Hadrian, the pope at the time, was orchestrated to avoid any suggestion that Charlemagne enjoyed rights of kingship within Rome. Although the pomp was considerable, the high officials of the city of Rome sent to greet Charlemagne were instructed to do so at an unprecedented thirty miles beyond the city walls. Another diplomatic party composed of papal officials greeted Charlemagne one mile beyond the walls, as dictated by the protocol appropriate for a visiting *patricius*, while Hadrian waited to receive the king at the steps of St Peter's. The subsequent meetings between the pope and Charlamagne were held at the basilica and therefore outside the city of Rome. Accommodation arrangements were similarly circumspect during both Charlemagne's reign and that of his successors. At that time the palace on the Palatine hill which had been the official residence of Rome's ancient emperors remained largely intact. Constans II, the last emperor of Byzantium to visit Rome, stayed there in 663, and the *exarch* of Ravenna, the Byzantine emperor's representative on Italian soil, used the building on his visits. But although Charlemagne was emperor from 800 onwards neither he nor any other Carolingian ruler stayed in the Palatine palace while in Rome. They used instead the purpose-built Carolingian residence, probably created by Charlemagne himself, which was adjacent to St Peter's in the city's then suburbs and near the modern Vatican.

By 800, therefore, there was a long history of mutual respect in the observation of their rights, honours and dignity which were appropriate to the popes and the Frankish kings. The monarch who knelt before Pope Leo on that Christmas morning was also king of the Lombards – a title appropriated by Charlemagne following his defeat and occupation of the northern Italian kingdom in 774. He ruled the region through the local aristocracy but took care to safeguard his authority by introducing the comital system, a form of government which gave power to specially appointed Frankish counts whose presence in the region was intended to ensure that the king's will was done. The contrast with the situation in the papal territories is revealing, since their history records no such intrusion by the agents of Frankish government either before or after 800, and the coins issued by Hadrian bore exclusively his own name and image. If therefore there was so much continuity in the relationship between the papacy and the Frankish kings, what positive difference did an imperial title make to Charlemagne's position in Rome?

The fact that he pronounced a sentence of death on those accused just a few days after Christmas Day reveals much of the reasoning behind the coronation. After 25 December 800 Charlemagne, now emperor, possessed what he did not have before: the right to sit in judgment on Roman soil and issue a sentence. Leo's attackers, it was decided, had committed a *crimen laesae maiestatis*, although it remains uncertain whether Charlemagne actually delivered his judgment according to Roman law or in a more personal capacity as Leo's ally and friend. The imperial coronation lent itself naturally to pan-European expectations, and the ambitions of subsequent medieval rulers harked back insistently to the great event. But Leo's action was a solution to a local problem which had plagued him in the winter of 799–800 and in the months that followed: how could he deal with his attackers legally and how could he secure for his ally Charlemagne the legal competence to intervene on his behalf? The idea that Charlemagne ought to be emperor had been circulating among the intelligentsia of Francia, its clerics and policy-makers, for quite some time before 800, but it had taken a papal crisis to make it happen and it was only the attack on Leo which had brought the king to Rome.

REASONS FOR A CAROLINGIAN'S CAUTION

Imperial ambition was therefore real enough, but so also was the need for diplomatic caution. This is the context for the famous reservation recorded by Einhard, the author of a celebrated work, the *Life of Charlemagne*, which was completed by the late 820s. Einhard was a counsellor of note and fully signed up to the imperial project as it evolved in the years after 800. This is the first detailed biography of a medieval ruler and its literary model was Suetonius's *Lives of the Emperors*, although Einhard may well have been influenced too by *Agricola*, Tacitus's biography of the general. The Charlemagne of Einhard's pages is intended to be a ruler who can stand in that same august lineage. Here then is an author who might have been expected to highlight any available evidence in order to establish Charlemagne's imperial credentials and the legitimacy of such an ambition. And yet Einhard tells us quite explicitly that if Charlemagne had known what was going to happen he would not have gone to mass on that Christmas morning. He was taken by surprise and, once the deed was done and a crown placed on his head, he had to go along with a papal plan that was not his own. The circumstantial evidence goes against the idea of a scheme being hatched without Charlemagne's foreknowledge. He had taken care to dress beforehand in imperial and Roman garb (including the *chlamys*). Moreover, Charlemagne had been considering how best to respond to the papal crisis for the last eighteen months. Long-term speculation about the imperial office's revival had culminated in the gossip, negotiations and rumours circulating in Rome ever since his arrival there four weeks previously. There was of course a biographical and literary tradition of the reluctant ruler, one whose probity was established by his unwillingness to assume office. But Einhard's statement goes beyond that redundant platitude and, since he was a courtier with a privileged access to Charlemagne, it is necessary to ask what he could possibly have meant.

The mystery deepens when we look at the relevant section of the *Annals of the Kingdom of the Franks* (*Annales Regni Francorum*), compiled by contemporary scribes as a public and authoritative account of Charlemagne's reign and that of his successors. The entry for 801 describes how: 'having ordained the affairs, both public, private and ecclesiastical, of the Romans and of the apostolic city and of the whole of Italy – indeed throughout the winter the emperor did nothing else – he again sent an expedition under his son Pippin against the Beneventans and he himself, after Easter [25 April 801] set out from Rome for Spoleto'. Problems with the Lombard dukes of Benevento had been a recurring feature of the Frankish engagement with Italy, and in 801 Duke Grimoald was leading a movement to restore his territory's independence from Frankish rule. But before he left Rome that spring Charlemagne pronounced judgment, on 4 March, on an ancient dispute between Siena and Arezzo, towns which lay beyond the papal territories and within his Italian kingdom. Crucially, the diploma that he issued for Arezzo contains no mention of his new imperial office and it only refers to his titles as a king. Over two months had passed since the momentous coronation, but the emperor was either still uncertain about how to refer to himself or unwilling to define his new title.

It took at least another two months of deliberation and research to provide an answer, and the formula, which made its first appearance in a diploma issued in Bologna on 29 May 801, was the one used for the remainder of Charlemagne's reign. He was now '*Karolus serenissimus augustus a Deo coronatus magnus pacificus imperator Romanum gubernans imperium, qui et per misericordiam deo rex Francorum atque Langobardorum*'. The long-windedness reflects the care taken by his chancery officials while seeking to define a novel situation with as much precision as possible. But the prolixity goes some way to explaining what Charlemagne himself thought had happened on Christmas Day.

THE MEANING OF THE IMPERIAL TITLE

Charlemagne was, in the first place, a legitimate emperor whose authority was derived from the fact that he had been crowned by God (*a Deo coronatus*). Leo had been no more than a conduit for the operation of divine grace and the imperial office was of divine, not papal, origin. There was a continuity here with his kingly title, which had always been referred to in previous documents as having been bestowed on Charlemagne through God's grace (*rex Dei gratia*), and it was that kingship which remained the foundation of his rule. 'Roman emperor governing the empire' (*imperator Romanum gubernans imperium*) was a phrase probably discovered by rummaging around in the archives at Ravenna where the surviving documentation illustrated its occasional use during classical antiquity. The formulation is an odd one but its significance lay in what it did not assert, since it specifically excludes any claim to be ruling 'the Roman empire'. Care had to be taken not to offend the surviving eastern half of the ancient empire since the Byzantine Greeks habitually described themselves as '*Romaioi*' and the emperors who ruled in Constantinople regarded themselves as the sole rulers of the Roman empire. Charlemagne's empire, by contrast, had become Roman in the more restricted sense that it now included the populations of the city of Rome and the associated papal territories. But that did not mean that he was now ruling a Roman empire, and his new title made it clear that the basis of his empire was Christian and Frankish. He worked hard during the next twelve years to persuade Byzantium that he was not trespassing on the prerogatives of the eastern emperors, and eventually won their recognition of his title as an imperial equal.

In 806 Charlemagne would allocate different parts of his realm to his three surviving sons and thereby set in place the arrangements for his succession. But this was an allocation of specific responsibilities and areas of rule within a Frankish kingdom which he clearly continued to regard as a unity, and the emperor was therefore following the venerable Frankish tradition of partible inheritance. His sons were commanded to support one another and to take joint action when it came to defending the interests of the Church. And Charlemagne clearly did not think that the imperial title itself, that supreme expression of Frankish power, was just a personal honour, since in 813 he made his surviving son Louis the Pious emperor after the deaths of the two elder brothers, Charles and Pippin. The Byzantine emperors had now conceded a diplomatic recognition of the new empire of the west, and the way was made clear for a public declaration of the Frankish empire's line of continuity. In a ceremony held in the palace chapel at Aachen and attended by the Frankish nobility Louis lifted the imperial crown which had been placed on the altar. He placed it on his head, and was formally acclaimed by the assembled aristocrats just as the Romans congregated in St Peter's had acknowledged his father thirteen years previously. This was the ceremony that really guaranteed the succession, and it needed no pope to conduct it. Carolingian rulers became emperors as a result of the will of God and the declared wish of the Franks whom they ruled. This then was the reason for Charlemagne's reservations about the papal and Roman circumstances of his own coronation, and it is significant that he waited for the Byzantines to recognize his title's legitimacy before bequeathing it to his son. He undoubtedly believed that he was a true emperor, but the reservation recorded by Einhard was Charlemagne's way of demonstrating that he wanted nobody to think that his title's legitimacy depended exclusively on the desires of popes and the acclaim of local Romans.

As a result of the coronation the papal territory became part of the Frankish empire, but the actions of both Charlemagne and Pope Leo indicate that it was treated to all intents and purposes as an autonomous region within the enlarged imperial domain. The emperor's judgment on Leo's attackers is the only surviving example of a legal verdict arrived at by him on Roman soil. He neither levied troops nor minted any coins there, and no Carolingian taxes were raised in the papal territories. He did send his *missi* into Ravenna, and was roundly condemned for doing so by the papacy, but avoided any such extension of his administration elsewhere on Roman soil, and papal officials were subjected to no Frankish interference. Charlemagne's capitulary of 802 provided for an administrative reordering of his entire empire but it made no reference to the papal lands, and his revisions of various legal codes towards the end of his reign, just like his imperial programme of Church reform, seem to have left the pope's territories well alone. The titles of official documents once again provide an indication of the reality of power. Leo did date his documents according to Charlemagne's regal years, but it was the pope's name that came first, thereby showing that his was the relevant authority within the papal lands. Coinage supplies yet more evidence. Until 800 the coins issued by Leo bore only his own name. After that date they carried Charlemagne's name on the reverse but the words *Sanctus Petrus* and the papal monogram were both carried on the obverse. These were practices which would never have been tolerated either by a Byzantine emperor or an ancient Roman one, and they show the degree of effective independence which was allowed to continue.

Although Charlemagne had a new title, he treated the papal territories much as he had done before 800, and the pope remained a friend and ally rather than a subject.

CAROLINGIAN EMPERORS AND THE CHURCH IN ROME: PROTECTION AND OBLIGATION

An imperial coronation had therefore had the theoretical effect of incorporating the papal lands within the Frankish empire, but without changing the actual dynamics of power. It fell to Charlemagne's heir Louis, a less effective figure than his father in military and political terms but an altogether more sophisticated thinker, to resolve some contradictions. Louis brought brevity to the imperial title, calling himself simply *Imperator Augustus,* and he termed his office a *munus divinum* or 'divine duty'. The subjects he ruled were, in his view, no mere collection of different ethnic groups but a collective *populus Christianus* whom he was duty-bound to protect. This was a real political theology and a more explicit justification of the basis of government than had been achieved by any previous Carolingian ruler. In the first few years following his accession in 814 Louis embarked on a whole series of political, institutional and religious reforms with the aim of defining the basis of his power. The election of a new pope, Stephen IV, in 816 was an opportunity to clarify papal–Frankish relations, and later that year the pope travelled to Francia to meet Louis. The result of their negotiation, the *Pactum Ludovicianum,* spelt out the terms of the relationship and gave it a new theoretical basis. This was, importantly, a treaty and therefore an agreement arrived at between two rulers rather than a negotiation between a ruler and his subject. An alliance dating back to 754 was confirmed along with its obligations of mutual support, although by now the papal lands were no longer the independent entity they had been in the mid-eighth century. While he was in Francia Stephen crowned Louis at Reims in a ceremony which highlighted and confirmed the Christian nature of the imperial office he already held.

The negotiations between pope and emperor were held in early October 816 and the *Ludovicianum* which followed was declared by its drafters to be a *pactum confirmationis* and a *confirmationis decretum.*

Those descriptions matter because they show that an agreement was being renewed rather than being created anew. The Franks' obligation to defend the papal lands was defined, and the document also listed the various titles to lands held within those territories. All later papal territorial claims would refer to this document, which demonstrated the privileged position enjoyed within the empire by the papacy as an institution and by the territories under its government. Louis confirmed that no Carolingian ruler would intervene in Rome without being asked to do so and agreed that, except in highly unusual circumstances, any fugitives from Roman justice who sought refuge within Francia would be returned to papal jurisdiction. The lands ruled by the pope were part of his *'potestate et ditione'*. Stephen and his successors could therefore 'hold and dispose' of them as they wished. A large number of individual churches within Francia had already received diplomas from Louis recording and confirming their immunity. The entire papal lands of central Italy enjoyed a similar status and were subjected only to a vague imperial overlordship.

Internal Roman politics was, however, a rough and often violent affair, and unruly passions evaded the neat categories of legal logic. Local aristocrats threatened Leo again in 815, and the murderous events of eight years later left the *Ludovicianum* looking rather lame. Sometime between 28 June and 27 July 823 the emperor Louis learnt that two senior papal officials, Theodore the *primicerius* and Leo the *nomenclator*, had been blinded and beheaded, and that at least two others had suffered the same fate. It was their loyalty to Lothair, Louis's son, which had apparently led to the murder of these men, and there were strong indications that Pope Paschal was implicated. The *missi* sent by Louis to Rome to investigate encountered papal stonewalling. Paschal and other senior clergy had purged themselves by oath of any wrongdoing, and the delegation subsequently sent by the pope to the emperor declared that the perpetrators of the crime would not be handed over. In any event, so went the official message, Theodore and Leo had committed a *crimen laesae maiestatis* and been lawfully condemned. The phrase itself – 'majesty breaking' – is highly revealing. This was an offence in Roman law, one that only applied to an attack on the emperor himself and was therefore tantamount to treason. Paschal, in other words, was behaving like a sovereign ruler.

Theodore and Leo were senior officials of the Lateran, the palace and basilica which were the seat of the popes as bishops of Rome, and its hierarchy was deeply divided. From the middle of the eighth century onwards Rome's senior ecclesiastics and its noble families were an exceptionally fractious elite. Within that nexus of power different groups competed against one another for predominance, and especially in regard to land rights and the manipulation of the law. Those who stood accused of murdering Theodore and his colleagues were described as members of the *familia sancti Petri*, the farmer-soldiers to be found on the rural *domus cultae*, and the conflict had evidently spilt over into these great estates owned by the papacy. One Frankish report said that a total of thirty-four bishops in the entire Roman region had taken an oath denying responsibility for the murders. Since the city had seven bishops within its immediate suburbs, that leaves possibly twenty-seven bishops in the rural areas who were somehow involved in the wider conflict as supporters of Paschal. Those papal officials who opposed the pope could well have turned to Lothair, and thereby ultimately to Louis as emperor. Lothair and his most intimate retinue of advisers were often in Italy between 822 and 824, and in 823 this eldest son of the emperor had been himself crowned emperor by Paschal in a ceremony similar to Louis's own coronation at Reims in 816. Since the *Ludovicianum* did allow for an exceptional appeal to the emperor in cases of violence and oppression it would have been perfectly possible for those Romans who opposed Paschal to turn to Lothair and to Louis. The faction in power responded brutally, and the subsequent trail of violence and murder supplies the background to the issue in 824 of the *Constitutio Romana*, the document which records Lothair's negotiations on behalf of his father. In the same year Paschal died and was succeeded by Eugenius II, a reforming figure and the Franks' own preferred candidate for the papal office.

The *Constitutio* shows the empire and the papacy hard at work and trying to resolve some fundamental questions about how power should operate in Rome. It stated that papal elections had to be free of outside interference, and it confirmed that the franchise in such contests included not just the clergy but also the people of Rome which, in this context, meant in effect the local nobility. Two additional requirements were made explicit: anyone who interfered unlawfully with such an election would be exiled by the emperor, and a new pope had to confirm the Franco-papal alliance before he could be consecrated. There was no suggestion, though, that the Frankish emperors could impose their own preferred candidate on the electorate, and the relationship between the Holy See and the Frankish throne was still one of mutual rights and obligations. One major novelty was the requirement that all Romans had to swear an oath to the emperor, with one important safeguarding clause. Each Roman swore fidelity to the emperor 'save for that loyalty [*salva fide*] which I have promised . . . to my apostolic lord'. Fidelity was therefore owed to the pope in the first place, and only secondarily to the emperor. This was a conventional enough form of words and had been used in the past when Carolingian emperors set out the arrangements for their succession while also seeking to secure their own position during their remaining lifetimes. When Charlemagne had issued the *Divisio Imperii* in 806 he had inserted a similar safeguard clause to the effect that until his death he was to continue to receive all imperial rights and prerogatives. His son Louis inserted the same '*salva*' clause relating to his own imperial rights when drafting his own succession instrument, the *Ordinatio Imperii* of 817.

The tumultuous nature of Roman politics in the early 820s had made life difficult for the Frankish throne in terms of its relationship with the Romans and with the popes. It had been easy enough to agree on a common anti-Lombard front, and arrangements had been in place since the mid-eighth century to protect the papal state from its external enemies. But when the local clergy and nobility of Rome began attacking each other, the question of just how the imperial prerogative ought to be operating became a good deal more difficult. Now the people of Rome needed to be protected against themselves. The new oath, that of a subject of the imperial power of the Frankish monarchy, was a provision designed to supply exactly that degree of effective protection which would be needed when things turned nasty and an emperor was needed to sort out the mess. Pope Eugenius himself did not swear a subject's oath, but he had promised in writing to uphold the Frankish–papal alliance. The oath of fidelity required of the empire's subjects in Rome included a statement that in future they would not allow a pope to be consecrated until he had agreed to uphold the Franco-papal alliance, a commitment already made by Eugenius.

The Frankish crown had some past form when it came to the question of extracting oaths, and Charlemagne had imposed oaths of explicit fidelity on all his subjects for the first time in 789. Three years earlier a Thuringian noble named Hardrad had led a rebellion against the crown, and the aristocrats who supported him claimed that they had the right to resist because they had never sworn fidelity to Charlemagne. The oath of 789, which was again imposed on his subjects in 802 following the imperial coronation, enabled Charlemagne to demand loyalty and punish disobedience. Its effects were nonetheless very broad rather than specific, and the king was not prescribing the details of how his subjects ought to behave. What he wanted was loyalty and an acknowledgment that he had the right to expect his subjects not to harm him or one another. This was the kind of oath that was now expected of the Romans as well from 824 onwards, and its effect was to remove that wall of silence which had frustrated previous investigations by Charlemagne, Louis and their officials into the causes of Roman mayhem. Suspects would now be forced to answer the questions they were asked and could no longer evade investigation by saying that they had already sworn those all too convenient oaths of exculpation as Pope Paschal and his friends had done. By swearing an oath to the emperor those being investigated had already brought themselves within his legal framework, and they would have to behave accordingly.

The violence of local Romans had forced the Frankish authorities to intervene, and the *Constitutio* made certain truths of power more explicit than they had been in the past. But although the document represented an imperial intervention, its provisions were intended to provide the papal authority with a more effective support structure. It decreed that all Roman dukes and officials were to be obedient to the pope, and Louis had no right either to appoint or to dismiss them. The emperor did place a permanent *missus* in Rome and he required the pope to do the same, since there was a clear need to protect the local population against any future maladministration. This Frankish protectorate was therefore introducing a new safeguard, but those who had complaints to make against the papal government had first of all to appeal to the pope who would then appoint one of the two *missi* to adjudicate on the case.

Back in 754 Stephen II had sought better protection for himself and the Roman population, and now in 824 Louis was defining the means by which that support and defence could be upheld and continued. Germanic, Roman and ecclesiastical components had created a unique blend, that spiritual kinship between Carolingian kings and the papacy which was underwritten by certain specific mutual obligations to protect and aid each other. The Franks originally had to defend the popes from the Lombards externally and there was a continuing need to protect them from the Roman mob internally. Frankish kings were also duty-bound to sustain the faith of Catholic Christianity against attack. In return they received two forms of protection from the papacy. Intercessory prayers delivered on their behalf might be intangible but were nonetheless a highly valued resource in a society which thought that God could be induced to declare his hand and back natural-born winners. The Carolingian dynasty was also protected by more tangible, and distinctly political, declarations of papal support: rival claimants to the throne of the Franks were rejected, Charlemagne's incorporation of the Bavarian dukedom was supported, and the military campaigns waged by Carolingian rulers received papal blessing.

THE VIEW FROM ROME

The process of establishing the true implication of Charlemagne's coronation in these explicit terms was therefore a long-term affair, and the best part of a quarter of a century passed before the event acquired a real focus and a definitive meaning in the politics and culture of early ninth-century Europe. These details were hammered out in Rome because the city's contemporary significance and the themes of its history were intrinsic to the imperial title coveted by, and bestowed upon, Charlemagne and his Carolingian heirs. The relationship between Europe's Germanic north and its Latin south is a recurring leitmotif of Charlemagne's reign while also being central to the ambitions of the dynasty to which he belonged. And it is to Rome therefore that we must now return as we envisage the condition of the city in the year 800 and trace the impact upon it of the Christian Church and of the barbarian or 'Germanic' peoples who include the Franks. Charlemagne was himself the product of the fusion of those two mighty forces, and the early medieval history of the city shows that interplay between the Germanic legacy, the classical imperial heritage and the Christianity of the Church of Rome which lies at the heart of western Europe's Latin culture. What, therefore, did the city look like at this stage in its history, and what would the emperor have seen as he moved around the streets of Rome on that Christmas Day? Embedded within the statues, fountains, masonry, mosaics and frescoes there was a history which went beyond the story of evolution in artistic and architectural taste. For by the late eighth century the stones of Rome, its churches, temples and palaces, were Europe's profoundest illustrations of the transition from classical antiquity to Christian culture which had transformed the ancient societies centred on the Mediterranean. A king from the north whose emperor's crown had been gained in the south would have had much to think about, and perhaps much to guide his ambitions, while looking at such magnificence.

CHARLEMAGNE AND THE LEGACY OF CHRISTIAN ROME

The Rome in which Charlemagne arrived in the late summer of 800 had been a Christian city for almost half a millennium, and it was the emperor Constantine who had started the long process of its transformation and conversion to the new religion following his victory in battle over his co-emperor Maxentius on 28 October 312. That cavalry battle, which had started at a defile on the Cassian Road before continuing downhill to the Tiber and across the Milvian Bridge, had ended in the conquest of the capital, and Constantine attributed his success to the Christian God who in a vision had shown him the Cross. In 324 Constantine went on to conquer the empire's eastern half and he proved to be a zealous defender of the interests of the Christian Church, not least in the scale of his ecclesiastical building projects within Rome and in its immediate environs. He is the ruler who supplies the context for

Charlemagne, and Constantine's legacy as warrior and emperor provided the king of the Franks with his frame of reference.

The most ambitious and long-lasting of all Constantine's architectural programmes lay of course in the east, in the city of Constantinople that he founded on the shores of the Bosphorus, and which became the imperial capital following the inaugural solemnities that marked its formal dedication to the Virgin Mary on 11 May 330. Rome's political significance dwindled accordingly from the early fourth century onwards, but the decision to divide the empire had already been anticipated by the reforms inaugurated by the emperor Diocletian (285–305). The four co-emperors of the tetrarchy had moved between the imperial residences built at Nicomedia, Antioch and Thessalonica, at Milan, Trier and York, and no emperor from that time onwards had spent much time at Rome. Nonetheless, its symbolic significance remained immense, and the city visited by Paul and where Peter had preached would be embellished by Constantine to honour its Christian significance.

Pagan Rome had achieved some of its finest architectural expressions in the late third century, including the imposing sight of the Aurelian Walls, built by the emperors Aurelian and Probus in the 270s to enclose a city greatly expanded since the age of the Republic, and the Baths of Diocletian built on the Esquiline were on a monumental scale which rivalled even the vast cylindrical mausoleum of the emperor Hadrian raised by the banks of the Tiber just outside the city walls. By 800, then, such buildings were already venerable on account of their age, but the pilgrims who were now visiting the city came not as tourists curious about classical antiquity but as Christians who wanted to visit the tombs of martyrs and thereby establish a connection with the spiritual power which would sweep aside the pagan culture.

ROME'S EARLY CHRISTIAN WITNESSES

By Constantine's time perhaps as many as a third of the city's total population of some 800,000 were already Christian. Belonging mostly to the poorer and middling classes they were to be found crammed in Rome's inner-city slums, in the tenement houses located in the narrow and insanitary streets adjacent to the great public buildings of the Fora and the Capitol, by the foot of the Palatine, and in the area surrounding the Pantheon. Their places of worship were of course private places, as befitted the adherents of a faith which was intermittently subject to public persecution, and these centres were very different from the temples which were consecrated to the traditional gods and paid for by the state. Christians congregated to worship in buildings which were identified by the name of the original owner of the title, as in *titulus Clementis* or *titulus Anastasiae*, and these were often remodelled apartment houses. Perhaps no more than some twenty-five of these *tituli* or community centres existed in the Rome of Constantine's time and, with their numbers growing, many Christians must also have been meeting in one another's private houses for worship. By the third century these congregations were being joined by professional men such as lawyers and government officials, as well as by some aristocratic women, but the majority remained of modest origins.

There were Christian buildings outside the city walls too, such as the cult centres laid out around the graves of their venerated martyrs, and the Christian community retained for its own use a small plot within a cemetery on the Vatican Hill just beyond the city walls. Many Roman Christians were buried here but the cemetery's chief significance was as a devotional centre since it contained the grave of St Peter. The celebrated underground networks of tombs called catacombs were to be found further away in the Roman countryside, and these many-layered constructions were dug into the land bought by Christian freedmen and slaves from their landlords or donated to them by the same landowning class. It was in these catacombs that the Christian community met for their private funerary meals to mark the anniversaries of those who had died, occasions whose seclusion demonstrated the domesticity of this young religion and the privacy of its rituals. Constantine the Christian sympathizer transformed the Church's prospects and status by endowing it with estates in Rome and Italy, and later in Sicily and Sardinia, north Africa and Greece, to which were later added extensive holdings in Egypt, Syria and Cilicia. The Church derived a total annual income from such estates of some 25,000 gold *solidi* in Constantine's time, and the emperor's donation was intended to enable the Church to pay its clergy and to help maintain his Roman church foundations. Christianity's original phase of anonymity was over.

The basilica was a long-established form of Roman public architecture, and this large timber-roofed hall, with or without its apses and clerestory windows, was a pattern followed in the building of law courts and bazaars, reception halls and throne rooms. It proved also to be easily adaptable as a style of Christian architecture, and was much favoured by Constantine's architects as a way of demonstrating quickly and with maximum visibility the emperor's goodwill towards a previously minority faith. These churches, founded by Constantine and the devout female members of the imperial family, spread right across the empire, and in Rome itself Constantine started work straight away. In the winter of 312–13 he decided to build a cathedral for Rome's bishop, and the barracks of the imperial horseguards which stood on the Lateran were razed to the ground – a decision which may owe something to the fact that these soldiers had apparently been loyal to Constantine's rival Maxentius.

On the site of the barracks there rose a longitudinal hall, just over 300 feet long and almost 200 feet wide, whose nave was flanked by double aisles, both supported by columns. The nave ended in an apse whose vault shimmered in gold and on the chord of the apse a canopy, sheathed in silver, carried statues of Christ, the Apostles and angels. Within both chancel and nave there were gold and silver lighting fixtures as well as seven silver tables, while behind the church was built the baptistery which stands to this day. Known as St John Lateran by the eighth century, the church marked the first, and decisive, break with the private Christianity of the Roman past. But the Lateran, along with S. Croce in Gerusalemme, which was installed in the early third-century Sessorian Palace, was the only church building raised by the imperial family within the city walls of Rome. Rome might have a large, and increasingly self-confident, Christian population, but Constantine still had to respect the pagan sentiments of the overwhelming majority of the local aristocracy. Christians were among his closest advisers, and bishops were now ranked in the court calendar alongside the highest government officials, but when it came to the business of running an empire Rome's supreme rulers were dependent on the support of the great Roman families, and in Constantine's time such aristocrats were still tenacious in their attachment to the old gods.

Constantine's own private ambitions may be guessed at from the fact that in the first year of his reign he raised a statue of himself carrying the *labarum*, an ensign marked with the X cross, within the civilian Basilica Nova which had been recently built inside the ancient Forum, the very heart of Republican and Imperial Rome. This was an audacious public gesture, but that religious ostentation would never be repeated by Constantine and he kept his Christian building programme well out of the centre of Rome. He more than fulfilled an emperor's traditional role as a builder of great secular edifices. Constantine completed the colossal hall of the Basilica Nova which is still the greatest of the Forum's ruins. He built a complex of baths on the Quirinal and also raised the great triumphal arch which bears his name and stands near the Colosseum. But the churches he founded in Rome were plain from the outside and situated on imperial estates found on the edge of the city.

Beyond the walls Constantine could afford to be more explicit. The basilicas he raised in the Roman countryside would later become churches, but they were originally intended to be covered cemeteries and, adjoining the catacombs and the graves of martyrs, they provided new burial grounds for the Christians who now came here for their banquets in honour of the departed. St Peter's too was first used as a covered cemetery and funerary hall, though here the martyr's shrine was to be found inside the structure and was the focus of the new basilica. The building in which Charlemagne was crowned was raised on a large terrace created by filling in the pagan necropolis which, along with its small area reserved for Christian use, lay on the Vatican Hill. St Peter's shrine, however, remained above the floor level of Constantine's church which, though again consisting of a nave and double aisles, was considerably larger than the Lateran cathedral. Although the Lateran was the cathedral of Rome and the place where the bishop was provided with a residence and offices, St Peter's was the great pilgrimage church and its size reflected the number of visitors for whom it was designed. As with Constantine's other church buildings, a good deal of pilfering from older buildings went into the making of Old St Peter's, and that process would continue in the centuries of Christian building up to the age of Charlemagne. The king of the Franks, when he came to visit Rome, could inspect a Christian city whose victory over paganism was evidenced in the physical dismantling of old structures and their incorporation as fragments within new churches.

One of the first objects from the classical past that Charlemagne would have seen when walking towards the west front of St Peter's was the *pigna*, a huge pine cone which had been placed under a canopy in the atrium extending in front of St Peter's. From the very start of the basilica's history a long portico existed to shelter the approaching pilgrims from the elements, and this structure ran all the way from the eastern façade to the Aelian bridge (now the Ponte Sant' Angelo) which crossed the Tiber at a point near the Mausoleum of Hadrian. The devout came in ever-increasing numbers but, whether at St Peter's or the other Christian buildings erected by Constantine and his family in Rome and in the countryside, the pilgrims were visiting places which had been raised by private initiative. These were monuments to the private convictions of the ruling circle and, being built on imperial land, they therefore stood outside the control of the public authorities as constituted by Rome's civil service and its municipal administration. When Constantine turned his back on Rome and left for Constantinople he was leaving a place whose public image, just like the majority of its population, remained pagan – a fact which explains in large measure his disillusion with the city.

Right to the end of the fourth century Rome would remain a stronghold of the old paganism, a diffuse but tenacious faith with deep roots in the social practices of the ancient aristocracy. But the lavish new churches which were raised in the post-Constantinian era showed the vitality of an emerging Christian ascendancy. Many of the *tituli* of old survived but some were now replaced by churches whose construction was financed by the richer parishioners and by the bishops of Rome. Churches such as SS. Giovanni e Paolo, built on the Caelian Hill in about 410, were raised in this way, and Christianity's public face started to penetrate into the old inner city as well. The great basilica of S. Clemente, built in the late fourth century near the Colosseum and the gladiators' barracks, rose on the site of what had probably been a community centre, and its apse was set over a small mansion which had been converted into a sanctuary of Mithras in the early third century. The form of these churches remained that of the basilica, and with their columns, capitals and bases pilfered from classical buildings they were meant to make a public and visible statement. The pagan shrines continued to do brisk business up until the prohibition of public pagan worship throughout the empire in 346. The temples were closed in 356 and their revenues subsequently confiscated in 364, while another decree, in 408, declared that they should be put to new, probably secular uses. Nonetheless, the temples were preserved by state command as public monuments testifying to the glory of the Roman past.

CHRISTIAN ASCENDANCY AND PAGAN SURVIVALS

Even as late as the year 500 Cassiodorus, a Roman and also chancellor to the Ostrogothic king Theoderic who ruled the Italian peninsula at that time, was admiring the Theatre of Pompey whose vaulted caves seemed to him to 'resemble more the grottoes of a huge mountain than anything wrought by human hand'. When Procopius visited the city some thirty years later he found Rome filled with statues such as the shrine of Janus whose seven-and-a-half-foot statue stood in the Forum – an area he describes as containing many statues attributed to Phidias and Lysippus. By then these monuments to the pagan past were fast decaying, and they could be safely admired as the remnants of a cultural milieu which no longer posed a threat to Christianity. But throughout the fourth century the religious struggle remained real. An enlightened paganism was still attached to an eclectic mixture of cults and philosophies: the cult-like secretiveness of Gnosticism, the neo-Platonic worship of eternal Forms, the Pythagorean attachment to mathematical order, as well as oriental mystery cults transplanted to the Roman milieu. Worship of the Roman gods had long since been considered an essential part of a citizen's duties, and the observance was therefore associated with the greatness and prosperity of both city and empire. This is why Christianity was originally regarded as a form of treason, but with the emperors now established in Constantinople there were new and political reasons for the anti-Christian sentiments of a local aristocracy which feared that it was being shunted into a provincial obscurity.

There was also a cultural dimension to the Christian–pagan divide, since it was only from the fifth century onwards that Christianity started to adopt a positive attitude to the classical past and to incorporate the best of the classical tradition into a new religious aesthetic. Before then Christians were at best indifferent to the established canons of good taste, and the pagan aristocracy must have been appalled by the frequent crudity of new Christian buildings which disregarded the classical architectural orders, and by the roughly executed sarcophagi of the Christians. Much of this would change as a result of the conversion of great families, and especially after the final suppression of paganism in Rome by official decree in 395. The Roman patricians who staffed a Christian and aristocratic civil service helped to ensure the incorporation of an elevated classical culture within the Christian consensus. And a new generation of Christian intellectuals, such as Ambrose of Milan whose family belonged to the senatorial aristocracy and Augustine of Hippo whose early career was that of professor of rhetoric, absorbed much of the classical thought of the past while directing it to a new religious definition.

Jerome too had been a key figure in Rome's Christian high society as a fashionable director of souls and spiritual adviser to a number of aristocratic Christian women in Rome, before leaving for Palestine where he established a lay religious community in Bethlehem. That withdrawal was prompted by the onset of a spiritual crisis after a dream in which he saw himself condemned to hell for following Cicero rather than Christ, and his questioning shows a mind prepared to abandon the classical intellectual tradition root and branch: 'What has Horace to do with the psalter, Virgil with the Gospels, Cicero with Paul?' In the fastness of the Judaean desert Jerome would develop a new and powerful form of the Latin language, pared down and directly expressive in order to appeal to the masses. It is that *sermo humilis* which pervades his revision of the Latin Bible, the Vulgate, and thereby shaped the early medieval mental outlook at so profound a level. But the extremity of Jerome's reaction marked him out, and the pontificate of Damasus, the son of a high Church dignitary and elected in 366, represented the more mainstream, socially smoother, attitudes of a time when the Church was adopting pagan learning.

A circle consisting of patrician clerics and the lay leaders of the great

Christian families now dominated the Church, and it was this grouping which elected popes who, thoroughly absorbed in the Roman social and intellectual milieu, tended to be diplomats and jurists. The mosaic in the apse of the church of S. Pudenziana, raised c. 390, shows the new classicizing trend: Christ sits enthroned in shimmering gold, and the Apostles to either side are clad in the togas worn by Roman senators. This is one of the moments when we can see the Church playing down its eastern roots and presenting itself as a Roman institution, despite the fact that as late as the third century its official language and leadership had been Greek rather than Latin. One of the many poems written by Damasus echoes the theme with an account of how Peter and Paul, though coming from the east, had become Roman citizens by right because they had died for Christ in the city. Popular veneration of heroes had now shifted from those of pagan antiquity to the locally buried martyrs who were spiritual athletes for Christ's sake, and Peter and Paul, the princes of the Apostles, had replaced Romulus and Remus in a process which had led to Rome's rebirth – a true *renovatio urbis*.

THE ROMANIZATION OF CHRISTIANITY

The idea that Rome was *caput orbis* and as such the very source of all civilized order had been a key theme for those late fourth-century pagan circles who devoted their energies towards the cause of imperial revival. And the same idea, translated into a Christian context, was now taken up by the Roman Church. Constantine's theologians had already established the view that the empire, having been renewed by the emperor in Christ's name, was a kingdom of God on earth. Ambrose in his time returned to the theme and saw the Christian empire as the fulfilment of Augustus's *Pax Romana*, and in 384 work started on the construction of the basilica of S. Paolo fuori le mura, a building which exemplifies this powerful new current of thought.

As Rome's first bishop it was Peter and his memory that had predominated in the agenda of the Constantinian Church. The idea of an apostolic succession was meant to be the rock on which the Roman Church was founded – and Peter's supposed successors as bishops of Rome therefore claimed precedence over all other sees in the western half of the Roman empire. But in the earlier Church Peter had always been conjoined with Paul, the more philosophical and intellectual figure among the early Apostles. The revival of Paul's reputation paralleled the resurgent Christian intellectuality of the late fourth century and found an architectural expression in the basilica raised over his probable grave. Here the forty columns were specifically designed for the church rather than being taken from older buildings, and when it became necessary to repair the basilica in the 440s the decoration was executed on a lavish scale, with stucco adornment covering the arcades, frescoes of biblical scenes adorning the nave walls, and a mosaic on the triumphal arch which showed the four and twenty elders offering their wreaths to Christ. The balance of these proportions showed the impact of the classicizing revival in Rome, and the elegant proportions of the church of S. Sabina raised on the Aventine c. 425 make it the most graceful of all surviving early Christian churches in Rome. Superbly carved columns and capitals exemplify the new presentation of Christian themes in a classical setting, and one of the original mosaics still survives with its figures of the Church of the Jews and that of the former pagans who are represented by a series of Roman matrons.

The political and military context of these great achievements was, however, one of danger. In August 410 a military force of Visigoths led by Alaric had broken through the Aurelian Walls and sacked the city for three days. The empire had been formally divided since 395 and Honorius, based in Ravenna as emperor of the west, was unable to mount a resistance. Some of Rome's greatest mansions went up in flames and in the course of the looting some of the silver furnishings donated by Constantine to the Lateran basilica were seized. There was no massacre, though, and, since warning was given to the population beforehand, a good deal of private treasure was hidden away and asylum was provided in St Peter's and St Paul's. But although the damage was limited the shock to Roman and imperial self-confidence was immense.

'It's the end of the world,' said Jerome, 'words fail me, my sobs break in; I cannot dictate.' This was the first successful attack on Rome since its foundation, and some pagans saw it as a judgment delivered by the old gods who were angry at not being worshipped. Others simply wanted to ignore the event as an aberration, while for some rigorist Christians it was a divine punishment delivered against the lingering remnants of paganism within the city. Augustine's response, as we have seen, was to counsel Christian detachment towards all forms of earthly government since human attempts at the expression of power were intrinsically flawed. Successive leaders of the Church in Rome, however, returned to the imperative task of building a Christian city. Rome in fact recovered quickly from the Visigothic attack, its economic base was unaffected and at an ideological level the sack in fact strengthened the Church's prospects. Neither the emperor of the west nor his equal in Constantinople had been able to defend the city, and that task would therefore have to be performed by the only relevant power left standing, namely the Roman Church whose Christian culture had absorbed the classical past and taken the place of ancient Rome. St Peter's see was its representative quintessence and Rome's bishop was resolute in contesting, so far as the west was concerned, the claims of the Church of Constantinople.

Leo the Great, who was pope from 440 to 461, expressed the new power politics to perfection: 'Rome has become the Head of the World through the Holy See of Saint Peter.' *Caput orbis*, a phrase long since used to describe Rome, was now deployed to novel effect and the decorative arts reflected that theme. The interior of the Lateran basilica's octagonal baptistery, built by Constantine, was redesigned and its walls sheathed by colourful marble plaques. But it was the great basilica of S. Maria Maggiore on the Esquiline, built in the 420s and 430s, which provided the most eloquent testimony to an ancient tradition's infusion with new meaning. The Forum of Trajan, erected just over three centuries earlier, had been the last Roman building to show the Ionic orders and pilasters, and these now reappeared in the basilica's two rows of twenty columns, all crowned by Ionic capitals, and on the upper walls of the nave which are articulated by a classical order of tall pilasters. The mosaics in the nave and on the apse were simultaneously Christian and imperial: the Christ who appears on the arch of the apse is enthroned looking like a young emperor and the angels who attend him could be mistaken for deferential courtiers, while the Virgin, who is seen to the right of the apse opening, is a regal figure waited upon by a suite of angels who look like her ladies-in-waiting.

Leo was a figure of enormous influence as a teacher of his flock and he may well have inspired the biblical cycles which were painted on to the nave walls at St Peter's, at S. Paolo fuori le mura and in the Lateran basilica. Building activity in Rome was now centrally planned by the papacy, rather than being left to the initiative of individual parishes, and many basilicas were being built alongside the great covered cemeteries in the nearby countryside. By the early sixth century Rome had acquired a real ecclesiastical suburbia: each of the martyrs' graves had its own church – some forty in all – and the countryside was dotted with monasteries. Inside the city, the Lateran continued to be the political, religious and administrative centre of Christianity in Rome, and its refurbishment reflected that importance. In 428 figural mosaic replaced the gold foil of the apse vault and in the mid-fifth century biblical murals were painted on the nave walls. Constantine's baptistery, having been remodelled in the 430s, was expanded thirty years later with the addition of attached and adjoining oratories, and provided with a courtyard and fountain. The pope was now Rome's de facto ruler, and the bureaucrats who staffed his expanded administration were accommodated within the Lateran palace which, with their needs in mind, had been extended to the south and east of the basilica. But although genuine administrative needs drove some of these changes, they were also a symbolic affirmation of the Lateran's status vis-à-vis the popularity of St Peter's. The Apostle's shrine was a crowd-puller as the Lateran could never hope to be, and throughout the Middle Ages the contest for primacy between the two great centres never really ended. It was the prevailing pagan ethos of early fourth-century Rome which had forced Constantine to choose a site so remote from the centre, but the location proved to be a real inconvenience, especially since the population was starting to move westward into the area of the Campus Martius and the Tiber bend. A tide of humanity was engulfing the theatres and temples of a district which would become the core of medieval Rome.

SIXTH-CENTURY THREATS AND ROME'S RECOVERY

The early medieval Rome seen by Charlemagne had been profoundly influenced by Gregory the Great, who was pope from 590 to 604 and an administrator of genius. He belonged to the ancient and rich clan of the Anicii, one of the few aristocratic families who had decided to stay in Rome rather than transplant themselves to Constantinople. Educated in the classics and the works of the early Fathers of the Church, Gregory had an early career as a civil servant before withdrawing to the monastic community that he established in the family mansion sited on the west slope of the Caelian Hill. He then took Orders and went as a legate to the imperial court at Constantinople before returning to Rome. He was charged with the security of Rome and of the possessions of the Church in central Italy – known as the Lands of St Peter – as well as its vast landholdings in Sardinia and Sicily, at a time of exceptional danger. Gregory also had to contend with the claims of Byzantium which, since 552, was in legitimate occupation of Italy, while also dealing with the threat posed by the Lombard invaders from the German north who from 568 onwards were in possession of large areas of north and central Italy. The pope might be de facto ruler of Rome but he was still a subject of the emperor based in Constantinople, and in Ravenna there was a viceroy or *exarch* who represented the empire's imperial interests. Gregory negotiated a deal with the Lombards in the form of a truce which had to be renewed annually and in the course of a lengthy career he also effected no less important a change in the intellectual presentation of Christianity. He was a characteristic product of the fusion of Christianity and classical antiquity which had been evolving from the fifth century onwards but he also recognized its limitations, especially from the point of view of a proselytizing faith. Not only were pagan images and concepts too evident within that synthesis, it was also remote from the needs of the masses and expressed in a style they would have found affected and obscure. Gregory by contrast addressed them in the Latin of their daily lives, and his sermons were meant for intellectuals and non-intellectuals alike. That renewed burst of missionary enterprise associated with Gregory did nonetheless retain some specifically Roman features of the classical tradition: a clarity of reasoning and a practical instinct about how to get things done were adapted to Christian use.

This is the background to the Roman Church's great mission to convert its immediate neighbours the Lombards, the Visigoths who had now settled in Spain, and the Anglo-Saxons. Gregory also had to fix the details of day-to-day life in Rome, since the city's physical fabric was visibly decaying by the early seventh century following a century of massive disruption in the Italian peninsula as a whole. Following the Ostrogoths' invasion of north Italy in 488, their leader Theoderic ruled the entire peninsula as its king (493–526) and asserted his effective independence from the Byzantine emperors who, until his emergence, had been the region's nominal rulers. However, in 534 the emperor Justinian launched his military campaign to reconquer the west for the eastern Roman Empire. There was a twofold justification for the offensive: the usurpers were not just Germanic invaders but also attached to an Arian form of Christianity and therefore deemed to be heretics by Catholic Christianity. Rome was retaken two years later by Belisarius, Justinian's general, then lost again, retaken, and lost a second time. The city was finally captured for good by Narses, Belisarius's successor, in 552. The Byzantine period of re-established peace was then disrupted by the arrival of the Lombards who from 568 onwards were able to occupy large areas of northern and central Italy.

The impact of this prolonged warfare on the city, just like its wider effect on the devastated countryside of the Italian peninsula, was disastrous. Rome's economy collapsed and its population levels plummeted. In the year 400 Rome had a population of about 800,000. By the early seventh century it is doubtful if more than 90,000 people lived there, and many of them were refugees from the despoiled rural areas. Rome's population levels never recovered much beyond that figure during the Middle Ages, and the numbers were frequently even fewer. Regular incursions of pilgrims would have masked some of this depopulation, but the monumental quality of the new Christian architecture must often have made the streets of Rome look very empty by comparison. War had provided the tipping point but Rome's economy had been in decline for many decades before the arrival of these later calamities. From the third century onwards the agricultural estates near the city were being abandoned and fields which were no longer tilled and drained turned quickly into malarial swamps. Imports of foodstuffs from overseas were also imperilled for more than one reason. Production of agricultural goods in the massive estates, or *latifundia*, established in Rome's colonies had always been dependent on the existence of large numbers of slaves, and that was a dwindling source of labour in an era of population decline. The fifth-century occupations of north Africa by the Vandals, of Gaul by Burgundians and Franks, and of Spain by Visigoths removed whole areas of supply. Rome was now entirely dependent for its food on Sicily, whose sea lanes were threatened by Vandal pirates, and on southern Italy, where communications were imperilled by Lombard offensives and the effects of the Gothic wars.

The result was poverty and unemployment in Rome; and regular famines, along with epidemics of cholera, bubonic plague and malaria, afflicted both the city and the surrounding area. Rome's increased vulnerability to flooding from the Tiber was a measure of the city's structural decline, and its problems in this regard continued well into the Carolingian era. The *Liber Pontificalis* records a major flood in 791, just nine years before Charlemagne's imperial coronation, and there were similar inundations recorded for 716, 856 and 860. By 600 many of Rome's great mansions had been abandoned and their ruins, especially in the form of column shafts, bases and capitals as well as marble, would be reused in the building of Christian churches. Much remained, however: the city walls still stood as did the public baths, the aqueducts worked for the most part and the palaces on the Palatine were kept in reasonable repair. There was something for Gregory and his Church to work on.

The Byzantine government, established in its enclave in Ravenna, was powerless: it was just about able to keep garrisons in Rome and Ravenna, Naples and Rimini, and in the stretch of inland territory linking Rome with Ravenna. Rome's chief secular authority was meant to be the Senate as reconstituted in 554, but that was a merely ceremonial institution and after 603 was replaced by an informal advisory council. The Church, by contrast, though shorn of its eastern, Spanish, north African and Gaulish estates, retained Sicily and Sardinia. Its most important lands were in central Italy, and these comprised a loose chain of possessions extending from Rome across to the Adriatic coast and up into Tuscany, Liguria and Romagna. Gregory's negotiation had preserved these estates from the Lombard threat, and most of the area was directly controlled from Rome where a papal chancery had emerged with a developed accounting system. The funds thereby gained had already enabled the Church to embark on its ambitious fifth-century building programme including S. Maria Maggiore and the extended Lateran complex. And these same financial resources could now be used to subsidize the local welfare programme urgently needed because of the impact of famine and disease.

At Gregory's accession the papal treasury was the only public financial body still functioning in Rome, and it was the Church therefore which had to pay the local troops. He inherited a situation in which the Church had emerged to take on the functions and duties of a temporal power in Rome and in the central Italian 'Lands of St Peter' as well as in Sicily. Gregory helped the further evolution of this process with the Church taking over the public buildings, and many private mansions became monasteries and churches. The supreme example of this process was the Christianization of the Pantheon, once a temple dedicated to all the gods and which, following its handover from the empire to the papacy in 609, became the church of S. Maria Rotunda. Although over 200 years had passed since the enforced closure by law of the pagan sanctuaries, the Pantheon was the first such building to be converted to Christian use. A long time would pass before that initiative was repeated with the Christianization of the temple of Fortuna Virilis in the 870s. The widespread belief that evil spirits haunted these ancient consecrated centres may have inhibited the local Roman Christians, although in the east there were many examples of pagan temples which had become Christian churches. Gregory eventually rejected the superstition and instructed the mission to England to consecrate that country's pagan sanctuaries to Christian purposes, and in Rome itself Hadrian's Mausoleum became the Castel S. Angelo.

Throughout the seventh century the process of Christianizing the Fora, the Via Sacra and the Palatine gathered pace. This was the heart of imperial and pagan Rome, and since its buildings had fallen into disrepair there was an opportunity to consecrate an entire area to the Christian God. There was precious little parochial need for the new churches that emerged in this depopulated part of the city, whether in the form of new building or as structures converted from old ones. But it was the triumphalist symbolism that mattered in a district which

Constantine had been forced to leave well alone so far as any public Christian statement was concerned. Between 625 and 638 the churches of S. Adriano and S. Martina were installed in the former Senate buildings on the Forum, and later on a *diaconia* or welfare centre was set up near the Temple of Concord. The Roman population needed of course to be fed literally as well as spiritually, and Gregory's reorganization of the Church lands into various regions, as in the case of the patrimony of Sicily, resulted in a renewal of Rome's grain supplies.

THE ARRIVAL OF THE PILGRIMS

An influx of new pilgrims from the recently Christianized north of Europe meant that the city's sacred authority was evident as never before in the age of Gregory. It was the desire to stand near the martyrs' graves, and especially that of St Peter, which drew these visitors to Rome, and the associated veneration of relics grew in intensity. The removal of particles of bone for the purposes of veneration had been a feature of the eastern Church from a very early date, but the western Church disapproved of the practice, not least because it was contrary to Roman law. In Gregory's view the eastern trafficking in relics was both superstitious and ridiculous. When the empress of Byzantium pleaded with him to send her the head of St Paul he frightened her off with a scare story: when the tomb of St Lawrence was accidentally opened during some building renovations the Roman workmen who saw the body had all died within ten days. The pope was happy to send the empress some filings from St Peter's chains but that was as far as he was prepared to go in satisfying her relic-hunger. Linen strips lowered into the grave were just about acceptable in his eyes, and Gregory made a concession to Queen Theodelinda of the Lombards who received from him small bottles of the oil taken from lamps burning near the tombs of martyrs. The pope's distaste for the relic trade was very much the official line of the western Church until well into the seventh century, but the popular devotion proved to be uncontrollable and western Europe was amassing huge numbers of bone relics despite the disapproval of the Church hierarchy.

From the sixth century onwards pilgrim numbers were so great that special hostels were set up in Rome to cater for the more indigent of these travellers, and the conversion of western Europe to the Roman Church brought a whole new flood of Franks and Visigothic Spaniards, Frisians and southern Germans, British, Irish and Anglo-Saxons, as well as Lombards from nearer home. The pilgrims arrived in town in order to accrue spiritual merit, and a hazardous or lengthy journey was considered to be especially worthy although, as many churchmen recognized, motives may well have been as mixed as in any other area of human ambition. The Englishman Boniface, the apostle to the Germans, thought in 749 that a good many 'sex-hungry and ignorant Swiss, Bavarians, or Franks' mingled with the devout. But whatever brought them to Rome, the pilgrims would have found accommodation in the *diaconiae*, the welfare centres run by the Church and serviced by the monastic congregations. The first such buildings may have been raised in the late sixth century, and their original task of providing and distributing food, and catering generally to the sick and poor, was later extended to include the provision of facilities for pilgrims. In the early ninth century there were twenty-four *diaconiae*, and many were to be found within those compounds for foreign communities called *scholae*.

S. Maria in Cosmedin, which would be transformed into a church in the eighth century, started life as a *diaconia* catering for the Greeks of southern Italy who included traders settled in Rome as well as pilgrims from the area. The first specifically northern *schola* was that of the Saxons, established perhaps as early as 726 and its name, the *burgus Saxonum*, survives in the term Borgo to describe the area by the Tiber leading up to St Peter's. By the mid-eighth century the entire district surrounding the basilica was heavily colonized by northerners, and all such colonies of foreigners would eventually incorporate both rich and poor, pilgrims and more long-standing residents. In about 770 the Lombards established their *schola* at a site just north of St Peter's, and in the late eighth century that of the Franks was to be found just south of the basilica's atrium. The Frisian compound was on the site of S. Michele in Borgo, on the top of the hill to the south-east of where Bernini's colonnade now stands. By 799, on the eve of Charlemagne's coronation, all these *scholae* were organized as autonomous civilian and military entities, and they would only be absorbed within Rome at a much later stage.

The pilgrims formed part of Rome's early tourist trade, and the three earliest guides to Christian Rome date from the seventh century. Visitors were an important conduit for the spread of Romanization, and from the late sixth century onwards Frankish bishops were making regular trips to Rome in order to learn the Roman liturgy which was replacing the older Gallican rite in their dioceses. Boniface was always in close touch with developments in Rome and, as leader of the English mission to the Germans, he helped to carry the Roman liturgy to the newly Christianized areas. It was in 754 that Pippin declared, following his meeting with Pope Stephen II, that the Roman version of the liturgy was the only one allowed in the Frankish kingdom. But the king's proclamation followed more than a century's policy evolution in that direction. The economic impact of the visitors on Rome was no less profound and long-lasting. Both the building trade and the tourist industry benefited from the need to cater for the visitors who needed to be accommodated. And the redecoration of Roman churches can be seen as huge projects of capital expenditure calculated to attract devout sightseers as well as designed to encourage them in their faith. In the first decades of the seventh century St Peter's was continuing to evolve and the new furnishings it acquired in that period were meant to awe: a gilded coffered ceiling was placed over the nave, the main doors were covered with silver, and the basilica's roof was covered with bronze tiles removed from the temple of Venus and Roma. All this opulence shows that the papacy was continuing to extract significant amounts of money from its lands. But the seventh century would turn out to be a time of trial and contraction for the Church of Rome. As with the rest of the ancient civilization of the Mediterranean, its prospects would be profoundly affected by an Arab culture transformed into an expansionist power by the influence of a new missionary religion: Islam.

ROME'S SEVENTH-CENTURY CRISIS

In 635 Arab forces conquered Syria and Palestine; Jerusalem fell in 640 and Egypt was taken in 641, with Mesopotamia and Iran succumbing shortly afterwards. North African territories came under Arab domination and Spain, having been invaded in 711, was swiftly overrun apart from a mountainous enclave in the north. Byzantium shrank in the face of an onslaught from Islam to its south as well as being threatened by Slavs and Bulgars in the Balkans and by the Lombards in Italy. Constantinople's remit now extended only as far as Asia Minor, Greece and the southern Balkans, with its hold on southern Italy, Sicily and Ravenna becoming increasingly precarious. Rome, however, remained subject to the emperor's rule as exercised from Constantinople and there was a series of attempts at strengthening Byzantium's hold on the city and on the Roman Church. An early eighth-century reform turned Rome into a duchy ruled by a Byzantine *dux* who was intended to be a governor in both civil and military affairs. Although that particular attempt failed, the emperor and his viceroy in Ravenna, the *exarch*, remained in theory the ultimate source of authority in Rome. Up until 731, and as a matter of form, papal elections required imperial confirmation, and the Roman Church was deeply involved in the theological disputes that embroiled Byzantium. But the tensions between east and west were rarely far from the surface, and Byzantium imposed heavy taxes on the Church estates in southern Italy. The emperor Constans was received with all due ceremony when he came to Rome in 667 for a twelve-day visit. But on leaving he took away with him the bronze tiles of the Pantheon, a building which by then had been Church property for sixty years. Common interests, and especially the threat from Islam, might oblige Rome and Constantinople to co-operate, but their relations were ambivalent.

The economic impact of the Islamic advance was disastrous for the west and the Mediterranean looked as if it might become a Muslim lake. North Africa's grain supplies were lost, and both the Italian coastline and the Mediterranean sea lanes were threatened. Provisioning Rome, always a problem, became extremely difficult, and the Church policy, initiated by Honorius I (625–38), of leasing central Italian lands to private landowners led to the alienation of many such properties. The dwindling of economic resources accompanied a series of public health crises – especially as a result of insanitation – and in 680 Rome witnessed an outbreak of bubonic plague. One consequence of the loss of the east was the arrival in Rome of a number of refugees fleeing from the Arab armies, and many of these, together with their families, became influential figures. Of the thirteen popes who occupied the see of Peter from 678 to 741 eleven were either Syriac or Greek in origin, with many of them having been brought up in southern Italy. Their immigrant origins meant that they were eager to assimilate by identifying themselves with the Roman Church, and their familiarity with eastern languages permitted them to combat Byzantine claims in an authoritative manner. Monastic refugees also came to Rome in large numbers and by 645 a group of monks from the community of St Sabbas in the Judaean Hills had established themselves in a mansion on the Little Aventine. Towards the end of the seventh century many of these now fully Romanized refugees from Islamic lands were influential in spreading Roman doctrine and liturgy in western Europe. These include the two emissaries sent to England in 664 to strengthen the fragile local Church there: Hadrian's family origins lay in north Africa and Theodore came from Tarsus in Cilicia.

Martyrs' bones, long an object of eastern devotion, now arrived en masse in Rome as a result of these eastern influences and the objects were no longer frowned upon by Church officialdom. Pope Leo II, a Sicilian and therefore subject to Byzantine influences, transferred martyrs' relics from the catacomb of Generosa on the Via Portuense to a side-chapel at S. Bibiana. And the seventh century is also the time when the sermon became a regular feature of services in the western Church, as it had long since been in the Churches of Byzantium, Syria and Palestine. The icons which begin to appear in Roman churches from the early seventh century onwards are evidently eastern in their style and inspiration, as in the case of the Virgin and Child which was placed in the Pantheon following its 609 consecration as a church. Rome became a major centre for the production and veneration of icons after iconoclasm swept the eastern Church from the early eighth century onwards. That new policy, formulated in 726 and pursued until 843 (save for the thirty-year interruption of 786–816), prohibited the veneration of images and was the cause of a major dispute with the Roman Church. Many hundreds of monks and hermits fled its persecutory impact and arrived in the Greek-speaking territories of southern Italy and Sicily.

Byzantine artistic style acquired a great patron in John VII, both before and during his short pontificate of 705–7. His father, called Plato, had been a long-serving official in the civil service of Byzantium and ended his career as *curator palatii* or governor of the imperial palaces on the Palatine, which were still the property of the emperors. John installed a shrine in St Peter's against the inner façade wall of the outer north aisle, and the mosaic above the door showed a huge figure of the Virgin framed by seven scenes from her life. Gregory III (731–41) and his successor Zacharias (741–52) resumed the tradition of lavish donations. Gregory placed six vine-scrolled columns in St Peter's along with many silver furnishings, and Zacharias's restoration of the papal palace at the Lateran made an immense impression on contemporaries. He both enlarged the palace and decorated it with mosaics, marble and murals, along with a map of the world and explanatory verses which adorned the *triclinium* on the upper floor.

From the sixth century onwards, and right up to the emergence of the Carolingian dynasty as a major European power, the papacy found itself torn between east and west. In order to resist the Lombards it had to arrive at some kind of accommodation with Byzantium. But guaranteeing the security of the city of Rome and of the papacy's central Italian territories might come at a cost: the eastern emperor's intervention in Italian affairs and an accompanying threat to the doctrinal claims of the Roman Church. From the early eighth century onwards the papacy was increasingly self-confident about its ability to deal with these problems. A new landholding class emerged which was centred on Rome and her various landed institutions, including monasteries and *diaconiae* as well as the churches, and it was this grouping which provided local militias able to defend the papacy and uphold Rome's independence. The emergence of a Roman militia is a late seventh-century development and, along with the clergy and the lay leaders of the local great families, it would play an important role in papal elections. Nor was this just a local and Roman development: the Ravenna militia sent to arrest Pope Sergius I c. 680 mutinied and decided instead to rescue him.

Byzantium made strenuous attempts at asserting its countervailing power: Pope Gregory II (715–31) was the victim of repeated assassination attempts planned in Constantinople, and heavy taxes were imposed on Church estates in Sicily and southern Italy, which were finally confiscated. But Rome's de facto independence was fast becoming an irreversible fact of European politics. It was Gregory who persuaded the Lombard king Liutprand to withdraw his invading force from central Italy and on the renewal of hostilities ten years later Pope Zacharias negotiated a similar peace deal, taking over in person the frontier towns which were returned by the enemy. The papacy, Rome's effectively independent ruler, was a power on the rise both diplomatically and militarily, and when the Lombards once again threatened Ravenna in 743 the *exarch* and his population appealed to Zacharias for protection.

FRANKS TO THE RESCUE

753 is the crunch point, the year which tested the idea of Roman independence. Lombard forces had taken Byzantine Ravenna and then besieged Rome while demanding her surrender. Pope Stephen II negotiated and succeeded in getting the siege lifted, but at the same time the Byzantines made a personal appeal to him and requested that he regain those imperial territories in Italy which were now being occupied by the Lombards. Stephen's solution involved turning to the Frankish monarchy as the only European power capable of dealing with the Lombard threat, and in the winter of 753 he decided to make the hazardous journey across the Alps to Francia. As we have already seen, he anointed both the sons of Pippin and the king himself who had usurped the throne with papal approval just three years previously. Pippin's legitimacy was upheld and the king promised in return to protect the safety both of Rome and of her Church's territorial possessions. The king of the Franks now became, by papal appointment, 'patrician of the Romans', a symbolic title borrowed from Byzantine court ceremonial but one which nonetheless showed the depth of the papacy's regard for its new protector. What happened subsequently determined much of the future course of European medieval history.

Pippin extracted a promise from the Lombards that they would restore to the Church those of its territories occupied by them, and would also donate to 'St Peter and the Holy Roman Church' the formerly Byzantine lands in Italy they had seized. The legal status of these Byzantine territories remained undefined, and the same is true of the position of

Rome itself. But the situation as it obtained on the ground was clear enough: Byzantium had been knocked out of Italy north of Naples and was no longer a player of any significance in the politics of western Europe. Rome, as represented by her Church and great families, was now a major power in its own right within the Italian peninsula. The formal ratification of these arrangements in 756 was known as the Donation of Pippin and the document provided a legal basis for the papacy's new territorial power in Italy. Pope Hadrian I was able to appeal to Pippin's son and successor Charlemagne when the Lombards returned to the attack in 773, threatening Rome and the towns securing the route to Ravenna. As a direct result the Frankish army moved over the border into Lombardy and occupied Pavia, and Charlemagne annexed the kingdom of the Lombards to Francia in 774. Charlemagne, himself now accorded the title of 'patrician of the Romans', became the most significant protector of the Church and of the city of Rome, and all of central and northern Italy was ruled by the Franks and the papacy.

The power which had now emerged represented a fusion of the Church, the city of Rome and the symbolic figure of St Peter. The deeds of territory granted by Pippin and Charlemagne were made out to 'St Peter' since Rome was his city, and those who lived on the Church's lands were his *peculiaris populus*. From the time of Gregory the Great onwards the Church estates in central Italy, an area comprising the ancient Roman region of Latium as far as southern Tuscany, were fictitiously the property of St Peter and therefore termed the *patrimonium Petri*. Its strongholds were the *castra Petri*, the Apostle's castles. The papal administration's writ ran within the territory, and Rome was the capital of this de facto state. Militias were raised in the city and its adjacent territories, and the papal administration handled foreign relations and the civil government. Ecclesiastical, military and civilian affairs were thoroughly interfused with the same families producing the personnel of the clerical, administrative and military elites. These also were the people who elected popes, and despite the frequent infighting between the families as they jockeyed for position there was a cohesive quality to this self-perpetuating administration.

This Roman oligarchy might, as circumstances dictated, ally itself either with or against the Lombard kingdom, but the goal of removing the last traces of Byzantine rule in Italy was pursued consistently. Collective memories of ancient Rome were deployed to political effect: foreigners were thereby put in their place and the longevity of Roman identity was adduced to demonstrate its legitimacy. Ancient titles such as that of *consul* were therefore revived, and from the early ninth century onwards the term *senatus* was collectively used to describe the great families. These co-existed with the Byzantine titles of *dux* and *comes*, and this latest arrival among the constellation of powers that emerged out of the interplay between the barbarian Germanic kingdoms and the Roman imperial legacy called itself the *res publica* or *Sanctae Dei ecclesiae res publica Romanorum*. It was an aristocratic republic run by an elective monarchy, and it had discovered a protector in the Frankish kingdom which, although its key ally, was also capable of pursuing ambitions which did not always coincide with papal interests.

THE RESURGENT PAPACY

Hadrian I, whose pontificate (772–95) coincided with the first half of Charlemagne's reign as sole king of the Franks, was Roman to the core, and his aristocratic family had provided the Church with many of its most significant lay officials and clerical leaders. His biographer stressed Hadrian's *romanitas* and the associated qualities he brought to the defence both of the faith and of the *patria*. The association between them was a close one, but Hadrian is also the pope who made sure that Charlemagne had to respect the traditional forms and ask for permission in order to cross from St Peter's – outside the city walls – into the city proper when he visited in 774. Securing the safety of the city and making it a place in which Romans could live decent and comfortable lives was once again a priority. Rome had been besieged twice by the Lombards during 752–5 and its countryside ravaged in the process, and the first years of the pontificate had witnessed a resumption of their attacks. These depredations had dealt a setback to the economic advances which had been such a feature of the period leading up to the mid-eighth century. The city was crowded with refugees whose numbers included monks forced to flee the countryside, and many aqueducts had to be either repaired or rebuilt. Among the major ecclesiastical buildings, St Peter's and St Paul's as well as the church of St Lawrence needed major repairs, and the catacombs were in a poor state since many of them, once the Lombards had raided and carried off the bones as relics, were being used by farmers as shelters for their cattle and sheep.

Increased security after the removal of the Lombard threat meant that Hadrian could set to work on maximizing revenue from the Church's central Italian estates, and he therefore developed the *domus cultae*, large estates which were run by the Church and obliged to deliver set quotas for the maintenance of churches, clergy, the papacy and welfare institutions. Pope Zacharias had developed the first four of these *domus cultae* in the Campagna of the 740s, and they differed markedly from previous Church farms which were widely scattered and far from Rome. These new estates were large holdings bequeathed to the Church and then built up into huge estates by the additional purchases of adjoining land. They were located near the city and declared to be inalienable according to the terms of the charters issued for the 'apostolic farmland', *constituta apostolicae exarationis*, with a corporation of clergy established on each farm as part of its regulatory supervision. Hadrian founded an extra seven of the *domus cultae* and the produce of one of them was set apart to feed one hundred of the poor every day at the Lateran. Combined with the increased number of *diaconiae* under both Hadrian and his successor Leo III, the initiative revived the welfare system and thereby helped the Church to retain its hold on the affections of the urban poor and of needy pilgrims. Quite as importantly, the *domus cultae* provided the Church with a political and economic power base in the Roman countryside, a resource comparable to the landholdings already possessed by the abbeys and the established familial clans.

Like Gregory before him, Hadrian was a vigorous renovator of the aqueducts, including the Sabbatina which had been cut in the Lombard siege of 755. It was this aqueduct which fed the mills on the Gianicilo, the fountain in the atrium of St Peter's, as well as the nearby bath which was intended to keep the pilgrims clean, and Hadrian also ensured that the lead pipes which conveyed the water to St Peter's were repaired. The entire Lateran complex, including its bath and baptistery, could also rely on a resumption of its regular water supply once the Aqua Claudia, which crossed the Caelian Hill, had been repaired. The Aurelian Walls, being now almost five centuries old, needed repairs, and Hadrian's pontificate saw an extensive rebuilding of the walls and towers. There were immense technical challenges to be overcome in the course of this major programme of development right across the city: new beams eighty feet long were put in place spanning the nave of St Peter's, and more than 12,000 blocks of stone were used to strengthen the Tiber's embankment near the Castel S. Angelo. Schemes such as these also demanded a large workforce and this was provided by levies drawn from the countryside, a method of securing labour not seen in Rome since late classical antiquity. Church building repairs were of course on a lavish scale, and it was Charlemagne who made sure that the forests of Spoleto yielded the huge beams spanning the naves of the major churches of Rome: fourteen for St Peter's and twenty for S. Maria Maggiore, fifteen for the Lateran basilica and no fewer than thirty-five for St Paul's. He also provided the 1,000 pounds of lead needed for the roof of St Peter's, and when visiting the city he did so at least partly as the latest in a long line of patrons who demonstrated their piety through their munificence and care for the buildings of Christian Rome.

The redecoration programme extended to most of the major churches and included the provision of textiles in purple silk and embroidered gold which were designed to hang in front of doors, to cover triumphal arches and to be placed in between nave columns. St Peter's reached a new pinnacle of magnificence: silver paving extended from the chancel doors to the foot of the high altar, all 365 lights of the cross-shaped chandelier were lit at Easter and Christmas, and sixty-five curtains were hung between the columns of the nave. Lombard looting is one reason why the Church relented its former policy on relics, and whole cartloads of them arrived in the city churches from the time of Paul I's papacy to that of Paschal. These were no longer mere dry bones but spiritually potent and politically useful reminders of the link between Roman Christianity's glorious past and its contemporary renaissance. A relic of Sylvester was placed at S. Silvestro in Capite and was especially emblematic of the idea of a Christian empire since he had been pope during the age of Constantine. A similar significance attached itself to the remains of a Roman noblewoman, Aurea Petronilla. Local legend in Rome insisted that she was the daughter of St Peter, and during the late 750s her sarcophagus was removed from the main body of St Peter's to the rotunda which, attached to the south transept, served as an imperial mausoleum. In 760 this mausoleum was dedicated to 'St Petronilla' as the chapel of the kings of the Franks, and it would retain that status right up to the demolition of the old basilica and the building of New St Peter's in the sixteenth century. These stones were therefore a concrete proof of the bond between the royal house, the Apostle himself, and Peter's successors as bishop's of Rome. The fact that St Peter's, from the early years of Hadrian I's pontificate onwards, was being referred to as an *aula* rather than just an *ecclesia* or *basilica*, showed that the building as a whole had acquired an imperial dimension. Previously, that term had only been used in dedicatory inscriptions of the most solemn kind and it could be read therefore on the various gifts given by Constantine to St Peter's: the arch of the apse, the triumphal arch between nave and transept, and the gold cross. In those cases there was an analogy with the term's appearance on the Arch of Constantine, that monumental record of imperial and military success. But now the entire basilica was itself an *aula* and a signal example of a later triumph: a resurgent Rome sacralized and justified through its association with Christian power.

This then is the context for the writing of one of the most famous forgeries in history, the Donation of Constantine, a document which was concocted by officials of the papal chancery either in 754 while Pope Stephen II was visiting Francia or at various stages during the second half of the eighth century. The Donation claimed to be a decree addressed by Constantine to Pope Sylvester and for many centuries it would be used to justify the more extravagant papal claims. On his departure for the east and his new capital of Constantinople, the emperor was supposed to have granted to the pope and his successors the imperial honours, incomes, regalia and insignia which signified a status higher than Constantine's own 'secular throne'. Not only the Lateran palace and the rest of the city of Rome but also 'all provinces, places and towns of Italy and the Western regions' were ceded to the papacy. Papal supremacy was explicitly asserted over the eastern patriarchates, and the effect of the Donation was to relegate the Byzantine emperor's de facto rule to the eastern territories. The pope's imperial status co-existed alongside his spiritual supremacy over the whole of Christendom, and the claim to temporal rule over Rome, Italy and the entire west, though couched in vague generality, was the Church of Rome's attempt at defining the relation that ought to obtain between the popes and the Frankish kings. These monarchs were to be subject to the imperial authority invested in the person of the pope of the day, and the role allotted to them was that of loyal defenders of the papal interests. The Donation's terms of reference were the power arrangements that obtained in Italy at the time of its actual composition: the Church's rule in the city of Rome and within its Italian territories (the 'Lands of St Peter'), including the former Byzantine-controlled areas of central Italy. This was the concrete reality, and the Donation tried to give a theoretical underpinning to the situation.

Hadrian preserved that balance of power between the Franks, the Byzantines and the papacy which is the political context of the Donation and its claims. It was this configuration of forces which was thrown off balance by his successor when Pope Leo III, expelled from Rome by local aristocratic factions, returned to the city and crowned Charlemagne emperor on Christmas Day 800. On approaching the city the king had been accorded the formal reception worthy of a Roman or Byzantine emperor rather than, as in the past, that of a *patricius*, the title conferred on him by the papal chancery from 754 onwards. The Romans assembled in St Peter's, including clergy, lay administrators, the local military and aristocracy, acclaimed him as '*Augustus*' (or Majesty) in a well-choreographed manner. But the exact nature of this new imperial sovereignty was left undefined, partly because of the wish to spare Byzantine feelings but also because of the lack of general agreement about what a Christian empire actually meant in practice.

ILLUSTRATING THE CHRISTIAN EMPIRE

Papal diplomats may well have envisaged an empire of and for the Romans – the *imperium Romanorum* of the title eventually adopted – an institution which was meant to be in the gift of the papacy and whose chief purpose was the defence of Rome and of the Roman Church. This is indeed the view which is represented visually in the mosaic which was once in the *triclinium* (or dining hall) of the papal palace at the Lateran and which dates from 798–9. To the right an enthroned St Peter hands the *pallium* to Pope Leo and the *labarum* (a standard or banner) to Charlemagne, who is still represented as a king rather than as the emperor he would shortly become, while on the left Christ hands the *labarum* to Constantine and the keys to the Kingdom of Heaven to St Peter. In the half-dome of the apse there is a representation of the Apostolic Mission: Christ is flanked by the eleven disciples who will be charged with the conversion of the world. The Church's role in the spreading of the faith is therefore here related to the supportive roles of both Constantine and Charlemagne, with the former being conceived of as a role model for the latter. This was also the job specified for the kings of the Franks according to the Constantinian Donation, but the dynamics were changed as a result of Charlemagne's coronation. Perhaps Leo and his advisers only thought of the ceremony as some kind of ratification of an alliance which was already some half-century old. But the creation of an imperial title also meant the arrival of some kind of empire to match it, and subsequent history would demonstrate the dangers as well as the advantages of such an institution where the papacy was concerned.

Byzantium's claim to be a legitimate ruler in the west might now be a fiction but it had never been explicitly challenged before 800. Moreover, this new western emperor was also claiming to be the successor to the Roman emperors of antiquity, both pagan and Christian. Charlemagne was in fact ruling large parts of what had been their empire at its widest extent, in Gaul, Italy and Germany. The Frankish king-emperor and his successors would also use the titles of Caesar and Augustus, terms revived to Carolingian effect for the first time on Christmas Day 800. The documents of this imperial dynasty were dated in consular years according to the Roman style, and the emperors' seals, which bore the legend *Renovatio Romani Imperii*, framed a symbolic image of Rome, a city which could therefore be interpreted as being the capital of this Carolingian empire. Papal diplomacy, as evidenced in the Donation of Constantine, did of course actively promote the revival of a Christian empire and related Constantine to Charlemagne with that end in view.

It was thought that Constantine and Pope Sylvester had exercised a kind of condominium and that they had done so at a time when Christianity and the empire were coterminous. It is not just the mosaics in the Lateran *triclinium* which show that the papacy wanted Charlemagne to revive and continue Constantine's role as the Church's protector. Documents issued by the papal chancery refer repeatedly to Charlemagne as the 'new Constantine', and when Louis the Pious, Charlemagne's son, was crowned in 816 it was supposedly Constantine's own crown that was used. Yet that revival posed new dangers for both parties to the deal: imperial pretensions could discomfit the papacy and a closer involvement in Italian affairs might not always suit the imperial agenda.

Charlemagne and Louis were in fact respectful of the papal territories' de facto autonomy, but the notion of a Christian empire contained contradictions which could lead to conflict. The year 843 provided a test case when the empire claimed the city of Rome and the 'Lands of St Peter' as a fief subject to its newly created sub-kingdom of Italy. Charlemagne's grandson Lothair tried to enforce what he took to be his imperial rights by sending a military expedition led by his own son, the king of Italy. On that occasion the breach in relations was healed: imperial confirmation of papal elections continued and so did the papal swearing of an oath of allegiance to the emperor. But the weakening of central authority within the Carolingian empire in the second half of the ninth century meant that the papacy could no longer rely on it as a source of military defence, and the close relationship of Charlemagne's reign diminished accordingly.

The coronation of Charlemagne in 800 therefore both contained and acquired layers of meaning, and the myriad differing accounts of its significance reflected ambiguities which were always latent within the idea of an imperial title. Rome was the city of the martyrs and the see of St Peter, the goal of pilgrims and the administrative capital of the vast patrimony ruled by the pope as Peter's successor. At the same time she was an imperial capital in two inherently contradictory senses of that phrase. She had been granted, as the Donation's forgers in the papal chancery claimed and as many believed, by Constantine to Pope Sylvester. The fact that the pope possessed the city as its ruler was therefore taken to be part and parcel of his own imperial standing. But at the same time the new western emperor, Charlemagne, claimed to be the heir to Constantine and to all Roman emperors, and therefore he too had a legitimate title to Rome as his capital. Future popes and theorists of papal power in the Middle Ages would contend that his coronation derived its legitimacy from the fact that it was conducted in St Peter's and by a pope. But that, as we have seen, was not Charlemagne's view of the matter, and neither was it that of his own dynastic successors as emperors. The Carolingian title to imperial rule also conflated Rome's present and her past, the age of Charlemagne with that of the Caesars. 'Rome' had become an idea which meant different things to different people and was therefore interpreted variously by popes and emperors. In addition, there was an entirely separate 'Rome' on the Bosphorus, and Constantinople was often described as a 'second Rome'.

Architecture reflected these various facets of meaning. The records and surviving illustrations of the original complex of buildings at the Lateran, demolished in the 1580s, show that from the early eighth century onwards the popes were intent on building a palace which could be compared with that of the Byzantine emperors. Pope Zacharias in the middle of the century built an entrance tower whose bronze gate was surmounted by a portrait of Christ, a structure which evoked the two-storied *Chalke* at the entrance to the imperial palace in Constantinople. And the details of the *triclinium* built by Leo III just before 800, and whose apse carried the mosaic already referred to, was equally Byzantine in scale and ambition: marble sheathed the walls while porphyry columns supported the entrance. The second *triclinium* he built a few years later on the upper and main floor of his palace was even more magnificent and extended for 220 feet. An apse at the end and five conchs on either side of the hall held tables and dining divans where, on particularly grand occasions, the guests reclined. From the anteroom a canopied balcony overlooked the area facing the palace and it was here that successive popes delivered the blessing *urbi et orbi* until well into the thirteenth century. Leo had built a similar dining hall adjoining the steps ascending the atrium of St Peter's, but the one in the Lateran palace was clearly intended to parallel the Hall of the Nineteen Divans in Constantinople's imperial palace.

Church buildings in the late eighth and early ninth centuries show yet another facet to the meaning of Rome, and here there was a decided return to early Christian, and very Constantinian, themes. This was a version of contemporary Rome whose strength was derived from its identification with Rome's Christian past, and elements of pagan antiquity were Christianized in the process. Churches such as S. Prassede were in no small measure a political statement and their revival of the Christian monumental art of late antiquity showed that this Rome wished to be seen as the centre of a genuinely pan-European civilization and not just as the focus of a Mediterranean power. The return of mosaic art to Rome just before 800 may show the desire to compete with contemporary Constantinople, but the mosaicists used glass *tesserae*, the material current in Rome three or four centuries previously, rather than the marble and glass of Byzantine artists. Their themes also revert to the iconography typical of that earlier period, such as the Second Coming of Christ which is portrayed at S. Prassede, and the architectural plan of the church's side-chapel dedicated to S. Zeno is similar to that of a late antique mausoleum. And there were distinct signs too of northern influences in eighth-century Rome: the wooden tower which, gilded and silver-plated, was added to the roof of St Peter's in the 750s was typically Frankish, and the massive tower over the entrance gate of the atrium at SS. Quattro Coronati is a distinctively north European feature.

By the last two decades of the eighth century the Carolingian renaissance, a literary and artistic movement which was rooted in northern Europe and enjoyed the patronage of Charlemagne's court, was establishing its own distinctive fusion of Christian thought with the traditions of classical antiquity. Visual elements of both traditions can be seen in the illuminated manuscripts produced at the Carolingian court and at such great centres of learning as the convents at Trier, Reims and Tours, and also in the ivory carvings produced at Aachen and Metz. It was the bronze casters at Aachen who produced the classical designs of the local palatine chapel's railings and doors. Workmen in the same city produced the tomb plaque of Pope Hadrian I which, with its delicate frame of classical tendrils, can be seen in St Peter's. These were the Frankish testimonies to the classical revival which was taking place north of the Alps, and the emergence of a western empire in the early ninth century gave that renaissance a political focus. It followed its own, very northern, path and its literary achievements, especially in the work of the north Briton Alcuin and of Einhard, born in Seligenstadt in eastern Francia, find few echoes in Rome. The Roman renaissance by contrast was rooted in the visual arts and in a recovery of the artistic styles associated with the city's history during the period of late antiquity. There was a distinctive political agenda at work here: the recovery of an imagined Constantinian past now revived to serve the needs of the papal court from the mid-eighth century onwards and embodied to monumental effect in the designs and the decoration of its greatest achievements: St Peter's and the Lateran basilica, S. Paolo fuori le mura and S. Maria Maggiore.

These buildings and the aspirations embedded within them showed that there were two kinds of empire and that although their interests might at times coincide, as happened on 25 December 800, the one was not the equivalent of the other. A coronation whose meaning was originally uncertain did, as we have seen, acquire definition to the mutual satisfaction of both the papacy and the Frankish monarchy within the generation that followed the events of 25 December 800. But that consensus did not last beyond the first few decades of the ninth century. Imperial aspiration stirred passions, inspired imaginations, and fired ambitions at so profound a level that it could not but separate kings and popes, courtiers and priests, writers and artists, the theorists and the practitioners of power. And the fundamental divide in all these cases was between those who thought that success in gaining an earthly crown was itself a sign of God's grace and those who maintained that the authority of the keeper of the keys to the Kingdom of Heaven had been divinely ordained to bring order to the hearts of men, peace to the peoples of earth, and supremacy to Peter's see. The crown placed on Charlemagne's head by Pope Leo disappeared soon after the event, but that which it came to represent loomed over the long centuries of Europe's Middle Ages. Its power lay in the fact that it could be interpreted so variously, and its true legacy was the piercing intensity wrought by the collision between differing forms of idealism.

CHAPTER 5

Aristocratic Power and Carolingian Calculation

How did Charlemagne rule his kingdom? What methods did he use to implement his policies, and what were the obstacles that had to be overcome? How did he gain assent for his reforms, and in what way did the kingdom's evolution into an empire change the distribution of power within Francia? Charlemagne the warlord must now give way to Charlemagne the domestic ruler, though here too he showed the same kind of resoluteness that gained him his military successes. These questions will also take us into the period of Charlemagne's successors since it was his legacy that now framed Frankish expectations and set a daunting standard of achievement for the ninth-century Carolingians. The institutional basis of the new order, its assemblies and scribes, its myriad counts and agents charged with communicating the royal will and enforcing it, will be described in the following chapter. Here, however, our concern will be as much social as political, and we shall be observing the relationship between the Frankish aristocracy and their king. They were the raw material with which he had to work in order to reform and renew the kingdom, and without their support he could not have achieved as much as he did. The great preoccupations of this elite were evident in the lives that were lived at court, within the royal household, and in the Carolingian palaces. This was the milieu of Charlemagne's closest relatives, the royal family itself, and we now take the opportunity to introduce ourselves to some of their senior courtiers.

A DOMESTIC SCENE

Much of the evidence we have about the society of the palace and court is literary in form, and the poets who benefited from the king's patronage repaid him with effusive accounts of a civilized monarch surrounded by his cultured family. The eminent diplomat Angilbert, who became an influential abbot of St-Riquier, celebrates the king's love of poetry and describes some of Charlemagne's children – Charles, Rotrud and Bertha – as well as the king's sister Gisela. He also names some of the key officials of the royal household: Audulf, who was the seneschal, Meginfred the chamberlain, and Hildebold, the priest who was head of the palace chapel. Alcuin's verse invokes Charlemagne the ruler in a typically enthused manner and also describes those who served the king in his chapel. The nicknames he invented for various members of the household shows Alcuin at his ingratiating worst. A priest with a particularly resonant singing style therefore becomes 'Jesse', and Charlemagne himself was 'David'.

Theodulf of Orléans's poem gives a more rounded portrait of the court and of the king who presides over it. Here we have Charlemagne the just ruler, a figure who stands in the lineage of his mighty predecessors and who guards the treasure gained by his kingdom as a result of mighty victories won over its enemies. He dispenses justice to the ordinary people who travel to the palace in order to seek an audience with their king, and he distributes patronage in the form of *honores* – those grants of land and office allocated to Charlemagne's more socially elevated subjects. Courtly society is portrayed in some detail in the context of a feast attended by major officials. Meginfred and Hildebold reappear, and the chamberlain and chaplain are joined by figures such as the notary, steward and cupbearer, who all listen to a public recitation of Theodulf's poem before retiring to their own chambers after dinner. Theodulf also provides a family portrait: Charlemagne is surrounded by his sons Charles and Louis, and by his daughters Bertha, Rotrud and Gisela (named after her aunt), Hruodhaid, Hiltrud and Theodrada. The fact that Queen Liutgrad, whom Charlemagne married in 794, is not mentioned may mean that this poem describes the household at some date after 800 since she had died by that year.

Hruodhaid's presence in the group is an interesting commentary on the extended royal family since, born in 775, she was the king's daughter by his liaison with a concubine called Madelgard and went on to have a distinguished career as abbess of Faremoutiers in the Île de France until her death in 810. Her half-sister Theodrada would also become an abbess, and she presided over the convent of Argenteuil whose location was some miles beyond the then boundaries of Paris. Both Theodrada and Hiltrud were the daughters of Charlemagne's queen Fastrada whom he married in 784 and who died ten years later. All the other royal children mentioned in Theodulf's group portrait were the product of Charlemagne's marriage to Hildegard, a union contracted in 771 at the beginning of his reign and which lasted until the queen's death in 783. That was perhaps the most emotionally significant of all his marriages, and it was certainly the most important in political and dynastic terms. Charlemagne had married Hildegard immediately after setting aside the Lombard princess Desiderata as his wife, and she provided him with three male heirs: Charles the Younger (c. 772–811), Carloman (773–810), who would be rechristened Pippin, and Louis (778–840), who succeeded his father on the throne since Charlemagne's two eldest sons predeceased him.

Charlemagne's procreative energy was an important aspect of the dynamism that he brought to the whole business of being a creative ruler. While still a youth he had also probably been married to Himiltrude, the mother of 'Pippin the Hunchback' (c. 769–811) who joined a conspiracy against his father in 792. The total number of his legitimate children was thirteen, and to these must be added at least seven children who were known to be the offspring of his liaisons with an officially acknowledged series of five concubines who succeeded one another chronologically in the royal bed. Two of these illegitimate children would go on to be politically influential in the first half of the ninth century: Drogo (801–55) as the bishop of Metz and his full brother Hugh (802–44) as arch-chancellor of the empire during the reign of their half-brother Louis the Pious. During this period illegitimacy was by no means the important social issue that it became at a later stage in medieval history when clerical views on the sanctity of marriage became more influential. Charlemagne's unmarried daughters Rotrud and Bertha took as their respective lovers Count Rorigo and Angilbert, a layman who was the abbot of St-Riquier, and the three children produced by these partnerships were brought up at court. Louis, who was the son of Rotrud and Rorigo, is another figure who shows the family connection at work across the generations since he became Louis the Pious's arch-chancellor and then carried on doing the same job for Charles the Bald.

The degree of control exerted by Charlemagne over his progeny is without parallel in the annals of medieval European kingship. He had thirty-six children and grandchildren, and almost all of them, whether legitimate or otherwise, were brought up at courts that were presided over either by Charlemagne or by his queens. The only exceptions among this group are Louis the Pious, the seven children who were born to Louis before 814, Pippin of Italy and his son Bernard. In 781 Charlemagne had established Pippin and Louis, then aged just four and three, as sub-kings in Aquitaine and in Lombardy. Both regions were only recently assimilated and the arrival of the two boy-kings, along with their courtiers and advisers, was meant to encourage the development of a local sense of loyalty to the Carolingian cause. Both boys were anointed kings in a ceremony conducted in Rome by Pope Hadrian I, and it was then that Pippin, previously called Carloman, acquired his new name through papal baptism. These two sons of Charlemagne were therefore brought up within their own courts. But they were special in another way as well. Of the entire brood of children and grandchildren, and within the period leading up to the death of the emperor in 814, only Louis, Pippin and Pippin's son Bernard were allowed to marry. Most of the unmarried royals were either steered towards an ecclesiastical career or ended up in a monastery – either voluntarily or because events dictated their removal from the halls of power.

Charlemagne may have wanted to keep his daughters unmarried because he had no consort after 800. The princesses could therefore help their father out by performing those public duties which were traditionally part of the role of a queen. But an even more fundamental reason for keeping so many of these male and female children unmarried is the king's wariness of the complications that might arise as a result of a marital alliance with a powerful and ambitious aristocratic family. Nonetheless, it still seems strange that Charles the Younger was not allowed to marry since he was Charlemagne's eldest legitimate son. He had been crowned king in St Peter's by the pope during the same ceremony of Christmas Day 800 in the course of which Charlemagne was crowned emperor. Charles was a renowned military figure as a result of his many campaigns both in Saxony and on the border area with Brittany. He died, however, childless and unmarried, in 812 at the age of forty or thirty-nine, and his brother Pippin of Italy had died two years earlier. Charlemagne's line was therefore carried on by Louis the Pious whose legitimate issue included the three sons who ruled the kingdoms into which the empire was divided in 843: Charles the Bald of west Francia, Louis the German of east Francia, and Lothair, who ruled the middle kingdom. There was therefore an imperial succession within the Carolingian direct line, but Charlemagne had still taken a risk by keeping his family so close to him and in 814 Louis was his sole legitimate son.

COURTIERS AND PALACES

Public authority in early medieval Europe was concentrated in and around the royal household, its members and various officers of state. This was the nerve centre of the kingdom and the place where political and military decisions were made. It was also where a good deal of a ruler's wealth was kept. Control of the household and court was therefore central to the maintenance of power in the realm as a whole, and questions of personality loomed large in this close-knit environment. Friendships and the ties of kinship, tidal waves of jealousy and ambition, of suspicion and love, were all to be found in the hothouse society of the court and played their part in deciding who had, or ought to have, power and influence. The personal was therefore also the political. Early medieval Europe records a wide variation in the size of such royal households. The larger ones, as in the case of Charlemagne's, could employ specialist courtiers whose jobs and responsibilities were carefully defined.

The clergy of the Frankish court were organized as a distinct body, the *capellani* who guarded the collection of relics, chief among which was the *cappa*, or *capella*, the cloak torn in half by St Martin of Tours which he then shared with a beggar to relieve his distress. This was spiritual wealth in material form, while the royal bedchamber was the place where the kingdom's treasure was stored. This was guarded by the official who became known as the chamberlain as well as by the queen, and it was they who arranged for the treasure's annual distribution in the form of gifts made to the warriors who waited in attendance on the household. The constable was the official who looked after the king's horses while also organizing the king's military retinue in times of war, and the ushers who guarded the doors of the palace thereby controlled access to the royal presence. To this list of major officials we should add the royal foresters, falconers and huntsmen. Organized sport helped to feed the household but hunting was not just about obtaining meat. It was a highly ritualized affair and participation in the royal hunt gave young aristocrats the opportunity to bond with the king.

The chief post in each of these divisions of the household was given by the king to an aristocrat whom he favoured, and that nobleman in turn would place his own clients and favourites in the lesser posts. Medieval courts would develop further arcane rituals and a fantastical elaboration of offices but this Carolingian model was the basis to which they all harked back. Despite the stress on hierarchy Charlemagne's court was also a youthful place, since it teemed with young nobles who had been sent there in order to learn the arts of war, gain social finesse and master political skills. The court was the place where they cultivated, and sought to influence, those older than themselves in an environment of boisterous, touchy and competitive masculinity.

This milieu also included specially selected non-noble youths whose ambitions may well have been used by kings as a way of spurring on their noble contemporaries. The *Gesta Caroli*, attributed with high probability to Notker the Stammerer ('Balbulus'), a monk of the Benedictine monastery of St-Gall in Switzerland, contains a story of how Charlemagne would praise non-aristocratic youths in order to shame lazy noble ones into activity. Notker compiled his notoriously unreliable book of anecdotes about Charlemagne in the early 880s, and some seventy years had elapsed by then since the death of the king. But the story may nonetheless amount to something more than folk memory. Notker's sources would have included the memories of his teacher Grimald of Reichenau, the abbot of St-Gall who, as Alcuin's pupil, would have been a conduit of valuable information about the palace. Out of this nexus at court a king could fashion his *fideles* and bestow his gifts accordingly. Louis the Pious, for example, gave the men of his household a new suit of clothes each year. Alongside the young nobles who hoped in time for such tangible rewards as land or an heiress, a countship or a lay abbacy, there were also youthful clerics who hoped for their own rewards. Memories of intimate friendships formed at court in the days of youth helped to create an integrated elite, one which was united in the service of the crown.

The *littérateurs* of the age make much of the parallels between this palace society and the Roman past. An eclogue written by the churchman and poet Modoin sometime between 804 and 810 uses the evocative phrase *caput orbis* (the head of the world) to describe the glory of a New Rome established in the kingdom of the Franks. Two anonymous works also pursue the theme of Roman renewal: *Karolus magnus et Leo papa*, written c. 800, famously describes Charlemagne as the father of Europe, and the *Lament* on the king's death, composed sometime after 814, states that he is mourned in Rome as well as in Francia. Sophisticated allusions of this kind were a literary reflection of the imperial ideology which underpinned Carolingian warfare, diplomacy and politics.

But the assumption that all the works of literature describing life at the palace refer to Aachen is one we should be wary of since it is only the anonymous *Lament* which actually refers to the palace by name. *Karolus magnus et Leo papa* gives a particularly romantic account of palace architecture, and since it also describes the meeting between the king and pope at Paderborn in 799 it refers in all probability to the palace and church built there rather than to Aachen. These works are therefore best seen as composite idealizations of the Carolingian court, with the authors drawing on their experience and knowledge of a very wide variety of locations. The offices that they describe, and those who held them, certainly existed, and other sources reveal a large number of other jobs at court which convey something of the flavour of that busy and intense world. These include the *mansionarius* who was the master of the lodgings, a *dispensator* who distributed alms, the *sacellarius* or treasurer, and the *scapoardus* who was the keeper of the vessels.

The needs of the aristocratic hunt are indicated by the presence of the *bersarii* who were the wardens of the forest, of the *veltrarii* who looked after the kennels, and the *bevarii* who hunted down beavers, while a specific department of the household looked after the interests of the falconers or *falconarii*. Dogs had long since been a special enthusiasm of the Franks, and regulations concerning their welfare had been included in the *Lex Salica* of the early sixth century.

Charlemagne's chancery consisted of a small team of scribes headed by the *cancellarius* or chief notary. The charters produced by this administrative office recorded grants of land to individuals and to institutions such as monasteries, as well as royal judgments on such matters as the settlement of disputes, manumission and freedom from tolls. Some of the notaries may well have accompanied the king on his travels but the central team, located in various palaces, could and did carry on with their work in his absence. There may well have been an overlap of personnel between the notaries and the clergy officiating in the chapels of the various palaces. The term *aprocisiarius* is sometimes used to designate the chaplain to the royal court who was also head of the palace chapel, and the word's usage reflects the Franks' antiquarian delight in establishing their continuity with the past. Later Roman emperors from Constantine onwards were supposed to have employed an *aprocisiarius* at their courts. The Franks liked to think that the job and the term used to describe it had existed continuously in the courts of their own kings from Clovis onwards. That may well be a hyperbole typical of the Franks but the claim does illustrate how fond they were of using, or inventing, history in order to bolster their own authority. A few chaplains, just like the notaries, would travel with the king on his palace visits and they also accompanied him on military campaigns. Each of the different palace chapels, however, was staffed with enough clerical personnel to perform the liturgy regularly.

Charlemagne's daily and domestic life was spent at a variety of *villae* as well as palaces. These manor houses were located on the royal estates, also known as *villae*, whose agricultural produce and craft specialisms were exclusively devoted to supporting the life of the royal household. This was where the palace got its provisions of vegetables, grain, wine, fish and meat, as well as shoes, saddles, weapons and tools. Each such estate had its own royal *villa*, and it was the duty of the *mansionarius* to make sure that the buildings were fully equipped with kitchen utensils, bedding and tableware, and therefore ready to accommodate the king whenever he chose to arrive. These arrangements may have been particularly useful when Charlemagne was on the move during military campaigns. Estate produce could then be loaded on to carts for transportation and used to provision the army. The *villae* may well have been used also as convenient stopping places when the king was travelling between two palaces which were far apart.

Aachen dominates the story of Charlemagne and his court largely because of the influence of Einhard's *Vita Karoli*. He tells us that the king liked to swim and was appreciative of the hot springs at Aachen where, therefore, he built the palace in which he spent most of his time towards the end of his life. His sons and courtiers were invited to join him in this favoured recreation, so that there might be up to a hundred members of the Frankish nobility splashing around together in the thermal baths. Congregational exercise of this kind evokes the pleasures of the Roman aristocracy of the past, and Einhard's picture is another element designed to illustrate Charlemagne's *renovatio* of an ancient imperial order. Even so, the details he gives reveal a fairly small royal household so far as its central officials are concerned, and the palace needs to be distinguished from the numerous houses which surrounded it in Aachen and where various individuals linked to the court and its business were accommodated. These would have included palace servants and merchants as well as bishops, abbots and counts.

In architectural terms it is the chapel which really captures Einhard's attention. It remains a dominating building, and the liturgy celebrated within its walls is basic to his authorial view of Charlemagne's role as a Christian king and emperor. He attended the chapel services daily, both in the morning and the evening, and took an informed interest in the way lessons were read and psalms were sung. The collection of tales about Charlemagne collated by Notker 'Balbulus' (c. 840–912) contains the comment that 'no new arrival dared to join the emperor's choir unless he could read and chant'. That might be a folk memory transmitted across two generations since the king's death. Nonetheless, the story does convey a core truth: it was Aachen's role as a religious centre which made it significant for Charlemagne, and the liturgical reforms pioneered within its chapel were subsequently diffused throughout his empire.

Charlemagne is buried in Aachen and its real importance as a focus for Carolingian government developed after his death and during the reign of Louis the Pious who was crowned there on two occasions, first in 813 and then again by Pope Stephen IV in 816. Its strong association with Charlemagne may explain Aachen's centrality at a time when his ninth-century successors were trying to preserve the Carolingian legacy in the face of political and military discord within the Frankish empire. Aachen had now become a symbol of the glory of a past for which there was much nostalgia. Louis held at least seventeen of his major assemblies there and Aachen was his capital city and administrative centre, with Ingelheim, though also important for the king, playing a secondary role. His father is recorded as having held five general assemblies of the Franks in Aachen, in 789, 802, 809, 811 and 813. The palaces at both Ingelheim and Nijmegen were built by Charlemagne, again according to Einhard's testimony, and they joined a large number of such buildings in which some of the great events of the reign were played out. In the case of diplomatic embassies, of which there were very many as Charlemagne's authority grew and his fame spread, there are records of their being received at the palaces in Paderborn and Nijmegen, Thionville and Reims as well as in Aachen.

Both Charlemagne and his father Pippin before him inherited a large number of palaces which had been built and used by the Merovingian kings. After the coup of 750–51 Pippin was able to start using the palaces at Compiègne and Berny, Ponthion and Soissons, and both he and his son would also establish new palaces of their own at Attigny, Corbeny and Samoussy. The palace at Clichy had been a major Merovingian centre and in 741 it was given to the abbey of St-Denis where Charles Martel was buried. Paris seems to have declined in importance during the reigns of both Charlemagne and his son Louis, but St-Denis retained much of its symbolic significance because of its association with Frankish regal power, and the monks there may well have raised a special building to accommodate any royal visitors.

The pattern of Charlemagne's visits to his many palaces tends to reflect

the contemporary military and political agenda, as well as his own physical capacity with the passing of the years. The palaces he visited most
regularly, apart from Aachen, were Thionville and Mainz, Worms, Ingelheim and Herstal. But there were also frequent trips to Compiègne, Ver,
Verberie and Quierzy, centres which were located within the historic
core of the Franks' territories and therefore strongly identified with the
memory of the Merovingian kings. Charlemagne needed to make his
presence felt in these areas in order to demonstrate his continuing
authority and the legitimacy of his title. The palace at Worms was burnt
to the ground in the winter of 790–91 but before then, and just like the
palace at Frankfurt, its Rhineland location led to Worms performing an
important role as a link between the western and eastern parts of Charlemagne's kingdom. Long-term campaigning against the Saxons meant
that the king needed a reliable base within their territory, and the residences at Eresburg and Herstelle were used by him for that purpose
during the winter months. But it was Paderborn, right in the heart of
Saxony, which was the region's major Carolingian centre. Both a church
and a palace were built here, and we have already seen how important
Paderborn became as a place of assembly for Charlemagne's army and
his courtiers in the course of the long struggle to conquer and subdue
the native population.

The palace complexes built and embellished by Charlemagne were
major assertions of dynastic strength and religious mission, and the surviving architectural and archaeological evidence shows the degree to
which these buildings were intended to inspire awe and instil respect.
The coloured glass, mosaics and painted plaster recovered at Paderborn
are indicators of its magnificence, and the group of buildings at the site
included a great *aula* or hall as well as the three-aisled basilica which
later became a cathedral on the creation of the episcopal see in 805.
Charlemagne would have presided over meetings and assemblies held
within the *aula*, an architectural feature which recurs in his other complexes and which may well have been inspired by the one raised by Constantine in Trier. Later Roman emperors in general used an *aula* for
purposes of official deliberation and public meetings, and Charlemagne's
imitation of that precedent would have been appreciated by well-informed
members of his audience.

The portraits of rulers painted on the walls of the palace at Ingelheim, which are described by Ermold the Black in his poem *In Honour of Louis the Pious*, were replete with historical parallels linking Charlemagne and his predecessors with the emperors and conquerors of antiquity. Augustus, Constantine and Theodosius join Charles Martel, Pippin III and Charlemagne on the apse of the *aula* at Ingelheim. The palace walls were decorated with portraits of Ninus, the king of the Assyrians who conquered Babylon, Phalaris, the Greek ruler of Sicily in the sixth century BC, and the Persian king Cyrus, as well as Alexander the Great, Hannibal, and Romulus and Remus. Some of these illustrations may have been intended as a warning of the dangers of excessive pride; indeed the established historical record available to the Franks gave Phalaris a reputation for unusual cruelty. But the chief effect of these portraits was to place Charlemagne and his dynasty within a distinguished tradition of creative leadership, and one which was particularly associated with the establishment of new centres of world civilization. The Franks are thereby raised to the same status as the founders of Rome and Constantinople, and the refinement of the palace society presided over by Charlemagne and his successors is indicated by the evidence of ceramic tableware and tapestries discovered in Paderborn.

Charlemagne therefore had a whole network of palaces at his disposal, and he used them as part of his governmental apparatus to a degree which seems co-ordinated and impressive in its total effect. He certainly travelled a lot, but that is not the same thing as a pattern of 'itinerant kingship' whose routes would be calculated to show the ruler to as many people as possible right across his territories. The history of Charlemagne's military campaigns when considered in isolation might suggest that the king was almost continuously on the move at least until the late 790s, and that his court was therefore an itinerant one since its personnel were dependent on the monarch whom they served. That is indeed the traditional picture which has been presented of this king of the Franks. He is often supposed to have been a monarch who needed to show himself to as many of his subjects as possible in order to emphasize the personal nature of his kingship. Such a version of Charlemagne's *modus operandi* would therefore establish a continuity with the Ottonian rulers of the tenth century, those dukes of Saxony who rose to greatness as the first Holy Roman Emperors and thereby revived many features of the Carolingian empire. Otto I, along with his son and grandson who succeeded him and who bore the same name, certainly adopted itinerancy and made it an established feature of the government they conducted across the territories they acquired beyond the original power base in Saxony. Charlemagne's style of kingly conduct in the earlier years of his reign also tends to be contrasted with the more settled and later period, a time of imperial consolidation of the new frontiers following the end of the great military campaigns of territorial expansion. These were the years of the king's later maturity and old age, and there is little doubt that by then Charlemagne was spending most of his time in Aachen.

But there were a large number of palaces quite apart from the one at Aachen, and the fact that it was the one which acquired predominance from the 790s onwards should not blind us to the importance of the palace societies which operated at centres such as Ingelheim and Nijmegen. Charlemagne, moreover, not only made extensive use of his other palaces during the first quarter-century or so of his reign, he also tended to be settled in them for a considerable period of time once he had arrived. Classic itinerancy, however, as practised by some medieval monarchs and especially by the Ottonian emperors, was a much more regularly mobile affair. When a king travelled his court always went with him, and the journeys were therefore institutionalized as a permanent feature of regal control and authority. Charlemagne the warrior-king had to fight his battles, and those campaigns involved long-distance travelling, but the pattern of his biography in its more domestic periods reveals a style of settled existence which is strongly reminiscent of the palace society presided over by the Roman emperors of classical antiquity.

Charlemagne could rely, as we shall see later, on a sophisticated method of administration in order to make his views known, and his will was therefore effective even when he was not physically present. In any event, the palaces that he visited the most and where he ran his government and presided over the court were concentrated in certain well-defined areas between the Seine and the Rhine. Military campaigning of course took him beyond this region, and most importantly to Aquitaine and Saxony, Bavaria, Lombardy and northern Spain. But where the government of a palace society and the arts of peace were concerned, Charlemagne's itinerary was mostly restricted to the two areas which comprised the Frankish heartland: the Meuse–Moselle region and that of Rhineland–Main. The former region predominated as the focus of his activities the older he got, and Aachen is an important part of that story. Charlemagne spent Christmas there for the first time in 768 but did not return to celebrate the feast at Aachen for another twenty years. It is known that he wintered there in 795 and 796, 798 and 799, 802 and 804, and from 806 until his death. A reliable estimate suggests that he spent just under a third of his time in Aachen between 794 and 814, and that he was there for almost two-thirds of the time in the last ten years of his life. In 810–14 he seems to have been there almost continuously. There was much to detain him at Aachen, a place which was beginning to acquire a reputation as one of the great centres of Carolingian culture. Nonetheless, its architectural development was still work in progress during Charlemagne's latter years. In the 790s and for at least a decade afterwards builders must have been as evident as courtiers, and by as late as 825 the town of Reims was still being obliged to provide labourers for the Aachen construction works.

A *villa*, or perhaps a small *palatium*, was to be found in Aachen during the reign of Pippin III and that was where Charlemagne had spent his Christmas in 768. There was also a small church, and the baths had been established on the site since the later Roman empire. The fact that the forests of the Ardennes, an excellent area for hunting as well as a fertile source of game and fish, could be reached in just three or four days' travelling made Aachen an attractive place from the point of view of palace provision and sporting opportunity. Charlemagne hunted regularly until well into old age, and his last recorded ride to hounds occurred in the Ardennes in 813. There were also a large number of royal estates near Aachen, and that was always an important consideration when it came to the location of a Carolingian palace. Its easy access to the Roman road system and the major waterways placed the town at the centre of an excellent communications network, and the main road linking Cologne with Maastricht and the river Meuse were both nearby. The chapel or *capella palatina* was completed by about 796, and work on the great *aula*, measuring 56 x 144 feet, was completed between 792 and 804. A covered passageway connected the *aula* with the chapel, and in its middle lay a two-storied building which was probably the royal residence. The destruction of the palace at Worms as a result of the fire of 790–91 is probably one reason behind the decision to extend the old palace at Aachen, and the monumental scale of the project is a testimony to the quality of Charlemagne's continuing ambition as a ruler despite the fact that he had been on the throne for over twenty years when work started on the complex.

There are no traces left of the palace or the *aula* but they can hardly have been less impressive than the chapel. The entire complex illustrates the elevated authority Charlemagne was claiming for his imperial style of kingship and it also implies the standard against which he was measuring himself. Aachen was a royal residence, a place of worship and also a space where subjects could approach the ruler. That architectural conception invited comparison with the Lateran palace and cathedral in Rome, the court of the Abbasids in Damascus and that of the Byzantine emperors in Constantinople. Those who saw the king-emperor seated on his throne in the gallery of the chapel at Aachen could have had few doubts that Charlemagne had joined a very select group of rulers. The octagonal structure of the chapel links it by association with San Vitale in Ravenna and the Lateran baptistery, and beyond its impressive bronze doors, in Charlemagne's time, there was a sumptuous interior decorated with coloured paving as well as antique columns imported from Italy and containing shafts of marble and porphyry. In the cupola above, the worshipper would have seen mosaics portraying Christ surrounded by the twenty-four Elders of the Apocalypse. An equestrian statue of Theoderic, Italy's Ostrogothic king, had been removed from Ravenna to adorn the palace precincts. And perhaps it was a memory of the *pigna* that Charlemagne would have seen outside St Peter's in Rome which explains the presence in Aachen of a similar antique Roman pine-cone sculpture.

RULING THROUGH NOBLES

The evidence of charters and the wording of capitularies, the building and the embellishment of abbeys, cathedrals and palaces, the quality of military leadership and the *réclame* of papal confirmation: all seem to demonstrate the Carolingian rulers' easy predominance over the aristocratic retinue which surrounded them daily, whether in the society of the palace or on the field of battle. But concentration on the undoubtedly glittering nature of this new monarchical style should not lead us to ignore the way in which these kings were in fact often dependent on the aristocrats who supported them.

Tribal assemblies were a thing of the past, no more than a dimly recollected bit of folklore about Germanic origins and ancestral virtue. That does not mean, however, that the Frankish aristocracy had become merely passive recipients of royal favour, neutered worshippers before the Carolingian alliance of throne and altar. There might not be a constitutional forum in which the agreement or dissent of these nobles could be formally expressed in debate. But at a more implicit level and in the day-to-day conduct of affairs it was aristocratic assent which enabled Pippin III, his predecessors and his heirs, including Charlemagne himself, to govern in the way that they did. Aristocratic power was the context out of which the Carolingians had emerged and it supplied the dynasty with its frame of reference both before the coup of 750–51 and for long afterwards. The marriage of Pippin II to Plectrude, for example, sometime before 668–70, was an important recognition of noble power rather than just a gracious bestowal of royal favour. Plectrude belonged to a great Austrasian noble family and she brought with her to the marriage estates whose wealth were badly needed at that time by a cash-strapped Pippin. Such families were as much allies as they were followers of the Carolingians.

Aristocratic status in early medieval western Europe was a result of birth, with status and titles being transmitted, then as now, from one generation to the next. This may today seem to be an obvious fact of noble life since it was the way in which the future history of these families would be played out. But heredity as the basis of title did not apply right across Europe. In the Byzantine empire to the east it was only at the end of the eighth century that an aristocracy emerged which was truly hereditary, and before that time titles lapsed with the death of their holders. Even in the early medieval west the fact of a hereditary title did not carry with it an automatic presumption that nobility should entail influence. Those who were talented but of lowly birth could be ennobled by the kings who promoted them in the service of the royal house.

Western aristocracies, therefore, were not closed 'caste' systems and could be quite strikingly open in their recruitment, a fact which the Carolingians took full advantage of in building up their authority. This does not mean, however, that the dynasty were entirely free agents. The Carolingians did frequently exercise their prerogative rights in favour of the nobility of Austrasia, a grouping to whom they were particularly close since their family origins were to be found in that territory. But their strategy could not rely merely on elevating the Austrasian nobility and using them as pliant agents of the royal will at the expense of other regional aristocracies, as has sometimes been portrayed. Francia's kings needed to co-operate with the entire Frankish aristocracy, and regional aristocracies therefore survived as the dominant fact of power within their own particular areas.

In Alsace, for instance, the ducal house of the Etichonids went into decline after the mid-eighth-century rise of the Carolingians, but its members re-emerged during Charlemagne's reign as figures of high authority in the imperial service. The connection moreover between the royal house and the aristocracies of those new areas which had been absorbed within the empire was very close. Charlemagne's queen Hildegard, for example, was descended from Gotefridus, who had been the *dux* of Alamannia in c. 700. As a result of these strategies the native aristocracies were not displaced but given instead a novel role, with competition for royal favour becoming the new focus and expression of the traditional rivalries between local noble houses. This is why Hildegard's brother and uncle exercised the option of calling on Charlemagne's support in their successful bid to recover the authority that they had once enjoyed in Alsace but had lost to the Etichonids decades previously.

The emergence of a Carolingian empire gave these regional aristocrats immense new opportunities since imperial power led to the creation of more jobs, which they filled as office-holders. They now represented the royal will and they were charged with the duty of implementing kingly commands. Even here, however, we can see the persistence of noble solidarity.

THE IMPERIAL ARISTOCRACY: A COLLECTIVE IDENTITY

The *Reichsaristokratie*, the truly imperial aristocracy who governed the empire in the king's name and who held lands and offices right across that vast territorial expanse, was a novel, and distinctively Carolingian, development. But the solidarity displayed by the members of this rich and influential noble elite, together with the pride they displayed in that shared identity, was a new form of traditional aristocratic linkage. These were the *Königsnahe*, the families who became powerful because of their closeness to the dynasty in a relationship of convenience which benefited both parties. An influential and reliable analysis of this group's membership as it operated at the height of its prosperity under Charlemagne lists 111 men belonging to forty-two families. At first sight this seems a tiny elite, and especially when one considers the geographical spread of its responsibilities and power. That first impression, however, is a misleading one since each member of that elite was provided with a support structure in the form of familial relationships. Such tentacles of power, reinforced by the fact that both paternal and maternal lines of descent counted when establishing noble ancestry, could spread right across the empire. The kinship groups of those associated with the *Königsnahe* were therefore both extensive and elaborate, and the consciousness of interconnected family membership was one of the resources used by the *Reichsaristokratie* to discharge the duties devolved upon them by the king.

It was indeed royal favour which enabled some men to advance at the expense of others, and to be counted as being among those who were closest to the king. As a result the imperial aristocracy was not a closed system of power. Great nobles had relatives who were never advanced and whose days were spent in a rural and provincial obscurity. It is also the case that not all the royal offices were monopolized by men of the very highest birth. Carolingian patronage produced a remarkably flexible system of government, one which adapted to the needs of the moment and which could recognize the talents of exceptional individuals. The government of the Ottonian emperors in tenth-century Germany seems strikingly rigid in its structures and formulaic in its recruitment policies compared to the creativity displayed in both respects by the Carolingian rulers. Nonetheless, the dynastic choice of those who deserved honour and jobs was not made in a vacuum and there were real limits to a Carolingian king's freedom of action. Social tradition and political pressure obliged him to rely to a very great extent on the Frankish aristocracy, and its highly developed sense of identity, when making appointments.

JOB-HUNGRY NOBLES ON THE MOVE

Royal patronage meant that aristocrats now became more mobile than they had been before. Adela von Pfalzel (660–735) was one of the most significant figures of her age, a sister-in-law of Pippin II as well as founder, and the first abbess, of the important monastery of Pfalzel, located on the Moselle at a site near Trier. Her upbringing and family connections meant that she was very well connected in Austrasia, but by the first half of the eighth century Adela's grandchildren were working for Charles Martel in Burgundy and Provence, having moved there from their native land between the Meuse and the Moselle. The mobility was not just a question, either, of the Austrasian nobility moving outwards. The retinue of Charles Martel in the Trier of 722 included Abbo, a great Gallo-Roman magnate in Provence and a key figure in establishing Carolingian authority in that region.

This readiness to uproot oneself and work in a very different territory from one's native region is a testimony to the development of a common Carolingian civilization across the component parts of the empire. At the level of the literate and governing elites there was undoubtedly an awareness that they shared something of a common culture. It was this frame of reference which informed the structures of authority and which made it possible for aristocratic office-holders to move across the borders. The subject peoples whom they governed remained sharply distinguished from one another in cultural terms. But the consolidation of the elite meant that this governing class, absorbed within the milieu of their equals, could feel at home wherever they found themselves within the empire.

That degree of mobility would remain a key feature of the imperial office-holders right up until the dissolution of the empire. Take, for example, Bernard of Septimania, so called because he was an official in the old Visigothic domain in south-west France which now formed part of the officially designated Spanish March, the empire's border territory to the south. His career shows the central importance of Aachen, the town where he was married in 825 and whose palace society shaped the lives of those who, like Bernard, wanted to play a role in the high politics of their age. In 829 he became guardian of the young Charles the Bald but had to flee Aachen's court in the following year after a rebellion broke out, caused partly by his own arrogant behaviour. In 832 we find him back at Aachen. But in the following year he pops up in Burgundy before settling down back in Septimania for the rest of the 830s.

Those family connections of the *Reichsaristokratie* are also all-important in explaining the ease of their mobility. An aristocratic family grouping, for example, has been discovered in the area between the Rhine and the Meuse; their members have such distinctive names as Heriricius, Albericus, Wernharius and Hunfridus. This group consisted of a number of families who combined with one another to form a larger entity, and the documentation of the region shows them exercising power there for over a century, from about 760 to 870. They in turn were associated with some of the more important kinship groupings who enjoyed links with such significant elements within the *Reichsaristokratie* as the Adalhard and Unruoch families.

A grandee such as Adalhard 'the Seneschal' was therefore able to move with comparative ease from one Carolingian centre of power within the empire to another because in each of its component territories there was a local network of relatives, who could welcome him when he arrived and advise him subsequently. In the second half of the 840s Adalhard left the court of Charles the Bald and established himself in that of Lothair I where, we are told, he gained *honores* (offices). In 853 we know that Adalhard met an individual called Heriricius, whose name indicates that he was a member of the seneschal's kinship group and whose absence otherwise from the surviving records suggests a humble status within that grouping.

This is the practical side of Carolingian government as it actually operated on the ground, far away from the refined claims to sacral power and the parallels drawn between the Aachen of Charlemagne and the Jerusalem of Solomon or David. Adalhard was typical of important aristocrats who owed their position to royal patronage but who in turn communicated and expressed that patronage locally by directing it towards their relatives. If the relationship between the *Königsnahe* and the Carolingian dynasty was one of mutual obligation and reciprocal advantage, then so also was the one which obtained between these great aristocrats and their humbler kinsmen. Moving from one centre of power to another in pursuit of *honores*, these stars of the Carolingian firmament could rely on a network of individuals whose support was the expression of their loyalty to the wider kinship group.

When we try to imagine what it was like to live the life of an early medieval aristocrat in western Europe, and especially that of the *Königsnahe*, it is important to distinguish between them and their successors, the nobility of the 'high' Middle Ages who from c. 1100 onwards were established in the castles where they exercised their lordship. With the emergence of castles in the landscape of western Europe aristocratic families start to be concentrated around those local centres of power. As a result those families became smaller in size, and this led to the fragmentation of the very wide clientage networks previously sustained by kinship. Aristocratic inheritance was by then universally restricted to a smaller number of heirs than in the past and the emphasis on the patrilineal line had become more or less exclusive. Territoriality was the expression of this new degree of concentrated family power and is reflected in the adoption of a place-name as an aristocratic surname, a custom which is unrecorded in the history of the early medieval nobility.

Royal patronage and kinship groups alike resulted, as we have seen, in the mobility of the high aristocracy in the eighth and ninth centuries. But they also seem not to have had a fixed family seat, a place where they and those close to them could congregate. Owning lands which were scattered across wide areas, as well as exercising responsibilities whose theatre of operation might be similarly imperial in scale, the ambitious members of the higher Carolingian nobility could not be rooted in localities as their twelfth- and thirteenth-century successors would be. Dhuoda, the wife of the itinerant Bernard of Septimania, was based at Uzès in the Languedoc when she wrote the *Liber Manualis* in order to guide her son in the details of family history. But the focus of her account is not Uzès but the Burgundian inheritances of Bernard's brother, Theudericus, and also the court at Aachen since it and the king were the source of all *honores*.

Nobles were not allowed to hold office in more than one kingdom after the Treaty of Verdun in 843 divided the empire into the kingdoms of the eastern Franks, the western Franks and the 'middle kingdom'. But they could still hang on to the lands they owned right across the new boundaries. And, crucially, they might also hand them on to their heirs. Eberhard of Friuli, a Frankish noble who had married into the Carolingian dynasty and gathered *honores* from the hands of Louis the Pious, retained all the many properties he owned in the three kingdoms after 843. This is perhaps what we might expect given his stature as a key magnate. But Eberhard was also able to bequeath his territories to his children, and those lands crossed the new boundaries. His son Unruoch, therefore, inherited estates in Alamannia and Italy, the two areas which were now ruled respectively by Louis the German and Louis II, and he would retain his lands by cultivating the patronage of both these rulers.

LIMITS TO FAMILY LOYALTY

The fact that early medieval aristocrats belonged to kinship groups, and used them to consolidate their advancement, does not mean that these clientage systems operated in a monolithic way. Fluidity and dynamism are the keynote qualities of this system of power, and family links therefore are not always reliable predictors of behaviour and views. If we go to the border with Brittany in 834 we find there two brothers, Lambert and Wido, who fought on opposing sides in the local clash between the supporters of Louis the Pious and those who sided with his son Lothair. This was a key defensive region in the empire's western approaches. The office of *praefectus* of the Breton March had been held by no less a person than Hruodland, the historical figure whose death in 778, at the head of a Frankish army retreating from Spain through the Basque region, would, as we have seen, acquire a heroic dimension in the eleventh-century French *Song of Roland*. The extension of Carolingian authority to the Breton border area, with the old Roman province of Armorica lying to the west, had only been achieved with great difficulty. Frankish forces always found it a hard region to control. The breakdown of order here in the 830s anticipated the more widespread revolt of the 840s which re-established Breton independence. At such a time of conflict it may well have made sense for families to divide their allegiances in order to safeguard their collective interest. Perhaps some such strategy lay behind the decisions taken by Lambert and Wido, since their family had a long tradition of office-holding in Brittany. But if that was the deal, its terms did not last long. Wido's death in a pitched battle conducted against his brother's forces showed the reality of interests and allegiances which transcended family loyalty.

Sharp divisions within families are very evident in the conflicts of the early 840s, a period when Charlemagne's successors were forced to conclude that they could no longer sustain Carolingian order on an imperial scale. Adalhard 'the Seneschal', for example, opted to support Charles the Bald at this time, while his brother Gerard committed himself to Lothair's cause. Civil war conditions of this kind may throw up extreme and untypical examples of conflict between relatives, but even in periods of peace we can find family quarrels dividing the kinship groups. At some time between 754 and 782, for example, we find Bishop Megingoz of Wurzburg striving strenuously to stop his niece from succeeding his sister as abbess of the convent of Wenkheim because he thought her an unworthy candidate for that high office. His failure in this regard may show the power of family connections. But, equally, the fact that so senior and well-connected a figure as this aristocratic bishop had such strong views on the issue, and that he was ready to mount a campaign against his own niece, showed that claims made as a result of family connection could indeed be challenged.

We are not dealing here, therefore, with clans, a social system in which all the members of an individual grouping may be presumed to share a common interest. The great Carolingian nobles served both the dynasty and their own interests. But the forces which moved them to act as they did went beyond mere awareness of family loyalty. Religious beliefs, the claims of friendship, political alliances: all could and did cut across the ties of kinship.

ARISTOCRATIC OPTIONS: CHOOSING A LINEAGE AND FAVOURING RELATIVES

Moreover, at this stage in western European history the structure of an aristocratic family's collective identity remained very flexible. In the event, for instance, of a man improving his social status through marriage it was the wife's kin who provided the name pool used for their offspring. There was the very highest authority for this practice since the Carolingians themselves most often took their names from the family of Pippin, whose daughter Begga had married Ansegisel, the son of Bishop Arnulf of Metz from whom the dynasty was descended in patrilineal terms. Only rarely did that genealogy in the male line provide the Carolingians with their names.

On occasions, therefore, a family might choose to emphasize the role of a powerful female ancestor. It was convenience and need, rather than any fixed principle, which dictated that decision. When Thegan of Trier (d. 850) sat down to write his biographical account of Louis the Pious (*Gesta Hludowici Imperatoris*) in c. 835 he gave a very full account of Hildegard, the emperor's mother, and he linked her through a maternal line of descent to the relatives of Duke Gotefridus of Alamannia. In doing so he was probably reflecting the imperial family's own current view of the more important elements in its immediate ancestry. When describing Charlemagne's descent, however, Thegan opted for a strictly patrilineal presentation and traced the king's lineage back to Arnulf in a direct line of male inheritance. That lack of complication may have been Thegan's way of presenting the transition of power in the generations before Charlemagne as a smoothly inevitable process, one which culminated in the king's greatness. Louis, by contrast, presiding over an empire in disarray, was a ruler whose authority needed buttressing, which is why his mother's powerful connections are described by Thegan in such detail.

This fluidity of the family structure allowed for a wide variety of inter-pretation about which of its members mattered the most, as Dhuoda's choice of terms shows in her manual. She commemorates eight dead members of her son William's kin as belonging to his *genealogia*, while other relatives, being less important, are categorized as his *stirps*. Her decision to emphasize William's paternal uncle Theodericus reflects the importance of cultural considerations as well as genealogical linkage, since he was the boy's godfather and also his guardian (*nutritor*). These relationships mattered enormously because they involved the transmis-sion of property and the defence of those territorial rights. Dhuoda therefore tells William that he should pray for the *parentes* of his father Bernard, relatives who have bequeathed him property. This is a heritage which is in the custodianship of William's family but still needs to be safeguarded, which is why her son should offer prayers for the souls of those ancestors who are counted as his patrons. Dhuoda reflects here the turbulence of the 830s and 840s, a period which saw her husband leading a rebellion against Charles the Bald in 842 and his consequent execution in 844. If he was to hang on to his inheritance William clearly needed all the help he could get, both in this world and the next. Nonethe-less, Dhuoda's careful inclusion of some relatives (and her relegation of others) also shows that aristocratic kinship could be a very tightly con-structed group when it came to the preservation and inheritance of land.

The family unit which counted in 867 when Eberhard of Friuli drew up his will was very small, despite his extensive ties of kinship: he and his wife bequeath properties to their four sons and three daughters, with no mention being made of anyone else. Abbo of Provence is a partic-ularly interesting example of the linkage between land inheritance and kinship since he had no heirs. He had helped Charles Martel to estab-lish the Franks' control of the lower Rhône valley and was therefore granted many of the lands confiscated from his regional opponents as well as the office of *patricius*. The will that Abbo drew up in 739 gets straight to the point with its statement that there is only one group of individuals whom he regards as his kin, namely those persons from whom he has inherited property.

Western European nobles during our period were therefore antici-pating their twelfth-century successors in at least one respect. Even at this early stage they were already starting to restrict rights of inheritance and they were doing so in favour of their immediate family. Frankish law codes, some of them of great antiquity, supported this practice. The *Edictum Chilperici* dates from the late sixth century and it says that land should go to sons and, in their absence, to daughters. An intriguing late ninth-century legal dispute involving Ingeltrude, the daughter of Count Manfred of Orléans and therefore a member of the high Frankish nobility, proves the point. Ingeltrude had left her husband Boso and then drawn up a will which arranged for her properties to be inherited by her own kin. This arrangement excluded the daughters of her marriage to Boso and the contested case went to Rome for a final adjudication. Pope John VIII decided against Ingeltrude on two counts: her will was invalid because she had drawn it up while under sentence of excommunication and it also went against the principle that 'in matters of inheritance children take precedence over all other types of relative'.

THE INFLUENCE OF ARISTOCRATIC WOMEN

As the papal judgment made explicit, a tight definition of who could inherit often benefited women and privileged them as immediate members of the family circle. Count Waltbert was a Saxon noble who, with his wife Aldburg, had founded the monastery of Wildeshausen in the 860s as an *Eigenkirche*. Family monasteries of this kind, endowed and controlled by the nobility, were important centres of aristocratic wealth throughout the Carolingian period. The count's will specified that he wanted Wildeshausen to be run by his own immediate descendants after his own time: his son Wibert was to be the *rector* and should be succeeded by the son of Waltbert's brother or, in the event of that being impossible, by the son of Waltbert's sister. This, as it turned out, proved to be the order of succession in the running of Wildeshausen. The clerical status of these particular heirs made direct patrilineal succession an impossibility in any event, but Waltbert's provisions for the inheritance envisage a tight group, and its exclusivity embraces the right of inheritance through the female line.

The inheritance rights of daughters born to the Frankish nobility may in fact have been fairly extensive, and have gone further than the official law codes' record of a right of female inheritance which is subordinated to that of their brothers. We know, for example, that c. 700 the Neustrian noblewoman Erminetrude drew up a will which bequeathed vineyards and slaves to her granddaughter and daughter-in-law, as well as leaving substantial properties to her grandson. The eighth century in fact produces many examples of women inheriting noble properties and by no means all of them were widows without children or daughters without brothers. Nor was this a new development. Even in the late seventh century there are examples, drawn from charter evidence, of women inheriting property alongside their brothers. Their rights in this regard may not have been as secure as those of their male relatives but could well have been reinforced by that major cultural phenomenon of the eighth and ninth centuries, the celebration of female aristocrats whose lineages were long and distinguished.

Dhuoda used her *Liber Manualis* in order to construct her family's true identity – a role which was performed by many other Carolingian noblewomen. Often highly educated, such women were well placed to pass on their knowledge, which would have included an expertise in family history and traditions, both to their children and to the wider milieu of their aristocratic society. Religious foundations provided some female heirs with a distinctive opportunity to preside over the long-term celebration of their families and the remembrance of their ancestors. Aadorf, for example, was one of the greatest of the Carolingian family monasteries, having been founded by Count Udalrich at its site in Alamannia during the mid-ninth century. This was intended to be the family's necropolis, and after the count's death it was run by his daughters since they, along with their brother, were named as Udalrich's direct heirs in a will whose provisions therefore combined spiritual duty with secular property rights. A similar combination of motives can be seen at work in the abbey of Andlau in Alsace. Richardis, consort of the emperor Charles the Fat (r. 881–8), helped the abbey to expand so that it could be a focus of her own family's power and so rival the prestige of nearby Erstein, a foundation associated with the Etichonid family. Not even marriage into the Carolingian royal house itself, therefore, could obliterate this noblewoman's awareness of her own family origins and its particular imperatives.

GETTING A JOB FROM THE KING

Throughout the history of their order the members of the Carolingian aristocracy were engaged in intense competition for the public offices and clerical benefices that were both categorized as *honores*. Here there are two strands at work and the interplay between them is one of the great constant themes of the eighth and ninth centuries in western Europe. On the one hand the nobles knew that they had to demonstrate to the king that they were fit to hold jobs which brought with them such great prestige and political power. But the aristocracy also thought that they in fact deserved these *honores* because of their noble status. Some families indeed claimed that their members had the exclusive right to fill certain specific posts from one generation to the next.

The increased authority of the Carolingian dynasty often accompanied, and even benefited from, the ability of some families to monopolize some of the comital offices. This seems to have been a particular feature of the government of Neustria during the period when this area of north and western France was being increasingly drawn within the Carolingian orbit. From 744 to 813, for example, the countship of Meaux was held in turn by Helmgaudus, who transmitted it to his son Gauzhelmus, who was then succeeded by his son, another Helmgaudus. The countship of Paris remained in the hands of the descendants of Count Gerard for over a century between 753 and 858. In 877 Charles the Bald issued a capitulary which recognized the hereditary right to counties and benefices, a ruling which has been seen as a landmark decision and a demonstration of the dynasty's loss of authority. The Neustrian examples, however, show that the nobility could exercise control over certain offices and in certain areas even when the dynasty was at the height of its power in the previous century, and that this was a development which coincided perfectly happily with the Carolingians' interests.

The fact, however, that there were invariably more candidates than there were *honores* did give Carolingian kings a freedom of manoeuvre. In 816 the emperor Louis appointed Ebbo, born a serf and then educated at Charlemagne's palace school in Aachen, to be archbishop of Reims. This was a spectacular instance of the Carolingian readiness to promote the humbly born and to ignore the traditional sources of recruitment when it served the kingly interest to do so. And even during the reign of Charles the Bald half a century later, when the dynasty's power had long since passed its zenith, we can still find a Carolingian king deciding that certain *honores* should not be transferred from father to son. During the intervening period there had of course been a civil war which had resulted in the partition of Charlemagne's empire. But it is possible to view even that catastrophe as a result of noble need rather than of regal debility, since the aristocracy were in fact desperate for more *honores* than were available. This was certainly the view arrived at by Archbishop Hincmar of Reims when he described the civil war's origins: 'the magnates of the realm began to fight among themselves for *honores*, to see which of them might obtain the lion's share.'

WHICH WAY TO JUMP?

Why did Carolingian nobles invest such effort into gaining these offices and, quite as crucially, why did they fear so greatly the consequences of losing them? Intense ambition for public recognition and a desire not to lose face provide part of the answer. But the need to protect oneself against the hostility of rivals was also an important motivation. Matfrid of Orléans lost the king's favour, and therefore his job, in 828. The following year Louis the Pious announced that he was setting up an investigation into Matfrid's past conduct as Count of Orléans and encouraged those who wished to make allegations to come forward. Matfrid, however, bided his time, and when Louis's sons rebelled against the king he seized the chance to attack Odo, the noble who had replaced him in office. He then lost the countship of Orléans once again when Louis defeated his rebellious sons and reinstated Odo. Matfrid and Odo would engage in a further bout of fighting, and this particular phase of the conflict ended in Odo's death. The definitive re-establishment of Louis on his throne in 834, however, led to Matfrid's final and lasting expulsion from the office of Count of Orléans and his subsequent exile. This had been a six-year struggle and one whose extremes showed the intensity of the aristocratic attachment to *honores*. Possessing these offices could make a noble, and their loss could break him. A clever Carolingian king understood this fact of political life and could exploit it to enhance the aristocracy's dependence on his unique prerogative.

The Frankish aristocrats needed their *honores* because they felt insecure without them. But times of instability right at the top of dynastic politics meant that the hunt for office and honour carried with it its own forms of insecurity. Whom should an aristocrat back when the Carolingians were divided among themselves? In such circumstances there were knife-edge decisions to be made about who was most likely to come out on top and which Carolingian it might be safest to support. The bonds of allegiance might also mean that a Frankish noble could in fact exercise no choice in these matters, in which case he had to go with the flow of events, and that turbulent current might either cast him into darkness or ensure his prosperity.

A number of key aristocrats had to make calculations of this kind in 771 when Carloman, Charlemagne's brother, died suddenly. For the past three years the two had reigned as joint kings of the Franks in a sometimes uneasy partnership, and they had ruled the component parts of Francia allocated to them by their father's will. The claims of Carloman's infant sons to rule as his successors in their father's former territories were plausible enough in dynastic terms. The idea was also completely unrealistic given their uncle's ambition. Some of Carloman's former supporters, among them the nobleman Warin, a future *comes palatii* or count of the palace, Wilichar, archbishop of Sens and Abbot Fulrad of St-Denis, switched sides and invited Charlemagne to annex Carloman's territories. But a number of Carloman's noble retinue left for the Lombard court at Pavia. For them this was not so much a question of contested legitimacy as a decision about the likelihood of *honores*. Those who went into exile knew that Charlemagne had a large number of followers to reward and that there was therefore no room for them in the newly consolidated Frankish kingdom. Similar calculations would have been made in 817 by the noble followers of Bernard of Italy after it was revealed that Louis the Pious planned to exclude him from the line of succession. This relegation of their Carolingian patron threatened their own self-interest and they therefore decided to follow Bernard in open rebellion.

Periods of conflict and rebellion showed just how fundamental the possession of an *honor* was to the whole aristocratic enterprise and way of life. Threatened at such times with its withdrawal, Frankish nobles immediately felt denuded of significance and would act in self-defence. But at all times, whether the political climate was calm or turbulent, one of the most important aspects of *honores* for the aristocracy was the fact that these posts provided a regular source of income. A countship, for example, involved not just the possession of land but also the right to collect the profits which accrued in the settlement of judicial disputes. We have seen how the aristocracy were restricting the rights of inheritance to smaller numbers, but primogeniture did not apply in early medieval Europe and the persistence of partible inheritance was a real threat to the prosperity of the Frankish nobility. This division of inherited lands did not amount to equal shares for all children, and sons, as was seen above, generally gained more than daughters. There were also important regional differences at play. To the west of the Rhine certain sons, and sometimes one son alone, could be favoured above others. But the custom did mean that one generation's fortunes could decline swiftly compared to those of its predecessor. This was of course a particular problem for the minor nobility but it affected the high aristocracy in an acute form since their estates were so widely scattered.

Acquiring an *honor* and defending it might involve the Frankish nobility in a lot of hard work, but the comparative economic security that it represented was highly prized. The rewards that came to those who played and won this particular game could be spectacular, and that good fortune might separate them quite sharply from the lives of those close relatives they left behind. Charles the Bald's right-hand man Boso, for example, started life as a Lotharingian noble before travelling west to serve the king, and the west Francian territories that he eventually administered constituted a vast power network which extended from Cambrai to Pavia. His brother Bivinus meanwhile stayed at home and contented himself with pursuing hereditary claims to the lands which surrounded the family's local power base at the abbey of Gorze.

Aristocrats with an eye to the main chance, or just seized with insecurity about the family future after calculating what their progeny actually stood to inherit, were ready to uproot themselves. Those who prospered substituted new problems for old ones because their grandeur and success inevitably attracted a retinue of supporters whose loyalty, in turn, was dependent on the great aristocrats' ability to provide them with land. In order to satisfy such demands these magnates usually had to petition the king for the grant of territories which they could then redistribute to their retinue. Even if they themselves retained their prosperity, the high nobility of the Franks could not rely on its continuance in the time of their heirs. The history of Alamannia in the eighth century records two administrators whose influence carried all before them: Ruthard and Warin. But of the two only Ruthard's descendants were able to put down roots in the region once dominated by their father. Warin's son Isanbard succeeded him as a count in Thurgau but aroused the hostility of the local nobility, and by 779 he had been forced to leave the region. The two generations illustrate the two constant themes in the history of the Frankish aristocracy as a whole. Insecurity, either real and present, or anticipated and feared, is one. The other is the presence of a dynasty that knew how to profit from the tidal ebb and flow of noble grandeur and of noble anxiety, qualities which were calculated by the Carolingians in full and equal measure.

KEEPING IT IN THE FAMILY: WHY MARRIAGE MATTERED

Aristocratic and royal marriages, and the pattern of alliances created in their wake, were at the heart of the ruling elites' economic calculations. They also show how important women could be within the courtly politics of Carolingian Europe. The family values of the ruling dynasty embraced mistrust, tension and rebellion as well as the loving relationships sanctified by the rite of marriage. Charlemagne's edict, the *Divisio* of 806, expressly forbade his sons 'to kill, blind, mutilate their nephews, or force them to be tonsured against their will'. Royal nephews were often regarded with suspicion since their ambitions might undermine the authority of the main dynastic line and act as a focus for dissidence. Royal women, by contrast, were fundamental to the dynastic authority. They were the means by which the Carolingians were able to expand their properties and power, and women could play an important role in the internal politics of the court.

Aristocratic marriages in general bonded together not just two individuals but also the wider groups of their respective families. The implications of such an alliance in terms of the distribution of power were naturally of particular concern to a Carolingian monarch. Family rows would therefore be referred to the king, as in the case of the Lady Northild who, after deciding that she had had enough of her husband's sexual perversions, appealed to Louis the Pious. He referred the case to a court of bishops who pleaded that they lacked the necessary expertise to adjudicate. The issue was then passed on to a court of laymen who decided that the unfortunate wife had to remain married to her husband.

A royal marriage was a major political event in the early medieval west and tantamount to a declaration of public policy. Partners marrying into a royal house were chosen by and large from the aristocracy of the king's realm or from that of neighbouring kingdoms, and it was very rare for two royal families to contract a marriage alliance. Female spouses were placed at the apex of palace society as befitted their rank but could still find themselves exposed to the eddying currents of dynastic calculation. Plectrude, for example, the wife of Pippin II, brought with her to the marriage her family's substantial estates between the Meuse and the Moselle. This region was very much the Carolingian heartland and his possession of lands in his area helped to confirm Pippin's authority. But Charles Martel, Pippin's son by another woman, undermined Plectrude's authority after Pippin died and advanced the interests of his own mother's kin who were located in the region of Liège. When Martel's son, Pippin III, became king of the Franks he derived some of his authority from the high, and quite possibly Merovingian, birth of his wife Bertrada who had also inherited great riches. The case of the king's sister, Chiltrude, shows how the actions of an independent-minded woman could pose a threat to Carolingian calculations. Her decision to marry the duke of Bavaria went against the advice of her royal relations, and the son of that marriage, Duke Tassilo, would clash with Pippin's son Charlemagne.

The women of the Lombard royal house played an especially important role in fulfilling the ambitions of King Desiderius. Tassilo of Bavaria, Arichis the duke of Lombard-controlled Benevento, and Charlemagne all married princesses who were Desiderius's daughters. A fourth sister exercised an important influence as abbess of the convent of San Salvatore, a foundation established by Desiderius and his wife at the king's home town of Brescia. Charlemagne's decision to set aside his Lombard bride was keenly resented by her sisters and after the death of Arichis his widow was well to the fore in organizing Lombard resistance to the Frankish takeover.

Bavaria provides another example of the interplay of female status and dynastic power politics. After Charlemagne ousted Tassilo in 788 he tonsured both the duke and his son, and carried off Tassilo's daughters and wife (Charlemagne's own former sister-in-law) into captivity. The arrangements for Bavarian government remained a family matter since the man Charlemagne put in charge was Gerold, brother of Hildegard whom he had married after rejecting his Lombard bride. Hildegard had died in 783, but the fact of a royal connection ensured Gerold's continued high status; and Pippin, the son of the queen's marriage to Charlemagne, would have inherited Bavaria as his own domain had he lived.

ROYAL WOMEN AS A FOCUS OF NATIONAL IDENTITY

Hildegard's authority shows therefore how a royal female, even in death, could be an important focus for loyalty within the Carolingian family. Her status also reveals how such women played a key role in the formation of a national identity. This was an especially important process in those areas east of the Rhine which had been assimilated to the Frankish kingdom and whose national amour propre required some careful massaging as a result. Hildegard was chosen by Charlemagne because on her mother's side she was descended from the ducal rulers of Alamannia, and the marriage might have appeased those Alamanns who continued to resent the local dynasty's displacement. It was only a generation since the slaughter of the Alamannian nobility by Charlemagne's own uncle Carloman in 746. Hildegard certainly more than fulfilled her duties as a provider of heirs: the years of marriage (771–83) produced eleven children. Her successors as queen, Charlemagne's wives Fastrada (d. 794) and Liutgard (d. 800), were less prolific but, like Hildegard, they were intimately involved in the business of running the estates which provided sustenance for the royal household. Carolingian queens also had an important role to play as patrons, since the household was an organization which educated young aristocratic warriors and it was queens who decided how annual gifts should be distributed among those scions of the nobility. The supposed 'cruelty' of Fastrada in this regard was one of the reasons adduced for the two major rebellions of Charlemagne's reign, those of 786 and 792. A queen had unique access to the monarch and the opportunities she had to benefit her own kinsmen were correspondingly extensive. That pattern is particularly obvious in the careers of those kings who remarried after the death of an earlier wife.

Civil war erupted in Francia when Louis the Pious favoured the son of his new wife Judith over the sons of his first wife. When Judith was accused of adultery both she and her brothers were banished to monastic imprisonment. Similar discord erupted in Wessex in 855 when King Aethelwulf, then in his fifties, married Judith's granddaughter, a fourteen-year-old girl who bore the same name as her ancestor. The princess was the daughter of Charles the Bald, king of the Franks, and was instrumental in securing an alliance between Wessex and the Franks. A common exposure to the Viking threat had brought the two kingdoms together, and Aethelwulf was in any event well connected at the Frankish court, having probably been born in the palace at Aachen. It was indeed at the palace that he first met young Judith, while staying over on the return journey from Rome where he had been on pilgrimage. As part of the deal Judith was crowned queen of Wessex, a ceremony which ran counter to the kingdom's royal traditions. But Aethelbald, the son of Aethelwulf's earlier marriage, rebelled when confronted by a teenage queen who might bear his father more heirs, and the king subsequently retired from public duties. By 858 Aethelwulf was dead but, intriguingly enough, Aethelbald married his young stepmother soon afterwards, a move which outraged the Church but helped to cement good relations between Wessex and the kingdom of the Franks.

The Carolingian custom of marrying into the local aristocracies of the lands they governed helped them to control the various sub-kingdoms and regions. Louis the German's three sons married noble heiresses in, respectively, Bavaria, Saxony and Alamannia during the 860s. Charles the Bald's two eldest sons took the initiative and chose their own brides, against their father's wishes, in Neustria and Aquitaine. Queens mattered because Carolingian kingship was centred on the court, and it was female sovereigns who ran the royal household as a whole. They invariably had a household of their own as well, and that was a major institution equipped with its own key officers. A royal divorce therefore signified not just marital discontent but also a deep political divide. This is why the breakdown of King Lothair II's marriage became such a cause célèbre, though the details of the case were notorious enough in themselves: the king accused his childless wife Theutberga of incest through an act of anal intercourse with her brother Hubert, and Lothair's ambition was to marry Waldrada, the mistress by whom he already had children. The case divided his uncles, with Charles the Bald opposing the divorce while Louis the German supported it, and the two rulers split Lothair's Lotharingian kingdom between them on his death in 869.

STRATEGIES IN COPING WITH AMBITIOUS RELATIVES

Royal marriages, and the issues of government to which they gave rise, reflected that inclusive view of kinship which was current in early medieval Europe. A king shared his father's kin with his brothers and his wife's kin were also regarded as his own. If a ruler's kin on either his father's or his mother's side threatened to rebel, he could therefore call on his in-laws for support. The emperor Lothair's father-in-law Hugh of Tours and Charles the Bald's brother-in-law Boso of Provence helped both rulers to survive political challenges in the 870s. Marriage's consequences, however, were also unpredictable and the advantages, both materially and politically, could be reversed dramatically if the marriages of royal daughters produced numerous in-laws with onerous claims on the patrimony. This was probably why Charlemagne kept his daughters unmarried, but that policy in turn had its own dangers since the princesses' sexual adventures caused scandal both at court and in Francia at large. The solution, imposed on almost all the daughters of Carolingian kings in the ninth century, was to place them in convents. That way, at least, the number of thrusting sons-in-law claiming their place at court and a share of the patrimony could be limited. The strategy brought in its wake, however, the possibility of the royal line of descent becoming too narrow. The chronicler Regino of Prum, writing c. 880, struck a resonant chord when he noted how 'the sterility of their wives' posed a threat to Carolingian rulers.

Few members of the Carolingian dynasty could be kings themselves and the lives of brothers were often precarious as a result. We have seen how difficult relations were between Charlemagne and Carloman. The annals give no information about what happened to Carloman's sons. But the fact that the king went out of his way to tell his own sons what not to do to their own nephews suggests that the boys' fate weighed on his conscience. One nephew who rebelled openly was Bernard, after his uncle Louis the Pious excluded him from any inheritance in favour of the king's sons. Bernard was first of all blinded and then died. Louis had to perform a very public penance in 822 in order to atone for this crime since Bernard had been a popular and well-supported public figure. One rebellion which came very close to the throne was that of Charles the Bald's son Carloman. His aristocratic associates did eventually abandon Carloman's cause but only after he had been blinded following a show trial.

There were many strategies that could be adopted in order to try to avoid such conflict and regnal divisions. West Saxon kings arranged fraternal pacts. These were legally binding agreements arrived at before the death of the reigning monarch, and it was also the kingdom's policy to downgrade the status of those kings' wives who might produce rival lines of descent. The Carolingians attached particular importance to the names that they gave their sons as a way of establishing who counted in the pursuit of power and who was excluded from it. The names of two of Charlemagne's sons linked the new dynasty with its predecessor. Louis was a later version of Clovis, and his twin brother who died in infancy was called Lothair, a name with ancient Merovingian association. The name Bernard may have been reserved for illegitimate sons, as in the case of Louis the Pious's nephew, whom Charlemagne nonetheless recognized as king of Italy in 813. Charlemagne's eldest son was baptized Pippin, a name which signified his status as heir to the full dynastic glory. This, however, did not stop the king from excluding him from the succession in c. 790 in order to privilege Pippin's half-brothers. The former heir was tonsured and sent to the monastery of Prum following the crushing of his revolt two years later.

Tonsuring was a very effective, because so public, method of excluding certain individuals from the line of succession. Many ninth-century Carolingian rulers resorted to it. Hugh and Drogo, the illegitimate sons born to Charlemagne in his old age, were tonsured by their half-brother Louis the Pious 'lest they should solicit the people', according to Nithard, the Frankish court historian writing in the early 840s. Charles the Bald, Louis's son, went so far as to tonsure his legitimate younger sons while they were still children, and he did the same to his nephews when they were adults. Charles's position as king of the western Franks was initially precarious because of Viking raids and until at least the early 860s many of his vassals were disloyal to him. But by careful custodianship of his lands as well as through a close relationship with the Church Charles was able to hang on to his authority and actually enhance it. By the time of his death in 877 it seemed as if much of the original Carolingian renaissance had been revived and Charles's rigorous policy of tonsuring had helped to preserve his kingdom. Tonsuring, therefore, was a good way of sidelining some royals who were either awkward already or were thought to have the potential to cause trouble in the future. Many of those born on the wrong side of the royal bed ended up being tonsured. But illegitimacy of itself was no disqualification when it came to a royal succession. And even the tonsured could gain a constituency of supporters when a crown was in sight. What really mattered in those stakes was effectiveness and a reputation for getting things done. Despite his illegitimacy, Arnulf was acknowledged king of east Francia in 877, a time when the royal line there was in danger of extinction, and in 870 Charles the Bald's son Carloman, though tonsured since childhood, was a popular candidate for a kingdom.

Kingly power, endowed with its new resources at both a material and an ideological level, was Francia's very own revolution in government. Regal rituals and the role of courtiers, the palatial context in architecture and the diffusion of power's commands from the household of the king: Charlemagne's legacy in these matters shaped the conduct of European monarchs during a millennium of recorded history. Managing the nobility and organizing patronage would be the constant preoccupations of kings who wanted to retain their thrones, and here too there were lessons to be drawn from the Carolingian past. Successive French royal houses, Capetian, Valois and Bourbon, considered themselves to be Charlemagne's successors, and the execution of Louis XVI in 1793 proved to be a decisive blow not just to the monarchy in France but also to the notion that a king's person was hedged with divinity. But in the long centuries before the falling of the axe European monarchs never ceased to look back to Charlemagne. His story and the history of his dynasty supplied those precedents and traditions which confirmed the authority of kings and made the quality of their power appear as natural a fact of life as the air breathed by their subjects.

CHAPTER 6

Charlemagne and the Institutions of Carolingian Government

AN ELEPHANT AT AACHEN

In July 802 an African elephant which had been given the name of Abul-Abaz arrived at Charlemagne's court in Aachen. The possession of so fabulous a creature had been a symbol of the authority of a ruler in the courts of the ancient Near East from Hellenistic times onwards, but hardly any of Charlemagne's subjects can have seen an elephant with their own eyes. Abul-Abaz was the gift of Harun al-Rashid, the Caliph of Baghdad (786–809) whose Abbasid dynasty had supplanted the Umayyads in the eastern Mediterranean and Middle East half a century earlier. The Franks referred to him as '*Rex Persarum*' and Harun's gift was part of a diplomatic initiative since he was keen to gain Charlemagne's support in his continuing struggle against those members of the Umayyad dynasty and its supporters who had fled west to Spain and taken over the emirate of Cordoba. He may also have been keen to draw Charlemagne into a confrontation with the Byzantines. They were Harun's neighbours and adversaries, and the Caliph would have been eager to exploit any divisions that might have arisen between the Franks and the Greeks as a result of the recent imperial coronation in Rome.

An elephant can be a fast-moving creature capable of achieving a top speed of twenty-five miles per hour, and many of the old Roman roads in Charlemagne's kingdom were in good condition. Even so, it must have taken many months for Abul-Abaz to complete his journey from the east, and the wonder aroused by his arrival in the Aachen menagerie lasted for a very long time. He played a full role in the court's outdoor ceremonials and joined the Frankish army on military campaigns in a strictly decorative capacity during the summer months. Abul-Abaz was a ruler's trophy and he enjoyed eight years of celebrity until his death in 810. It had been a bad year for animal sickness in Charlemagne's kingdom. A cattle pest killed off the herds brought together to feed the army which was then assembling for a projected expedition against the Danes, and this bovine disease had spread throughout Francia. But while Abul-Abaz lived, Charlemagne's subjects took a rare delight in this impressive tribute to their king's international prestige. A scribe working at the abbey of St-Denis near Paris drew an elephant's head in the initial B of the copy he produced of Cassiodorus's *Commentary* on the Psalms in the early ninth century, and the impact of the animal's exoticism on the Franks' imagination ensured his posthumous reputation. Drawings of two elephants appear in the spandrels of a page of a bible produced at Tours in the mid-840s, and an elephant also features in a work of ivory depicting the Garden of Eden which was carved at the same time in the Loire valley.

INTERNATIONAL RECOGNITION: TRIBUTES AND GIFTS

Abul-Abaz survives in the historical record because Charlemagne's successes were recognized at an international level, and the king certainly knew how to use the channels of diplomacy in order to enhance his authority. He had taken the initiative with regard to Harun al-Rashid by sending three envoys to Baghdad in 797, and these emissaries may also have established contacts with the Patriarch of Jerusalem who sent his own representatives to Charlemagne in 799 and 800. The Patriarch would in all probability have acted with the permission of al-Rashid when he sent Charlemagne the keys to Jerusalem since the city was at that time part of the Caliphate. This was a powerfully symbolic gesture and one that established Charlemagne's status as a protector of Jerusalem's Christian shrines. Al-Rashid's first set of envoys to Charlemagne presented themselves in 801 while the king, now a newly crowned emperor, was still in Italy, before his return to Aachen in the autumn of that year. These ambassadors included the Caliph's viceroy in the west, Ibrahim ibn al-Aghlab, who was based in Tunisia, and his high-level presence signifies the importance al-Rashid attached to good relations with Charlemagne.

Two of the ambassadors Charlemagne sent to Baghdad in 797 died during the mission but the third, called Isaac the Jew, survived. The Baghdad diplomats who met Charlemagne in Italy in 801 reported that Isaac was now returning to Aachen and that an elephant was among the many gifts he had been commanded to deliver to the king. If al-Rashid's aim was the establishment of a permanent rift between the Frankish monarchy and the Byzantine empire, then he failed. There were Frankish–Greek military hostilities over the issue of Venice, and the Byzantines' oscillation on the question of icons troubled Charlemagne. He was dismayed by the iconoclastic fury which had convulsed the Greek Church, but the way in which that campaign was suspended can hardly have improved his temper. The Council of Nicaea (787) restored image worship but it also excluded Charlemagne from its deliberations. His own *via media* on icons is recorded in the capitulary or edict known as the *Libri Carolini* composed in 791–2. Icons, it says, can be used as decoration but are not to be worshipped. The document goes on to assert that the Council held at Nicaea was just a Greek synod rather than a body with universal authority. Nonetheless, these Byzantines remained the heirs to the *romanitas* that Charlemagne both believed in and identified with. They were a part of his mental world as no Caliph of Baghdad could ever hope to be. Al-Rashid, however, proved to be a persistent diplomatic suitor, and the envoys he sent to Charlemagne in 806 brought some spectacular gifts: pavilion and entrance tents made of linen and dyed in different colours, perfumes and ointments, bales of silk, and a brass water clock whose bells, struck by twelve tiny balls, marked the hours as did the appearance of twelve horsemen in the mechanism's twelve windows.

The authority of Frankish rulers had been gaining international renown even before Charlemagne's reign and in 757 Pippin III received the gift of an organ which had been dispatched from Constantinople. Byzantine diplomacy had a reputation for sophistication and calculation, and the Greeks were characteristically quick off the mark in recognizing that a formidable power was emerging in western Europe. But it is Charlemagne's reign which witnessed the most striking diplomatic recognition of Frankish power. The pattern of his achievements along with the range of his ambitions meant that he was at the centre of a diplomatic network which extended right to the very boundaries of the world as it was known in his time.

This international theme is well to the fore in the history of the Carolingian dynasty which was produced towards 806 at the monastery of Chelles under the direction of Gisela, Charlemagne's sister. This history is known as the *Annals of Metz* and it is Pippin II, Charlemagne's great-grandfather, who is there described as receiving a profusion of embassies: 'Delegations of the nations living round about him, that is, the Greeks, Romans, Lombards, Huns, Slavs and Saracens, poured in to him. And the fame of his victory and triumphs so went out among all peoples that, deservedly on account of his virtue and prudence, all the nations round about sought his friendship with great gifts and rewards.' The *Annals* set out to justify the Carolingian ruling house, and a stress on the continuity of the dynastic glory was part of that same project. Arrangements for an anticipated division of the empire (*Divisio Regnorum*) between his three legitimate sons in the event of Charlemagne's death were being finalized at the time of the *Annals'* compilation. It was all the more important, therefore, to stress the unity and continuity of the dynastic line. It may indeed be true that Pippin II was the centre of much diplomatic activity. But the list of embassies described in the Metz *Annals* surely draws on the author's knowledge of more recent history. Charlemagne's international successes were being projected backwards in time to the late seventh century.

We know that Charlemagne sent ambassadorial envoys to Spain and Byzantium, to Jerusalem and to Rome, while also receiving delegations from Spain's rulers (both Christian and Arab), successive popes, emperors of Byzantium, the kings of Denmark, Mercia and Northumberland, and the rulers of the Avars and the Slavs. Many of these emissaries came bearing varying forms of the recognition considered to be Charlemagne's due. In 799 the governor of Huesca in northern Spain sent him the keys of the city, and 'King Sadun', the warlord of Barcelona, was sent in chains to Charlemagne in 803 after the city's capture by a Frankish army. The Frankish–Greek peace negotiations of 802 saw an exchange of ambassadors between Constantinople and Aachen, and the envoys sent by the emperor Nicephorus to Charlemagne in the following year arrived bearing a draft peace agreement. The Byzantine nobleman Nicetas negotiated peace in 807 on the issue of Venice with Charlemagne's son Pippin, who at that time was king of Italy. In the following year, after King Eardwulf of Northumbria's arrival in Nijmegen, Frankish envoys were sent to his kingdom in the north of England.

In 812 envoys from Byzantium arrived with the news that the court at Constantinople now recognized that Charlemagne was an imperator. It was easy enough, from Byzantium's point of view, to recognize a ruler as exercising an *imperium* since the term meant something fairly simple and uncontentious: power and influence exercised over more than one people or *gens*. But an imperator was a very different kind of ruler, one who could claim that level of universal authority which had hitherto been the sole prerogative of the rulers of the Greek empire. This Byzantine concession was perhaps Charlemagne's most substantial diplomatic achievement. The military involvement in northern Spain in the late 790s brought its own forms of tribute, and especially in the context of the alliance with Alfonso, king of the Asturias and Galicia. In 797 Alfonso's envoys Froia and Basiliscus arrived at the Carolingian court bearing gifts which included Moorish prisoners, a pavilion tent, coats of mail and mules. Embassies such as these opened up Francia to the rest of the world and the *imperium* enjoyed by its king gained new horizons as a result. Unusual goods and new technologies arrived in Charlemagne's kingdom, and the eyes of his emissaries were opened to novel forms of human experience and culture in the course of their travels. The members of a Frankish embassy to the Caliphate returned home in 806 having had to negotiate their way through the Greek-occupied regions of Dalmatia on the eastern Adriatic coast. They were accompanied on their way back by two monks from Jerusalem who were the Patriarch's emissaries to Charlemagne and whose knowledge of Greek would have been useful in ensuring the party's safe passage.

These diplomatic gifts and tributes, the reception of envoys and the sending of embassies to foreign lands, the formal negotiations relating to peace and war, had two related consequences. They ministered in the first place to the Franks' sense of their own importance and to the reputation of their king. But the international dimension also led to a greater self-knowledge among the Franks about the necessary limits to their own culture and polity. The greatest number of diplomatic exchanges during Charlemagne's reign, and the ones that were most extensive in geographical terms, took place from the late 790s onwards. This is the period when we can see the Frankish kingdom defining itself in relation to other societies and political organizations. The territorial expansion was reaching its limits and it was important therefore to consider how best to ensure *defensio patriae* – that defence of the fatherland which resonates in the documentation issued by Charlemagne's officials.

Incorporation of conquered territories meant that an expanded Francia acquired new boundaries. And that entailed having new neighbours whose numbers included those who were hostile to the Franks as well as peoples who wished to establish some kind of accommodation with them. To the west there was a Breton 'march' or border region, and to the south there was a Spanish one. An alliance with the Slavic Abodrites meant that the Franks could turn the area of Saxony which lay to the north and the east of the river Elbe into its colonized border territory. The question of what was and was not really 'Frankish' acquired a new focus as a result of this novel and imperial dimension to the government of the Carolingian realm.

Diplomacy in all its forms displayed the respect due to a ruler whose instruments of government had given a new definition to his kingdom and thereby raised it to predominance as the greatest power in western Europe. What, therefore, were the political and institutional means used by Charlemagne and his dynasty in order to achieve these domestic goals?

Charlemagne was involved in the business of government on an intimate and detailed basis. Palace architecture, as we have seen, was designed to enable his subjects to approach the king in order to present their requests and grievances. This personal element to his administration was an important piece of symbolic ritual. Access to the king who was the fount of all justice and honour was part of the collective memory of the Franks, and Charlemagne's preservation of that custom confirmed his authority by linking him with his regal precursors. But the governing will which emanated from the royal palaces was a sophisticated mechanism whose expertise in the gathering of information and the enforcement of order had evolved beyond the personalized nature of kingship as exercised originally within a tribal society. The right of his subjects to be heard was still a feature of Charlemagne's government, and he extended that right to the populations of the conquered territories as well as to those living within the original Frankish territories. But for most of them, as opposed to courtiers and nobles, being 'heard' in this new context usually meant access to the officialdom operating in the king's name rather than talking directly to Charlemagne himself.

There were four major elements to Charlemagne's institutions of government. The assemblies of the Franks, together with the documentation consisting of clauses or *capitula* and therefore known as capitularies, were the means by which the royal will was expressed. *Missi dominici* operated in Charlemagne's name and were personally charged with the implementation of his commands. Counts concerned themselves with the day-to-day issues of administration within their different areas and this included the business transacted in courts of law. How therefore did each of the elements of this system of government work in practice? An answer to that question involves a comparison with what was happening elsewhere in Europe at the same time while bearing in mind, too, how the king's system evolved in the successor Frankish kingdoms of the ninth century.

THE ASSEMBLY OF THE FRANKS

The Frankish national assembly was convoked by the king of the day and it was an opportunity for him to invite all those who really mattered to attend on him. It was usually held at a palace and legal business was frequently transacted during this great event. A scribe, writing in c. 870, captures what must have been the general tone in the description he gives of a collection of capitularies drawn up during one such assembly: 'Capitula of Bishops, Kings, and Especially All the Noble Franks'. The equivalent body in Wessex was called the *witan* or 'wise men', and in all such assemblies kings seized the opportunity to combine general policy declarations with the resolution of particular issues of the day. The assembly that Charlemagne convened in Frankfurt in 794 was unusually significant and its agenda was impressively wide-ranging: the restoration of order after the 792 rebellion, consideration of how to distinguish between the loyal and the faithless, confirmation of the downfall of Tassilo of Bavaria, measures dealing with the consequences of a major famine (including price-fixing and punishment of profiteers), and debate on the establishment of an orthodox code of belief for Latin Christendom. The Edict of Pires, proclaimed in June 864, is the most far-reaching document of administrative law produced by any Carolingian assembly, its ambitious measures including anti-crime legislation, coinage reform, regulations applying to the management of royal estates, army reforms, and steps to ensure the edict's widest possible diffusion and effectiveness.

The assembly of the Franks was therefore the most regular and public vehicle available to Charlemagne as a way of demonstrating his authority and of establishing the terms on which it could be exercised. Following the rebellion of his son 'Pippin the Hunchback' he summoned an assembly at Regensburg in 792: 'and there the whole Christian people present with the king judged that Pippin as well as those who were his accomplices in this abominable plot should lose both their estates and their lives . . .' Since the king did not wish Pippin to lose his life, 'the Franks judged that he must be subjected to God's service' and the erring son was therefore sent to the monastery of Prum in the Rhineland where he died some twenty years later. Those who met at Regensburg were discussing the political consequences of an armed threat, and the combination of military questions with civilian ones is a recurring feature of Charlemagne's assemblies. This was a society with a militarized ethos and an assembly was in part an opportunity for the gathering of intelligence in relation to both the demands of war and the requirements of peace. Hincmar tells us that each individual who took part in an assembly 'was to collect information concerning any relevant matter . . . not only from his own people but from strangers and from both friends and enemies'. Discussions both formal and informal, feasting and drinking, secular rituals such as the hunt and liturgical ones such as the celebration of the mass: all of these features of the varying assemblies showed the Frankish leadership coming together in order to assert its political and military solidarity.

Both laity and clergy attended these meetings and there were two kinds of assembly. Ever since the mid-eighth century it had been customary to hold the general assembly of the Franks in May, but the assemblies which were convened to discuss specific issues could take place at any time of the year. Examples of the latter include the assembly held in 773 to discuss whether to agree to Pope Hadrian's proposal of a campaign against the Lombards, the 806 meeting which debated Charlemagne's proposed division of the kingdom (the *Divisio Regnorum*), the witnessing of the king's will at the 811 assembly, and the agreement of the 813 assembly that Louis the Pious should be Charlemagne's successor. Charlemagne needed these assemblies, both the annual events and the more occasional ones, in order to consult the *optimates* of his kingdom and to gain their approval for his proposals. But the initiative to summon the meetings came from the king and from no one else, although there are a few examples of the participants at a general assembly deciding where the following year's meeting should be held. Charlemagne would send out letters notifying the participants where and when they were expected to congregate, and many an assembly would coincide with preparations for the summer's military offensive. We have already seen how in 806, for example, the king informed Abbot Fulrad of St-Quentin in Picardy that he was to travel to eastern Saxony, to a point near present-day Magdeburg, where that year's general assembly would be held. Fulrad was to bring his men with him, and they should be armed and equipped to join the army which would convene at a point to be determined. A journey from western France to Saxony's furthest reaches was demanding enough in itself, but Charlemagne also told the abbot that he should load his carts with enough provisions for three months and that he should reckon on the total expedition lasting some six months in all. He and his men should take nothing from the land while travelling to Saxony, apart from firewood, grass and water. Since the letter received by Fulrad was a circular, we can assume that all those travelling to the 806 assembly received copies of the same document, and the arrangements which are implied by its contents argue for a highly effective communications network operating right across Charlemagne's territories.

What went through the mind of one of the *potentes* while expecting a summons to such an assembly? The letters of Abbot Lupus of Fer-rières, written in c. 850, give some clues. Lupus was keen for an invitation and awaited the king's messenger impatiently but he also knew that attendance brought its own costs since the demands of a king could be burdensome. Still, refusal was a practical impossibility for any of the *potentes* even though, as Lupus wrote, the king's smile might well be just a mask. Alfred of Wessex, writing from a top-down perspective in one of his letters, communicates a similar noble apprehension when he describes the rationale for a palace assembly in his own kingdom: 'not all are similarly at ease when they get there. Some are received with greater respect and familiarity than others, some with less; some with virtually none, except for the one fact that he [the king] loves them all.' The 'love' allowed for gradations and the fact that it could never be presumed upon was a source of kingly power.

The numbers of those attending a Frankish assembly in the age of the Carolingians varied. Winter assemblies were mostly small-scale affairs, perhaps no more than a handful of key nobles and counsellors. The one held in Savonnières in November 862 was exceptional since there were three kings involved, and a participant estimated that 'nearly 200 *con-siliarii*, bishops and abbots as well as laymen, were under one roof'. These numbers begin to approach those more typical of summer assemblies which were major occasions of state attended by the lesser as well as the greater nobility and clergy. *Consiliarii* would arrive with retinues whose numbers, however, were carefully limited by kings, and only those nobles who were exceptionally favoured, and very reliable, could turn up with large numbers of followers. One bishop had the presumption to turn up at a Carolingian assembly with 'the whole company of his men'. This may have been an insurance policy on his part since he had already fallen out of favour and may well have been suspected of planning to defect. Royal officials told the bishop that a maximum of ten or twelve retainers (*casati homines*) were more than enough, plus attendant clergy and servants, and we know that fifty or so was considered an average number for the retinue accompanying most bishops when they went on an official tour round their dioceses. There is one, very rare, document which survives from the great assembly held at Verdun in 843 and which names a hundred Bavarian nobles who were there. Nobles from all three Carolingian kingdoms would have been represented at this exceptionally important event and an extrapolation from the Bavarian figures suggests the presence at Verdun of over 1,000 assembly members, a figure to which we should add the bishops who would have been there representing the imperial episcopate.

These, then, were large-scale gatherings and the buildings in which they were held needed to be correspondingly spacious. The *capella palatina* at Aachen, built by Charlemagne, saw quite a few assemblies and it can squeeze in a maximum of 7,000 people. Archaeological investigations have revealed the foundations of a hall nearby which is nearly 164 feet long, and that *aula* would have come in very useful during an Aachen assembly. Similar work at Ingelheim has uncovered a hall 115 feet in length which dates from the time of Louis the Pious. Frankish kings were not alone in needing large buildings where they could hold assemblies, conduct business and perform rituals. The church of St Julian at Oviedo in the kingdom of the Asturias, dating from the reign of Alfonso II, and the palace complex of Ramiro I which stands nearby, both reveal something of the monumental scale of public building required by early medieval kings in order both to impress and be effective. Even so, there must have been an overspill at some of the summer assemblies, and tents would have been used to accommodate those surplus numbers. These could be magnificent structures, and the ones received and given by kings as diplomatic gifts show how tents were an essential part of monarchy's panoply. The presence of many hundreds of horses, who all needed to be groomed under the supervision of constables and marshals, and whose ordure had to be disposed of in vast quantities, would have added its own flavour to the gathering.

Hincmar, archbishop of Reims, gives a detailed description of how a typical assembly was supposed to work in *De Ordine Palatii* and, having been a senior adviser to both Louis the Pious and Charles the Bald, he would certainly have had plenty of experience in the practical running of such events. The archbishop stood at the apex of his society and we need therefore to make allowances for his establishment smoothness. Hincmar is not the man to go to for evidence of quarrelsome debates and the striking of deals. Still, his description of what ought to take place surely reflects the aspirations of Carolingian kings and may stand as an informed account of what did actually happen at least some of the time.

Potentes, Hincmar tells us, first of all conferred together in private on an agenda which had been drawn up by the king. Meanwhile, lesser figures had their own discussions. A king only joined in these early meetings if his presence was requested. Otherwise he concerned himself with demonstrating regal bonhomie: 'he would be occupied with the rest of the assembled people, receiving gifts, greeting the more important, exchanging news with those he did not see often, expressing sympathy with the old, sharing their pleasures with the young'. Sociability of this kind reflected the personality of a monarch, and his possession of the 'king-becoming graces', or lack of them, was all-important in establishing his authority. The *auctoritas* of Charlemagne's personality is evident in Einhard's *Life*, and Charles the Bald had something of the same élan. It mattered, by contrast, that Charles's son Louis, who succeeded him briefly on the throne of west Francia (877–9), had a speech impediment, and it was contemporaries, not posterity, who felt bold enough to name that unhappy monarch 'the Stammerer'. Alfred of Wessex's own pen tells us that he took care to address his bishops 'in a loving and friendly manner' and in a style modelled on phrases used in Pope Gregory's famous *Regula Pastoralis* (*Pastoral Care*), a book translated by the king himself. There was therefore a formula involved but Alfred, like any other king of the period, also needed to be personally convincing when using his chosen words. Such moments of self-disclosure are, necessarily, difficult to trace in the surviving sources but in relation to the aristocracy in particular a king needed to demonstrate that he was both self-confident and prepared to confide in them. By these means he could persuade the nobility to participate in government in ways that benefited both the crown and themselves. A king, we can suspect, might confide less than frankly and would need to keep his own counsel as well. But in consulting his *potentes* no monarch could afford the appearance of just going through the motions.

Once the counsellors had finished deliberating and, in Hincmar's phrase, 'found counsel', the agreed results would be written down in *capitula*. The archbishop stresses the way in which 'the less important heard that counsel' as well, 'sometimes deliberated on it, and confirmed it, not because they were forced to do so but from their own understanding and freely expressed opinion'. His emphasis on consensus is clearly intended to sideline the possibility of dissent, and the requirement that counts and *missi* should take copies of the agreed *capitula* back to their regions shows a similar preoccupation on the part of Carolingian kings. This was the political nation at work and it was important that all should be bound by its settled agreements. There is a striking example of this process to be seen in 802 when Count Stephen, a *missus* operating in a group of counties in the region of Paris, returned home after an assembly in Aachen had agreed on some additions to the *Lex Salica*. The relevant capitulary states that the count made the new laws 'manifest in the *civitas* of Paris in the public assembly, and . . . read them out before the judgment-finders [*scabini*]' with the result that 'all consented together. Further, all the *scabini*, bishops, abbots and counts confirmed these *capitula* by writing beneath in their own hands'.

It was therefore a local assembly, like the one in Paris, which confirmed and helped to enforce the decisions of the central assembly. Bodies such as these, known in Francia as the *mallus* and called the *moot* in Wessex, also played an important role in settling local disputes. Their powers as local courts of law were extensive. Charlemagne's capitulary dealing with the government of the conquered Saxony left the region's legal infrastructure in place, and cases here were settled 'through local men [*pagenses*]' who sat 'in local courts . . . according to custom'. Any appeals were 'brought to the palace' in the words of the king, whose authority or *bann* now applied to the Saxons quite as much as it did to the Franks. But there is a clear impression here of the royal will deciding that its purposes were best served by working through the local structures when it came to fining miscreants and punishing criminals. It was, for example, a Saxon custom to burn the houses of criminals and Charlemagne decreed that that punishment should continue 'for coercion to judgment on our behalf'.

Carolingian conquests and the dynasty's acquisition of lands by marriage meant that royal administration became more demanding and therefore more specialized. Lay aristocrats and churches in possession of grants of land and other privileges bestowed on them by the king needed charters in order to prove legality of title. In Charlemagne's time, and during the reigns of his ninth-century successors, a team of notaries (never more, probably, than some three or four) worked on charter-writing, and they were headed by the chancellor, the official who looked after the royal seal. With so many petitioners coming to court in order to obtain appropriately worded charters and prepared to make gifts to secure that end, there were plenty of opportunities for these notaries to enrich themselves. Their most important job, however, was to produce the capitularies.

THE CAPITULARIES: AN INSTRUMENT OF THE ROYAL WILL

Carolingian legislation was recorded in capitularies, documents which recorded the details of a king's command and whose effect was intended to extend right across the realm. Not a single one of these documents survives in its original form and quite possibly very few of them were in fact ever produced in such an official way. Instead, drafts may have been produced by those who had influence at court and these were then used as a basis for the public proclamation of legislation. Royal agents, especially in areas to the west and south of the Rhine, also made their own copies of the capitularies. Master-copies may well have been held in the royal archive – at least during the more sedentary period of Charlemagne's later years and during the reigns of his successors Louis the Pious and Charles the Bald. The court in Wessex had similar arrangements where Aethelwulf had imported a Frank to be the chief notary, and the Christian kingdom of the Asturias, though so beleaguered, must have been serviced by a fair number of notaries since it produced a large number of charters.

Hincmar's account reflects a later ninth-century evolution of the Carolingian administration, and his words have been interpreted to imply that most of Charlemagne's capitularies were records of decisions arrived at in an assembly. Some did indeed do that job. It was an assembly held at Herstal in 779 which led to the issuing of a capitulary in that same year whose provisions established regulations for court administration, tithe payments, and the sentencing policy for the crimes of perjury and robbery. The synod held at Frankfurt in 794 was an important event in the history of Christian doctrine, and Charlemagne presided over it in much the same way that Constantine had overseen the Council of Nicaea just over four and a half centuries earlier. But the synod also qualifies as an assembly and, quite apart from the condemnation of the heresy of 'adoptionism', it produced the major rulings on coinage and weights and measures which are recorded in the subsequent capitulary. And the details of the *Divisio Regnorum* are recorded in the capitulary which was issued following an assembly specially convened to discuss that issue.

But these are the exceptions, and recent work has shown that less than four per cent of the total number of capitularies which can be dated to Charlemagne's reign are the result of business transacted at an assembly. This startling fact makes Charlemagne even more central to the business of government than was previously supposed. It is now clear that the authority of a royal capitulary was derived from the fact that it had been issued by the king himself. The conventional idea that the assemblies operated as some kind of proto-parliamentary forum, and that their assent was needed in order for the capitularies to be issued, is therefore wide of the mark. Capitularies cannot be seen as the kind of legislation which might be produced by a deliberative body. They were effective simply because Charlemagne decided that they should be so. The 110 capitularies of Charlemagne's reign expressed the royal will, and those who copied these documents and sent them to the *missi* who enforced the relevant provisions did so as subjects who were obedient to the king's command. These documents, regardless of whether or not they reflected an antecedent assembly discussion, mattered because they expressed Charlemagne's views and wishes. Compared to that basic fact the distinction conventionally made between the king's oral command and its written expression is an unimportant one. Both were equally important – and for the same reason. Charlemagne's authority gave force to any oral pronouncements he made at an assembly. Equally, the written records of an assembly over which he presided had to be obeyed precisely because Charlemagne had been there.

One of the defining features of the reign and its associated cultural renaissance is an emphasis on literary accuracy and the correct expression of thought through the written word. The history of the capitulary record demonstrates this same scrupulousness since the documents needed to express with maximum fidelity the details of what Charlemagne thought and decided. Sometimes we can almost hear him at work. Some of the clauses of the Frankfurt capitulary are introduced with phrases such as 'the king also stated', 'he recommended also' and 'our most pious lord decreed, with the approval of the holy synod'. Yet others take us even closer to the king's presence, with the royal first person plural expressing the initial assertion 'We have heard' and 'We and the holy synod have decreed', and the document as a whole is a striking example of Charlemagne's view that religious and political order are indistinguishable from each other. *Coniurationes* or conspiracies against the king are condemned, bishops need to have detailed knowledge of how monasteries are run, 'deacons, monks and clerics are not to drink in taverns', and 'the Lord's day is to be observed from evening to evening'. Bishops' courts of law are to try cases which involve the clergy, with archbishops functioning as a court of appeal. If a case cannot be settled at that higher level then the parties to the dispute may appear before the king for a final judgment.

The *Admonitio generalis* issued in capitulary form by the king five years earlier in 789 shows the same combination of secular and spiritual authority at work. It is doubtful that any assembly preceded the *Admonitio* although it does reflect Charlemagne's consultations with a number of his advisers, and Alcuin may have played a role in drafting the provisions. Just as in the case of the Frankfurt document there are clauses relating to correct weight and measures, and the *Admonitio*'s prescriptions for a Christian society are formidably detailed. Rules are set out on the singing of the Roman version of the chant in Church liturgy, and there are even proposals on the appropriate content of sermons. The question naturally arises of the degree to which the capitularies were actually enforced. The *Admonitio* in particular reflects that heightened sense of Christian mission which emerged in the late 780s, but it would be wrong to view the ambitious aims which recur in Charlemagne's capitularies as merely idealistic and aspirational rather than practical. The very large number of copies which were made, and the fact that these were distributed across so many regional centres, argue for a fairly effective implementation. In the case of the *Admonitio* alone there are forty manuscript versions, and their geographic spread extends not just across the core Carolingian domain but also into newly assimilated territories in Italy and Bavaria.

Charlemagne's concern with the principles of an orderly government is evident in the capitularies he was issuing even before the 780s. The capitulary of Herstal, issued in 779 following an assembly, contains clauses which affirm the provisions of Pippin III's assemblies and synods, and which ensured that those earlier decisions should now be re-expressed in written form. Charlemagne's concern here would have been to ensure continuity with the administrative details of his father's reign. The same aim explains the issuing of a capitulary for Aquitaine in 768 (or possibly 769) when the then very young king confirmed Pippin's arrangements for the government of that territory. Even at this early stage we can see the emergence of some of the themes that define the reign as a whole. So far as Aquitaine was concerned, the king set out fundamental principles for the reorganization of the Church, confirmed that his subjects enjoyed the right of legal appeal to the king, and gave a job specification for *missi dominici* working in the region. And his concern with the operation of the law courts and with Church discipline in the so-called *Capitulare primum* of c. 770 represents an initial foray into areas of policy and government to which he would return time and again in the decades ahead. Charlemagne's exalted conception of a king's duty is therefore evident right from the word go, and the charters he issued in 769–75 state that a ruler needs to protect both the clergy and the buildings of the Christian Church. His ambitions were formed early and those aims were pursued with a remarkable consistency and tenacity.

THE CHAIN OF COMMAND: *MISSI DOMINICI* AND COUNTS

The king's government remained personalized in the sense that it took its cue from Charlemagne. He was the *fons et origo* of the measures enacted in his name, and he made sure that his officials acted in full knowledge of that fairly intimidating fact. A series of undated notes survives in which Charlemagne records his intention to send letters to the *missi dominici* and the counts telling them where and when they are to congregate for the next assembly. Complaints about the way in which the *missi* and the counts are discharging their official duties should, Charlemagne adds, be reported to him. The capitulary drawn up in 802 states that the *missi*, once having been sent to the different parts of the Frankish empire, should send written reports on their work to Charlemagne, and the document lays stress on the need to keep him regularly informed: 'We wish to know by means of our *missi* now sent out throughout our entire realm . . . how laymen are observing the order for the assembly of the army.' It was not enough therefore just to report that the king's will had been done. Charlemagne wanted an interpretation and a judgment on those bare facts – not just the 'what', then, but also the 'how'. The same capitulary states that in relation to his subjects, and especially the clergy, counts and 'hundredmen', Charlemagne needed to know 'the nature of their obedience to our command and will and also how they have observed our *bannus*, and above all how each is striving to keep himself in God's holy service'.

Hincmar's *De Ordine Palatii* stresses how a Carolingian king used both oral messages and written ones when compiling a list of topics for discussion with his senior courtiers, and the same combination of means was used to instruct the notaries who produced the royal charters. There is certainly every indication in Charlemagne's case that the letters exchanged between the king or his senior officials and other dignitaries were supplemented by oral commands which were communicated in strict confidence to the messengers bearing those documents. Pope Hadrian, for example, sent Charlemagne a letter, carried by two senior clergy, which said that he had provided his envoys with oral instructions about what the king should be told by them concerning the pope's views. Incriminating letters might also be destroyed. Bishop Arn sent Alcuin a letter in 799 which contained a summary of his investigation into the charges of immorality levelled against Pope Leo III. Alcuin told the bishop later that year that he had been careful to burn the letter.

An emphasis on both oral and written instructions is also evident in the circular letter which was drawn up by four of Charlemagne's *missi* in March 806 and then sent to a number of counts who were told that Adalhard and Fulrad, Unruoch and Hrocculf depended on their information in order to compile the written reports expected by the king. The counts should 're-read their capitularies' in order to check that they had done what was expected of them, and they also needed to remember what they had been told orally. The names of rebels and dissidents should be listed by the counts, and that intelligence could be either sent in writing or communicated verbally to the *missi*. If there were any further questions, the counts could send their own envoys to the *missi* who would then provide clarification. Further up the chain of command lay the king himself who, in another document, tells one of the *missi* that questions relating to legal procedure which cannot be answered by consulting the textbooks of either Roman or Frankish law should be raised at a general assembly.

Missi were therefore an important link between the king and his counts who, nonetheless, could and did make their views known to the king directly. In 811 some of them complained to Charlemagne that they were experiencing difficulties in enforcing military conscription and that too many of his subjects were going directly to the *missi* rather than to the counts when seeking redress of grievances. This may reflect the particular circumstances at the end of the reign when Charlemagne was more or less settled in Aachen. The *missi* were always in regular contact with the king, and by this late stage they were therefore a much more reliable channel of communication for those who needed to present their case to Charlemagne than the counts based in the various regions of the Carolingian empire.

The role played by the *missi dominici* in Charlemagne's government was further defined in the years immediately following the imperial coronation of 800. He had made use of their offices since the beginning of the reign but the arrival of an imperial title may account for the desire to explain in some detail the pattern of their contribution to the king's success. One annalist commented on how the standing of these high officials meant that they did not need to solicit gifts, and he judged that the presence of the *missi* at the heart of government showed Charlemagne's determination to fight bribery. The administrative capitulary issued in 802 is a justly celebrated document and represents Charlemagne's programmatic view of his kingdom's government. Its preamble states that the *optimates* whom he sent out as *missi* were a means by which the king 'confirmed to all his subjects the right to live according to the appropriate body of law'. That confirmation could clearly involve some pretty direct action. The Herstal Capitulary of 779 stated that if a count was accused of failing to administer justice he was to receive an extended visitation from a *missus dominicus* and 'he is to have the needs of our *missus* provided for from his household until justice has been done'. Administration of justice entailed that the *missi* acted as appeal judges. They delivered sentences in the king's name and administered oaths, but the *missi* were also meant to keep an eye on local officials and clergy, and to make sure that secular and spiritual duties were properly performed. Armed with copies of the king's capitularies and his letters, and charged with the duty of implementing the commands expressed in those documents, the *missi* were the single most important element in Charlemagne's network of communications.

The arrangements outlined in 802 involved a major development with the creation of an administrative unit termed the *missiaticum*, and within each such area two *missi*, one lay and one clerical, were to operate in tandem. Rouen comprised one such *missiaticum*, and the maintenance of the area's coastal defence system and harbour was part of the duties expected of Count Madelgaud and the local archbishop, Magenaud.

The 802 capitulary associated Charlemagne with the general cause of justice as so many of its predecessors had done, but it was also highly specific in some of its commands. The explicit way in which cases involving murder were said to be reserved for the courts, for example, may well indicate Charlemagne's awareness of the danger of vengeance killings, and there is a strong personal flavour to certain other clauses too. Charlemagne complains, for example, about the way poachers have been stealing game from the royal forests. The king's personal recollection of how a man called Fricco had committed incest with a nun may explain why that detail is included in the clause specifying punishment for incest. Individual capitulary clauses such as these show the king's mind at work, interpreting justice, clarifying policy goals, and cajoling in a highly individual way. But there were many other means, quite apart from the capitularies, which could be used by Charlemagne when he wanted to express his views and assert his command. Like any other king in the early medieval west Charlemagne relied on mandates which instructed individual agents as well as the letters and seals which communicated the royal intention and were sent to the nobility.

The oral command of kings was another important feature of early medieval government in general, and that practice was linked to the monarch's function as a declaratory law-giver on the Solomonic model. Charlemagne was the supreme example of both. No one who had eyes to see and ears to hear could doubt the royal will, having been in the presence of the king when he gave expression to the law of his realm, and that personalized fiat was particularly relevant for a society in which only a tiny minority were literate. Oral messages must also have been the basis of the daily activities that were carried out at Charlemagne's court. The annalists and notaries who worked there, as well as the royal agents who waited at the palace for their instructions, were all dependent for their information on the couriers (*veredarii*) and envoys who arrived at court and told them what was going on in the other parts of the realm.

The kings of this period had indeed a whole network of agents who worked on their behalf and were located in regions far away from the palace. Controlling them could be a problem, though. Alfred had only a small kingdom to run in Wessex but even so he had to work hard to get his ealdormen, thegns and royal estate managers to do what was expected of them, and he often complained about their tardiness. Charlemagne, in one of his capitularies, urged that the heads of villages (*maiores*) be recruited 'not from among the *potentiores*, but from the middling ranks [*mediocres*] who are faithful'. Estate managers in Charlemagne's realm had to report to the village heads three times a year and present accounts, but this requirement did not stop complaints of corruption. Many such officials were related to local nobles who might have made illegal financial demands on their kin and creamed off some of the profits from land cultivation.

Counts formed an important layer of Carolingian government as intermediaries between king and people, a role which was largely continuous with the origins of the office in the later Roman empire when the *comites* were the emperor's personal agents. Carolingian counts were meant to keep the peace locally by presiding over courts and prosecuting crimes. They were also charged with looking after the royal estates located within their areas and with assembling the local soldiery when the king went to war. They had their equivalents elsewhere. The ealdormen of Wessex and other Anglo-Saxon kingdoms raised armies on behalf of the king. That same duty was discharged in Lombardy by dukes (*duces*), a rank of officialdom distinguished from the *gastaldi* who looked after the estates of Lombard kings.

Whether beyond Francia's boundaries or within it, the reality of power on the ground could be pretty murky. In 811, for example, some of the Carolingian counts complained of a widespread refusal to obey their summons to war and alleged that many of the king's subjects preferred to obey their local lords. Countships themselves differed widely. Those located east of the Rhine, where there was no antecedent structure of Roman *civitates*, were Carolingian creations. Lands which constituted an individual countship in this area were often widely scattered and existed alongside the component parts of other, similarly dispersed, countships. Some counts were real magnates while others were merely local lords, and some countships could be held in plurality by a single great aristocrat. On the boundaries of the empire several counts could share responsibility for the frontier area (the march or mark) and these *marchiones* are the ancestors of the later marquesses.

Carolingian kings tried hard to persuade counts that they were royal office-holders first and foremost, but countships tended to become hereditary and power was exercised therefore through local dynasties. Those chosen to be counts usually already owned lands in the relevant area. The additional territories they were allocated, and in which they exercised power on behalf of the king, tended to become assimilated to their own. This privatization of what had once been public was a significant aspect of Carolingian history in the eighth and ninth centuries, with the counts allocating lands in turn to the various subordinates (viscounts) who were often their relatives. This safeguarding of the local nobility's position was especially noticeable in the newly assimilated territories. The aristocracies of Alamannia and of the Lombard kingdom were allowed to keep their regions' laws, and Bavarian law actually gained a new authority as a result of its incorporation in a written code. Things changed in this regard towards the end of our period. Western European law became increasingly territorial in expression in the course of the ninth century, and it therefore applied to all those living within a certain area. Before then, however, the idea persisted that law was the possession of a people and, since it was the local nobility who provided that *gens* with its leadership, legal codes and customs retained a strongly personal flavour.

Counts needed watching, therefore. When appointing a count's successor Carolingian kings could hardly ignore the claims of male heirs or, in their absence, the rights of close kin. But the *missi dominici* were very useful to kings in this regard and could be used to check up on what the counts and their families were getting up to. As members of the higher nobility who already had a track record of service as counts, the *missi* would often arrive armed with local knowledge as well as the king's authority. That was a powerful combination. Charlemagne's *missi* ensured that reliable people were chosen to serve in comital courts, and he also used them to recruit the personnel who considered the redress of grievances in legal cases involving counts who had abused their powers. Even more strikingly, those nobles who failed to attend local assemblies convened by the *missi* were placed on a blacklist which was then sent to Charlemagne himself. A particular feature of *missi* investigations was the *inquisitiones* which were held on the spot and involved locals giving sworn testimony. This is what probably happened in 865 in Alamannia when the *missi* overrode the decision of a local count who had confiscated property on the grounds of a landowner's incest.

Bishops could also be selected as *missi* and their duties in that role often included the supervision of mints and the organization of oath-taking ceremonies. Abbots, whether they were laymen or clergy, enjoyed immunity on the lands under their control and so they presided in person at court sessions held to settle disputes which had arisen on the territories within their jurisdiction. Bishops, abbots and abbesses also supplemented the counts' efforts in the business of raising armies. Senior clergy would muster troops on their lands, provision them with military equipment, and then send them off to fight for the king. Archbishops were magnates in their own right and exercised powers over the counts who operated within their regions.

Another category of individuals helpful to Carolingian rulers was their *vassi*, men whom they had endowed with lands and who therefore stood in a relation of personal obligation to them. *Vassus* originally meant a boy but the word also came to describe this particular kind of royal agent. That derivation may record the Franks' idea of a joke. The *vassi* were clearly distinguished from counts either great or small, and the absence of any overlap suggests that most *vassi* were recruited from an intermediate social grouping, that of the *mediocres*. These men's activities suggest that they were often in attendance on Carolingian kings, since the *vassi* helped them make legal judgments and were frequently used as diplomatic envoys. We have an account, for example, of six of them swearing on behalf of Lothair II in 863 that he would treat his wife 'as a king should a queen'. But these agents were also at work in the provinces: in 869 Charles the Bald asked his *vassi* in each county to check up on the number of benefices (or lands) held by counts in order to calculate contributions to the cost of building fortifications on the Seine.

A count who was not up to the job was in practice difficult to get rid of although in times of real crisis a king could strip him of his lands and send him into exile. But the political situation had to be grave for this to happen since so extreme a *dishonoratio* might be taken to demonstrate a king's weakness rather than his strength. The only examples of such reprisals that survive in the historical record were imposed because of outright rebellion and treason: Charlemagne after 792, Louis the Pious after 818 and 833, Charles the Bald after 858, Louis the German in 861, and Charles the Fat in 883. Alfred may have done something similar after 878, the year in which he had been threatened simultaneously both by a Danish army and by noble dissidence in Wessex. But royal caution meant that kings had to justify such extreme actions. Einhard is noticeably keen to point out that the rebels who were killed on Charlemagne's orders in 786 only suffered their fate because they resisted arrest and drew swords. Charles the Bald ensured the execution of rebels and went so far as to blind the bishop who was of their number, but was careful to follow the correct legal form appropriate to treason 'by judgment of the Franks'.

THE KING'S JUSTICE: LAW, CRIME AND PUNISHMENT

Alfred's kingdom of Wessex, because of its tiny size, is one of early medieval Europe's best examples of a royal domain where legal force was fused with kingly presence. People here stood a good chance of actually seeing their king. But Francia was a different matter and with the Carolingian empire spreading over 463,000 square miles at its greatest extent during the first half of the ninth century, most of those territories were never visited by the kings who ruled them. There are a few examples of itinerant hyperactivity: in the three months of autumn 852 Louis the German travelled from Bavaria to Mainz in order to settle local disputes, returned to Bavaria, went north through the Rhineland to Saxony to adjudicate in more local disputes, and then returned to Regensburg in time for Christmas. This, though, was a wholly exceptional period of extensive travel in Louis's life and for the rest of his reign he hardly ever visited Saxony. Brittany, although an extreme example, shows the remoteness of Carolingian power since here the dynasty devolved jurisdiction to regional princes who were, effectively, sub-kings. By stages between the 830s and the 860s their titles changed, and advanced, from that of *missi* to *reges*. These local Breton rulers acknowledged the Carolingians as their overlords but within that overall structure they exercised their own rights of public jurisdiction. A similar situation existed east of the Rhine where the Carolingians had to reconcile themselves to the persistent power of the local lords who exercised public jurisdiction, albeit doing so in the king's name. A *missus* who sat in his capacity as a judge in his own local county had the power to issue judgment in a case brought against himself. A common enough such case might involve a serf who was trying to persuade the court that he was of free, and not servile, status. The plaintiff would have been presenting his case to a court filled with community leaders who were beholden in various ways to the local magnate, and the judgment can rarely have been in doubt. What steps, therefore, did Charlemagne take to ensure the operation of the king's justice, and how did the administration of his law buttress the king's authority?

Discontented plaintiffs and defendants could console themselves that the most important court of all was the one held in the palace itself, a building most easily defined as the place where one might find the king. Pressure of judicial business, according to Einhard, meant that Charlemagne started on the work of hearing cases as soon as he got out of bed in the early morning. The palace was a public space, which is why access to it was made available to the many individuals, including peasants, who came there seeking the redress of grievances. Those seeking to understand what they meant by the word palace often harked back to Rome. Hincmar in his *De Ordine Palatii* said it was 'nowadays in normal use to mean [what in antiquity had been called] the *praetorium*', the term signifying the headquarters of a Roman military commander and which then evolved to describe both the emperor's headquarters and the residence of a provincial governor (*procurator*). The word's military and civilian connotations are equally important and a king's failure to maintain order in this space betokened a wider loss of authority. The palace murder in 893 of a major noble who was close to Arnulf of east Francia was considered shocking because it was done without royal authority, and the disorder of Louis the Pious's palace reflected, in the estimation of the time, the king's lack of authority in the Frankish empire. Charlemagne's rigorous control of his own palace and court was a crucial aspect of his reputation for consistent judgment and firm command.

One remarkable feature of Charlemagne's government in relation to the conquered territories is the extent to which he allowed the native population to keep their legal systems. We have already seen how that helped to support the position of the local aristocracies, but this form of legal devolution also had a wider social application. The policy set out for Aquitaine in 768–9 stated that all those living there, whether they were immigrant Franks or members of the original Roman population, were to be allowed to use their own laws. This was a far-reaching concession and the principle underlying it is usually referred to as that of the 'personality of the law': a legal code was the possession of the entire people among whom it had originated and who were bound by its provisions. The validity of the principle, still very much alive and kicking in Charlemagne's time, was unaffected by the geographical fact of where an individual subject happened to be at any one time. If he travelled from his native region to live in another area he still had the right to use the laws of his own people. Those of Charlemagne's Franks who had moved to Aquitaine were therefore bound by the laws of their own people and not by the Roman law which prevailed in the territory where they had now settled. That particular application might seem to benefit the Franks, but the principle would be extended to apply right across Charlemagne's enlarged kingdom.

The native population of Aquitaine, the Lombards, Bavarians and Saxons, were among Charlemagne's newly acquired subject peoples who continued to be governed according to their established laws in their own native territories. Crucially, those who belonged to such *gentes* could still use these same law codes even though they might have moved to another area within the Carolingian kingdom and empire. Charlemagne also made provision for the updating of these local laws and he clearly regarded the maintenance of pre-existing legal systems as a way of consolidating the unity of his enlarged kingdom. By this process of renewing the local laws Charlemagne was also ensuring that, in many cases, they were also being written down for the first time in their history. If this was a recognition of what was appropriate in particular circumstances and places, its effects were also cleverly inclusive and assimilationist. Having been revised and issued anew, these codes were now also Charlemagne's laws and a testimony to the authority of his kingdom.

The extent to which the king and his administrators intervened to support legal rights as they existed before the introduction of a Carolingian regime is particularly striking in the case of Bavaria. Some local aristocrats had sought to benefit from the political uncertainty in the duchy during the period of Charlemagne's takeover and they had encroached on the rights of some of the region's monasteries and episcopal foundations. Charlemagne and his officials ensured, however, that these establishments were issued with charters confirming their pre-existing legal rights. Saxony is something of a test case of the Franks' willingness to tolerate established legal customs and practices, given the notorious brutality displayed in conquering the region. And yet, they seem to have respected the antecedent legal customs of the Saxons. That was a fairly remarkable concession although it is also fair to note that the Franks enforced those pre-existing provisions with conqueror's zeal.

The first Saxon capitulary has been dated to 785 and is notorious for a tough-minded determination to extirpate paganism. Even so, the document allowed for the continuance of some native customs such as the penalties which were due for perjury according to Saxon law. A successor document dealing with government in Saxony was issued in 797, and that capitulary followed on from an assembly which had been held in Aachen on 28 October of that year. Saxons had been included by the Franks in those discussions. One clause, for example, states that the Saxons had themselves consented to a new scale for legal fines: where Franks had to pay fifteen *solidi*, aristocratic Saxons would pay twelve, freemen had to pay six and the more dependent class of *liti* or peasants paid three. The arrangements relating to the Saxons' fines reaffirmed the provisions of their own laws, and the prescribed penalties could only be changed as a result of a direct appeal to the king himself.

Carolingian kings also relied on provincial power-brokers when they were trying to ensure good order within Francia itself. An oath taken in the west Francia of 853 by the hundredmen (*centenarii*) reveals the existence of a category of freemen, the *Franci homines*, who undertook to report on criminal activity and hunt down the guilty. Charlemagne asked his *missi* to provide him with lists of reliable locals who would deliver miscreants up to justice in this way. Alfred in Wessex similarly stressed the keeping of oaths and he decreed that those involved in a feud should seek a legal resolution before attacking their adversaries. Our period is one in which it became a king's duty to uphold the peace within his realm, and sovereigns tried to co-opt subjects who might become their effective allies in that challenging enterprise. In military matters as well, and in the declaration of war, there was a striking series of equations made between the commands of kings, the safety of the nation and the needs of subjects. In 864 Charles the Bald laid down the death penalty for those who failed to 'come to the defence of the fatherland'. Alfred's Laws are particularly relevant to this theme of patriotic defence since they imposed a double compensation for attacks made on the fortified residences of a king or an archbishop, of bishops, ealdormen, nobles and ceorls, 'when the army had been called out'. Kings had to protect their subjects' properties at all periods but wartime imposed on them an additional obligation, one which recognized the development of a new identity which bonded king and people, the ruler and the ruled.

No account of government in early medieval Europe would be complete without an assessment of the Church's increased authority and its impact on how kings ruled their subjects. Ecclesiastical power meant greater social influence and from the eighth century onwards it was, for example, the Church itself as a body which legislated on marital questions rather than individual holy men. There were now definitions of the degree of kinship within which marriage was impermissible, and that sacrament had to be administered publicly. A wedding was therefore a very social occasion and one which could hardly take place without the knowledge of the wider family and the local community. With so many people being informed and involved there was thus far less risk of a marriage turning out to be an incestuous alliance.

The Church's prohibitions applied equally to nobles and non-nobles, and the private lives of kings therefore changed in order to conform to new norms of sexual behaviour. Members of the royal family in Merovingian times had kept concubines and repudiated their wives, practices which were increasingly condemned by Church councils. Kings were now expected to observe monogamy as well as advocate it to their subjects. Church canons relating to sexual restraint were incorporated by kings into their own legislation, and the fact that both rulers and ruled were bound by the same prohibitions was one aspect of the new bond which united them. Charlemagne's concubines are therefore something of a throw-back to ancient customs as well as illustrating the latitude the king allowed himself in his private life. Nonetheless, the dynasty's authority was intimately bound up with its acceptance of Church teaching, and its readiness to promulgate those counsels gave Carolingian kings the right to act as leaders of Latin Christendom.

Acceptance by kings of a new authority over their subjects also implied a new duty to protect them. This reciprocity is an important feature of Charlemagne's reign and it is very evident in the oaths that were sworn by his subjects. We shall see later on what the king expected of them in this regard, but his side of the bargain did nonetheless carry its own obligations. The oath imposed in 793 made it clear that acceptance of lordship, on Charlemagne's terms, also meant the protection of freedoms. *Missi* were sent to explain to his subjects that the king was 'well aware that many complain that their law had not been kept for them; and that it is totally the will of the lord king that each man should have his law [*lex sua*] fully kept'. The king asked for a further oath of fidelity in 802, two years after accepting the imperial title's responsibilities. It was perhaps those new circumstances which now impelled him to explain in greater detail what exactly he meant by *lex sua*. The oath, said Charlemagne, meant that his subjects accepted that they should do nothing that might harm 'the *honor* of the realm' and that they had to be faithful 'as a man in right ought to be to his lord'. A further document of about the same time contains Charlemagne's prohibition against anyone abandoning his lord once the gift of a shilling, a symbol of lordship, had been accepted. But it is the document's definition of exceptions to that rule which make it so interesting and revealing of the king's attitudes. A subject was absolved of his duties if 'his lord seeks to kill him, or assaults him with a stave, or debauches his wife or daughter, or takes away his allodial property'. A man's *lex*, in other words, gave him a right to life, immunity from violence against his person, power over his immediate female relatives, and the right to protect his patrimony.

One notable feature of the reign is the rarity of rebellion in the core Frankish territories that comprised the original kingdom and also in most of the contiguous areas (with the exception of Saxony) which were conquered and assimilated. Charlemagne's regime was frequently intrusive, as we have seen, and there was surely therefore plenty of scope for the kind of grievances which might have led to large-scale rejection of his authority. Count Hardrad seems to have led a significant rebellion in 785 since it is described in the sources as a *coniuratio*, and so oaths would have been sworn by the dissidents involved. But there is little indication of the plot having much of an effect, and the same is true of the 792 rebellion involving 'Pippin the Hunchback', Charlemagne's eldest son by his first wife Himiltrude. The *Annales Regni Francorum* do not even bother to give any details of Pippin's scheming, though another source claims that he was reacting against the cruelty of his stepmother Fastrada who was Charlemagne's queen at the time. That claim is a reliable pointer to a family quarrel, and the fact that Charlemagne changed the name of his second son by Queen Hildegard from Carloman to Pippin in 781 would have been resented by 'the Hunchback' since this clear act of favouritism threatened his rights of inheritance. One annalist claims that Pippin rebelled because he wished to seize the throne for himself. But a personal grudge, if that is indeed what motivated him, failed to elicit much support. A Lombard noble called Fardulf discovered the plot and, having informed the king, he was rewarded with the office of abbot of St-Denis. Pippin's co-conspirators were arrested and those who were not beheaded were hanged. He himself was sent off to Prum abbey where he died eighteen years later. It is doubtful whether Pippin would have agreed with Einhard who tells us, in his summary of these events, that the rebel always did have an inclination towards the monastic life.

The revolt mounted in 786 by a group of nobles based in Thuringia was an altogether more serious affair, and the treatment meted out to the ringleaders shows that there was a dark side to the Carolingian idea of justice. The Thuringians were first of all tried in a court of law, found guilty, and then forgiven by the king. Accompanied by some of Charlemagne's *missi*, they were then sent by him to various locations: 'some into Italy and to St Peter and some into Neustria and Aquitaine . . . to the tombs of saints so that they might swear fidelity to the king and his children. And this they are attested to have done.' The anonymous narrator may have been a Thuringian and there is more than a hint of sympathy in his description of the grim fate that awaited these unfortunate men. 'Several of them were arrested on their return journey . . . Their eyes are known to have been torn out. Some however reached the city of Worms and were arrested there and sent into exile and their eyes are known to have been torn out there. And all their possessions and estates are known to have been confiscated by the crown.' There is no surviving record of why these Thuringians decided to take up arms against Charlemagne, though the report of what one of them said to him is vivid enough: 'If my confederates and associates had proved to be of my sentiments, never again would you have been seen crossing this side of the Rhine alive.'

What happened in Thuringia was exceptional. The Frankish bureaucracy did of course control the official history of Charlemagne's reign. And that iron grip ensured that what survives is for the most part a series of acclamations for the spread of Carolingian justice and an acceptance by Charlemagne's subjects of a governing dispensation which was benign in its effects and well ordered in its structures. Even when we have allowed for this smoothing out of the historical record, however, it is surely remarkable that the reign did not witness any more serious rebellions other than the ones just described, especially given the length of Charlemagne's reign and the geographical spread of his territories. The success was real enough and so was the orchestration of assent, that whole panoply of legitimacy which surrounded Charlemagne and which made any alternative to his rule seem increasingly improbable the longer he sat on the throne of the Franks. Oaths which were sworn to the king in explicit acknowledgment of his right to rule were fundamental to that process, and these explicit rituals can be seen as the highest expression of the authority attained by Charlemagne as king and emperor.

HOW TO BE OBEYED: THE USEFULNESS OF OATHS

The idea that oaths of loyalty should be expected of all Charlemagne's leading subjects, both lay and clerical, seems to have surfaced for the first time in March 789. The king and his officials had found the issue of Duke Tassilo's supposed breaking of oaths to be politically expedient when arranging for the takeover of Bavaria in the previous year. This may explain why the idea gained favour as a way of enhancing Charlemagne's authority in general. But although the wording of a text was agreed upon, little seems to have been done to enforce it.

Pippin's conspiracy of 792 would have concentrated minds and in the spring of the following year, following an assembly held at Regensburg, it was agreed that an oath of fidelity should be sworn to the king and his sons. The *missi* were charged with the duty of administering the oath in their particular areas and they were also provided with notes which they could refer to when explaining the necessity of this ritual. Frankish antiquarianism played a useful role in this regard, and the *missi* were instructed to say that oaths of loyalty were an ancient custom of the tribe. A more relevant explanation was also contained in these notes:

some recent conspirators had pleaded in their defence that they had never been obliged to swear an oath to Charlemagne, and that they were therefore innocent of any *infidelitas* when organizing their dissent. The oath which was subsequently imposed in 793, and whose necessity was reiterated after the Frankfurt assembly and synod of the year following, applied to the upper ranks of Carolingian society: the counts and also those landowners who were the king's vassals, since they had received their estates or 'benefices' directly from him. It also applied to bishops, abbots and some of the lesser clergy such as archdeacons.

The decision to impose another oath was taken in 802 and its details are contained in the great capitulary issued in that same year. This general oath was imposed on the great majority of Charlemagne's subjects and its wording makes this one of the most astonishingly rigorous of all his instruments of government. All those who had promised fidelity in 793 to Charlemagne as king now had to repeat a comparable oath to him as emperor. And the oath also now applied to a whole new category, namely all freemen over the age of twelve. Charlemagne was thus expecting all males within his kingdom and empire who were capable of swearing an oath of loyalty to do so. The requirement that this should be done on saints' relics intensified the Christian symbolism which runs through this highly explicit exaltation of the king as a focus, under God, of the kingdom's unity. The capitulary details the oath's implications, and those administering the oath were expected to explain those same details to Charlemagne's subjects. Fidelity meant protecting the emperor's life, not giving help to his enemies, and not keeping silent when aware of treacherous plots. It also meant avoiding cheating the emperor financially and involved an agreement not to obstruct the payment of those rents and dues which were properly his. Those who took the oath were not to neglect any benefice received from Charlemagne. They were equally bound not to evade military service, not to oppose or ignore any of the emperor's commands and intentions, and not to impede the implementation of his justice. Fidelity involved the service of God, and not harming any churches, widows, orphans or pilgrims.

The 802 oath also entailed a commitment by each subject 'to maintain himself in God's holy service, according to God's command and his own promise; for the lord emperor cannot himself provide the necessary care and discipline for each man individually'. This latter notion seems particularly extravagant, even by the standards of early medieval Christian kingship. The emperor declared himself to be responsible for the spiritual welfare of his subjects. Being a busy ruler, however, he could not be relied upon to be on hand to guide their spiritual development. Any back-sliding in Christian conduct signified nonetheless a betrayal of the king, and those guilty of such a transgression had committed an act of treason.

The oath devised and administered in 802 identified Charlemagne's commands with God's will, and its framework of political and moral obligation was based on divine sanction. Religious duties were politicized to a degree never before seen in western Europe. The requirement to protect the Church was now an aspect of the fidelity owed to Charlemagne by his subjects. Previous rulers such as the Roman emperors of classical antiquity had inveighed against treasonable acts and conspiracies. They had as a matter of course enforced oaths to protect themselves in that regard. But this latest initiative of Charlemagne's was the first oath which made *not* doing something into an explicit act of treason. It was now disloyal not to look after property which had been Charlemagne's gift, and any acts of commission or of omission which harmed his economic interests were deemed to be treachery. The preservation of his rule and kingship had now become completely fused with the need to protect all aspects of social, political, moral and religious order within the imperial domain. Anyone who harmed any aspect of that order was therefore attacking Charlemagne personally and would be punished accordingly.

We have seen the importance of Constantine's legacy as a guiding inspiration for the Carolingian achievement in the arts of government. But not even the example of that great precursor could furnish Charlemagne with precedents for the 802 oath and its complete identification of an emperor's rights and duties with those of his subjects.

It is conventional enough to portray Charlemagne as a ruler who stood at the apex of a hierarchical society which was composed of different orders and strata, but the relationship that he achieved with his subjects was more intimate than the one suggested by such an analogy.

Only a very small number of them of course ever set eyes on him, but that hardly mattered since he entered their lives in so many other powerful ways. Counts and *missi dominici* explained his views and decisions when they were administering Charlemagne's justice and enforcing his oaths. The solidarity of his subjects was maintained and furthered through their loyalty to a ruler who was the embodiment and guarantor of the political and social order. Prayers were said for him in the liturgy of the Frankish Church. Special masses were said and collective fasts observed when extraordinary threats, such as famines, endangered the entire realm. Prayer associations organized by the Church authorities had existed in Francia since the reign of Pippin III, and in Charlemagne's time they assumed increasing importance as a way of bringing people together and affirming his subjects' collective identity. Institutional power and social practices alike showed the monarchy bonding with the nation. This would prove to be the most vital aspect of Charlemagne's achievements in government.

CHARLEMAGNE'S LEGACY: THE NEW EUROPEAN NATIONS

In 843 Charles the Bald gave his own interpretation of what oaths meant. His *fideles*, he said, had promised to uphold the king's *honor* and, consequently, Charles would deprive no man of his *honor* without due cause. Each of his *fideles* would keep his own due law according to his rank and status: '*lex competens . . . in omni dignitate et ordine*'. Other documents from the mid-ninth century record the importance of this idea that different social ranks share the obligations and rights which correspond to their status. Carolingian kings who are also brothers are defined as '*pares*' (peers) and the *fideles* are described as having their own peers, individuals on whose support they could rely if any one of them was imperilled by the king's actions. There is a clear sense here of political action as a collective enterprise, and that notion acquires an increasingly explicit expression in the ninth-century vision of how the different social orders come together to participate in public life. Their commitment in that regard carries with it both responsibilities and benefits, and Hincmar's description of a collective body, the *universitas*, which acts through assemblies and kings for the good of the realm as a whole, shows we are now in a different world from that of the eighth century.

Charlemagne had told his subjects that 'everyone should personally strive to maintain himself in God's service, because the lord emperor cannot himself provide the necessary care and discipline for each man individually'. But his son Louis the Pious had a far more ambitious plan in view when he committed 'ourself, our sons, and our colleagues [socii] in the administration of this realm' to the task of ensuring that 'peace and justice be kept among our whole people [generalitas]'. The king was quite clear about the ministerium or office which 'rests in our person'. Both the 'divine authority' and the governmental structures (ordinatio) of the day, he says, support that exalted status. But Louis also went on to argue that the ministerium was 'divided into shares so that each of you in his place and in his own ordo, has a share in our office, so that I am the adviser of you all, and all of you need to be my assistants'. These remarks may have been addressed in particular to the king's counts since he refers to an oath they have taken and which obliges them to be 'the ruler's helper and the people's preserver'. But Louis has all his subjects in mind when he tells them to observe mutual 'love and peace, and to show honour to his representatives [missi]'.

The king's declaration stressed therefore the need for mutual support among the governing orders and the idea of a common good which was served by that co-operation. Louis's successors made similar noises about the communis utilitas later in the ninth century. Quite frequently the context was one in which co-operation was endangered and therefore had to be emphasized through public statements. The conflicts of the early 840s led directly to the Strasbourg Oaths. This extraordinary series of documents records the aristocracy's resolve to underwrite the oaths made by Carolingian kings to one another, as well as their threat to withdraw obedience on a collective basis if the monarchs broke those same oaths. Later on in the 850s we find Charles the Bald and his entourage referring to the political advice and military support (consilium et auxilium) which ought to be the concern of all faithful people who concerned themselves with the honor of the kingdom as a whole. That concept of the regnum is what was uppermost by now in the minds of the royal circle rather than just the duties which individuals owed their king. *Societas* has emerged as a key word and a distinctive idea, the basis of a notion of statehood which looked backwards for its authority as well as anticipating future developments. It was the Theodosian Code which inspired Charles to declare in 861 that 'all without exception had to come to the defence of the *patria*'. If the king decided instead to yield and pay tribute to attackers, then that too involved a common obligation, and all Charles's subjects, he declared, should contribute to the payment. The comprehensive spread of that financial burden among urban dwellers and countrymen, Jews and Christians, traders, peasants and serfs, reflected the wider conception of the nation which was now taking root as the basis of government.

Beside the new assertiveness we must also place the reality of political and military danger. Charles had to make these novel demands on his subjects because of the external threats and internal dissidence which plagued him persistently during his reign as king of the western Franks, problems which his grandfather Charlemagne did not have to contend with. But if Charles's position was, in one sense, weaker than that of his Carolingian predecessors, it was also, in another way, stronger since he clearly felt able to call on new resources of national loyalty in order to meet the challenges of his time. A strengthened public authority was now justified in terms of its capacity to serve the nation, and the aristocratic pursuit of *honor* had veered in the same direction since it too had become linked with the public good.

Honor had originally meant high office in the gift of the king and the word was subsequently used to describe the lands which had been granted by the ruler. But the word's association with royal patronage remained constant and that linkage of ideas reinforced the primary meaning of *honor* as signifying rank or status. Royal authority, the maintenance of order and social ambition: all these forces combined together to ensure that it was the public authority of king and government which legitimized the social standing of the ambitious. The *Vita Ermelandi* makes the point rather well when it describes the motivations of the saint's parents. They introduced Ermelandus to the court 'and commended him to the king of the Franks to serve in the military household with great *honor* so that by the pathway of this service he could attain the due *honor* of his ancestors'. Ermelandus is a seventh-century figure but his life was written in the west Francia of c. 800 and its vocabulary reflects the contemporary aristocratic acceptance of the idea that *honor* was gained by public service.

The business of government for a ninth-century Carolingian king was still dominated by the needs of war although consolidation of frontiers meant that warfare was not the constant preoccupation it had been for earlier kings of the Franks. Louis the Pious's official portrayal as a soldier of Christ, *miles Christi*, records an important change in this regard since the image shows him holding the Cross standard rather than a sword. This was one aspect of the increasing specialization within the elite. Kings retained overall direction of military strategy, and they were the only ones with the right to declare public war (*bellum*) – a concept sharply distinguished from the private conflicts (*werrae*) which it was also their duty to suppress. But they now had generals to whom they might delegate the actual business of fighting. There were occasions when Charles the Bald led his armies into battle, just as Charlemagne had done in the past, but on the whole Charles was more concerned with royal government's political, judicial and courtly aspects. The *Annales Bertiniani* for 865 describe how Count Robert, having defeated a Viking army, handed over to Charles the standards and weapons of the conquered, and the king's role, in a scene such as this, corresponds to a later Roman emperor's mostly civilian status.

Martial imagery continued to provide royal government with resonant motifs and the sword was the most important symbol of a nobleman's *honor*. A Carolingian capitulary prescribed that each horseman had to be equipped with a sword, and a fresco painted on the walls of a church at Mals in the Dolomites shows the noble patron offering his sword to Christ. Swords were a visible definition of status and the Bretons who surrendered to Charlemagne in 799 handed theirs over, with their names inscribed on them, 'for it was by these weapons that each one of them yielded himself, land and people'. A nobleman found guilty in a court of law might be subject to a range of penalties but the one that perhaps hit him hardest was the symbolic stripping of his noble status by being deprived of his sword and belt – a punishment which was prescribed for a variety of offences, including homicide.

Ritual was no mere question of form but an assertion of power, a means of social control, and a technique of fundamental importance to the practice of Carolingian government. Some of the ninth-century capitularies prescribe the *harmscar*, a public humiliation involving the carrying of a saddle on the miscreant's shoulders, as a penalty for non-performance of public duties. The great political occasions of that period paid an increasing attention to ritual. Bishops, being both liturgical specialists and public figures, played a prominent role at such events. After the battle of Fontenoy, fought in 841 between Louis the Pious's heirs, and a prelude to the Carolingian partition at Verdun two years later, bishops were asked to perform rites of reconciliation. And it was an episcopal pronouncement of 842 which declared that Lothair had forfeited his kingship since he lacked the 'knowledge for governing the state'. Ordeals – a specialized and theatrical blend of religious and political ritual – were performed under ecclesiastical supervision in order to ascertain God's will. Louis the Younger, king in east Francia, resorted to them when he was threatened by his uncle Charles the Bald in 876.

Rituals performed by the clergy helped the Carolingian dynasty therefore to defuse the consequences of its own internal divisions. God having, as it were, spoken, quarrels had to be shelved. But rituals also had a more positive role to play and a king's authority could be enhanced by court feasts and processions as well as by the prescribed order of the assemblies. Carolingian kings turned to senior churchmen to help them invent such ceremonies, and one of the most significant is Charles the Bald's inauguration in 869 when he acquired the 'middle kingdom' of Lothair II, an area west of the Rhine and extending from the North Sea to the Alps. This is the first king-making ceremony whose details survive in full, and its rituals were designed to remind Charles's subjects of their common Frankish identity. Hincmar of Reims consecrated the king with the oil that Remigius, that great apostle to the Franks, was supposed to have used when he baptized his most significant convert, Clovis. From that moment onwards, say the *Annales Fuldenses* for 869, Charles 'ordered himself to be called emperor and *augustus* as one who was to possess two kingdoms'. On Christmas Day 875 he was crowned emperor by the pope in Rome in the course of a ceremony whose details, timing and location recalled in the most self-conscious manner possible his grandfather's coronation seventy-five years previously.

The kingdoms of western Europe as they emerged in the course of the ninth century were new creations and their boundaries corresponded to cultural identities which were clearer than they had been a century previously. It was now possible to distinguish between the civilizations of Scandinavia and those of the Germans who, in turn, were clearly different from their Frankish cousins to the west, the French. Within the British Isles the cultures of England, Wales and Scotland were becoming almost as distinctively different as that of the island of Ireland. Iberian and Italian civilization was divided into a profusion of autonomous polities, and the same is true of what would later be called 'France' and 'Germany'. Language, that key denominator of national identity, was playing an important role in all such European regions. Here again the mosaic was immensely varied but by the middle of the ninth century it is clear that Latin had ceased to be a spoken language and was now growing into the different Romance languages which are the ancestors of modern French, Spanish and Italian.

Because they were so new, west European kingdoms had to claim that they were old. The governments of kings were self-conscious about their novelty, especially when compared to the ancient Roman *imperium* which tended to be the standard by which they measured themselves. Ritual was helpful because it masked the reality of a recent arrival. The birth of nations was therefore attended by ceremonies which proclaimed them to be already venerable. Such an assertion of antiquity amounted to more than mere antiquarianism since it was used by the governing orders to try to persuade the governed that they shared a common identity which was both ancient and vital, historic and contemporary. That was why Charles the Bald harked back to Charlemagne's *renovatio*, a progressive programme which nonetheless claimed to be restoring an order which had been lost and now was found. Alfonso III, king of the Asturias, had a similar motive in mind when, a few years after Charles's coronation, he tried to get hold of a crown which had been found in Tours and was rumoured to be somehow 'imperial' in its origins. The political uses of a recovered Christian antiquity had already been seen in the Asturias during the reign of Alfonso's father: the discovery of the supposed tomb of St James the Apostle at Compostela meant that the kingdom was now the guardian of a major shrine, and the self-confidence which came with that new status helps to explain the Asturias' territorial expansion.

Alfred provided an English example of the uses of tradition when in 886 he celebrated his conquest of London, previously a Mercian city, by issuing a coin which recalled the Londinium of Roman Britain and, in the vainglorious tone adopted by the *Anglo-Saxon Chronicle*, 'all English-kind bowed to him'. The *Chronicle*'s authors are anonymous but their work was inspired, perhaps even directed, by the king himself, and the record that was transcribed was also an interpretation since it wished to emphasize the continuity of a national story and its culmination in the achievements of Alfred's government. But it was the Franks who enjoyed priority when it came to constructing a history which could be used by the political present, and those of their aristocrats who delighted in the ten books of Gregory of Tours's *Historiae* in the late ninth century were being inspired by a work which was already three centuries old. The institutions of government in which these nobles served were infused with that Frankish sense of identity which had evolved by using the testimony of the past in order to symbolize the present. Charlemagne's decision that the *antiquissima carmina* (most ancient songs) of the Franks be written down and recorded for posterity's sake reveals his grasp of that powerful dynamic, one whose force shaped both his own destiny and that of his people. His legacy in this regard was not confined to his Carolingian successors who sat on the thrones of the Frankish kingdoms, since other western European rulers had been influenced so profoundly by Charlemagne's achievements in the arts of government. He was the exemplar, and all who sought to emulate this king of the Franks were his heirs.

Chapter 7

The Economic Basis of a Civilization

Some of his subjects could have familiarized themselves with the idea of Charlemagne the man by looking on the grandest coin issued during his reign and scrutinizing the facial features which were there displayed. Following his coronation of 800 Charlemagne decided to issue a coin whose details would express the new title's significance, and the imperial coinage is therefore an important indicator of the emperor's own interpretation of his new role. The bust of Charlemagne inscribed on these coins portrays him as a Roman emperor crowned with laurels, and they carry the inscription KAROLVS IMP(erator) AUG(ustus). He was clearly identifying himself with the Roman past. And the style adopted to express his *maiestas* associated him especially with the emperor Augustus whose recasting of Rome's ancient institutions adapted them to serve the needs of an age of imperial expansion. Money as a means of exchange was a vital aspect of Charlemagne's kingdom as it too evolved into an empire, and the coins produced at his command are an important aspect of the royal authority.

Pippin III and Charlemagne built on the foundations of their ancestors who, as mayors of the palace in the later Merovingian period, established central control over the process of minting. The silver denier or penny which was introduced in the late seventh century replaced gold coinage. A pound was divided into 240 of these deniers (*denarii*) and a *solidus* had a value equivalent to twelve *denarii*. The mayors ensured the uniformity of the denier's weight and design. Like these predecessors, Charlemagne and his father understood that coins reflected power and that effective government presupposed the state's monopoly over the production of coinage. A statement of the link between the dynasty and the coinage issued in its name was an important part of this policy, and during Pippin's reign coins started to be issued bearing the royal inscription. Such was the effectiveness of that policy within Francia that it also affected areas neighbouring the empire. After 800 and up until about 970, all the papal coinage produced in Rome carried either Charlemagne's name or his monogram, and since the Franks' trade with Venice was so significant, they insisted that the coinage produced there should be of a standard acceptable to themselves.

From 793–4 onwards the obverse (or front) of the coins struck in Francia carried the royal monogram whose design inscribed the four letters KRLS around a lozenge shape. That symbol contained all the letters of the name Karolus (with u being represented as a v) and its cruciform shape associated the king with the religious basis to his authority. This was particularly effective, because so readily understandable, symbolic statement as well as being a vivid assertion of Charlemagne's credentials as a restorer of Roman ideas of authority. The emperors of old had issued coins inscribed with their names and features, and Roman order had enforced the principle that it was only the imperial government which could issue coins. That key element of state authority, which had been lost in western Europe during the centuries following the dissolution of Rome, was now once again asserted by Charlemagne, and the deniers which circulated right across his vast territories were the single European currency of the age.

Exchange and barter, rather than money, were of course the predominant means by which most people bought and sold goods in Carolingian Europe. But although the silver penny which circulated in Charlemagne's kingdom was worth a significant amount, its value was not such as to place it beyond the daily experience of the majority of his subjects. Four *denarii*, for example, would have been enough to buy a sheep or a pig, and a record survives of a cobbler being paid seven *denarii* for two pairs of shoes with new soles. The coin would therefore have been seen and used by large numbers, and its value made it an important symbol of the king's order.

The location of the mints that produced the Carolingian coinage reflects the patterns of trade within a kingdom which had evolved into an empire. There were over a hundred of them in operation until the reforms of 793–4. The subsequent reduction in the number of mints to about forty reflects the increasingly consolidated degree of royal control over their operations, with monastic and comital mints (run by monasteries and by counts respectively) being brought within Charlemagne's remit. Coins bearing his name were minted from 768 onwards, and in about 771 an important reform ensured the standardization of the style adopted to reproduce his name. In 793–4 this coinage was replaced by heavier and larger coins bearing a cross on one side and the monogram Karolus on the other. The imperial coin's introduction has been dated to 812, the year when Charlemagne was recognized by the Byzantines as emperor of the west. Mints were to be found in the more important towns and trading centres located within the entire region stretching from the Loire to the Rhine, as well as in such southern centres as Uzès and Arles, and the imperial absorption of northern Italy brought the major mints at towns such as Milan, Pavia, Lucca and Pisa under the control of the Carolingian administration.

The introduction of the silver denier was a reflection of the increased pace of economic activity as witnessed especially in the markets held in the towns of Francia, and that expansion continued during the period when Charlemagne sat on the throne of the Franks. What therefore are the key features of this economic growth and how are they related to the Carolingian dynastic achievement?

EUROPE'S LANDSCAPE: A DISTRIBUTION OF POWER

The pursuit of power, as practised by the kings, princes and aristocrats of early medieval western Europe, was related to their wealth, and in about 750 there were two striking aspects to the region's economy. A vast land mass stretching from the Pyrenees to the central areas of Germany produced agricultural goods, while the exchange of goods in general was concentrated on the great rivers which drain that territory and run into the northern seas. Were we to compare this picture with the situation some four centuries earlier, western Europe might seem to have regressed in terms of the volume of goods produced and the extent of their exchange. Early medieval rulers, including the Carolingians, had to make do with far fewer resources than the ones available to Roman emperors, who could rely confidently on an expansionist economy – one whose wealth they were able to plunder and consume. The mid-eighth-century picture, however, was showing signs of economic recovery both in the core Carolingian domains and within Francia as a whole, and there was also a distinctive economic advance which went beyond the boundaries of the old Roman world.

The economy of classical civilization had been centred on the Mediterranean but the rise of Islam had blocked off access to eastern markets and thus disrupted that ancient southern base. Nonetheless, in the course of the eighth century a new economic dynamism began to emerge along what had been the northern peripheries of the Roman empire. The development of a Scandinavian economy as well as one centred on the British Isles ensured a new context for the return of prosperity to many parts of the old Roman world. Just as in its culture, so too in its economy, Carolingian Europe was witnessing a progressive *renovatio*.

It was the possession of land which determined European power in the eighth and ninth centuries. The authority of a king, and the influence of his realm as a whole, depended on the location and also the quality of the lands under direct regal control. These were the royal domains (*demesnes*) and the centrality of their importance was both political and economic. In the late sixth century, for example, the cities of the Po valley had passed directly from the control of the empire to that of the Lombard rulers, and became the consistently loyal power base of Lombard kings during the next two centuries until the Carolingian takeover. The Somerset estates of the west Saxon kings had been seized by their ancestors from the Britons in the fifth and sixth centuries, and the antiquity of that possession meant that these lands were recognized as *principalior* (more royal) than Kent, Surrey and Sussex, territories which were only seized by Wessex at a later date.

The royal lands of Francia were often called the *fisc*, an old Roman term, and comprised those Roman *civitates* and imperial lands which had been taken over by the Merovingian dynasty. After 751 the Carolingians added their own family territories in the valleys of the Meuse and Moselle to this ancient *fisc*. The preservation of this core territory was a constant, and highly successful, preoccupation of Frankish royal policy, with kings labouring hard to ensure that this inheritance went to a single heir. But even when they failed in that struggle, and were either deposed or assassinated, the *fisc* itself survived. The Merovingian palaces located in the Seine basin are a particularly good example of this continuity since they disappear from the official records in the early eighth century and then reappear after 751, by which time they are under Carolingian control. Compiègne, having been the residence of the late Merovingian kings, was subsequently occupied by their usurper Pippin in the 750s and over a century later it was the favourite palace of Charles the Bald. When partitions of royal lands did have to take place, as happened in the case of Charlemagne and his brother Carloman in 768, and then between the three sons of Louis the Pious in 843, a careful survey would be made of these estates and their resources.

Land was not just for display. It was worked in order to support the king's war band with provisions and to provide them with horses. Kingship's frequently itinerant nature should not blind us to the fact that rulers spent most of the winter settled in their palaces, and those centres of power were mostly located in areas where royal land happened to be concentrated most intensely. Produce from this domain was needed in order to support the household, and kings were zealous enforcers of their forest rights, since a regular supply of meat was an especially important requirement of the household during the winter. The number of palaces at which a king stayed was in fact quite small. Lombard kings might have problems controlling their aristocracy but Pavia was the undoubted centre of their palace government throughout the eighth century. Charlemagne's travels were indeed frequent but his more extensive journeys were mostly related to the needs of military campaigning. Within Francia itself we have seen how his journeys tended to follow a well-worn path between certain palaces that were familiar to Charlemagne, and it is important to remember that most of his empire was in fact never visited by the king. From the 790s onwards he was increasingly based in Aachen whose palace was the recognized seat of his realm, the *sedes regni*.

Inheritance or donation of land, as well as its acquisition by conquest, could extend a *fisc*. Its confiscation (as the term suggests) was a punishment meted out to the disloyal, and a good deal of an early medieval king's power depended on his capacity to act as a conduit transferring confiscated lands to his reliable followers. Conquest involved the most significant transfers of all, as in the case of the Carolingians' wholesale acquisition of Lombardy and Bavaria. As we have seen, Charlemagne's empire at its greatest extent covered an area of 463,000 square miles and communication systems had to operate across this vast territory. There were of course the great rivers and these could be used, just as in Roman times, as a transportation system linking the coast with inland areas. Roman roads, and even their old staging posts, survived in many areas, but Charlemagne's regime needed to adopt strenuous measures in order to enforce its authority across huge distances. The arrival of the king with his army was a spectacular event in the history of a dissident area but, having restored order, that military force had to move on and problems in the peripheral areas could persist. A good many of the lands granted by kings were to be found in outlying regions where it was hoped that they might buttress the royal authority.

This instability is the source of a major paradox since it was also the origin of any early medieval monarch's authority. Raiding and the taking of tribute expanded the realm's boundaries and showed that a king was on the way up. This was particularly true of the Frankish kings. 'Have a Frank as a friend and not as a neighbour' is a proverbial saying of the period. Einhard repeats it in the form: 'If a Frank is your friend, he is certainly not your neighbour.' The fact that he describes it as 'a Greek proverb', as well as the remark's rueful tone, suggest that it may refer to the Franks' activities in Byzantine southern Italy. But the challenge and opportunities of such border expansion typified all successful monarchies during this period. Kings wanted lands which they could then redistribute and thereby maintain the loyalty of aristocratic followers while also satisfying the ambitions of potential rivals within the royal family. Smaller kingdoms could grow to comparative greatness in this way. The kingdom of the Asturias started life as a precarious Pyrenean outpost which was vulnerable to Moorish attack. But its eighth-century rulers responded to the challenge by leading their armies south, where they plundered the towns of the Douro valley, and they eventually succeeded in extending their authority over Galicia. Competitive jostling between the rulers of the Anglo-Saxon kingdoms shows the same pattern at work, with the more powerful gaining lands at the expense of their weaker neighbours and allocating territories within the conquered areas to their followers. Wales to the west provided a particular and diplomatic application of the principle. From the time of Offa onwards rulers of Mercia had tried to expand into Wales, whose princes therefore turned to Alfred of Wessex, Mercia's rival, and swore allegiance to him.

Sub-kingdoms might be created, as in the case of Aquitaine which was bestowed on the three-year-old Louis the Pious in 781. This was a substantial royal domain whose boundaries were extended to include Gascony and Septimania, but it was hardly an independent one. Charlemagne intervened there in order to prevent misappropriation of royal estates by the local nobility, and he reorganized the Aquitanian *fisc* in order to provide his son with four palaces where Louis could spend the winter months: Chasseneuil and Doue in Poitou, Angeac in the Saintonge, and Ébreuil in southern Berry. There were also important royal residences in the regions' ancient *civitates* such as Limoges and Clermont, Toulouse and Bourges. Having been ruled by the Carolingians as a subordinate kingdom from 781 to 838, Aquitaine was eventually absorbed by Charles the Bald within the wider Francia. A succession of royal representatives, mostly either very young or frail, were sent to live in Aquitaine. Settled either in the areas of the *fisc* owned by the dynasty (mostly within *civitates*) or in ecclesiastical centres, their presence was a witness to the Carolingian supremacy.

Gascons were beyond Frankish control, but Septimania's nobility, exposed as they were to the Muslim threat on the Spanish border, valued the Carolingian connection which helped to protect them. Alamannia was another territory acquired by the Carolingians. Here again they could find accommodation on the royal *fisc* as well as in the ecclesiastical centres which, as in Aquitaine, provided an infrastructure for government and whose clerics could be used as royal personnel. Alamannia would become strategically important for the Carolingians as a distinctive east Frankish zone of influence emerged in the early ninth century. The palace of Bodman on the Bodensee provided Louis the Pious with a base for several weeks during 839 and he also used the resources of the great royal abbey of Reichenau which was located nearby.

Frankish kings could look back to the example of Charles Martel when it came to the acquisition of Church lands. That mighty progenitor had, in the words of Einhard, set out to 'crush the tyrants', and Martel granted to his followers the ecclesiastical territories seized from the bishops in ancient Gaul. A pleasing fable, taking its cue from Einhard, portrays a ruler who laid the basis for the feudal system itself by granting to his vassal cavalrymen the lands stolen from the Church. But the reality is both less simple and more interesting. Martel was doing nothing new and his attitude was not that of a nineteenth-century anticlericalist. He did not attack the Church that vigorously and his real concern was to dispossess those bishops who were building up ecclesiastical principalities in key strategic centres such as Auxerre and Orléans, and who therefore represented a real political threat to him. Nor did he set out to 'reform' the Church in Gaul. He gave the two sees of Trier and Reims to Milo, a famously unreformed character but a cleric whose loyalty to Martel was undoubted.

Merovingian kings continued the policy of placing pliant churchmen in key positions and of distributing Church lands to favoured supporters. It was in fact Martel's son Pippin III who was responsible for a real *Einstaatung* of the Frankish Church right across the territory of what had been Gaul. This was after all a ruler who had been consecrated by the pope, and he behaved accordingly. Pippin appointed Gaul's most important bishops and abbots personally, a procedure which a century later the Frankish kings would claim to be their traditional royal custom, and he summoned them to attend his councils and assemblies in order to ensure the Church's endorsement of dynastic policy. He demanded military service from the relatives and retinue of such senior churchmen, and the king granted ecclesiastical lands to those he wished to reward.

With this in mind, any realistic analysis of the material resources available to the Carolingians has to include the Church's properties and its clergy. Pippin's easy access to the lands of the bishopric of Auxerre helped him to secure control of Burgundy in the 750s, a move which was vital for the subsequent assertion of his authority in Aquitaine. Frankish acquisition of other regions was a means of solidifying the Church–State connection, as in the case of Alamannia where, following the takeover, extensive grants of the *fisc* which had once belonged to the duchy were made to Abbot Fulrad of St-Denis, the abbey where Pippin wished to be buried. After the annexation of the Lombard kingdom Charlemagne endowed St-Denis, as well as St-Martin in Tours, with lands in the Val d'Aosta.

Church policy bolstered public authority and although ecclesiastical foundations such as monasteries might be granted jurisdictional immunity they nonetheless remained firmly under the wider royal control. They therefore had to meet the often highly explicit Carolingian demands. Charles the Fat made his grant of lands to St-Gall on condition that they were used to commemorate his father. Charles the Bald's grant of over 2,000 *manses* to the see of Laon was linked to the expectation that these benefice-holders would be chosen by him and consequently obliged to perform military service for the king. The peasants who worked on the estates of the royal abbey of St-Germain-des-Prés had to hand over a fixed quantity of produce, known as the *hostilicium*, which was reserved for troop provision. Most Carolingian armies, especially in the ninth century, would have included a large number of benefice-holders who worked on Church property and were organized to take part in military campaigns by the bishops, abbots and abbesses who oversaw those territories.

This was par excellence the system which had emerged in that part of Francia which comprised the old Roman province of Gaul. In the newly acquired territories where well-endowed churches were of much more recent foundation, things may not have run quite so smoothly. There seems to have been no ecclesiastical contribution to the king's army in the Lombard kingdom, and the patriarch of Aquileia, that very ancient see at the head of the Adriatic, wrote to Charlemagne in 789–90 asking the king for permission 'to serve only in the camps of the Lord' since 'no man can serve two masters'. This was an echo of an ancient Augustinian theme and, as such, the very opposite of the Carolingian regime's guiding ideal which involved the dual service of God and king.

Anglo-Saxon churches had particular difficulties of their own in relation to the royal power, and archbishops of Canterbury proved doughty defenders of Kentish autonomy after the Mercian defeat of the kingdom in the eighth century. It was the Viking onslaught on archiepiscopal territories in the late ninth century which weakened Canterbury's position vis-à-vis the claims of Wessex and which enabled Alfred to embark on his imitation of the Carolingian Church–State arrangements. The northern English see of York had consistent difficulties with the claims of Northumbrian kings, and the conflicts here could lead to physical attacks. That level of insecurity and violence is the major reason why Alcuin, the brother of an archbishop of York, decided to flee to Aachen. Trapped within this breakdown of authority, the Northumbrian Church was unable to resist the aristocratic takeover of its lands, and Bede thought that many of the kingdom's monasteries were fake institutions set up by the aristocracy in order to evade its military obligations.

England's churches could offer their kings nothing comparable to the institutional support which the Frankish Church leadership gave to its kings in a deal whose advantages cut both ways. Ecclesiastical office holders, bolstered by the prestige of royal support, were strikingly loyal – more so than many secular ones. The Carolingian dynasty relied on the Church's ability to provide it with military service, but it also wanted its prayers, and these became a kind of loyalty test calculated to boost dynastic self-confidence. When Louis the Pious drew up a list of duties which he was owed by monasteries there were three relevant categories: gifts, military service and prayers. Monasteries in the former Lombard kingdom were expected to offer public prayers for Charlemagne, and the example of St-Denis, where there were royal endowments for specific feasts, shows how communal eating could be a form of prayer on behalf of the dynasty. Carolingian power at its height absorbed such monasteries into its support structures, and the decline of that power is measured by the extent to which these foundations came under aristocratic control. In the late ninth century St-Vaast was taken over by the counts of Flanders, St-Denis was transferred to Odo, Count of Paris, and St-Martin in Tours, another Frankish spiritual power house, fell into the hands of Odo's brother Robert. This is the time when Fulk of Reims was able to build up a regional power base in the very heart of west Francia and in the city which was a nerve centre of the Carolingian enterprise. The kings of the eastern Franks, however, retained their ecclesiastical power base, a fact of crucial importance since it enabled their successors, the tenth-century Ottonian emperors, to develop a Church–State alliance whose authority justified their claim to be Charlemagne's true heirs.

The land-grant system operated by the Carolingians, especially in relation to the Church, diminished the royal *fisc* but did not represent a squandering of their material resources. This was in fact the way in which the kings of the Franks built up their authority. Times of political and military crisis witnessed a decline in the number of such grants, and their renewed occurrence in the sources is usually a sign that such difficulties have been resolved. But a king's authority also depended on his possession of material wealth, goods which could be distributed among his supporters. Plunder and tribute were an especially important part of the royal income during Charlemagne's reign. The *Annales Laureshamenses*, partly compiled at the abbey of Lorsch near Worms, contain an entry for 793 describing how the king rewarded those who had not defected in the recent rebellion by giving them 'gold and silver and precious cloths'.

Einhard describes the cartloads of treasure which came to Aachen after the defeat of the Avars and which made the Franks so rich 'it seemed as if they had been almost paupers before'. Much of this loot was distributed to churches, but some of it was given to other rulers. Such largesse was a popular early medieval means of demonstrating the royal donor's authority, and we know that Offa of Mercia was given a sword which had formed part of the Avar loot. Tribute from territories which had been either conquered outright or forced to acknowledge Carolingian supremacy supplemented this hoard. The Beneventans, for example, were not conquered but had to pay a substantial tribute in recognition of their submission. The loot of empire constituted Charlemagne's treasure trove and survives in Einhard's breathlessly itemized account of the three great silver tables, the hangings, carpets and silks, gold and silver vessels, vestments, bullion and cash, as well as the richly illuminated books. To these we must add prestige items such as the king's clock and organ, and the gem-encrusted reliquaries made of gold and silver.

Possession of treasure on its own was not enough to guard a kingdom against decline. Denmark proves the point. Here was a kingdom which posed a serious late eighth-century threat to the Carolingians, but the assassination of King Godfrid in 809 was the trigger for a prolonged succession dispute which also depleted royal treasure. In 845 the exceptionally successful Danish warlord Ragnar raided Paris, and on his return to court he displayed his loot before King Horik. He did so as an assertion of his own warrior prestige and shared none of this treasure with his sovereign. Horik's problems were compounded by Denmark's persistent paganism, despite the many attempts at evangelization made by Frankish missionaries. Had a Danish Church existed, its resources might have been a useful source of kingly support. Within a decade of Ragnar's ostentatious display another outbreak of dissidence concerning the succession led to Horik's death and the slaughter of most of the Danish nobility. If we look to the lands on the Carolingians' eastern theatre of operations there is another salutary example, that of Moravia. Here there is a real black hole in terms of documentary information although archaeology helps to fill in some of the gaps. Moravian kingship in its origins was similar to the Frankish version. Here again was a kingdom whose raison d'être was expansion, and the fact that there were just three kings who reigned for most of the ninth century meant that Moravia prospered. Between c. 830 and c. 894 the kingdom expanded to include, in all probability, the territories of the present-day Czech republic and Slovakia as well as embracing a large area to the south of the Danube. But Moravia failed to maintain its earlier momentum and internal dynastic disputes enabled the kingdom's weakness to be exploited by the Hungarians.

Denmark and Moravia in their different ways define by contrast the nature of the Carolingian success. But there came a point at which the expansion had to stop, and 804, the date of the final subjugation of the Saxons, marks the furthermost extension of boundaries. When Charlemagne died in 814, the hoard of treasure which was a visible token of his kingdom's imperial stretch was dispersed. Imperial longings survived, especially when Charlemagne's successors looked south and contemplated intervention in Spanish affairs. In 826 the king of the Franks wrote to the citizens of Merida and urged them to revolt against the emir of Cordoba. Diplomacy, though, seems to have gained the upper hand in Frankish–Iberian relations, and in the 850s Zaragoza's Muslim governor granted safe conduct to a group of Frankish monks who were allowed to fetch relics of Christians who had been martyred recently in Cordoba. But not only were the rulers of the Franks unable to gain extra territories in either Spain or Italy during the ninth century, they also failed to stop the Saracens from raiding Mediterranean coastal areas. *Nach Osten* as well there was a real sense of the frontier being consolidated. In 805 Charlemagne issued a capitulary declaring that trade with the Slav peoples could only take place in eight specified border posts located on the frontier running from Saxony to Austria. Only here could Frankish merchants export swords and coats of mail, and even then they needed royal licences in order to do so.

If they thought they could get away with it, Carolingian kings would continue to plunder and exploit the peoples beyond their boundaries. The ninth-century situation, however, differed profoundly from the past, and the *exterae gentes* were now mostly a source of military recruitment, a trading opportunity and a mission field. On the face of it the story of the Carolingian dynasty in this era is one of dissolution – the *Auflösungsprozess* which is stressed in the conventional narrative. But if we look at what they actually owned, the story of Charlemagne's immediate successors includes a good deal of preservation and consolidation. The external expansion ended but in its place came the redistribution of wealth among dynastic members. Despite the division of the empire in 843 (and then again in 855) into its constituent Carolingian kingdoms, the brothers, uncles and nephews who sat on these thrones felt that they still belonged to a single and overarching *regnum*, a familial patrimony in which they all had a stake. Inheritance rights helped in this regard. Louis the German expanded his kingdom because a nephew's consort was infertile, and Charles the Bald gained territories because one of his nephews had no sons. Church land and resources continued to be available and were exploited rigorously. The ninth century is a period when Carolingian kings granted to their followers ever more temporal lordships over abbeys and benefices held on Church lands while also receiving gifts from Church treasuries.

There is plenty of evidence that the kings of this period were managing their own *fisc* lands more rigorously by extracting more labour from their peasants and increasing dues owed in kind as well as in cash. Hincmar of Reims used his spiritual authority to tell Louis the German and Charles the Bald that their estate managers' demands were oppressing the peasantry. As long as these royal lands were being run properly they were perfectly capable, he thought, of supporting the royal household's needs without making peasants' lives miserable. Moreover, kings ought not to be making such unreasonable demands for hospitality on bishops and abbots, abbesses and counts. That only made a difficult situation worse, wrote the archbishop, by forcing these clerical and secular lords in turn to make heavy demands on the peasantry. Hincmar's complaints show how royal authority was maximizing its own resources and turning to strenuous landlordship (*Grundherrschaft*) instead of relying on the easy plunder.

Aristocratic elites were also expected to help foot the bills for kingship. Carolingian rulers – like early medieval ones generally in Europe – could not tax in the way the Roman imperial government had been able to do. The expectation, however, of 'annual gifts' was effectively an annual levy imposed on the aristocracy. This was a major source of gold and silver for the royal coffers and also, very importantly, of horses. Jobs in the king's gift had carried a price tag ever since the sixth century, and Carolingian rulers developed this source of income to new heights as well as sharing with the aristocracy the proceeds of fines imposed through the justice system.

More intensive exploitation of already available sources of revenue is far from being the whole story of the Carolingian economy. The total volume of coinage circulating in the lands west of the Rhine (including the Frankish lands and the Anglo-Saxon kingdoms of England) may well have amounted to millions of coins in the early eighth century. The same may be true a century later, and those facts argue for a pretty healthy level of trade. Having been so quick off the mark in establishing a ruler's monopoly over the minting of coins, the Carolingians were well placed to exploit these trading developments to their own advantage. Pippin and Charlemagne's coinage reforms, rather like those of Offa in Mercia, show how the revived royal authority paralleled trade expansion. Protection of the coinage against debasement benefited not just kings but also traders, and the existence of reliable coins stimulated a trading process which produced in turn more toll contributions to the royal treasury. Kings therefore benefited from the economic stimulation but they also contributed to the means of its creation. Godfrid of Denmark, according to one chronicler, 'destroyed the *emporium* on the Baltic sea coast at Reric [probably the site of Old Lübeck] whence he used to extract a large benefit from tolls, and putting the traders on board ship, he made for the *portus* of Schleswig [in eastern Denmark], which he then decided to protect with a rampart'. Better protection meant greater opportunity to exploit, and kings like Godfrid who protected the merchants and other patrons of such emporia stimulated economic exchanges whose consequences, in terms of consumption and exaction of tolls, benefited the crown.

Markets which were more domestic than those of the emporia must have flourished as well. Charlemagne's famous prohibition of Sunday markets suggests that the peasantry were economically active on this local scale, and here again there were direct benefits for kings as the landlords of markets and their regulators. The Scandinavian warriors recruited by Charles the Bald in 860 to fight against their countrymen were paid for in part by taxing traders. Although they played no direct role in economic activity, monarchs consistently acted on the assumption that they had a right to a share of commercial profits, and their coinage policy reflected that fiscal claim. The recoinage ordered by Charles the Bald in 864 for the west Frankish kingdom was the most ambitious of any Carolingian ruler since it involved calling in all current coins and replacing them with coins of purer quality using new standardized dies. Those who delivered the old debased coins to the country's mints received fewer coins in exchange and this amounted therefore to a substantial form of taxation – perhaps some ten per cent – which was shared between the king and those who ran the mints (both the moneyers themselves and the local count or viscount).

Charles's success in this complex enterprise argues for the existence of a well-organized treasury team, as does his imposition of a nation-wide land tax in order to help pay for his Scandinavian warriors. Alfred the Great, in his Wessex kingdom, carried out a similarly successful remonetization in the 860s and the money that he had to give to the

Vikings was raised by means of a tribute imposed throughout his realm. Alfred and Charles are two of the greatest success stories in the ninth-century history of royal administration but even they had to tread warily in dealing with the aristocracy when it came to money. Alfred had to exert pressure on his *potentes* in order to get the necessary tribute money and the west Frankish aristocracy rebelled when Charles tried to increase their taxation in 877. The expansion of Wessex parallels in miniature the earlier Frankish rulers' ability to raise more money by conquering other regions and plundering them. Alfred and his heirs had an advantage in this respect which was denied Charles the Bald and his successors. But kings in all parts of western Europe during the ninth century needed to husband their resources carefully and to be alert to whatever economic opportunities came their way.

AGRICULTURE: PLENTY AND PROGRESS

Europe's population growth during the Carolingian period is well attested, and that increase was related to a widespread reclamation of land which led to the establishment of new estates and farms. The area surrounding Paris records some of the greatest advances in both respects and evidence drawn from the polyptych of the abbey of St-Germain-des-Prés, a document which catalogued the abbatial estates, suggests population densities of a hundred inhabitants per square mile on a number of abbey estates in the southern Parisian region during the early ninth century. Friesland's most densely populated area may have matched this high figure by about 900. These are exceptionally high statistics for the period, and other regions of reclaimed land would have supported much lower numbers, probably between thirteen and thirty-one per square mile. Areas where the processes of reclamation and consequent arable advance were most marked include southern Gaul and the Île de France, the area of the Rhine–Moselle, and the territories between the Scheldt and the Dender in Belgium. The contrast between such major zones of development and thinly populated areas – northern Belgium and the south-west and western parts of France, for example – was very sharp. Areas of economic progress, however, did record a remarkable population increase, and a fair estimate suggests that the numbers of those living on estates in these territories doubled over a period of 150 years during the eighth and ninth centuries.

The growth rate is even more striking since it occurred despite the famines which hit northern France at the end of the eighth and the beginning of the ninth century. These natural disasters led to major government interventions such as Charlemagne's attempts to control the inflationary rise in bread and grain prices, his new units of measurement, weight and currency, and the emergency operations designed to help the hardest-hit. These famines, however, may themselves have been a result of the economic growth since it was that process which had led to the rising population levels. The rigid structures of the rural economy found it difficult to adjust to such expansion, resulting in certain areas becoming overpopulated in relation to their food-producing capacity. Famine's effects were severe, but they were soon overcome and economic dynamism, assisted by the youthfulness of the population, reasserted itself after each such trauma.

Western Europe's new population was being fed because of a major agrarian revolution. In large parts of the region, most noticeably in Switzerland and south-west Germany, north-east France and southern Belgium, two kinds of grain, winter-sown corn and spring-sown corn, were being grown in regular rotation side by side during the same harvest year. This was an eighth-century innovation and as a result the fields that had produced spring corn during the previous year were left fallow for a year before being sown again, first with winter corn and then with spring corn during the appropriate seasons. The three-year crop rotation system had first appeared in various localities between the Alps and the North Sea, and it replaced a system in which the land was allowed to remain fallow for much longer periods, with individual territories sustaining the same grain crop without any rotation.

This was a major economic advance and as a result two kinds of grain crop could now be cultivated: spelt, rye and wheat were raised for human consumption as the constituent grain for bread; barley and oats by contrast were used as animal feed. Fallow land had been reduced from a half to a third and this led to a more intensive use of arable soil, with consequent major gains in productivity.

There was, though, an important limit to the spread of the new system

since it was effectively confined to large complexes of territorial holdings such as the demesnes of ecclesiastical landlords, which were where
this crop rotation system first appeared. It was the class of dependent
farmers who cultivated these demesnes on behalf of the landowners,
but it is very unlikely that they used the rotation system on the lands
they farmed for their own benefit. Their plots of land were often widely
scattered and intermingled with one another, whereas those owned by
their territorial lords were located within the same field complex, a fact
which promoted consistency of tillage right across them. It is important to remember, though, that these were complexes of fields and not
open ones. Demesne lands, the best example of such complexes, did not
yet form continuous open areas and they were still separated by woods,
heathland and other uncultivated plots. It is only within the complexes
themselves that the plots corresponded to a small-scale version of the
open field which came to typify the agrarian landscape of later European history. These fields would in time be divided into narrow strips,
a practice which probably resulted from the division of inherited free-
hold property as well as from the various partitions to which demesne
land was subjected over time. That division into strips, however, must
also reflect the more widespread use in the eighth and ninth centuries
of the heavy asymmetrical plough equipped with its mould board, a
form of technology which contributed to the economic expansion (as
well as being stimulated by it).

Which animals could be seen grazing on the lands of western Europe
during the Carolingian period? Cattle were far less common than smaller
domestic animals such as pigs and sheep, a situation which holds true
for both northern and southern Europe, and the general impression is
of an agricultural economy which concentrated on the production of
grain. There were some northern areas, however, where cattle-raising
was more important than other forms of agriculture. In Fulda, for
example, the local abbey recorded the units of land that it owned in
terms of the numbers of animals – cattle as well as sheep and pigs –
that its pasture could sustain. On either side of the North Sea, in East
Anglia and the coastal areas of the Low Countries, there were huge
flocks of sheep whose wool production was far in excess of what was
needed for local consumption by the abbeys who owned them. The

development of a specialized trade in the production and processing of wool was not just a rural affair but, as witnessed in the towns of Flanders, also an urban one, and its spread was an example of the period's increasing economic sophistication and specialization of labour.

On the whole, however, it was grain production which was Europe's major agricultural pursuit. That fact holds true even for Italy, although the contemporary opinion there was that the roughly equal division between wild and cultivated areas in its central northern area led to a proportion of arable which was too high. Here again the three-crop rotation was in evidence, and cultivated Italian land was paying less attention to summer grain than to the winter grains – especially spelt and rye. Spelt, that very ancient European crop, accounted for between fifty and eighty per cent of all grain production in south-west Germany, north-east France and southern Belgium. Elsewhere in Europe, however, spelt was being overtaken by rye – a crop which would become the chief bread grain in Italy during the ninth and tenth centuries. Europe's built environment was also showing the importance of grain with the arrival on the landscape of large numbers of watermills which specialized in its treatment. Many were built by laymen, and in parts of north-east Spain and northern Italy the grain mills were owned collectively by village communities. But in the Frankish empire they were owned by substantial ecclesiastical landowners as part of their demesne, and the people who actually operated the mills were tenants who paid rent in order to be able to do so.

OWNING AND WORKING THE LAND: THE MANORIAL SYSTEM

From the mid-eighth century onwards there were profound changes at work in the pattern of land-ownership within most of the territories which comprised the central Frankish empire, and also in the north and centre of Italy. Central to those changes is the introduction of the *villa*, a unit of ownership which was divided into two parts: the demesne which was cultivated directly for its lord by the farmers who divided among themselves the other constituent part of the *villa*, the tenements or holdings. Tenants worked these holdings for themselves in exchange for the services, goods and payments they rendered to the lord and his demesne.

This model emerged first of all in the region between the Seine, Meuse and Rhine, and it then spread outwards from this Carolingian heartland at uneven rates of development. On the edges of the Frankish kingdoms, in areas such as the delta of the Meuse and the Rhine, this bipartite system was still evolving in the middle of the ninth century. But in a central region, such as the one surrounding Paris, it was already in decline by the beginning of that century. The only Mediterranean region where it left its mark was in the Italian territories after 774, and even here it was only Lombardy which witnessed an effective operation of the system. These facts of geography, allied to the way in which this manorial system was mostly to be found operating on royal estates, on Church lands acquired as royal gifts and on the territories of the high nobility, all suggest that this agricultural regime was the invention of Frankish kings and their advisers.

The manorial system's introduction involved a massive shift in the structure of economic power, leading, for example, to the more effective integration of big farms previously worked directly by slaves, as well as to the absorption within large estates of previously small, by and large independent, parcels of land. Various pre-existing developments helped the process along and made it appear more inevitable. The reclamation, for example, of wooded and very fertile soils had already enlarged the demesne's amount of arable land and these quite compact units were called *culturae* or *territoria*. The people who performed this work of land clearance were sometimes the serfs who lived on the demesne (and who did not have farms of their own to cultivate), but quite often it was also done by free, and semi-free, individuals who arrived as newcomers on the *demesne*. As payment for the work done they were granted the right to cultivate a small part of the unexploited demesne which they were then allowed to keep as a holding while also making payments and services to the demesne's lord. This arrangement, therefore, conformed to what would be a central feature of the bipartite manorial system and contributed to its spread. Manorial developments could only really take place on large estates, territories which were overwhelmingly owned by kings and bishops, the nobles and the monasteries. Wherever it took root the bipartite system represented a significant concentration of power for those ruling orders, and the newly ordered lands were located near their main centres of power: royal palaces, abbeys and cathedral cities.

If there was a certain basic structure, there was also an immense variety. A lord's direct control might be limited by the survival of older rights among groupings such as freemen, the half-free *coloni*, and slaves. The demesne comprised arable land which could extend to several hundred hectares as well as various kinds of uncultivated land, and those estates with larger areas of arable land needed a correspondingly greater body of manpower. On these estates the lord probably had to use slaves who lived on his land in order to supplement the services of his tenants. On the Staffelsee estate of the bishop of Augsburg slaves provided a minimum service each of three days a week in the period between 800 and 820, and on the abbatial estate of Montierender in north-eastern France, shortly before 843, each demesne contained an average of thirteen slaves. Nonetheless, the chief characteristic of these large estates, which were mostly territories either owned by the king or donated by him to the nobility and to ecclesiastical landowners, was the exploitation of the demesne using the services of tenants.

As the system developed a new term started to be used to describe the services which were due to a lord: the *mansus*. As evolved by the Frankish kings, the term meant a unit of assessment on which payments, due in kind and in money and also rendered as services, were calculated. The unit on which the assessment was calculated consisted of houses, other buildings and land. And a single *mansus* was supposed to be capable of supporting the needs of one family. It was also used to express rough estimates of the value of a piece of land or that of a whole region, and royal circles also deployed the *mansus* as a basis for various taxes and military obligations. But its major function was related to the demesne and to the structure of obligation which applied to all who lived there, whether they were slaves, tenants who were half-free or ones who were free.

The scale of services that was expected varied of course according to the status of the order of society to which one belonged, but *mansi* also meant different things in different areas. East of the Rhine, in Italy, and also in some outlying areas of the western part of the empire, the services imposed on free and half-free tenants were quite limited: some transportation duties, occasional agricultural services lasting two weeks a year, and the cultivation of a plot on the demesne. This light regime was made possible by the fact that there were still large numbers of slaves in the areas concerned and they were therefore available for the bulk of the work. But most areas of the western empire witnessed a drastic reduction in the number of slaves in the course of the ninth century, largely because most of them had been settled on holdings. As a result, the social distinction between these ex-slaves and the tenants (free and half-free alike) was not as clear as it had been in the past. Large demesnes in these areas required a lot of work, and both kinds of tenant were now performing labour which was practically indistinguishable from that expected of slaves in other parts of the empire. Labour may have become easily exploitable because of the population increases in economically advancing regions, which may have made it easier to effectively downgrade the status of tenants in this way. Even so, the process shows the immense reserves of power enjoyed by both the Frankish crown and the Church as well as the ease with which they could impose their will.

Other forms of the manorial system existed in parallel with the standard model and some of these harked back to earlier periods. The standard Merovingian manor was a unit which persisted well into the Carolingian age and, known as the *curtis*, consisted of no more than about 40 to 150 hectares of arable land which would have been directly cultivated by slaves who lived on or near the estate. Some land holdings, limited in number, may have been administered from this manorial centre and were often to be found in areas whose territories were only just beginning to be cultivated. At the beginning of the ninth century, the abbeys of Fulda and Montierender owned lands of this kind in, respectively, central Germany and north-eastern France's Argonne forest. Within Italy, the abbey of Farfa owned similar lands in the central Apennines, the mountainous Piemonte region, and at the Po estuary.

The *curtis* was really no more than a large farm. Nonetheless, it did include some land holdings and these may even have increased in number.

One way in which this might be done was by assigning elements of the demesne to slaves or ex-slaves, as happened in parts of Italy as early as the eighth century. Those parts of the demesne which had not yet been developed could also be assigned to new holdings, as happened, again, in Italy during the second half of the ninth century. A *curtis* which had evolved in this way had become a manor consisting of two component parts, and since this was the distinguishing characteristic of the *villa*, that was the term now used to describe it. The evidence, though, does not all point in the same direction since many of the newly created holdings consisted of lands which were widely scattered over several villages where they existed cheek by jowl with the lands of other lords. In these instances the demesnes' contact with their holdings was a remote one and mostly confined to the collection of rent, as happened to many of the lands owned by the abbeys of Corvey and Fulda.

The manorial system, considered as a whole, was intended to maximize efficiency and increase productivity, and its effects included the promotion of small-farm enterprise and a reduction in slave numbers as a result of the introduction of services. The major institutions of the age were the court, the Church and the army, all of which had increasing needs in the delivery of agricultural supplies. Productivity gains helped to satisfy those needs as well as speeding the production process in manual crafts. The manorial system's widespread introduction was a process associated with the rise in royal authority, and the onset of its decline in the late ninth century paralleled the diminished effectiveness of kings during that same period.

The areas that were assimilated into the empire as a result of the late eighth-century Carolingian expansion contained most of southern and western France, and landownership here was very different from the manorial system of the central Frankish territories. In Charente, Poitou, the Limousin and Provence, small farms predominated, and most of these were owned as allodial property, which meant that they were held absolutely and without any encumbrance in the form of services. The Auvergne was another area dominated by small farms but here they were held as tenements. Throughout these French areas the demesne was also a small-scale affair, being cultivated directly for the local lord by his slaves. Land holdings did exist but, apart from producing rental

income, they had no close links with the demesne and they did not produce services for it.

Even in the eighth century these southern and western French property structures were regarded as ancient, and the origins of the small
allodia are to be found in the period of the later Roman empire, though
some did evolve during the land reclamations of the Carolingian era.
Most of the land holdings were also ancient and probably originated as
the possessions of late Roman *coloni*, with their numbers being boosted
later by the grant of lands to former slaves: the principal obligation on
such lands was that of paying a levy in kind which amounted to about
a tenth of the harvest. The oldest tax list of the abbey of St-Martin in
Tours dates to the early 670s and the obligation is described in that
document as the *agrarium*, a term which recurs in the seventh-century
Formulae Wisigothorum. At a later stage the obligation became a fixed
payment, and *colonicae* also had to pay for the right to pasture: this
pascuarium, as it was called, consisted of one-tenth of the yield of cattle-
raising, chickens and eggs. The *colonicae* also yielded a sum of money,
the *tributum*, as a token of dependence. An individual *colonica* consisted of about 40 acres, and therefore corresponded in size to the
northern European *mansus*, a term which started to be used south of
the Loire (and mostly in the Auvergne) only during the ninth century.
Here, however, the meaning of the term *mansus* was limited to the calculation of the right to exploit buildings and gardens in the immediate
vicinity of *colonicae* lands, and the word did not signify an obligation
to render agricultural services.

Catalonia and Roussillon recorded different developments and here,
from the tenth century onwards, the allodial lands of the free peasantry
would be sold and, in exchange for part of the yield, became part of the
holdings of large landowners such as the new abbeys of the area. Brittany supplies another example of the same profound shift from a society
of small peasant properties owned as *allodia* to one dominated by large
estates which, again, included new abbeys. English evidence for land-
owning at this period is extremely thin but there was probably a large
number of slaves who cultivated the demesne without much help from
the rent-paying tenants known as the 'ceorls' and whose half-free status
corresponded to that of *coloni* within the Frankish empire. The 'hide'

was the predominant unit of English land measurement and, since it was used to assess land values and was also meant to be enough to support one family, the term is roughly comparable to the continental *mansus*. One of the rare pieces of evidence we have for Anglo-Saxon taxation is a charter granted by Edward the Elder at Winchester in 900, and that document shows the hide being expected to produce not only money but also supplies of beer and bread, of barley, wood, sheep and lambs.

MANUFACTURES AND INDUSTRIES, MARKETS AND TRADERS

Textiles and iron-working were the two main forms of industrial production within the Carolingian countryside and both activities evolved in order to meet demand from beyond the locality. Most tenants engaged in textile production as a sideline, and landlords delivered to them the woven pieces of linen cloth, the raw wool or flax which were used to manufacture shirts. Production of coats and capes made of wool (*pallia* and *saga*) was also a major aspect of textile production. From the eighth century onwards, and especially in the Low Countries and Germany, in France and Italy, workplaces reserved for women (*gynaecea*) start to appear on the demesnes of estates. It was here that female slaves and the wives of the half-free *coloni* had to do work that corresponded to the services required of their menfolk on the demesnes. It is a fair guess that most of the weaving was done in the *gynaecea*, and these workplaces also existed on the royal *fisc*. Sheep, as we have seen, were put to pasture in their many thousands along the North Sea coast of the Low Countries, and great abbeys which were located in other areas, such as St-Wandrille, Fulda and Lorsch, either owned many of these flocks or had woollen monks' clothes and other woven materials delivered to them from the region. This was the origin, therefore, of the Low Countries' long history as a textile centre and also of their Europe-wide reputation for high-quality manufacture in that sector.

The Carolingian miner (*fossarius*) who extracted iron ore from surface furrows, pits and funnel shafts seems to have been a peasant farmer engaged in a side activity, although excavations in the Franconian Alps have revealed the existence of a whole settlement of artisans located near one Carolingian iron mine. Iron-working in general was developed to serve rural needs, and smiths were highly specialized artisans whose high status within their local community reflected a long tradition and one whose pre-Christian origins credited the blacksmith with magical powers. Iron-working on an industrial scale and serving markets at a distance from the locality may well have been particularly associated with the royal *fisc*, and the *Capitulare de Villis* makes special mention of the iron objects (*ferramenta*) which the royal government commanded to be supplied to the army. A similar royal connection exists in the inventory of the estates of the bishopric of Chur which records the income from one complete *ministerium* as consisting mainly of iron products which were paid as *census regis* to the king's representative. Abbeys were, as we might expect, the other main sources of demand for iron. Documents from major foundations such as St-Remi of Reims, Weissenburg, Lorsch and St-Gall record the delivery of iron which might be either in the form of ingots or as finished products such as ploughshares, horseshoes and weapons. These objects were delivered as rents due from the peasants who worked the abbeys' lands and they show the extent to which peasant farmers were involved in the digging of iron and its manufacture.

Capitularies dating from 779 onwards prohibited the export of weapons and of military equipment such as the metal shirt or *brunia*. Glass and ceramics, however, continued to be exported throughout the Carolingian period and have been discovered on sites excavated in Scandinavia. The industry was an ancient one in Francia, and Scandinavia has also produced abundant evidence of glassware which had been produced and exported during the Merovingian era. But the earliest evidence so far discovered of an actual location where glaziers produced glass, the wooded area of the Hochwald near Trier, belongs to the Carolingian period. This too was an industry which was related to royal needs, and another workshop has been found in the remains of the Carolingian palace at Paderborn.

Pottery production in the Francia of the eighth and ninth centuries was on a scale and of a quality which far exceeded the Merovingian manufactures. Here we can surmise the effects of the manorial system at work with its more efficient production techniques. High-quality pottery needed not just the raw elements of clay and sand but also the ready availability of local wood and water which were used as sources of energy in the production process. The Frankish kingdoms led the field in pottery production, and although the England of the time contained two important centres of such production in Ipswich and Hamwic (Southampton) most of the pots used in the country were imported from the continent.

Salt was an essential commodity in the early medieval economy because it was used not just as a flavourer but also as a preservative of fish and meat. Salt production had been a major feature of western European industrial activity from the earlier Roman empire onwards, and in our period it was the abbeys which played a major role in the industry's organization. The lands in Lorraine owned by the abbey of Prum contained waters which were rich in salt, and abbatial documentation shows that it was Prum's tenants who boiled the water and obtained the salt by a process of crystallization. They received in exchange the grant of their holdings. Many other substantial abbeys with a high demand for salt also owned lands in this region so that they too could extract and crystallize the local water. Prum's salt arrived at the abbey having been transported through Metz and along the Moselle on a journey organized by other tenants who provided a transportation system. Other abbeys got their supplies by owning salt basins filled with sea water, and these salines were mostly located along the coast at the estuaries of rivers such as the Loire and the Seine. There is good evidence for the existence of local groups of manual workers who operated these works, and salt production in the lagoons of Venice and at the head of the Po estuary was on such a scale that it led to the development of a major interregional trade network along the river Po. This was also, however, an inland business and there were salt mines both at the Salzkammergut and at Reichenhall in southern Bavaria.

Large abbatial communities had major economic needs and it is therefore unsurprising that abbeys such as Fulda, Lorsch and St-Gall contained substantial communities of manual workers working under institutional supervision. This involved a variety of craftsmen including blacksmiths and weapon-makers, woodworkers and furriers. St-Riquier's artisans were housed in a settlement specifically developed for that purpose near the abbey site and they were grouped together in its various streets according to their specialism. Workers of this kind were a cut above the mere *provendarii*, the ranks of the unskilled who would also live near the abbey. Nonetheless, their artisan independence was limited by the fact that they were part of the abbey's unfree, or half-free, *familia*, and they would have had few opportunities to work for themselves.

It was the manorial system, and the range of transportation services required of its tenants, which enabled the exchange of goods and trade to develop along the local roads and waterways of western Europe during the Carolingian period. By these means, the surpluses of agrarian and industrial production (especially those on the demesnes within the larger manorial centres of the king and the Church) were taken either to regional estate centres or directly to the palace and the abbey. The agrarian and craft products which represented payment in kind by estate tenants also used this communication system in order to arrive at the same destinations. Specialized products such as salt, oil and wine could be sent very long distances, but a product such as corn tended to be sent just to the local abbey.

Markets operated under royal permission and an increasing number of them, usually located in or near certain estates, appear during the ninth century. This was where local surpluses could be sold, and if there was a particular demand elsewhere for a certain commodity, then those goods might be taken to markets which were further away. The new markets were sometimes located near large abbeys, as in the case of the ones established at St-Vaast (867) and St-Bertin (874). But a large number were to be found in the countryside, and those established at Faverolles (774) and Saclas (814), both in the region of Paris, were on estates owned by the abbey of St-Denis. There were older markets too, and the ones which operated in or near local *civitates* of Roman origin such as Nantes and Angers, Troyes and Orléans, dated from well before the ninth century. Coins were often minted at these market towns and when a new market was opened the king might grant coinage rights on those sites as well, as happened in the regional markets established at Rommersheim (861) and Munstereifel (898) on the Eifel estates of the abbey of Prum.

Traders would certainly have been present at these weekly events but it was mostly the producers themselves – the peasants, craftsmen and unfree tenants – who came to market and offered their own produce for sale. Craftsmen would have bought chickens, eggs and corn with the money obtained by selling their own products. Peasants for their part bought from these same craftsmen the tools needed for their own work. We can assume a fair degree of bartering also going on between these two groups and it was the passing traders from further afield who provided them with a chance to buy goods which might not be local, as in the case of salt, oil and wine. These individuals were sometimes foreigners and by the late ninth century we know that Russian and Czech merchants were operating a flourishing salt trade along the middle Danube in Bavaria. The buying and selling of wax and honey, horses and slaves, was necessarily an international business but most trade within the Carolingian empire operated on a local and regional basis. The one exception is northern Italy whose markets were concentrated in the region's towns, and the historic continuity of these settlements extended back to the late Roman empire. Markets here were organized by churches and monasteries, as well as by abbeys, and many of those established from the ninth century onwards, in small towns like Bobbio (860), as well as in such major centres as Volterra, Piacenza and Mantua (894), were annual fairs operating within an international trading net-work concentrated in the north and north-east of the peninsula. The surplus products, mostly corn and oil, of these regions' abbatial estates would be transported along the Po and its tributaries to towns such as Pavia, Milan and Mantua, Parma, Cremona and Piacenza, where the abbeys' daughter foundations then took charge of the goods and arranged for their sale.

Centres located at the estuary of the Po, just like Venice to its north, produced hardly any agrarian goods of their own, but the large amounts of salt that they crystallized became the centre of a major trade which moved the commodity inland by travelling up the Po. By the mid-ninth century this business was being run by traders from Venice and Cremona, and its international aspect is revealed in the documents recording the pepper and cinnamon owed by Venetian traders to the great abbey of Bobbio, located near Piacenza.

The activities of Arab pirates (Saracens) made coastal navigation to the Provençal ports a hazardous enterprise during the Carolingian period, and Italy's international trade along the Mediterranean routes was therefore mostly restricted to the Adriatic in the eighth and ninth centuries. Venice was the major beneficiary of this shift, and a treaty of 812 between Charlemagne and the Byzantine emperor Michael gave the Venetians new access to eastern Mediterranean trade. Their economic interests were also well served by the *pactum Lotharii* of 840 which exempted the city from paying toll and berthing taxes in an arrangement which benefited both the *Serenissima* and the Franks. The continental kingdoms of the latter would now be opened up to Venetian economic enterprise, and Frankish traders were granted concessions in the Venetian shipping businesses. Goods such as the spices and textiles imported from the east, and furs from the Black Sea region, would be transported from Venice and the Po valley cities across the Alps to the Frankish empire; slaves from the Balkans and regions east of the Elbe were mostly conveyed by the Venetians to the south of the peninsula and to Sicily, where they would then be sold to Arabs.

The cities of what had once been southern Gaul were a melancholy sight in the eighth century. Major *civitates* of Roman origin such as Aix, Narbonne, Arles and Nîmes were much reduced, having been occupied or destroyed by Muslims, and their military function had suppressed the once flourishing economies associated with the towns. This Provençal decline would last until the end of the tenth century, but northern Europe by contrast was emerging as an important zone of international trade during the Carolingian era. Economic activity was especially evident along the Frankish kingdoms' frontier regions: along the coast of the Channel and that of the North Sea's southern reaches, on the Danish frontier, along the Elbe which divided the Franks from the Slavs, and also along the Danube. The growth in trade meant that major royal tolls were established in these areas, and international trade could be transported inland using the Rhine, Meuse and Danube.

Quentovic, Dorestad and Domburg, located on the southern coastline of the North Sea, and Hedeby, on the border with Denmark, were the major frontier emporia of the Carolingian age. These settlements traded with similar sites such as the English ones at Hamwic and

Lundenwic, the island of Birka near Stockholm, Kaupang near Oslo, and a large number of trading centres scattered along the Baltic region and extending as far as north-west Russia. The coastal emporia imported and exported a wide variety of mostly luxury goods: Dorestad and Domburg sent Rhenish wine to England and Scandinavia, and other goods sent from there included ceramics produced in Cologne and Bonn, millstones from the Eifel and glassware made in Kordel, near Trier. The major inland emporia along the Elbe included Magdeburg, conquered by Charlemagne and subsequently a nerve centre for the Slavs' Germanic colonization, and Bardowiek, whose name recalls its history as a Lombard centre before the tribal movement to the south and Italy. Once Saxony and the Danubian region had been conquered there was a regular flow of slaves, furs and wax across the Elbe–Saale–Danube border area from Saxony and eastern Europe. Slaves could be transported to the Arabs who were their eager buyers either through Venice, or along the Meuse and then the Rhône to southern France and, subsequently, to north-east Spain.

This extensive international and interregional trade required the services of a large number of agents. Kings, bishops and abbeys employed individual traders who worked on their behalf and received special protection in return. Their numbers included Jewish traders who worked together in groups, especially in the Rhône valley and Septimania. The Jewish merchants known as the Radanites, a word which could refer to a specific tribal grouping or may be the Carolingian term for Jews who traded internationally, were based in the Rhône valley and were celebrated on account of the length of their travels and their trading expertise. One Abbasid governor in eastern Persia wrote admiringly of the Radanites' mastery of 'Arabic, Persian, the languages of the Roman Empire, of the Franks, the Spanish, and the Slavs' and he went on to describe their method of operation. On occasions they would 'ship out from Frankish territory on the Mediterranean Sea' and then travel over the Suez land bridge before sailing down the Red Sea to Mecca and Medina. On other occasions they would sail across the Mediterranean to Antioch and then travel on the Euphrates to Baghdad. As non-Christians the Radanites were able to dominate their local trade in slaves, both male and female, as well as the one in eunuchs. And like a few other Carolingian traders

The octagonal cupola of Aachen's Palatine Chapel. The design of the chandelier, given by Frederick I Barbarossa in 1168, alludes to the Book of Revelation's description of the heavenly Jerusalem's towers.

Carolingian art arrives in Rome: S. Prassede's mosaics of the 820s are Byzantine-influenced but emphasise the city's own heritage. The triumphal arch illustrates the heavenly Jerusalem, frequently treated in Rome's earlier Christian art.

A reconstruction of the early-fourteenth-century Lateran complex, including the basilica and papal palace whose architectural forms had survived since the age of Charlemagne.

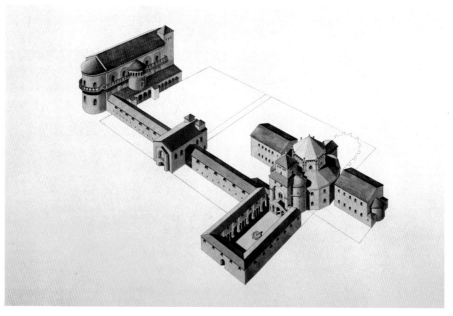

A modern reconstruction of the palace complex at Aachen, showing the *aula* or hall on the left, the chapel on the right, and connecting offices. The two-storied building intersecting the covered passage way was probably the royal residence.

The Crown of the Holy Roman Empire, first used at the imperial coronation of Otto I ('the Great') in 962, and fought over by successive monarchs who laid claim to Charlemagne's legacy.

Charlemagne's courtiers buried him in this late-second-century Roman sarcophagus which illustrates Proserpina's rape. The goddess has been gathering flowers with Minerva, and is abducted by Pluto. The matronly figure on the left is Ceres, goddess of fertility, who searches for her lost daughter.

Carolingian cavalry: a miniature from the Golden Psalter of St. Gall which dates from the 890s and was produced either in the monastery of St. Gall, Switzerland, or possibly at Soissons in the west Frankish kingdom.

The dedicatory page of *De Laudibus Sanctae Crucis*, a verse collection praising the Cross by Hrabanus Maurus (c.776-856), portrays Louis the Pious, Charlemagne's son and imperial successor (814–40), as Christ's soldier (*miles Christi*). A poem is superimposed.

The Lorsch Gospel's ivory cover, like the manuscript itself, was produced at Aachen by c. 810. This classicising treatment of the archangels and of Christ who treads on the beasts shows late Roman art's impact on Charlemagne's court.

Lesson for a ruler: the ivory cover produced in Reims for Charles the Bald's psalter in the 860s shows Nathan the prophet rebuking King David and comparing the rich man's flock with the poor man's single lamb.

The dedication page of Charles the Bald's Bible. Charlemagne's grandson, king of the western Franks (843–77), receives from Count Vivian, lay abbot of St. Martin, Tours, the luxurious illuminated Bible produced by the abbey's monks.

Charlemagne's grandson Lothair I, Holy Roman Emperor (840–855), and ruler of the 'middle kingdom' created by the treaty that divided the Carolingian empire in 843. These confidently sweeping forms mark a high point in Carolingian art.

Slavic, German, French and Roman personifications of Europe's civilisation pay homage in c. 998–1000 to the emperor Otto III whose dynasty revived the Carolingian imperial tradition.

Otto III's large-eyed stare recalls Constantine. Clergy and nobility are subordinated to the young emperor (996–1002) in his purple tunic. Otto wears a huge crown and is enthroned before a magnificent cloth of honour.

prepared to risk the Saracen-infested sea lanes of the Mediterranean, they also exported highly valued furs and swords to the Islamic east. A further journey into northern India and China would yield the spices and perfumes which were in great demand in the Christian west. The trading rights which underpinned these merchants' work would have been negotiated by the envoys sent by Charlemagne to the Caliph Harun al-Rashid at the time when the emperor secured some form of protectorate over the Christian holy sites in Jerusalem. Luxury goods moved in and out of Charlemagne's empire as a result of these import and export trading activities, but the threat of Arab piracy in the Mediterranean meant that this was a precarious and small-scale business. Europe's north and west offered not only new economic opportunities but also a more secure means of travel for goods and for those who dealt in them.

Traders employed by abbeys were more often than not unfree, although the evidence of Louis the Pious's *Praeceptum Negotiatorum* shows that they were nonetheless able to trade on their own account. There were also, however, some independent free merchants who were not just agents in the exclusive service of an individual or institution, and many of these were Frisians who operated mostly along the Rhine and also in England. The abbey of St-Maximin in Trier used the services of a Frisian merchant called Ibo in the early ninth century and he must have been very prosperous, since the maritime journey he made to (probably) England in association with other traders required six ships.

The coastal emporia of the Carolingian age did not, on the whole, outlive the dynasty. They were places invented for a particular purpose and, being so heavily dependent on the dynasty's inspiration and patronage, they mostly disappeared from the map with the final dissolution of Carolingian authority in the late ninth century. The settlements they traded with across the seas also tended to disappear at the same time since they had only existed in order to serve the Carolingian emporia. Hamwic was an exception in this regard, as was Lundenwic, a trading area which stretched across what is now the Strand in London. This coastal decline, however, was not the end of the story and the Carolingians' inland trading centres survived to become major centres of urban life and of European civilization in the later history of the

Middle Ages. In the eighth and ninth centuries these places, often called a *portus*, were overshadowed in importance by the coastal emporia, but sites such as Cologne and Mainz, both on the Rhine, as well as Ghent, Tournai and Valenciennes, all sited along the Scheldt, had an exciting future ahead of them in the year 900.

The trading patterns of the Carolingian economy were, as we have seen, predominantly local, regional and interregional, and they had evolved to meet the agrarian, craft and industrial needs of western Europe's rural estates. Luxury goods might excite the senses of the few but their economic consequence was dwarfed by the trade in food which helped to satisfy the daily needs of the many. Moreover, those engaged in trade of any kind were still for the most part acting as agents on behalf of the great landowners: the kings and nobles, the bishops, abbeys and monasteries.

Nonetheless, the signs of a greater economic independence and variety were clearly visible in many European areas and in many European lives during the age of Carolingian power. Traders who occasionally operated on their own accounts were starting to resemble the professional merchants who were already beginning to make their presence felt in western Europe and whose numbers would grow during the centuries of the high Middle Ages. The structures of the Carolingian economy, and the enterprise of those who operated within it, were renewing the material fabric of European existence, and the quickened tempo of the economic advance was the material expression of that sense of optimism which defined the civilization of the age.

CHAPTER 8

The Carolingian Cultural Renaissance

THREE MAPS: DIRECTIONS OF TRAVEL

From the late eighth century onwards western Europe's intellectual and artistic life was transformed by the Carolingian renaissance. Charlemagne's personality and interests shaped that revival, and his view of Carolingian culture determined the course taken by the renaissance during its ninth-century evolution. What were the ideas that shaped this great cultural movement and why did they matter so much to this warrior ruler? Some clues may be found in the details of the three engraved silver tables that he owned and which are recorded in Einhard's account of Charlemagne's will. We have already come across the table on which a map of the world was engraved, and this object was bequeathed to Charlemagne's royal heirs. The one which portrayed Rome was bequeathed to the see of Ravenna and a contemporary source records its arrival there, while the table whose map depicted Constantinople was destined for the papal court in Rome. None of these objects survives, although it has been speculated that the table depicting the known world was the one inherited by the emperor Lothair from his father Louis the Pious. We know that the map on Lothair's table showed not just the world's geographic details but also the planets and the interrelation of their movement. It rather suited the conceit both of the Franks and of the dynasty to interpret their own kingdom's earthly order in the context of that wider cosmology which revolved around it. This was the table that Lothair cut up into the separate pieces which he then distributed among some of his leading supporters, presumably as a way of affirming his solidarity with them, during the civil wars of 840–42. Its dismantling speaks volumes for the dwindling of imperial authority at that time.

Einhard says that Charlemagne's table map presented the world within three concentric circles, and this may have been a way of structuring the relationship between the three known continents of Europe, Asia and Africa, with possibly some cosmological detail added for good measure. There is no way of knowing exactly where the king kept these furnishings but his allocation of them in the royal will shows a keen appreciation of their symbolic worth. Constantinople was the second Rome, and the maps delineating those two cities would have been a daily reminder to Charlemagne and his household of the classical legacy in its imperial form. He wanted the Frankish elite to assimilate that tradition and make it part of their own identity. The Roman past would therefore live on in the Frankish present. These maps might give the king, his courtiers and his generals some reliably practical information about locations and the probable length of journeys. But they were also intended to demonstrate the Franks' mastery of the world and the breadth of their king's vision. Victories in battle had given them not only the power to exert territorial command in the here and now but also the right to lay claim to the most august cultural lineage of the past.

This was a renaissance with a compulsive desire to get things right, to dot the i's, cross the t's and leave no room for ambiguity. That obsession with orthodoxy, definition and classification lent a twitchy quality to the culture, and its controlling attitudes can seem claustrophobic. Take, for example, the Franks' preoccupation with the *filioque* clause of the Nicene Creed in the form they had adopted. Did the Holy Spirit, the Trinity's third person, proceed not just from the Father but also from the Son? The clause stated that it did and the Franks agreed. But the Church leaders of the Greek east pointed out that the clause had been added to the original text as agreed at the Council of Nicaea (325), and they wanted nothing to do with it. The how and the why of the clause's insertion remain uncertain, but it may have been invented in Spain during the late sixth century. That was a time and a place with a special interest in elevating the role of Christ the Son. Spain's Visigothic leaders were turning to Catholic Christianity and abandoning their old Arian ways. Arianism notoriously had denied the equality of the Son with the Father and had emphasized instead Christ's human nature. The *filioque* clause may therefore have been a particularly Spanish way of asserting orthodoxy by nailing Arianism. But whatever its origins may have been, by the eighth century the clause was being recited as part of the Creed right across western Europe. It had become the conventional religious wisdom of Latin Christianity, much to the annoyance of the Greek Churches. The Frankish lay and clerical intelligentsia brought their typical zealotry to the defence of the *filioque* clause, and Charlemagne's personal support for it at the Synod of Frankfurt in 794 is one of the many reasons why the Latins and the Greeks drifted apart.

Happily there is more to the Carolingian renaissance than the lethal game of hunt the heresy, and the movement's push towards the more effective Christianization of western Europe had important consequences for the region's languages. Charlemagne's mother tongue was probably Old High German and he may well have spoken this oldest form of the language in the Rhenish–Franconian dialect which was current in such centres as Speyer, Mainz and Frankfurt. The way the dialects of Old High German were written had been much influenced by Latin, and that fact would have helped Charlemagne to become bilingual. Einhard tells us that he spoke Latin fluently, and the evidence of the king's close involvement in the preparation of government documents supports that claim. But the Latin that was spoken and written in the seventh and eighth centuries in western Europe varied considerably. The Latin heard and read in regions of Spain, Italy and southern France was evolving into the differing forms of the Romance languages, and the Latin current among the Franks was similarly diverse.

A king who was keen on unity and eager for his commands to be understood by as many people as possible had a problem on his hands. Latin was the only language which was common to most of Charlemagne's territories, but when he came to the throne it was hardly a *lingua franca*. Grammarians and scholars who enjoyed Charlemagne's patronage, such as Paulinus of Aquileia, were therefore set to work to produce the rules which had to be followed in order to get Latin back to its earlier uniformity. Alcuin's *De Orthographia* set out the correct spelling and was based largely on Bede's work of the same name. This revived Latin provided Charlemagne with an instrument for his *Sprachen-politik*, and it may have been too formal by half. We shall return to that criticism later, but the fact that literacy was so highly valued was of immense importance. Major jobs in the secular administration and the Church went to those who could read and write proficiently, and from the 790s there was a dramatic improvement in the orthography, grammar and spelling of the Latin language. That standardization was a direct result of the king's resolve and its achievement shows just how effective Charlemagne was as an administrator. His actions gave Latin a new lease of life as the official language of the Frankish government and the Carolingian empire, and its predominance in education, law and religion gave a structure to Charlemagne's cultural project. Latin had become once again a tool of empire and its introduction to conquered areas where it was previously unknown, such as Saxony, promoted their assimilation.

In about 786 Charlemagne described the 'vigilant zeal' necessary in order 'to repair the ... learning, almost destroyed by the sloth of our forefathers'. The texts of the Old and New Testaments, 'corrupted by the ignorance of copyists', were now being corrected, but there was a continuing need 'to master the studies of the liberal arts'. Those arts were grammar, rhetoric and logic – collectively termed the *trivium* – and they were supplemented by the *quadrivium* which consisted of arithmetic, geometry, music and astronomy. These were the *artes liberales* of late antiquity, so called because it was men who were free who studied them rather than slaves, and the curricular grouping of the subjects had enjoyed widespread currency from the sixth century onwards. Charlemagne's interest in them had a typically disciplinarian edge. He had received letters from certain monasteries, he complained in about 784, and 'in most of these writings their sentiments were sound but their language was uncouth . . . because of their neglect of learning their unskilled tongues could not express it without fault'. A good deal of the Carolingian cultural programme can be summarized as a rejection of the idea that it was enough just to be well-meaning. Indeed, a rough and ready approach to expression was positively dangerous since careless talk and shoddy writing created misunderstanding. Hence Charlemagne's minatory conclusion: 'those who seek to please God by right living may not neglect to please him also by right speaking. We are well aware that, although verbal errors are dangerous, errors of understanding are more so.' He considered it his duty to get his subjects to think straight. So let us turn to the ambitious details of the Carolingian curriculum for the nation.

BUILDING THE NATION

The Carolingian venture was an experiment in the arts of government, the result of a co-ordinated attempt at framing the laws and at influencing the beliefs of a whole society. The revival inaugurated by Charlemagne, and continued by his ninth-century heirs and successors, issued in legislation whose ambitious scope sought to govern human conduct in ways that were both novel and, compared to the immediate Germanic past, highly intrusive. Being comprehensive in its ambitions, the scheme was directed towards the renovation of a society's collective mentality, its framework of assumptions about what might or might not be admirable, as well as prescribing the external conduct of the king's subjects. There was therefore a pragmatic, utilitarian and ideological aspect to the work of the educated and literate individuals who were attracted to Charlemagne's court, and the undoubted glories of the Carolingian renaissance in arts and letters were meant to be 'socially useful'.

The Church–State axis was all-important to this programme of reform and the diocesan structure provided a framework for its implementation. Charlemagne had already reigned for over a quarter of a century when the movement was gaining pace, and as a result most of the bishops had assumed office during his time on the throne. They were therefore the king's men, sympathetic to his aims and administratively adroit in delivering what Charlemagne wanted. His instincts were also theirs, and the Church structure had already benefited from the king's preoccupation with order, hierarchy and orthodoxy. The arrangements decreed by the king for Church affairs in 779, after bishops, abbots and counts had been consulted, were typically rigorous in their combination of the bureaucratic with the ethical. Tithe collection would now be under episcopal control and there were limits to criminals' rights to claim sanctuary in a church building. The rules to be followed in monasteries were defined, as was the jurisdiction of bishops over their diocesan clergy and in relation to lay people who committed incest.

Charlemagne wanted a well-organized Church, rigorous in its self-discipline and zealous in its invigilation of the laity's conduct. He was also eager to tell the clergy what they should be reading. He never let up, and in the year before he died, during a series of Church councils held at Reims, Tours, Mainz, Arles and Chalon-sur-Saône, he was still issuing reading lists for the clergy. They were to study not just the Gospels, the Epistles of Paul and the Acts of the Apostles but also patristic texts and canon law, and the laity had to be taught the Creed and the Lord's Prayer. An immense amount of effort went into the royal definition of details such as these, and the intensity of that concern shows the way in which civil order and religious experience were so inextricably interfused that it is impossible to separate 'Church' from 'State' in this society. Charlemagne would not have regarded himself as 'intervening' in Church affairs. Rather, he was the ruler of a realm whose population was being turned into a Christian people, and whose salvation was therefore his urgent concern. His militancy on this question may seem surprising. Christianity, after all, was hardly a new arrival in eighth-century Francia, and the sees located in the south of what had been Roman Gaul already had centuries of history behind them. But so far as Charlemagne was concerned Christianity still needed to conduct itself within the kingdom of the Franks as if it was a missionary religion. He wanted it to be distinctive, dynamic and uncompromising – rather like the Franks themselves, in fact. The congruence is not accidental. This austere form of Christianity was both Charlemagne's personal faith and at the same time a creed whose missionary rigour made it particularly useful in building up the national identity. The longer he sat on the throne, the more distinctive that identity became in the eyes of others as well as in those of the Franks themselves. War and conquest pushed them to new frontiers where they encountered non-Christians such as the Avars, the Saxons, and the Muslims in Spain. Confronted with cultures that were entirely alien to them, the Franks gained a keener appreciation of their own difference and came to exult in that distinctiveness.

Despite the intensity of the Frankish propaganda about being a chosen race and one which was a fit heir to the Greeks and the Romans, the Francia of the early to mid-eighth century was nonetheless a comparatively backward place in terms of the intellectual and cultural standards which obtained at court. It had, as we shall see, certain advantages in terms of its access to manuscripts which were both many and varied, profane and sacred. But Francia's political leaders, those whose beliefs and conduct furnished the Carolingian world with its exemplars, still occupied a rebarbative warrior milieu which compared badly with such centres of contemporary sophistication as the courts of Visigothic Spain or those of the Anglo-Saxon kingdoms of Northumbria and Kent. Nonetheless, the fact that he was starting more or less from scratch in terms of governmental cultural policy also worked in Charlemagne's favour when it came to the propagation of his programme and its typical mix of classical Roman and Catholic Christian influences. Francia offered him and his advisers among the Carolingian intelligentsia a *tabula rasa* – a population which could conceive of no alternative to the cultural experiment imposed upon them from above.

In order to staff his initiative Charlemagne had to turn to the Church since that was the body which enjoyed by and large a monopoly of education and literacy, and he needed to recruit in large numbers given the scale of his ambitions. His own kingdom could not supply him with enough educated clerics and he therefore had to look to the more advanced cultures that lay beyond Francia's boundaries. Regions which had been conquered by the Franks, as Lombardy had been; countries occupied by hostile powers, as in the case of Visigothic Spain which was now under Islamic rule; royal domains such as Anglo-Saxon England which enjoyed good relations with Francia: all supplied a mix of individuals suitable to the king's purposes. Whether they were imported to the imperial heartland from its newly acquired provinces, provided with refuge from a hostile occupying force, or simply invited to cross the national borders and offered employment, the Carolingian intelligentsia found themselves members of a movement which took its lead from the king himself.

The personal imprint is shown in Charlemagne's republication in 802 of the *Dionysia-Hadriana*, a document which set out the rules governing the Church and clergy. This framework of canon law had originally been compiled by the Syrian monk Dionysius Exiguus in the early sixth century, and was handed to the king by Pope Hadrian I when Charlemagne visited Rome in 774. Reissued as a governmental edict, the regulations provided the king with a legislative authority in Church affairs and the power to oversee the work of the clergy – including those who were working on his cultural programme. Biblical study was basic to that project and Charlemagne was an enthusiast for the Scriptures, which were interpreted as providing a convenient basis for his own authority and a portrayal of the way in which 'the superiors should act towards their subjects and the subjects towards their superiors'. The last twenty years of the reign, a period which saw a vast expansion and consolidation of the imperial territory, are also a time which sees an accelerated rate of production of biblical texts by the copyists working under ecclesiastical supervision in the *scriptoria*. The king's new subjects had to be educated in the virtues of obedience, and biblical studies, like other areas of Carolingian scholarship, followed that utilitarian imperative.

The planned national renewal took its cue from the papacy, an institution which had decided that, in the words of eighth-century papal officials, 'of all the kingdoms the Frankish shines forth in the sight of the Lord'. Nation-building therefore involved the Franks' identification with papal policy and a break with the tribal past. No longer was the Frankish kingdom to be seen as a mere collection of individual units, of families and tribes, of conquered areas brought together under the crown as a result of fortuitous victories won on the field of battle. These aspects of the Germanic past would now be overlaid by something stronger and deeper: the principle and the idea of a holy nation.

Just as the individual Christian was directed from his past and emerged, through baptism, into a new life, so too an entire society was to be consecrated to a new and higher purpose as a result of a collective baptism. The key terms repeated in the official documents issued by Charlemagne and written by his officials make this very clear. *Renovare, emendare, revocare, reformare, renasci*: those who read or heard these words would have been familiar with them as a description of the processes which had turned individuals into the new kind of people called Christians. The terms were now being used in a social and governmental sense, and the Carolingian renaissance was a cultural programme directed towards the reformation, renewal and rebirth of a society. The clerics and scholars who had been recruited to ensure these aims were therefore part of the governmental machine, and since universities did not exist at this time the notion of an independent-minded intelligentsia is irrelevant to the Europe of the eighth and ninth centuries. A vocationally directed programme placed scholarship and learning at the service of the ruler, and the kind of literature which was studied served to enhance the ruler's status.

The set texts favoured by this renaissance were overwhelmingly written in Latin, and the movement by and large ignored Greek works. Books by Tertullian and Cyprian, Jerome, Boethius and Cassiodorus transmitted a Christian culture which had been recast in terms of Roman ideas of law and government, and the notion of imperial authority informed these authors' attitudes. Early Christian writers such as these had also often absorbed the influence of the Hellenistic milieu with its own distinctive emphasis on the ideology and cult of the ruler. It was by these means that an originally Germanic society was wrenched from its own past and reinterpreted so that it could adapt to a cultural framework which had originally been alien to it. The Roman, Latin and Christian culture of southern Europe and the eastern Mediterranean which was transplanted to Europe's north and west acquired a new definition, and that formulation obliged rulers by providing them with new justifications for their political power. A nexus of ideology provided classical culture with a new rationale, and that fact ensured its continuing dominance in shaping the beliefs of the educated and the powerful up to and beyond the more inclusive renaissance which originated in the Italian city-states of the fourteenth century.

A renaissance communicated through the Latin language had the ability to transcend Europe's various regions. In this respect the movement reflected a time when the continent's internal boundaries were ill-defined, and the idea that distinctively separate national groupings even existed had yet to be expressed at the beginning of our period. But beside this cosmopolitan quality the Carolingian renaissance was also typified by two kinds of narrowness. It was, in the first place, the creation of an intellectual elite which consisted overwhelmingly of the higher clerical class, and this resulted in a certain preciosity of style and rigidity of thought. The mental preoccupations of that elite and its way of life were infinitely removed from the material circumstances and concerns of the mass of the population who were simply viewed as the raw material which had to be moulded into an appropriate shape by the privileged few. The consequences of that fact would loom large in the intellectual life of the later medieval centuries, framed as they were by so much of the Carolingian legacy.

This separation was further emphasized by the intelligentsia's concentration on Latin as its written form of expression at a time when the speech of western European peoples was rapidly evolving from vulgar or popular Latin into the earliest forms of the Romance languages. The parochial clergy had to preach in the vernacular if they were to communicate with their flock, but this was a tenuous cultural link with the wider Carolingian project and the local priests were in any event mostly unlearned men. An emphasis on Latin also indicates the depth of another divide, the one that separated western Europe from the Greek-speaking east. The Carolingian renaissance elevated Latin as the language of its high culture, but in doing so it reinforced the earliest example of an east–west divide in the continent's history.

That division, however, was hardly one invented by Charlemagne or by the Carolingians. Its roots lay in the breakup of late antique culture, and the distinctive nature of the Carolingian renaissance can only be understood by appreciating its relationship to that background.

LATE ANTIQUE CULTURE: STRATEGIES FOR SURVIVAL

From the mid-fifth century onwards the last schools of classical antiquity disappeared from the territories of the former western Roman empire. In the eastern empire, however, the cultural scene remained a lively one for another 200 years and it was the seventh-century onslaughts by Persians and Avars, Slavs and Arabs which eventually led to a major disruption in the communication of antique culture in these areas. The Greek empire survived these onslaughts, but did so in part by emphasizing its Hellenic identity as the bond which united Byzantium's subjects and distinguished their culture from that of the barbarians at its gates. Latin–Greek bilingualism, an important feature of the eastern empire before this crisis, was abandoned, and as a result the political, military and diplomatic differences between the Latin west and the Greek east were reinforced by a linguistic divide.

The Germanic tribes which came into contact with the culture of late Roman antiquity in the west lacked any kind of public educational institutions. But the history of culture, like that of politics and warfare, shows that it would be wrong to interpret the period as one in which massive waves of invading barbarians overwhelmed an enfeebled empire. There had been long-term contacts between these two kinds of human society on the imperial frontiers, and even after the empire's western collapse there were various ways in which the culture of the written word survived. The Roman nobility in the towns and provinces responded to the crisis by educating their children domestically, and at an institutional level the bishoprics and monasteries of the Christian Church provided an education for its future clergy as well as for those who had been baptized. The large estates and towns might now fall within the boundaries of barbarian kingdoms, but they contained centres of cultivation, where children were educated to read and write in Latin and where the manuscripts of the ancient authors were still being copied.

A traditional class of literate Roman professionals also found employment at the courts of the new rulers who needed them in order to administer their new territories and to draw up the documents which governed relations between the new settlers and the native population. The barbarian invaders were heavily outnumbered by the original inhabitants of the areas they now ruled and as a result there was a substantial assimilation of the newcomers to Latin culture. Peoples such as the Goths had in any event a long history of close involvement with Roman civilization, but even the leaders of those tribes which lacked that kind of experience tended to defer to the cultural superiority of Rome's civilization, a fact which also led to assimilation.

The greatest single cause of the transformation in classical culture's aims and means had been at work centuries before the empire's breakup, and its consequences continued to develop after the imperial dissolution. It was Christianization which had changed the process of classical education, and it did so by directing it towards a spiritual end and a religious goal: the knowledge of God and instruction in the means of salvation. The Church was certainly the means by which much of the learning of classical antiquity was preserved, but it also changed the way in which the authors of that past were supposed to be understood. Ancient culture had now been co-opted into the Christian providentialist scheme, and virtuous pagans were interpreted as anticipating the fuller wisdom inaugurated by Christ's birth and confirmed by the arrival of a Church which expounded his teachings. The Church's pedagogic and scholarly institutions continued to develop these themes long after, and despite, the violent breakup of the fifth century.

The debate about the relationship between Christianity and the classical past acquired a new focus towards the end of the sixth century. Political and military events explain why that discussion suddenly became more urgent. After the end of Justinian's reign in 565 Byzantium went into a sudden decline, and in the 620s the empire came under sustained attack from both the Persians and the Slavs. This is also the period when the Burgundian and Ostrogothic kingdoms, both of them Arian in belief, disappeared, and in 589 Spain's Visigothic rulers decided to abandon Arianism and embrace orthodox Catholicism. These events increased the authority of the western Church's version of Christianity, and that process is reflected in the writings of four men of genius: Gregory of Tours working in Francia, Cassiodorus in Italy, Pope Gregory the Great, and Isidore of Seville, the writer whose zealous organization of knowledge has led to his early twenty-first-century status as patron saint of the internet. The encyclopaedias of knowledge written by Isidore and Cassiodorus show the self-confidence of a Christian intelligentsia which believed that it could produce a kind of *summa* of human knowledge, while both Pope Gregory and Gregory of Tours showed great skill in adapting Christianity to different levels of understanding, and communicating the truths of faith in a way appropriate to often uneducated audiences. All four of them reflect a western Christian consensus that providence was showing its hand and rewarding faith with success.

This is a period when the shift from the Mediterranean towards the European north, west and north-west gathers pace. Byzantine north Africa had been showing signs of economic stagnation even before it was conquered by Islam. Southern Italy had fallen victim to the quar-

rels between the Lombards and Byzantium. And the Merovingian kingdoms were still at this stage rent by internal divisions. The south and
the centre of what had been the western Roman empire were therefore
stagnating politically and economically, and that regression was reflected
in these areas' cultural life. Cultural progress was instead concentrated
in northern Italy, the abbeys of northern France, and in the monastic
schools of north-west Spain as well as in the Iberian south, and especially in Baetica and Toledo, where Isidore's influence would lead to a
true renaissance of learning. It was, however, the British Isles that provided some of the most startling evidence of cultural take-off.

Ireland was in a unique position since both Christianity and the Latin
language arrived there at the same time, and the missionary impulse
which characterized the Irish scholars, monks and priests from the fifth
century onwards owed much to that fact. They exported first to England, and then to Gaul and Germany, a Christian culture which was
rooted in scholarship and literary refinement. The Christian civilization
of the Anglo-Saxons ensured the rebirth of Latinity in the southern half
of the country, and then secured its introduction to Northumbria whose
finest mind, the Venerable Bede, produced works of scholarship that
gained a European reputation for the culture of the English.

Justinian's attempt at reconquering the western parts of the Roman
empire had important consequences for sixth-century cultural life. He
tried to restore the public scholastic institutions on a widespread basis,
but this initiative met with lasting success only in the imperial capital
cities of Carthage, Rome and Ravenna. The reconquest of north Africa
from the Vandals, however, did lead to a resumption of literary and
scholarly life. It was in this province that the grammarian Flavius Cresconius Corippus produced the last Roman epic devoted to a military theme,
the *Johannide* whose Virgilian hexameters praise the victories won by
General John Troglytus over the Berber tribesmen. In Spain, though,
the cultural scene was very different. Justinian's armies succeeded in
occupying only a narrow coastal strip of land, and there were few signs
of a literary and artistic revival. It was the conversion of the Visigoths
to Catholic Christianity which made the difference here, and which also
supplies the context for the emergence of Isidore in the last years of the
Byzantine occupation. That conversion oriented the Spanish kingdom

away from Byzantium, and in 624 Isidore would celebrate (in his *Historia Gothorum*) the expulsion of the last Greek soldiers from Spanish soil. Isidore's brand of Spanish nationalism meant that he distrusted oriental Christianity and, knowing very little Greek, his works are overwhelmingly based on Latin sources. He is a powerful witness to the growing east–west divide across the European continent, a historic fissure which would be consolidated by the Carolingian renaissance.

The intervention of Justinian's armies had a disastrous impact on cultural life in Italy, just as it did on the peninsula's politics. A long war (536–55) ended in the ruination of the Ostrogothic kingdom and also destroyed the earlier co-operation between Gothic rulers and Italian natives. Spain would eventually see the benefits of an assimilation between its Visigothic rulers and the Hispano-Roman population, but Italy would experience no comparable process. This was a protracted crisis which continued into the second half of the sixth century when the peninsula's north, and then parts of its south, were occupied by the Lombards, a race which took a long time to adapt to Latin culture. The Lombard dynasty centred at Pavia did eventually convert to Catholic Christianity, a fact which helped its local assimilation from about 650 onwards, but it was only in the succeeding century that Italy's written culture showed any signs of revival.

Two solitary examples from early sixth-century Italy show the significance of what was lost. Boethius and Cassiodorus were Italian senators and both were unusually open to the influence of Greek culture. Any list of 'makers of the Middle Ages' has to include Anicius Manlius Severinus Boethius whose grand lineage connected him with the eminent Roman *gentes* of the Anicii and the Symmachi. He wrote four treatises on the four mathematical arts and called these the *quadrivium*, a term and an organization of disciplines which would prevail in European education for almost a thousand years. He also started on the work of translating the whole of the Aristotelian corpus, and though his execution in 525 left the project uncompleted, he had managed to finish his translation of Aristotle's book on logic. As a direct result Aristotelian logic dominated the curriculum of western education and the work of western philosophers for centuries, and Aristotle's other works would only become known to the west from the twelfth century onwards as a result of the work of Arab translators. Boethius fell victim to King Theoderic the Great's suspicion that he was conspiring with the Byzantines, and it is a striking paradox that it was the intervention of a Byzantine emperor, Justinian, which created the Italian dislocation that secured the effective removal of Greek culture from western Europe. The book that Boethius wrote during his imprisonment, *The Consolation of Philosophy*, is a synthesis of Greek thought with Christian sensibility, and its profound meditation on how the philosophic spirit enables the afflicted to endure misfortune made it one of the most widely read works of the Middle Ages.

The decision taken by Benedict of Nursia and by Cassiodorus, both of whom were Boethius's contemporaries, to withdraw from the world was a reaction to the turbulent circumstances of the early sixth century. Flavius Magnus Aurelius Cassiodorus Senator was a member of the ancient senatorial aristocracy and became the Ostrogothic kingdom's senior administrator as *magister officiorum*, the office in which he had been preceded by Boethius, and he subsequently became the praetorian prefect for Italy. The collapse of the Ostrogothic government led to his departure for Constantinople where he stayed for some two decades immersing himself in theological studies, and on his return to the peninsula he established the monastery of Vivarium on his family's Calabrian estate in southern Italy. He was a significant collector of manuscripts for the monastery's library, and a very active *scriptorium* also translated works from the Greek. Vivarium represented Cassiodorus's attempt at bringing together Latin culture and Greek thought, both Christian and classical, and its success was a major western European phenomenon: some of the manuscripts in the Vivarium library as well as copies of Cassiodorus's own translations can be shown to have travelled to the Aachen of Charlemagne and to Northumberland.

The title of his two books of *Institutions* recalls Cassiodorus's training in Roman law: *Divine Institutions* is devoted to the sacred Scriptures and discusses their correct chronological sequence, while *Human Institutions* gives an abridgment of the seven liberal arts as the basis of secular culture. Many literate individuals in late antique civilisation enjoyed copying and correcting manuscripts. But it was Cassiodorus who, seeing that such work was necessary for the transmission of a

Christian culture, made sure that it became more than just a hobby for the cultivated. He organized the lives of the copyists he employed, looked after the material needs of this cadre of scholars, and Vivarium at its site on the shores of the Ionian Sea can be described as Europe's first post-Roman institute of advanced study. The example of those who worked there, and the widespread diffusion of their works, meant that these techniques of copying supplied Christian monks of the future with the professional basis of their manuscript expertise, and that work in turn would become an element in the armoury of medieval Christian apologetics and spiritual combat.

Benedict's disavowal of the world was more inward-directed than that of Cassiodorus, an ambitious man whose luck had run out, and the emphasis of the movement that he founded was single-mindedly Christian. In c. 500, when he would have been about twenty years old, this son of a Roman nobleman embarked on the hermetic life and withdrew to a grotto near Subiaco in central Italy. The *Rule* that Benedict wrote for the monks of Monte Cassino in the mid-sixth century would be followed by the monasteries associated with his name, and its last chapter is a prescribed reading list including the Old and New Testaments, patristic literature and the lives of the Fathers of the desert – those Middle Eastern figures who had established the first monasteries in the Egyptian desert. Study of some of the early Church Fathers enabled Benedict's monks to know a little about Greek Christianity, but classical authors were irrelevant to the founder's aim: a mental training suitable for those engaged in spiritual warfare in a west which was going through a crisis.

Outside the ranks of the religious clergy or monks stood the secular clergy who served in parishes and also needed to be educated. Caesarius of Arles, a figure of major intellectual importance and the town's bishop from 503 to 542, was a pioneer in training his clergy to use a kind of pared-down Latin (the *sermo humilis*) when preaching to their mostly rural congregations. Like so many bishops before him, Caesarius lived a communal life with his clergy, taught them personally, and questioned them on their understanding of what they had read. During the sixth century a number of new institutions designed to educate the clergy emerged in southern Gaul, Spain and Rome. A Church council which met at Vaison-la-Romaine in 529 stipulated that parish clergy, 'following the customs, already old, of Italy', should educate those destined for a clerical career. Two years later the Council of Toledo prescribed the form of that education and stipulated that it should take place 'in the house of the Church in the presence of the Bishop, by a person appointed to that post', and that the training should last until the age of eighteen when the young made their final choice between the Church and a worldly career. Cassiodorus's ambitious attempt at establishing a school of higher studies in Rome in 535 followed the model of the *Didascaleion* of Alexandria, a major centre for scriptural exegesis and the study of early Christian history, and the institution where Origen had worked in the early third century. A Christian university is what Cassiodorus had hoped for, and although the plan did not succeed in Rome, some of its essential features were incorporated in the aims of the monastery he went on to establish at Vivarium.

The way in which the classical culture of late antiquity evolved into that of early medieval Christianity reflected therefore the political changes in western Europe, and it also varied according to the pace and nature of those developments. Gaul's division into two civil dioceses during the later Roman empire acknowledged the differences between the north and a more profoundly Romanized south. The density of the Frankish occupation in the north accentuated that division and produced a sixth-century civilization which blended the Gallo-Romanic written culture with the more utilitarian skills associated with the Germanic courts, in areas such as land surveying, architecture and medicine, while to the north-west the British Isles at this same time were gaining their reputation for literature written in an affectedly elegant form of Latin. *De Excidio et Conquestu Britanniae* (*On the Ruin and Conquest of Britain*), written by the priest Gildas, conforms to that style and is an extended jeremiad against the local princes and clergy who are held responsible for a collapse of British civilization by the mid-seventh century. Byzantium was enduring its prolonged crisis from the late sixth century onwards and its north African territories were being subjected to intensive attacks from the Berbers of the interior. The paralysis of authority in Italy deepened further as a result of the Lombard invasions from the north, the first wave of which can be dated to 568.

Gaul's evolution into early Merovingian Francia was marked by severe conflicts and a breakup into its new constituent kingdoms, but the Frankish nobility nonetheless displayed a striking commitment to their common, and literate, culture even while they were killing one another. Chilperic I of Neustria (c. 539–84) led his kingdom into a prolonged, and treacherously conducted, war against his brother Sigebert, ruler of Austrasia, but he was also noticeably cultured, a competent musician, a decent poet and a reformer of the Germanic alphabet – as well as the author of an anti-Trinitarian polemic, a fact which earned him the enmity of Gregory of Tours.

There were about 200 monasteries spread across the Merovingian domains, and the early Frankish Church was a determined and cultured institution whose resolve on reform and high standards is recorded in the Acts, written in decent Latin, recording the thirty Church councils held in Gaul between 560 and 637. The literary work of Gregory, bishop of Tours from 572 to 594, is one of the most vivid examples of that Frankish cultural evolution in the central Gaul of this period. Tours contained St Martin's tomb and it was therefore something of a spiritual centre for the Franks. Its bishop was a well-connected figure, a member of the province's senatorial aristocracy, and Gregory was educated in the *domus ecclesiae* of his uncle Gallus, the bishop of Clermont-Ferrand. That social status explains why he was able to stand up to King Chilperic whose depredations of Church lands, as well as his unorthodox theology, were a source of tension between the two men.

Personal knowledge and experience give real life to Gregory's account of the disruptions and chaos of Merovingian dynastic history between 580 and 591, the subject of the last four books in his ten-volumed *History*. He lamented the decline of his own age in something of the conservative spirit of a *laudator temporis acti*, though the Latinity of his own prose style corresponded to present needs and was therefore decidedly rough and ready. But it is his connection with his audience and his readership which lends authority and interest to Gregory's works, especially in the numerous works of hagiography that he wrote recounting the lives of confessors, saints and martyrs of the past. There was an immense appetite for this kind of literature in seventh-century Francia, and Gaul as a whole would produce more hagiographical texts than any other part of the previously Roman world. Whether read in private, or listened to in an almost liturgical setting, these texts showed how Christianity was acquiring deeper roots. Caesarius of Arles once described how he used to lock the church doors to ensure that his flock did not leave during the sermon, and Christianity's reception, especially in rural Gaul, was a long-term and patchy affair. But the half-century that divides the age of Caesarius from that of Gregory had made a difference, and there were popular roots to the Frankish conviction that theirs was an especially effective and privileged form of Christianity.

Spain's recovery was perhaps the most remarkable of any of the old Roman provinces and was well established even before the conversion of King Reccared to Catholic Christianity in 587 followed by that of the entire Visigothic nobility at the Third Council of Toledo two years later. Recarred's father, Leovigild, had unified almost the entire peninsula between 567 and 586, and his approval of mixed marriages had led to the Romanization of the Visigoths. A distinctive Hispano-Gothic nation had therefore emerged by c. 600, and Isidore of Seville's enthusiastic scholarship of the early seventh century is its greatest single adornment. The Isidorean renaissance, just like that of the Carolingians which it anticipates in so many ways, was polemical in its aims, and the kind of knowledge that it celebrated was designed to be politically useful in the task of building up national identity.

Leander, Isidore's brother who was also his predecessor in the metropolitan see of Seville, had been an effective propagandist against Arianism among the peninsula's aristocratic circles. The fusion of Catholic Christianity with a Spanish national identity, itself the synthesis of Goths with Romans, of the Germanic with the Latin, was a momentous affair, and its cultural consequences changed the cultural map of Europe. Works such as his *In Praise of Spain* and *History of the Goths* show Isidore at work as the supreme ideologist of that new identity, an achievement which he saw as a blueprint for the future Christian history of the continent as a whole.

The capital of the province of Toledo became a major cultural centre and it was there that the children of the nobility were taught. Toledo's court became a significant source of literary and cultural patronage, and several of Isidore's successors as archbishop were prolific authors of works of grammar and history, of theology and poetry. *The Rebellion of Paul against Wamba*, written by Julian who was Seville's bishop from 679 to 690, is an animated work of Visigothic history, and several other works of theology, biblical criticism and poetry flowed from his pen. This rich cultural idealism would, however, come unstuck in the Spain of the late seventh century when noble anarchy and anti-Semitism disfigured the country's politics. But it was little wonder that Carolingian scholars rediscovered Isidore and revived his relevance to their own project of the *reformatio* of a society in which Church and government were thoroughly interfused. Isidore's comprehensive aims and wide scholarship are seen to best effect in his extraordinary *Etymologies*, an encyclopaedia devoted to 'the origins of certain things' and a repository of knowledge borrowed from ancient and patristic sources. Definitions, synonyms and accounts, often highly fanciful or just speculative, of the origins of words are jumbled together in the twenty books of the *Etymologies*, which became a key reference work for Europe's literate classes in the long centuries of its continent-wide influence.

Isidore's authority helped to fix the meaning of words and as a result early medieval Europe's fledgling culture could deploy Latin vocabulary and grammar in a newly confident way. The educated populations of the British Isles found the *Etymologies* especially useful since Christianity and Latinity marched hand in hand both in Ireland and in the Anglo-Saxon kingdoms. An emphasis on correct Latin was therefore associated with the correct definition of Christianity in insular societies, and both stood apart from the pagan milieu of a native population, who had their own languages, and who were to be converted to the new faith. This was a missionary enterprise conducted in the evangelists' own countries, but the Irish, or *Scotti* as they were called by contemporaries, also showed a remarkable zeal for the continental mission, which for them included the Anglo-Saxon kingdoms as well as the European mainland. Their journeys had a direct cultural impact since they so often carried with them the manuscript copies of texts, many of which had been produced in Irish monasteries. This was one of the means by which Isidore's *Treaty of Nature*, for example, was diffused through continental Europe in the seventh century. The Irishman Columbanus was a notable monastic itinerant and the journey that he took in the early seventh century from Burgundy and across the Alps was marked by the foundation of monasteries which would play a major role in the culture and politics of subsequent centuries, such as Luxeuil, St-Gall and Bobbio. The Northumbrian abbot Benedict Biscop, who made six journeys to Rome between 653 and 668, must have been a physically resilient character. He carried back from Rome a large number of important manuscripts, and on one occasion he persuaded a member of St Peter's choral staff to return with him in order to teach Gregorian chant to his monks.

Such a diffusion of texts and manuscripts helps to explain the refined quality of insular Latin, and the literature produced in these regions was often of a high and distinctive quality. The mingling of pre-existing Irish and Celtic literary tradition with the new Latin influence can be seen in the rhythmic lines of Irish hagiographies, works which often also sought to show off the authors' learning by using words borrowed from Greek and Hebrew. Insular Britain's other original culture, that of the Romano-Britons who were pushed west and north by the Anglo-Saxon invaders, produced its own heroic age of poetry from the early seventh century onwards. Poems such as *Y Gododdin*, composed in the British kingdom of Strathclyde c. 600, were composed in Welsh, a language which was profoundly influenced by the Latin of Roman Britain's earlier rulers as well as by that of the contemporary seventh century.

England's cultural formation of course included not just the Celtic–Roman influences which arrived from across the Irish Sea but also the direct transmission of Catholic Christianity from Rome to southern England. The cosmopolitan nature of this evangelization was shown by the arrival in Canterbury in 669 of the African abbot Hadrian, who had been bishop of Naples, and of the eastern monk Theodore of Tarsus. Friendships sustained through correspondence and maintained through the formation of small groups of the learned were at the heart of scholarly Christianity, as can be seen in the career of Aldhelm, who was abbot of Malmesbury from 683 until his death in 709. He was probably a member of the royal family of Wessex but was sent to Canterbury to be educated personally by Hadrian, who was now abbot of St Augustine's. Aldhelm returned to Wiltshire where he joined a community of scholars under the direction of Maeldulph, but Hadrian was a strong influence on him and he rejoined the abbot for a further period in Canterbury before eventually committing himself to the group established in Malmesbury.

Maeldulph's original circle of monks and scholars seems to have been a fairly informal grouping and the idea of a common rule only emerged later when Aldhelm's scholarly fame attracted foreign students, including ones from Francia. In c. 683 this collection of individuals came together to form a religious community following the rule of Benedict, and Aldhelm, gifted in Greek, Latin and Hebrew and a significant poet in his own native tongue, became their abbot. The abbey's reputation for learning, aided perhaps by Aldhelm's family connections, meant that it was richly endowed by the Wessex royal family, and Aldhelm's fame outlasted his own time. Alfred the Great regarded him as the first of the major Anglo-Saxon poets, though Aldhelm also composed verses in Latin, and his ballads, according to William of Malmesbury, were still being sung in twelfth-century England. He was an important royal agent in King Ine's attempts at persuading the remnants of the ancient British Church in Cornwall to accept Anglo-Saxon ecclesiastical disciplines. But Aldhelm's reputation, especially as a result of his ferocious treatise in defence of virginity, was also a European one, and we know that he made at least one journey to Rome at the invitation of Pope Sergius I.

From the mid-seventh century onwards a remarkable confluence of Roman, Gallo-Roman and Irish influences spread to the north of England, and achieved its greatest expression in the religious foundations of Northumbria. Aidan of Iona had already established Lindisfarne in 635, but it was the twin monasteries of Wearmouth and Jarrow, founded in 674 and 685 respectively, which were the beacons of Northumbrian learning and provided Alcuin of York with his most immediate cultural heritage. The historian Bede, whose *Ecclesiastical History of the English People* is the dominating achievement of his country's culture in this period, joined the monastery of Jarrow in 685 and stayed there for the next fifty years of his life. He not only immersed himself in the manuscript sources but also worked at achieving the limpid and elegant Latin prose which makes him one of the great artists of the early Middle Ages. Apart from this scrupulous literary refinement, however, Bede was a figure who was resolutely hostile to the culture of antiquity. He scorned rhetoric, dialectic and ancient cosmology as decadent sciences produced by a profane culture whose time was past. Ancient cosmography and astronomy were useful in constructing the daily monastic timetable, but in all other respects it was the Bible, and it alone, which was regarded by Bede as the basis of any intellectual authority.

The monastic rules devised by Columbanus, combined with those of Benedict, produced the 'mixed' Rule which was so influential in the continental monasteries of the seventh and eighth centuries. But it was not so easy to export the polish of insular Latin from Britain to the rest of Europe. Those Irish and Anglo-Saxons who had mastered the language and wrote it with such authority were in command of a literary medium which they had acquired, and one which had no connection with their own maternal languages whose roots were Celtic in its Goidelic form for the Irish and Germanic in the case of the English. Seventh- and eighth-century Irish monasteries were particularly adept at producing Latin grammars to be used by non-native speakers of the language. As a result they were far removed from the situation in Spain, Gaul and Italy where Latin was still the popular literary and spoken language, but in a form which was showing a rapid evolution into the various kinds of Romance. Insular Latin's influence certainly helped to consolidate the language's authority as a written medium on the continent. But it did so at a cost, since, though so polished and correct, this form of Latin could also appear stiff and remote from the needs of daily life. A gap therefore emerged between the written and the vernacular, and the accelerated rate of divergence between the two speeded up the development of the continental Romance languages.

In the seventh century many continental preachers were still following the precepts of Pope Gregory the Great, who had counselled the clergy to develop a simpler style of Latin which could be more easily understood by their congregations. The *Life of St Eligius*, written after his death in 660 by his friend Bishop Audouin of Rouen, shows how in northern Gaul the priest could still be understood as long as he gave 'his pronunciation as rustic an inflection as his style'. But in the wider scheme of things the bastardization of Latin was yet another nail in the coffin of east–west relations, with a wall of incomprehension dividing the Greeks from an increasingly varied linguistic scene. Political differences were already acute, and Justinian's expansionist policies had resulted in western suspicion of the Greek empire. Latin ceased to be an official language in Byzantium during the reign of Heraclius, a decision which was a cultural reflection of the political chasm.

Enclaves of Hellenism survived in the west, but only as privileged centres which were extrinsic to mainstream developments. Braga in north-west Portugal, for example, had a school of monastic translators, and the presence of Theodore of Tarsus gave Canterbury more than a whiff of Greek culture. But even the Byzantine officials who were administering the Exarchate of Ravenna, the centre of imperial power in the peninsula's north-east, seem to have been uninterested in advancing the cause of Hellenism. Sicily retained its lively Greek culture, so much so that the emperor Constans II contemplated removing himself and his government there in 660 when the empire was threatened by both Islamic and Slav attack. But Sicily's contacts with the mainland were exiguous, and the island could supply no bridgehead for a Hellenic revival. The Arabs' occupation of Carthage in 695 was the culmination of their conquest of Byzantine north Africa, and from 711 onwards they were in occupation of most of Spain. The Greeks had been expelled from most of their continental western Mediterranean possessions, leaving only Ravenna which survived precariously until it was conquered by the Lombards in 750–51.

These conquests in the west had a major cultural consequence. Arab rule had now spread across territories which were formerly part of the Roman empire, and whose culture also showed the continuum that had once existed between *romanitas* and Byzantium. Many of these regions' scholars responded to the occupation by choosing exile and, carrying their manuscripts with them, left for the more congenial Christian ambience of north-western Europe. In a sense they formed the vanguard of the Carolingian renaissance since so many of them responded to the new cultural opportunities which opened up as a result of Pippin II's victory at the battle of Tertry in 687. The victory of the forces of Austrasia over those of Neustria unified northern Francia, and confirmed that Pippin's family were the real source of authority in a royal domain where the Merovingian kings reigned rather than ruled. The affiliation of his dynasty with the abbatial culture was a strong one. Most of its members were educated at the great abbey of St-Denis near Paris and their patronage was directed towards the abbeys located in the dynasty's heartlands within northern and eastern Gaul. It was here that the Irish had established the monastery of Peronna Scottorum in commemoration of their compatriot St Furney after his death in c. 650, and the foundation would be the most important base for Irish missionary activity both east and west of the Rhine.

There were signs of revival too in north Italy, a region where literary Latin culture was making a comeback in the late seventh century. King Cunipert of the Lombards welcomed a Latin grammarian to his court at Pavia in the 680s, and the *Origo Gentis Langobardorum* with its fanciful interpretation of Lombard origins can be dated to c. 671. Byzantium's crisis was deepening in its own geopolitical centre of gravity at this time. Between 673 and 677 Constantinople was besieged five times by Arab armies, and the cities of the once Christian Middle East, together with the scholastic institutions located within them, went into steep decline as a result of military attacks and the massacres inflicted on the local populations. But western Europe was witnessing the first signs of that cultural spring which would lead to the flowering of the Carolingian renaissance.

FRANCIA: THE ROOTS OF A CULTURAL SURPRISE

Throughout the first half of the eighth century, and for some time afterwards, Frankish Gaul offered few parallels with the scholarly advances recorded in Anglo-Saxon England. Boniface's missionary activities on the continent had helped to establish his countrymen's reputation for learning, and his many pupils in the monasteries he founded there often wrote to him for advice about their Latin style as well as asking for guidance on theological issues. England's religious communities of both men and women were notably learned, none more so than the school at Canterbury where Theodore and Hadrian, according to Bede, instructed 'not only in the books of holy scripture but also in the art of metre, astronomy and *computus*'. Aldhelm tells us that Roman law was also taught there, and this would probably have been done from copies of the *Digest* of Justinian. The glosses which survive from the school at

Canterbury show the rich variety of books kept at that intellectual power house, and which formed the thought-world of the English Church as a whole. They include, as we might expect, Church canons and papal decretals, but also the *Ecclesiastical History* of Eusebius, works by Isidore, Athanasius's *Life of St Anthony*, Jerome's *De Viris Illustribus*, Orosius's *Historia*, Augustine's *Sermons*, grammars by Donatus and Phocas, the *Dialogues* and *Regula Pastoralis* of Gregory the Great. There was, moreover, no scholar in the Frankish Gaul of the period comparable to Bede, Aldhelm or Theodore.

When we compare the intellectual resources available to these two societies, however, a different picture emerges. A little over one hundred English manuscripts survive from before the ninth century and they were mostly produced at Canterbury and in the northern centres of Lindisfarne, Jarrow and Wearmouth. Although they include some important commentaries by authors such as Gregory the Great, Cassiodorus and Jerome, as well of course as works by the local luminaries Bede and Aldhelm, the majority are Gospel texts or other books of the Bible. English scholars and writers had to make do with a distinctly meagre range of works to inspire their pens. What is more, the script types of the Northumbrian manuscripts differ markedly from those produced in the south of England, a fact which confirms the poor state of communications between the north and the rest of the country. This was not a society which was producing a particularly cohesive culture.

Francia, however, produced some 500 manuscripts during this same period before the ninth century, and 400 of these can be dated to the eighth century alone, with 200 being written during its last two decades. Survival rates may well have improved during that time, but the impression of a greatly accelerated rate of literary production is overwhelming. The appeal issued by Charlemagne in 780 for copies of remarkable or rare books was made to a society where many such texts were already in circulation, and the ones which made their way to the library in Aachen inspired in turn the production of a large number of other texts at the court during the ninth century. It is true that Merovingian Gaul offers no comparison with the enormous number of Gospel texts produced in Anglo-Saxon England before the mid-eighth century. But the region's real literary riches lay in its many sacramentaries (or Mass Books) and in the availability of a huge range of classical, literary and patristic works.

Lyons, a city which had been an important centre for the book trade since classical antiquity, illustrates the cultural resources available in Merovingian Gaul, and the texts copied in early eighth-century Burgundy include Jerome on the Psalms, the *Vetus Latina* compilation of canon law, works by such major Church Fathers as Augustine, Origen, Ambrose and Gregory the Great, as well as the Gallo-Roman authors Hilary of Poitiers and Eucherius of Lyons, in whom there would have been a lot of local interest. The *scriptorium* at Luxeuil wrote for export as well as for its own scholarly and liturgical needs, and it was at a peak of production in the late seventh century. Biblical commentaries and theological treatises, works of canon law, grammar and liturgy, were all produced here, including Augustine's commentary on Genesis, the sermons and letters of both Augustine and Jerome, and Isidore's *Synonyma*. Nuns working in the convents of the Seine basin produced copies of such major works of patristic literature as Augustine's *De Trinitate*, as well as works by Isidore and Eusebius, and Gregory of Tours' *Historiae*.

The abbey at Corbie, located near Amiens, was an immensely significant late Merovingian centre of scholarship, and its library contained not just the standard range of patristic and exegetical texts but also works by Cassiodorus and John Chrysostom, Tertullian, Ambrose and John Cassian. The library at Fleury was richly stocked with patristic works, and in the course of the ninth century it would be celebrated for its major collection of classical texts. The newer centres of learning established in Merovingian Francia included early eighth-century foundations in the Loire valley, Picardy and along the Seine. Some of the books produced here were highly individual, such as the *Cosmography*, a miscellany of fantastical information compiled by the Irishman Virgil, bishop of Salzburg. Hugeburc, an English nun working at Hildesheim in Germany, produced a similar collection of strange lore in her *Hodoeporicon*, a work which purports to describe the travels of Willibald in Palestine and Asia Minor. Manuscripts of a less wayward kind include the Mass Books which contain new prayers and a reformed liturgy, work which in this earlier period was particularly associated with the partnership between Pippin III and Chrodegang of Metz, and which looks forward in turn to the major liturgical reforms implemented by Charlemagne in association with Benedict of Aniane.

There was another anticipation of the Carolingian future in the form of *De Libris Recipiendis et Non Recipiendis*, a list which distinguishes between approved and unapproved books, and whose earliest manuscript form was produced in north Francia c. 700. That concern with authority and orthodox belief would be a key feature of Carolingian culture, but the cosmopolitan nature of that later renaissance is also prefigured in the links that these manuscripts demonstrate between work done in Francia and the scholarship of Spain and Italy.

Lyons, for example, had links with Spain, while north Italian monasteries, among them Bobbio and Verona, had important connections with Frankish centres such as Luxeuil. Manuscripts surviving from such major centres as Ravenna, Vercelli and Monte Cassino show that Lombard intellectuals shared the interests of the Franks and that they were particularly active in the field of canon law. Italian centres display the usual preoccupation with patristic and exegetical literature, but there is an additional fondness for classical texts, and works by Virgil and Juvenal survive in the sixth-century manuscripts of Italian monastic libraries.

The *Liber Pontificalis*, a work containing biographical details of the popes and possibly written in Rome, emerged in two editions during the sixth century and, regularly updated right through to the end of the ninth century, the book shows a novel interest in historical facts and events. Intellectual curiosity is also a feature of the massive commentary on the Apocalypse which was compiled by Ambrosius Autpertus of San Vicenzo al Volturno in the period 758–67. This exposition also contained a number of patristic interpretations of the Book of Revelation, and the author's ability to compare these different studies marks a new sophistication in biblical scholarship. It also shows the degree of teamwork that must have been involved in the production of such major feats of scholarship, with copyists, extractors and compilers all working together to a common end. Scribal discipline is another feature of the Italian evidence, as it is of the Frankish, and in both Rome and north Italy there are observable improvements in legibility: the uncial script was becoming more consistent and pre-Carolingian forms of the minuscule were attaining greater clarity.

Spanish Christianity was largely confined in the eighth century to the kingdoms of the north and the Mozarabic communities of the centre. But although fewer manuscripts were produced here than in other European Christian centres they include some striking historical documents. The Arabic–Byzantine *Chronicle* of 741 and the *Mozarabic Chronicle* of 751 are the product of a peninsular sensibility which was keenly aware of Spain's idiosyncratic cultural development and which wished to communicate it to non-Spaniards. Cross-border cultural fertilization can also be seen in the many areas where the English established new monasteries – in Hesse and Franconia, Thuringia, Bavaria and the northern Rhineland. Foundations such as Fulda, Echternach and Wurzburg showed the continuing depth of identification between the Anglo-Saxon civilization and its Germanic cousin. Alamannian and Bavarian foundations, however, showed the influence of Irish and Frankish missionaries, as in the case of St-Gall and Reichenau, Regensburg, Salzburg and Freising, all of which would be major centres of learning during the Carolingian renaissance. The lives of the saints which were written during the eighth century are a rough and ready affair in strictly literary terms, but they nonetheless show not just a devotion to the better-known early Christian saints but also the energetic celebration of sacred individuals associated with particular local areas. Northern Francia was a particularly rich source of these provincial hagiographies whose subjects include Lambert of Liège and Hugobert, Arnulf of Metz and Rigobert of Reims. Local concentrations of power, including members of the saints' own families and the monasteries associated with those celebrated, wished to promote the knowledge of these individuals' sanctity and to gain prestige by association. This kind of promotion of the locality was also a motive for the more significant historical works of the age such as the *Metz Annals*, the *Continuations* added to the *Chronicle* of Fredegar, and the *Liber Historiae Francorum*.

In a more secular vein this was also an important period in legal history, with an increasing number of cases being settled by reference to written records. The Lombards were especially active in this area, with their eighth-century rulers Liutprand and Ratchis adding to the impressive compilation of laws formulated by their mid-seventh-century pred-ecessor Rothari. Roman law seems to have had a continuing influence in the Lombard-ruled territories, quite noticeably in the distinction between the public and the private as well as in the application of laws of property, possession and inheritance. Frankish rulers were particu-larly aware of the importance of legal forms, since the *Lex Salica* was a prized document dating from the earliest sixth-century history of their race, and Pippin III's officials compiled a revised version of that docu-ment. Another Frankish document, the *Lex Ribuaria*, was drawn up in Austrasia in the mid-seventh century and, in its revised form of a cen-tury later, its provisions governed the conduct of official business by the Austrasian nobility and the Carolingian mayors of the palace. Other codes of law were useful in formulating resistance against the Franks, as in the case of the *Lex Baiuuariorum*, formulated by Duke Tassilo of Bavaria in the 740s. This was a sophisticated document which distin-guished between custom and law, and its prologue referred to the ancient laws of the Hebrews and Greeks, the Egyptians and the Romans. Legal invocations, however, were of little use when Charlemagne had decided on an expansionist plan, as Tassilo discovered.

The *Liber Iudiciorum* of the Visgothic kingdom was first compiled in the mid-seventh century and, added to by subsequent rulers, has a justly celebrated role in legal history. This was early medieval Europe's first territorial law code and it therefore applied to all those living under the king's jurisdiction regardless of their ethnicity, race or culture. It also protected subjects against a possible abuse of power by the sovereign as well as safeguarding personal property, and it subjected kings to the rule of law. This extraordinary document, a unique Visigothic bequest to European thought and culture, made Roman law redundant within the kingdom and was still being applied in the northern Christian king-doms of the Asturias and Leon after the Arabs had conquered the rest of the Iberian peninsula. Elsewhere in Europe, there is evidence that Roman law continued to be used. The *Breviary of Alaric* was compiled in the southern Gaul of the early sixth century, and this convenient digest of the Theodosian Code continued to circulate well into the ninth century. Roman law principles were followed in many of the earliest Germanic codes of jurisprudence, and this accommodation is even evident in the laws of the very first kings of Kent, Wessex and (perhaps) Mercia despite the fact that they were written in the Germanic vernacular rather than in Latin.

Charlemagne's concern with the right ordering of a Christian society, with renewal, hierarchy and discipline, did not arise out of a vacuum. Seventh- and eighth-century sources show that western European intellectuals were already well used to thinking about these issues, and legal documents of this nature could not have existed without some kind of legal training having been made available to those who compiled them. From the point of view of the development of kingship, that ideology and practice which would be so crucial to Carolingian culture, the production of legal codes was one of the many ways in which Germanic kings could gain credibility by showing that they were the true heirs to Roman and Judaeo-Christian culture, civilizations with highly developed systems of jurisprudence. Here, therefore, as in so many other respects, Merovingian Francia supplied the Carolingians with a basis on which to work.

CHARLEMAGNE'S AIMS AND CAROLINGIAN CONSEQUENCES

Charlemagne's cultural campaign was not an antiquarian exercise. The king and his immediate circle looked to the present and the future, and the wisdom of the past was to be studied less for its own sake than as a means to ensure effective political control. Two documents, the *Admonitio generalis* and the *Epistola de Litteris Colendis*, define the aims of a programme which sought to ensure that the clergy, 'the soldiers of the Church', were equipped to lead 'the people of God to the pasture of eternal life'. The military metaphors are revealing of the king's attitudes. It was only in the reign of his son, Louis the Pious, that the iconography of the ruler as a *miles Christi* (soldier of Christ) took root, and Louis was the first Carolingian ruler to be portrayed in manuscripts as holding the Cross rather than the battle standard. But it was the example of his father which had established the naturalness of thinking about the ruler as a militant whose battles were culturally directed towards the creation of a Christian society.

The poorly written letters sent to the court by the clergy had shown, said Charlemagne, that they needed to be educated, and he believed that their linguistic clumsiness revealed an even more fundamental problem, a lack of mental capacity. No longer was it enough for the people just to see their clergy at work, so ran a key formulation in the *Epistola de Litteris Colendis*, it was also vital that they be instructed through the words which were spoken and sung by priests and monks. Charlemagne for his part compared his role to that of King Josias who was described in the second Book of Kings (22:11) as correcting and admonishing the people of Israel in order to bring them back to God. But a reformed and cultured clergy was also necessary if Charlemagne was to achieve his goal: 'For although it is better to do what is right than to know it, yet knowledge comes before action.'

This was, therefore, bound to be a very long-term programme, and one which required consistency and determination in order to see it through. Charlemagne's longevity, highly unusual for the time, helped to give it a continuous impetus, as did his personality. Einhard describes a man who was talkative to the point of verbosity (*dicaculus*), and the confidence Charlemagne displayed as a military leader was also evident in his brisk dealings with the scholars, bishops and abbots who attended the court. He knew what he wanted from the intelligentsia of his time, and they were keen to obey him, all the more since Carolingian policy entailed a significant improvement in the social standing of intellectuals. Scholars, poets and artists rubbed shoulders with the influential, not just at Aachen but in all the other palaces where Carolingian kings exercised their power, and that fact gave a new authority to the appeal of arts and letters.

The enterprise carried on long after Charlemagne's own time since the sons and grandsons who were his heirs continued to emphasize the importance of scholarship and learning, and these ninth-century continuities were reinforced by the clergy in their episcopal councils and statutes. Louis the Pious and Charles the Bald were especially active in attracting scholars to their courts, and Carolingian patronage in general covered a very wide field, including verse (mostly panegyrical in tone), biblical exegesis, works of history, translations of Greek patristic works into Latin and the financing of scholastic institutions.

This renaissance's centres of influence, we should remember, extended not just to the court life of royal princes but also to the cathedrals, abbeys and monasteries associated with such great Church figures as Claudius, bishop of Turin, Theodulf, bishop of Orléans, Hraban Maur who was abbot of Fulda and archbishop of Mainz, Lupus, bishop of Ferrières, and Hincmar, archbishop of Reims. The sophistication and influence of such men meant that they too were, in effect, running their own local courts. Abbots did not have to be ordained and the ones who were laymen, as in the case of Angilbert of St-Riquier, included figures whose significance was both cultural and political. Angilbert had been a high official at the Aachen court and was at the king's side when he was crowned emperor in 800. An accomplished poet, he enjoyed an unmarried relationship with Bertha, the king's daughter, and their son Nithard wrote a history of the empire in four volumes covering the turbulent period of dissension between the sons of Louis the Pious.

Production of manuscripts leapt up as a result of the Carolingian initiatives, and *scriptoria* became ever more active at courts as well as in monasteries and cathedrals. As many as 50,000 may have been circulating in the Francia of the ninth century, and books became valuable objects which could be used as diplomatic gifts to be exchanged between Frankish princes. As part of the peace deal with his brother Charles in 849 the emperor Lothair entered into an association with St-Martin, Tours, one of the greatest monasteries within his brother's domain. One of the consequences of this agreement was the production of the Lothair Gospels, one of the most lavish Gospel Books of the Carolingian age and a work whose copying costs were paid for by the emperor. A neverending quest for books which could be added to their libraries was one of the ways in which monasteries, abbeys and courts sought to demonstrate their power and influence during the Carolingian age, and many of the libraries in turn supported schools which gave employment to two or three generations of masters. These scholastic intellectuals were as productive as the professional scribes employed in the *scriptoria*, and the manuscripts they worked on included multi-layered revisions of biblical texts, compilations of patristic texts, and treatises on more secular arts which could be followed by their students.

The Carolingian renaissance would never have happened without the formal encouragement and dictates which issued from the courts of

Charlemagne and his successors. That having been said, the cultural pattern which actually emerged was more varied, and often more interesting, than the one envisaged and commissioned by the central policy-making machine. Charlemagne's own cultural aims were fairly simple: increased rates of literacy which would make for better government and a more effective implementation of the royal will. But not even this first of the Carolingian Kaisers was immune to the unintended consequences which are a regular feature of governmental initiatives. He might prescribe, but the intellectual resources that were available varied immensely in the different parts of his kingdom and in the conquered territories, and no amount of prescription could smooth away the fact that different scholars had different interests and could not always be expected to write exactly to order.

We have already seen how misleading it is to think of either Christianity or classical antiquity as monolithic systems of thought. There were many different Christianities in eighth- and ninth-century Europe, younger missionary ones as well as versions which already seemed venerable, and whether newly arrived or older, both forms of the faith were capable of criticizing kings rather than just being grateful to them. Classical culture had its own internal differences, and some versions of it were more easily Christianized than others. Some scholars enjoyed Christianizing the arts, others thought that this would lead to a back-door revival of pagan culture. In Charlemagne's own time there was certainly an immense amount of literature written which flattered him personally and elevated his authority. But the following generation of court intellectuals knew how to rebuke kings and political leaders, as Louis the Pious learnt to his cost. This kind of pluralism was not Charlemagne's intention but it was certainly a Carolingian consequence. Polemical literature is an important ninth-century phenomenon, with scholars taking sides on political and theological issues, and it is that adversarial vigour which explains the advent of literary forgery, a skill which required commitment, flair and knowledge on the part of its more successful practitioners.

GOING TO SCHOOL

Schools took many different forms in Carolingian society. The palace school was a phenomenon of court society and was a result of the way in which all Carolingian monarchs, but especially Charlemagne, Louis the Pious, Lothair I, Lothair II and Charles the Bald, attracted scholars to their courts. It would be wrong to think of this as a particularly structured institution, and the masters had to fit in the teaching of royal and aristocratic children among their many other advisory tasks, as well as writing books which were often dedicated to their patrons.

The heyday of the palace school was the 780s and 790s, after which time its scholars tended to leave for the many cathedrals and monasteries where they established more formal schools. It was the legislation of that late eighth-century period which had assigned to monasteries and cathedrals the task of educating the future clergy. The lines between the two kinds of establishment, however, were blurred, and in many of the missionary and frontier regions monks had for a long time worked as secular clergy in charge of parishes. Progress in this area involved specialization of function, and when Louis the Pious and Benedict of Aniane set out to reform the monasteries they were exercised by the dangers of having so many non-monks within the monastic precincts. The two councils that were held in Aachen in 816 and 817 therefore sought to separate those training to be monks from future parish priests, and from 817 onwards only the oblates intended for the religious life were meant to receive a monastic education. Nonetheless, it may well have been very difficult to enforce a plan which contradicted tradition and one which also went against aristocratic self-interest. Many nobles – Angilbert, Einhard and Dhuoda are particularly eminent examples – had been educated to a very high standard by monks and nuns, and monastic schools offered the best education available.

Louis the Pious tried to get the bishops to assume responsibility for educating the secular clergy but these maids of all work had enough to do elsewhere, and the financial cost of organizing such provision was beyond them in most cases. Further down the scale, it was usually the parish priest's duty to maintain a local school, but this too was a difficult requirement to enforce. Bishop Theodulf of Orléans, an émigré

Spanish Visigoth and a key figure at Charlemagne's court as both poet and theologian, sought to persuade his priest to offer instruction free of charge in the network of schools he was trying to establish in his diocese. Most priests, however, needed the extra income if, that is, they were capable of running schools at all. Bishop Herard of Tours (855–66) and Bishop Walter of Orléans (?869–91) could only express the aspirational hope that priests might find it possible to establish schools. At the end of the ninth century Fulco, archbishop of Reims and Hincmar's successor, had to call in two monks to help him reform his diocese's two schools for clerical education, foundations which were both in a very poor way when he arrived in the diocese.

The local schools run by the parish priests were at the front line in the battle for literacy. We know that the priests had to make sure that godparents knew the Lord's Prayer and the Creed before sponsoring a child for baptism, and rural parishes' inventories for the ninth century record the existence of modest libraries which would have been used to teach reading and writing to children. These were the measures adopted in order to secure obedience to the injunction of the *Admonitio generalis* that the children both of free parents and of peasants were to be educated, and a fair degree of participation in the liturgy would have developed as a result.

Angilbert of St-Riquier assumed that the seven communities near his abbey would be able to take part in the great liturgical processions that marked Rogation Days, singing as they went along and following banners bearing legends. Paschasius Radbertus wrote of how the local peasants lamented the death of Abbot Adalhard of Corbie in their own local tongues and then joined with the clergy in a Latin antiphonal lament. Both these men were shrewd observers and not prone to fantasizing. Their evidence shows that Charlemagne's edicts on literacy must have had important practical effects in at least their own areas. But moving beyond basic, or functional, literacy to anything more demanding must have been a real problem within the ranks of the parochial clergy. They would have been educated as boys to a level at which they could master the service books, but a good deal of their priestly competence would have been learnt by imitating their teachers' liturgical movements when celebrating the Mass. Later in the ninth century Hincmar was very sceptical about whether the priests who taught in his diocese's schools could actually read, and Bishop Sigemund of Meaux was similarly doubtful about the literacy of his own diocesan clergy.

Moving on from the local schools to the monastic and episcopal ones involved a big jump – and one which often required some good connections. Hincmar of Reims's nephew, the younger Hincmar, got on in life as a result of that family link, but there are examples of the talented and lowly born also securing a step up. Walahfrid 'Strabo' ('the squint-eyed'), a scholarly monk and poet who wrote the standard *Life* of St Gall as well as a curious poem which criticizes Charlemagne for his sexual incontinence, was humbly born, and Ebbo, archbishop of Reims, was the son of a serf.

Women's educational opportunities were real though limited. Hincmar recommended that girls should not be taught in the same place as boys, a fact which argues at least implicitly for the existence of female schooling, and Carolingian scholars who admired patristic writers were also being introduced thereby to a world of female intelligence. Jerome, for example, was much read by Francia's ninth-century scholars, and that saint's circle of educated female companions would have been familiar to these Carolingian *litterati*. The treatise on the Assumption of Mary, composed by Paschasius Radbertus for the nuns of the community at Soissons, is written in the style of a letter from Jerome to his pupils Paula and Eustochium. And when Charlemagne's sister Gisela and his daughter Rotrud were trying to persuade Alcuin to write a commentary on John's Gospel especially for them, they quoted in support the example of Jerome and his female circle. Jerome, they pointed out, had dedicated many of his works on the prophets to women and had always responded to the intellectual needs of his female friends. Nor should we forget the way in which women who had entered religious communities were, in a way, specialists in religious knowledge, and therefore had to be literate enough to be able to read prayers and biblical texts as well as knowing how to perform the chant.

Who taught these women to be literate in the first place? It is a fair assumption that it was other women who were the educators since a capitulary of 802 barred all men from female monasteries except for priests who were allowed in just to perform Mass, or visit the sick, and then had to leave quickly. The evidence for the existence of circles of intellectual women is in fact fairly extensive. Paschasius Radbertus had been raised as an orphan by the Soissons community, was educated by its members, and wrote two other works at their request as well as the treatise on the Assumption. Gisela and Rotrud had turned to Alcuin for help after they had tried to tackle the Fourth Gospel on their own, and there are also examples of women who were not members of religious communities working as teachers. Wilborada, a cave-dwelling anchoress, taught Oudalricus, a young monk from the nearby monastery of St-Gall. Some kind of folk memory of her instructional prowess may survive in the story that Wilborada warned the monks that the Magyars were on their way to attack St-Gall, and that they paid the price for ignoring her.

We know too that in the communities surrounding St-Riquier there were women who specialized in preparing children for participation in liturgical processions. Educated laywomen of the Carolingian period also include Dhuoda who, as we have already seen, was engaged in teaching her son William. Judith, the second wife of Louis the Pious, was an intellectually lively figure in court life, and her granddaughters, the daughters of Eberhard of Friuli, inherited part of their father's extensive library. These were aristocratic women and it is not surprising that so many were educated, but an increasing amount of evidence shows that there were female scribes at many religious communities, and they would often have been of humbler birth. Recently discovered female writing centres include Chelles, Jouarre, Remiremont, Sackingen, Poitiers, Herford, Soissons and Brescia. Copying was after all a kind of manual labour, and formed therefore something of a natural continuum with the crafts of embroidery and working with cloth, both of which were traditionally identified as women's work both inside and outside the community walls. In addition, a number of collectively written histories produced at this time, many of which remain unattributed, could well have involved female scribes. These include the *Liber Historiae Francorum*, the *Annales Mettenses Priores* and the *Annales Quedlinburgenses*. It is also inconceivable that all the *Lives* of the various founders of female monastic houses were written by men, and of these there are a very large number.

How did boys and young men live while being educated for a clerical life? They would have arrived in the monasteries at the age of seven, and at about ten in the case of the cathedral schools. From then on they lived continuously in a milieu which taught them the naturalness of their separation from the secular world, and perhaps the fact that there were often so many of them gathered together in one place made for a convivial atmosphere, one in which the separation may not have been experienced as hardship. The lists that survive from the monasteries associated with Fulda as dependencies suggest that at any one time these students, both boys and youths, comprised between a quarter and a half of the total population. Perhaps the atmosphere would have been more claustrophobic in some of the smaller monasteries and cathedrals, and here the students lived with a *magister* or *grammaticus* who would have had to perform several roles – as teacher, librarian and director of the *scriptorium*. Greater specialization is observable in larger foundations, and here there would have been different masters for the chant, copying, grammar and biblical study.

But whether the community was larger or smaller, the relationship between master and pupils could be closely personal and spiritual, as well as academic. Alcuin of York indulged himself with laments that his pupils came and went but that the 'old man' remained behind. His habit of giving pet names to his students must have been irritating to many, and the fact that he did so with the royal family as well (Charlemagne was 'David', for example) shows his desire to be on familiar terms with the powerful. Less contrived attitudes are recorded in the case of Heiric of Auxerre who wrote a poem in praise of his masters, Lupus of Ferrières and Haimo of Auxerre. He also published parts of the lectures delivered by them as an act of *pietas*. Ercanbert of Fulda wrote touchingly that he had to write down the lectures of his *magister*, Rudolf, since he thought that the words of his preceptor might otherwise be lost to history.

The *magistri* had a keen sense of professional solidarity, a fact which comes through in their correspondence. They wrote to exchange personal news, to check up on what might be the latest authoritative answers to difficult intellectual questions, and also to borrow books from one another as well as to pass on suitably talented pupils for further training.

Heiric of Auxerre spent some years at Soissons before returning to Auxerre, and Lupus of Ferrières sent some of his monks to Prüm in order
to learn German – an interesting indication of the demands of the mission
field. Archbishop Fulco recruited Hucbald of St-Amand and Remigius
of Auxerre to Reims, and teachers of quality and proven scholarship
were a pool of talent who could be used by leading churchmen, nobles
and kings when they needed a specific book written, such as a *Life* of
a local saint or a commentary on a Gospel. It was a good career choice
for the ambitious and one with fine prospects, as was demonstrated by
Hraban Maur, Lupus of Ferrières and Paschasius Radbertus, all of whom
started their careers as schoolmasters.

The majority of schools were concentrated in the four areas where
intellectual activity was at its most intense: the region north of the Loire;
the former Lombard kingdom in northern Italy; those parts of Germany which had seen the most intense missionary activity in the eighth
century – including especially the areas of Boniface's mission – and the
Spanish March along with Septimania. Links between teachers as well
as the influence of Carolingian courts resulted in the establishment of
informal groupings among certain schools. Theodulf of Orléans and
Hincmar of Reims exercised some central powers of organization over
the schools in their areas. In 823 Lothair I tried to implement an
ambitious scheme which would have concentrated northern Italian
education in nine major towns: Pavia, Ivrea, Turin, Cremona, Cividale,
Florence, Firmo, Verona and Vicenza. The Council of Paris (829) saw
an episcopal attempt at persuading Lothair's father, Louis the Pious, to
establish three schools under direct royal patronage. Neither of these
initiatives was successful and they were in any event undermined by
the political and military attacks on Louis's authority in the 830s.
Throughout the decade that followed both Lothair and Louis were preoccupied with issues of war and peace rather than with cultural revival,
and Carolingian scholarship and education as a consequence had to fall
back on local initiatives.

It is a striking fact about the schools, and a sign of their progressive
agenda, that antiquity was irrelevant to their success or failure, and it
was often the most recent foundations which had the highest reputa-
tions. Fulda, for example, was a new ninth-century establishment, and

its reputation swiftly rivalled such antique centres as Milan and Pavia. Culturally speaking, Rome had fallen behind quite badly in the ninth century despite some attempts at reform. Pope Eugenius gathered together sixty-two bishops from the province in 826 for a meeting which discussed the problem of abandoned churches and illiterate priests. A plan of action was formulated on broadly Carolingian lines and included the establishment of new schools. But the fact that much the same scheme had to be announced again in 853 shows the depth of the problem, and Rome was effectively off the ninth-century map of significant intellectual centres.

Availability of high-quality books and a reputation for equally demanding teaching: these were what established the reputation of a scholastic centre. Auxerre enjoyed such a prominence, and the careers of its great masters, from Murethach and Haimo to Heirie and Remigius, span the whole of the ninth century. The distinction of Hadoard and Ratramnus lent a similar lustre to Corbie. St-Gall was associated with three scholars who bore the name Notker, and with no fewer than four who were each called Ekkehard. Martin Scottus taught at Laon for twenty-five years until his death in 875 when he was succeeded by Bernard and Adelhelm. The teaching and scholarship of such men established the notion of a common body of knowledge in European scholarship, and as luminaries in their own time they also prepared the way for the great system builders of European thought in the twelfth and thirteenth centuries. Having seen where these *magistri* worked and how their lives were organized, we must now turn to the question of what they actually taught and how European letters were changed as a consequence.

CHANGING MINDS

Reforming the way supposedly educated people spoke, as well as wrote, Latin was basic to the Carolingian project. It applied especially to the clergy, as we have already seen. What the reformers called 'unskilled language' (*lingua inerudita*) was more than just a matter of making mistakes and being infelicitous. Accurate expression was the only way in which correct belief, truth itself, could be communicated. Ethical comportment in this life and salvation in the next depended, therefore, on correct speech and grammar.

There was, however, a danger associated with a programme which tried to get the clergy to sound like Augustine and Ambrose. If it was too successful it might well end up distancing the clergy from the people themselves who, right across the Carolingian domain, were now speaking a whole variety of vital, albeit often rustic, dialects and tongues. Alcuin was the great advocate of this reform programme but his personal experience and formation surely meant that he underestimated the problems involved. He was a Briton who had learnt Latin from scratch as a foreign language, and the Anglo-Saxon which was his native tongue bore no relation to Latin. So it was easy for him to be alert to what did, or did not, constitute accurate Latinity. But those to whom he preached about precision in the Carolingian Europe of his day had no such clear frame of reference since the linguistic riot of vernacular Latin was their native speech. What is more, even if the clergy were to become faithful imitations of the early Fathers of the Church they ran the risk of not being understood by the people. Pragmatism seems to have often won the day and in 813 three Church councils held at Mainz, Reims and Tours all urged bishops to preach in the language spoken by their flock, either a form of early German (*Theotiscam*) or rustic Latin (*rustica Romana lingua*). Another council held at Mainz in 847 repeated the injunction.

Nonetheless, for the sixty or so recognized authors who wrote during the Carolingian period, as well as the numerous unknown masters in the various schools, correct pronunciation and case endings really did matter. Lupus of Ferrières was one major scholar who thought that the movement veered in the direction of a merely formal and abstract precision. Some of his colleagues, he wrote, were more interested in correcting errors in language than in reforming their own lives. But most scholars and writers thought that precision mattered because it permitted the real meaning of words thereby to be grasped and some of the thickets cleared from the path that led to truth.

Aspiration was one thing, but what were the tools which could be used in order to guide minds which had to be purged of error? Some of the most popular books will be already familiar: Augustine's *De Doc-*

trina Christiana, a hugely influential book since it expressed so elo-
quently the basis of a Christian education, Cassiodorus's two *Institutiones*, and of course the *Etymologiae* of Isidore. These were *the* handbooks
that mattered, especially since they showed how secular learning could
be harnessed to sacred wisdom, and to them we should add Martianus
Capella's eloquent allegory of the arts, *De Nuptiis Philologiae et Mercurii*.

The attempts at producing a synthesis between Christian purposes
and the liberal arts programme of antiquity were many and various, and
they often took a poetic form in order to help students learn through
imagery. Wetti, a monk of Reichenau who died in 824, was particularly
active as a poet whose regard for the liberal arts achieved a near-
mystical expression, and there were many *magistri* who compiled their
own manuals or anthologies of texts on these arts in order to teach their
pupils.

But the question of just how the arts, an expression of antique and
profane culture, were to be Christianized remained a thorny issue
throughout our period. Alcuin tried to smooth things over by describing
grammar as the handmaiden of theology, and his picture of Christian
wisdom as a temple supported by the seven columns of the arts was
doubtless useful to those who did not want to investigate the foundations too closely. John Scottus Erigena, an Irishman working at the west
Frankish court in the mid-ninth century, is the major philosopher of
the period between Boethius and Anselm, and his knowledge of Greek
made him an unusual figure in the western Europe of his age. The
Irishman's philosophical system is imbued with an understanding of
how neo-Platonism influenced the thought of Greek Christian writers,
and his translation into Latin of the works of the Pseudo-Dionysius, a
Syrian and Christian neo-Platonist of c. 500, would influence later Christian scholastics. Erigena described the arts as the tributaries of a stream
whose flow of influences combined to form Christian understanding.
But this again was imagery which postponed some real difficulties and
Erigena's use of dialectic as a way of understanding predestination
attracted the stringent criticism of Bishop Prudentius of Troyes.

There were other voices which also expressed scepticism about the
influence of the liberal arts, and Agobard of Lyons criticized the

specialized study of music which produced singers who in his view combined personal conceit with intellectual ignorance. Right at the end of
the ninth century Ermenric of Ellwangen had a dream in which the
ghost of Virgil appeared, and he was invariably tense about the possibility of a rapprochement between Christian philosophy and antique
culture. Interestingly enough, Jerome had had the same troubled dream
and shared the same doubts five centuries earlier, for these were disson-
ances which tended to recur within the culture.

Less reflective types could turn to Hraban Maur and his *De Institutione Clericorum* for a cheerful assurance that all wisdom conspired to
a common end. This was a handbook for the training of young men
destined for the priesthood and it gave them as much knowledge as
they needed in order to achieve a bare competence in the liberal arts:
grammar, rhetoric and logic, arithmetic, geometry, music and astronomy.
Works by Cassiodorus, Isidore and Gregory the Great would have
supplied a Christian superstructure to these foundations. This of course
assumes fluency in written Latin on the part of the students, who would
have made their first acquaintance with the language by writing out
letters and words on wax tablets and pieces of slate. However, even at
quite an advanced stage in their studies many needed special guidance.
Hildemar was a monk at Corbie and the author of a commentary on
the *Rule* of Benedict which was specially written with the needs of Latin
learners in mind. He describes how Corbie's abbot would question his
monks on their Lenten reading and often assign a simpler book to those
who had been given too difficult a text by the abbey librarian. Learning
correct Latin was also an aural affair, with the liturgy and communal
readings imprinting correct sounds on the minds of the young. The
Psalms were especially important in this respect and the Psalter was a
regular reference point for Carolingian scholars both doctrinally and
artistically.

Of all the liberal arts it was grammar that mattered most in the
Carolingian period. It ordered, of course, language and syntax, but its
rules in this regard were also used to explain the categories of thought
in areas such as equivalence and contradiction. The works of Latin
grammarians, supplemented by Irish and Anglo-Saxon treatises and also
by Carolingian commentaries such as those by Alcuin and Donatus,

were the equivalent of primers in philosophy and logic. To these exercises we should add the numerous glossaries, word-lists which defined a single word often by supplying a synonym, and the most important of these was the *Liber Glossarum*, a massive work consisting of over 500,000 entries.

However expert these students might become in Latin they all remained thoroughly bilingual, a fact which had important cultural consequences for Carolingian culture. Bilingual Latin–vernacular glossaries existed to help these men explain to their congregations the substance of what they themselves had learnt, and we can surmise that these works would have been especially useful in the new mission fields of the conquered territories in the ninth century. Glossaries of Greek words and terms also survive from this period, which indicates that there was some modest revival in the knowledge of Greek and that Erigena was not as solitary a figure in this regard as used to be supposed.

Given the fact that this culture was so deeply imbued with references to the Old Testament, as well as containing within it some important Jewish communities, the absence of any evidence of Hebrew learning seems strange. Carolingian Jews intermingled freely with other groups, and at a high level as well. Agobard of Lyons was unusual in his hostility, but his anti-Semitic tracts nonetheless show that Jews played a role at the court of Louis the Pious. It was here that Bodo, a palace deacon and an Alamannian by birth, had established a major scholarly reputation, and he found the Jews that he met at court so persuasive that he decided in 839 to convert to Judaism. He changed his name to the Jewish Eleazar, married a Jewish woman, and travelled to Spain along with his nephew who had also converted. Reports arrived back at the Frankish court of Bodo-Eleazar's attempts at persuading Spanish Christians to convert to Judaism or to Islam, and he engaged in dialogue with Paul Alvar, a Cordoban Jew who had converted to Christianity. According to the *Annales Bertiniani* Louis the Pious was disturbed by these events, but Christian–Jewish relations do not seem to have suffered. Hraban Maur, Paschasius Radbertus and Amalarius of Metz are among the many scholars who continued to consult Jews, but without bothering to learn Hebrew.

Carolingian scholars and masters developed a particularly straightforward literary style in order to write their commentaries on the secular and sacred texts. They knew their readership well enough to grasp that a direct, literal and historical interpretation was what was needed rather than anything more elaborate, mystical or allegorical, and they also became expert in blending the works of several other, often Irish, commentators with their own writings in order to supply a variety of interpretations. These commentators excerpted, combined and paraphrased from the works of their predecessors, but far from being unoriginal, what they ended up producing was genuinely authoritative, and it was in the ninth century that patristic scholarship in particular first became an important discipline in western Europe. Grammar's primacy in Carolingian letters extended to both secular and sacred literature since it was the key to intellectual order itself. Its techniques could be used to explain and comment on all kinds of texts, and the relationship between grammar, rhetoric and dialectic was a close one, since all revolved around the proper use and understanding of words.

Rhetoric had been one of the central disciplines of classical education, with its various techniques being designed to help the speaker win over his audience. Its sophistication made it pretty irrelevant to the writing of sermons, given the kind of congregations who were listening to most Carolingian priests. But when it came to their own skills of literary self-expression the scholars and the literary elite were eager to use rhetoric's literary tropes, and the writers of biblical commentaries were especially keen to point out how rhetorical figures of speech and metaphors recurred in the sacred texts. Most of those who studied rhetoric, however, did not go on to become professional scholars, and the usefulness of the discipline in their case was that it helped them to write different kinds of letters adapted to varying circumstances. The much-studied letters of Lupus of Ferrières were particularly influential in this respect, and the Carolingian student of rhetoric had to master such set exercises as the writing of a letter of condolence and the methods involved in expressing praise and flattery. It is not surprising therefore that Carolingian literature abounds in certain standard phrases which were learnt in youth and endlessly repeated thereafter. The use of reliable works of literature as stylistic models falls into the same category of study, as in the case of Einhard's *Life* of Charlemagne, a literary exercise which follows the biographical techniques of Suetonius and, possibly, Tacitus.

The definition that Isidore of Seville gave of rhetoric, in his *Etymologies*, pinpointed its political function. It was a 'skill in speaking well on civil matters and a flow of eloquence intended to persuade men to do what is just and good'. Carolingian authors, taking their cue from this thought, developed a whole genre of works which linked rhetoric with rulership and sought to advise princes on the models of good government. Alcuin was first in the field here and his *Disputatio de Rhetorica et Virtutibus* was dedicated to Charlemagne. A large number of authors followed his example in the succeeding decades. Smaragdus of St-Mihiel wrote *Via Regia* for Louis the Pious, Jonas of Reims composed his *De Institutione Regia* for Louis's son Pippin, and Hincmar of Reims wrote the typically accomplished *De Regis Persona et Regio Ministerio* for Charles the Bald.

Dialectical studies, another verbal discipline, flourished in the ninth century. John Scottus Erigena was the great master of its techniques, but it is increasingly clear that there were a large number of other *magistri* and students who were also exercised by the problem of essence and universals, and who could apply Aristotle's categories and his syllogistic reasoning to theological enquiry. Aristotle's *Categories* was now back on the reading list of the educated and, joined by Boethius's *Opuscula Sacra* and Augustine's *De Trinitate*, was the basis of dialectical investigation.

Alcuin's *De Dialectica* might have been typically self-serving in adopting the style of a dialogue between the author and Charlemagne, but he was once again the first to see an intellectual opportunity here, and his teaching spread the message about the uses of dialectic. His lecture notes on the subject survive as a collection of manuscripts, the *Dicta Albini*, so called because they consist of statements (*dicta*) about such topics as the Trinity, God's existence, and also the creation of God before the beginning of time. The statements exist in relation to one another and in the form of question and answer – a dialectical style which would become widespread in other areas of Carolingian culture, though there is some evidence of a backlash against its popularity. Theodulf of Orléans, Benedict of Aniane and Prudentius of Troyes all objected to dialectic's over-reliance on syllogism, a feature they attributed to the influence of Irish masters and which they thought resulted in a mechanistic way of reasoning. But despite the reservations of these influential critics dialectic went from strength to strength, as is shown by the existence of numerous glosses to the school texts on the subject, and especially in the case of the *Categoriae Decem*, a Latin summary of Aristotle's work on the categories.

The study of numbers, a science whose significance was both practical and abstract, took the Carolingian student beyond words, and the *Admonitio generalis* prescribed mastery of the *computus*, early medieval Europe's method for calculating time and dates. A society whose economy and Church were so dependent on the tithe needed professionals, usually clerics, who knew how to calculate the harvest and compute the rents due from farmers. This was also a culture which had embarked on a vast building programme – an architectural enterprise which required the study of ratio and geometry. And as ninth-century chant became ever more elaborate, so the need developed for a musical science which understood harmony and measure in a sophisticated way. Carolingian students and intellectuals also saw numbers as a way of understanding God, and the mastery of measures, numbers and weights could be seen as an intuition of the divine order. They could see how biblical allegory was often expressed through numbers – as with the seven days of Genesis and the dimensions of Noah's Ark – and that precision tied in with the typically Carolingian concern with correctness of speech, thought and action. Numbers were charged therefore with a divine significance, and a religion which was centred on God's incarnation in time and space celebrated that fact in the order of its liturgy and in the succession of its feast days, both of which needed to be computed.

Astronomy stirred curiosity at several different levels, as an object of wonder and as a source of scholarly investigation. Both Alcuin and Dungal, an Irish scholar who had been placed in charge of the school at Pavia, were asked by Charlemagne to explain the movements of the heavenly bodies, and the eclipse of the sun in 810 stirred the king's interest greatly. The *computus* taught in schools was technically rigorous and could be used to measure the movements of the planets and the stars, as well as calculating more mundane arithmetical needs. Authoritative texts in this area of study included Boethius's *De Arithmetica*, the relevant works of Euclid and Bede, and also the computistical manuals and tables which existed in a wide variety of forms. A conference of computists was held at Aachen in 809 in order to regularize the great variety of opinions which had emerged on these issues, and two enormous collections, the 'Three-Book Computus' and the 'Seven-Book Computus', subsequently integrated arithmetic, *computus* and astronomy.

But the most important single development in this Carolingian science was the rediscovery of Pliny, since at some time early in the ninth century a *magister* gathered together the writings on astronomy that he had extracted from the second book of Pliny's *Naturalis Historiae*. These selections discuss the movements and position of the seven planets, the intervals between their circular orbits, and their travel through the bands of the zodiac. The Plinian observations aroused wide interest and would have a long scribal history: they appear in thirty-eight manuscripts at various dates between the ninth and the twelfth centuries. Pliny gave the Carolingian masters a theoretical framework which was lacking in other early medieval treatises on astronomy, and they could now offer their students lucid explanations of the variety and complexity of the planetary movements. Their enthusiasm led them to draw diagrams which illustrate the Plinian system, and these pictorial aids to astronomy, which exist in the form of circular, tabular and grid formats, lend a remarkable beauty to these masters' surviving manuscripts.

Notions of harmony and measure, of number and order, were also fundamental to the Carolingian study of music, a subject which met a practical and liturgical need by instructing students in the chanting of the Psalms. The spread of Roman chant to northern and western Europe during the eighth and ninth centuries is one of the great chapters in the history of music, and its adoption reflects the Carolingian striving towards regularity and order. Roman chant's eloquent and measured harmonies were intended to serve as the musical reflection of the Carolingian political order, which is why the *Libri Carolini* claimed that the chant followed in the wake of the conquests. Its attractions to the dynasty dated back to the 750s when Chrodegang of Metz urged Pippin III to encourage the adoption of Roman chant in his realm. The *schola cantorum* established by the bishop in Metz was modelled on the one he had seen on a visit to Rome, and both Pippin and his son Charlemagne supported the bishop's campaigning efforts.

Charlemagne was deeply affected when he heard the chant on his visits to Rome, and was struck by its superiority to the versions of chant sung in his own kingdom. According to one story, the king compared the difference between the two sounds to that between the clear waters of a well and the muddy waters of a creek, a simile which reveals one aspect of his cultural ambitions. Authenticity was the goal here, and its recovery meant returning *ad fontes*. Once this prior truth had been grasped, the accumulated detritus which separated Charlemagne's age from that of Pope Gregory the Great, the Roman chant's supposed originator, could then be cleared away. An antiphonary and a responsorial were sent north from Rome to help Charlemagne and his advisers achieve their goal, and there were many who responded eagerly enough to the challenge. Archbishop Arn of Salzburg ordered his bishops to establish schools of chant which followed the Roman method, and the *schola cantorum* established by Archbishop Leidrad of Lyons was run by a monk who had been educated in Roman chant at Metz.

This attempt at a musical reformation was undoubtedly idealistic, but there was also a naive strain to it and that fact led to frustration and suspicion. Carolingian intellectuals, clergy and princes had embraced a certain vision of authenticity, one which dictated that the Roman chant had to be immutable. But the musical scene in Rome, and in most of the rest of Italy, was both evolving and varied, and by c. 800 the chant differed quite markedly from its notation in the seventh, and earlier in the eighth, centuries. The cantors from Metz who visited Rome soon discovered that many features of the chant as sung by them, and which they regarded as the authentic sound, had now been abandoned. This fluidity is what one would expect from a musical tradition which depended on oral transmission from masters to pupils over many generations. But Germanic suspicion of Italian wiles had been aroused. Notker Balbulus, the monk of St-Gall who wrote in the late ninth century, speculated that the musical chaos of Charlemagne's day must have been the result of sabotage by the twelve Roman monks sent by Pope Stephen to Francia. These cantors, he thought, were surely 'envious of the glory of the Franks' and had therefore set out quite deliberately to teach different systems of chant in the twelve centres to which they were sent. A uniform chant remained the Carolingian goal, and a New Hymnal was issued during the reign of Louis the Pious. But the 'Gregorian' chant, as it evolved during the next two centuries, was in fact a synthesis composed of Carolingian elements, ancient Roman melodies and features of the Gallican plainchant which had prevailed in Francia under the Merovingians.

Musical theory is an area in which the Carolingian notion of a renaissance is particularly evident, for this was a subject whose ancient sources and authorities were revived to great effect during the ninth century. The idea that music's quasi-mathematical ordering gave it a cosmological significance was Pythagorean in its origins, and Boethius's *De Institutione Musica* was the Carolingians' great guide to ancient Greek musical theory. Writings by Augustine, Cassiodorus and Isidore were also referred to, and all these authors supplied a suitably Christian gloss to the antique theme of music's transcendent powers. Texts such as these take us to the very heart of the Carolingian imagination with their lyrical accounts of singing angels, their description of the musical harmonies which reflect the created order and also regulate the movements of the planets, and their portrayals of music's ability to raise the spirits of warriors as well as its capacity to soothe the otherwise dangerous beasts.

The ninth section of Martianus Capella's fifth-century work *De Nuptiis* was devoted to music, and the numerous Carolingian commentaries on his *De Harmonia* show how Martianus helped his readers to understand Greek musical theory and also technical musical terms. Musical study, just like *computus* and astronomy, was a subject whose applications were both practical and abstract. It regulated the daily chanting of the choirs while also instructing the mind in the divine harmonies of the cosmos. For the great masters of the Carolingian age who wrote on the subject there could be no doubt about music's special status. John Scottus Erigena and Remigius of Auxerre produced glosses of the *De Nuptiis*, and both of them accorded musical study an honoured place within the curriculum of the liberal arts. But their evaluation of music's significance may also remind us more generally of the strongly theoretical bias which typified the Carolingian renaissance as a whole. Their pages show the great gulf which divided the *cantor* who taught his pupils how to sing from the *musicus* who understood ratios, rhythms and mathematical proportions. In the 840s Aurelian of Rome produced early medieval Europe's first complete treatise on musical theory, and the simile he uses in *Musica Disciplina* is highly revealing. Singing was like reading, and the study of music was akin to mastering grammar: the one was a form of manual labour, while the other was the real thing – reasoning. The remark captures the idealism of the Carolingian intellectual ambition. But its delight in the abstract also goes some way towards explaining why the goal of cultural uniformity which inspired this renaissance remained so elusive, and why its frustrations are quite as revealing as its achievements.

CHAPTER 9

The Survival and Revival of Empire

MORTAL REMAINS AND IMMORTAL LONGINGS

In 806 Charlemagne was nearing sixty and his thoughts turned towards the question of how best to safeguard his legacy. The arrangements he prescribed in the *Divisio Regnorum* which was drawn up in that year provide us with an insight into Charlemagne's own view of his achievements as king and emperor. A good deal of pomp surrounded the *Divisio*, whose terms were agreed to at an official assembly of the Franks held at Thionville, and Einhard then took a copy of the document with him to Rome so that it might gain papal approval. Charlemagne's three eldest sons by Hildegard were all still alive at the time and they are the beneficiaries of the provisions envisaged as coming into effect on their father's death. Louis and Pippin were already ruling as sub-kings in Aquitaine and Italy respectively and the kingdoms they were allocated therefore consolidated arrangements which had been in place since 781. The kingdom of Louis was defined to include not just Aquitaine proper but also its southern frontier area of Gascony as well as Provence and the westernmost parts of Burgundy. Pippin's kingdom comprised central and northern Italy, as well as Bavaria with the exception of a frontier territory known as the Nordgau on the duchy's northern frontier. Charles the Younger's envisaged possession of the Nordgau was dictated by military strategy: in the event of war it would have given his troops a convenient access to Bohemian-occupied territories. He was the major beneficiary under the division and as his father's successor Charles was meant to rule in the core Frankish territories of Austrasia and Neustria, as well as in Saxony and Frisia, most of Burgundy, all of Thuringia and most of Alamannia (part of which went to Pippin).

Charlemagne's continuity of aim as revealed in the *Divisio Regnorum* is the document's single most striking feature. He was confirming arrangements which had been made a quarter of a century earlier when sending his then infant sons to rule at the courts established for them in Italy and Aquitaine. The power base of the Reich was still the core territories of the Frankish kingdom, which is why they were allocated to the emperor's principal heir along with Thuringia and Alamannia – areas of Germanic population which had been central to the Franks' cultural and political project ever since first coming under their hegemony in the sixth century. The allocation of Saxony to Charles indicates that this region, only recently conquered in its entirety, was earmarked for complete assimilation within the kingdom of the Franks. The terms of the division also show that it was thought important for Charles and Louis to have access through the Alps to Italy via, respectively, the Aosta and Susa valleys.

This was designed to be an allocation of Carolingian responsibilities rather than a breakup, and the division is very much a family affair. The three sons are enjoined 'to maintain peace and amity' with one another, and to defend the rights of the Church, 'just as it was once assumed by our grandfather Charles [Martel] and by our father of blessed memory'. Charlemagne's daughters were told that they could either enter a monastery or choose to live with one of their brothers. The removal by death of his patriarchal control meant that they could even marry, said Charlemagne, if they wanted to. One notorious clause highlights the emperor's recognition that his immediate relatives were more than capable of mistreating one another. None of his sons are to put to death, mutilate, blind or tonsure against their will any of Charlemagne's grandsons and nephews without a fair trial and an enquiry having first been held into any possible offences that might have been committed. 'Rather it is our will that they be honoured by their fathers and uncles and be obedient towards these with all the deference which is fitting in such a blood relationship.' The precision of Charlemagne's allocation of certain amounts of treasure and specified valuables to his children and grandchildren in his will of 811 shows that here too he was anxious to avoid a family quarrel about who should get what.

The *Divisio* envisaged, then, a consensual and tripartite scheme for the government of the Carolingian empire. Pippin of Italy's death in 810, followed by that of Charles the Younger in 812, frustrated that goal and left Louis the Pious as the sole heir. Charlemagne persevered, however, with arrangements designed to secure the Italian kingdom's future as an autonomous region within the Carolingian empire. Pippin's son Bernard was formally recognized as his father's successor at the general assembly which was held in Aachen in 812, and the boy, who was then about twelve years old, was sent to rule in Italy as king. Bernard's young sisters meanwhile returned from Italy to Francia and were cared for as part of the extended royal family presided over by their grandfather. In the following year Louis was summoned from Aquitaine and crowned emperor by his father during the general assembly held at Aachen in September. In true Carolingian and Frankish style there was a formal acclamation of the crowned co-emperor by the aristocrats, abbots, bishops and other dignitaries of the realm who had gathered to witness this great event. We are told that Charlemagne specifically commended three of Louis's half-brothers to his care and service. Drogo, who was then aged about twelve and whose mother was the concubine Regina, would have a distinguished career as bishop of Metz and imperial arch-chaplain. His slightly younger brother Hugh, another son of Regina, became arch-chancellor of the empire and abbot of St-Quentin. Six-year-old Theoderic was the issue of Charlemagne's liaison with a concubine named Adalind and died in youth sometime after 818.

There may have been a period in the late summer and early autumn of 813 when Charlemagne spent some time instructing Louis in his new responsibilities while the new co-emperor was still in Aachen. But by the winter Louis must have returned to Aquitaine since it was there that he learnt that his father had died on 28 January 814. Having reigned as *Rex Francorum* for forty-five years and three months, Charlemagne was buried in the palace chapel at Aachen. A highly reliable medieval tradition maintained that at his funeral Charlemagne's body was placed in the late second-century Roman marble sarcophagus which is now kept in Aachen's cathedral treasury. In that event, the sarcophagus must have already arrived at Aachen since Charlemagne was buried on the day of his death. The aged emperor would therefore have had an opportunity to familiarize himself with its decorative details: Proserpina is being abducted by Pluto, the god of the underworld, and behind them we see Ceres, the goddess of fruitfulness, who searches for her lost daughter. A rape scene being played out by the pagan deities is surely an unexpected presence at the obsequies of this ostentatiously orthodox Christian emperor. Augustine's *City of God*, frequently read aloud after dinner to the imperial circle at Charlemagne's court, describes the myth of Proserpina in disgusted detail, and Books VI and VII of that work castigate the classical gods *tout court* as 'unclean demons'. The courtiers and clergy may just have wanted to use the most magnificent item they could lay their hands on in order to honour their emperor. If these mourners were aware of any discordancy, then they must have decided that imperial prestige needed to take priority over Christian theology on this occasion, and they therefore chose not to look too closely at what those figures carved on the Carrara marble were actually doing.

It was a whole month before the new king of the Franks arrived at Aachen. '*Vivat Imperator Ludovicus*,' shouted the nobility who had gathered to see Louis crown himself as his father's successor. This, though, may not have been the prevailing sentiment among his unmarried sisters, since one of Louis's first acts was to drive them from the palace and into the various nunneries, where they spent the rest of their days. Charlemagne's household had been dispersed. His wider legacy, however, was destined to have an enduring influence in the history of European nations.

CHARLEMAGNE'S HEIRS: DYNASTIC CONCLUSIONS

Louis the Pious (778–840), Charlemagne's heir and successor, struggled to keep the imperial show on the road in the face of successive rebellions by his disloyal sons. In 833–4 he was briefly deposed and a period of civil war (840–43) followed immediately after Louis's death. His sons were already established in different parts of the empire and the formal recognition of their authority within those territories by the terms of the Treaty of Verdun (843) ended the warfare between them. Louis the German (806–76) was guaranteed the rights of kingship in all the imperial lands lying to the east of the Rhine and to the north and east of Italy. The title by which he was known showed that a real cultural shift had occurred, and one moreover that was obvious to contemporaries. Louis's kingdom included Saxony whose ruler Duke Otto I would be crowned emperor in 962, and that duchy was the stem out of which the Holy Roman Empire emerged in the tenth century. Charles the Bald (823–77) received the lands west of the Rhine and retained supreme authority in Aquitaine. His kingdom of west Francia is therefore the precursor to the kingdom of France. Lothair I (795–855) received the imperial crown, as befitted a ruler whose territories included the cities of Aachen and Rome. His 'middle kingdom' included much of present-day Belgium and Holland, Lorraine, Burgundy, Provence and north Italy.

Lothair's kingdom, however, would enjoy only a brief history and its components were divided between his three sons: Louis II became king in Italy, Charles of Provence gained Burgundy, and the rest went to Lothair II (835–69) – hence its subsequent name of *regnum Lotharii* or Lotharingia. It was the territory of that *regnum*, comprising the Rhineland and the Low Countries, which would be fought over by subsequent Carolingian rulers and their later successors on French and imperial thrones.

After Lothair II died, his uncles Louis the German and Charles the Bald partitioned Lotharingia between them in 870, with the result that the Rhineland and Alsace became part of the eastern Frankish kingdom. Charles the Bald's successors found it difficult, however, to maintain their authority in west Lotharingia, and in 880 they ceded the area to Louis the Younger (835–82), who had succeeded his father Louis the German as king in east Francia. For centuries to come the westernmost area of Lotharingia would be the accepted boundary between the French kingdom and the Holy Roman Empire. The foreign policy of Louis XIV, however, revived the question of what should be the 'natural' French border to the east, and the treaty arrangements of 880 once again became a major diplomatic and military issue.

Louis the German had to deal with sons whose dissidence rivalled that displayed by himself and his own two brothers in earlier years, and his lands had to be divided in order to gratify the ambitions of his heirs. Louis's eldest son Carloman (830–80) became king in Bavaria in 876, and he also enjoyed a period as king of Italy from 877 until he was incapacitated by a stroke in 879. Louis the Younger was the middle son but his rule over Saxony and Thuringia, the heartlands of east Francia, meant that he considered himself to be the true *Rex Francorum*, a title that he enjoyed using. The youngest son was Charles the Fat (839–88) whose sobriquet, bestowed on him by twelfth-century annalists, is a reference to his supposed lethargy. His regular bouts of sickness may in fact have been the result of epilepsy, and in periods of good health Charles could be a perfectly competent ruler.

Charles the Fat became king of Alamannia when his father's kingdom was formally divided in 876, and three years later he succeeded his brother Carloman as king in Italy. As a result of this Italian involvement Charles received a plea for assistance from Pope John VIII following an invasion of the papal states in the summer of 880 by the forces of Guy II, duke of Spoleto. A pope troubled by a neighbouring power and appealing to a Frankish king to come to his aid was a venerable enough diplomatic exercise, though this particular initiative seems to have borne little fruit. In any event, the troublesome Guy died soon afterwards in 882–3. But there was one relevant, if somewhat nostalgic, conclusion since on 12 February 881 Pope John, keen to get Charles's support, crowned him emperor as Charles III. Charlemagne's memory clearly mattered to Charles. He had a lively sense of the imperial title's significance and the palace that he started to build in the Alsatian town of Selestat was consciously modelled on the one in Aachen. The death of his brother Louis the Younger, leaving no legitimate male issue, meant that in 882 Charles succeeded to the east Frankish throne, and he was an effective enough consolidator of the realm's boundaries in the face of Viking attacks. Hopes of a dynastic revival must have been aroused right at the end of 884 when Charles found himself king in western as well as in eastern Francia. A ruler who was already emperor seemed to have reunited the territories of his great ancestor's realm. This, however, proved to be the prelude to the last act in the Carolingian story.

*

Carloman II (c. 866–84) was a distant cousin of Charles, since his grandfather was Charles the Bald. Carloman and his brother Louis III were the sons of Louis the Stammerer (846–79), Charles the Bald's son and ineffective successor on the throne of west Francia, and in 879 the two boys were elected joint kings by the local nobility. The idea of a dual kingship was controversial and the brothers' condominium met serious opposition, most significantly from the nobleman Boso who renounced his allegiance and was then elected a king by the magnates of Provence. Although Boso was a usurper and a rebel, his period as monarch in Provence (879–87) is a highly significant episode since he was the first non-Carolingian to become a king on Frankish soil since Childeric III, the last Merovingian ruler.

Carloman II struggled on as sole ruler after his brother's death in 882, but the teenage king was unequal to the enormous challenge posed by the incursions of Norman raiders on his kingdom. Charles the Fat succeeded to the throne of west Francia, but it was that same threat from the north, and the failure to mount an adequate response, which did for him in both Frankish kingdoms.

Towards the end of 887 Charles was formally deprived of his throne in east Francia by the nobility. He was replaced as king by his nephew Arnulf of Carinthia (850–99), whose son Louis the Child (893–911) would be the last Carolingian to rule in east Francia. The dissolution of Charles's authority had been equally rapid in west Francia during 887, although here there would be a final Carolingian twist to events. The great man of the kingdom was Odo, count of Paris (860–98), whose vigorous leadership in resisting the Viking advance had gained him a wide following. He was therefore elected by a majority of the nobility to be king of western Francia and duly crowned at Compiègne in February 888. There was another contender to the throne, however, and a genuinely Carolingian one at that, since Carloman II did in fact have a perfectly legitimate heir in the form of his half-brother. This prince was recognized as being direct in manner, which is why he was called Karolus Simplex (879–929). The historical record, however, has perpetuated an original mistranslation, which is why this particular Charles is still sometimes referred to as 'the Simple'. Born in September 879, he was Louis the Stammerer's posthumous son since his father had died in April of that year, and his claim to the throne had therefore been disregarded twice, first on the occasion of Charles the Fat's accession and then again when Odo was elected.

Dissident aristocrats took up the cause of Charles the Simple and crowned him king in 893. Five years later he entered into his full inheritance and, as Charles III, was west Francia's sole king after Odo's death. His directness was not the only Carolingian thing about him. Charles's kingdom might well be evolving as a more distinctively French civilization, but he himself surely harked back to his family's roots in north-western Europe's Germanic culture. His marriage to Eadgifu, the daughter of King Edward the Elder of England, would have strengthened that sense of a northern solidarity and the couple chose to call their daughter Gisela, a thoroughly Carolingian name and the one borne by Charlemagne's sister, daughter and granddaughter. The deal that Charles struck with the Viking leader Rollo also shows his appreciation of the northern dynamic at work in Europe's geopolitics. Although he had defeated Rollo in battle in 911 Charles nonetheless realized that the force represented by these men of the north had to be somehow accommodated. He therefore granted Rollo the territories along the lower Seine which the Viking first held as a royal fiefdom, and it was these lands that became the basis of the subsequent dukedom of Normandy. The deal included Rollo's conversion to Christianity and Gisela's hand in marriage. This might have been prudent realpolitik but it may have cost Charles the support of west Frankish nobles who were reared in the ancestral tradition of martial resistance to the Vikings. Following the baronial rebellion against him in 922 he was deprived of his throne and West Francia's subsequent Carolingian kings survived only precariously until Hugh Capet's dynastic takeover in 987.

The career of Charles the Simple ended in personal defeat but his policy with regard to the Vikings would prove to be irreversible, and their force of arms was transmuted into the Norman civilization in the decades after his death. Vitality and renewal could also be seen at this time in the kingdom of the Germans, as the congeries of territories comprising the old eastern Francia were beginning to be called. The Carolingian line of rulers had died out here in 911, but in 919 Saxony's Duke Henry I (876–936) was elected to the German kingship by the nobility of his own region and by that of Franconia. Swabia's duke soon followed suit, and two years later Henry took military action to ensure that the Bavarians also recognized his kingship. By the time Lotharingia's duke swore fealty to him in 925 Henry had created a powerful federation the like of which had not been seen in German lands since the time of Charlemagne. Henry's successor as both duke and king was his son Otto I the Great (912–73) and the history of the Holy Roman Empire is usually dated from the year of Otto's coronation as emperor in 962. Otto's son and grandson, who shared his name, were also crowned emperors and all three rulers were Charlemagne's heirs in the whole business of constructing a European and imperial order blessed by the Church and intent on further expansion to the east. This dynasty, sometimes called the Ottonians, took the Carolingian legacy and ensured its survival at a time when the continent was being subjected to immense strains from the east, most obviously in the form of Magyar incursions. It was therefore during the tenth century that Charlemagne experienced the first of his many posthumous renaissances.

ETHNIC INVENTIONS AND NATIONAL CONSEQUENCES

Of all the various peoples termed Germanic or barbarian, and who established themselves in Europe during the period following the Roman empire's fifth-century dissolution, it was the Franks who stayed the course and mattered the most. Charlemagne enjoyed unparalleled success as their ruler partly because his interests and ambitions mirrored those of his people. His own achievements, and those of his dynasty, in warfare, diplomacy and politics, in the vitality of religious life and the extension of cultural progress, need no further rehearsal. None of this, however, would have happened without the Franks' keen sense of their own identity. They chose of their own accord to think of themselves as a people set apart and destined for greatness. Frankish missionary zeal was based on that supreme self-confidence and artful self-invention. At the beginning of our period it was not at all obvious that Europe's future history would conspire to reward such ethnic audacity. Many others, after all – Spanish Visigoths and Italian Lombards among them – had also thought that they were travelling on the high road to success and international recognition. By the year 814, however, the Franks were the ones that were left standing. They were the masters of the western European scene and all other parts of the continent recognized, with varying degrees of willingness, the reality of that hegemony.

There are therefore two related aspects to the legacy of Charlemagne and of the dynasty that ruled the Franks. The story of the Carolingian empire's survival after 814, of its division in 843 and eventual replacement by the kingdoms of eastern and western Francia will already be familiar. That division of interests and territories would lend shape and give substance to Europe's geography of power for over a millennium. There was, however, another bequest. All European nations and their leaders were affected by that psychological bounciness of the Franks in one way or another. Some disliked it. Others tried to ape it in the hope that success might come their way as well. And many of those who fought the Franks also imitated their assertiveness. If 'good Europeans' can claim Charlemagne as their godfather, then so can the continent's assorted nationalists of varying stripe.

None of Charlemagne's family members contested the terms of his will so far as we know. But the argument about who should be the true heirs of his vision has been intense from the ninth century onwards, and that debate reflects the disagreement about Charlemagne's true goals. In this conclusion it is Charlemagne the Frankish nationalist who will predominate because that label's brand of ethnic pride proved to be the most vital aspect of his legacy. The *Reges Francorum* who ruled in a Carolingian imperial context would be consigned to history by the beginning of the tenth century, but that which made them great would live on in the ruling passions of those German kings who revived and directed the imperial ideal in the decades that followed, as Europe braced itself to mark the grand climacteric of the year 1000.

It was quite an achievement for the Franks to establish themselves in their own minds and those of others as a single people, since to begin with, at least, they were many and not one. In the eighth and ninth centuries the Franks were nonetheless presenting themselves to the world as a single ethnically related people or *gens*, and they were also claiming to have a continuous history in that regard. They enjoyed such success in doing so that most nineteenth-century historians and a good many twentieth-century ones fell for the idea that the original history of all European nations could be seen as the playing-out of the struggle between distinct races, each of which could be clearly defined in biological terms. Race and ethnicity obviously matter in the history of the Franks, but only as categories which were invented and then used by them to justify their sense of self-worth. The Franks needed to be imagined before they could come into being as a cohesive people, and that is a truth which may well apply in the wider history of nations as well. Once invented, a national identity will often need to be subsequently sustained by fables about shared origins and through stories which celebrate supposedly common experiences. It was not just love of a good yarn that led Charlemagne to order that the Franks' most ancient songs be written down and recorded for posterity.

The legacy we are dealing with therefore includes the idea that a people is a kind of community, racially connected and endowed with certain typical attributes and defining forms of cultural expression. Franks have the dubious honour of priority in the successful playing of this particular game in the history of medieval and modern Europe. The history of words certainly records the emergence between 400 and 1000 of the names that are still used today to describe the peoples of Europe. Angles turned into the English and some of the Franks into the French. Danes, Bulgarians, Croats, Serbs, Poles, Czechs, Hungarians and a host of others acquired their contemporary national labels during this period. European regional names can also claim an ancestry going back to the early Middle Ages, as in the case of Burgundy, Lombardy, Bavaria and Saxony. Alamannia survives in the Welsh and the French words for Germany (*Yr Almaen* and *Allemagne*). In the case of barbarian or Germanic peoples the words denoting them suggest, as in the case of the Franks, a long line of continuity and a happy responsiveness to new opportunities which accommodated long-term ambitions. Angles and Saxons therefore become the English, and those who lived in the Germania of the ancient Romans turn into Germans. Italy seems the odd man out since there the Lombards and Ostrogoths were seen for the most part as outsiders.

But the nations had invented the kind of history that suited their contemporary purposes, and the words they used to describe themselves can therefore be misleading guides to their history. None of them started out with a clear-cut identity. That was something which had to be acquired through many generations of adjustment to changing circumstances. The Franks set the standard but even here the process was prolonged. When Clovis established his Frankish kingdom in the Gaul of c. 500 his people spoke a variety of Germanic languages and dialects, and they were a very small minority compared to the Romanized population and the other groups of barbarian peoples who were already settled in the province. It took well over 300 years for this minority to assimilate itself to the language of the majority, and the process by which the natives learnt to accept that they too were now Franks was very long drawn out.

Extreme discontinuity and substantial changes in the mixture of populations were the norm across large parts of Europe towards the beginning of the period described in this book. It would be rather odd if the continent's peoples and nations were each still possessed of some core identity after going through so profound a change, even if the assumption is accepted that they started out in full possession of that supposedly blessed biological condition. What is surprising is that so many have been taken in by the propaganda which claimed that a clear-cut ethnic identity existed in the first place. The stories are vivid enough and undercut the ideology. The Roman diplomat Priskos arrived at the court of Attila, king of the Huns, and there he met a warrior who seemed at first sight to be a thoroughly Hunnish type. It turned out that he was a former Roman merchant and he described to Priskos the advantages of his present existence with some enthusiasm. The two conducted their conversation in Greek. The native populations of Italy thought the Lombards were alien intruders but that does not mean that the invaders shared a common identity. Paul the Deacon, the Lombard exile who became a member of Charlemagne's circle while living in Francia, wrote a history of his people. His *Historia Langobardorum* describes the many others who joined King Alboin's expedition of 568 into northern Italy. The Germanic peoples known as the Gepids and the Suevi, the Sarmatians and Bulgars who were both originally peoples of the steppe, as well as some Roman provincials from Noricum and Pannonia (modern Austria and Hungary): all were part of what is usually called a 'Lombard invasion'.

Can clothes, fashions and customs be used as evidence to distinguish peoples from one another? Early medieval authors desperate to establish the distinctiveness of nations certainly wanted to think so, and historians have seized on the evidence provided. And so we learn that the Lombards had beards, that Avars wore their hair in braids, and that the Franks went into battle carrying the axe known as the *francisca*. Details such as these are hardly distinctive enough to ensure a separate national identity. Besides which, fashions change. In about 790 Paul the Deacon decided to go to Monza near Milan. The famous Iron Crown of the Lombard kings was kept at the local cathedral, but would the town yield any evidence of the continuity of Paul's people? He went to Monza's royal palace, looked at some frescoes dating from the time of Queen Theodelinda (c. 600), and concluded that the Lombards' dress sense had changed completely in the past 200 years. Only a naif would expect anything else.

Archaeology helps us to trace the development of some Frankish customs between the fifth and seventh centuries. Women's clothes change, graves start to be organized in rows, and objets d'art cease to be placed in the tombs of the dead. None of these customs of themselves pinpoint the distinctive Frankish identity. All the barbarian invaders changed their way of life once they were settled in what had been the Roman provinces. But long before then they had already been changed as a result of an often prolonged exposure to Romanizing influences on the northern frontier. The Vandals who were settled in the former Roman province of north Africa in the early sixth century seem to have adopted the creature comforts of the late Roman aristocracy with some aplomb. If the Byzantine historian Procopius is to be believed, they lived in villas with gardens, enjoyed going to the circus and the theatre, and employed musicians and dancers to entertain them. Perhaps these Vandals were still claiming to be the same kind of people as their remote ancestors who in the mid-third century had been attacking the Romans in the middle Danube valley. If so, they were surely very much mistaken. Vandal history shows how a culture can change entirely while the name of its people remains the same.

In early medieval Europe barbarian peoples ended up being Romanized, and originally Roman populations were affected by barbarian customs. The period also shows how the leaders of these societies and the literate classes who were on their side recoiled fastidiously from the truth about their past and tried to contain a shifting scene within fixed categories. Historical writing served political and military ambitions in a very specific way. It was designed to show that different peoples had different histories which corresponded to their separate ethnic identities. Perhaps rulers believed it was easier to control subjects who thought in this way. And attitudes like that are certainly helpful when people are being encouraged to go to war. Tidy minds therefore got to work. And the titles they gave their books give the game away by preaching rather too loudly. Jordanes's *History of the Goths*, Paul the Deacon's *History of the Lombards* and Bede's *Ecclesiastical History of the English*: all tried to convince their readers and listeners that these were the categories that mattered now, and that they had also mattered for a very long time previously. The authors needed to labour the ethnic point in broad-brush headlines because it was not in the least obvious that this was actually the truth of the matter. European rulers and authors enjoyed great success in this flawed enterprise. The idea that peoples had core identities whose collective origins were lost in the mists of time, or at any rate perhaps buried within the undergrowth of ancestral Germanic forests, acquired a great vogue. This might have been nonsense, but it was historically significant nonsense because so many subjects of so many kings started to believe that it was true and acted accordingly.

Towards the end of the first millennium most Europeans had sorted out their mental furniture when it came to the question of national identities – or at any rate those furnishings had been arranged on their behalf. Whether they were, for example, English, French and Germans in the west, Danes and Norwegians in the north, or Poles, Czechs and Hungarians in *Mitteleuropa*, they had become convinced that they ought to hang together and distinguish themselves from their neighbours. That conclusion of popular psychology was an all-important element in the development of the national monarchies which claimed the allegiance of their subjects. Rulers could now tax and spend and go to war because it was thought that they represented a national identity. This successful attribution of a fixed and coherent identity was, in its way, a huge imaginative achievement. It is still important to remind ourselves that it was just that – an invention.

When it comes to the question of how and why the Franks were so spectacularly successful in the invention of an identity it is those graves of theirs that provide a clue. Conversion to Christianity meant that other European peoples also stopped burying horses with their fallen warriors and ceased to deposit decorative objects in the tombs of those who once were powerful and now were dead. The way the Franks chose to be buried does not of itself separate them from a host of other populations who were Christianized from the sixth century onwards. Conversion was nonetheless the single most important element in the fabrication of identities right across Europe. Whether it was from straightforward paganism, or from Arianism to Catholicism, that religious change could scarcely fail to transform the way individuals thought about themselves and the group to which they belonged. As a way of defining a culture it clearly goes rather deeper than hairstyles or axes – however expert the design might have been in either of those instances.

In the case of the Franks the Christian conversion was unusually intense in its effects. This does not mean that they were more devout than other converts, but the Franks did establish a brand of Christian nationalism which asserted that it was God's will that they should be special and successful. And in our period nobody else managed to get away with that trick for quite as long as the Franks, or performed it with quite such élan. The Visigoths of seventh-century Spain did something similar with their own Catholicized and nationalistic milieu, and at a time when their culture was immensely more sophisticated than that of the Franks. A pattern of Muslim conquest, however, extinguished Spain's Visigothic civilization in the early eighth century, and the onward march to the Pyrenees of armies who blessed the name of the Prophet was also the supreme moment of Frankish opportunity. The Frankish sense of an ethnic identity defined in Christian terms was given a huge boost by that new status of theirs as front-line warriors in the battle against Islam. The engagement that Charles Martel fought in 732 against a Muslim force which had advanced to a point between Tours and Poitiers may indeed have been no more than a skirmish. But Frankish chroniclers and propagandists made sure that Martel's victory was recorded to so grandiloquent an effect that it became in retrospect a defining moment in the history of Frankish religious nationalism. It was certainly used in order to help invent the nation that existed by the time Martel's grandson Charlemagne came to the throne two generations later. Memories of the 1939–45 war have played a very similar role in the development of a British identity during the decades after that conflict. Nations need their enemies, and national identities are built on the graves of foes.

TOWARDS THE TENTH CENTURY

The imperial coronation and its consequences dominate the question of Charlemagne's legacy. With papal approval, a king of Germanic descent was crowned emperor in 800 and he became the sovereign of a renewed Roman empire in the west. That event was the fusion of two forces which had originally provoked major challenges to the old empire's authority from the second century onwards: Christianity and barbarian power. Having transformed the Roman world, these two mighty influences now found themselves united in the cause of a renewed empire which was Christian in its inspiration and whose authority extended over many differing peoples in western Europe. The Church of Rome had been consecrating Christian emperors since late antiquity but now, and for the first time, it had crowned one who was a representative of the barbarian *gentiles*. For many centuries the leaders of the barbarian peoples had thought that this was an impossible ambition. Arbogast, the Frank who served as a general in the late fourth century; Stilicho, who as *magister militum* became the empire's commander-in-chief in the late 390s and whose father was a Vandal; the Germanic general Odoacer who was the first non-Roman to rule Italy after the deposition of the last emperor of the west in the 470s: all of them had the chance to seize the imperial crown but were held back by their own judgment that it could not be worn by those of barbarian lineage. Theoderic, the Ostrogothic king of Italy, thought the same during the early sixth century. Charlemagne's coronation meant goodbye to all that inhibition. His imperial status was at one and the same time Roman, Germanic and Catholic Christian. He never lost sight of the fact, however, that first and foremost he was *Rex Francorum*, and was at pains to establish that he did not owe his imperial crown to any act of papal largesse. It was the will of God and of the Franks that he should be king, and the same was true of the imperial honour.

Charlemagne's military victories created the largest conglomeration of territories to come under the authority of a single sovereign in western Europe since the fall of the Roman empire. The imperial title also meant that these lands were more than just a collection of kingdoms, duchies and regions delivered into Charlemagne's hands by the fortunes of war. His goal was administrative uniformity and he had a very specific pro-gramme for government. Charlemagne subdivided his empire into dif-ferent areas and he appointed functionaries who sought to establish legal observance and fiscal obedience within those territorial units. He cre-ated a single currency and the laws that he issued were meant to apply right across the Carolingian empire. Both clerical and secular govern-ment show the decisive impact of Charlemagne's mind and personality on the course of events and the transaction of business. He took a close and informed interest in the education and training both of the clergy in general and of the laymen who served his administration. In both areas he stressed the importance of an accurate use of a revived Latin language and culture. The Roman liturgy was imposed on the entire empire, and so was the Carolingian script which was destined to have a long, and continuing history. Enthusiastically rediscovered and adopted by the humanist scribes of renaissance Italy, the script became the basis of the typographical font that was developed for the first printing presses and which is now known as 'Venetian'.

That is quite some record of achievement. All Europeans are surely Charlemagne's heirs – some, however, more directly than others, and if we stand back a little from the map of the continent in 814 we can see why. The Carolingian empire consisted essentially of what we would nowadays call France, Germany, Belgium and Holland, with some southern appendages in the northern regions of Spain and Italy. Large parts of Christianized Europe lay beyond its boundaries including, most significantly, the entire British Isles with its mosaic of kingdoms both Celtic and Anglo-Saxon, the kingdom of the Asturias in north-west Spain, and the Lombard-ruled areas of southern Italy. Greece and the coastal regions of the Balkan peninsula were areas of Christian Europe which owed their political allegiance to the emperors of Byzantium, and the Church which claimed the religious loyalty of the populations of these areas refused to recognize the primacy of Rome. Vast regions of Scandinavia, central Europe and the Balkan interior remained pagan and also lacked stable forms of government. All of these non-Carolingian regions and countries would play a role in the making of Europe, and their influence in that regard is at the very least the equal of Charlemagne's own.

The Carolingian power bloc did of course influence those European areas that lay beyond its boundaries, and its long-term cultural impact was especially profound. Alfred's court, for example, in the Wessex of the late ninth century witnessed an artistic and intellectual *renovatio* which was centred on the person of the king and achieved thereby an Anglo-Saxon reflection of the Carolingian renaissance. But the story of continental progress is something more than just a question of influences emanating from the Carolingian heart of Europe and being diffused to the peripheries by means of evangelizing Christian mission supported by military power. Charlemagne wanted his empire to endure, and we have seen how his heirs seated on their various ninth-century thrones often saw themselves as members of the same family with interconnecting interests and ambitions. But the fragility of the Carolingian empire was increasingly evident after 814, and the contrast between the ideals that had inspired Charlemagne and the customs of the societies he had sought to reform grew ever sharper once he was no longer around to cajole, invigilate and inspire. Fifty years after the coronation in Rome the Carolingian empire was divided into a number of kingdoms whose horizons were limited and whose ambitions diverged quite as often as they converged. Charlemagne's campaigns in Saxony and against the Avars were the last Carolingian dynastic ventures to enjoy any real success in the Christianization and military conquest of pagan territories. His successors' attempts in that line of work were intermittent and largely unsuccessful. From the time of Louis the Pious to that of Charles the Fat many of these *epigoni* called themselves 'Emperor'. The truth is that none of them were quite up to the job.

If the Carolingian legacy was fast disintegrating within its territorial nucleus there were nonetheless some very fast-moving developments which were visible to the north and east of the empire. From the eighth century onwards the Scandinavian world had been seeing increasingly lively patterns of trade along the North and Baltic Seas that connected the British Isles and northern France with Denmark, Sweden and the north coast of Russia. These latter areas in turn supplied a contact with the trade travelling west from the Islamic Middle-East and the Greek empire, with important trading centres emerging along the coastal areas of Poland, Sweden, Denmark, eastern Britain and the French Channel. Coinage boosted trade and Charlemagne's single currency, the denier, had made a big difference. But the coins of the Anglo-Saxon kingdoms and the Islamic lands were, together with silver ingots, another major element in the currency exchange which vitalized these commercial contacts. The northern reaches of the Carolingian empire benefited from the new trading opportunities, with Danes and Swedes playing a central role in their evolution. It was those people who, together with the Norwegians, produced the warrior class known as the Vikings, and their devastating impact on the western European scene in the ninth century is also part of the story of commercial progress during this era.

Domestic leaders, sometimes bearing the title of king, were trying to impose political and fiscal control over large tracts of economically buoyant Scandinavian territory. Different war bands clashed violently and commanders had to pay their followers in order to ensure loyalty. Since land in these societies was still mostly owned communally those payments needed to be in cash, and leaders therefore needed regular access to huge amounts of liquid wealth. Scandinavian society's commercial prosperity also made it unusually rich in the flow of currency which could be seized by the war bands and used to subsidize their own activities. It was a heady dynamic and one which was cyclical in both its creativity and its destructiveness. Some of the conquered populations decided not to submit and this is what led to the Viking movement, with large-scale expeditions of piracy being launched from Scandinavian shores and then directed towards the coastal areas of Britain and the Carolingian-ruled territories. Those areas were already familiar to many of these warriors as a result of trading contacts, and the aim was to extract enough cash and booty which would allow them to return home and resume their political and military struggles.

Viking incursions undermined Charlemagne's legacy and compounded the difficulties experienced by Carolingian government during the ninth century. But the northern warriors were also laying the basis of new kinds of political and economic partnership as well as of renewed means of communication across northern Europe. In time they established stable colonies, and the Vikings of the tenth century would settle in northern France, eastern regions of both England and Ireland, south Wales, Iceland and Greenland. Warriors became courtiers and administrators who were keen to exploit the institutional powers of royal governments within the conquered regions. By the beginning of the eleventh century the kings of Denmark were also ruling in England and in Norway, and the duchy of Normandy was closely linked to that same axis of power. Sweden at the same time was seeing a very significant extension of royal authority over areas which had once been run by local communes, and the country's commercial colonies could be found on the southern Baltic shores and by the side of the rivers that flowed across the Russian plain down to the Black Sea. Scandinavian populations might still be pagan but their kings were becoming Christian, and the introduction of an ecclesiastical infrastructure into their territories gave rulers a new tool which could be deployed in the exercise of their regal command. There is a cultural story here as well as a political one, since the Scandinavian mission was directed by the German archdioceses which had emerged during the age of the Carolingians. It was that institutional structure which enabled many of the Carolingian renaissance's most distinctive achievements to be diffused northwards, with liturgical and legal reforms, Latin texts, as well as southern European architectural and artistic styles, emerging within the Scandinavian milieu.

Towards the east of the Carolingian empire lay the Slavic populations, and the ninth-century history of those of their number who were settled to the south of the Danube supplies another example of princely power. Dalmatia's Croat tribes were united under a duke whose title by the century's end would become that of king, and the government of the Moravians had extended its influence into Bohemia and Pannonia. The boundaries of these principalities were fluid, and there were frequent border disputes along the zone connecting them with the Carolingian-ruled territories. These skirmishes, however, cannot be compared to the ferocity of the Viking onslaught to the north, which had been driven by the hunger for land, plunder and booty. The militarized aristocracies of the Slav principalities lacked that kind of motivation since their territories, unlike those of Scandinavia, were agriculturally prosperous. Their material needs were therefore well provided for locally, and the region's economy was also well integrated with the flow of trade which ran from the Baltic to Bavaria and Dalmatia, and then down the Danube to the Black Sea and the Greek empire of Byzantium. These ninth-century Slavic societies, though keen to protect their political autonomy, proved receptive to the Carolingian culture which was largely filtered in the south through Bavaria, although Moravia bucked that westernizing and Latin trend by inviting missionaries from Byzantium to evangelize the region. Into this scene of comparative peace came the Magyars, whose arrival heralded decades of conflict along the eastern frontier of an emergent Christendom.

The Magyars were pagans whose lineage was Mongolian and they practised an economy of nomadic herding. From their base in what is now Hungary they attacked Europe continuously during the first half of the tenth century. The Moravian principality collapsed as a result of their incursions, and for the German territories, southern France and northern Italy they were a terror equivalent to the one visited upon northern France and the British Isles by the Vikings. Real heroism was needed to confront the nomadic techniques of slash and burn that the Magyars brought to the art of war, and this tenth-century conflict was surely the making of medieval European civilization. It was a crucible. And within it were fashioned the mental attitudes and the martial techniques which enabled that culture to define itself, to survive, and then to win.

Confronted by these dangers, the Slavic lands to the north showed themselves to be not only resilient but also ready to consolidate their political position within the imperilled continental centre. During the tenth century Bohemian princes extended their influence to the southern reaches of Poland and embraced the Christian evangelization of German missionaries. Prague played an important role within the central European network of commercial traffic and the city was also the power base of the Premyslid princes whose dynastic hegemony over the other Bohemian magnates laid the basis of a Czech kingdom. At the same time central and northern Poland witnessed the rise to greatness of the Piast dynasty, who created a state infrastructure buttressed by a regional network of fortified settlements run by royal appointees charged with the duty of governance and defence. Both Bohemian and Polish princes were strongly committed to the development of the Christian mission within their territories, and by the second half of the tenth century they were running well-evolved administrations which could coin reliable units of currency and impose taxation on both agricultural produce and commercial trade.

This dynamic northern and eastern European milieu had enjoyed strong links with those European centres of power that had emerged to their west in the post-Carolingian age of the late ninth and early tenth centuries. Among these was one that would rise to a position of awe-inspiring primacy. The ducal house of Saxony – the territory which had been strong-armed into Christian faith and political submission by Charlemagne and his armies – started its march to greatness by exercising royal authority over the other German territories. These German kings then became the hub of a tenth-century network of European power which extended from north to south as well as from west to east. It was therefore the Ottonian dynasty of Saxon rulers who revived the Carolingian imperial tradition and redirected it in the service of their own ambitions.

Power was following the money. German territories were experiencing strong and sustained rates of economic growth during the tenth century, with their markets extending into the Baltic in one direction and across to Venice in another. The major trade routes which crossed the German lands connected the Slavic areas with France and Spain, and the region's shipping lanes communicated with Scandinavia to the north. In the case of Saxony there was one additional boon in the form of the silver deposits which had been discovered locally in the Harz mountains during the 930s. The produce of the mining operations filled Ottonian coffers and it was Harz silver which paid for those triumphalist ceremonies and magnificent buildings which demonstrated the dynasty's regality and authority. This wealth also subsidized the expansion of Ottonian territorial influence and enabled the dynasty to produce a currency whose worth and weight were valued right across the European markets.

Otto I used both his army and the Church to extend his influence in the territories surrounding the German kingdom. He sharp-elbowed his way into Burgundy whose weak king came under his formal protection, and in the Czech lands he forced the Prague princes to pay him formal tribute. Following his invasion of Italy in 951 Otto called himself king of the Lombards – as Charlemagne had done before him – and bestowed the title of Italian king on his local peninsular vassals. Towards the north and east there was another resumption of that thrusting *Weltanschauung* which had typified the Carolingians while at the height of their influence. Otto instituted three missionary bishoprics in Jutland and two others in the territories between the Elbe and the Oder where the Slavic populations were still pagan. The defeat he inflicted on the Magyars in 955 at the battle of Lechfeld was so shattering that they never really recovered from its impact and were forced afterwards to opt for a settled existence on the Pannonian plain. Otto had demonstrated the crushing superiority of his Germanic army and earned the right to be regarded as the greatest, because most militant, defender of the rights of Latin Christianity since Charlemagne a century and a half earlier. On gaining the victory, Otto's warriors are said to have raised him on their shields in celebration – a gesture evocative of both ancient Roman and ancestral Germanic precedents on the field of battle.

In 962 Otto was summoned to Rome by Pope John XII who, just like his predecessor Leo III in 799–800, had run into serious difficulties with the local Roman and Italian nobility. On 2 February of that year the king of the Germans was crowned emperor by John, and a few days later the two of them ratified the *Diploma Ottonianum* which committed Otto to the defence of the papal states' independence. The new emperor also had a papal mandate now to spread Christianity among the Slavs, a project he turned to with special enthusiasm. Otto created a new ecclesiastical province, which meant that the existing bishoprics strung along the Elbe came under the authority of an archbishop located at Magdeburg, a site which was commercially important as well as strategically significant. Here again there were strong Carolingian associations since the town had been founded by Charlemagne in 805, and Otto's father

King Henry I had fortified Magdeburg to protect it against both Magyars and Slavs. The emperor spent a good deal of his time at Magdeburg's palace and would be buried in the local cathedral, which was also the final resting place of his first wife Edith, the daughter of the Anglo-Saxon king Edward the Elder. Border disputes with Poland's princes were resolved in Otto's favour, and he established a bishopric at Poznan to further the country's conversion. And the defeated Magyars, now quiescent, accepted the German missionaries that Otto sent into Hungary to further the cause of Christian evangelism.

Otto I's successors continued his policy of extending the German kingdom's influence and control over the lands that surrounded it, and the entire dynasty, together with the lay and clerical intelligentsia at its disposal, gave to the imperial dignity those connotations of sacred and universal authority which had been the hallmarks of Charlemagne's own ambitions and achievements. The Danish king Harald Bluetooth, who was baptized a Christian during Otto I's reign, became the emperor's vassal and allowed German priests to establish three bishoprics as missionary centres in his realm. Harald would rebel against both Otto I and his son Otto II – unsuccessfully on both occasions – but he never gave up on the Christianizing project and his reign saw the widespread conversion of the Danish nobility.

The emergence of a national Hungarian monarchy was a development closely associated with the evangelism of German priests among a people whose ancestors had been terrorizing central Europe barely two generations previously. Geza the Grand Prince of the Magyars was baptized by a German missionary sometime during the 970s, and although he is said to have continued to worship the old gods, Hungarian aristocrats nonetheless embraced Christianity in large numbers during the late tenth century. Geza's son was a more convinced convert and chose to be known by his baptismal name of Stephen or Istvan, a Christian version of his birthname Vajk. Stephen's accession as his father's eldest son marked a significant break with the Magyar tribal custom which dictated that it was the eldest close male relative who should succeed a Grand Prince. He had to fight his uncle, a powerful pagan chieftain, for the right to inherit and Stephen did so as the representative of Christian dynastic kingship – a principle and an idea which the Ottonians' pervasive influence helped to diffuse among the Magyars. The substantial military aid that Stephen received from the German rulers enabled him to carry the day, and his coronation as Hungary's first king in c. 1000 was a victory both for Latin Christianity and for the imperial dynasty which had supported his cause.

Ottonian hegemony was secured through often violent military interventions and the imperial system of tribute payments was intended to remind defeated princes of the reality of their subjection. Nonetheless, not even these German dynasts could put a stop to the long-term development of national states in the territories that surrounded them. And rather similarly, German Christianity's missionary impact did not inhibit the establishment of autonomous national Churches once the new faith had been consolidated in those same territories. Otto III (980–1002) was his dynasty's most far-sighted ruler in this regard despite his tender years, and he seems to have actively sponsored these developments. The archbishoprics of Gniezno in Poland and of Gran in Hungary were both established during his reign, and as a result both the Polish and the Hungarian Churches were withdrawn from the ecclesiastical jurisdiction of Ottonian bishops. Otto made a special pilgrimage to the cathedral at Gniezno in order to pay homage at the shrine of Adalbert, the missionary killed by pagan Baltic Prussians in 997, and he was an active supporter of the papacy's decision to bestow a royal crown on Stephen I of Hungary. It may have been his Greek ancestry that explained Otto's fresh pair of eyes. His mother was Theophanu, the Byzantine noblewoman who had married Otto II (955–983), and their son had clearly moved away from that German-dominated form of imperial rule which had typified his dynasty's previous history. Otto III made Rome his capital, represented himself on his imperial seal as a Greek *basileus* with a full beard, and encouraged a system of alliances with the princes of Poland, Hungary, Moravia and Bohemia. He may well have envisaged Europe's unity as an imperial federation of nations extending right across the continent from east to west, and this youthful ruler certainly spent a lot of time thinking about Charlemagne and his legacy. He had been crowned at Aachen and in the year 1000, that time of apocalyptic visions which included that of Christ's anticipated return to sit in judgment, Otto returned there in order to pay his respects to Charlemagne's memory.

One medieval story claims that he opened the tomb in which the body was by now enclosed, and found that the corpse had lost none of its members apart from the tip of the nose which Otto replaced with gold. Two years later he himself would be dead as a result of a fever contracted in Ravenna's marshes. Otto's soldiers carried his body back to Aachen where he was then buried and thereby joined his imperial forebear in death.

The brief and intense drama of Otto III's reign is a reminder of the reality of European disunity as well as of the persistent aspiration towards continental unity. His parents' marriage had been arranged in order to promote a diplomatic rapprochement between the Greek east and the Latin west, but despite the yearnings of their son that division within Christendom would persist and deepen. Already by the year 1000 there was too much history that separated those two cultures. The processes of Christianization and state formation which had been experienced by the Slavic societies to the European north from the ninth century onwards had also been evolving at the same time in the southern Balkans, the region to the south of the lower Danube and the Ukraine. But the Bulgarian, Serbian and Russian magnates and princes who contested for power in these regions had strong links with the Byzantine empire, and they operated within its sphere of influence not just politically and militarily but also culturally. The evangelizing missions sponsored by these rulers were conducted by the clergy of Byzantium, who proved adept in the promotion of Christianity by using the local Slavic languages for the liturgy. And the invention by these missionaries of the Cyrillic alphabet was a major cultural breakthrough since it enabled sacred Greek texts to be translated into characters that corresponded to the sounds of the Slavic tongues. Those parts of southern Italy which remained Greek-controlled were directly adjacent to the Ottonians' own newly acquired areas of peninsular influence, and the German armies were invariably routed by the Byzantines in the repeated military confrontations that occurred within the region. Southern Italy would not be integrated within a westernizing ambit of influence until the eleventh-century arrival of the Norman invaders who were the descendants of the Viking warriors who had settled in northern France.

These conflicts of interest recalled disputes which were familiar to

Charlemagne two centuries previously, and they harked back to an even more ancient division – the one between the eastern and western halves of the ancient Roman empire. By the end of the first millennium, however, the nature of his legacy was subsumed by the pattern of Europe's political, cultural and military developments as they had evolved in the almost two centuries that had elapsed since his death. The Charlemagne that now mattered and whose legacy could be exploited most effectively in the centuries to come was the one whose ambitions and achievements seemed most consonant with those of successive German rulers, who once again dreamed of European hegemony and were prepared to act in militant pursuit of that imperial goal. Those who came to pay tribute at Aachen and to stand in that imperial shade were powerful witnesses to an affinity which stretched across the centuries. In 1165 the emperor Frederick I Barbarossa, who had been excommunicated five years earlier by Pope Alexander III, secured Charlemagne's canonisation by the dissident Antipope Paschal III. The emperor's bones were disinterred and, at a great service in Aachen attended by the German nobility and episcopate, Paschal consecrated these mortal remains 'to the honour and glory of Christ and the strengthening of the Roman Empire.' Three years later Barbarossa donated the massive bronze chandelier which hung over the new saint's shrine and which can still be seen within the cathedral. Towards the end of July 1215 Frederick II, the grandson of Barbarossa, arrived in Aachen to be crowned king of the Germans and thereby take his seat on Charlemagne's throne. The ornate reliquary of silver and gold designed to provide the emperor with his latest place of rest was now ready. On the day after his coronation Frederick laboured alongside the cathedral workmen as the body of his mighty precursor was re-interred within the new shrine which would become an object of mass veneration. The final nails were driven into the reliquary lid. Charlemagne had become Kaiser Karl, a German emperor.

Primary Source References

ABBREVIATIONS

Annales fuldenses *Annales fuldenses sive Annales regni francorum orientalis*, ed. F. Kurze, *MGH SRG* 7 (Hanover, 1891).

Annales laureshamenses (Lorsch annals) *Annales laureshamenses*, ed. G. Pertz, *MGH SS* 1, (Berlin, 1826).

Annales mettenses priores *Annales mettenses priores*, ed. B. von Simson, *MGH SRG* 10 (Hanover, 1905).

ARF *Annales regni francorum unde ab a. 741 usque ad a. 829*, ed. F. Kurze, *MGH SRG* 6 (Hanover, 1893).

Codex epistolaris carolinus *Codex epistolaris carolinus*, ed. W. Gundlach, *MGH Epp.* 3, *Epistolae merowingici et karolini aevi*, 1 (Hanover, 1892).

*DKar.*1 *Die Urkunden der Karolinger*, 1: *Urkundens Pippins, Karlmanns und Karl der Grossen*, ed. E. Muhlbacher, *MGH Diplomata karolinorum* (Hanover, 1906).

Fredegar J. Wallace-Hadrill (trans.), *The Fourth Book of the Chronicle of Fredegar with its Continuations* (London, 1960). *Chronicorum quae Dicuntur Fredegarii Scolastica Libri IV, cum continuationibus*, ed. B. Krusch, *MGH SRM* 2 (Hanover, 1888).

GH *Gregorii Turonensis Episcopi Historiarum Libri Decem*, ed. B. Krusch and W. Levison, *MGH SRM*, 1 (rev. edn, Hanover, 1951).

HE *Historia Ecclesiastica Gentis Anglorum*, ed. and trans. B. Colgrave and R.A.B. Mynors, *Bede's Ecclesiastical History of the English People* (Oxford, 1969).

LP *Liber pontificalis*, ed. L. Duchesne, *Le liber pontificalis: texte, introduction et commentaire*, 2 vols (Paris, 1886–92).

MGH *Monumenta Germaniae Historica.*

MGH AA *Auctores Antiquissimi*, 15 vols (Berlin, 1877–1919).

MGH Cap. *Capitularia, Legum Sectio II, Capitularia regum francorum*, ed. A. Boretius and V. Krause, 2 vols (Hanover, 1883–97).

MGH Conc. *Concilia, Legum Sectio III, Concilia* II, ed. A. Werminghoff (Hanover, 1906-08); III, ed. W. Hartmann (Hanover, 1984).

MGH Epp. *Epistolae* III–VII. *Epistolae merowingici et karolini aevi* (Hanover, 1892–1939).

MGH Epp. Sel. *Epistolae selectae in usum scholarum*, 5 vols (Hanover, 1887–91).

MGH Fontes *Fontes iuris germanici antique in usum scholarum ex monumentis germaniae historicis separatim editi*, 13 vols (Hanover, 1909–86).

MGH Formulae *Formulae merovingici et karolini aevi* (Hanover, 1882–6).

MGH Poet. *Poetae latini aevi carolini*, ed. E. Dummler, L. Traube, P. von Winterfeld and K. Strecker, 4 vols (Hanover, 1881–99).

MGH SRG *Scriptores rerum germanicarum in usum scholarum separatim editi*, 63 vols (Hanover, 1871–1987).

MGH SRL *Scriptores regum langobardicarum et italicarum* secs. VI–IX, ed. G. Waitz (Hanover, 1898).

MGH SRM *Scriptores rerum merovingicarum*, ed. B. Krusch and W. Levinson, 7 vols (Hanover, 1885–1920).

MGH SS *Scriptores in folio*, 30 vols (Hanover, 1824–1924).

PL *Patrologia Latina*, ed. J.-P. Migne. *Patrologiae cursus completus, series Latina*, 221 vols (Paris, 1841–64).

VK Einhard, *Vita Karoli*, ed. L. Halphen, 2nd edn (Paris, 1947).

CHAPTER 1: GODS, KINGS AND FRANKS

Adomnan, *Vita Sancti Columbae*, ed. and trans. A. Anderson and M. Anderson, *Adomnan's Life of Columba*, Oxford Medieval Texts, 2nd edn (Oxford, 1991).

Alcuin, *Epistolae*, ed. E. Dummler, *MGH Epp.* IV (Berlin, 1895), *Epp.* 84, 154, 195, 226; pp. 127, 29, 322–33, 359–60.

Alcuin, *Vita Sancti Willibrordi*, ed. W. Levison, *MGH SRM* 7 (Hanover, 1920), pp. 81–141.

Annales mosellani, ed. I. Lappenberg, *MGH SS* 16 (Hanover, 1859), 781, p. 497.

Augustine, *De Civitate Dei*, Book XIX.

Boniface, *Epistulae*, ed. M. Tangl, *Die briefe des heiligen Bonifatius und Lullus, MGH Epp. Sel.* 1 (Hanover, 1916), *Epp.* 22, 23 24, 28, 36–8, 63, 86, 130, 165, 193, 63, 36–8, 50.

Cassiodorus, *Variae*, ed. A. J. Fridh, Corpus Christianorum Series Latina, 96 (Turnhout, 1973), pp. 1–499. Eng. trans. S.J.B. Barnish, *Cassiodorus: Variae. Translated Texts for Historians* 12 (Liverpool, 1992).

Chronicon moissacensis, ed. G. Pertz, *MGH SS* 2 (Berlin, 1829), pp. 282–313.

Codex epistolaris carolinus, ed. W. Gundlach, *Epp.* 6, 45–6, 85; pp. 488, 563–5, 621–2.

Constantine Porphyrogenitus, *De administrando imperii*, ed. G. Moravcsik, trans. R. Jenkins. Dumbarton Oaks Texts, 1 (Washington, DC, 1967).

Constantin VII Porphyrogenete, *Le Livre des cérémonies*, ed. A. Voigt (Paris, 1935–40).

DKar. 1, nos 7, 8, 16, 22, 23, 25, 26, 27, 43, 44–6, 53, 57–9, 60–61, 79, 149.

Diplomata chartae epistolae, leges ad res gallo-francicas spectantia, ed. J. M. Pardessus, 2 vols (Paris, 1843).

Epistolae variorum Carolo magno regnante, ed. E. Dummler, *Ep. 7, MGH Epp. IV*, pp. 501–5.

Fredegar, c. 53, p. 121.

HE V. 10; II, 12; III, 18.

Isidore of Seville, *Isidori Hispalensis Episcopi Etymologiarum sive Originum Libri XX*, ed. W.M. Lindsay. 2 vols (Oxford, 1911), IX, iii, 4–6.

Isidore of Seville, *Historia Gothorum, Vandalorum et Suevarum*, ed. T. Mommsen, *MGH AA* 11, *Chronica Minora* II (Berlin, 1894), pp. 241–303.

Justinian, *Corpus Iuris Civilis*, ed. T. Mommsen and P. Kreuger, 3 vols: I, *Institutiones, Digesta*; II, *Codex Justinianus*; III, *Novellae* (Berlin, 1872–95), 14th edn (1967). *Digest*, trans. C. H. Munro, *The Digest of Justinian*, 2 vols (Cambridge, 1904, 1909).

Karolus magnus et Leo papa, ed. E. Dummler, *MGH Poet.* I (Berlin, 1881), pp. 366–79.

LP, Life, 97, cc. 31 and 34, ed. L. Duchesne, 1, pp. 395–6.

Maurice, *Das Strategikon des Maurikios*, ed. and trans. G. Dennis and E. Gamillscheg, *Corpus Fontium Historiae Byzantinae*, 17 (Vienna, 1981). Eng. trans. G. Dennis, *Maurice's Strategikon. Handbook of Byzantine Military Strategy* (Philadelphia, PA, 1984).

MGH Leges nationum germanicarum, ed. K. Zeumer (*Lex Visigothorum*); L.R. de Salis (*Leges Burgundiorum*); F. Beyerle and R. Bluchner (*Lex Ribuaria*); K.A. Eckhardt (*Pactis Legis Salicae and Lex Salica*); E. von Schwind (*Lex Baiuuariorum*), 6 vols. In 11 parts (Hanover, 1892–1969).

H. Mordek, *Biblioteca capitularium regum Francorum manuscripta. Überlieferung und Traditionszusammenhang der frankischen Herrschererlasse*, MGH Hilfsmittel 15 (Munich, 1995).

Paul the Deacon, *Historia Langobardorum*, ed. L. Bethmann and G. Waitz, *MGH SRL* 48 (Hanover, 1878); W.D. Foulke (trans.), *Paul the Deacon's History of the Lombards* (Philadelphia, PA, 1907).

Poeta saxo, Annales de gestis Caroli: magni imperatoris, ed. P. von Winterfeld, *MGH Poet. IV* (Berlin, 1899), pp. 1–71.

Regum francorum genealogiae, ed. G. Pertz, *MGH SS* 2, pp. 304–14.

Tacitus, *Germania*, ed. M. Winterbottom, *Cornelii Taciti Opera Minora* (Oxford, 1975), I, 55–68; II, 9–17, 26, 44–6, 62–3, 88.

Vita Alcuini Abbatis Turonensis, ed. W. Arndt, *MGH SS* 15:1 (Hanover, 1887), pp. 182–97.

Vita Bonifatii, ed. W. Levison, *Vita Sancti Bonifatii*, *MGH SRG* 57 (Hanover, 1905), pp. 62–78.

VK c. 18, p. 54; c. 19, pp. 58–60.

Walahfrid Strabo, *Visio Wettini*, ed. E. Dummler, *MGH Poet.* II, pp. 301–33.

CHAPTER 2: FROM PRINCE TO KING

Annales fuldenses, anno 752, ed. F. Kurze, *MGH SRG*, p. 6.

Annales mettenses priores, ed. B. von Simson, *MGH SRG* 10, 754, p. 47; 755, p. 49; 771, p. 57.

ARF, 749–50, pp. 8–10; 755, p. 12; 756, p. 14; 761, p. 18; 769, p. 28; 771, p. 32; 773, pp. 34–6.

Clausula de unctione Pippini Regis, ed. B. Krusch, *MGH SRM* 3, p. 465.

Codex epistolaris carolinus, ed. W. Gundlach, *Ep.* 6 (755), p. 488; *Ep.* 44, pp. 558–60; *Ep.* 45, pp. 561–3; *Epp.* 47–8, pp. 565–7; *Ep.* 85, pp. 621–2.

Codice diplomatico langobardo, 1 and 2, ed. L. Schiaperelli (Rome, 1929–33); 3, ed. C. Bruhl (Rome, 1973).

*DKar.*1, nos 43–6, 47, 48, 49, 50, 52, 54, 57, 58, 59, 60, 61, 79.

Fredegar, c. 22, p. 96; cc. 25–6, pp. 98–9; c. 36, p. 104; c. 37, p. 106; c. 39, p. 109; cc. 53–4, pp. 120–21.

Leges Langobardorum, 643–866, ed. F. Beyerle (Witzenhausen, 1962).

Liber historiae Francorum, ed. B. Krusch, *MGH SRM* 2 (Hanover, 1888), pp. 214–328.

LP 1, 405, 407–9, 420–21, 426, 432, 434, 442, 444, 446–7, 451, 453–4, 463, 469–70, 471–3, 477, 486–8, 489, 490–91, 493, 496, 498.

Paschasius Radbertus, *Vita Adalhardi*, *MGH SS* 2, p. 252.

Paul the Deacon, *Hist. Lang.*, 5. cc. 56–7, *MGH SRL*, p. 185.

VK, c. 3, pp. 13–15; c. 6, p. 20; c. 16, p. 50; c. 33, p. 102.

CHAPTER 3: THE KINGDOM AT WAR

Alcuin, *Epp.* 6, 107, 111, ed. E. Dummler, pp. 31, 153–4, 159–62.

Annales Bertiniani, 834, ed. F. Grat, J. Vieillard and S. Clemencet, *Annales de Saint-Bertin* (Paris, 1964), p. 14.

Annales laureshamenses, ed. G. Pertz, *MGH SS* 1, 788, pp. 33–4; 793, p. 35; 796, p. 37; 797, p. 37; 798, p. 37; 799, p. 38.

Annales mettenses priores, ed. B. von Simson, *MGH SRG* 10, 746, p. 37; 791, p. 79; 803–4, pp. 90–1.

Annales mosellani 777, 781, ed. I. Lappenberg, *MGH SS* 16, pp. 496–7.

Annales Sancti Amandi, Annales Tiliani, Annales Laubacenses, Annales Petaviani, ed. G. Pertz, *MGH SS* 1, pp. 6–7.

Anskar, *Miracula Willehadi*, ed. G. Pertz, *MGH SS* 2, pp. 379–84.

ARF   The earlier Saxon wars: 741, p. 2; 747, p. 6; 753, pp. 10–11; 758, p. 16; 772, p. 34; 775, pp. 40–41; 777, pp. 48–51; 778, p. 52; 782, pp. 58–65; pp. 62–3; 785, pp. 69, 71.

ARF   The Italian and Spanish campaigns: 753, pp. 10–11; 754, p. 12; 773 and 774, pp. 34–41; 776, pp. 42–5; 777, p. 48; 778, p. 51; 780 and 781, pp. 54–9; 800–802, pp. 110–17.

ARF   The Bavarian assimilation: 743, pp. 4–5; 748, p. 8; 757, pp. 14 and 16; 763, pp. 20 and 22; 778, p. 50.

ARF   The Avars: 788, p. 82; 791, p. 88, pp. 88–9; 792, pp. 92–3; 793, p. 93; 795, p. 97; 796, pp. 98–9; 799, pp. 108–9; 805, pp. 119–20; 811, p. 135; 811, p. 135.

ARF   Later Saxon wars: 789, pp. 84–7; 794, pp. 94–7; 795, p. 96; 797, pp. 100–03; 798, pp. 102–5; 799, pp. 106–7; 802, p. 117; 804, pp. 118–19; 805, p. 120; 806, p. 122; 808, p. 125, p. 126; 809, pp. 128–9; 810, pp. 131–2; 811, p. 135; 828, p. 176.

Boniface, *Epp.* 21, 46, 47, *S. Bonifatii et Lullii epistolae*, ed. M. Tangl, *MGH Epp. Sel.*

Chron. Moissac, ed. G. Pertz, *MGH SS* 1, 802, pp. 306–7; 808, p. 308; 809, pp. 308–9.

Codex epistolaris carolinus, ed. W. Gundlach, *MGH Epp.* III, *Epp.* 57, pp. 582–3; 82, pp. 615–16; 83, pp. 616–19; 84, pp. 619–20.

Epistolae Austrasicae 8, ed. W. Gundlach, *MGH Epp.* III, pp. 119–22.

Erchempert, c. 4, *Historia Langobardorum Beneventanorum*, ed. G. Waitz, *MGH SRL*, p. 236.

Fredegar, c. 12, p. 90; c. 19, p. 93; c. 25, p. 98; c. 26, p. 99; c. 27, p. 99; c. 31, p. 101; c. 32, pp. 101–2; c. 35, pp. 103; c. 38, p. 31; c. 52, p. 43; c. 54–5, pp. 44–5; c. 74, p. 63; c. 75, pp. 63–4; c. 78, pp. 65–7; c. 87, p. 73.

GH 2, c. 9; 4, c. 14; 3, c. 3; 5, c. 26.

LP 1, 33, p. 499.

MGH Cap. 1, no. 81, pp. 115–17; no. 82, p. 118.

Paul the Deacon, *Historia Langobardorum*, ed. G. Waitz, *MGH SRL* (Hanover, 1890), 6, c. 54, p. 237; 3, cc. 10 and 30, pp. 118 and 133–5; 4, cc. 7 and 39, pp. 146 and 167.

Rimbert, *Vita Anskarii* 55, ed. G. Waitz, *MGH SRG*, pp. 30–7.

VK, 9, p. 30; 11, p. 34.

CHAPTER 4: CROWN IMPERIAL

Agnellus of Ravenna, *Liber Pontificalis Ecclesiae Ravennatis*, ed. D. Deliyannis, Corpus Christianorum, Continuatio medievalis 199 (Turnhout, 2006).

Alcuin, *Epistolae*, ed. E. Dummler, *MGH Epp.* 2, Epp. 92, pp. 135–6; 93, pp. 136–8.

Annales mettenses priores, ed. B. von Simson, *MGH SRG* 10, 754, pp. 46–7; 755, p. 48.

ARF, 753, p. 10; 755, p. 12; 757, pp. 14–16; 770, p. 31; 771, p. 32; 773, pp. 34–6; 773–4, pp. 38–9; 786, p. 73; 787, p. 74; 796, p. 28; 800, p. 112; 801, p. 114; 810, p. 112; 813, p. 138; 815, pp. 142–3; 816–17, pp. 144–6; 823, p. 161; 827, pp. 173–4.

Astronomer, *Vita Hludowici*, *MGH SS* 2, c. 25, p. 619; c. 27, p. 621.

Boniface, *Epistolae*, ed. Tangl, *MGH Epp. Sel.*, 12, 50, 58, 61.

Constitutum Constantini, ed. H. Fuhrmann, *MGH, Fontes iuris germanici antiqui* (Hanover, 1968), cc. 3–7, pp. 59–71; c. 12, pp. 82–4; cc. 14–19, pp. 86–96.

Fredegar, c. 33, p. 102; c. 36, p. 104; c. 37, p. 105; c. 38, p. 108; c. 39, p. 109; c. 40, p. 109.

Gregory of Rome, *Dialogues*, ed. A. de Vogue and P. Antin, 3 vols (Paris, 1978–80).

Hadrian I, *Ep.* no. 2, *Epistolae Selectae Pontificum Romanorum*, *MGH Epp.* 3, p. 6.

John the Deacon, *Vita Gregorii*, *PL*, 75, 1, cc. 36 and 42, cols 78 and 80; 2, c. 53, col. 110.

Leo III, *Epp. X*, *MGH Epp.* 3, *Ep.* no. 1, p. 88; *Ep.* no.2, p. 91; *Ep.* no. 9, p. 100; *Ep.* no. 10, p. 103.

LP I, pp. 371–4, 390–3, 403–5, 420–21, 423, 428–9, 442, 444, 446–7, 451, 463, 468–9, 470–1, 487–8, 498. II, pp. 1, 28, 49, 52, 69, 73, 86, 134, 151, 356, 385.

Mansi, *Sacrorum Conciliorum Nova et Amplissima Collectio* (Florence and Venice, 1758–98).

MGH Cap. 1, no. 33, pp. 91–9; no. 34, p. 101; no. 44, c. 15, p. 129; no. 45, c.15, p. 129; no. 45, c. 20, p. 130; no. 90, pp. 190–91; no. 136, c. 17, p. 273; no. 161, p. 324; no. 172, p. 354; no. 172, pp. 354–5.

MGH Conc. 2.1, pp. 74–92; 2.1, pp. 81–6.

Paul the Deacon, *Historia Langobardorum, MGH SRL,* 6, c. 11, p. 168; 6, c. 31, p. 175; 6, c. 27, p. 174; 6, c. 44, p. 179–80; 6, c. 54, pp. 183–4; 6, c. 56, p. 185; 5, c. 56–7, p. 185.

VK, c. 3, pp. 13–15; c. 6, p. 20; c. 16, p. 50; c. 18, p. 54; c. 19, pp. 58–60; c. 30, p. 84.

Willibald, *Vita Bonifatii,* ed. W. Levison, *Vitae Sancti Bonifatii, MGH SRG* 57 (Hanover, 1905), pp. 1–58.

CHAPTER 5: ARISTOCRATIC POWER AND CAROLINGIAN CALCULATION

Annales Bertiniani, ed. G.Waitz, *MGH SRG* 5 (Hanover, 1883).

Annales Mosellani, ed. I. Lappenberg, *MGH SS* 16 (Hanover, 1859), pp. 494–9.

ARF, 774, p. 40; 777, p. 48; 780, p. 56; 787, p. 76; 793, p. 92; 816 and 817, pp. 144–5.

Astronomer, *Vita Hludowici Pii Imperatoris,* ed. G. Pertz, *MGH SS* II (Berlin, 1829), pp. 604–48.

Capitulare de villis, MGH Cap. 1, no. 32, pp. 82–91.

Concilium Francofurtense 794, MGH Conc. II, I, p. 171.

Dhuoda, *Liber Manualis,* ed. and French trans. P. Riche (Paris, 1975); III.4, VIII.15, X.5.

*DKar.*1, nos 55, 56, 98–101, 102, 108–9, 110, 126, 138, 163–7, 204.

L. Duchesne, *Fastes épiscopaux de l'ancienne Gaule,* 3 vols (Paris, 1907, 1910, 1915).

Fredegar, c. 13, p. 10; c. 24, p. 16; c. 52, p. 43; c. 54, p. 45; c. 87, p. 73.

GH, 2, c. 12; 3, c. 14; 3, c. 23; 5, c. 3; 4, c. 39; 5, c. 18; 6, cc. 11, 12, 20, 26; 7, cc. 19, 22, 27, 34; 8, cc. 21, 26, 39; 9, cc. 9, 12, 27, 35; 10, cc. 2, 28.

Hincmar of Reims, *De ordine palatii,* c. 21, ed. T. Gross and R. Schieffer, *MGH Fontes* 145 (Hanover, 1990), pp. 70–72.

Isidore of Seville, *Etymologiae,* 10.185; 10.147

MGH Cap. 2, no. 188, p. 10.

*MGH Poet.*1, pp. 360–63, 245–6, 483–9, 385–6, 435–6.

Nithard, *Historiarum Libri IV,* ed. E. Muller, *MGH SRG* 44 (Hanover,

1907), I.c. 5, p. 20; II.c. 3, p. 44; III. c. 2, p. 84; IV, c. 3, p. 128 and c. 5, p. 138.

Notker Balbulus, *Gesta Karoli Magni Imperatoris*, ed. H. H. Haefele, *MGH SRG* NS 12 (Berlin, 1959). I, cc. 4, 5, 7, 11, 19, 30–33 and II, cc. 7, 8; pp. 5–10, 16, 25, 40–6, 58–62.

Paul the Deacon, *Liber de episcopis mettensibus*, ed. G. Pertz, *MGH SS* 2 (Berlin, 1829), pp. 260–70.

Regino of Prum, *Chronicon*, ed. F. Kurze, *MGH SRG* 50 (Hanover, 1890).

Thegan, *Gesta Hludowici Imperatoris*, ed. G. Pertz, *MGH SS* II (Berlin, 1945–53), pp. 585–604.

VK, c. 17, pp. 26, 33, 50–52, 77–8, 98.

CHAPTER 6: CHARLEMAGNE AND THE INSTITUTIONS OF CAROLINGIAN GOVERNMENT

Alfred the Great: Asser's Life of King Alfred and other Contemporary Sources, ed. S. Keynes and M. Lapidge (Harmondsworth, 1983).

Annales Bertiniani, trans. J. Nelson, *The Annals of Saint-Bertin* (Manchester, 1991), 831, 834, 839, 860, 865, 867, 870–71, 872, 873, 876; pp. 23, 31, 45, 92, 124, 138, 167, 171–5, 177, 180–81, 196.

Annales Laureshamenses, ed. G. Pertz, *MGH SS* 1, 791, 798, 802; pp. 34, 37, 38–9.

ARF 757, p. 14; 772, p. 34; 773, p. 35; 776, p. 44; 777, p. 48; 778, p. 50; 787, p. 78; 788, p. 84; 791, p. 88; 794, p. 94; 795, pp. 98–100; 797, p. 100; 798, pp. 102–4; 799, pp. 106; 803, p. 118; 804, p. 118; 807, p. 123.

Chronicle of Moissac, ed. G. Pertz, *MGH SS* 1, p. 307.

Codex epistolaris carolinus, ed. W. Gundlach, *Epp.* 20, 47, 55, 57, 67, 72, 92; pp. 520–52, 565–6, 578–80, 582–3, 594–7, 602–3, 629–30.

*DKar.*1, nos 93, 94.

Hincmar, *De ordine palatii*, ed. T. Gross and R. Schieffer, *Hinkmar von Reims, De ordine palatii*, *MGH Fontes* 3 (Hanover, 1980), c. 25, c. 34, c. 36; pp. 78–9, 90–92, 94–6.

Lupus of Ferrières, *Epistulae*, ed. P. K. Marshall (Leipzig, 1984). *Epp.* 17, 41, 45, 58, 67.

MGH Cap. 1, no. 16, c. 1, p. 68; no. 18, pp. 42–3 (cc. 6 and 8, p. 43);

no. 20 (*Capitulary of Herstal*), p. 47; no. 20, c. 21, p. 51; no. 21, p. 52; no. 22 (*Admonitio Generalis*), pp. 52–62; nos 23 and 24, pp. 62–6; no. 23, cc. 18, 27, pp. 63 and 64; no. 25, cc. 1, 4–6, pp. 66–7; no. 26, cc. 2, 26, 29–31, 33–4, pp. 67–70; no. 27, cc. 1, 3 and 11, pp. 71–2; no. 28, pp. 73–8; no. 32 (*Capitulare de villis*), pp. 82–91; no. 33 (*Capitulare missorum generale*), cc. 1, 2–9, 14, 25, 28 and 40, pp. 92–3, 94, 96 and 98; no. 34 (*Capitulare missorum speciale*), cc. 13, 18, pp. 100–101; no. 36, c. 15, p. 36; no. 39, pp. 111–12; no. 40, c. 3, p. 115; no. 44, cc. 7, 9 and 10, pp. 123 and 124; no. 45 (*Divisio regnorum* of 806), c. 18, pp. 129–30; no. 48, pp. 134–5; no. 49, cc. 2 and 3, p. 136; no. 49, c. 4, p. 135; no. 50, pp. 137–8 (c. 8, p. 138); no. 52, pp. 139–40; no. 58, pp. 145–6; no. 61, c. 8, p. 149; no. 67, p. 136; no. 69, pp. 158–9; no. 70, cc. 6 and 8, p. 163; no. 72, pp. 162–4; no. 73, pp. 164–5; no. 74, pp. 166–7; no. 75, p. 168; no. 77, cc. 9 and 10, p. 171; no. 77, cc. 1 and 14, pp. 170 and 172; no. 80, c. 2, p. 176; no. 85, pp. 183–5; no. 124, pp. 245–6; no. 150, c. 26, p. 307; no. 181, pp. 377–8.

MGH Cap. 2, no. 32, p. 88; no. 188, c. 3, p. 10; no. 205, c. 3, p. 72; no. 218, c. 4, p. 96; no. 243, p. 165; no. 254, c. 3, p. 255; no. 260, p. 274; no. 264, c. 4, p. 284; no. 271, pp. 301–2; no. 272, p. 323; no. 273 (*Edict of Pitres*, 864), pp. 310–28; no. 278, p. 281; no. 279, pp. 349–50; no. 281, c. 31, p. 361.

*MGH DKar.*1, no. 16.

MGH Epp. IV, nos. 96, 100, pp. 140, 146.

Thegan, c. 44, *Gesta Hludovici Imperatoris*, ed. G. Pertz, *MGH SS* II (Berlin, 1829), p. 599.

VK, c. 16, p. 50; c. 33, p. 98.

CHAPTER 7: THE ECONOMIC BASIS OF A CIVILIZATION

Aldhelm, p. 18, *Opera*, ed. R. Ehwald, *MGH AA*, 15 (Berlin, 1919), ll. 70–71.

*DKar.*1, nos. 145, 179, 217.

GH, 3, c. 19; 4, cc. 27–8; 5, c. 3, c. 17, c. 28, c. 48; 6, cc. 5, 7, 11, 17, 31–2; 7, c. 2, c. 46, c. 29; 8, c. 33; 9, cc. 9, 12, 22; 10, c. 9, c. 26.

HE II, 3; V, 10.

Liutprand of Cremona, *Antapodosis*, ed. J. Becker, *Liudprandi Opera*, *MGH SRG* 41 (Hanover, 1915), pp. 1–158.

MGH Cap. 1, no. 28, pp. 73–8; no. 32, pp. 82–91; no. 46, p. 132; no. 52, p. 140; no. 90, p. 191; no. 147, p. 299.

MGH Cap. 2, no. 273, pp. 310–28.

Isidore of Seville, *Etymologiae*, XVII, 8.8; XX, 3.

Praeceptum negotiatorum, ed. F. Ganshof, *MGH Formulae* 37 (1937), pp. 101–12.

Procopius, *History of the Wars*, ed. and trans. H. Dewing, 5 vols (Cambridge, Mass., 1914–28), 3. 16. 10–11; 3. 20. 5; 4. 23. 18.

Rimbert, *Vita Anskarii*, ed. G. Waitz, *MGH SRG* (Hanover, 1884), pp. 13–79.

Synodus Francofurtensis (794), c. 9. *MGH Cap.* 1, no. 90, p. 191.

Urkundenbuch des Klosters Fulda 1, ed. E. Stengel (Marburg, 1958), nos 149, 169, 213, 261, 237, 246, 278.

CHAPTER 8: THE CAROLINGIAN CULTURAL RENAISSANCE

Adrevald of Fleury, *Miracula Sancti Benedicti*, *PL* 124, cols 909–48, ed. G. Waitz, *MGH SS* 15: I (Hanover, 1887), pp. 474–97.

Agobard of Lyons, *Opera*, ed. L. von Acker (CCCM 52) (Turnhout, 1981).

Agobard of Lyons, *De Antiphonario*, ed. L. von Acker (CCCM 52), (Turnhout, 1981), pp. 335–51.

Alcuin, *Carmina*, ed. E. Dummler, *MGH Poet. I* (Berlin, 1881), pp. 160–351.

Alcuin, *De Dialectica*, *PL* 101, cols 949–76.

Alcuin, *Disputatio de Rhetorica et Virtutibus Sapientissimi Regis Karli et Albini Magistri. The rhetoric of Alcuin and Charlemagne*, ed. and trans. W. S. Howell (New York, 1965).

Alcuin, *Epistulae*, ed. E. Dummler, *MGH Epp.* IV (Berlin, 1893).

Alcuin, *De Grammatica*, *PL.* 101, col. 833.

Alcuin, *Vita Sancti Willibrordi*, ed. W. Levison, *MGH SRM* 7 (Hanover, 1920), pp. 81–141.

Aldhelm, *Opera Omnia*, ed. P. Ehwald, *MGH AA* 15 (Berlin, 1919).

Angilbert of Saint-Riquier, *Institutione de Diversitate Officiorum*, ed.

K. Hallinger, M. Wegener and H. Frank, Corpus Consuetudinum Monasticarum I (Siegburg, 1963), pp. 283–303.

Aurelian of Rome, *Musica Disciplina*, ed. L. Gushee, Corpus Scriptorum de Musica 21 (1975).

Bede, *Ecclesiastical History of the English People*, ed. and trans. B. Colgrave and R.A.B. Mynors, Oxford Medieval Texts (Oxford, 1969).

Bede, *De Temporibus*, ed. T. Mommsen and C. Jones, Corpus Christianorum, Series Latina 123C (Turnhout, 1980), pp. 585–611.

Bede, *De Temporum ratione*, ed. C.W. Jones. CCSL 123B (Turnhout, 1977), pp. 463–544.

Benedict, *Regula Benedicti*, ed. A. de Vogue, *La Règle de St Benoit*, 7 vols, Sources Chrétiennes 181–6, 260 (Paris, 1971–2, 1977).

Benedict of Aniane, *Institutio Sanctimonialium Aquisgranensis (Concilium Aquisgranense a. 816)*, ed. A. Werminghoff, *MGH Conc. II:I* (Hanover, 1906), pp. 312–456.

Boethius, *Consolation of Philosophy*, ed. and trans. H. F. Stewart et al., Loeb Classical Library (Cambridge, Mass., 1918).

Boniface, *Epistolae*, ed. M. Tangl, *Die Briefe des Heiligen Bonifatius und Lullus, MGH Epp. Sel.* I (Berlin, 1916).

Capitula ad Quibus Convocati Compositae Interrogati Fuerint, ed. E. Dummler, *MGH Epp.* 4 (Hanover, 1895), pp. 565–6.

Capitulare Missorum Generale, c. 18 MGH Cap. 1, p. 93.

Cassiodorus, *Institutiones*, trans. R.A.B. Mynors (Oxford, 1937).

Concilium Romanum a. 853, ed. W. Hartmann, *MGH Conc.* III (Hanover, 1984), pp. 317–39.

Eddius Stephanus, *Vita Wilfridi*, ed. and trans. B. Colgrave, *The Life of Bishop Wilfrid by Eddius Stephanus* (Cambridge, 1927).

Epistola de Litteris Colendis, MGH Cap. 1, p. 79.

Gisela and Rotrud of Chelles, *Epistulae*, ed. E. Dummler, *MGH Epp.* 4 (Berlin, 1895), pp. 323–5.

Gottschalk of Orbais, *Oeuvres théologiques et grammaticales de Godescalc d'Orbais*, ed. C. Lambot (Leuven, 1945).

Gregory of Rome ('the Great'), *Liber Regulae Pastoralis*, ed. B. Judic, F. Rommel and E. Dekkers, trans. C. Morel, *Règle pastorale*, Sources Chrétiennes 381, 2 vols (Paris, 1992).

Hildemar of Corbie, *Expositio Regulae Sancti Benedicti*, ed. R.

Mittermuller, *Vita et Regula SS. P. Benedicti, Una cum Expositione Regulae a Hildemaro Tradita* (Regensburg, New York and Cincinatti, 1880).

Hilduin of Saint-Denis, *Gesta Dagoberti*, ed. B. Krusch, *MGH SRM* II (Hanover, 1888), pp. 396–425.

Hincmar of Reims, *Collectio de Ecclesiis et Capellis*, ed. M. Stratmann, *MGH Fontes* 5 (Hanover, 1990), XIV, c. 100.

Hincmar of Reims, *De Regis Persona et Regio Ministerio, PL* 125, cols 833–56.

Hraban Maur, *De Institutione Clericorum, PL* 107, cols 293–420.

Hraban Maur, *Epistulae*, ed. E. Dummler, *MGH Epp.* 5 (Berlin, 1899), pp. 381–515.

Hraban Maur, *Liber de Computo*, ed. W. M. Stevens. Corpus Christianorum, Continuatio Mediaevalis 44 (Turnhout, 1977).

Isidore of Seville, *Etymologiae sive originum libri XXX*, ed. W. M. Lindsay (Oxford, 1989).

Isidore of Seville, *Historia Gothorum, Vandalorum et Suevorum*, ed. T. Mommsen, *MGH AA* 11, Chronica Minora II (Berlin, 1894), pp. 241–303.

Lupus of Ferrières, *Epistulae*, ed. P.K. Marshall (Leipzig, 1984).

Martianus Capella, *De Nuptiis Mercurii et Philologiae*, ed. J. Willia (Leipzig, 1983).

Nithard, *Historiarum Libri*, ed. E. Muller, *MGH SRG* 44 (Hanover, 1907), ed. and trans. P. Lauer, *Histoire des fils de Louis le Pieux* (Paris, 1926).

Notker Balbulus, *Gesta Karoli Magni I*, 1–2, *MGH SS* II, p. 731.

Orosius, *Historiarum adversus Paganos Libri* VII, ed. C. Zangmeister (Vienna, 1882).

Paul the Deacon, *Historia Langobardorum*, ed. L. Bethmann and G. Waitz, *MGH SRL* 48 (Hanover, 1878).

Remigius of Auxerre, *Commentarium in Martianum Capellam*, ed. C. Lutz (Leiden, 1962–5).

John Scottus, *De Praedestinatione*, ed. G. Madec CCCM 50, (Turnhout, 1978).

Theodulf of Orléans, *Erstes Kapitular*, ed. P. Brommer, *MGH Capitula Episcoporum* I:I (Hanover, 1984), pp. 73–142.

Theodulf of Orléans, *Libri Carolini*, ed. H. Bastgen, *MGH Conc. II*, Supp. (Hanover, 1914).

Theodulf of Orléans, *De Libris Quos Legere Solebam*, ed. E. Dummler, *MGH Poet.* I, (Berlin, 1881), pp. 543–4.

Theodulf of Orléans, *De Septem Liberalibus Artibus in Quadam Pictura Depictis*, ed. E. Dummler, *MGH Poet.* I (Berlin, 1881), pp. 544–7.

VK, c. 23, p. 74.

Walahfrid Strabo, *Visio Wettini*, ed. E. Dummler, *MGH Poet.* II (Berlin, 1884), pp. 301–33.

Willibald, *Vita Bonifatii*, ed. W. Levison, *Vitae Sancti Bonifatii, MGH SRG* 57 (Hanover, 1905), pp. 1–58.

CHAPTER 9: THE SURVIVAL AND REVIVAL OF EMPIRE

Alcuin, *Epistulae*, ed. E. Dummler, *MGH Epp.* 4 (Berlin, 1895), *Epp.* 7, 20, 81; pp. 32, 57, 124.

Annales Fuldenses, ed. F. Kurze, *MGH SR* 7 (Hanover, 1891), 857, pp. 49–50; 872, pp. 74–6; 876, pp. 87–9; 888, p. 94.

Annales Lauershamenses, ed. G. Pertz, *MGH SS* 1 (Berlin, 1826), 793, p. 15.

Annales Quedlinburgenses, ed. G. Pertz, *MGH SS* 3 (Hanover, 1839), 929, p. 54; 991, p. 68; 994–5, p. 72; 996, p. 73; 1000, p. 77; 1003, p. 78.

Annales Vedastini, ed. B. von Simson, *MGH SRG* 12 (Hanover, 1909), 879, p. 44; 882, p.52; 884, p. 56; 888, p. 65; 889, p. 67; 892, p. 72.

ARF, 806, p. 121; 810, p. 132; 811, p. 134; 812, pp. 136–7; 813, p. 138; 814, p. 140.

Augustine, *De Civitate Dei*, ed. B. Dombart and A. Kalb, Corpus Christianorum Series Latina 48 (Turnhout, 1955).

Chron. Moissac, ed. G. Pertz, *MGH SS* 1 (Berlin, 1829), 813, pp. 310–11.

Flodoard, *Les Annales de Flodoard*, ed. P. Lauer. *Collections de textes pour server à l'étude et à l'enseignement de l'histoire* 39 (Paris, 1905), 949, pp. 121–8; 958, p. 146.

Hrotsvitha, *Gesta Ottonis*, verses 66–124, *Hrotsvithae Opera*, ed., P. Winterfeld, *MGH SRG* 34 (Hanover, 1902), pp. 206–8.

Liudprand of Cremona, *Antapodosis: Liudprandi Opera*, ed. J. Becker.

MGH SRG 40 (Hanover, 1915), 1. c. 13, p. 15; 4. cc. 24–6, pp. 117–22; 4. c. 25, p. 119; 5. cc. 20–22, pp. 141–4.

MGH Cap. 1, no. 45 (*Divisio regnorum*), pp. 126–30; no. 136, p. 270; no. 136 (*Ordinatio imperii*, 817), pp. 270–73.

MGH Cap. 2, no. 246, pp. 168–70; no. 251, pp. 193–5; no. 252, pp. 196–249; no. 281, pp. 355–61; no. 301, pp. 453–5.

MGH Epp. 2, 775, p. 503; 793, p. 51.

Nithard, *Historiarum Libri*, ed. E. Muller, *MGH SRG* 44 (Hanover, 1907), 2. c. 10; 4. cc. 1, 6.

Notker Balbulus, *Gesta Karoli*, ed. H. Haefele, *MGH SRG* NS 12 (Berlin, 1959), 1. c. 27, pp. 37f.; 2. c. 6, pp. 54–7.

Orosius, *Historiarum adversum Paganos Libri VII*, ed. C. Zangemeister, Corpus Scriptorum Ecclesiasticorum Latinorum 5 (Vienna, 1882).

Priscus, *Prisci fragmenta*, ed. L. Dindorf, *Historici Graeci Minores* (Leipzig, 1870), pp. 275–352.

Regino of Prum, *Chronicon*, ed. F. Kurze, *MGH SRG* 50 (Hanover, 1890), 867, pp. 92–3; 877, p. 113; 878, p. 114; 882, p. 118; 883, p. 121; 887, pp. 125–6; 888, p. 129; 891, p. 136.

Thietmari Merseburgensis Episcopi Chronicon, ed. R. Holtzmann, *MGH SRG* NS 9 (Berlin, 1955), 2. cc. 2, 5, 9, 28, pp. 40, 44, 48, 74; 4. cc. 2, 9, 44, 47, 49, pp. 132–4, 140, 182, 184, 188.

VK, c. 15, pp. 17–18; c. 19, p. 61; c. 31, pp. 86–8; c. 33, pp. 92–102; c. 34, p. 96.

Widukindi Monachi Corbeiensis Rerum Gestarum Saxonicarum libri tres, ed. H.-E. Lohmann and P. Hirsch, *MGH SRG* (Hanover, 1935), 1. c. 15, p. 25; 1. c. 16, p. 26; 1. cc. 18–19, p. 29; 1. c. 25, p. 38; 1. c. 36, p. 52; 1. c. 38, p. 55; 1. c. 39, pp. 57 f.; 1. c. 41, p. 60; 2. c. 11, p. 75; 2. c. 15, p. 79; 2. cc. 24–5, p. 87; 2. c. 36, p. 95; 2. c. 36, p. 97; 3. c. 2, pp. 104–6; 3. c. 9, p. 109; 3. c. 33, p. 120; 3. c. 43–4, p. 124; 3. c. 46, p. 127; 3. c. 49, p. 128f.; 3. c. 69, p. 145; 3. c. 75, p. 153.

Secondary Source References

ABBREVIATIONS

CHR	*Catholic Historical Review*
DA	*Deutsches Archiv für Erforschung des Mittelalters*
DOP	*Dumbarton Oaks Papers*
EHR	*English Historical Review*
EME	*Early Medieval Europe*
HJ	*Cambridge Historical Journal*
JDAI	*Jahrbuch des Deutschen Archäologischen Instituts*
Med.S	*Medieval Studies*
MIOG	*Mitteilungen des Instituts für Österreichische Geschichtsforschung*
NCMH	*The New Cambridge Medieval History*, vol. 1, ed. P. Fouracre (Cambridge, 2005); vol. 2, ed. R. McKitterick (Cambridge, 1995)
P&P	*Past and Present*
PBA	*Proceedings of the British Academy*
PBSR	*Papers of the British School at Rome*
RBPH	*Revue Belge de Philologie et d'Histoire*
RQSCHR	*Römische Quartalschrift*
SSCI	*Settimane di studio del Centro Italiano di studi sull'alto medioevo*
TRHS	*Transactions of the Royal Historical Society*
ZKG	*Zeitschrift für Kunstgeschichte*
ZSRG	*Zeitschrift der Savigny Stiftung für Rechtsgeschichte, Kanonische Abteilung*

INTRODUCTION

A. Barbero, *Carlo Magno: un padre dell'Europa* (Rome, 2000).

A. Barbero, *Charlemagne: father of a continent* (New Haven, CN, 2004), trans. from the Italian edn of 2000 by A. Cameron.

M. Becher, *Karl der Grosse* (Munich, 1999); Eng. trans. D. Bachrach, *Charlemagne* (New Haven, CN, 2003).

W. Braunfels (gen. ed.), *Karl der Grosse. Lebenswerk und Nachleben: I, Personlichkeit und Geschichte; II, Das Geistige Leben; III, Karolingische Kunst; IV, Das Nachleben* (Düsseldorf, 1965–7).

D. Bullough, *The Age of Charlemagne* (London, 1965).

R. Collins, *Charlemagne* (London, 1998).

M. Costambeys, M. Innes and S. Maclean, *The Carolingian World* (Cambridge, 2007).

G. Faber, *Das erste Reich der Deutschen* (Munich, 1980).

J. Favier, *Charlemagne* (Paris, 2000).

H. Fichtenau, *Das karolingische Imperium: soziale und geistige Problematik eines Grossreiches* (Zurich, 1949).

H. Fichtenau, *The Carolingian Empire*, trans. P. Munz (New York, 1964).

R. Fossier, *Enfance de l'Europe* (Paris, 1982).

P. Fouracre, *The Age of Charles Martel* (London, 2000).

F. L. Ganshof, *The Carolingians and the Frankish Monarchy* (Providence, RI, 1971).

M. P. J. Geary, *The Myth of Nations: the medieval origins of Europe* (Princeton, NJ, 2002).

P. Geary, *Before France and Germany: the making and transformation of the Merovingian world* (New York, 1998).

D. Hagermann, *Karl der Grosse, Herrscher des Abendlandes: Biographie* (Munich, 2000).

L. Halphen, *Charlemagne and the Carolingian Empire*, trans. Giselle de Nie (Amsterdam, New York, 1977).

P. Heather, *The Fall of the Roman Empire: a new history* (Oxford, 2004).

E. H. Kantorowicz, *Karl der Grosse oder Charlemagne? Acht Antworten deutscher Geschichtsforcher* (Berlin, 1935).

P. D. King, *Charlemagne: translated sources* (Kendal, 1986).

J. Le Goff, *The Birth of Europe* (Oxford, 2005), trans. from the French by J. Lloyd.

P. Llewellyn, *Rome in the Dark Ages*, 2nd edn (London, 1993).

H. Loyn and J. Perceval, *The Reign of Charlemagne* (London, 1975).

R. McKitterick, *Charlemagne: the formation of a European identity* (Cambridge, 2008).

J. L. Nelson, *The Frankish World, 750–900* (London, 1996).

B. Scholz, *Carolingian Chronicles* (Ann Arbor, MI, 1972).

J. Story (ed.), *Charlemagne: empire and society* (Manchester, 2005).

J. R. Strayer, *On the Medieval Origins of the Modern State* (Princeton, NJ, 1970).

C. Wickham, *The Inheritance of Rome: a history of Europe from 400 to 1000* (London, 2009).

CHAPTER 1: GODS, KINGS AND FRANKS

A. Ben Abed and N. Duval, 'Carthage, la capitale du royaume et les villes de Tunisie à l'Époque Vandale', in G. Ripoli and J. M. Gurt (eds), *Sedes Regiae* (Barcelona, 2000), pp. 163–218.

À l'aube de la Gaule: la Gaule de Constantin à Childéric. Exhibition catalogue. Musée de Luxembourg, 26 February–1 March 1981 (Luxembourg, 1981).

A. Alfoldi, *A Conflict of Ideas in the Late Roman Empire* (Oxford, 1952).

P. Amory, *People and Identity in Ostrogothic Italy, 489–554* (Cambridge, 1997).

A. Angenedt, 'Karl der Grosse als "Rex et Sacerdos"', in R. Berndt (ed.), *Das Frankfurter Konzil von 794. Kristallisationspunkt karolingischer Kultur*, 2 vols (Mainz, 1997), pp. 255–78.

C. J. Arnold and J. L. Davies, *Roman and Early Medieval Wales* (Stroud, 2000).

H.-X. Arquillière, *L'Augustinisme politique: essai sur la formation des théories politiques du moyen âge*, 3rd edn (Paris, 1955).

H. Atsma (ed.), *La Neustrie* (Sigmaringen, 1984).

J. P. V. D. Balsdon, *Romans and Aliens* (Chapel Hill, NC, 1979).

R. Bartlett, 'Symbolic meanings of hair in the Middle Ages', *TRHS*, 6th series, 4 (1994), pp. 43–60.

M. Beard, J. North and S. Price, *Religions of Rome* (Cambridge, 1998).

P. Beskow, *Rex Gloriae: the kingship of Christ in the early Church* (Uppsala, 1962).

D. A. Binchy, *Celtic and Anglo-Saxon Kingship* (Oxford, 1970).

J. Blair, *The Church in Anglo-Saxon Society* (Oxford, 2005).

I. Bona, *Das Hunnenreich* (Stuttgart, 1991).

A. Borst, *Medieval Worlds: artists, Barbarians and heretics in the Middle Ages* (Cambridge, 1991).

C. A. Bouman, *Sacring and Crowning* (Gröningen, 1957).

W. Bowden and R. Hodges (eds), *The Sixth Century* (Leiden, 1998).

P. Brown, *Augustine of Hippo* (London–Berkeley–Los Angeles, CA, 1967).

P. Brown, *Religion and Society in the Age of Saint Augustine* (New York, 1972).

P. Brown, *The Cult of the Saints: its rise and function in Latin Christianity* (Chicago, IL, 1981).

P. Brown, *Power and Persuasion in Late Antiquity* (Madison, Wis., 1992).

P. Brown, *The Rise of Western Christendom: triumph and diversity, AD 200–1000* (Oxford, 1996).

F. J. Byrne, *Irish Kings and High-Kings* (London, 1973).

A. Cameron, 'How did the Merovingian kings wear their hair?', *RBPH* 43 (1965).

E. Campbell, *Saints and Sea-Kings: the first kingdom of the Scots* (Edinburgh, 1999).

E. Carpentier, *Les Batailles de Poitiers. Charles Martel et les Arabes* (Poitiers, 2000).

J. Cavadini, *The Last Christology of the West: adoptionism in Spain and Gaul, 785–820* (Philadelphia, PA, 1993).

T. Charles-Edwards, *Early Christian Ireland* (Cambridge, 2000).

J. J. Chifflet, *Anastasis Childeric I Francorum Regis* (Antwerp, 1655).

R. Collins, *Early Medieval Spain: unity in diversity, 400–1000* (London, 1983).

R. Collins, *Law, Culture and Regionalism in Early Medieval Spain* (Aldershot, 1992).

R. Collins, *Visigothic Spain* (Oxford, 2004).

P. Courcelle, *Histoire littéraire des grandes invasions germaniques* (Paris, 1964).

C. Courtois, *Les Vandales et l'Afrique* (Paris, 1955).

W. Davies, *An Early Welsh Microcosm* (London, 1978).

W. Davies, *Wales in the Early Middle Ages* (Leicester, 1982).

W. Davies, *Patterns of Power in Early Wales* (Oxford, 1990).

E. Demougeot, *La Formation de l'Europe et les invasions barbares* (Aubier, 1979).

Fischer Drew, *The Lombard Laws* (Philadelphia, PA, 1973).

H. F. Drinkwater and H. Elton, *Fifth-century Gaul: a crisis of identity?* (Cambridge, 1994).

S. Driscoll and M. Nieke (eds), *Power and Politics in Early Medieval Britain* (Edinburgh, 1988).

M. Dubuisson, 'Barbares et barbarie dans le monde Gréco-Romain: du concept au slogan', *L'Antiquité Classique* 70 (2001), pp. 1–16.

F. Dumas, *La Tombe de Childéric, père de Clovis* (Paris, 1982).

D. Dumville, 'Sub-Roman Britain: history and legend', *History* 62 (1977), pp. 173–92.

J. DuQuesnay Adams, *The Populus of Augustine and Jerome: a study in the patristic sense of community* (New Haven, CA, 1971).

E. Emerton, trans., *The Letters of Boniface* (New York, 1940).

M. Erdrich, *Rom und die Barbaren* (Mainz am Rhein, 2001).

E. Ewig, 'Zum Christlichen Königsgedanken im Frühmittelalter', in T. Meyer (ed.), *Das Königtum* (Constance, 1956), pp. 7–73.

J. Favrod, *Histoire politique du royaume Burgunde (443–534)* (Lausanne, 1997).

J. Favrod, *Les Burgundes: un royaume oublié au cœur de l'Europe* (Lausanne, 2002).

A. Ferreiro (ed.), *The Visigoths: culture and society* (Leiden, 1999).

I. M. Ferris, *Enemies of Rome: Barbarians through Roman eyes* (Sparkford, 2003).

R. Fletcher, *The Conversion of Europe: from paganism to Christianity, AD 371–1386* (London, 1997).

M. Fleury and A. France-Lanord Albert, *Les Trésors mérovingiens de la basilique de Saint-Denis* (Klopp, 1998).

J. Fontaine, *Isidore de Séville et la culture classique dans l'Espagne wisigothique* (Paris, 1959).

S. Foster, *Picts, Gaels and Scots: early historic Scotland* (London, 1996).

P. Fouracre, 'Observations on the outgrowth of Pippinid influence in the "regnum Francorum" after the battle of Tertry (687–715)', *Medieval Prosopography*, V.2 (1984), pp. 1–31.

P. Fouracre, 'Merovingian saints and Merovingian hagiography', *P&P* 127 (1990), pp. 3–38.

P. Fouracre, *The Age of Charles Martel* (Harlow, 2000).

P. Fouracre, 'The long shadow of the Merovingians', in J. Story (ed.), *Charlemagne: empire and society* (Manchester, 2005), pp. 5–21.

P. Fouracre and R. Gerberding, *Late Merovingian France: history and hagiography, 640–720* (Manchester, 1996).

M. Garrison, 'The Franks as the new Israel? education for an identity from Pippin to Charlemagne', in Y. Hen and M. Innes, *The Uses of the Past in the Early Middle Ages* (Cambridge, 2000), pp. 114–61.

M. Gelling, 'Why aren't we speaking Welsh?', *Anglo-Saxon Studies in Archaeology and History* 6 (1993), in W. Filmer-Sankey (ed.), *Anglo-Saxon Studies in Archaeology and History* 6 (Oxford, 1996).

H. W. Goetz, J. Jarnut and W. Pohl (eds), *Regna and Gentes: the relationship between late antique and early medieval peoples and kingdoms in the transformation of the Roman worlds* XIII (Leiden–Boston, 2003), pp. 571–95.

Walter Goffart, *The Narrators of Barbarian History* (Princeton, NJ, 1988).

W. Goffart, 'Foreigners in the histories of Gregory of Tours', in his *Rome's Fall and After* (London, 1989), pp. 275–91.

W. A. Goffart, *Barbarian Tides: the migration age and the later Roman empire* (Pennsylvania, 2006).

P. Grierson, 'Election and inheritance in early Germanic kingship', *HJ* 7 (1941), pp. 1–22.

P. Gros, *La France Gallo-Romaine* (Paris, 1991).

D. M. Gwynn, *The Eusebians: the polemic of Athanasius of Alexandria and the construction of the Arian controversy* (Oxford, 2007).

P. Heather, *Goths and Romans, 332–489* (Oxford, 1991).

P. Heather, 'Theoderic, king of the Goths', *EME* IV (1995), pp. 145–73.

P. Heather, 'The Huns and the end of the Roman empire in western Europe', *EHR* CX (1995), pp. 4–41.

P. Heather, *The Goths* (Oxford, 1996).

L. Hedeager, *Iron Age Societies: from tribe to state in northern Europe* (Oxford, 1992).

Y. Hen, 'The Annals of Metz and the Merovingian past', in Y. Hen and M. Innes, *The Uses of the Past in the Early Middle Ages* (Cambridge, 2000), pp. 175–90.

Y. Hen and M. Innes (eds), *The Uses of the Past in the Early Middle Ages* (Cambridge, 2000).

R. Hitchcock (ed.), *Christian–Islamic Interaction in Medieval Spain* (London, 1991).

D. Horspool, *Why Alfred Burned the Cakes* (London, 2006).

J. Howard-Johnston and P. A. Hayward (eds), *The Cult of Saints in Late Antiquity and the Early Middle Ages: essays on the contribution of Peter Brown* (Oxford, 1999).

P. Hulten, *The True Story of the Vandals* (Vanarmo, 2001).

M. Innes, '"Teutons or Trojans"? The Carolingians and the Germanic past', in Y. Hen and M. Innes, *The Uses of the Past in the Early Middle Ages* (Cambridge, 2000), pp. 227–49.

E. James, 'Cemeteries and the problem of Frankish settlement in Gaul', in P. Sawyer (ed.), *Names, Words and Graves* (Leeds, 1979), p. 58–59.

J. Jarnut, U. Nonn and M. Richter (eds), *Karl Martell in seiner Zeit* (Sigmaringen, 1994).

B. Jaski, *Early Irish Kingship and Succession* (Dublin, 2000).

A. H. M. Jones, *The Later Roman Empire, 284–602*, 3 vols (Oxford, 1964).

R. Kaiser, *Die Burgunder* (Stuttgart, 2004).

J. N. D. Kelly, *Jerome: his life, writings and controversies* (London, 1975).

P. D. King, *Law and Society in the Visigothic Kingdom* (Cambridge, 1972).

W. Klingshirn, *Caesarius of Arles* (Cambridge, 1994).

G. Lacam, *Ricimer: un Barbare au service de Rome* (Paris–Lille, 1986).

G. B. Ladner, 'On Roman attitudes towards Barbarians in late antiquity', in *Viator 7* (1976), pp. 1–26.

R. Lane Fox, *Pagans and Christians* (London, 1986).

S. Lebecq, 'The two faces of King Childeric: archaeology, history, historiography', in W. Pohl and M. Diesenberger (eds), *Integration und Herrschaft* (Vienna, 2002), pp. 119–32.

R. Le Jan, 'Convents, violence and competition for power in

seventh-century Francia', in M. de Jong and F. Theuws (eds), *Topographies of Power in the Early Middle Ages* (Leiden, 2001).

N. Lozovsky, 'Roman geography and ethnography in the Carolingian empire', *Speculum* 81 (2006), pp. 325–64.

B. Luiselli, *Storia culturale dei rapporti tra mondo Romano e mondo Germanico* (Rome, 1992).

R. McKitterick, *History and Memory in the Carolingian World* (Cambridge, 2004).

N. McLynn, *Ambrose of Milan* (Berkeley, CA, 1994).

O. Maenchen-Helfen, *The World of the Huns* (Berkeley, CA, 1973).

J. Y. Marin (ed.), *Les Barbares et la mer: les migrations des peuples du nord-ouest de l'Europe du V au X siècle* (Caen, 1992).

R. A. Markus, *The End of Ancient Christianity* (Cambridge, 1990).

R. A. Markus, *Sacred and Secular: studies on Augustine and Latin Christianity* (Aldershot, 1991).

J. R. Martindale (ed.), *The prosopography of the later Roman empire*, II (AD 395–527) (Cambridge, 1980).

M. Mass (ed.), *The Cambridge Companion to the Age of Justinian* (Cambridge, 2005).

R. W. Mathisen and D. Schanzer (eds), *Society and Culture in Late Antique Gaul* (Aldershot, 2001).

T. Mayer (ed.), *Das Königtum: seine geistigen und rechtlichen Grundlagen. Vorträge und Forschungen*, vol. 3 (Sigmaringen, 1956).

H. Mayr-Harting, *The Coming of Christianity to Anglo-Saxon England* (3rd edn, London, 1991).

A. H. Merrills, *Vandals, Romans and Berbers* (Aldershot, 2004).

R. Miles (ed.), *Constructing Identities in Late Antiquity* (London, 1999).

Y. Moderan, 'L'établissement territorial des Vandales en Afrique', *Antiquité Tardive* X (2002), pp. 87–122.

Y. Moderan, *Les Maures et l'Afrique romaine (IV–VII siècle)* (Rome, 2003).

A. Monigliano (ed.), *The Conflict between Paganism and Christianity in the Fourth Century* (Oxford, 1963).

K. E. Morrison, *The Two Kingdoms: ecclesiology in Carolingian political thought* (Princeton, NJ, 1964).

A. C. Murray, *Germanic Kingship Structure* (Toronto, 1983).

A. C. Murray, 'From Roman to Frankish Gaul', *Traditio* XLIV (1988), pp. 59–100.

A. C. Murray (ed.), *After Rome's Fall: narrators and sources of early medieval history. Essays presented to Walter Goffart* (Toronto, 1998).

L. Musset, *Les Invasions: les vagues Germaniques* (Paris, 1994).

J. Nelson, 'Queens as Jezebels: Brunhild and Bathild in Merovingian history', *Studies in Church History* (Woodbridge, 1986).

J. Nelson, 'Kingship and royal government', in *NCMH* II (1995), pp. 383–430.

F. S. Paxton, *Christianizing Death: the creation of a ritual process in early medieval Europe* (Ithaca, NY, 1990).

W. Pohl, *Die Völkerwanderung: Eroberung und Integration* (Stuttgart–Berlin–Cologne, 2002).

W. Pohl (ed.), *Kingdoms of the Empire: the integration of Barbarians in Late Antiquity* (Leiden, 1997).

T. Reuter, 'Saint Boniface and Europe', in T. Reuter (ed.), *The Greatest Englishman* (Exeter, 1980), pp. 69–94.

T. Reuter (ed.), *Alfred the Great* (Aldershot, 2003).

P. Riche and P. Le Maître, *Les Invasions barbares* (Paris, 1989).

M. Richter (ed.), *Ireland and Its Neighbours in the Seventh Century* (London, 1999).

J. Scheid, *Religion et piété à Rome* (Paris, 1985).

J. Scheid, *Quand faire, c'est croire: les rites sacrificiels des Romains* (Paris, 2005).

T. Schieffer, *Winfrid-Bonifatius und die Christliche Grundlegung Europas* (Freiburg, 1954).

K. A. Schondorf, *Die Geschichtstheologie des Orosius* (Munich, 1972).

P. E. Schramm. *Kaiser, Rome und Renovatio*, I–II, *Studien der Bibliothek Warburg* 17 (Leipzig, 1929).

O. Seeck, *Geschichte des Untergangs der antiken Welt*, vol. VI (Stuttgart, 1920).

I. R. Simek, *Religion und Mythologie der Germanen* (Darmstadt, 2003).

P. Sims-Williams, *Religion and Literature in Western England, 600–800* (Cambridge, 1990).

P. Sims-Williams, *Britain and Early Christian Europe* (Aldershot, 1995).

H. Sivan, 'The appropriation of Roman law in Barbarian hands:

Roman–Barbarian marriage in Visigothic Gaul and Spain', in W. Pohl (ed.), *Strategies of Distinction: the construction of ethnic communities, 300–800* (Leiden, 1998), pp. 189–203.

H. Steuer, *Die Franken in Köln* (Cologne, 1980).

R. Stocking, *Bishops, Councils and Consensus in the Visigothic Kingdoms, 589–633* (Ann Arbor, MI, 2001).

J. Straub, *Vom Herrscherideal in der Spätantike* (Stuttgart, 1939).

U. Sussenbach, *Christkult und kaiserliche Baupolitik bei Konstantin* (Bonn, 1977).

E. Taayke, J. H. Looijenga, O. H. Harsema and H. R. Reinders (eds), *Essays on the Early Franks*, Gröningen Archaeological Studies I (Gröningen, 2003).

C. H. Talbot, *The Anglo-Saxon Missionaries on the Continent* (London, 1954).

E. A. Thompson, *The Early Germans* (Oxford, 1965).

E. A. Thompson, *Romans and Barbarians* (Madison, Wis., 1982).

R. Turcan, *La religion romaine. I. Les dieux. II. Le culte* (Leiden, 1988).

R. Van Dam, *Saints and Their Miracles in Late Antique Gaul* (Princeton, NJ, 1993).

K. van Welck (ed.), *Die Franken: Weghereiter Europas*, 2 vols (Mainz, 1996).

A. von Domaszewski, *Die Religion des römischen Heeres* (Trier, 1895).

J. M. Wallace-Hadrill, *Early Germanic Kingship in England and on the Continent* (Oxford, 1971).

J. M. Wallace-Hadrill, *The Merovingian Church* (Oxford, 1983).

B. Ward-Perkins, 'Why did the Anglo-Saxons not become more British?', *EHR* CXV (2000), pp. 513–33.

P. S. Wells, *The Barbarians Speak: how the conquered peoples shaped Roman Europe* (Princeton, NJ, 1999).

C. Wickham, *Early Medieval Italy: central power and local society, 400–1000* (Totowa, NJ, 1981).

G. Wirth, *Attila* (Stuttgart, 1999).

G. Wissowa, *Religion und Kulturs der Römer* (Munich, 1912).

H. Wolfram, *Die Germanen* (Munich, 1977).

H. Wolfram, *History of the Goths* (Berkeley, CA, 1987).

H. Wolfram, *Das Reich und die Germanenz zwischen Antike und Mittelalter* (Berlin, 1994).

I. Wood, *The Merovingian Kingdoms, 482–51* (London, 1994).

I. N. Wood, 'Roman law in the Barbarian kingdoms', in A. Ellegard and G. Akerstrom-Hougen (eds), *Rome and the North* (Jonsered, 1996), pp. 10–11.

I. Wood (ed.), *Franks and Alemanni in the Migration Period* (Woodbridge, 1998).

I. Wood, 'Missionaries and the Christian frontier', in W. Pohl, I. Wood and H. Reimitz (eds), *The Transformation of Frontiers from Late Antiquity to the Carolingians* (Leiden, 2001), pp. 209–18.

I. Wood, *The Missionary Life: saints and the evangelization of Europe, 400–1050* (London, 2001).

P. Wormald, 'Lex Scripta and Verbum Regis: Legislation and Germanic Kingship from Euroic to Cnut', in P. H. Sawyer and I. N. Wood (eds), *Early Medieval Kingship* (Leeds, 1977), p. 108.

P. Wormald, 'Bede: the Bretwaldas and the making of the gens Anglorum', in Wormald et al. (eds.), *Ideal and Reality in Frankish and Anglo-Saxon Society* (Oxford, 1983), pp. 99–129.

P. Wormald, 'Kings and Kingship', in *NCMH* 11 (2005), pp. 571–604.

P. Zanker, 'I barbari, l'imperatore e l'arena: immagini di violenza nell'arte Romana', in I. M. Ferris, *Enemies of Rome: Barbarians through Roman eyes* (Sparkford, 2003), pp. 54–6.

G. Zecchini, *Attila* (Palermo, 2007).

CHAPTER 2: FROM PRINCE TO KING

M. Becher and J. Jarnut, *Die Dynastiewechsel von 751* (Münster, 2005).

C. Bertelli and G. P. Brogiolo (eds), *Il futuro dei Longobardi. L'Italia e la costruzione dell'Europa di Carlo Magno* (Brescia, 2000).

O. Bertolini, *Roma e i Longobardi* (Rome, 1972).

D. Bullough, 'Germanic Italy: The Ostrogothic and Lombard kingdoms', in D. Talbot Rice (ed.), *The Dawn of European Civilization* (New York, 1965), pp. 157–74.

E. Caspar, *Geschichte des Papsttums, 1–11* (Tübingen, 1930–33).

P. Chiesa (ed.), *Paulo Diacono e il friuli altomedievale* (Spoleto, 2001).

R. Christlein, *Die Alemannen* (Stuttgart, 1978).

R. A. Gerberding, *The Rise of the Carolingians and the 'Liber Historiae Francorum'* (Oxford, 1987).

D. Geuenich, *Geschichte der Alemannen* (Stuttgart, 1997).

M. McCormick, *Eternal Victory: triumphal rulership in late antiquity, Byzantium and the early medieval west* (Cambridge, 1986).

R. McKitterick, *Perceptions of the Past in the Early Middle Ages* (Notre Dame, 2006).

G. C. Menis (ed.), *I Longobardi* (Milan, 1990).

H. L. Mikoletzky, 'Karl Martell und Grifo', in *Festschrift E.E. Stengel* (Münster, 1952), pp. 130–56.

D. H. Miller, 'Papal–Lombard relations during the pontificate of Pope Paul I: the attainment of an equilibrium of power in Italy, 756–767', *CHR* 55 (1969), pp. 358–76.

I. Moreira, *Dreams, Visions and Spiritual Authority in Merovingian Gaul* (Ithaca, NY, 2000).

M. Rouche, *L'Aquitaine des Wisigothes aux Arabes, 418–781* (Paris, 1979).

P. E. Schramm, *Beiträge zur allgemeinen Geschichte, I: Kaiser, Könige und Papste. Gesammelte Aufsätze zur Geschichte des Mittelalters*, I (Stuttgart, 1968).

F. Siegmund, *Alemannen und Franken* (Berlin, 2000).

J. M. Wallace-Hadrill, *The Long-haired Kings and Other Studies in Frankish History* (London, 1962).

J. M. Wallace-Hadrill, *The Chronicle of Fredegar* (Ann Arbor, MI, 1972).

C. Wickham, 'Aristocratic power in eighth-century Lombard Italy', in A. C. Murray (ed.), *After Rome's Fall* (Toronto, 1998), pp. 153–70.

C. Wickham (ed.), *The Lombards from the Migration Period to the Eighth Century* (Woodbridge, 2007).

I. Wood, *The Merovingian Kingdoms, 450–751* (Harlow, 1994).

CHAPTER 3: THE KINGDOM AT WAR

S. Airlie, 'Narratives of triumph and rituals of submission: Charlemagne's mastering of Bavaria', *TRHS* 6th series 9 (1999), pp. 93–119.

E. Albu, 'Imperial geography and the medieval Peutinger map', *Imago Mundi* 37 (2005), pp. 136–48.

P. Amory, *People and Identity in Ostrogothic Italy, 489–554* (Cambridge, 1997).

H. H. Andersen, H. J. Madsen and O. Voss, *Danevirke* (Copenhagen, 1976).

B. Anke, *Studien zur reiternomadischen Kultur des 4 und 5 Jahrhunderts* (Weissbach, 1998).

H. Arhweiler, *L'Idéologie politique de l'empire byzantin* (Paris, 1975).

B. Bachrach, *Early Carolingian Warfare: prelude to empire* (Philadelphia, PA, 2001).

B. Bachrach, 'Charlemagne and the Carolingian general staff', *Journal of Military History* 66 (2002), pp. 313–57.

B. Bachrach, *Religion and the Conduct of War, c. 300–1215* (Woodbridge, 2003).

A. Barbero, *Barbari, immigrati, profughi, deportati, nell' impero romano* (Bari, 2006).

I. Barbiera, *Changing Lands, Changing Memories: migration and identity during the Longobard invasions* (Florence, 2005).

P. S. Barnwell, 'War and peace. Historiography and seventh-century embassies', in *EME* 6 (1997), pp. 127–39.

R. Bartlett, *The Making of Europe: conquest, colonization and cultural change 950–1350* (London, 1993).

M. Becher, *Rex, Dux und Gens: Untersuchungen zur Entstehung des Sachischen Herozogtums im 9 und 10 Jht* (Husum, 1996).

K. Bosl, *Gesellschaftsgeschichte Italiens im Mittelalter, Monographien zur Geschichte des Mittelalters*, vol. 26 (Stuttgart, 1982).

C. Bowlus, *Franks, Moravians and Magyars: the struggle for the Middle Danube, 788–907* (Philadelphia, PA, 1995).

D. Breeze, 'The edge of the world: the imperial frontier and beyond', in P. Salway (ed.), *The Roman Era* (Oxford, 2002), pp. 173–200.

T. S. Brown, *Gentlemen and Officers: imperial administration and aristocratic power in Byzantine Italy, AD 554–800* (Rome, 1984).

W. Brown and P. Borecki (eds), *Conflict in Medieval Europe* (Aldershot, 2004).

T. S. Burns, *Rome and the Barbarians, 100 BC–AD 400* (Baltimore, PA–London, 2003).

C. Carroll, 'The bishops of Saxony in the first century after Christianization', *EME* 8 (1999), pp. 219–45.

R. Collins, *The Basques* (Oxford, 1986).

R. Collins, *The Arab Conquest of Spain, 710–797* (Oxford, 1989).

F. Curta, *The Making of the Slavs: history and archaeology of the Lower Danube region, ca AD 500–700* (Cambridge, 2001).

F. Curta (ed.), *Borders, Barriers and Ethnogenesis: frontiers in late antiquity and the Middle Ages* (Turnhout, 2005).

F. Curta (ed.), *East Central and Eastern Europe in the Middle Ages* (Ann Arbor, MI, 2005).

G. Dagron, *Empereur et prêtre: étude sur le 'césaropapisme' byzantin* (Paris, 1996).

C. Diehl, *Études sur l'administration de l'exarchat*, in *Bibliothèque des Écoles Françaises d'Athènes et de Rome*, 53 (Paris, 1888).

F. Drinkwater, *The Alamanni and Rome, 213–496* (Oxford, 2007).

B. Effros, 'De partibus Saxoniae and the regulation of mortuary custom. A Carolingian campaign of Christianization or the suppression of Saxon identity?', *RBPH* 75 (1995).

J. A. S. Evans, *The Age of Justinian: the circumstances of imperial power* (London–New York, 1996).

G. Fasoli, *Carlomagno e l'Italia*, vol. 1 (Bologna, 1968).

H. Frolich, *Studien zur langobardischen Thronfolge von den Anfangen bis zur Eroherung des Italienischen Reiches durch Karl den Grossen*, 2 vols (Tübingen, 1980).

F.-L. Ganshof, *Le Moyen Age: histoire des relations internationales*, 1 (Paris, 1958); trans. R. Hall, *The Middle Ages: a history of international relations* (New York, 1971).

S. Gasparri, *I Duchi Longobardi*, Instituto Storico Italiano per il Medio Evo, vol. 109 (Rome, 1978).

S. Gasparri and P. Commarosano (eds), *Langobardia* (Udine, 1990).

F. Graus, *Die Nationenbildung der Westslaven im Mittelalter* (Sigmaringen, 1980).

D. H. Green and F. Siegmund (eds), *The Continental Saxons from the Migration Period to the Tenth Century: an ethnographic perspective* (Woodbridge, 2003).

J. T. Hallenbeck, *Pavia and Rome: the Lombard monarchy and the papacy*

in the eighth century, Transactions of the American Philosophical Society,
vol. 72, no. 4 (Philadelphia, 1982).

G. Halsall (ed.), *Warfare and Society in the Early Medieval West* (London, 2002).

G. Halsall, *Violence and Society in the Barbarian West, 450–900* (London, 2003).

M. Hardt, 'Hesse, Elbe, Salle and the frontiers of the Carolingian empire', in W. Pohl, I. Wood and H. Reimitz (eds), *The Transformation of Frontiers from Late Antiquity to the Carolingians* (Leiden, 2001), pp. 219–32.

M. Hardt, 'The *limes Saxoniae* as part of the eastern borderlands of the Frankish and Ottonian–Salian empire', in F. Curta (ed.), *Borders, Barriers and Ethnogenesis: frontiers in late antiquity and the Middle Ages* (Turnhout, 2005), pp. 35–50.

P. J. Heather, 'The late Roman art of client management and the grand strategy debate', in W. Pohl and I. N. Wood (eds), *The Transformation of Frontiers from Late Antiquity to the Carolingians. Proceedings, European Science Foundation Transformation of the Roman World Project* (Leiden, 2001), pp. 15–68.

Y. Hen, 'Charlemagne's jihad', *Viator* 37 (2006), pp. 33–51.

J. Herrmann (ed.), 'Griechische und Latinische Quellen zur Frühgeschichte Mitteleuropas', in *Schriften und Quellen der Alten Welt*, 37 (Berlin, 1988–92), pp. 1–4.

J. D. Howard-Johnston, 'The two great powers of late antiquity: a comparison', in A. Cameron (ed.), *The Byzantine and Early Islamic Near East 3: resources and armies* (Princeton, NJ, 1995), pp. 123–78.

M. Innes, 'Franks and Slavs, 700–1000', *EME* 6 (1997), pp. 201–16.

L. Jorgensen, B. Storgaard and L. Gebauer Thomsen (eds), *Sieg und Triumpf: der Norden im Schatten des römischen Reiches* (Copenhagen, 2003).

H. Keller, *Adelsherrschaft und stadtische Gesellschaft im Oberitalien, 9–12 Jht.* (Tübingen, 1979).

B. Kreutz, *Before the Normans: southern Italy in the ninth and tenth centuries* (Philadelphia, PA, 1991).

P. Laederich, *Les Limites de l'empire: les stratégies de l'empire romain dans l'œuvre de Tacite* (Paris, 2001).

C. La Rocca (ed.), *Short Oxford History of Italy in the Early Middle Ages, 476–1000* (Oxford, 2001).

Friedrich Lotter, 'The crusading idea and the conquest of the region east of the Elbe', in R. Bartlett and A. MacKay (eds), *Medieval Frontier Societies* (Oxford, 1989), pp. 267–306.

M. McCormick, 'The liturgy of war in the early Middle Ages: crisis, litanies, and the Carolingian monarchy', *Viator* 15 (1984), pp. 1–23.

H. Mayr-Harting, 'Charlemagne, the Saxons and the imperial coronation of 800', *EHR* 111 (1996), pp. 1113–33.

O. Mazal, *Justinian I und seine Zeit: Geschichte und Kultur des Byzantinischen Reiches im 6. Jahrhundert* (Cologne–Weimar–Vienna, 2001).

G. Mengozzi, *La città Italiana nell' alto medioevo* (Florence, 1973).

K. Modzelewski, *L'Europe des Barbares: Germains et Slaves face aux héritiers de Rome* (trans. from the original Polish) (Paris, 2006).

J. Moorhead, *Theoderic in Italy* (Oxford, 1992).

G. Ostogorsky, *A History of the Byzantine State*, rev. edn trans. J. Hussey (New Brunswick, NJ, 1969).

W. Pohl, *Die Awaren. Ein Steppenvolk in Mitteleuropa, 567–822* (Munich, 1988).

W. Pohl, 'The role of the steppe peoples in eastern and central Europe in the first millennium AD', in Przemyslaw Urbanczyk (ed.), *Origins of Central Europe* (Warsaw, 1997), pp. 65–78.

W. Pohl, I. Wood and H. Reimitz (eds), *The Transformation of Frontiers from Late Antiquity to the Carolingians, The Transformation of the Roman World* (Leiden, 2001).

M. Redde (ed.), *L'armée romaine en Gaule* (Paris, 1996).

T. Reuter, 'The end of Carolingian military expansion', in P. Godman and R. Collins (eds), *Charlemagne's Heir: new perspectives on the reign of Louis the Pious (814–840)* (Oxford, 1987), pp. 391–404.

P. Sawyer and B. Sawyer, *Medieval Scandinavia* (Minneapolis, MI, 1993).

E. Schallmayer, *Der Limes: Geschichte einer Grenze* (Munich, 2006).

D. S. Sefton, 'Pope Hadrian I and the fall of the kingdom of the Lombards', *CHR* 65 (1979), pp. 206–20.

G. Tate, *Justinien, l'époque de l'empire d'orient* (Paris, 2004).

S. Teillet, *Des Goths à la nation gothique: les origines de l'idée de nation en occident du Ve au VIIe siècle* (Paris, 1984).

P. Urbanczyk (ed.), *Early Christianity in Central and East Europe* (Warsaw, 1997).

F. Vallet and M. Kazanski (eds), *L'Armée romaine et les Barbares du IIIe au VIIe siècle* (Saint-Germain-en-Laye, 1993).

A. Vlasto, *The Entry of the Slavs into Christendom* (Cambridge, 1971).

G. V. B. West, 'Charlemagne's involvement in central and southern Italy: power and the limits of authority', *EME* 8 (1999), pp. 241–67.

C. R. Whittaker, 'Les frontières de l'empire romain', in *Annales littéraires de l'université de Besançon*, 390 (1989).

C. R. Whittaker, *Frontiers of the Roman Empire: a social and economic study* (Baltimore, 1994).

I. Wood, 'An absence of saints? The evidence for the Christianization of Saxony', in P. Godman, J. Jarnut and P. Johanek (eds), *Am Vorabend der Kaiserkrönung* (Berlin, 2002), pp. 335–52.

I. Wood, 'Beyond satraps and ostriches: political and social structures of the Saxons in the early Carolingian period', in D. H. Green and F. Siegmund (eds), *The Continental Saxons from the Migration Period to the Tenth Century: an ethnographic perspective* (Woodbridge, 2003), pp. 271–86.

CHAPTER 4: CROWN IMPERIAL

M. Alberi, 'The evaluation of Alcuin's concept of the *Imperium Christianum*', in J. Hill and M. Swann (eds), *The Community, the Family and the Saint* (Turnhout, 1998), pp. 3–17.

A. Alfoldi, *The Conversion of Constantine and Pagan Rome* (Oxford, 1948).

H. Amirav and B. H. Romeny (eds), *From Rome to Constantinople: studies in honour of Averil Cameron* (Leuven, Paris, Dudely (Mass.), 2007).

P. Amory, *People and Identity in Ostrogothic Italy, 489–554* (Cambridge, 1997).

Matthia Becher, *Eid und Herrschaft: Studien zum Herrscherethos Karls des Grossen* (Sigmaringen, 1993).

H. Beck, D. Ellmers and K. Schier (eds), 'Germanische Religionsgeschichte: Quellen und Quellenprobleme', in *Reallexicon der*

Germanischen Alterumskunde, Erganzungsband V (Berlin–New York, 1992).

O. Bertolini, 'Carlomagno e Benevento', in W. Braunfels (ed.), *Karl der Grosse: Lebenswerk und Nachleben*, 5 vols (Düsseldorf, 1965), I, pp. 609–71.

O. Bertolini, 'Osservazioni sulla "Constitutio Romana" . . . dell' 824', in *Studi . . . in onore di A. de Stefano* (Palermo, 1956), pp. 43ff.

C. A. Bouman, *Sacring and Crowning: the development of the Latin ritual for the anointing of kings and the coronation of an emperor before the eleventh century* (Gröningen, 1957).

L. Brehier, *Les Institutions de l'empire byzantin* (Paris, 1949).

L. Brehier and R. Aigrain, *Grégoire le Grand, les états barbares et la conquête arabe, 590–757*, vol. 5 of A. Fliche and V. Martin (eds), *Histoire de l'église depuis les origines jusqu'à nos jours* (Paris, 1947).

R. Brentano, *Rome before Avignon* (New York, 1974).

P. Brown, 'The rise and function of the holy man in Late Antiquity', *Journal of Roman Studies* LXI (1971), pp. 80–101.

T. S. Brown, 'The Church of Ravenna and the imperial administration in the seventh century', *EHR* 94 (1979), pp. 1–28.

J. Burckhardt, *Rom unter Gregor dem Grossen*, written in 1857 and printed in his *Kulturgeschichtliche Vorträge* (Leipzig, 1930), pp. 20ff.

P. Classen, 'Romanum gubernans imperium: zur Vorgeschichte der Kaisertitulatur Karls des Grossen', *Deutsches Arche für Erforschung des Mittelalters* 9 (1951), pp. 103–21.

P. Classen, 'Karl der Grosse, das Papsttum und Byzanz', in W. Braunfels (ed.), *Karl der Grosse*, 4 vols (Düsseldorf, 1965), I, pp. 537–608.

P. Classen, *Karl der Grosse, das Papsttum und Byzanz* (Sigmaringen, 1988).

R. Collins, 'Charlemagne's imperial coronation and the annals of Lorsch', in J. Story (ed.), *Charlemagne: empire and society* (Manchester, 2005), pp. 52–70.

Y. Congar, *L'Ecclésiologie du haut moyen âge de Saint Grégoire le Grand à la désunion entre Byzance et Rome* (Paris, 1968).

R. Davis, *The Lives of the Eighth-century Popes* (Liverpool, 1995).

R. Davis, *The Lives of the Ninth-century Popes* (Liverpool, 1995).

C. Davis-Weyer, 'Das Apsismosaik Leos III . . .', *ZKG* 28 (1965), pp. 177ff.

C. Davis-Weyer, 'Die Mosaiken Leos III . . .', *ZKG* 29 (1966), pp. 111ff.

F. W. Deichmann, 'Frühchristliche Kirchen in antiken Heiligtümern', *JDAI* 54 (1939), pp. 105ff.

M. de Jong, 'Charlemagne and the Church', in J. Story (ed.), *Charlemagne: empire and society* (Manchester, 2005), pp. 103–35.

H. Dorries, *Das Selbstzeugnis Kaiser Konstantins* (Göttingen, 1964).

L. Duchesne, *The Beginnings of the Temporal Sovereignty of the Popes, AD 754–1073*, trans. A. Harris Mathew (London, 1908).

B. Dumezil, *Les Racines chrétiennes de l'Europe: conversion et liberté dans les royaumes barbares, V–VIII siècle* (Paris, 2005).

H. Fichtenau, 'Karl der Grosse und das Kaisertum', *Mitteilungen des Instituts für Österreichische geschichtsforschung* 61 (1953), pp. 257–334.

R. Folz, *The Imperial Coronation of Charlemagne*, trans. J.E. Anderson (London, 1974).

J. Fontaine, 'Un fondateur de l'Europe: Grégoire le Grand', in *Helmantica* 103–5 (1983), pp. 171–89.

H. Fuhrmann, 'Das Constitutum Constantini', in *MGH*, *Fontes Iuris Germanici* X (1968), text and commentary.

F. L. Ganshof, 'The imperial coronation of Charlemagne: theories and facts', in his *The Carolingians and the Frankish Monarchy: studies in Carolingian history*, trans. J. Sondheimer (Ithaca, NY, 1971), pp. 41–54.

P. Geary, *Furta Sacra: thefts of relics in the central Middle Ages* (Princeton, NJ, 1977).

W. Gericke, 'Wann entstand die konstantinische Schenkung?', *ZSRG, Kanon.* 43 (1957), pp. 1ff.

W. Gericke, 'Das Constitutum Constantini und die Sylvester-legende', *ZSRG, Kanon.* 44 (1958), pp. 343ff.

P. Godman, J. Jarnut and P. Johanek (eds), *Am Vorabend der Kaiserkrönung* (Berlin, 2002).

A. Grabois, 'Charlemagne, Rome and Jerusalem', *RBPH* 59 (1981), pp. 792–809.

F. Gregorovius, *Geschichte der Stadt Rom im Mittelalter*, vols 2 and 3. 7th edn (Stuttgart, 1922).

P. Grierson, 'The coronation of Charlemagne and the coinage of Pope Leo III', *RBPH* 30 (1952), pp. 825–33.

P. Gros, 'Le concept d'espace à Rome', in J. P. Genet (ed.), *Rome et l'état moderne européen* (Rome, 2007), pp. 97–114.

A. Guillou, 'Demography and culture in the exarchate of Ravenna', *Studi Medievali*, 3rd series, 10 (1969), pp. 201–19.

J. T. Hallenbeck, 'The election of Pope Hadrian I', *Church History* 37 (1968), pp. 261–70.

J. T. Hallenbeck, 'Pope Stephen III: why was he elected?', *Archium Historiae Pontifico* 12 (1974), pp. 287–99.

L. Halphen, 'Les origines du pouvoir temporel de la papauté', in his *À travers l'histoire du Moyen Âge* (Paris, 1950), pp. 39–50.

L. M. Hartmann, *Geschichte Italiens im Mittelalter*, 3 vols in 5 (Gotha, 1897–1911).

J. Herrin, *The Formation of Christendom* (Oxford, 1987).

J. Herrin, 'Constantinople, Rome and the Franks in the seventh and eighth centuries', in J. Shepard and S. Franklin (eds), *Byzantine Diplomacy* (Aldershot, 1992), pp. 91–107.

N. Huyghebaert, 'La donation de Constantin ramenée à ses véritables dimensions', *Revue d'histoire ecclésiastique* 71 (1976), pp. 45–69.

H. Jedin and J. Dolan (eds), *The Church in the Age of Feudalism*, trans. A. Biggs, vol. 3 of *Handbook of Church History* (New York, 1969).

A. H. M. Jones, 'Church finances in the fifth and sixth centuries', *Journal of Theological Studies* 11 (1960), pp. 84ff.

A. H. M. Jones, *The Decline of the Ancient World* (New York, 1966).

E. Josi, 'Liber Pontificalis', *Enciclopedia Cattolica 12* (Vatican City, 1949), pp. 152–8.

W. E. Kaegi, *Byzantium and the Decline of Rome* (Princeton, NJ, 1968).

W. Kamlah, *Christentum und Geschichtlichkeit*, 2nd edn (Stuttgart, 1951).

E. Kantorowicz, 'Oriens Augusti–lever du roi', *DOP* 17 (1963), pp. 117ff.

C. Kelly, *Attila the Hun: Barbarian terror and the fall of the Roman empire* (London, 2008).

R. Krautheimer, 'The Constantinian basilica', *DOP* 21 (1967), pp. 117ff.

R. Krautheimer, *Rome: profile of a city, 312–1308* (Princeton, NJ, 1980).

R. Krautheimer et al., *Corpus Basilicarum Christianarum Romae, I–V* (Vatican City–New York, 1973–7).

R. Lanciani, *Forma Urbis Romae* (Milan, 1896).

P. Lauer, *Le Palais de Latran* (Paris, 1911).

P. S. Leicht, 'Il feudo in Italia nell'eta Carolingia', *SSCI* 1 (1954), pp. 71–107.

C. Leyser, *Authority and Asceticism from Augustine to Gregory the Great* (Oxford, 2000).

F. Lot, 'Le concepte d'empire à l'époque carolingienne', *Mercure de France* 330 (1947), pp. 413–27.

P. Maraval, *Le Christianisme de Constantin à la conquête arabe* (Paris, 2005).

G. S. Marcou, 'Zaccaria (679–752): L'ultimo papa Greco nella storia di Roma altomedioevale. Note storico-giuridiche', *Apollinaris* 50 (1977), pp. 274–89.

R. Markus, 'From Caesarius to Boniface: Christianity and paganism in Gaul', in J. Fontaine and J. Hillgarth (eds), *The Seventh Century* (London, 1992), pp. 154–72.

R. A. Markus, *Gregory the Great and His World* (Cambridge, 1997).

H. Mayr-Harting, 'Charlemagne, the Saxons and the imperial coronation of 800', *EHR* III (1996), pp. 1113–33.

H. Mayr-Harting, 'Charlemagne's religion', in P. Godman, J. Jarnut and P. Johanek (eds), *Am Vorabend der Kaiser Krönung: das Epos 'Karolus Magnus et Leo Papa' und der Papstbesuch in Paderborn* (Berlin, 2003), pp. 113–24.

D. Miller, 'The Roman revolution of the eighth century: a study of the ideological background of the papal separation from Byzantium and the alliance with the Franks', *MedS.* 36 (1974), pp. 79–133.

W. Mohr, 'Karl der Grosse, Leo III und der Römische Aufstand von 799', *Archum Latinitas Medii Aevi* 20 (1960), pp. 39–98.

R. Morghen, *Medioevo Cristiano* (Bari, 1972).

W. Muller-Wiener, *Bildlexikon zur Topographie Istanbuls* (Tübingen, 1977).

J. L. Nelson, 'Kingship and empire', in J. H. Burms (ed.), *The Cambridge History of Medieval Political Thought* (Cambridge, 1988), pp. 211–51.

T. Noble and T. Head, *Soldiers of Christ* (London, 1998).

T. F. X. Noble, *The Republic of St. Peter: the birth of the papal state, 680–823* (Philadelphia, PA, 1984).

W. Ohnsorge, 'Orthodoxus Imperator: Vom religiosen Mot für das Kaisertum Karls des Grossen', in *Abendland und Byzanz: gesammelte Aufsätze zur Geschichte der byzantinisch-abendlandischen Beziehungen und des Kaisertums* (Darmstadt, 1958), pp. 64–78.

P. Partner, *The Lands of St Peter: the papal state in the Middle Ages and in the early Renaissance* (Berkeley, CA, 1972).

G. Pepe, *Le Moyen âge barbare en Italie*, trans. J. Gonnet (Paris, 1956).

C. Pietri, *Roma Christiana. Recherches sur l'église de Rome . . . 311–440*, in Bibliothèques des Ècoles Françaises d'Athènes et de Rome, 224 (Rome, 1976), pp. 405ff.

A. Pigagnol, *L'Empire chrétien (325–395)* (Paris, 1972).

W. M. Plochl, *Geschichte des Kirchenreichs*, vol. 1. 2nd edn (Munich, 1960).

F. Prinz, *Frühes Monchtum im Frankreich* (Munich, 1965).

F. Prinz, *Klerus und Krieg im frühen Mittelalter* (Munich, 1974).

J. Ramackers, 'Die Werkstattheimat der Grabplatte Papst Hadrians 1', *RQSCHR* 59 (1964), pp. 36ff.

J. Richards, *The Popes and the Papacy in the Early Middle Ages, 476–752* (London, 1979).

J. Richards, *Consul of God: the life and times of Gregory the Great* (London, 1980).

C. Rohault de Fleury, *Le Latran au moyen-âge* (Paris, 1877).

R. Schieffer, 'Charlemagne and Rome', in J. M. H. Smith (ed.), *Early Medieval Rome and the Christian West: essays in honour of Donald A. Bullough* (Leiden, 2000), pp. 279–75.

C. Schneider, *Geistesgeschichte des antiken Christentums* (Munich, 1956).

P. E. Schramm, 'Karl der Grosse als Kaiser im Lichte der Staatssymbolik (800–814)', in his *Beiträge zur Allgemeinen Geschichte*, I: *Kaiser, Könige und Papste. Gesammelte Aufsätze zur Geschichte des Mittelalters*, I (Stuttgart, 1968), pp. 264–302.

J. Shepard, 'Information, disinformation and delay in Byzantine diplomacy', *Byzantinische Forschungen* 10 (1985), pp. 233–93.

J. M. H. Smith, 'Old saints, new cults: Roman relics in Carolingian Francia', in J. M. H. Smith (ed.), *Early Medieval Rome and the Christian West: essays in honour of Donald A. Bullough* (Leiden, 2000), pp. 317–40.

J. Straub, 'Christliche Geschichtsapologetik in der Krisis des römischen Reiches', *Historia* 1 (1950), pp. 52–81.

J. Straub, 'Konstantins christliches Sendungsbewusstsein', in *Regeneratio Imperii* (Darmstadt, 1972), pp. 70ff.

R. E. Sullan, *The Coronation of Charlemagne: what did it signify?* (Boston, Mass., 1960).

P. Toubert, *Les Structures du Latium mediéval: le Latium méridional et la Sabine du IX siècle à la fin du XII siècle*, 2 vols, Bibliothèques des Écoles Françaises d'Athènes et de Rome, vol. 221 (Rome, 1973).

C. N. Tsirpanlis, 'Byzantine reactions to the coronation of Charlemagne (780–813)', in *Byzantina* 6 (1974), pp. 354–60.

W. Ullmann, 'The origins of the Ottonianum', *HJ* 11 (1953), pp. 114–28.

W. Ullmann, 'Leo III', in *Lexicon für Theologie und Kirche* 7 (Freiburg, 1963), pp. 947–8.

W. Ullmann, *The Growth of Papal Government in the Middle Ages: a study in the relation of clerical to lay power* I, 3rd edn (London, 1970).

R. Vieillard, *Recherches sur les origines de la Rome chrétienne* (Rome, 1959).

M. Vitiello, *Il Principe, il filosofo, il guerriero: lineamenti di pensiero politico nell'Italia ostrogota* (Stuttgart, 2006).

J. M. Wallace-Hadrill, *The Frankish Church* (Oxford, 1983).

B. Ward-Perkins, *The Fall of Rome and the End of Civilization* (Oxford, 2005).

J. Zettinger, 'Rompilger aus dem Frankreich', *RQSCHR* Suppl. 11 (Rome, 1900).

CHAPTER 5: ARISTOCRATIC POWER AND CAROLINGIAN CALCULATION

S. Airlie, 'The aristocracy', in R. McKitterick (ed.), *NCMH*, vol. II (Cambridge, 1995), pp. 431–50.

S. Airlie, 'The palace of memory: the Carolingian court as political centre', in S. Rees Jones, R. Marks and A. Minnis, *Court and Region in Medieval Europe* (York–Woodbridge, 2000), pp. 1–20.

S. Airlie, 'Towards a Carolingian aristocracy', in M. Becher and J. Jarnut,

Der Dynastiwechsel von 751: Vorgeschichte, Legitimationsstrategien und Erinnerung (Münster, 2004), pp. 109–28.

S. Airlie, 'Charlemagne and the aristocracy: captains and kings', in J. Story (ed.), *Charlemagne: empire and society* (Manchester, 2005), pp. 90–102.

G. Althoff, *Verstande, Freunde und Getreue: zum politischen Stellenwert der Grüppenbildung im frühen Mittelalter* (Darmstadt, 1990), trans. C. Carroll, *Family, Friends and Followers: political and social bonds in early medieval Europe* (Cambridge, 2004).

R. Balzaretti, '"These are things that men do, not women"', in G. Halsall (ed.), *Violence and Society in the Early Medieval West* (Woodbridge, 1998), pp. 175–92.

G. Binding, *Deutsche Königspalfzen von Karl dem Grossen bis Friedrich II (765–1240)* (Darmstadt, 1996).

J. Blair, *The Anglo-Saxon Church* (Oxford, 2006).

F. Bougard, 'Les palais royaux et impériaux de l'Italie carolingienne et ottonienne', in A. Renoux (ed.), *Palais royaux et princiers au moyen âge* (Le Mans, 1996).

K. Brunner, *Oppositionelle Gruppen im Karolingerreich* (Vienna, 1979).

P. Buc, *The Dangers of Ritual* (Princeton, NJ, 2001).

D. Bullough, 'Aula renovata: the Carolingian court before the Aachen palace', *PBA* 71 (1985), pp. 267–301.

A. Cabannis, *Charlemagne's Cousins* (Syracuse, 1974).

D. Claude, *Adel, Kirche und Königtum im Westgotenreich* (Sigmaringen, 1971).

M. Claussen, 'God and man in Dhuoda', *Studies in Church History* 27 (1990).

L. Cracco Ruggini, 'Les généraux francs aux IV–V siècles et leurs groupes aristocratiques', in M. Rouche (ed.), *Clovis: histoire et mémoires. I Clovis et son temps: l'événement* (Paris, 1997), pp. 673–88.

C. Cubitt (ed.), *Court Culture in the early Middle Ages* (Turnhout, 2003).

K. Dark, *Civitas to Kingdom: British political continuity, 300–800* (Leicester, 1994).

M. de Jong, *In Samuel's Image: child oblation in the early Middle Ages* (Leiden, 1996).

A. Demandt, 'The osmosis of late Roman and Germanic aristocracies', in E. K. Chrysos and A. Schwarcz (eds), *Das Reich und die Barbaren* (Vienna, 1989), pp. 75–86.

J. Durliat, *Les Finances publiques de Dioclétien aux Carolingiens (184–888)* (Sigmaringen, 1990).

J. Fleckstein, *Early Medieval Germany*, trans. B. S. Smith (Amsterdam, 1978).

P. Fouracre, 'The origins of the nobility in Francia', in A. Duggan (ed.), *Nobles and Nobility in Medieval Europe* (Woodbridge, 2000), pp. 17–24.

M. Garrison, 'English and Irish at the court of Charlemagne', in P. L. Butzer, M. Kerner and B. Oberschelp (eds), *Karl der Grosse und sein Nachwerken, 1200 Jahre Kultur und Wissenschaft in Europa. I. Wissen und Weltbild* (Turnhout, 1997), pp. 97–124.

M. Garrison, 'The social world of Alcuin: nicknames at York and at the Carolingian court', in L. A. J. R. Houwen and A. A. MacDonald (eds), *Alcuin of York: scholar at the Carolingian Court* (Gröningen, 1998), pp. 59–80.

P. J. Geary, *Aristocracy in Provence: the Rhône basin at the dawn of the Carolingian age, Monographien zur Geschichte des Mittelalters* 31 (Stuttgart, 1983).

R. Gerberding, *The Liber Historiae Francorum and the Rise of the Carolingians* (Oxford, 1987).

M. Heinzelmann, *Gregory of Tours: history and society in the sixth century* (Cambridge, 2001).

M. Innes, 'A place of discipline: aristocratic youth and Carolingian courts', in C. Cubitt (ed.), *Court Culture in the Early Middle Ages* (Turnhout, 2004), pp. 59–76.

R. Le Jan, *Famille et pouvoir dans le monde franc* (Paris, 1998).

R. Le Jan (ed.), *La royauté et les élites dans l'Europe carolingienne: début du IXe siècle aux environs de 920* (Lille, 1998).

K. Leyser, 'Early medieval canon law and the origins of knighthood', in L. Fenske et al. (eds), *Institutionen, Gesellschaft und Kultur im frühen Mittelalter* (Sigmaringen, 1984), pp. 549–66.

R. McKitterick, 'The illusion of royal power in the Carolingian annals', *EHR* 115 (2000), pp. 1–20.

S. Maclean, 'Queenship, nunneries and royal widows in Carolingian Europe', *P&P* 178 (2003), pp. 3–38.

J. Matthews, *Western Aristocracies and (the) Imperial Court, 364–425* (Oxford, 1975).

P. Munz, *The Origin of the Carolingian Empire* (Leicester, 1960).

J. Nelson, 'The Lord's anointed and the people's choice: Carolingian royal ritual', in D. Cannadine and S. Price (eds), *Rituals of Royalty* (London, 1988), pp. 137–80.

J. Nelson, *Politics and Ritual in Early Medieval Europe* (London, 1986).

J. L. Nelson, 'Women at the court of Charlemagne: a case of monstrous regiment?', in J. C. Parsons (ed.), *Medieval Queenship* (Stroud, 1993), pp. 43–61; repr. in J. L. Nelson, *The Frankish World, 750–900* (London, 1996), pp. 223–42.

J. L. Nelson, 'Aachen as a place of power', in M. de Jong, F. Theuws and C. van Rhijn, *Topographies of Power in the Early Middle Ages* (Leiden, 2001), pp. 217–42.

J. L. Nelson, 'Was Charlemagne's court a courtly society?', in C. Cubitt (ed.), *Court Culture in the Earlier Middle Ages* (Leiden, 2001), pp. 39–57.

C. F. Odegaard, 'Carolingian oaths of fidelity', *Speculum* 16 (1941), pp. 284–96.

C. F. Odegaard, *Vassi and Fideles in the Carolingian Empire* (Cambridge, Mass., 1945).

A. Orchard, 'Wish you were here: Alcuin's courtly poetry and the boys back home', in S. Rees Jones, R. Marks and A. J. Minnis, *Courts and Regions in Medieval Europe* (New York–Woodbridge, 2000), pp. 21–44.

J. C. Parsons (ed.), *Medieval Queenship* (Stroud, 1993), pp. 43–61.

S. Rees Jones, R. Marks and A. J. Minnis (eds), *Courts and Regions in Medieval Europe* (New York–Woodbridge, 2000).

A. Renoux (ed.), *Palais médiévaux (France–Belgique): 25 ans d'archéologie* (Le Mans, 1994).

T. Reuter (ed. and trans.), *The Medieval Nobility: studies on the ruling classes of France and Germany from the sixth to the twelfth century,* Europe in the Middle Ages Selected Studies 14, general editor R. Vaughan (Amsterdam–New York–Oxford, 1979).

B. Rosenwein, 'The family politics of Berengar I, king of Italy (888–924)', *Speculum* 71 (1996), pp. 247–89.

J. Smith, 'The problem of female sanctity in Carolingian Europe', *P&P* 146 (1995), pp. 3–37.

E. Stengel (ed.), *Urkundenbuch des Klosters Fulda*, 2 vols (Marburg, 1913–58).

G. Tellenbach, 'Vom karolingischen Reichsadel zum deutschen Reichsfurstenstand', in *Adel und Bauer im Deutschen Staat des Mittelalters*, Theodore Mayer (ed.) (Berlin–Leipzig, 1943).

P. Toubert, 'The Carolingian moment (eighth–tenth century)', in A. Burguiere et al. (eds), *A History of the Family*, I (Cambridge, 1996), pp. 379–406.

K. F. Werner, 'Important noble families in the kingdom of Charlemagne: A prosopographical study of the relationship between king and nobility in the early Middle Ages', in *The Medieval Nobility: studies on the ruling classes of France and Germany from the sixth to the twelfth century*, ed. and trans. T. Reuter (Amsterdam–New York–Oxford, 1978), pp. 137–202.

M. Werner, *Adelsfamilien im Umkreis der frühen Karolinger* (Sigmaringen, 1982).

P. Wormald, 'Bede, Beowulf and the conversion of the Anglo-Saxon aristocracy', in R. Farrell (ed.), *Bede and Anglo-Saxon England*, British Archaeological Reports British Series 46 (Oxford, 1978).

CHAPTER 6: CHARLEMAGNE AND THE INSTITUTIONS OF CAROLINGIAN GOVERNMENT

S. Abel and B. Simson, *Jahrbücher des Frankischen Reiches unter Karl dem Grossen*, 2 vols, 2nd edn (Leipzig, 1883–8).

S. Airlie, 'Talking heads: assemblies in early medieval Germany', in P. S. Barnwell and M. Mostert (eds), *Political Assemblies in the Earlier Middle Ages, Studies in the Early Middle Ages 7* (Turnhout, 2003), pp. 109–28.

S. Airlie, J. Jarnut and W. Pohl (eds), *Staat und Staatlichkeit im frühen Mittelalter* (Vienna, 2006).

G. Althoff, *Spielregeln der Politik im Mittelalter: Kommunikation im Frieden und Fehden* (Darmstadt, 1997).

G. Althoff, *Family, Friends and Followers* (Cambridge, 2003).

B. S. Bachrach, 'Was the Marchfeld part of the Frankish constitution?', *Med.S* XXXVI (1974), pp. 178–85.

P. S. Barnwell, *Emperors, Prefects and Kings* (London, 1992).

P. S. Barnwell and M. Mostert (eds), *Political Assemblies in the Earlier Middle Ages, Studies in the Early Middle Ages 7* (Turnhout, 2003).

S. Baxter, C. Karkov, J. Nelson and D. Pelteret (eds), *Early Medieval Studies in Honour of Patrick Wormald* (London, 2009).

J. W. Bernhardt, *Itinerant Kingship and Royal Monasteries in Early Medieval Germany, c. 936–1075* (Cambridge, 1993).

N. P. Brooks, 'Alfredian government', in T. Reuter (ed.), *Alfred the Great* (Aldershot, 2003), pp. 153–73.

K. Brunner, *Oppositionelle Gruppen im Karolingerreich. Veroffentlichungen des Instituts für Österreichische Geschichtsforschung*, vol. 25 (Vienna, 1979).

F. W. Buckler, *Harunu'l-Rashid and Charles the Great* (Cambridge, Mass., 1931).

A. T. M. Charles-Edwards, 'Law in the western kingdoms between the fifth and the seventh century', in A. Cameron, B. Ward-Perkins and M. Whitby (eds), *The New Cambridge Ancient History*, vol. XIV. *Late Antiquity: Empire and Successors, AD 425–600* (Cambridge, 2000), pp. 260–87.

S. M. Crosby, *The Royal Abbey of Saint-Denis from its Beginning to the Death of Suger, 475–1151*, ed. P. Blum (New Haven, CA, 1987).

R. R. Davies, 'The medieval state: the tyranny of a concept?', *Journal of Historical Sociology* 16, pp. 280–300.

W. Davies and P. Fouracre (eds), *The Settlement of Disputes in Early Medieval Europe* (Cambridge, 1986).

M. de Jong, 'Sacrum palatium et ecclesia: L'autorité religieuse royale sous les Carolingiens (790–840)', *Annales* 58 (2003), pp. 1243–69.

P. E. Dutton, *The Politics of Dreaming in the Carolingian Empire* (Lincoln, Neb.–London, 1994).

E. Ewig, *Spätantikes und frankisches Gallien*, 2 vols (Munich, 1976–9).

H. Fichtenau, *Das karolingische Imperium: soziale und geistige Problematik eines Grossreiches* (Zurich, 1949), trans. P. Munz, *The Carolingian Empire* (Oxford, 1957).

R. Folz, 'Charlemagne and his empire', in V. Mudroch and G. S. Couse (eds), *Essays on the Reconstruction of Medieval History* (Montreal, 1974), pp. 86–112.

P. Fouracre, 'Carolingian justice: the rhetoric of reform and the contexts of abuse', in *La giustizia nell' alto medioevo (scoli V–VIII), SSCI* 42 (1995), pp. 771–803.

F. L. Ganshof, 'Observations sur le synode de Francfort de 794', in *Miscellanea Historica in Honorem Alberti de Meyer*, pp. 306–18 (Louvain, 1946).

F. L. Ganshof, *Recherches sur les capitulaires* (Paris, 1959).

F. L. Ganshof, 'Charlemagne et les institutions de la monarchie franque', in W. Braunfels (gen. ed.), *Karl der Grosse, Lebenswerk und Nachleben*, vol. 1 (Düsseldorf, 1965) pp. 349–93.

F. L Ganshof, 'Charlemagne's programme of imperial government', in his *The Carolingians and the Frankish Monarchy*, trans. J. Sondheimer (London, 1971), pp. 55–86.

F. L. Ganshof, *Frankish Institutions under Charlemagne* (Providence, R.I., 1968).

P. J. Geary, 'Extrajudicial forms of conflict resolution', *SSCI* 42, pp. 569–605.

A. Gillett, *Envoys and Political Communication in the Late Antique West, 411–533* (Cambridge, 2003).

K. Glockner (ed.), *Codex Laureshamensis*, 3 vols (Darmstadt, 1929–36).

L. Halphen, *Études critiques sur l'histoire de Charlemagne* (Paris, 1923).

G. Halsall (ed.), *Violence and Society in the Early Medieval West* (Woodbridge, 1998).

W. Hartmann, *Die Synoden der Karolingerzeit im Frankreich und in Italien* (Paderborn, Munich and Vienna, 1989).

A. Hauck, *Kirchengeschichte Deutschlands*, 5th edn, vols 1 and 2 (Leipzig, 1935).

K. Heldmann, *Das Kaisertum Karls des Grossen: Theorien und Wirklichkeit* (Weimar, 1928).

R. Hodges, *The Anglo-Saxon Achievement: archaeology and the beginnings of English society* (London, 1989).

O. Hofler, 'Der Sakralcharakter des germanischen Königtums', in T. Mayer (ed.), *Das Königtum* (Constance, 1956), pp. 75–104.

H. J. Hummer, *Politics and Power in Early Medieval Europe: Alsace and the Frankish realm, 600–1000* (Cambridge, 2006).

M. Innes, *State and Society in the Early Middle Ages: the middle Rhône valley, 400–1000* (Cambridge, 2000).

A. H. M. Jones, *The Later Roman Empire, 284–602: a social and administrative survey*, 3 vols (Oxford, 1964).

F. Kern, *Kingship and Law in the Middle Ages*, trans. S. B. Chrimes (New York, 1970).

V. Krause, 'Geschichte des Instituts der Missi Dominici', *MIOG* 11 (1890), pp. 193–300.

W. Levison, *England and the Continent in the Eighth Century* (Oxford, 1946).

F. Lot, 'Le concept d'empire à l'époque carolingienne', in *Recueil des travaux historiques de Ferdinand Lot I: 338–52*, 3 vols (Paris, 1968–73).

H. R. Loyn, *The Governance of Anglo-Saxon England, 500–1087* (London, 1984).

R. McKitterick, *The Frankish Kingdoms under the Carolingians, 751–987* (London, 1983).

R. McKitterick (ed.), *The Uses of Literacy in Early Medieval Europe* (Cambridge, 1990).

H. Mitteis, *Der Staat des hohen Mittelalters*, 4th edn (Weimar, 1953), trans. H. Orton, *The State in the Middle Ages*, North Holland Medieval Translations I (Amsterdam–Oxford–New York, 1975).

W. Mohr, *Studien zur Charakteristik des karolingischen Königtums im 8. Jahrhundert* (Saarlouis, 1955).

W. Mohr, *Die karolingische Reichsidee* (Münster, 1962).

H. Mordek, *Bibliotheca capitularium regum Francorum manuscripta* (Munich, 1995).

H. Mordek, *Studien zur frankischen Herrschergesetzgebung: Aufsätze über Kapitularien und Kapitulariensammlungen ausgewahlt zum 60. Geburtstag* (Frankfurt am Main, 2000).

J. L. Nelson, *Politics and Ritual in Early Medieval Europe* (London, 1986).

J. L. Nelson, 'The voice of Charlemagne', in R. Gameson and H. Leyser (eds), *Belief and Culture in the Middle Ages: studies presented to Henry Mayr-Harting* (Oxford, 2001), pp. 76–88.

W. Ohnsorge, *Das Zweikaiserproblem im früheren Mittelalter* (Hildesheim, 1947).

H. Quaritsch, *Staat und Souveranität*, vol. 1 (Frankfurt, 1970).

T. Reuter, 'Assembly politics in western Europe from the eighth to the twelfth century', in P. Linehan and J. L. Nelson (eds), *The Medieval World* (London, 2001), pp. 434–50.

B. Rosenwein, *Negotiating Space: privileges of immunity in early medieval Europe* (Ithaca, NY, 1998).

P. E. Schramm, *Herrschaftzeiche und Staatssystem* (Stuttgart, 1954).

W. Sickel, 'Kirchenstaat und Karolinger', *Historische Zeitschrift* 84 (1900), pp. 385–409.

J. Story, *Carolingian Connections: Anglo-Saxon England and Carolingian Francia, c. 750–870* (Aldershot, 2003).

G. Tabacco, 'L'ambiguità delle istituzioni nell'Europa costruita dai Franchi', in G. Rossetti (ed.), *Forme di potere e struttura sociale in Italia nel medioevo* (Bologna, 1977), pp. 73–81.

W. Ullmann, 'The development of the medieval idea of sovereignty', *EHR* 64 (1949), pp. 1–33.

L. von Ranke, 'Zur Kritik Frankisch-Deutscher Reichsannalen', *Abhandlungen der Königlichen Akademie der Wissenschaften* (Berlin, 1854), pp. 415–56.

K. F. Werner, *Structures politiques du monde francque* (London, 1979).

P. Wormald, 'Lex scripta and verbum regis: legislation and Germanic kingship from Euric to Cnut', in P. Sawyer and I. Wood (eds), *Early Medieval Kingship* (Leeds, 1977), pp. 105–38.

P. Wormald (ed.), *Ideal and Reality in Frankish and Anglo-Saxon Society* (Oxford, 1983).

P. Wormald, '*Exempla Romanorum*: the earliest English legislation in context', in A. Ellegard and G. Akerstrom-Hougen (eds), *Rome and the North* (Jonsered, 1996), pp. 15–27.

P. Wormald, *Legal Culture in the Early Medieval West: law as text, image and experience* (London–Rio Grande, 1999).

P. Wormald, *The Making of English Law: King Alfred to the twelfth century*, I: *Legislation and its Limits* (Oxford, 1999).

P. Wormald, 'The *leges barbarorum*: law and ethnicity in the post-Roman west', in H. W. Goetz, J. Jarnut and W. Pohl (eds), *Regna and Gentes:*

the relationship between late antique and early medieval peoples and kingdoms in the transformation of the Roman world (Leiden, 2003), p. 41.

CHAPTER 7: THE ECONOMIC BASIS OF A CIVILIZATION

A. Avramea, 'Land and sea communications, fourth–fifteenth centuries', in A. E. Laiou (ed.), *The Economic History of Byzantium*, I (Washington, DC, 2002), pp. 57–90.

P. Ballet, 'De l'empire romain à la conquête arabe', in *La Céramique médiévale en Méditerranée* (Aix-en-Provence, 1997), pp. 53–61.

R. Balzaretti, 'Cities, emporia and monasteries: regional economics in the Po valley, 700–875', in N. Christie and S. Loseby (eds), *Towns in Transition* (Aldershot, 1996), pp. 213–34.

R. Balzaretti, 'Cities and markets in the early Middle Ages', in G. Ausenda (ed.), 'After Empire: towards an ethnology of Europe's Barbarians', *Studies in Historical Archaeoethnology* I (Woodbridge, 1996), pp. 113–42.

M. Banniard, 'Language and communication in Carolingian Europe', in R. McKitterick (ed.), *New Cambridge Modern History*, II, pp. 695–708.

J. Barbier, 'Le système palatial franc: genèse et fonctionnement dans le nord-ouest du regnum', *Bibliothèque de l'École des Chartes* 148 (1990), pp. 245–99.

S. Barnish, 'Taxation, land and barbarian settlement in the western Empire', *PBSR* LIV (1986), pp. 170–95.

S. Barnish, 'The transformation of classical cities and the Pirenne debate', *Journal of Roman Archaeology* II (1989), pp. 383–400.

P. S. Barnwell, *Kings, Courtiers and Imperium* (London, 1997).

M. Bloch, *Les Caractères originaux de l'histoire rurale française* (Oslo, 1931).

M. Bloch, *Feudal Society* (London, 1961).

P. Bonnassie, *From Slavery to Feudalism in South-western Europe* (Cambridge, 1991).

M. Borgolte, *Geschichte der Grafschaften Alemanniens im Frankischer Zeit* (Sigmaringen, 1983).

A. Borst, *Die karolingische Kalendarreform*, *MGH* Schriften 46 (Hanover, 1998).

G. P. Brogiolo (ed.), *Early Medieval Towns in the Western Mediterranean* (Mantua, 1996).

G. P. Brogiolo (ed.), *La fine delle ville romane* (Mantua, 1996).

G. P. Brogiolo and A. Chavarria Arnau (eds), *Archeologia e societa tra tardo antico e alto medioevo* (Mantua, 2007), pp. 193–204.

G. P. Brogiolo and B. Ward-Perkins (eds), *The Idea and Ideal of the Town between Late Antiquity and the Early Middle Ages*, *The transformation of the Roman World 4* (Leiden, 1999).

G. P. Brogiolo et al. (eds), *Towns and Their Territories between Late Antiquity and the Early Middle Ages* (Leiden, 2000).

W. Brown, *Unjust Seizure: conflict, interest and authority in an early medieval society* (Ithaca, NY, 2001).

C. Bucker and M. Hoeper, 'First aspects of social hierarchy of settlements in Merovingian southwest Germany', in C. Fabech and J. Ringrved (eds), *Settlement and Landscape* (Hojbjerg, 1999), pp. 441–54.

E. Campbell, 'The archaeological evidence for external contacts', in K. R. Drak (ed.), *External Contacts and the Economy of Late Roman and Post-Roman Britain* (Woodbridge, 1986), pp. 83–96.

A. Carandini, *Schiavi in Italia* (Rome, 1988).

E. Champion, *Moulins et meuniers carolingiens* (Paris, 1996).

N. Christie (ed.), *Landscapes of Change: rural evolutions in late antiquity and the early Middle Ages* (Aldershot, 2004).

N. Christie and S. Loseby (eds), *Towns in Transition* (Aldershot, 1996).

R. Corradini, M. Diesemberger and H. Reimitz, 'The construction of Communities in the early Middle Ages: texts, resources and artefacts', *The Transformation of the Roman World 12* (Leiden–Boston–Cologne, 2003), pp. 123–48.

W. Davies and P. Fouracre (eds), *The Settlement of Disputes in Early Medieval Europe* (Cambridge, 1986).

J. M. de Jong and F. Theuws, with C. van Rhijn (eds), *Topographies of Power in the Early Middle Ages*, *The Transformation of the Roman World 6* (Leiden, 2001).

P. Delogu, 'Reading Pirenne again', in R. Hodges and W. Bowden (eds), *The Sixth Century* (Leiden, 1998), pp. 15–40.

J.-P. Devroey, 'Men and Women in early medieval serfdom: the ninth-century north Frankish evidence', *P & P* 166 (2000), pp. 3–30.

J.-P. Devroey, *Études sur le grand domaine carolingien* (Aldershot, 1993).

A. Dopsch, *Die Wirtschaftsentwicklung der Karolingerzeit* (Cologne, 1962).

G. Duby, *L'Économie rurale et la vie des campagnes* (Paris, 1962).

G. Duby, *Rural Economy and Country Life in the Medieval West* (London, 1968).

S. Epperlein, *Herrschaft und Volk im karolingischen Imperium* (Berlin, 1969).

E. Ewig, *Trier im Merowingerreich* (Trier, 1954).

P. A. Février, *Le développement urbain en Provence de l'époque romaine à la fin du XIV siècle* (Paris, 1964).

R. Fossier, 'Les tendances de l'économie: stagnation ou croissance?', *SSCI* XXVII (1981), pp. 261–74.

P. Fouracre, '"Placita" and the settlement of disputes in later Merovingian Francia', in W. Davies and P. Fouracre (eds), *The Settlement of Disputes in Early Medieval Europe* (Cambridge, 1986), pp. 23–43.

P. Fouracre, 'Eternal light and earthly needs', in W. Davies and P. Fouracre (eds), *Property and Power in the Early Middle Ages* (Cambridge, 1995), pp. 53–81.

R. Francovich and R. Hodges, *Villa to Village* (London, 2005).

P. Freedman, *Images of the Medieval Peasant* (Stanford, CA, 1999).

P. Galetti, *Abitare nel medioevo* (Florence, 1997).

I. H. Garipzanov, 'The image of authority in Carolingian coinage', *EME* 8 (1999), pp. 197–215.

M. Garrison, '"Send more socks": on mentality and the preservation context of medieval letters', in M. Mostert (ed.), *New Approaches to Medieval Communication* (Turnhout, 1999), pp. 69–99.

M. Ghilardi, C. Goddard and P. Porena (eds), *Les Cités de l'Italie tardo-antique, IV–VI siècles. Institutions, économie, société, culture et religion, Collections d'École Française de Rome*, 369 (Rome, 2006).

H.-W. Goetz, 'Serfdom and the beginnings of a "seigneurial system" in the Carolingian period', *EME* II (1993), pp. 29–51.

P. Goubert, *Byzance avant l'Islam*, 2: *Byzance et l'Occident sous les successeurs de Justinien* (Paris, 1956).

N. Gradowicz Panzer, 'Degendering female violence: Merovingian female honour as an "exchange of violence"', *EME* 11 (2002), pp. 1–18.

P. Grierson and M. A. S. Blackburn, *Medieval European Coinage, 1: The Early Middle Ages (5th–10th centuries)* (Cambridge, 1986).

H. Grieser, *Sklaverei im Spätantiken und Frühmittelalterlichen Gallien (5–7.Jh.)* (Stuttgart, 1997).

J. F. Haldon, 'The feudalism debate once more', *Journal of Peasant Studies* XVII (1989), pp. 5–39.

G. Halsall, *Settlement and Social Organization in the Merovingian Region of Metz* (Cambridge, 1995).

G. Halsall (ed.), *Violence and Society in the Early Medieval West* (Woodbridge, 1998).

I. L. Hansen and C. Wickham (eds), *The Long Eighth Century: production, distribution and demand, The Transformation of the Roman World* II (Leiden, 2000).

D. Harrison, 'The development of elites: from Roman bureaucrats to medieval warlords', in W. Pohl and M. Diesenberger (eds), *Integration und Herrschaft. Ethnische Identitäten und soziale Organisation im Frühmittelalter* (Vienna, 2002), pp. 289–300.

L. Hedeager, 'Migration period Europe: the formation of a political identity', in F. Theuws and J. L. Nelson (eds), *Rituals of Power* (Leiden–Boston–Cologne, 2000), pp. 15–58.

M. F. Hendy, 'From public to private: the western Barbarian coinages as a mirror of the disintegration of late Roman state structures', in *Viator. Medieval and Renaissance Studies* (Berkeley–Los Angeles–London, 1988), pp. 43–59.

D. Hill et al., 'Quentovic defined', *Antiquity* LXIV (1990), pp. 51–8.

R. Hodges, *Dark Age Economics: the origins of towns and trade, AD 600–1000* (London, 1982).

R. Hodges, *Light on the Dark Ages: the rise and fall of San Vincenzo al Volturno* (London, 1997).

R. Hodges, *Towns and Trade in the Age of Charlemagne* (London, 2000).

R. Hodges and B. Hobley (eds), *The Rebirth of Towns in the West, 700–1030* (London, 1988).

R. Hodges and D. Whitehouse, *Mohammed, Charlemagne and the Origins of Europe* (London, 1983).

H. Hummer, *Politics and Power in Early Medieval Europe: Alsace and the Frankish realm, 600–1000* (Cambridge, 2006).

M. Innes, *State and Society in the Early Middle Ages: the middle Rhône valley, 400–1000* (Cambridge, 2000).

M. Innes, *Introduction to Early Medieval Western Europe, 300–900: the sword, the plough and the book* (Oxford–New York, 2007).

J. Johns, 'The longue durée', in E. L. Rogan and T. Tell (eds), *Village, Steppe and State* (London, 1994), pp. 1–31.

A. H. M. Jones, *The Decline of the Ancient World* (London, 1966).

G. Kobler, 'Land und Landrecht im Frühmittelalter', *ZSRG*, gA 68 (1969), pp. 1–40.

R. Le Jan, *Famille et pouvoir dans le monde franc* (Paris, 1995).

S. Lebecq, 'The role of the monasteries in the systems of production and exchange of the Frankish world between the seventh and the beginning of the ninth centuries', in I. I. Hansen and C. Wickham (eds), *The Long Eighth Century* (Leiden, 2000), pp. 121–48.

C. Lepeley (ed.), *La Fin de la cité antique et le début de la cité médiévale* (Bari, 1996).

A. R. Lewis, *The Northern Seas: shipping and commerce in northern Europe, AD 300–1100* (Princeton, NJ, 1958).

K. Leyser and T. Reuter (eds), *Communications and Power in Medieval Europe: the Carolingian and Ottonian centuries* (London–Rio Grande, 1994).

J. H. W. G. Liebeschuetz, *The Decline and Fall of the Roman City* (Oxford, 2001).

C. Lorren and P. Perin, 'Images de la Gaule rurale au VI siècle', in N. Gauthier and H. Galinie (eds), *Grégoire de Tours et l'espace gaulois* (Tours, 1997), pp. 93–109.

S. T. Loseby, 'Marseille and the Pirenne thesis', I, II, in R. Hodges and W. Bowden (eds), *The Sixth Century* (Leiden, 1998), pp. 203–29.

F. Lot, *The End of the Ancient World and the Beginning of the Middle Ages*, Eng. trans. (London, 1931).

M. McCormick, 'New light on the Dark Ages: how the slave trade fuelled the Carolingian economy', *P&P* 177 (2002), pp. 17–54.

M. McCormick, *Origins of the European Economy: communication and commerce, AD 300–900* (Cambridge, 2001).

R. McKitterick, *The Frankish Kingdoms under the Carolingians, 751–987* (London, 1983).

J. R. Maddicott, 'Prosperity and power in the age of Bede and Beowulf', *PBA* CXVII (2003), pp. 49–71.

C. Mango, *Le développement urbain de Constantinople (IV–VIIe siècles)* (Paris, 1990).

K. E. Morrison, *Carolingian Coinage, Numismatic Notes and Monographs*, vol. 158 (New York, 1967).

V. Neri, *I marginalinell' occidente tardoantico: poveri, 'infames' e criminali nella nascente società Cristiana* (Bari, 1998).

P. Ouzoulias and P. Van Ossel, 'Dynamiques du peuplement et formes de l'habitat tardif', in P. Ozoulias et al. (eds), *Les Campagnes de la Gaule à la fin de l'Antiquité* (Antibes, 2001).

F. Panero, *Schiavi servi e villani nell'Italia medievale* (Turin, 1999).

H. Pirenne, *Medieval Cities* (Princeton, NJ, 1925).

H. Pirenne, *Mahomet et Charlemagne* (Brussels, 1937), trans. as *Mohammed and Charlemagne* (London, 1939).

K. Randsborg, *The First Millennium AD in Europe and the Mediterranean: an archaeological essay* (Cambridge, 1991).

E. Renard, 'Les *mancipia* carolingiens étaient-ils des esclaves?', in P. Corbet (ed.), *Les Moines du Der, 673–1790* (Langres, 2000), pp. 179–209.

T. Reuter, 'Plunder and tribute in the Carolingian empire', *TRHS*, 5th series, 35 (1985), pp. 75–94.

P. Reynolds, 'Trade in the western Mediterranean, AD 400–700: the ceramic evidence', *British Archaeological Reports I 604* (Oxford, 1993).

S. Reynolds, *Fiefs and Vassals* (London, 1994).

J. Rich (ed.), *The City in Late Antiquity* (London, 1992).

P. Riche, *Daily Life in the World of Charlemagne*, trans. J. A. McNamara (Philadelphia, PA, 1978).

M. Roblin, *Le Terroir de Paris aux époques gallo-romaine et franque*, 2nd edn (Paris, 1971).

W. Rosener, 'Zur Struktur und Entwicklung der Grundherrschaft in Sachsen in karolingischer und ottonischer Zeit', in A. Verhulst (ed.), *Le Grand domaine aux époques merovingienne et carolingienne* (Gent, 1985), pp. 173–207.

A. Rovelli, 'Monetary circulation in Byzantine and Carolingian Rome', in J. M. H. Smith (ed.), *Early Medieval Rome and the Christian East* (Leiden, 2000), pp. 85–99.

P. Sarris, *Economy and Society in the Age of Justinian* (Cambridge, 2006).

J. Schmitt, *Untersuchungen zu den liberi homines der Karolingerzeit* (Frankfurt, 1977).

P. Senac, *Le Monde carolingien et l'Islam* (Paris, 2006).

J.-P. Sodini (ed.), *Les Villages dans l'empire et le monde Byzantin (V–XV siècles)* (Paris, 2005).

H. Steuer, *Frühgeschichtliche Sozialstrukturen in Mitteleuropa* (Göttingen, 1982).

R. Van Dam, *Leadership and Community in Late Antique Gaul* (Berkeley, CA, 1985).

A. Verhulst, 'Karolingische Agrarpolitik: das Capitulare de Villis und die Hungersnote von 791 und 805/806', *Zeitschrift für Agrargeschichte und Agrarsoziologie* 13 (1965), pp. 175–89.

A. Verhulst, *Rural and Urban Aspects of Early Medieval Northwest Europe* (London, 1992).

A. Verhulst, *The Rise of Cities in North-west Europe* (Cambridge, 1999).

A. Verhulst, *The Carolingian Economy* (Cambridge, 2002).

B. Ward-Perkins, *From Classical Antiquity to the Middle Ages: urban public buildings in northern and central Italy, AD 300–850* (Oxford, 1984).

B. Ward-Perkins, 'Continuists, catastrophists and the towns of post-Roman northern Italy', *PBSR* 45 (1997).

K. F. Werner, 'Missus-marchio-comes: Entre l'administration centrale et l'administration locale de l'empire carolingien', in W. Paravicini and K. F. Werner (eds), *Histoire comparée de l'administration IV–XVIII siècle, Beihefte der Francia* 9 (Munich, 1980).

C. Wickham, *The Mountains and the City* (Oxford, 1988).

C. Wickham, 'La chute de Rome n'aura pas lieu', *Le Moyen Âge* 99 (1993), pp. 107–26.

C. Wickham, 'The development of villages in the West, 300–900', in C. Morrisson and C. Wickham, *Land and Power* (London, 1994).

C. Wickham, 'Early medieval archaeology in Italy: the last twenty years', *Archeologia Medievale* XVI (1999), pp. 7–19.

C. Wickham, 'Le forme del feudalesimo', *SSCI* XLVII (2000), pp. 15–51.

C. Wickham, 'Italy at the end of the Mediterranean world system', *Journal of Roman Archaeology* XIII (2000), pp. 818–24.

C. Wickham, *Framing the Early Middle Ages: Europe and the Mediterranean, 400–800* (Oxford, 2005).

H. Wolfram, *Die Geburt Mitteleuropas* (Vienna, 1987).

P. Wormald, *Legal Culture in the Early Medieval West: law as text, image and experience* (London, 1999).

CHAPTER 8: THE CAROLINGIAN CULTURAL RENAISSANCE

S. Airlie, 'The anxiety of sanctity', *Journal of Ecclesiastical History* 43 (1992), pp. 372–95.

S. Allott, *Alcuin of York* (York, 1974).

E. Amann, *L'Époque carolingienne: histoire de l'Église depuis les origines jusqu'à nos jours*, A. Fliche and V. Martin (eds), vol. 6 (Paris, 1947).

H. H. Anton, *Fürstenspiegel und Herrscherethos in der Karolingerzeit, Bonner Historische Forschungen*, vol. 32 (Bonn, 1968).

B. Bastert (ed.), *Karl der Grosse in der Europäischen Literaturen des Mittelalters: Konstruction eines Mythos* (Tübingen, 2004).

G. A. Beckmann, 'Aus den letzten Jahrzehnten des Vulgarlateins in Frankreich', *Zeitschrift für Romanische Philologie* LXXIX (1963), pp. 305–34.

B. Bildhauer, *Medieval Blood* (Cardiff, 2006).

B. Bischoff, *Manuscripts and Libraries in the Age of Charlemagne* (Cambridge, 1994).

B. Bischoff, 'Das thema des Poeta Saxo', in *Mittelalterliche Studien*, III (Stuttgart, 1981), pp. 253–9.

A. Bowman and G. Woolf (eds), *Literacy and Power in the Ancient World* (Cambridge, 1994).

A. Bryer and J. Herrin (eds), *Iconoclasm* (Birmingham, 1977).

D. Bullough, *Alcuin: achievement and reputation. Being part of the Ford Lectures delivered in Oxford in the Hilary term 1980* (Leiden–Boston, 2004).

D. A. Bullough, *Carolingian Renewal: sources and heritage* (Manchester, 1991).

P. L. Butzer, M. Kerner and W. Oberschelp (eds), *Karl der Grosse und sein Nachwirken: 1200 Jahre Kultur und Wissenschaft in Europa* (Turnhout, 1967).

C. Chazelle, *The Crucified God in the Carolingian Era: theology and art of Christ's passion* (Cambridge, 2001).

M. Claussen, *Chrodegang of Metz and the reform of the Frankish Church* (Cambridge, 2005).

R. Collins, *Fredegar, Authors of the Middle Ages* 13 (Aldershot, 1996).

J. J. Contreni, *Carolingian Learning, Masters and Manuscripts* (Aldershot, 1992).

J. J. Contreni, 'The pursuit of knowledge in Carolingian Europe', in Sullivan, *'The Gentle Voices of Teachers': aspects of learning in the Carolingian age* (Columbus, OH, 1995), pp. 106–41.

S. Coupland, 'The rod of God's wrath or the people of God's wrath', *Journal of Ecclesiastical History* 42 (1991), pp. 535–54.

W. Davies, 'Clerics as rulers', in N. P. Brooks (ed.), *Latin and the Vernacular Languages in Early Medieval Britain* (Leicester, 1982), pp. 81–97.

M. de Jong (ed.), *The Power of the Word: the influence of the Bible on early medieval politics*, special issue of *EME* 7 (1998).

D. M. Deliyannis, 'Charlemagne's silver tables: the ideology of an imperial capital', *EME* 12 (2003), pp. 159–78.

R. Deshman, '"Christus rex et magi reges": kingship and Christology in Ottonian and Anglo-Saxon art', *Frühmittelalterliche Studien* 10, ed. K. Hauck (Berlin–New York, 1976).

P. Dronke, *Women Writers of the Middle Ages* (Cambridge, 1984).

P. E. Dutton, *Charlemagne's Courtier: The complete Einhard* (Peterborough, Ont., 1998).

P. E. Dutton, *Carolingian civilization: a reader* (Peterborough, Ont., 2004).

P. E. Dutton, *Charlemagne's mustache and other cultural clusters of a dark age* (New York, 2004).

J. Fleckenstein, *Die Hofkapelle der deutschen Könige. 1 Teil: Grundlegung. Die karolingische Hofkapelle. Schriften der MGH*, vol. 16, pt. 1 (Stuttgart, 1959).

P. Fouracre, 'The origins of the Carolingian attempt to regulate the cult of the saints', in J. Howard-Johnston and P. Hayward (eds), *The Cult of Saints in Late Antiquity and the Early Middle Ages* (Oxford, 1999), pp. 143–65.

R. Gameson (ed.), *The Early Medieval Bible: its production, decoration and use* (Cambridge, 1994).

R. Gameson and H. Leyser (eds), *Belief and Culture: studies presented to Henry Mayr-Harting* (Oxford, 2001).

F. L. Ganshof, 'Alcuin's revision of the Bible', in his *The Carolingians and the Frankish Monarchy: studies in Carolingian history*, trans. J. Sondheimer (Ithaca, NY, 1971), pp. 28–40.

D. Ganz, *Corbie in the Carolingian Renaissance, Beheifte der Francia* 29 (Sigmaringen, 1990).

D. Ganz, 'The preface to Einhard's "Vita Karoli"', in H. Schefers (ed.), *Einhard: Studien zu Leben und Werk* (Darmstadt, 1997), pp. 299–310.

A. Giardina, *Cassiodoro politico* (Rome, 2006).

P. Godman, *Poetry of the Carolingian Renaissance* (London, 1985).

P. Godman, *Poets and Emperors: Frankish politics and Carolingian poetry* (Oxford, 1986).

M. M. Gorman, 'The encyclopedic commentary on Genesis prepared for Charlemagne by Wigbod', *Recherches Augustiniennes* 17 (1982), pp. 173–201.

M. Gorman, *Biblical Commentaries from the Early Middle Ages, Millennio Medievale* 32, Reprints 4 (Florence, 2003).

D. H. Green, *Language and History in the Early Germanic World* (Cambridge, 1998).

C. Heltz, *L'Architecture religieuse carolingienne* (Paris, 1980).

Y. Hen, *The Royal Patronage of the Liturgy in Frankish Gaul to the Death of Charles the Bald (877)* (London, 2001).

M. Innes, 'The classical tradition and Carolingian historiography', *International Journal of the Classical Tradition* 3 (1997), pp. 265–82.

M. Innes, '"He never even bared his white teeth in laughter": the politics of humour in the Carolingian renaissance', in G. Halsall (ed.), *Humour, Politics and History in Late Antiquity* (Cambridge, 2002), pp. 131–56.

E. H. Kantorowicz, *Laudes Regiae: a study in liturgical acclamations and medieval ruler worship* (Berkeley, CA, 1946).

S. Keefe, *Water and the Word: baptism and the education of the clergy in the Carolingian empire* (Notre Dame, 2002).

E. Kitzinger, *The Art of Byzantium and the Medieval West: selected studies* (Bloomington, Indiana, 1976).

T. Klauser, *A Short History of the Western Liturgy*, trans. J. Halliburton, 2nd edn (Oxford, 1979).

W. Kohler, *Die karolingischen miniaturen*, II. *Die Hofschule Karls des Grossen* (Berlin, 1958).

R. Krautheimer, 'The Carolingian revival of early Christian architecture', *Art Bulletin* 24 (1942), pp. 1ff, and repr. in his *Studies in Early Christian, Medieval and Renaissance Art* (New York, 1969).

A. Kupfer, 'Medieval world maps – embedded images, interpretative frame', *Word and Image* 10 (1994), pp. 262–88.

V. Law, *Grammar and Grammarians in the Early Middle Ages* (London, 1997).

R. Le Jan, 'Espaces sauvages et chasses royales dans le nord de la France', *Revue du Nord* 62 (1980), pp. 35–57.

K. Levy, *Gregorian Chant and the Carolingians* (Princeton, N.J., 1998).

J. H. W. G. Liebeschuetz, *Barbarians and Bishops* (Oxford, 1990).

H. Lowe, 'Salzburg als Zentrum literarischen Schaffens im 8. Jahrhundert', in H. Koller and H. Dopsch (eds), *Salzburg im 8. Jahrhundert* (Salzburg, 1975), pp. 99–143.

K. Lowith, *Weltgeschichte und Heilgeschehen* (Stuttgart, 1953).

S. G. MacCormack, *Art and Ceremony in Late Antiquity* (Berkeley, CA, 1981).

R. McKitterick, 'Charles the Bald and his library', *EHR* 95 (1980), pp. 28–47.

R. McKitterick, *The Carolingians and the Written Word* (Cambridge, 1989).

R. McKitterick, *Books, Scribes and Learning in the Frankish Kingdom, 6th–9th centuries* (Aldershot, 1994).

R. McKitterick (ed.), *Carolingian Culture: emulation and innovation* (Cambridge, 1994).

R. McKitterick, *The Frankish Kings and Culture in the Early Middle Ages* (Aldershot, 1995).

J. Marenbon, *From the Circle of Alcuin to the School of Auxerre: logic, theology and philosophy in the early Middle Ages* (Cambridge, 1981).

H. Marrou, *A History of Education in Antiquity* (Madison, Wisc., 1982), trans. from the original French edition of 1948.

H. Mayr-Harting, 'Charlemagne as patron of art', *Studies in Church History* 28 (1992), pp. 43–77.

R. Meens, 'The nature and frequency of early medieval penance', in P. Biller (ed.), *Handling Sin* (York, 1998), pp. 35–61.

A. Momigliano, *The Classical Foundations of Modern Historiography* (Berkeley, CA, 1990).

L. Nees, *The Tainted Mantle: Hercules and the classical tradition at the Carolingian court* (Philadelphia, PA, 1991).

F. Paxton, *Christianizing Death: the creation of a ritual process in early medieval Europe* (Ithaca, NY, 1989).

C. Possel, H. Reimitz, and P. Shaw (eds), *Texts and Identities in the Early Middle Ages* (Vienna, 2007).

G. Post, *Studies in Medieval Legal Thought* (Princeton, NJ, 1964).

C. Ricci, *Mysterium Dispensationis: tracce di una telogia della storia in Gregorio Magno* (Rome, 2002).

P. Riche, *Education and Culture in the Barbarian West*, trans. J. J. Contreni (Columbia, SC, 1976).

P. E. Schramm, *Die deutschen Kaiser und Könige in Bildern ihrer Zeit*, 1 (Leipzig–Berlin, 1928).

P. E. Schramm, *Die zeitgenossischen Bildnisse Karls des Grossen, Beitrage zur Kulturgeschichte des Mittelalters und der Renaissance*, vol. 29 (Leipzig, 1928).

P. E. Schramm, *Kaiser, Könige und Papste: gesammelte Aufsätze zur Geschichte des Mittelalters* 1: 215–63, 4 vols (Stuttgart, 1968–71).

P. Sims-Williams, *Religion and Literature in Western England, 600–800* (Cambridge, 1990).

W. Stevens, 'Astronomy in Carolingian schools', in P. L. Butzer, M. Kerner and W. Oberschelp (eds), *Charlemagne and His Heritage: 1200 years of civilization and science in Europe* (Turnhout, 1997), pp. 417–88.

C. Stiegemann and M. Wemhoff (eds), *799 Kunst und Kultur der Karolingerzeit: Karl der Grosse und Papst Leo III in Paderborn*, 3 vols (Mainz, 1999).

R. L. Stocking, *Bishops, Councils and Consensus in the Visigothic Kingdom, 589–633* (Ann Arbor, MI, 2000).

S. Tanz, 'Aspekte der Karlsrezeption im Frankreich des 19. Jahrhundert', *Das Mittelalter* 4/2 (1999), pp. 55–64.

L. Tondelli, *Il disegno divino nella storia* (Turin, 1947).

C. Treffort, *L'Église carolingienne et la mort* (Lyons, 1996).

R. Turcan, *L'art romain dans l'histoire: six siècles d'expression de la romanité* (Paris, 1995).

F. W. Unger, *Quellen der byzantinischen Kunstgeschichte* (Vienna, 1878).

C. Verlinden, *Les Origines de la frontière linguistique en Belgique et la civilisation franque* (Brussels, 1955).

M. Weidemann, *Kulturgeschichte der Merowingerzeit nach den Werken Gregors von Tours*, 2 vols (Mainz, 1982).

R. Wright, *Late Latin and Early Romance in Spain and Carolingian France* (Liverpool, 1982).

R. Wright (ed.), *Latin and the Romance Languages in the Early Middle Ages* (London, 1991–Philadelphia, PA, 1996).

CHAPTER 9: THE SURVIVAL AND REVIVAL OF EMPIRE

S. Airlie, 'After empire: recent work on the emergence of post-Carolingian kingdoms', *EME* 2 (1993), pp. 153–61.

S. Airlie, 'Private bodies and the body politic in the divorce case of Lothar II', *P&P* 161 (1998), pp. 3–38.

Gerd Althoff, *Otto III* (Darmstadt, 1996), trans. P. G. Jestice (Pennsylvania, 2003).

P. Boitani, *Letteratura Europea e medioevo volgare* (Bologna, 2007).

R. Boyer, *Le mythe Viking* (Paris, 1986).

D. Bullough, '*Europae pater*: Charlemagne's achievement in the light of recent scholarship', *EHR* 85 (1970), pp. 59–105.

R. Collins, 'The Carolingians and Ottonians in an anglophone world', *Journal of Medieval History*, vol. 22 (1994), pp. 227–47.

R. Coroneo, *Scultura altomedievale in Italia: materiali e tecniche di esecuzione, tradizioni e metodi di studio* (Cagliari, 2005).

E. R. Curtius, *European Literature and the Latin Middle Ages* (Princeton, NJ, 1991).

G. Declerq, *Anno Domini: les origines de l'ère chrétienne* (Turnhout, 2000).

M. de Jong, *The Penitential State: authority and atonement in the age of Louis the Pious, 814–840* (Cambridge, 2009).

M. de Jong, 'Power and humility in Carolingian society: the public penance of Louis the Pious', *EME* 1 (1992), pp. 29–31.

Philippe Depreux, *Prosopographie de l'entourage de Louis le Pieux (781–840)* (Sigmaringen, 1997).

J. Devisse, *Hincmar, archevêque de Reims*, 3 vols (Paris, 1975).

A. Dierkens, 'Le tombeau de Charlemagne', *Byzantium* 61 (1991), pp. 156–80.

R. Folz, *Le Souvenir et la légende de Charlemagne dans l'empire germanique médiéval* (Paris, 1950).

R. Folz, *The Concept of Empire in Western Europe from the Fifth to the Fourteenth Century* (London, 1969), trans. S. A. Ogilvie from the 1953 French edition.

R. Folz et al., *De l'antiquité au monde médiéval* (Paris, 1972).

J. Fontaine, *Isidore de Seville et la culture classique dans l'Espagne Wisigotique*, 3 vols (Paris, 1983).

S. Foot, 'Angelcynn: English identity before the Norman conquest', *TRHS* 6 (1996), pp. 25–49.

A. Fraschetti, *La Conversione. Da Roma pagana a Roma Cristiana* (Rome–Bari, 1999).

F. L. Ganshof, *Histoire des relations internationales* I: *le Moyen Âge* (Paris, 1953).

F. L. Ganshof, 'Louis the Pious reconsidered', in his *The Carolingians and the Frankish Monarchy: studies in Carolingian history*, trans. J. Sondheimer (Ithaca, NY, 1971), pp. 261–72.

F. L. Ganshof, 'Some observations on the "Ordinatio Imperii" of 817', in his *The Carolingians and the Frankish Monarchy: studies in Carolingian history*, trans. J. Sondheimer (Ithaca, NY, 1971), pp. 273–88.

P. J. Geary, 'Ethnic identity as a situational construct in the early Middle Ages', *Mitteilungen der anthropologischen Gesellschaft in Wien* CXIII (1983), pp. 15–26.

P. J. Geary, *Aristocracy in Provence: the Rhône Basin at the dawn of the Carolingian Age* (Stuttgart, 1985).

P. J. Geary, *The Myth of Nations: the medieval origins of Europe* (Princeton, NJ, 2002).

P. Godman and R. Collins (eds), *Charlemagne's Heir: new perspectives on the reign of Louis the Pious (814-40)* (Oxford, 1990).

E. Goldberg, 'Frontier kingship, martial ritual and early knighthood at the court of Louis the German', *Viator* 30 (1999), p. 41.

E. Goldberg, *Struggle for Empire: kingship and empire under Louis the German, 817-876* (Ithaca, NY–London, 2006).

G. Halsall, *Early Medieval Cemeteries* (Glasgow, 1995).

W. Hartmann (ed.), *Ludwig der Deutsche und seine Zeit* (Darmstadt, 2004).

H. Hoffmann, 'Zur Geschichte Ottos des Grossen', *DA* 28 (1972), p. 42.

M. Innes, 'Charlemagne's will: piety, politics and the imperial succession', *EHR* 112 (1997), pp. 833–55.

H. Jantsen, *Ottonische Kunst* (Munich, 1974).

K. Jarausch, 'Normalization or renationalization?: On reinterpreting the German past', in R. Alter and P. Montreath (eds), *Rewriting the German Past: history and identity in the new Germany* (Atlantic Highlands, NJ, 1997).

G. Jones, *A History of the Vikings* (Oxford, 1968).

H. Keller, 'Das Kaisertum Ottos des Grossen im Verständnis seiner Zeit', *DA* 20 (1964), p. 325.

R. Kopke and E. Dummler, *Kaiser Otto der Grosse, Jahrbücher der Deutschen Geschichte* (Leipzig, 1876).

M. P. Laffitte and C. Denoel (eds), *Trésors carolingiens: livres manuscrits de Charlemagne à Charles le Chauve* (Paris, 2007).

K. Leyser, 'The battle at the Lech, 955: a study in tenth-century warfare', *History* L (1965), pp. 1–25.

K. Leyser, 'The German aristocracy from the ninth to the early twelfth century: a historical and cultural sketch', *P&P* 41 (1968), pp. 25–53.

K. J. Leyser, *Rule and Conflict in Early Medieval Society: Ottonian Saxony* (London, 1979).

K. Leyser, *Communication and Power in Medieval Europe: the Carolingian and Ottonian centuries* (London–Rio Grande, 1994).

F. Lot, 'Les derniers Carolingiens: Lothaire Louis V.–Charles de Lorraine 954–991', *Bibliothèque de l'École des Hautes Études* 87 (Paris, 1891).

B. Luiselli, *La formazione della cultura Europea occidentale* (Rome, 2003).

R. McKitterick, 'The scriptoria of Merovingian Gaul: a survey of the evidence', in H. B. Clarke and M. Brennan (eds), *Columbanus and Merovingian Monasticism* (Oxford, 1981), pp. 173–207.

S. Maclean, *Kingship and Politics in the Late Ninth Century: Charles the Fat and the end of the Carolingian empire, Cambridge Studies in Medieval Life and Thought* (Cambridge, 2003).

K. Maund, '"A turmoil of warring princes": political leadership in ninth-century Denmark', *Haskins Society Journal* 6 (1994), pp. 29–47.

H. Mayr-Harting, *Ottonian Book Illumination: an historical study*, 2 vols (London, 1991).

E. Muller-Mertens, *Karl der Grosse, Ludwig der Fromme, und die Freien* (Berlin, 1963).

L. Musset, *Les Invasions: le second assaut contre l'Europe chrétienne (VII–XI siècles)* (Paris, 1965).

J. L. Nelson, 'Kingship, liturgy and law in the political thought of Hincmar of Reims', *EHR* 92 (1977), pp. 241–79.

J. L. Nelson, 'Public histories and private history in the work of Nithard', *Speculum* 60 (1985), pp. 251–293.

J. L. Nelson, *Charles the Bald* (London, 1992).

T. F. X. Noble, 'The monastic ideal as a model for empire: the case of Louis the Pious', *Revue Bénédictine* 86 (1976), pp. 225–50.

A. D. Nock, 'Cremation and burial in the Roman empire', in his *Essays on Religion and the Ancient World* (Oxford, 1972, first edn, 1932), pp. 277–307.

F. Oswald, L. Schaefer and R. Sennhauser (eds), *Vorromanische Kirchenbauten*, I–III (München, 1966–71).

W. Pohl, 'Zur Bedeutung ethnischer Unterscheidungen in der frühen Karolingerzeit', *Studien zur Sachsenforschung* 12 (1992), pp. 193–208.

W. Pohl with H. Reimetz, *Strategies of Distinction: the construction of ethnic communities, 300–800* (Leiden, 1998).

S. A. Rabe, *Faith, Art and Politics at Saint-Riquier: the symbolic vision of Angilbert* (Philadelphia, PA, 1995).

K. Randsborg, *The Viking Age in Denmark: the formation of a state* (London, 1980).

R. Rau (ed.), *Quellen zur Karolingischen Reichsgeschichte*, 3 vols (Darmstadt, 1972, 1974, 1975).

T. Reuter, *Germany in the Early Middle Ages, 800–1056* (Harlow, 1991).

P. Riche, *Éducation et culture dans l'occident barbare, 6–8 siècles* (Paris, 1962).

P. Riche, *Écoles et enseignement dans le haut moyen âge de la fin du V siècle au milieu du XI siècle* (Paris, 1979).

P. Sawyer, *Kings and Vikings* (London, 1982).

W. Schlesinger, 'Die Auflösung des Karlsreiches', in W. Brannfels (gen. ed.), *Karl der Grosse, Lebenswerk und Nachleben* I, *Personlichkeit und Geschichte* (Düsseldorf, 1965), pp. 792–857.

A. D. Smith, *The Ethnic Origins of Nations* (Oxford, 1986).

A. Smyth, *Scandinavian Kings in the British Isles, 850–880* (Oxford, 1977).

E. E. Stengel, 'Die Entwicklung des Kaiserprivilegs für die römische Kirche, 817–962', in his *Abhandlungen und Untersuchungen zur Mittelalterlichen Geschichte* (Cologne, 1960), pp. 214–48.

M. Wallace-Hadrill, 'History in the mind of Archbishop Hincmar', in R. Davis and M. Wallace-Hadrill (eds), *The Writing of History in the Middle Ages* (Oxford, 1981).

H. Wolfram, *Österreichische Geschichte, 378–907: Grenzen und Raume. Geschichte Osterreichs vor seiner Entstehung* (Vienna, 1995).

M. Zimmermann (ed.), *Les Sociétés méridionales autour de l'an mille* (Paris, 1992).

T. Zotz, 'Carolingian tradition and Ottonian–Salian innovation: comparative perspectives on palatine policy in the empire', in A. Duggan (ed.), *Kings and Kingship in Medieval Europe* (London, 1993), pp. 69–100.

Index

Aachen 196, 198–9, 202, 203–4, 209, 229–30, 239, 275, 381
Aadorf monastery 216
Abbasid dynasty 229
abbeys
  communities of manual workers and artisans 296–7
  location of markets near 297
  and salt production 296
  sources of demand for iron 295
Abbo of Provence 208, 214
'Abd al-Rahman, 'Abdallah ibn 101–2
Abodrites 125, 126, 128, 132, 133–4, 234
Abul-Abaz (elephant) 229–30
Adalhard 65–6
Adalhard 'the Seneschal' 209–10, 212
Adaloald, King 104–5
Admonitio generalis 244, 245, 333
adoptionism 112
Aethelbald 224
Aethelred 30
Aethelwulff, King 224, 242
Agilolfing 84, 104–6
Agilulf, King 40, 44
Agobard of Lyons 345–6, 347
agriculture 285–8
  and manorial system 288–94
Aidan of Iona 324
Aistulf, King 58, 85
Aix-la-Chapelle 188, 299

Alamannia/Alamannians 48, 61, 65, 77, 221, 223, 233, 276–7, 365
Alaric II 42
Alboin, King of the Lombards 71, 83, 84, 366
Alcuin of York 60, 142, 142–3, 189, 244, 279, 324, 341, 344, 345, 349
  De Dialectica 349
  De Orthographia 305–6
Aldfrith 30
Aldhelm 323–4, 327
Alfonso II the Chaste 101, 233
Alfonso III, King 268
Alfred the Great 284–5, 324
Alfred of Wessex 238, 240, 249, 252, 253, 256, 269
allodia 293
Alsace 61, 206, 359
Alvar, Paul 347
Amalarius of Metz 347
Ambrose of Milan 163, 164
Andlau, abbey of 216
Angilbert of St-Riquier 191, 335, 338
Angles 70
Anglo-Saxon Chronicle 269
Anglo-Saxons 169, 173, 250, 276, 279, 283, 294, 309, 315, 322–3, 325, 328, 346, 373
Anicii 168
animals
  and farming 287–8
Annales Bertiniani 266, 347
Annales Fuldenses 267
Annales Laureshamenses 280

Annales Regni Francorum 53, 54, 65, 75, 108, 146–7, 258
Annals of Metz 232
Annals of Ulster 38
Ansegisel 9, 11, 213
Ansgar, St 66
Anskar 131
Anstrude 11
antrustiones 40
Apollinaris, Sidonius 42
aprocisiarius 197
aqueducts 181
Aquitaine 5, 6, 17, 59, 60–3, 91, 96–7, 100, 245, 276, 359
Arabs xiii, 174
  culture 326
  invasion of Spain 91–2, 100–1, 175
  spread of rule and countries conquered 174–5, 326–7
Arbogast the Frank 370
Ardennes 203
Arezzo 147
Arianism 19–20, 305
Arichis II 7, 88, 98
Arioald, Duke 105
Aripert I 105
aristocracy xii, 24, 45, 55, 205–23
  annual levy imposed on 283
  and Carolingian rulers 205–7, 210
  choosing a lineage and favouring relatives 213–15

concentration of family
power 210, 220
decision as to who to back
218–21
divisions within families
211–13
family connections and
networks 209
and family monasteries
215
heredity as basis of title
205–6
and *honores* 217–20
imperial 207–8
influence of women
215–16
and insecurity 220–1
and marriage 221–3
mobility of 208–11
relationship with Charle-
magne 190
Aristotle 22, 316, 349
Arius 19
armies, Frankish 68–9
Arn of Salzburg, Archbishop
120, 142, 246, 352
Arnulf of Carinthia 361
Arnulf of Metz 8, 9, 213, 331
artes liberales see liberal arts
Asparuch 28
assemblies xii, 235–42, 243
astronomy 350–1
Asturias 100–1, 275–6
Audouin of Rouen, Bishop
Life of St Eligius 325
Augustine of Hippo 18, 19,
20–2, 163, 166
The City of God 14, 17,
20–1, 22, 23,
358
De Doctrina Christiana
345
Augustus, Emperor 136, 137
aula 200
Aurelian of Rome 354
Aurelian Walls 157, 165, 182
Austrasia xvii, 1–2, 5, 6–9,
10, 30, 49, 70, 71, 72,
206, 208
Authari, King 84
Autpertus, Ambrosius 330
Auxerre 277, 343
Avars x, 28, 36, 112–22, 124,
128, 280
acquisition of treasure
from by Franks xiv, 118

background 113–14
Charlemagne's campaigns
against 112–13, 115–21,
123, 124
dissolution of dominion
and consequences of
117–21
khanate of 36
and Lombards 113
missionary work among 120
move to area south of
Danube 120–1,
128
origins and travel west-
wards 113
and paganism 115
resistance to assimilation
121
and Slavs 114, 121
wealth 114
Baghdad 230–1
Balbulus, Notker 198, 352
Balearic Islands 123
Balkans 28
barbarians, Romanization of
40–3
Barcelona 101, 102
Bardowiek 300
basilica 159
Basilica Nova (Rome) 160
Basques 93
Bavaria/Bavarians x, 12, 30,
50, 77, 102–8, 124, 223,
255
Agilolfing rulers 104
background to annexation
of 105–8
Charlemagne's campaign
against and assimilation
of into Frankish
kingdom (788) 12, 65,
103, 105, 108–12, 114,
123, 124, 135
church in 105–6
importance of to Francia
102–4
Lombardy connection
104–5
origins 103
salt mining 103
submission of Duke Tas-
silo 108–12, 114
bedchamber, royal 195
Bede, Venerable 52, 315,
324–5

*Ecclesiastical History of the
English People* 324
Begga 9, 11, 213
Belisarius, General 18
Benedict of Aniane 330, 337
Benedict of Narsia 317, 318
Benevento 88, 97, 98–100,
147
Berbers 91, 92
Bernard of Italy 219, 226,
357
Bernard of Septimania 209,
211, 214
Bertha (Charlemagne's
daughter) 192–3
Berthar 10
Bertrada, Queen (Charle-
magne's mother) 49, 59,
60, 63–4, 65, 108, 222
Biscop, Benedict 323
'Blood Court at Cannstatt' 48
Bodo 347
Boethius 316–17
De Arithmetica 351
*The Consolation of Philos-
ophy* 317
De Institutione Musica 353
Bohemians (*Beheimi*) 121–2
Boniface (Anglo-Saxon mis-
sionary) 12–13, 30, 48,
54, 73–4, 75, 106, 174,
327
Boniface (Roman governor)
17–18
book production 328–31, 335
see also manuscript
production
Bornhoved, battle at 126
Boso of Provence 220, 225,
361
Bourbons 25
Bremen 130, 131
Brenner Pass 103
Breviary of Alaric 332
British Isles 273, 315, 319,
322, 323–4, 371
kingship 30–1, 37
migration of Saxons to 72
see also Anglo-Saxons;
England; Scotland
Brittany 253, 293
Brunhilda 6, 7
Bulgars 28, 36, 114, 121
Burchard, Bishop 47
Burgundy 2, 5, 6, 8, 359, 377
burial objects 25

Byzantium 28, 54, 58, 84, 90,
    121, 148, 168, 175,
    178–9, 185, 231, 312
  and aristocracy 205–6
  and Avars 115
  crisis and decline in power
    179, 314, 319, 327
  and diplomacy 231–2
  and Lombards 178
  and papacy 175, 177–8
  peace negotiation with
    Franks (802) 233
  relations with Charle-
    magne 99, 231
  and Rome 175
  see also Constantinople

Cadwalla (Cadwalader) 52–3
Caesarius of Arles 318, 321
canals 123
canon law 309–10
Canterbury 279, 326, 327–8
Capella, Martianus 345, 353
capellani 194–5
capitula 240–1
Capitulare de Villis 295
Capitulare primum 245
capitularies xii 240–1, 242–5,
    248, 267
  (802) 149, 246, 247–8, 261
Carantanians 103–4
Carloman (Charlemagne's
    brother) x, 53–4, 62–7,
    219
Carloman (Charlemagne's
    uncle) 11, 12, 48–9, 74,
    81, 85, 106, 223
Carloman (Charles the Bald's
    son) 226, 227
Carloman II 361
Carloman (Louis the
    German's son) 360
Carolingian empire 371–2
division of xv, 232, 237, 282,
    372
Carolingian renaissance xiv,
    118, 188–9, 303–54
  aims of Charlemagne and
    Carolingian conse-
    quences 333–6
  book/manuscript produc-
    tion 317–18, 328–31,
    335, 340
  building the nation 307–
    12
  changing minds 343–54

  and Church 307–8, 309–
    10
  and dialectical studies
    349–50
  and education 337–43
  and education of clergy
    318–19, 333–4, 337–9,
    343–4, 371
  importance of grammar
    345, 346–8
  and intellectual elite 311–
    12
  and language 305–6
  late antique culture back-
    ground to 312–27
  and Latin 305–6, 311, 312,
    343–4
  and liberal arts 306–7
  and literacy 338–9
  music and musical theory
    351–3
  set texts favoured by
    Charlemagne 311
  table maps 303–4
Carolingian script 371
Carolingians 23–4
  and aristocracy 205–7, 210
  importance of names 226
  link between religious cul-
    ture and military policy
    of 131
  marriage 221–3, 224
  new power base of 568
  palaces 23–4, 199–200
  relationship with papacy
    56, 58–9, 63, 84, 89,
    150–5, 178, 180, 184
  religious and imperial
    sense of mission 23–4,
    57–8
  rise to power 9–13, 50–3
  strategies in coping with
    ambitious relatives 225–
    7
  women as focus of
    national identity 223–5
Carthage 18, 326
Cassiodorus 41–2, 162, 314,
    316, 317–18, 319
  Institutions 317, 345
  Variae 41–2, 44
castles 210
cattle 287
cattle pest 230
chamberlain 195
chancery 197

Chanson de Roland 93–4, 212
chant
  Gregorian 353
  Roman 351–2
Charibert I 5
Charlemagne, King of the
    Franks
  Domestic and Personal
    Life
  and Aachen 203–4
  ancestry 7–13
  appearance and physique
    140
  birth and early years x, 49,
    59–62
  birth name 140
  children and bringing up
    at court 191–4
  concubines and mistresses
    192, 257
  death and burial 357–8
  dress 140
  fitness and robust health
    140
  heirs of 358–63
  household and courtiers
    191–2, 194–7
  and hunting 203
  illegitimate children 192
  keeping many of his chil-
    dren unmarried 193–4,
    225
  and languages 305
  literary portraits of court
    and palaces 191, 196,
    198
  marriages and wives 65,
    192, 223
  name 140
  palaces of xii, 199–203
  remains 381
  and villae 197–8
  visual representations of xi
  King of the Franks
  abandonment of Lombard
    alliance after Car-
    loman's death and repu-
    diation of Desiderata
    65–6, 86, 192, 222–3
  achievements 371
  adopts Rex Francorum et
    Rex Langobardorum as
    formal ascription xi
  alliance with Lombards
    through marriage to
    Desiderata 63–4, 85–6

becomes sole king of the
Franks (771) x
and Christianity 308
coronation (800) xi-xii, 62,
139–41, 145, 155, 185,
186–7, 189, 370
debate over true identity
and aims xv-xvii
and diplomacy 230
hostility towards paganism
23
imperial style of leader-
ship 204
imperial title and meaning
of 147–50
intervention in Rome after
attack on Leo III 141–3,
145, 149
itinerancy of 201–2, 203
joint kingship with Car-
loman x, 62–7, 85, 219
legacy xvi-xvii, 263–9,
364, 381
and papal ritual 144
relationship with aristocracy 190
relationship with papacy
64, 86–7, 95, 143–4,
149–50, 180, 185–6
style of kingly conduct
201–2
succession and safe-
guarding of legacy
through *Divisio Reg-
norum* 95–6, 148, 243,
355–7, 364
Military Campaigns 201,
371
Avars 112–13, 115–21,
123, 124
Bavaria x 12, 65, 103, 105,
108–12, 114, 123, 124,
135
Denmark's challenge and
destabilization of 129–
35
development of effective
war machine 68
importance of river navi-
gation in land cam-
paigns 123
influence of Roman mili-
tary strategies 136–7
Lombardy x, 66, 86, 87–
90, 123, 124, 135, 145,
179

military pragmatism of
122–4, 135
naval policy and expedi-
tions 123
Saxony x-xi 23, 70–83, 88,
90, 102, 117, 123, 135,
136–7
Slav 122
southern Italy campaign
97–100
Spain 78, 91–4, 100–2
see also individual territories
Charles the Bald 194, 212,
217, 224, 227, 240, 252,
256, 263, 264–5, 266,
267, 284, 285, 359
Charles the Fat *see* Charles
II, King
Charles II, King (was Charles
the Fat) 216, 278, 360,
361
Charles III, King (Charles
the Simple) 361–2
Charles of Provence 359
Charles the Simple *see*
Charles III, King
Charles the Younger (Charle-
magne's son) 81, 96,
122, 132, 192, 193–4,
355–6, 357
charters 242, 245
Childebert the Adopted 8–9
Childebert I 5
Childebert II 6, 43, 84
Childebert III 29, 51
Childeric 1, 47
Childeric I xv, 4, 24–6
Childeric III 2, 11, 361
Chilperic I 5, 6, 320
Chilperic II 10, 11
Chiltrude (sister of Pippin
III) 50, 222
Chindasuinth 42
Chlodomer 5
Chlothar I 5, 71
Chlothar II 6, 7, 45
Chlothar III 9
Christian empire 184–9
Christianity 13–17, 58, 130,
304–5, 308, 336
adoption of by barbarian
kings 45
appeal of Arianism
18–20
and conquest 12

and Constantine 14–15,
16, 158, 159–60
conversion to 369
devotion of Franks to
Christian martyrs 58
early church building in
Rome 159, 160–1
evolution of late antiquity's
culture into 314–19
forced conversion of
Saxons x, 23, 52, 73–4,
77, 79–80, 83, 128, 130,
131, 141–2
and Gregory the Great 168
impact on education 313–
14
influence of Augustine's
City of God 20–1, 22
and militarization 13
and Roman Empire 14, 35
Romanization of 164–7
and Rome 156–7, 157–8
struggle with paganism in
Rome 162–3
used to justify power of
monarchs 14
and Wulfila 19–20
Christopher 63, 64, 65
Chronicle (741) 331
Chunoald II, Duke 61, 62
Church
acquisition of lands of by
Carolingians 277–8,
282
and Carolingian renais-
sance 307–8, 309–10
and *Dionysia-Hadriana*
309–10
education of the clergy
318–19, 333–4, 337–9,
343–4, 371
impact on how kings
ruled their subjects
257–8
reading lists for the clergy
308
welfare system 181
civil wars 71, 72, 136, 212,
218, 224, 304, 358
clergy, education of 318–19,
333–4, 337–9, 343–4,
371
Clichy, palace at 199
Clovis I 1, 4–5, 17, 24, 27,
40–1, 42–3, 45, 70
Clovis II 8–9, 45

coinage xi, 270–2, 283–4, 297, 373
colonicae 293
Columbanus 37, 322–3, 325
comites 249
Compostela 268–9
computus 350, 351
Concilium Germanicum 48
constable 195
Constans II, Emperor 144, 175, 326
Constantine the Great xii, 13, 14, 16, 22, 33, 35, 156–7, 158, 159–60
Donation of 183–4, 185
Constantine VI 95, 98
Constantinople 16, 18, 28, 31, 44, 157, 175, 327
Constitutio Romana 152–3, 154
Continuator of Fredegar, The 55–6
Corbie, abbey at 329
Cordoba 91–2
Corippus, Flavius Cresconius Johannide 315
Corpus Iuris Civilis 32–3, 34
Corvey (Westphalia) 66
counts 245–8, 249–51, 252, 263
court, Charlemagne's 194–6
courts of law xii, 248, 253–4
craftsmen 298
crop rotation system 286–7, 288
Crown Imperial 139–89
culture, late antique 312–27
Cunipert, King 28, 327
curtis 291–2
Cyrillic alphabet 380

Dagobert I xvi, 7, 8, 62
Dagobert II 8
Damasus 164
Danevirke system 129, 133
David, Jacques Louis
The Emperor Crossing the Alps xv
defensio patriae 234
demesne 273, 287–92, 294, 297
Denmark 30, 129–33, 281
campaign against Abodrites 132
challenge to Franks 129–33

and Danevirke system 129, 133
destabilization of 133–5
formal peace accord with Franks (811) 135, 136
internal discontent 135, 136
promotion of siege economy and closing of border by Godefred 133, 134
Desiderata 192
Desiderius, King 63, 64, 65, 85, 86, 87, 105, 222
Dhuoda 214, 340
Liber Manualis 211, 214, 216
diaconiae 173, 177, 181
dialectical studies 349–50
Didascaleion 319
Diocletian, Emperor 157
Dionysia-Hadriana 309–10
Diploma Ottonianum 377
Divisio Imperii (806) 153, 221
Divisio Regnorum 243, 355–7
domus cultae 181
Donation of Constantine 183–4, 185
Donation of Pippin 179
Dorotheus 34
Drogo (Charlemagne's illegitimate son) 10, 11, 49, 85, 192, 227, 357

Ebbo 217
Eberhard of Friuli 211, 214
Ebro valley (Spain) 91–2
Ebroin 10
Echternach, abbey at 130
economy 270–302
agriculture 285–8
annual levy imposed on aristocracy 283
coinage 270–2, 283–4, 297, 373
importance of plunder and tribune to royal income 280–2
industrial production 294–6
and manorial system 288–94
and markets 284
trade 272, 297–302

Edict of Milan (313) 14
Edict of Pires (864) 236
Edictum Chilperici 215
education 316, 337–43
of clergy 318–19, 333–4, 337–9, 343–4, 371
impact of Christianization on 313–14
and women 339–40
see also schools
Egica, King 29
Egypt xiii, 174
Einhard 23, 101, 137, 189, 198, 252, 259, 275, 280, 304, 334
Life of Charlemagne 50–1, 65, 146, 198, 240, 348–9
elephants 229–30
England 268, 374
churches 279
cultural formation 323–5, 327–8
kingship 30, 52–3
land-owning 293–4
and pottery 296
production of texts 327–8
relations with Francia 309
trade 300, 301
see also Anglo-Saxons
Epistola de Litteris Colendis 333, 334
Eresburg 76, 77
Eric, Duke of Friuli 117–18
Erigena, John Scottus 345, 349, 353
Ermelandus 265–6
Erminetrude 216
Ermold the Black 201
Etichonids 206
Eugenius II, Pope 152, 153–4, 343
European nations
Charlemagne's legacy and new 263–9
European Union xvi
Eusebius of Caesarea
Church History 22
Eusebius of Nicomedia 19

fairs, annual 298
famines 286
Fardulf 259
Fastrada, Queen (Charlemagne's wife) 192, 223, 224

fideles 263
filid 37
fisc (royal lands) 273–4
Fleury, library at 329
Formulae Wisigothorum 293
Forum of Trajan 166
France
   Charlemagne as national
     hero of xvi–xvi
Franci homines 256
Francia, term 2
Frankfurt Council (794) xi,
   112, 236, 243, 305
Franks 364–6
   assembly of the xii, 235–
     42, 243
   emergence of 70
   origin of name 1
   sense of their own excep-
     tional destiny and own
     identity 23–4, 24, 58,
     363–4, 365, 369
fraternal pacts 226
Fredegunda 6, 7
Frederick I Barbarossa 381
Frederick II 381
Frisia/Frisians 12, 23, 30, 72,
   74, 134, 301
Fritzlar 75
Fulco 338
Fulda, abbey of 74, 342–3
Fulrad, Abbot 47, 59, 69,
   237, 278

Galswintha 6
Garipald 104
Gascony 61, 276
Gaul 4, 25, 26, 29, 70, 319–
   20, 327,
   328–9
Genoa 97
geometry 350
Gepids 113, 366
Germanic kings
   distinctive power of 38–40
   Romanization of 40–3
Germany
   Charlemagne as national
     hero xvi
Gerold (Charlemagne's
   brother-in-law)
   111–12, 120, 223
Gerold, Count 65
Gildas
   On the Ruin and Conquest
     of Britain 319

Gisela (Charlemagne's sister)
   60, 232, 339, 340
glass industry 295
glossaries 347
Godefred, King 132, 133, 134
Godfrid of Denmark 281,
   284
Godoin 10
Gotefridus 206
Goths 25, 42, 313
Government and administration xii, 202, 229–69,
   371
   administering of law and
     justice 253–60, 371
   and assembly of the
     Franks xii, 235–42, 243
   capitularies xii, 235, 240–
     1, 242–5, 248, 267
   and counts 249–50
   diplomacy 230–5
   and mandates 248–9
   missi dominici 245–8, 251
   oaths of loyalty 154, 257–
     8, 260–2, 263
   and oral command of
     kings 249
   personal element of and
     access to Charlemagne
     43, 234–5, 263–4
   response to rebellions
     258–9
   tributes and gifts 230–5
grain production 286, 288
grammar 345, 346–8
Great Moravia 120
Greek (language) 39
Greeks 15, 34, 58, 84, 90, 98,
   99, 113, 121, 148, 312
   see also Byzantium
Gregory the Great, Pope
   167–9, 171, 172, 314,
   325
Gregory II, Pope 73, 177
Gregory III, Pope 177
Gregory of Tours 70–1, 314,
   320–1
   History of the Franks 41,
     269, 320
Grifo 11–12, 48, 49–50, 72,
   85, 107
Grimald of Reichenau 195–6
Grimoald I 8–9
Grimoald II 10, 11
Grimoald III 97, 98–9, 100
Gundiberga 104, 105

Guntram 5, 6
Guy II, Duke of Spoleto 360

Hadrian, abbot 323
Hadrian I, Pope 98, 144, 179,
   180, 184, 246
   baptizing of Pippin of Italy
     95
   and Bavaria 109–10
   and Lombards 65, 86, 88,
     89
   relationship with Charle-
     magne 86–7, 95, 180
   renovation and rebuilding
     works 181–2
   and southern Italy 98–9
al-Hakam I 102
Harald Bluetooth 378
Hardrad, Count 154, 258
harmony 351
harmscar 267
Heiric of Auxerre 341, 342
Hellenism 3, 311, 326
Hellenistic cities 33, 43
Helmgaudus 217
Henry I, Duke 362–3
Heraclius, Emperor 32, 34
Herstal assembly/capitulary
   (779) 242–3, 245, 248
Heruli 41
Hildebold 191
Hildegar, Archbishop 74
Hildegard, Queen (Charle-
   magne's wife) 65, 95,
   192, 206, 213, 223
Hildemar 346
Hildeprand, Duke of Spoleto
   94
Himiltrude 64, 95, 192
Himmler, Heinrich 81
Hincmar of Reims 267, 283,
   342, 349
   De Ordine Palatii 239–40,
     246, 254
Hisham I 100, 102
Holy Roman Empire xvi 363
honores 217–20
Honorius, Emperor 165, 175
honour 264, 265
horse burial 25
household, royal 191–2, 194–
   7
Hrodgaud, Duke of Friuli 88
Hruodhaid (Charlemagne's
   daughter) 191, 192
Hruodland 93, 212

Huesca 101
Hugeburc 329
Hugh (Charlemagne's illegitimate son) 192, 227, 357
Hugh of Tours 225
Hungarian monarchy, emergence of 378
Huns 26, 113
hunting 195, 197

iconoclasm/iconography 32, 40, 58, 89, 98, 176, 188, 231, 333
illegitimacy 192
industrial production 294–5
Ine, King of Wessex 52, 324
Ingelheim 111, 199, 201, 202, 203, 239
Ingeltrude 215
intellectual elite 311–12
Iran 174
Ireland 315, 322, 323, 327
  kingship 30–1, 37–8
Irene 98, 99
Irminsul 75, 80
iron-working 294, 295
Isanbard 221
Isidore of Seville 27, 42, 44, 314, 315–16, 321, 322
  Etymologies 322, 345, 349
  History of the Goths 321
  In Praise of Spain 321
  Treaty of Nature 322
Islam 30, 174, 175, 273
Islam's caliphs 35–6
Italy 94
  Charlemagne's southern campaign 97–100
  culture 316–17
  invasion of by Pippin III (755) 58–9, 85
  see also Lombards/Lombardy; Rome

Jerome 163, 165, 339, 346
Jerusalem 174, 230
jewellery xv
Jews 300, 347
John VII, Pope 176–7
John VIII, Pope 360
John XII, Pope 377
Jonas of Reims 349
Judith (Judith's granddaughter) 224
Judith (wife of Louis the Pious) 224, 340

Julian, Bishop of Seville
  The Rebellion of Paul against Wamba 321–2
Julian, Emperor 70
justice 248
Justinian I, Emperor 28, 32, 82, 169, 315, 317, 325–6
Jutes 70

Karolus magnus et Leo papa 196
Khagan 28, 117, 119, 120, 121
kings/kingship x, 40–5, 55
  appeal of 31–8
  and aristocracy 45
  development and spread of in western Europe after Romans 27–31
  distinctive power of Germanic 38–40
  in England 30, 52–3
  importance of anointment 53–6
  in Ireland 30–1, 37–8
  Islam's caliphs model for 35–6
  law codes 41–3
  paring-down of officialdom 43–4
  rituals 44
  and Roman emperor model 31–5
  Romanization of barbarian 40–3
  royal martyrs 45
  sacral x, 13–14, 45, 52, 55
Königsnahe 207, 210

Lambert 211, 212
Lament 196
land xiii, 273–8
  acquisition of by conquest 275
  acquisition of Church lands by Carolingian 277–8, 282
  confiscation of 275
  and manorial system 288–94
  royal 273–4, 283
land-grant system 280
language 305–6 see also Latin
Lateran basilica 159, 167,

177, 181, 182, 185, 187, 189, 204
Latin 305–6, 311, 312, 313, 322, 325–6, 343–4, 346, 347, 371
law 250–1, 253–8, 271, 331–2
  devolution of 254–6
  Roman 255, 332–3
  settlement of cases with written records 331–2
law codes 42–3, 56–7, 215, 331–3
law courts 245
Lecho 122
Leo I the Great, Pope 166
Leo II, Pope 176
Leo III, Emperor 58
Leo III, Pope xi, 120, 127, 139–40, 141–2, 149, 184, 246
Leo IV, Emperor 98
Leo (nomenclator) 151–2
Leovigild 44
letters 348
Lex Baiuuariorum 332
Lex Ribuaria 43, 332
Lex Salica 42–3, 56–7, 58, 241, 332
Liber Glossarum 347
Liber Historiae Francorum 9, 51, 331
Liber Iudiciorum 332
Liber Pontificalis 54, 170, 330
liberal arts 306–7, 345–7
Libri Carolini 231, 351
Libris Recipiendis et Non Recipiendis, De 330
literacy 306, 336, 338–9
literature 348–9
Liutgrad, Queen (Charlemagne's wife) 191, 223
Liutprand 105
Lombards/Lombardy 28, 42, 49, 58, 63, 83–90, 96, 123–4, 168, 169, 273
  abandonment of alliance with by Charlemagne 65–6, 86, 192, 222–3
  and Avars 113
  Bavarian connection 104–5
  and Byzantium 178
  and Catholic Christianity 84, 316
  conquering of by Charle-

magne and annexation of (774) x 66, 86, 87–90, 123, 124, 135, 145, 179
granting of limited devolution by Charlemagne 96–7
history of Frankish relations with 83–7
invasion of Italy and attacks on Rome 113, 178, 180–1, 319
and law 331–2
marriage alliance between Desiderata and Charlemagne 63–4, 85–6
and papacy 178
rule of by Charlemagne 145
Lothair Gospels 335
Lothair I 151, 152, 186, 194, 211, 303–4, 335, 359
Lothair II 225, 252, 359
Lotharingia 359
Louis the Child 361
Louis the German 194, 224, 253, 282, 359, 359–60
Louis II 359
Louis III 361
Louis the Pious (Charlemagne's son) 66, 95, 192, 218, 254, 266, 333, 358–9
children 194
civil war against sons 136, 211, 224, 358–9
coronation 150, 186, 193, 199, 357
and Crown Imperial 150–1, 155
and government 264
household 196
kingdoms allocated in Divisio 355
made emperor by Charlemagne 148–9
reform of monasteries 337
reforms embarked on after accession 150
as sub-king 101, 193, 355
Louis (son of Rotrud) 193
Louis the Stammerer 240, 361–2
Louis XIV, King 359
Louis XVI, King 228
Louis the Younger 267, 359, 360

Ludovicianum 150, 151, 152
Lupus of Ferrières 238, 344, 348
Lyons 329, 330

Magdeburg 300, 377–8
magistri 341–2, 343, 345
Magyars 120, 363, 375, 377
al-Malik, 'Abd 28
mallus 241
mandates 248–9
manorial system 288–94, 295–6, 297
mansus 290–1, 293
manuscript production 317–18, 328, 335, 340
Map of the World 137
maps, Charlemagne's table 303–4
Marchfeld 77, 78, 90
markets 284, 297–8
marriage 21–3
Martel, Charles ('The Hammer') 2, 10, 11–12, 23, 48, 50, 59, 61, 62–3, 71, 73, 74, 91, 106, 222, 277, 369–70
Martin, St 61
Matfrid of Orléans 218
Maur, Hraban 347
De Institutione Clericorum 346
Maurice, Emperor 36
mayors of the palace 2–3, 7, 10, 29, 41, 44
mediocres 252
Meginfred 116, 191
Megingoz, Bishop 212
merchants 298
Mercia 30
Merovech 4
Merovingian dynasty 26, 29–30, 50
blood feud 6–9
deposition of x, 2, 12, 47, 50, 59
history of 3–5
palaces of 274
representation of by Carolingian historians 3, 50–1
techniques to pacify unruly neighbours 77
Mesopotamia 174
Metz 2, 5
Metz Annals 331

miners 294–5
ministerium 54
mints 272
missi dominici xii–xiii, 55, 235, 243, 245–8, 251, 253, 258, 260, 263
missiaticum 248
missionaries 12, 74, 130
Modoin 196
monarchy see kings/kingship
monasteries 215, 216, 278, 279, 320, 323, 325, 337, 341
monastic schools 315, 337, 339, 341–2
Monte Cassino 66
Moravia/Moravians 281, 374, 375
Morgan ap Athrwys 30
mosaic art (Rome) 188
Mozarabic Chronicle 331
music 351–3
and Roman chant 351–2
musical theory 353–4

Nanthild 8
Napoleon xv–xvi
national identity 265–9
royal women as a focus of 223–5
navy 123
Nepos, Flavius Julius xi
Neustria 2, 5, 6–7, 8, 10, 217
Nicaea Council
(325) 19, 35, 304
(787) 231
Nicene Creed 304
filioque clause 304–5
Nicephorus, Emperor 121, 233
Nijmegen 199, 202, 233
nobility see aristocracy
Nordeludi 78
Normandy 111, 362, 374
north Africa 315
Arab conquest 175
invasion of by Vandals 17–18
Northild, Lady 222
Northumbria 30, 41, 52, 324
notaries 197, 242
Notitia Dignitatum 137
Notker the Stammerer
Gesta Caroli 195
numbers 250

oaths 154, 257–8, 260–2, 263
Odilo, Duke 12, 49–50, 106
Odo, Count of Paris 361
Odoacer 370
Old Testament 55, 57–8
Olisipo (Lisbon) 102
Ostrogoths 39, 44, 58
Oswald, King of Northumbria 45
Otto I 202, 359, 363, 377–8
Otto II 378
Otto III 379–80
Ottonians 363, 376–7, 378–80
Oviedo 101

Pactum Ludovicanum 150
Paderborn 77, 90, 200
paganism 14–15, 16, 25, 161, 162–3
palace school 337
palaces 23–4, 196–7, 199–202, 234, 274
Palestine xiii 174
Pantheon, Christianization of 171
papacy
    and Byzantium 175, 177–8
    and Charlemagne 64, 86–7 95, 143–4, 149–50, 180, 185–6
    and Donation of Constantine 183–4
    honours and rituals 143–5
    and Lombards 58, 84, 178
    relations with Carolingians 56, 58–9, 63, 84, 89, 143–4, 145, 150–5, 178, 180, 184
    rise of power 178
    territorial power in Italy 179
    see also individual popes
papal territories 143–4, 145, 148, 149–50, 151, 186
Paris 2, 5, 199
    Council of (829) 342
Paschal, Pope 151
Paterculus, Velleius 137
patronage 191, 207–8, 210, 227, 334
    and royal women 223–4
Paul the Deacon 104, 366, 367
Paul, St 165

Pavia 28, 44, 85, 86, 87–9, 179, 274
peasants 298
Peronna Scottorum, monastery of 327
Peter, St 56, 164–5, 179
Petronilla, Aurea 182–3
Pfalzel, Adela von 208
Piast dynasty 376
Picts 31
pigna 161
pigs 287
pilgrims
    arrival in Rome 172–4
Pippin the Hunchback 95–6, 192, 236, 258–9, 260
Pippin I 7–8
Pippin II (Pippin of Herstal) 2, 9–11, 12, 30, 71, 205, 222, 232
Pippin III (Charlemagne's father) 11, 12, 23, 84, 91, 143, 222, 231
    Aquitaine campaign 61
    Bavarian campaign 106, 107
    career 48
    and Church lands 277–8
    coup d'état x, 2
    death x, 59, 61–2
    declared 'Patrician of the Romans' 143
    education 60
    elected king and anointment of 47, 53–4, 57–8, 59
    Italian expeditions 58–9, 63, 85
    and palaces 199
    receives title Patricius Romanorum from papacy 95
    relations with brother (Carloman) 49
    road to becoming king 47–50
    Saxon campaigns 71, 72, 74
    Spanish campaign 91
Pippin of Italy (Charlemagne's son) 95, 99–103, 192, 193, 194, 226, 355, 357
Pirenne, Henri xiii
Plectrude 11, 205, 222
Pliny 351

poetry 323, 345
Poland 376
polemical literature 336
pottery production 295–6
Praeceptum Negotiatorum 301
Prague 375–6
Priskos 366
privatization 250
Procopius 39
Prum, abbey of 226, 236, 259, 296, 297
Psalms 230, 346
public buildings 239

quadrivium 316
Quaestors 33, 41–2
Quinisext Council (691–2) 35
Quran 36

Radanites (Jewish merchants) 300–1
Radbertus, Paschasius 338, 339, 340, 347
Radbod 30
Radulf, Duke 71
Ragnar 281
al-Rahman I, 'Abd 91–2, 100
al-Rashid, Harun 229, 230–1
Ravenna 84, 85, 89, 170, 178
rebellions (786 and 792) 224, 236, 252, 258–60
Reccared, King 20, 321
Reccesuith 42
reformatio 137–8
Regensburg assembly (792) 236
Reges Francorum 364
Regina 357
Regino of Prum 225–6
regnum 264–5
Reichsaristokratie 207, 209
Reims 5, 53
relics 172, 176, 182–3, 194
renovatio xiii, 24, 58, 137–8, 268
rhetoric 348–9
rituals xii, 267, 268
    and new European nations 267–9
    and Romans 34–5
river navigation 123
Rollo 362
Roman chant 351–2
Roman emperors 31–2, 33–5
    and campaigning 32

influence of Greek culture
34
as inspiration for early
medieval kings
31–2
and law 32–3
palace culture 34
and religious belief 35
and ritual 34–5
Roman law 255, 332–3
Romans/Roman Empire 26
army 136–7
barbarian invasions
17–18
civil law code (*Corpus
Iuris Civilis*) 32–4
culture 313
influence on barbarian
kingship 40–3
legacy of 138
and religion 14–16
Rome xii, 89, 155–6, 186–7
arrival of pilgrims 172–4
and Byzantium 175
centre of iconoclasm 176
Charlemagne and legacy
of Christian 156–7
Charlemagne's interven-
tion in after attack on
Leo III 141–3, 145, 149
church building 159, 160,
161–2, 171–2, 182,
187–8
and culture 343
decline 169–70
development of *domus
cultae* 181
early Christians in 157–8
impact of Arab advance
175–6
influence of Gregory the
Great on 167–9
Lombard attacks on 178,
180–1
and paganism 157, 159,
161, 162
refugees from Islamic
lands 175–6
and relics 182–3
renovation and rebuilding
works by Hadrian I
181–2
sacking of by Visigoths
(410) 14, 16, 165–6
seventh-century crisis
174–8

sixth-century threats and
recovery 167–72
struggle between
paganism and Christi-
anity in 162–3
transformation to Christianity 156–7, 158–9,
162–4
Rome, Treaty of xvi
Roncesvalles
massacre of Charlemagne's
army (778) 93–4, 102
Rothard, Duke 59
Rotrud (Charlemagne's
daughter) 95, 98, 99,
192–3, 339, 340
Ruthard 221
rye 288

S. Maria Maggiore (Rome)
166, 171, 182, 189
S. Paolo fuori le mura
(Rome) 164–5, 167,
182, 189
S. Prassede (Rome) 188
S. Pudenziana (Rome) 164
S. Sabina (Rome) 165
Sabbatina aqueduct (Rome)
181
sacral kingship x, 13–14, 45,
52, 55
St Julian, church of (Oviedo)
239
St Peter's church (Rome) 139,
144, 160–1, 167, 174,
177, 182, 183, 189
saints 331
Salians 1, 4, 70
salt production 296, 298
Samuel 55
San Salvatore, convent of 222
Santiago de Compostela 101
Saracens 123, 299, 301
Saxons/Saxony 70–83, 90,
359, 376
allocation of to Charles
the Younger by Charle-
magne 356
attack on the Irminsul
shrine 75
background to Frankish
conflict with
70–4
Charlemagne's campaigns
against x–xi, 23, 51, 75–
7

Charlemagne's efforts at
legislative renewal and
religious reform 124–5
Christian conversion cam-
paign x, 23, 52, 73–4,
77, 79–80, 83, 128, 130,
131,
141–2
colonization 77, 79–80
customs 73
defeat of in battle in
Suntel mountains battle
(782) 80, 82
expansion and increasing
mobility of 72
expelling of Saxons from
native territories by
Charlemagne and set-
tling of Frankish sol-
diers on lands 127–8
and First Saxon Capitulary
79–80
internal organization 124
law 255–6
long-term consequences of
campaign in
x–xi
migration to Britain 72
origins 70
and paganism 51, 72–3, 80
peace 124
policy of destruction of
property and land by
Charlemagne 81–2
rebellions against Frankish
rule and Widukind's
resistance to 77–81, 117
re-emergence of resistance
and Charlemagne's
campaign against 125–8
surrender and conversion
of Widukind 82–3
Verden massacre (782)
80–1
Scandinavia 373–4
scholae 173–4
schools 337
monastic 315, 337, 339,
341–2
palace 337
running of by the parish
priests 338
science, Carolingian 350–1
Scotland 268
kingship 31, 38
Scottus, Martin 343

scriptoria/scriptorium 310, 329, 335, 341
Septimania 91, 276
Sergius I, Pope 177
sheep 287, 294
Sicily 90, 99, 326
Sigebert I 5, 6
Sigebert II 7
Sigebert III 7, 8, 41, 71
Sigifrid, King 131
Sigismund, king of the Burgundians 45
slaves 290, 291, 292, 300
Slavs 36-7, 120, 131, 374-5
  and Avars 114, 121
  Charlemagne's campaign against (805) 122
  expansion of 121, 122
  and Great Moravia 120
  internal divisions within 131
Smaragdus of St-Mihiel 349
Smeldingi 134
societas 265
Soissons 2, 53-4
Spain 100-2
  Arab invasion and conquest of 91-2, 100-1, 175
  Charlemagne's invasion of and background to offensive 78, 91-4, 100-2
  and Christianity 331
  and culture 315-16, 321-2
  Islamicization of early medieval 29
  manuscript production 331
  massacre of Frankish soldiers at Roncesvalles (778) 93-4, 102
  speech and grammar 343-4
spelt 288
spices 299, 301
Spoleto 88
St-Denis (Paris) 45, 47, 60, 61-2, 199, 279, 326
St-Martin abbey (Tours) 293, 335
St-Maximin abbey (Trier) 301
Stephen, Grand Prince of the Magyars 378-9

Stephen II, Pope 49, 54, 56, 59, 143, 155, 174, 178
Stephen III, Pope 63, 64, 65
Stephen IV, Pope 150
Stilicho 370
Strabo, Walahfrid 339
Strasbourg Oaths 264-5
Strategicon 36
Swanachild 106
Sweden 374
swords 266
Syria xiii 174

Tacitus 38
  Germania 39
Tassilo I 104
Tassilo III of Bavaria, Duke 12, 50, 64, 105, 107-12, 114, 222, 236, 260
taxation 284, 285
tents 239
Tertry, Battle of (687) 10, 326
Teutoburg Forest, Battle of (AD 9) 136
textiles 295
Thegan of Trier 213
Theodelinda, Queen 104, 172
Theoderic the Ostrogoth 39, 44, 169, 370
Theoderic (Saxon leader) 77-8
Theodore (*Khagan*) 120, 121, 151
Theodosian Code 33, 265
Theodrada (Charlemagne daughter) 192
Theodulf of Orléans, Bishop 191, 337-8, 343
Theudebert I 70, 83
Theudebert II 6-7
Theuderic I 5, 70, 129
Theuderic II 6-7
Theuderic III 10
Theuderic IV 11
Theudoald 11
Theutberga 225
Thrasco 128, 133-4
Thuringia/Thuringians 8, 30, 61, 70, 71, 77, 259
tituli 158, 161
Toledo 17, 44, 321
  Third Council of (589) 20
tonsuring 226-7
Toulouse 17

Tournai 26
Tours 61, 268, 320
Toxandria 70
trade 272, 297-302
traders 298, 300, 301, 302
  Jewish 300-1
Tribonian 34
tributes 280
Tudun 117-19, 120

Udalrich, Count 216
Ulfila 39
Umayyad dynasty 27-8, 36, 78, 91-2, 229
universitas 263-4

Vandals 17-19, 20, 25, 170, 367
vassi 251-2
Venice 231, 233, 271, 296, 298, 299, 376
Verden massacre (782) 80-1
Verdun assembly (843) 238-9
Verdun, Treaty of (843) xv, 211, 359
Vetus Lex 57-8
Vikings 129, 362, 373-4, 375
villa 288, 292
villae 197
Virgil, *Aeneid* 19
Visigoths 14, 16, 17, 20, 28-9, 42, 54, 91, 165, 314, 332, 369
Vita Ermelandi 265
Vita Karoli Magni 51
Vouillé, Battle of (507) 17, 91

Waiofar, Duke of Aquitaine 59, 62
Waldrada 225
Wales 276
Waltbert, Count 215
Warin 65, 219, 221
weaving 294
Wends 71, 72
Wessex 30, 52, 224, 235, 242, 253, 285, 372
Wetti 345
Wido 211, 212
Widukind 66, 77-9, 80, 82-3, 129-30, 132
Wilborada 340
Wildeshausen, monastery of 215

Willehad 130–1
Willibrord 12, 130
Wiltzi 125, 132, 134
Winigis, Duke of Spoleto
    100, 115
Wittiza, King 29
women
    and education 339–40
    focus of national identity
        of royal 223–5

importance of in courtly
    politics 221–3
importance of as power-
    brokers 11
influence of aristocratic
    215–16
wool trade 288
Worms 87, 200
    assembly at (781) 108,
        110

destruction of palace at
    204
Wulfila 19

Y Gododdin 323

Zacharias, Pope 47, 53, 55,
    177, 178, 181, 187
Zaragoza 92–3
Zatun 101

List of Illustrations

1. Late antique sculpture of the god Freyr. Fourth century. Musee des Beaux-Arts, Arras. © Andrea Jemolo / Scala, Florence.

2. Head of Constantine the Great, National Museum, Belgrade. © Photo Scala, Florence.

3. The Ludovisi sarcophagus, of Carrara marble, dated to c. 250, and discovered at a site near the Porta Tiburtina, Rome in 1621. Museo Nazionale Palazzo Altemps, Rome. © akg-images / Rabatti – Domingie.
   The central figure on horseback, top centre, may be the emperor Decius's son, and co-emperor, Herennius Etruscus. This remarkable work may in fact record Roman wish fulfilment. Both father and son were killed by Goths at the battle of Abritus in the province of Moesia Inferior (modern Balkans) in 252, and the empire was plagued by political, miltary and economic instability in the ensuing two decades. The chain-mail shows the Romans' superiority to be technological as well as moral.

4. The Trier basilica, built in c.310 by Emperor Constantine. © akg-images.
   This is the largest single-roomed structure to survive from Roman antiquity.

5. Ceremonial plate, also known as 'The Achilles Shield'. Possibly made in Constantinople in c. 400. Engraved silver, gilded in parts. Found 1656 in the river Rhône near Avignon. Cabinet des Medailles, Bibliothèque Nationale. © akg-images.

6. The Probus diptytch. 406 AD. © The Art Archive / Tesoro del Duomo Aosta / Gianni Dagli Orti.
   Commissioned by the Christian nobleman Anicius Petronius Probus, the ivory diptytch marked his election as consul of the western Roman empire for the year 406. Probus donated it to the emperor Honorius (384-423) at court in

457

Ravenna. The banner (labarum) reads: 'In nomine/ X(h)r(ist)i vincas semper'
(May you always win in the name of Christ).

7. Treasures from the grave of Childeric including sword hilts and scabbards. The cloisonné work and use of gold and garnet is typical of Merovingian royal adornment. Fifth century. Discovered at a site near Tournai in 1653. Bibliothèque Nationale, Paris. © akg-images / Erich Lessing.
   The objects may have been made in Constantinople or Ravenna. The encased deep-red mineral is garnet.

8. Childeric's seal ring. This is a copy of the lost original. Ashmolean Museum, Oxford. © The Bridgeman Art Library.

9. The ivory throne of Maximianus, archbishop of Ravenna (546-556). The front shows John the Baptist with four evangelists; the backrest depicts Christological themes. Museo Arcivescovile, Ravenna. © akg-images / Cameraphoto.

10. Front view of the Mausoleum of Theodoric in Ravenna. © 2006 Alinari / TopFoto.

11. The throne of Dagobert (602/605? – 638) Bronze. Originally part of the treasure at the Abbey of St Denis. Seventh century, the armrests and back are late ninth century additions. Bibliothèque Nationale, Paris. © White Images / Scala, Florence.

12. The helmet of Agilulf. Gold leaf from Valdinievole, seventh century, Lombard King Agilulf is shown on his throne. © The Art Archive / Museo del Bargello Florence / Alfredo Dagli Orti.
    The helmet may have been Agilulf's gift to a Lombard warrior.

13. The Teuderic casket. Reliquary casket, abbey of Saint-Maurice. Seventh century. © akg-images / Erich Lessing.
    Possibly given to the abbey of Saint-Maurice (Switzerland) by Pope Eugene I (654-657). Gold plates, slender gold tracery set with glass paste and garnets embellished with an arrangement of cabochons, pearls and intaglios, and a medallion of spun glass with portrait in the centre.

14. Iron Crown of the Lombards. Cathedral of Monza, Italy. © akg-images.
    Pope Gregory the Great (590-604) may have sent the crown to Queen Theodelinda who influenced the conversion of her husband King Agilulf to Catholic Christianity. It was used at the coronation of Otto I as king of the Lombards, and the coronations of Frederick I Barbarossa and Napoleon Bonaparte as kings of Italy.

15. Votive crown of Visigothic King Reccesuinth (649-72). Gold and gemstones,

Originally held as part of the Treasure of Guarrazar. Seventh century. Museo Arqueológico Nacional, Madrid. © The Art Archive / Granger Collection.

16. Seal belonging to Emperor Charlemagne. Bust in profile. Archives Nationales, Paris. © Giraudon / The Bridgeman Art Library.

17. Seal depicting Charlemagne offering the Capella Palatina to the Virgin. © The Art Archive / Archives Nationales Paris / Kharbine-Tapabor / Coll. Jean Vigne.

18. Vellum document exempting the abbey of Saint-Germain des Pres from tax signed by Charlemagne with his monogram. AD 779. Archives Nationales, Paris. © Scala / White Images.

19. Reliquary bust of Charlemagne donated in 1349 by emperor Charles IV. Silver, part gilt, Aachen, Domschatz. © akg-images / Erich Lessing.

20. Charlemagne's throne. Composed of marble slabs, probably imported from Rome. Aachen, Germany. © Adam Woolfitt / CORBIS.

21. Fresco at Lateran showing St. Peter giving the standard to Charlemagne. Mosaic, dating from papacy of Leo III, 795-816, restored in the eighteenth century. Rome, Lateran, Triclinium of Leo III. © akg-images / Andrea Jemolo.

22. Interior of Capella Palatina looking up to the octagon and showing Barbarossa's chandelier. 788-805, erected from plans by Odo of Metz. Aachen. © akg-images / Erich Lessing.
The cupola is supported by columns taken from Rome and Ravenna, and its mosaics, now hidden by nineteenth century restoration, represented Christ in Majesty with the twenty-four elders of the Apocalypse.

23. The basilica of Santa Prassede, Rome, built in c. 780. The mosaics covering the triumphal arch and the apse were commissioned by Pope Paschal I in c. 822. © Photo Scala, Florence / Fondo Edifici di Culto / Min. dell'Interno.

24. Reconstruction of the Lateran complex in Rome, including the basilica and adjoining papal palace, as they would have looked in the early fourteenth century. The palace was the principal residence of the popes until that time. It was badly damaged by fire in 1307 and 1361, and demolished in the late 1580s. © INTERFOTO / Mary Evans Picture Library.

25. Watercolour reconstruction of the palace complex at Aachen. Twentieth century. Archives Larousse, Paris © Giraudon / The Bridgeman Art Library.

26. The Crown of the Holy Roman Empire.Consisting of eight hinged gold

plates studded with pearls and precious gems, and made by the mid-tenth century at a location in the German imperial territory. Kunsthistorisches Museum, Vienna. © akg-images / Nimatallah.

27. Antique marble Roman sarcophagus depicting the rape of Prosperina. Re-used in 814 as Charlemagne's sarcophagus. Second century, Aachen, Germany. © akg-images / Erich Lessing.

28. Carolingian soldiers, a miniature from the Psalterium Aureum in St. Gall monastery, Switzerland. Tenth Century. © ullsteinbild / TopFoto.

29. Louis the Pious (814-840) as depicted in an illumination on the dedicatory page of *De Laudibus Sanctae Crucis* by Hrabanus Maurus. © akg-images / British Library.
   This collection consists of thirty poems all of which are encrypted in a grid of 36 lines each of which has 36 letters.

30. Lorsch gospels ivory cover. Produced at Aachen by c.810. Bibliotheca Apostolica Vaticana. © The Bridgeman Art Library.
   Both the ivory cover of the Lorsch Gospels and the manuscript itself were given by Charlemagne to the monastery of Lorsch, near Worms.

31. Nathan's rebuke of David. Ivory cover of the Psalter of Charles the Bald. The cover shows Nathan comparing the cattle and sheep of the rich man with the single sheep of the poor man. Bibliothèque Nationale, Paris. © akg-images.

32. Charles the Bald receiving a bible from Count Vivian and the monks of Saint-Martin de Tours. From the First Bible of Charles the Bald, c.843-51. Bibliothèque Nationale, Paris. © The Bridgeman Art Library.

33. Vellum image of Lothair I, from the Gospels of Lothair produced at Tours in 849-51. Bibliothèque Nationale, Paris. © Giraudon / The Bridgeman Art Library.

34. Slavic, German, French and Roman personifications of Europe's civilisation pay homage to the emperor Otto III (980 – 1002) in c. 998-1000, from the Gospel Book of Otto III. Illuminated manuscript, produced at Reichenau Abbey. C. 998-1000. Bayr. Staatsbibl Munich. Photo of a colour lithograph. © akg-images.

35. Otto III enthroned with courtiers. From the Gospel Book of Otto III. Illuminated manuscript, produced at Reichenau Abbey. C. 998-1000. Bayr. Staatsbibl Munich Photo of a colour lithograph. © akg-images.